Theatre Is My Life!
Thoughts on Play Quotes:
A book of meditations for each day of the year

by
Barbara J. Sloan

Who Am I Arts
Birmingham, Alabama

The tre Is My Life!

Thou ts on Play Quotes:
A book of medi tions for each day of the year

ISBN
9 -1-959172-20-8

Library of Congre Control Number: 2022915348

Publish d by Who Am I Arts
Birn ngham, Alabama

Dedication

This book is dedicated to my families. First, my immediate family: Elin and David Glenn, Emmeline, George, and Arthur; Seth and Kim Olson and Teddy; Roger Conville; Bill Sloan and our late parents (Jean and Buck); and also to my expanded family, with vast numbers of cousins, aunts, and uncles. Second, to my theatre family: Samford University students and faculty; the University of Montevallo fellow students and our mostly deceased but beloved faculty; University of North Carolina theatre colleagues; The Seasoned Performers; and all my fellow theatre workers from over 250 productions. And finally, to my St. Andrew's church family, my American Village family, my Camp Winnataska family, and my Institute for Conscious Being family.

All of these folks and more show up on pages of this book, and I am indebted to their interactions with my life. I was lucky to be born into a wonderful family, and to find my way into amazing theatre and spiritual families throughout my life. Thank you, one and all.

Note: These meditations are based on quotes from plays, which are considered fair use for an author to cite. In the case of musical lyrics from which I constructed some of the pieces, a writer finds it hard to be awarded permission. I have given the title of the song that I used, and in each case, I include a note that asks you to listen to the work online or from your library. I highly recommend that you do so, as hearing all those wonderful words and tunes will enhance the reading immensely.

To the Reader

If you are a person who believes there is nothing quite like settling into a darkened theatre seat on opening night just as the curtain is rising, this is the book for you! If you are an audience member in that theatre, you are about to be taken into another world with beings very different from yourself. This arena is a place you grow and learn, empathize and develop different perspectives by witnessing other people's lives unfolding before your eyes. If you are a director or designer watching the houselights dim, you feel a mixture of queasiness, relief, wonder, joy — and terror! Here is your baby coming to life before a large group of friends and strangers. What will they think? What will the critics say?

The title *Theatre Is My Life!* comes from a funny saying my theatre students at Samford University in Birmingham, Alabama (as theatre people everywhere) would use. One of them would arrive on the stage or in my shop with a huge backpack in tow, after a grueling day of classes, fighting a winter rainstorm, tired and hungry. But at that very moment, this dear soul would start work rehearsing or lighting or costuming. And she would cry, "Theatre is my life!" With that expression, the students expressed both the intense joy of being folded into the theatre family, and also the wry observance that their chosen activity takes time, effort, time, talent, and time, a lot of time. Work on and off stage becomes their life. A wonderful, passionate, sensitive, and full life — filled with laughter and tears.

I believe that even the mundane in our lives is spiritual in nature, and although theatre is anything but mundane, viewing a play or working on one can be a sacred experience. This volume is a daybook of meditations based on play quotes. A vast majority of the plays I cite are ones that I designed or directed over an almost 40-year career teaching and working in the theatre. I have written this work over the last eight years, but I also pulled from former essays and ruminations. The writings involve my recollection of plays, and also of the incidents that the quotes invoke. Because memories are based on our cognitive state and emotional response at the time, other people who experienced some of these events may have different reminiscences.

Tennessee Williams is quoted as saying, "No one is ever free until they tell the truth about themselves and the life into which they've been cast. Write it down; tell it to a friend in need, or a stranger who needs diversion. We are all here to be a witness to something, to be of some aid and direction to other people."

I have taken Williams' advice by writing and offering to you these musings. I hope that as you journey through this year, and through these daily meditations that you find something that stirs your mind, breaks your heart open, and nourishes your soul. I hope my "witness to something" shows you how theatre, music, art, literature, and dance seep into your psyche and form and inform your life.

Barbara J. Sloan, 2022

Theatre Is My Life!
Thoughts on Play Quotes:
a book of meditations for each day of the year
by Barbara J. Sloan

January 1

"Therefore my age is as a lusty winter,
Frosty, but kindly."
Adam from William Shakespeare's *As You Like It*, Act II, Scene 3

It is the end of another "frosty, but kindly" old year. Early January is beginning with promise and hope, resolutions I long to keep — and wonder about the new day, new week, new month, new year. In this part of the world — yes, even in Alabama — "lusty winter" is in full force: it is cold. Even though the days are getting longer, afternoons are still brief and light is short. Holiday decorations are being laid to rest until next November. This time is ripe for contemplating beginnings and endings.

In 2008, my Christmas tree was huge — eleven feet tall and totally filled with light. I loved that tree — a Fraser cut fresh from Grandfather Mountain in North Carolina. I filled it with glittery medieval ornaments and twinkly lights. The reason I held such great affection for this evergreen is that on the day I was going to drag it inside all by myself, my daughter Elin called and said she would help me with the task, since she was coming by to give me a new decoration for the tree. When she delivered the ornament, a silver snowflake, she had me look closely at the engraving. It was inscribed "C and Ma-Ma." That is how she announced (Gabriel-like) the exciting news that she and her husband, David, were having a baby — my first grandchild. So the celebration of Mary's pregnancy, the birth of the Christ Child, and this happy announcement twined around and emanated from that brightly lighted Christmas fir all during the late Advent season through Christmas, and all the way into Epiphany. In fact, I was loath to take the tree down, and kept finding myself going to meetings, doing projects, and putting other trinkets and baubles to bed rather than undecorating my tree.

On January 10, I attended the funeral of the father of a good friend and coworker. The day was quite foggy, and I came home on the edge of tears. I was alone, and in this mood, I somehow and suddenly found myself able to put the tree away. The evergreen that started the season with the happy news of a birth ended with the poignant remembrance of a long, fruitful, "lusty" life. First I took off all the ornaments. Then starting at the top, with the lights still lit, I removed the bright star, then the first strand of lights. The top of the tree was dark. Light outside had also faded in the early dusk of a January evening. The next strand came down, then the next, and the next. Soon the whole tree was dim. The observation of the gradual extinguishing was startling as I contemplated how the finish of something so lusty and vibrant as this tree could still somehow warm my heart as it departed. The curtain was pulled, the decorations were down, the climax of the holidays had transpired. And yet, that tree contained, even as it left the house, the mysterious fullness of new life and eloquent death.

January 2
"Everybody should eavesdrop once in a while. There's nothing like eavesdropping to show you that the world outside your head is different from the world inside your head."
Malachi Stack in Thornton Wilder's *The Matchmaker* Act 3

Maybe what goes on inside your head is always organized, helpful, positive, and productive. Much hard work goes into keeping my mind from spinning. I have often pondered the difference between the brain and the mind, how they are different, which is inside the other, our mind after death, and many other related topics.

Raymond Tallis wrote a book called *The Kingdom of Infinite Space: A Fantastical Journey Around Your Head.* Kenan Malik of London's Telegraph has said that, "Ray Tallis is one of the hidden treasures of British intellectual life. Physician, philosopher, poet and playwright, former director of geriatric care in Manchester and an expert on the aging brain, he is a polymath who has never quite received the attention that his writing deserves, probably because so much of his work remains defiantly unfashionable."

In the book, Tallis writes: "Selves are not cooked up, or stored, in brains. Selves require bodies as well as brains, material environments as well as bodies, and societies as well as material environments." Tallis strives to decipher what being a human really means: are we divine creations? Beasts? Or what he terms "embodied subjects"?

Most of us have consciences that process matters, committees inside us that comment on what we are doing, music that accompanies our tasks, memories that intersect themselves at odd times, inner chatter that asks "what if?" Once I became conscious of the voice inside me, I began to realize that my thoughts and my self are two separate things. My own presence is beyond the cogitation going on in my brain – and identifying myself as my thoughts denies my essence or my true being.

Meditation is a wonderful way to calm my mind and rid it of all the incessant inner noise. But another thing that helps me get outside myself is the empathy I share in watching or working on a theatre performance. Reading a script getting inside the skin of the characters, or creating just the right clothing for them to wear for their part expands my mind outside myself and forces me to walk in others' shoes.

And then, when rehearsals are over and the audience is invited to watch, there – in the darkened auditorium – I can see the actors become different people. I can listen to them bemoan or rejoice over what is going in those lives. Theatre is always happening in the present, so it makes viewers encounter the only moment any of us humans really have: the now. So listen to Malachi Stac, and remember a great place to eavesdrop is the theatre!

January 3

In *"Finishing the Hat"* from Sunday in the Park with George, George sings about completing one small portion of his work. (Listen to the work online or from your library!)

George in Stephen Sondheim and James Lupine's *Sunday in the Park with George*

Whenever I hear Mandy Patinkin sing the words to this song, I cry because that one little scene has so impacted me. Sondheim and Lupine have, in that song, defined and verbalized what I do and how I have felt as an artist. Genesis opens: "In the beginning, God created the heavens and the earth. The earth was formless and empty. Darkness was on the surface of the deep and God's Spirit was hovering over the surface of the waters. God said, 'Let there be light,' and there was light. God saw the light, and saw that it was good."

As an artist, my purpose, like the Divine's, is to bring into physical existence what before was only a possibility, a vision imagined in my mind. So, it is not surprising that one of my favorite parts of any musical comedy is when Georges Seurat performs this song in *Sunday in the Park with George*. He is working on the magnificent painting "A Sunday

Afternoon on the Isle of La Grande Jatte." He muses about the way artists can rarely live the "conventional" life, doing things that lovers, friends, and relatives want them to do, because part of them is always involved in the creation they are working on.

I remember when I designed ten or more shows every year, and much of my time was spent in the costume shop or in the darkened theatre. The rest of the world outside would be watching it rain. Once we had a tornado come very near the campus, and those of us working inside never knew about it. The rest of the world outside would be celebrating Halloween, would be eating dinner at home, would be walking their dogs, would be taking that weekend trip.

Meanwhile in the theatre, we would be plotting out a sky, we would be painting the drop of the sky, and then, we would be lighting the night and the day of the sky. We would be designing and putting clothes on actors who would come to life underneath that firmament after rehearsing and rehearsing and finally getting blocking right, getting lights gelled, getting props handled – underneath that sky.

Sometimes I envied those "normal" people living outside the orb of the playhouse. But when the show opened, and the audience completed the work we had begun by watching and appreciating the play, I was satisfied. The process amazes me. A play or a piece of art is incarnated into corporeal form through the accomplishment of the actor and director – or sculptor or musician. Something has emerged seemingly out of thin air. "I created a costume where before, there was nothing!"

This concept from Steven Pressfield has become important to me: The artist, a human, in a very God-like way, is the agent of the change from nonbeing to being! God cannot create Westminster Abbey or dance like Martha Graham or act like Derek Jacobi. We are created to do that in this world for each other and for ourselves. Have you created something lately? Have you been able to say, "Look what I created!"? And that it was good?!

January 4

"Why, Amelia, it is a curio cabinet, and I am a curious little person; besides, Amelia, you got no secrets from me. You got secrets from me, Amelia?"
Cousin Lymon in Edward Albee's *Ballad of the Sad Café* adapted from the novella by Carson McCullers

One of the extraordinary things about working in the theatre day in and day out is that the words of the script of the play I am creating soak through my clothing, permeate my skin, penetrate my brain, and saturate my life. While I am laboring to get that play onto the stage, I hear lines from the mouths of the actors drilling in the Green Room, coming into the costume shop for fittings, rehearsing on stage over and over and over again. And that is not a bad thing. In fact, what seems like drudgery and repetitive action imparts vitality, meaning, and power to my existence. Days, weeks, months, yes, even years later, I can hear the voice of a particular actor in my head, echoing from the stage of that recent or distant past.

In the early 1990s, I was privileged to direct and design Edward Albee's eccentric and unconventional *Ballad of the Sad Café* and to actually talk to the playwright for two hours about this work. The play revolves around an intriguing love triangle: the manly and taciturn Miss Amelia, her lover and 10-day husband Marvin Macy, and the child-sized hunchback Cousin Lymon who suddenly appears in their lives. Miss Amelia owns the café in a small southern burg and the townspeople are intrigued by the arrival of this new relative — and even more fascinated by her affection towards Lymon, because the rugged six-foot woman is generally aloof and untouched by human emotion. There is much that is peculiar and surprising in this play, and I think often of many of the lines that permeated my soul while I created the production.

My fiancé Roger thinks I ask a lot of questions. In fact, he sometimes compares me to my inquisitive four-year old granddaughter Emmeline who asks, "Why?" or "How?" about everything. I like to think of myself as probing rather than nosy, searching rather than snoopy. I have been a journalist since the age of 15, along with being an artist and theatre designer, so asking questions is part of my nature. When Roger complains about my queries, I answer him that, like Cousin Lymon, "I am a curious little person."

Roger, where are you going tomorrow? Roger, what do you want to do for my birthday? Roger who was that you just made a coffee date with? Roger, "You got no secrets from me. You got secrets from me," Roger?

January 5: Twelfth Night
"What creature is in health, either young or old,
But some mirth with modesty will be glad to use...

For mirth prolongeth life, and causeth health;
Mirth recreates our spirits, and voideth pensiveness;
Mirth increaseth amity, not hindering our wealth...
The wise poets long time heretofore,
Under merry comedies secrets did declare,
Wherein was contained very virtuous lore,
With mysteries and forewarnings very rare."
Prologue from Nicholas Udall's *Ralph Roister Doister*

And so the merry mirth of Christmas is drawing to a close with Twelfth Night today and Epiphany tomorrow. What a shame that so often Christmas trees are seen lying in the gutter on December 26, and that some Americans believe it is bad luck to have decorations up at New Year. Despite the fact that we are all back at work and following fairly normal schedules now, the twelve days of Christmas are just now ending. Today and tomorrow, my family and some friends are still partying, giving small gifts, pub hopping, enjoying a few remaining twinkly lights and garlands, eating "King's Cakes," and drinking wassail. Why cut such a wondrous festival short and stop the festivities when they are really just beginning?

Probably the most memorable Twelfth Night I ever spent was a two-hour party in the Victoria and Albert Museum in London in 1989. For a small ticket price, around a hundred folks got to go into the cavernous building after closing! The experience was almost like being in the youth novel *From the Mixed-Up Files of Mrs. Basil E. Frankweiler* by E. L. Konigsburg. Still fragrant with evergreen decorations, we all began the celebration capering about a street-level room in the manner of Tudor dancers. We ate a King's Cake and two people who found beans in their slices were crowned King and Queen. After winding our way up some torch-lit stairways, we were treated to a short version of the farce *Ralph Roister Doister*, said to be the first comic play written in the English language. Then, there was more dancing accompanied by mulled wine, quiches, meat pies, and mincemeat desserts. The evening was frivolous, yet serious fun — made even more special by the surroundings of incredible furniture, glass, metalwork, paintings, photographs, prints, sculpture, and other objects in the museum's holdings.

Merriment, laughter, gaiety, jollity! Even the Mayo Clinic suggests that giggles and guffaws are just what the doctor ordered to relieve stress and do your heart good. Yes, we all need to extend our holiday celebration to include mirth-filled traditions that recreate our spirits, and void our post-holiday pensiveness.

January 6: Epiphany

"The rain won't matter much when you're off the ground. You know, it's amazing how quickly you can leave this English soup and have only the stars for company." John Wheeler in Lucille Fletcher's *Night Watch*

Night Watch is not my favorite play. I did have fun working on the piece at Parkway Playhouse, a barn-like summer stock theatre in the mountains, during graduate school at the University of North Carolina at Greensboro. The reason for that enjoyment was that I loved all the friends I made there and working on any play would have been spectacular. But this suspense thriller is not one I would choose to see or read on this feast day that celebrates the revelation of God the Son becoming a human being in Jesus Christ. The Holy Day revolves around the Magi's visit to the Christ Child, laden with gifts of gold, frankincense, and myrrh. *Night Watch* spins about the murder scheme of a fairly insane woman which in no way parallels or echoes the feast day.

However, I really appreciate this quote. I am infatuated with England, even with the rainy, foggy weather. When I have flown in an airplane at night, from London — or from anywhere for that matter — the ascent from pea soup to clear atmosphere is startling. Such a takeoff can be something like an epiphany, an experience of unanticipated and breathtaking realization. In the case of the airplane flight, there are stars beyond the clouds! I love the season of Epiphany, which can be five to nine weeks long. Every day I can deliberately encourage higher consciousness and develop new practices that lead to enlightenment. Out of such discipline, I can sometimes understand my life from new and deeper perspectives.

The Star of Bethlehem is problematic for some humans who want scientific proof for everything. But, whether that star was a comet, a planet, or a pure fabrication of the writer of the Gospel of Matthew, it can be a powerful symbol for what I might find if I search for light. I might believe sometimes that the world is raining on my parade. I might feel comfortable wandering about in a fog. But the rain doesn't matter when I encourage myself to get off the ground and enjoy "only the stars for company."

January 7:
"It is not we alone, it is not the house, it is not the city that is defiled,
But the world that is wholly foul.
Clear the air! clean the sky! wash the wind! take the stone from the stone, take
the skin from the arm, take the muscle from the bone, and wash them. Wash the
stone, wash the bone, wash the brain, wash the soul, wash them, wash them!
Chorus in T. S. Eliot's *Murder in the Cathedral*

A number of years ago now, I was in the midst of a hectic academic and theatrical career, bent on success in those arenas. It was a time before I had learned how to say, "no" to people who wanted me to serve on committees and teams. In the rush of my world, where I was also tending to the rearing of two children, I felt overwhelmed, unbalanced, and knew I needed to make a change. I was desperate for some time for myself. Cold turkey, I started by getting up at 5:00 in the morning (not easy for a night owl and theatre professional). The house was dark and still. Not for an hour would the sun rise. Everyone in the house was asleep. Finding time of my own restored equilibrium to my life.

Soon after, I read a book about a Rule of Life that involved a classic traditional discipline of spirituality: the sacrament of the present moment. The idea of this practice is to be mindful and immerse the total self in the moment. It requires control from a multitasker like me. But, I began to undertake the exercise, and I realized no matter what I was doing, I could focus my attention on the chore, be mindful of the objects I handled, be grateful for life that allowed me to participate in the job, and somehow by doing so, to let go of anxiety and melancholy.

I would find myself looking forward to the drive to soccer practice or vacuuming the house instead of reluctantly and begrudgingly procrastinating about such tasks. When it was time to do the dishes or the clothes, I would — and, in fact, still do — find myself saying, Just go on and *"wash them, wash them!"* I was part of a stunning production of T. S. Eliot's *Murder in the Cathedral* in 1980, so as I wash items, this one entire speech of the chorus always crashes back to me: *"It is not we alone, it is not the house, it is not the city that is defiled, But the world that is wholly foul. Clear the air! clean the sky! wash the wind!"* And, as I carefully tend the task of scrubbing, somehow I also *"wash the brain, wash the soul, wash them, wash them!"*

January 8:

13

Santiago: Get me a calendar, I said. What's today's date?
Cheche: The twenty-first.
Santiago: How can it be the twenty-first when you've already crossed out the twenty-first on the calendar?
Cheche: That's how I do it.
Santiago: You've already crossed out today's date!
Cheche: I know.
Santiago: You might have a problem, Cheche.
Cheche: And what kind of problem do you think I might have?
Santiago: You are crossing out the new day before you start taking part in it.
Characters in Nilo Cruz's *Anna in the Tropics*

So we are already a week into the new year. Is anyone crossing off days? I had friends all through my child-rearing years who would say, "If my son would just get through the terrible twos, I would be fine." Or "I can't wait till this awkward pre-teen phase is over." Or "My life will be normal again when my teenagers stop this insurrection. When will they grow up?"

That is one approach to life I struggled to avoid: wishing mine and my children's life away. And I did relish every second of every age my daughter Elin and son Seth went through. Not that some ages and stages were not difficult. I cried many tears for many reasons, but I never wanted those days to just disappear. And I laughed a lot, too.

As a single mother for some of my parenting career, I certainly had struggles — late night calls about the car being broken down in a place it shouldn't have been, calls from principals about questionable hand gestures in school photos, heartbreaking game losses, prom disasters, and on and on. I remember going round and round with Seth when he was in college about whether or not jumping into quarries in his birthday suit with his friend Will was exactly the best decision he had ever made. (Looking back, I think maybe it actually was a good step toward the bold audacity and spunkiness he needed at the time.)

We all encounter life in tiny portions, and only occasionally glimpse the overall pattern of our existence. Each day gives me gifts in its details if I can just abide in them, the joys as well as the weeping and gnashing of teeth: the sleepless nights of the infant, the sudden expert dexterity of the fast-moving two year-old, the smart mouth of the butt-cut twelve year-old, the white knuckled driving lessons of the fifteen year-old, the face-smashing bicycle accident of the twenty-something.

Instead of crossing out the new day before I start taking part in it, at least for a couple of moments, I can cherish and value even the seemingly meaningless bits that create that unimaginably special life with my children. Now that they are both grown and out of the nest, I miss the endless visitors' days at the dance studio, the numbing hours of scrubbing blackened soccer socks back to white, the banner proclaiming me "Best Mom in the World," the scribbled notes left on the back steps stating where they were going to be. I would not trade any of even the frightening and outrageous moments for anything.

January 9:
Millie Owens: When I graduate from college I'm going to New York, and write novels that'll shock people right out of their senses. I'm never gonna fall in love. Not me! I'm not gonna live in some jerkwater town and marry some ornery guy and raise some grimy kids. But just because I'm a dope doesn't mean you have to be.
Madge Owens: Millie.
Millie Owens: Go with him, Madge.
Madge Owens: Millie?
Millie Owens: For once in your life, do something right.
Madge and Millie in William Inge's *Picnic*

I am not generally a "woulda coulda shoulda" sort of person. I have had many options in my life when I might have taken a left instead of a right turn. And I realize that many times when I made a decision what happened and what I wanted to have happen were strikingly at variance.

Though I do not really regret or dwell on such choices, a couple of the "other alternatives" are intriguing. Like Robert Frost's road not taken, splits in the path represent the crux of destiny and autonomy. Are we really choosing freely? On this side, we never really know what we are settling on — or settling for. So, what we pick is a combination of chance and choice.

When I was an art student in high school, my design was selected for a Loveman's window display competition when downtown department stores were still at their zenith in Birmingham, Alabama. The time was the mid-1960s and fashions were dominated by the British mod style: Mary Quant mini skirts, Twiggy false eyelashes and pale lipstick, bell-bottomed trousers, and Beatle-girl-friend-Liberty-print dresses. I was

15

a shoe nut and filling my closet were patent leather heels, knee high go-go boots, and Mary Janes in vibrant colors.

Besides having my fashion display sketch actually come to life in one of the store windows, I got to spend my entire spring break "working" during a fashion week at the retail giant. One of the celebrities who was in residence that week happened to be my favorite shoe designer, Mr. Sbicca. His company, which originated in Philadelphia in 1920, had moved to California following World War II. The Sbicca Brand was wildly popular in the 1960s and I had two pairs. As I traveled throughout the store doing odd jobs with the fashion crew that week, I ran into Mr. Sbicca a number of times, and one day, we had a lengthy conversation. I showed him some of my artwork and he liked my creations. He invited me to come to California and join his shoe design team. It was a family business, he said, and there was no one coming up among his relatives who wanted to go through the ranks of the company.

Wow! I was sixteen years old. How could I have possibly said, "Yes"? But how could I have possibly said, "No"? Not being an adult, my father would have been hard to convince. He wanted me to go to college. He wanted me to have an education and a future. I had heard it a million times. But, what would my destiny have been if I had taken Millie's path and shunned the family life or that career in a faraway place? What if like Madge I had "gone with him" — in this case "him" being the big kahuna boss? With my choice not to go, did I do something right or wrong, perfect or detrimental for my life? I will never, ever know for sure.

January 10

"Why, thinks King Henry's son that Margaret's love
Hangs in th' uncertain balance of proud time!"
Margaret in Robert Greene's *Friar Bacon and Friar Bungay*

Some historians suggest that on this day, January 10, in 1587, London businessmen Philip Henslowe (a dyer) and John Cholmley (a grocer) signed an agreement to build a playhouse above an old rose garden on the Bankside, near the south shore of the Thames. What became the Rose Theatre was the third large, permanent playhouse in London, and at the time, the only one in Southwark. By October of that year, the building was open to the public, for records show a complaint about plays being acted on the Sabbath. A few of Christopher Marlowe's and William Shakespeare's plays were most likely produced here. And for sure, Edward Alleyn's Admiral's Men presented Robert Greene's *Friar Bacon and Friar Bungay* at the Rose in 1592.

"*Margaret's love/Hangs in th' uncertain balance of proud time!*" This quote is about tenuousness in coronations and associations, power and politics. But any sort of balance is a funny thing. The dictionary defines the word as: an even distribution of weight enabling someone or something to remain upright and steady.

Balance is so fragile, and it can be so uncertain. The even distribution of weight can suddenly become lopsided, causing the someone or something to waver unsteadily, to collapse, topple over, and end horizontal, on the floor. I have known several people who have died recently from plummeting down a set of stairs after losing their equilibrium, and it seems horrifying to me that something so unremarkable and mundane as steps can execute so quickly.

Every day, I work on my steadiness and physical poise through Yoga. But if I congratulate myself on my balance, we all know pride goes before a fall, and I really do not want to topple over. I took a couple of minor spills a year or so ago, and thankfully ended up with only a bruise or two. My most spectacular fall ever was, harkening back to the quote, in England at a London tube terminal. I was holding my then three-year old son Seth as we threaded through metal crowd control barriers at the Goodge Street Station. I could tell what was going to happen as it unfolded, but there was nothing I could do to prevent the adventure. A blind lady was on the other side of the railing methodically moving her white-tipped cane to keep her bearings, but she abruptly jabbed it through the rails and between my feet just as we passed each other.

This was London, so rain had been falling and the floor of the station was wet. I tripped, then slipped, lunged, and fell to my knees, sliding literally a good thirty feet. At the end of my skid, I triumphantly held Seth up in the air, having spared any injury to the child. A number of people who were watching wide-eyed applauded. My pants knees were blackened, but what could have been a terrifically embarrassing moment ended up as "th' uncertain balance of proud time!"

January 11
"It is true, I have looked at you all this evening. Your beauty troubled me. Your beauty has grievously troubled me, and I have looked at you too much. But I will look at you no more. Neither at things, nor at people should one look. Only in mirrors should one look, for mirrors do but show us masks."

Oscar Wilde follows the gruesome biblical tale fairly closely: Herod, ruler of Galilee and Perea, divorces his first spouse to marry Herodias, his brother's wife. John the Baptist condemns the action, and though Herod is fascinated by the prophet, he arrests the baptizer. Herodias particularly despises John and when Herod throws a big party, his stepdaughter Salomé dances for him and "pleases" Herod so much, he offers to give her anything he wants — even up to half of his kingdom.

"I would that they presently bring me in a silver charger . . ." she says charmingly.

Herod answers, "O sweet and fair Salomé, you who are fairer than all the daughters of Judaea? What would you have them bring you in a silver charger?"

Pleasing her mother greatly, Salomé replies, "The head of Jokanaan." Herod finds the request exceedingly disturbing and clearly has second thoughts, but he goes through with the deed because of his oath and because he is reluctant to disappoint his dinner guests.

In Wilde's play, Herod confesses he had watched his niece, I mean step-daughter, too closely and he desperately begs the princess to free him of the vow. Feeling guilty, he believes Salomé may be punishing him since her beauty has grievously troubled him throughout the evening. He decides he just won't look at anybody or anything anymore. *"Only in mirrors should one look,* he says, *for mirrors do but show us masks."*

I have read scholars who say that Herod here chooses to be narcissistically captivated by his image in the glass which reflects the endless mockery, pretense, and masquerade of life. But what if suddenly he has had a flash of inspiration? What if he at least realizes that there is a veneer he hides behind every day? What if his brush with John the Baptist, who he describes as "man who has seen God," has revealed to Herod his own little, small, scared, false self?

The end of the play is chilling. Herod calls Salomé a monster and Herodias "the incestuous wife." Surely, he cries, "Some terrible thing will befall. Manasseh, Issachar, Ozias, put out the torches." He wants the palace to be in total darkness.

Then, maybe because now he really "sees," he repeats his vow: "I will not look at things. I will not suffer things to look at me. Put out the torches! Hide the moon! Hide the stars! Let us hide ourselves in our palace, Herodias. I begin to be afraid."

January 12

"Gee whiz! Other people's wives go down in the cellar. Why is it you never want to do anything together? I come home worn out from the office and you won't even go down in the cellar with me. God knows it isn't very far – it isn't as if I was asking to go to the movies or some place."
Mr. Preble in *"Mr. Preble Gets Rid of his Wife"* from James Thurber's Thurber Carnival

It is January, a new year, and I am inviting divine order into my life. I have just spent several days cleaning out my basement. For six years, my daughter, my son, Roger – my fiancé – and his daughter Laura Catherine have all used my lower floor, closets, and cupboards for retaining items they treasured during moves, cleaning out of mini storage units, year long mission trips, marriage, seminary, and other such escapades. My adventures, meanwhile, consisted of moving their furniture and boxes approximately one million times to get to something of mine that was behind something of theirs.

But now, most of their precious items are gone! So after cleaning out a good portion of the basement and filling six or eight bags and boxes to go to recycling today, I invited Roger down to see my neat work. He was watching football and did not want to accompany me. These lines from *Thurber Carnival* always come to mind when I ask someone to go downstairs to check something out. I change the words a bit to fit the occasion: *"Gee whiz! Other people's **friends** go down in the cellar. Why is it you never want to do anything together? I come **upstairs** worn out from the **cleaning** and you won't even go down in the cellar with me. God knows it isn't very far – it isn't as if I was asking to go to the movies or some place."*

One of the most renowned humorists of the twentieth century, James Thurber had a distinctive talent for unveiling the foibles of modern life in a peculiar and acerbic style. When we produced this show at Samford University, the theatre – arena-style – was still in the basement of the chapel with seating all around the stage area, so we literally had to invite the entire audience to "go down in the cellar" to watch the play. Audience members were surprised that Mr. Preble resolves to run off with his stenographer and murder his wife. The part of Mr. Preble was hilariously played by George, an expertly droll student comedian, and when he asked his wife to go t the basement, viewers could envision him taking her down into a spook smelly crypt of some sort.

Sometimes basement are dark, dank, and full of spider webs, creepy crawlers, and all sorts f abandoned objects. When my children were small and misbehaving w ile staying with my parents, my dad would always ask if they wanted to g downstairs to the "locker room to have a chat." The question filled tl m with trepidation and corrected their behavior immediately, even t ough their lower floor held nothing that was frightening.

Unlike Mr. Preble, I d not have ulterior motives — or a shovel concealed in the basement t hit Roger over the head — when I asked him to accompany me. And, I ctually had something to show him in the cellar: a view of the walls we l dn't seen in years!

January 13

PIERROT: *My love, by yon blac moon, you wrong us both.*
COLUMBINE: *There isn't a si of a moon, Pierrot.*
PIERROT: *Of course not. There ever was. "Moon's" just a word to swear by.*
Pierrot and Columbine in Ed a St. Vincent Millay's *Aria da Capo*

There is a huge, glowi ʒ, heavy, orange, expressive moon hanging over the mountain outside y window tonight. It looks like a paper lantern that might be used in very nonrealistic theatre piece, so it is not Pierrot's *"yon black moon."* An yet, the lines from this production come floating back to me.

Edna St. Vincent Mi ly was a lyrical poet and playwright who wrote Aria da Capo fairly ear in her career in 1919. First performed in the wake of World War I at e Provincetown Playhouse, the play both overtly protests war and yet su tly reveals deep thoughts about power and the universal human conditio . Featuring Greek-inspired pastoral scenes and Italian *commedia dell'art* characters, the drama (a forerunner of absurdism) is very modern nd expressionistic, alternating between realism and stylized theatrical y. Millay was a fascinating woman, known for her many bisexual love aft irs, as well as her avid feminist activism.

I fortunately discov ed this one-act play in college when upperclassmen performed it uring my freshman year and I was thrust into a new, sophisticated, ed cated, artistic, refined culture I had only vaguely glimpsed before. Suc as when in high school, I used to visit a beatnik joint where poetry w read and we snapped our fingers instead of applauding. Or when I ate Italian food in a basement restaurant where the only lights were candles in chianti bottles.

A couple of years after the *Aria da Capo* performance, I went on a theatre trip with fellow students to New York City and I saw *Jacques Brel Is Alive and Well and Living in Paris*. It gave me the same sorts of vibrations as *Aria da Capo* does even now. Perhaps this feeling was, and still is, a call to the Greenwich Village lifestyle of artistic bohemianism from the beatnik days: small bars, art shows, jazz, the shabby coziness of a corner deli, people of all colors and ethnic groups, active minds, vibrant hearts, lovers of the offbeat life.

The moon is so full tonight I will not sleep. If the moon can affect ocean tides and induce births, it can certainly be blamed for my poor sleep at this point in the lunar cycle each month. In new psychiatric experiments, tests seem to confirm that when the moon is full, our deep sleep brain activity plummets thirty percent, though no one can yet say just why.

While I am awake tonight, perhaps I will pull out a beret, play Puccini's *La Boheme*, and smoke that last little cigar from my pantry. Really, I wish I could take Pierrot and Columbine's words to heart and just go to sleep by pretending the moon isn't there: *"There isn't a sign of a moon, Pierrot... Of course not. There never was. 'Moon's' just a word to swear by."*

January 14
"I didn't go to the moon, I went much further – for time is the longest distance between two places."
Tom Wingfield in Tennessee Williams's *The Glass Menagerie*

Back with the moon, Tom's line is a reaction to his mother's words, *"Go then! Then go to the moon, you selfish dreamer."* After he utters his profound statement, Tom tells the audience that he "was fired for writing a poem on the lid of a shoe-box. I left Saint Louis," he says. "I descended the steps of this fire escape and followed, from then on, in my father's footsteps, attempting to find in great motion what was lost in space."

Tom is an interesting character in this play about memory, perhaps speaking a bit for Tennessee Williams himself, a writer who spent some of his younger days in St. Louis with an eccentric mother and mentally ill sister – and a father missing. Tom feels imprisoned in his life, and feels he must take flight; but ironically in fleeing, he never eludes the memory of his sister, Laura — power of his mother either. The concrete space between them that he so passionately longed for is meaningless, for they are with him always. Tom never frees himself of his memories, and part of him is ever captured in that shabby apartment.

I have friends who lived in my neighborhood during my early adolescence and high school days. We shared so many daily details of growing-up-hood: crushes on the Beatles, wearing mini skirts, going out on first dates, being stood up or second dates, monopoly games, trips to town on the bus, overnights, the differences in our parents. I don't think I could — or would — have matured into the person I am today without those friends, especially the sisters Sandra and Susan.

After World War II, some American playwrights were influenced by psychoanalysis and the ideas about memory and dreams of Carl Jung and his predecessor Sigmund Freud. The playwrights used memory as a literary device, along with complex character evolutions and convoluted plots. The term "memory play" was actually coined by Tennessee Williams in describing The Glass Menagerie. I studied the play in high school and thought I would never do anything other than create more memories forever and ever with those fabulous high school friends.

I did not endeavor, like Tom, to leave my friends behind. But somehow, sadly, during college and early marriage life, we drifted apart. They actually live fairly close to me, in physical distance. And yet I am actually less connected to them today than if we lived in separate countries. And like Tom, my memory of the time I spent with them haunts me as much as his recollections. Perhaps I should write a play...

January 15
"The envious will die, but envy never."
Madame Pernelle in Moliere's *Tartuffe*, (Act V, Scene 3)

Today is Jean-Baptiste Poquelin's — stage name: Moliere's — 391st birthday. His *Tartuffe* was one of my favorite plays to produce, contained some of my best-loved costumes to create, and was filled with one of my dearest groups of students: Paul and Mariann, Theresa, Sammy, Charles, Andy, Tammy. The themes in the piece deal with hypocrisy and deadly sins such as lust, greed, and pride — and there is some jealousy, too. And Madame Pernelle speaks of this envy as never dying.

Over the last year, I have studied and actually been certified by the Institute for Conscious Being to teach the Enneagram, an ancient wisdom system that uses a nine-sided figure to illustrate the compass of possible personality types. It is used by people who want to develop their awareness of the complexity of human nature and relationships, and is a very deep and enlightening spiritual tool.

I have discovered that I am beginning to be an integrated Four. In my earlier days, I was what I might call a flaming and broken Four (The Creator, Individualist, Romantic), which means that I was sensitive, melancholy, self-conscious, and temperamental — along with being creative, expressive, and special.

An unbalanced Four is overwhelmed with the desire to be different, and yet never feels truly authentic. For a long time, I searched for my true self in my own quest for the Holy Grail. What I found in my Enneagram studies was hard to swallow at first: the passion or deadly sin of a Four is envy. I never thought of myself as jealous or covetous. But, as a Four what I yearned for was the wonderful, genuine life I felt others were leading. I desired that real experience I saw in some people's professional or domestic situations. Everyone else was so much luckier than I. I was discontent and I spiraled downward.

I had already begun balancing myself before I learned about the Enneagram. Thriving Fours want to analyze their experiences and by doing so, come to terms with who they really are. Through many spiritual practices, I realized that I have a wonderful life and I could let go of negative feelings from the past. So Madame Parnelle is right in one way, envy will never die all over the planet. But it has, for the most part departed, from my life.

January 16

"There is nothing either good or bad, but thinking makes it so."
Hamlet in Shakespeare's *Hamlet*, Act II, Scene 2

Happy Birthday, Edward Henry Gordon Craig, born on January 16, 1872! He was the love child of an English architect, Edward Gordon, and the famous actress, Ellen Terry. Craig was a visionary scenic designer and also worked as an actor, director, and theatre critic. He became a reformer of stage design and his ideas of form and light were startling, though rarely followed. In the early 1900s, he settled in Florence and became a great craftsman. Later, he inaugurated the first international theatre publication, *The Mask* (1908–29), writing for it under numerous pseudonyms. This work spread his ideas worldwide with such groundbreaking articles as "The Actor and the Übermarionette." He greatly influenced our Samford University Theatre production of *Murder in the Cathedral* which Kennet Paul Shorey, reviewer for The *Birmingham News* held in high regard. Shoey had actually formed a close relationship with Craig before coming to Birmingham and had stories to tell about this great theatre character.

Craig created moving screens for the Konstantin Stanislavsky presentation of Hamlet at the Moscow Art Theatre in 1908, so thinking of that production put thoughts into my mind about lines from one of my favorite plays. I like thi quote about beliefs and thoughts and imaginings and visions. "*Why, hen, 'tis none to you, for there is nothing either good or bad, but thinking mak it so. To me it is a prison,*" Hamlet tells Rosencrantz and Guildenster. Nothing is actually bad or good in itself unless a person puts a judg ent on it. "*To me,*" he tells his friends, "*Denmark is a penitentiary.*"

Our minds really do g caught up in determining our moods, our emotions, our outlooks, o r views. Rain, traffic, hunger, insect infestation, internet disconn ction, theft, drought, murder. All these things happen. They simply e. Some of them we might all call really bad. Perhaps they are. We n amend or fix some of them. We can empathize with people goin through suffering. But many good and wonderful things happen eve day as well.

Today on Facebook, friend posted a quote by Ralph Waldo Emerson: "A man is what he inks about all day long." Building on this, one of my favorite modern th nkers Wayne Dyer said, "Not only do you become what you think about ut the world also becomes what you think about. Those who think that he world is a dark place are blind to the light that might illuminate t eir lives. Those who see the light of the world view the dark spots as erely potential light."

Just for the record, I hink Edward Henry Gordon Craig and Hamlet are really, really good

January 17

In "*The (Senatorial) Roll C ll*" from *Of Thee I Sing*, Alexander Throttlebottom takes the ro call of US Senators and confirms their presence in the chamber. (List n to the work online or from your library!)

Alexander Throttlebo om and the Senators from George and Ira Gershwin's *Of Thee I Sing!*

When we were students at the University of Montevallo, my friend, Joe Taylor, played Throttlebottom and got to sing the "The (Senatorial) Roll Call" in the Gershwin's parody of American politics, *Of Thee I Sing!* Imagine someone wanting to make a mockery of the power struggle and the shenanigans of the people running (or running for) our governmental operations. The plot revolves around John P. Wintergreen, a candidate who, while contending for the Presidency on the "love" platform, becomes infatuated with the levelheaded Mary Turner instead of falling for the beauty pageant winner selected for him, landing in a difficult political position. Hmmmm. Sounds all too modern and familiar.

The play was directed by a real character himself, Mr. W. T. Chichester. Born in 1913, Mr. Chi as we fondly called him, was 55 by the time I met him when I was a freshman in college. He was a gravelly-voiced, eyebrow-raising, cigarette-rolling fireball of a man who had produced United Service Organizations shows while serving in the army in World War II. As he told us, by the end of the war the USO was involved with something around 500 shows a day all over the world. Though not the top favorite with our students, *Of Thee I Sing!* was the first musical to earn a Pulitzer prize for drama and Mr. Chi really loved the "old chestnuts" from the 1930s, '40s, and '50s. We worked on *Show Boat* while I was a student, after talking him out of *Finian's Rainbow*.

W. T. Chichester was one of those people in my life who linked me to an era that was fading very quickly: a theatre where scene paint was mixed with animal glue, makeup was actually grease paint, and lighting was dimmed by huge levers mounted above the side of the stage. Costumes seemed to have a fragile inner glow to them and dressing rooms were heated by a network of rattling old pipes. Chi was in his element in the scene shop, on the stage (acting or directing), and in the classroom.

And he taught me about more than theatre: he gave lessons on how to care deeply about the quality of a show, how to laugh at the funny things that happen every day, how to tell a great story out of the memories of a lifetime, how to speak my mind directly yet kindly, how to pepper speech with colorful expressions, how to simply not be bothered when the names don't rhyme. Ah, Chi, I miss you so!

January 18
"I always longed to leave the brittle glamour of cities and theatre and find rest in some old-world nook."

Judith Bliss in Noel Coward's *Hay Fever*

Judith Bliss is Englis . Noel Coward is English. *Hay Fever* is English. For about 15 years i the late 1980s through 2001, I was lucky enough to go to London almo every January to teach a mini-term course at a Study Centre run by the college where I taught. So at this time of year, I am always homesick or London and look for English plays, documentaries, movies, and items to assuage my distress at being separated from my second ho e and my ancestral cradle.

A couple of years ago, designed costumes for *Hay Fever*, and that helped alleviate a little pain Sometimes I leaf through my A to Zed London city map or trace tub routes on a coaster I have. Looking at the Liberty of London sales onlir pep me up (not like actually being there, but I can drool over the fabr s). I can watch *Monty Python, Topsy Turvy*, or *Great Expectations*, listen to Winston Churchill radio address, or read *The Hobbit*.

But on a scale of one t ten, they help at a two-level, tops. Looking at brochures about the top att actions in London will suggest the Tower, the British Museum, the Vict ia and Albert, and the National Gallery — and yes, those places are aw inspiring. What I miss about my yearly London trips are the little thir s like wandering in neighborhoods. I have heard that London taxi drivei spend three years of advanced navigation training to get a license. The reets are not laid out in a square grid, the numbering makes very little nse, and as you traverse blocks, you will find many different names. E t that can be adventurous and fun if you give yourself time. I miss goii into a Boots Apothecary (or drug store) and exploring the different ki ds of botanics and skin care. I miss being able to purchase a Cadbury ca dy bar from a tube stop machine or small vendor. I miss the wide array of food items at Sainsbury's or Waitrose Groceries (including tiny cor ectioner sugar dusted mincemeat pies). I miss hearing Choral Evenson at Westminster Abbey, getting half-price theatre tickets at Leicester S quare, shopping at the Portobello Road market, quaffing a bitter or al or stout at a neighborhood pub, eating ice cream at the interval (intern ssion) of a musical, strolling beside the Thames. I can physically tire i yself out just thinking of it all.

Unlike Judith Bliss, I uess I really long to go back to the brittle glamour of theatre now that m not teaching. If I were still at Samford, in January I would easily cros the Atlantic again to roam that old-world nook of a city where I love t be, whether I am resting or worn out. I agree with Samuel Johnson who said, "When a man is tired of London, he is tired of life; for there is in London all that life can afford." I think he meant women, too — and he did say, "tired of" not "tired in" London!

January 19
"Undoubtedly; words give wings to the mind and make a man soar to heaven."
Pisthetaerus in Aristophanes's *The Birds*

My mother died last August exactly one month before her 85th birthday. She loved crossword puzzles and she would sit for hours with her feet on the couch and a crossword puzzle book on her vertical thighs racing through the pages. She could usually guess the word or phrase on the Wheel of Fortune television game show and until her final decade, she was a voracious reader.

She gave me a love for words and guided me in my early writing in elementary school, as she was an expert speller and a definition specialist. I became an insatiable reader and learner under her tutelage. She and my dad gave me an *Oxford English Dictionary* for my college graduation and for years, one of my favorite Christmas gifts from my mom was a Word-a-Day calendar. I loved them so much, I stored them in a colorful box so I could peruse some of the words from bygone years at my leisure.

Mom could turn a colorful phrase herself. "TaDa!" was one of her favorite expressions as she entered a room, solved a mystery, discovered a lost object, or presented a new recipe piping from the oven. If the weather was freezing, it was *"colder than a witch's tit."* If an occurrence seemed impossible, she would lament *"that it will happen the day I stand on my head in the middle of 20th Street,"* Birmingham's busiest thoroughfare. If she had gone too long without a meal, she would reckon, *"I could eat the stuffed rear-end off a Raggedy Ann doll."* And if someone put a dint in a piece of silver or scratched some furniture, she would opine, *"Well, don't worry. That's just what memories are made of."*

So many of my memories of my mother revolve around words — words I now wish I could hear her voice utter. I love this quote from *The Birds*, a wonderful play that I directed and designed in 1984. *"Undoubtedly, words give wings to the mind and make a man (or woman!) soar to heaven,"* like a bird no less.

January 20

Milt: What did you get for break[fa]*st?*
Harry: At home?
Milt: At home.
Harry: A glass filled with two-thi[rd]*s water and one-third milk.*
Milt: Coffee-grinds, that's what I [g]*ot.*
Harry: With sugar?
Milt: Not on your life. I ate it st[ra]*ight, like oatmeal.*
Milt and Harry in Murray Sch[i]sgal's *Luv*

Talk about two peopl[e] with half empty glasses! Murray Schisgal's *Luv* is an absurdist dark com[e]dy about two old college buddies who re-bond when Milt Manville thw[a]rts Harry Berlin's attempt to jump from a bridge. The reason Milt wants [t]o save Harry is so that he can interest him in his wife Ellen, leaving Mil[t] the opportunity to flee with his mistress. Talk about dark Jewish humo[r]!

In the Jewish Old Te[st]ament, many of the psalms are dark and despairing; but many are ho[pe]ful and buoyant. Psalm 81 proclaims: "I am Yahweh, your God, who [b]rought you up out of the land of Egypt. Open your mouth wide, and I [w]ill fill it." This idea is quite different from the glass half empty, whether [t]hat glass is filled with wine, lemonade or two-thirds water and one-thir[d] milk!

I remember saying, ["]Yes!" when Don Sandley, the chair of Samford University Theatre, [a]sked me to design costumes for *Intimate Apparel*, a play he was directin[g] at our local Birmingham Festival Theatre. Even knowing that going thr[ou]gh this process would be hard — having not designed a show for a co[u]ple of years — I said, "Yes!" At the time, I worked long hours at The A[m]erican Village, and this costume project took up valuable evening and [w]eekend time. BFT is a community theatre, so the work was volunteer; [b]ut even so, I said, "Yes!" And with the sacrifice and effort that were [ne]cessarily a part of such creative work came intense satisfaction and delig[h]t. On opening night, the stage brimmed with apparel (both intimate [a]nd otherwise) that had only been in my mind just weeks before. Sayin[g] "Yes!" both drained me and filled me up.

To part my lips and fi[ll] my mouth overflowing is a metaphor for my life with the Divine. The [c]ommand suggests two things. The first is fairly obvious: I have to take [ac]tion to open my lips, and if I do so, I am then in relationship with the [L]ife Giver. If I open, God will fill. I can, on the other hand, refuse to f[ol]low the command, decline to open my mouth, and repudiate the bond. I could have said, "No!" to the director. I can say, "No!" to the Divine.

The second implication is subtler: If I do what the Lord asks (to open wide my mouth), I may find that orifice overflowing with all kinds of things. In other Psalms and Biblical passages, God satisfies the thirsty and fills the hungry with good things. But here is no promise that my mouth will overflow with Turkish Delights. And that is how life is: to fully experience existence on this earth, we have to open our eyes, our ears, our noses — and our mouths — to be filled by all encounters. But we never know what that openness will bring.

Let's not be afraid to also open our hearts, minds, and spirits with our mouths — and have them filled, maybe even with coffee-grinds!

January 21
"You bubble-mouthing, fog-blathering,
chin-chuntering, chap-flapping, liturgical,
Turgidical, base old man!"
Thomas in Christopher Frye's *The Lady's Not for Burning*

An interesting Old Testament story is Jeremiah's call. Jeremiah says God told him that even before he was formed in the womb, God consecrated him as a prophet to the nations. Jeremiah's response was to dodge the summons. He did not exactly say, *"You bubble-mouthing chap-flapping old man,"* but he did his best to opt out. "Behold, I don't know how to speak; for I am a child." But the Lord told him, "Don't say, 'I am a child;' for you must go to whomever I send you, and you must say whatever I command you." Some translations read something like "for I am just a boy."

This passage reminds me of a story from my past. In 1979, I had been designing costumes for three years at my university. Though I had worked in the theatre for ten years, my degrees were in art and English, and sometimes I felt "unqualified" for my job. The theatre department took *The Lady's Not for Burning* to Troy, Alabama for an American College Theatre Festival competition, directed by Harold Hunt, our longtime department chairman. Along with other state designers, I displayed my costume drawings for the play in the theatre lobby.

As faculty from Alabama's colleges gathered to chat with our nationally renowned adjudicators, we all introduced ourselves around a circle, and as some professors noted degrees from Yale and the Goodman

29

School, I felt out of my league. When my turn came, I said, "I'm just the staff costume designer at Sanford." One of the judges actually jumped up out of his seat and said, "No, my goodness! You are not just anything! Don't ever use the word 'just' again. Your designs are wonderful, and they would stand up to anything I've seen in New York. The word 'just' is now banished from your vocabulary!"

I have often remembered the scenario and have bitten my tongue to keep from saying, "I am just this," or "I am only that." If you think about it, Moses was just an adopted boy, and on top of that, he had a speech impediment. So did Winston Churchill and George VI of England, so how could they amount to anything? George Washington had only eight years of schooling. Shakespeare was just a country bumpkin from Stratford-on-Avon. Stephen Hawking is only a guy in a wheelchair with a motor neuron disease. Examples like this go on and on.

Too many people in all professions and walks of life introduce themselves as "just a chef," "just a vet tech," "just a librarian." Like Jeremiah, we are all called to consider orders God gave us before we were even formed in the womb. We might protest we are too tired or too busy, too old or even too young. I may be "only a girl." You may be "only a boy" — and from Birmingham, or Poughkeepsie, or Podunk at that. However, I can value my work, respect myself, give myself credit, and jubilantly say, "I am the costume designer of THAT show!"

January 22

"Oh, you unhappy man!

May you never find out who you really are!"
Jocaste in Sophocles's *Oedipus Rex*

When I used to go out on dates or excursions with friends in high school, my mother would caution me as I scooted out the door, "Remember who you are!" She meant by this expression that I was not to dare do anything that would bring shame, disgrace, embarrassment, or even discomfort to my parents or my preceding generations of ancestors, going back 15 generations in time. Jocaste's advice to her husband (or is it her child?) is the opposite: "*May you never find out who you really are!*"

Our Samford University production of *Oedipus Rex*, featuring Tom Key in the title role, was a haunting and ritualistic rendition, full of miasmic fog, a wailing chorus choreographed with beating staves, heroic costumes, and strong actors. It made the play one of my top five favorites of all time. Oedipus was a man who certainly thought he knew who he was. Through a series of conversations and events, the king finds that either cursed by destiny or plagued by his own rash actions and hubris, he has unknowingly murdered father and married his mother. This situation is not what any of us would care to discover.

Who am I? We all wonder that, right? Who am I and why am I on this earth at this time, in this place, in this body?

I used to tell my Theatre Appreciation students that the arts and this theatre class they were taking could help them answer the question: Who am I? One of the most disheartening moments of teaching was when a freshman girl came to me after the first class and assured me that she knew who she was. Her parents had firmly instructed her in her ancestry and what she should be doing with her life.

After we explored many characters in many plays, walked in their shoes, found empathy by exploring their lives, looked through their eyes, and experienced their joys and tribulations, she came to me at the class's end. One of the most remarkable moments of teaching was when she told me that she had been mistaken at the first of the semester. She was only beginning to realize what she had to learn about who she was, and she was thankful that I had helped open her eyes to that fact. Like Oedipus, she thought she knew. At least she did not have to be physically blinded to be able to see how little we all really know until we start to consider the questions.

January 23
"The past is the present, isn't it? It's the future too."
Mary Tyrone in Eugene O'Neill's *Long Day's Journey Into Night*

I was fortunate enough to see a "Broadway Preview" performance of this Eugene O'Nell play staged at Duke University in March of 1986. My former student, Sammy Ledbetter was working for Emanuel Azenberg (whom he called "Manny") and the company offered a soft opening of the New York production of *A Long Day's Journey Into Night* at the private North Carolina school. The show, directed by Jonathan Miller, starred Jack Lemmon and Kevin Spacey, and Lemmon's interpretation of Tyrone defied the traditional approach. He made the patriarch into a "decent man with some indecent traits" as he said, because he understood the character.

When I think about the play, now, it becomes very present. I recall many details of the show and the trip to see it. My 10-year old daughter was flying to meet my then-husband and me, because we had driven up to attend a theatre conference in a nearby city just before the preview. She wanted to see the play, and she wanted to see one of her favorite former student-friends, Sammy. While waiting for her arrival in the Raleigh-Durham Airport, we were paged: "Would the persons who are meeting traveler Elin Olson please report immediately to the passenger information desk? Would the persons who are meeting traveler Elin Olson please report immediately to the passenger information desk?"

I can feel the panic that swept over me at this instant: weak knees, pounding heart, dry mouth, spinning brain. Did her plane crash? Was she kidnapped? Did she fall and break a leg? No, upon arriving at the desk, we found her plane was delayed. The past is living in me now as I think of this incident. And the past is living in me as I look back on the time I had at Samford with so many of my students; but now I'm thinking of Sammy — selling tickets in the box office, working on headpieces in the costume shop, sorting mailings in the dressing rooms, sitting in the dark auditorium watching a production grow from sure disaster to unrestrained success, bringing to life Look Homeward, Angel, The Servant of Two Masters, Pilgrim, Oedipus Rex, The First and Second Shepherd's Plays, The Mousetrap, Oliver! The Skin of Our Teeth, Tartuffe, Murder in the Cathedral, The Lady's Not For Burning, The Artful Antics of the Disguised Gypsies, The Playboy of the Western World, Dracula. What a lineup we created together! I can hear lines, see costumes, recall lighting cues — and even bring to mind director's notes.

Frederick Buechner has said, "But there is a deeper need yet, I think, and that is the need - not all the time, surely, but from time to time — to enter that still room within us all where the past lives on as a part of the present, where the dead are alive again, where we are most alive ourselves to turnings and to where our journeys have brought us. The name of the room is Remember — the room where with patience, with charity, with quietness of heart, we remember consciously to remember the lives we have lived." The plays we have done, the characters we have brought to life, the Sammys who have touched us — the past which is the present.

January 24

"To lose one parent, Mr. Worthing, may be regarded as a misfortune; to lose both looks like carelessness."
Lady Bracknell in Oscar Wilde's *The Importance of Being Earnest*

Today is my birthday and just five months ago, I lost my mother. My father died in 2003, so this past Christmas and this birth anniversary are the first such holidays I have spent as an outright orphan. On the one hand, Lady Bracknell's pronouncement is hilarious, because it is a preposterous play on the word "lose" — as if Mr. Worthing has misplaced his parental units by inattentiveness or irresponsibility rather than death. But my situation, being deprived of both progenitors, makes her words cold-hearted, insensitive, and unconcerned. And well, that is Lady Bracknell, right? While she is funny and memorable, Wilde created her as a satire on Victorian upper-class superiority and callousness.

My dad faced two years of kidney disease and dialysis before his passing. A month before he died, my mom and I could tell he was giving up the good fight and his will to live. We took him to the beach for our usual family vacation and he was buried two weeks after we returned. My son Seth went off to college the day after the funeral, and I thus "lost" the two men most important to me in a 24-hour period.

My mother somehow ambled into dementia the last three years of her life. She caught pneumonia last spring and was hospitalized. Then, she fell and broke her hip at the end of May. When she was recovering in the rehabilitation wing of an assisted living facility, I visited her one day and realized she was no longer the person who gave birth to me, reared, coddled, pampered, tended, protected, and befriended me. I almost could not drive home, I was sobbing so violently. Gone were her planning trips to the Florida panhandle, wrapping Christmas presents in October, standing on her head to show off, cooking wondrous cheesy hot casseroles, peppering her dialogues with colorful expressions, performing funny little dances from room to room, adoring her grandchildren and great-grandchildren.

She still knew my name and that I was her daughter. She still knew all of our family members' names, and she even asked about people not present. But there was a blankness in her eyes and increased difficulty actually forming words to speak. And she loved words! There was a tottering in her gait and a propensity for falling or sinking. She simply was not Jean anymore. She was always infatuated with looking for shells

33

at the beach — and now she was like the shell of a conch that no longer has a critter living in it.

This day last year, she gave me a set of eggplant-colored dishes that she somehow found the ability to order from a catalogue. She was so very excited about her purchase, and though another set of dishes was not something I desperately needed, I adore them because they were the last gift she ever actually picked out for me. In my favorite color, purple. I think I will go set the table with them now and find some of her shells for a centerpiece.

January 25

"She should have died hereafter;
There would have been a time for such a word.
Tomorrow, and tomorrow, and tomorrow,
Creeps in this petty pace from day to day
To the last syllable of recorded time,
And all our yesterdays have lighted fools
The way to dusty death. Out, out brief candle!
Life's but a walking shadow, a poor player
That struts and frets his hour upon the stage
And then is heard no more: it is a tale
Told by an idiot, full of sound and fury,
Signifying nothing."
Macbeth in William Shakespeare's *Macbeth*, Act V, Scene 5

People in the theatre call this "the Scottish play," so a quote from this Shakespearean tragedy is appropriate on January 25, birthday of Scottish poet Robert Burns. When I was in high school, I was assigned this passage to memorize, so it has been stored in the banks of my mind for a long time.

Back then, I just called the play *Macbeth*. It wasn't until I started working in the theatre that I realized there is a superstition surrounding the tragedy. Theatre folks believe that speaking the name "*Macbeth*" inside a theatre (except during rehearsal or performance) will bring bad luck, if not catastrophe, upon the performance. Two theories exist to explain this. One is that Shakespeare used "actual" witches' curses for the three Weird Sisters, and in retaliation, real witches cast a spell on the play.

A more plausible explanation is that during the premier of *Macbeth* on August 7, 1606, Hal Berridge, the young boy who played Lady Macbeth, became feverish and died backstage. Tradition claims that Shakespeare himself took over the part. That death hexed the play and initiated a long line of disasters surrounding it. Many misadventures have been documented, including an accidental stabbing with a real (rather than stage) dagger, fire, violent storms, riots, scenery collapsing, actors' strikes, and muggings, to name a few.

I know a number of directors who are, therefore, wary to produce this play, which is a shame. Just hearing a fine actor give voice to one of the greatest soliloquies of all time would be worth the price of a theatre seat. In this speech, Macbeth has lost everything. Lady Macbeth has just committed suicide and enemies surround his castle signifying a sure defeat. His nihilist attitude is understandable, and he ponders what is, for him, the meaningless of life and the frenetic passing of time. He wanted to achieve greatness and power so much that he murdered and cheated and double-crossed for gain.

Macbeth believes that even if he did shine like a candle briefly, he is ultimately on his way to dusty death, with his wife's departure before him. He pictures his existence as cursory, with as little significance as a minor actor agonizing over his part, and who, after leaving the stage, is never heard of again.

Yet is our time on earth nothing more than empty illusion *"full of sound and fury,"* and devoid of meaning? While searching the internet for research on this monologue, I discovered a clip of Patrick Stewart's 2010 BBC delivery of the speech. That two minutes of performance by itself reveals that theatre has substance; in turn, just the meaning and such a force of talent coming from playwright and actor convinces me that life has significance. And, a moving spirit behind, beyond, and within everything gives us all value and greatness if we are willing to accept it. Unfortunately Macbeth had an aberrant agenda that numbed him to this kind of power.

January 26

"I remember a time when a cabbage could sell itself by being a cabbage. Nowadays it's no good being a cabbage – unless you have an agent and pay him a commission. Nothing is free anymore to sell itself or give itself away. These days, Countess, every cabbage has its pimp."
Ragpicker in Jean Giraudoux's *The Madwoman of Chaillot*

In the spring of 1985, I designed the quirky *Madwoman of Chaillot*, written by French playwright, Jean Giraudoux in 1943. It is filled with an odd conglomeration of characters, so it was fun to costume. In a way, the piece is dated and outmoded but in another way, the satiric message is perhaps fresher than the day it was written. Unfortunately Giraudoux died before he saw the play produced.

A group of corporate executives — strangers to each other — meet in the Café de l'Alma, in the Chaillot district of Paris, to form a company to dig under the streets of Paris. There, they believe they will discover oil. In doing so, they will basically destroy the city to achieve their goal (or is that gold?). Accidentally, their vile scheme is discovered by the eccentric Countess Aurelia, the madwoman of the Chaillot neighborhood.

A romantic dreamer bubbling with hope, the countess is advised by her confidant the Ragpicker that these wicked men might just ruin the entire world in their search for power and money. She resolves to get rid of such evil by having a tea party at her apartment which is filled with an accumulation of treasures. One by one, the wicked entrepreneurs are tempted to lunge into a bottomless pit that smells of oil, undoubtedly never to be seen again.

When this play was written in the 1940s, the world was encountering the advent of subliminal, manipulative advertising created to lure the public into spending money, buying products, and becoming brand loyal. *"Every cabbage has its pimp,"* as the character says.

Lately, I am largely ignoring advertising in an effort to cultivate contentment for what I have and reduce my personal consumption. Every day, I ask for simplicity and divine order to enter my life as I attempt to eliminate excess and waste. As I accumulate less "stuff," I am able to save money for charitable giving and projects, trips and the arts.

Most spiritual traditions assert that a human's value is inherent as a child of God, and not to be judged by wealth or possessions. People who have riches are encouraged to share them. Not that prosperity is bad, but hoarded money impedes energy. Dollars are best in circulation, benefiting many people as they go in and out of pockets. But American secular consumerism would have us believe that any extra money should be rapidly spent on high-fat hamburgers and teeth-whitening mouthwash, luxurious cars and insurance sold by a ridiculous lizard. And, if we don't have extra funding, then credit cards and debt are the perfect solution.

If someone were to ask me, "What is your life about?" I certainly don't want an answer that includes how much stuff I have rather than how many people or causes I have helped, books read, art experienced, music heard. Experts say that you can tell a person's priorities in life by looking at her checkbook. Lately, I have taken that observation to heart.

January 27
"On the page it looked nothing. The beginning simple, almost comic. Just a pulse – bassoons and basset horns – like a rusty squeezebox. Then suddenly – high above it – an oboe, a single note, hanging there unwavering, till a clarinet took over and sweetened it into a phrase of such delight! This was no composition by a performing monkey! This was a music I'd never heard. Filled with such longing, such unfulfillable longing, it had me trembling. It seemed to me that I was hearing the very voice of God."
Salieri in Peter Shaffer's *Amadeus*

Wolfgang Amadeus Mozart was born on this day in 1756, so as you are reading this, add up the years to see which birthday it is. SiriusXM satellite radio's Symphony Hall promises to have a Mozart Marathon and be "all about Mozart all day."

His middle name means *"God's love"* in Latin and Mozart really is an amazing example of being a creative conduit of the Holy Spirit. He was an audacious — even sometimes called an "obscene" — person who is still the vessel of God. So if Mozart wasn't "perfect" and could still be a conduit for the holy, that gives me a lot of hope.

In the play, Salieri is astonished as he looks over Mozart's original scores, with no touch ups and a perfection of melody, and the thought comes to him that Mozart is the proof that God exists. Mozart himself once said music, which arrived in whole compositions, came through, not to him.

Alfred Tomatis was an audio expert who used alternative medical theories of hearing and listening to support opera singers as well as autistic children. He employed the music of Mozart to target diverse disorders and described the composer as "endowed with a 'cerebral transistor' able to capture what the creation and the environment were dictating to him." Tomatis said Mozart used music to express himself — or really, even more remarkably, to convey what he received from somewhere else - and was able to deliver to the world from the depths of his own being. He called the music of Mozart "a celestial message" and he remarked that, "Mozart's musical phrases transport us and immerse us in a different state (trance-like) which is in fact our original state — a state in which this prodigious being lived in permanence."

I know I will never reach creative expression on the magnitude that Mozart did. But that is no reason to bottle up what is inside of me — or to block what is outside and comes through me — because I might fail, I might not measure up. So today as I listen to the Mozart Marathon, I will invoke holy spirits to be the kind of conduit Mozart was.

January 28
"It's cold."
Dinosaur and Wooly Mammoth in Thornton Wilder's *The Skin of Our Teeth*

An appropriate quote for today is: *"It's cold."* For the fourth or fifth time since the beginning of this month, the temperature has gone below 20 degrees — in Birmingham, Alabama! And today, on top of cold, we got snow, which was forecast north of us and south of us, but not here. Flakes began falling at 9:00 this morning while everyone was at work or school — and by noon, traffic was impossible with several inches of white precipitation on the roads. I am keeping my twin 11-month old grandsons as I do each Tuesday, and my daughter Elin had to walk two miles in the frigid weather to make it to my house. I guess we will be holed up here together for a day or so.

A two-year old Elin was terrified and yet fascinated by the Dinosaur and Wooly Mammoth when we produced *The Skin of Our Teeth* in 1978. How delightful to be able to create these glacial period animals to romp about in a play set in early twentieth century New Jersey! Wilder makes the point that history always cycles back around. Early in the action, the hero Mr. Antrobus is inventing things like the wheel, the multiplication tables, and the alphabet. And the weather is getting as cold as the Ice Age. The maid Sabina begins the play telling the audience: "Here it is the middle of August and the coldest day of the year. It's simply freezing; the dogs are sticking to the sidewalks." And the first act ends with refugees seeking shelter at the Antrobus house. Theatre seats are sacrificed to make a fire for such arrivals as the Old Testament's Moses, the Greek poet Homer, and women who embody the Muses.

I love the play just a little less than *Our Town*. It is even more theatrical, and it has a favorite theme of human endurance. Despite setbacks of wars, natural disasters, and other catastrophes, people stay on an upward spiral as we inch up the levels of consciousness development. Wilder had begun writing *Skin* just before Pearl Harbor and ended his work a few weeks after the attacks. He actually missed the New York premier of his show on November 18, 1942 because he was on overseas duty as an army intelligence officer.

The Antrobuses have to endure glacial temperatures, talks of divorce, a biblical flood, and a devastating war — in fact, the end of the world seems near — but the family lives on. Sabina repeats much of her opening dialogue and then comes down to the edge of the stage and says: "This is where you came in. We have to go on for ages and ages yet. You go home. The end of this play isn't written yet. Mr. and Mrs. Antrobus! Their heads are full of plans and they're as confident as the first day they began, — and they told me to tell you: good night." I love the fact that the action ends where it began. History is always repeating itself and despite one disaster after another, humans miraculously reconstruct their lives and help the world at least partly right itself again.

So here we are at the end of January. If there were any dogs outside in my neighborhood, they would definitely be sticking to the sidewalk. I wouldn't be surprised to see a Dinosaur and Wooly Mammoth in the yard. Elin, upon arriving at the house, would be enchanted — and a tiny bit scared.

January 29
In "On the Street Where You Live" from *My Fair Lady*, Freddy Eynsford-Hill sings about seeing a thoroughfare differently when he knows his beloved lives on the road. (Listen to the work online or from your library!)
Freddy Eynsford-Hill in Alan Jay Lerner's and Frederick Loewe's *My Fair Lady*, based on *Pygmalion*, a play by George Bernard Shaw

My Fair Lady is a favorite musical of mine — the story, the setting, the characters, the music. But today, after the snow of yesterday, and 24 hours with the twins, George and Arthur, we required diapers. I volunteered to plod to the closest drug store two miles away and make the needed purchases. I walk just about every single day of my life. But as I did so today, a novel use of some of Loewe's lyrics came to me and I sang about often walking this particular street I was trudging up, but hoping now that the street remained beneath my feet. "Please let it do so now!" I added, as I did not want to slip in the icy snow, fall, and have to call 911.

Unfortunately, most of us are not used to walking even short spans in our ordinary rounds. To get to my destination today, I had to cross a busy highway, so under normal circumstances, I would drive there. Today, I had to trust that the unskilled snow drivers would not skid into me as I carefully hoofed it across the frozen thoroughfare — and I made it home safely.

And we moderns rarely walk journeys of far distances. In medieval times, many people ambled days or weeks to arrive at special holy places to find solace or have illnesses cured. Many religions have such spots — birthplaces of saints, martyrdom sites, or "thin places" where the boundary between heaven and earth is dissolved. Beloved English Queen Eleanor of Castile died in 1290, and her husband Edward I had twelve wooden crosses erected in her memory. Later, they were replaced by grandly decorated stone monuments, three of which survive. They originally marked the spots of the nightly stops along the way when her body was transported to London from Harby where she fell ill. Tracing the sites of these twelve crosses is said to be the most romantic pilgrimage in England.

I would enjoy moving by foot more in my daily routine, but in contemporary suburbia, that is not easy. Around sunrise, I walk just about every weekday in my neighborhood as part of my morning practice. On weekends, I take longer strolls after driving to local gardens, hiking paths, and parkways. On several occasions I have tripped, but, seemingly bolstered by unseen angels, did not fall. Something about the experience of long strolls keeps me grounded.

I have decided to purposefully be a pilgrim even on everyday excursions. I look at my daily walking as first aid for the journey of life. On a walk, I can see what is wry, search for the holy, live in the now, sort through feelings, think out problems, create plans. And if my angels continue to accompany me, maybe the pavement will remain beneath my feet, whether the weather involves snow, ice, rain, or sun.

January 30
"Oh, the night it is cold,
And there's no one here to hold ~
Far away, oh, so far from my home.
Gone away, gone to stay,

For a thousand lonely days,
I'm so far, oh, so far from my home."
Male Singer in Edgar Lee Masters' *Spoon River Anthology*, conceived, adapted, and arranged by Charles Aidman

In the spring of 1984, I was full of life — two lives, in fact. I was pregnant with my second child Seth, and looking forward to the birth, and new vitality and animation in my life. In contrast, we performed the haunting *Spoon River Anthology* all about the dead citizens of the little town of Spoon River. In both the Edgar Lee Masters book and the stage adaptation, these people are energetic and verbal as they look back on their lives with a sort of longing for what might have been. Numerous townspeople recall triumphs and losses of their time on earth. And as they reflect on dreams, secrets, and regrets, they paint a realistic and unidealized view of existence in a small rural town.

Some of the folks talk about their village of Spoon River in an unflattering light, but others feel that the separation is too great, and they yearn for their home turf. A lovely 1899 painting by Portuguese artist José Ferraz de Almeida Júnior is called "*Saudade.*" This word really has no faithful English translation, but means something like "longing" — like the aching some of Masters' characters feel for their birthplace. In Júnior's portrait, a lady by an open window holds a black shawl to cover her mouth. Her other hand clasps a letter that is causing her to shed tears.

Wikipedia online encyclopedia says that the Portuguese and Galician word *saudade* "describes a deep emotional state of nostalgic or profound melancholic longing for an absent something or someone that one loves. Moreover, it often carries a repressed knowledge that the object of longing may never return. A stronger form of saudade may be felt towards people and things whose whereabouts are unknown, such as a lost lover, or a family member who has gone missing."

In Brazil, people actually celebrate a day of *Saudade* on January 30, and I think I will likewise begin to honor this feeling of "the love that remains" when someone or something has been buried or lost. With *saudade*, I can still recall wonderful emotions of joy and comfort that I once experienced with certain people, I can relive the enthusiasm and enchantment of special occasions from the past. If observed correctly, saudade can make that person or event live again. Though I might feel sad about the actual absence, at the same time I can sense contentment, not only from the original feeling, but also from the imagined reunion.

So today, I have sau ade of that spring in 1984 when I had camaraderie with a group of s me of my most delightful students, of the melancholic and moving pre duction of *Spoon River Anthology*, of the miracle of a life growing withi me, of spending the last few months with an eight-year old daughter as m y only child, of my prenatal class exercising to Boy George singing "Ka ma Chameleon," of fluffy hairdos and sneakers with slouch socks an leggings, of Doc Marten shoes and Laura Ashley dresses. There! I just i ade all of that alive again. I have intense gratitude not only for this n w word I have learned, but also for the experiences and people I will l e able to revisit with a just a little intention and some *saudade*.

January 31
"Cowards die many times before t eir deaths; The valiant never taste of death but once.
Of all the wonders that I yet ha e heard, it seems to me most strange that men should fear;
Seeing that death, a necessary en , will come when it will come."
Caesar to Calphurnia in W liam Shakespeare's *Julius Caesar* (Act II, Scene II).

This quote has intrigu d me since I studied *Julius Caesar* in high school. I have never been a pa ticularly fearful person, but I do not know how courageous I am on a un versal scale. For a while, I thought Caesar was surely talking about imp ortant people like himself, who invaded England and fought battles an l crossed the Rubicon. But, then I realized we common folk need courag as well.

Last year was a hug growth spurt for me, spiritually and emotionally. I learned more a bout being brave than maybe ever before. Sometime in early March, got introduced to the Oprah Winfrey Network's *Super Soul Sunday* eekly program, and I encountered Brené Brown during two of Oprah's nterviews. She was talking about her book *Daring Greatly: How the Coura e to Be Vulnerable Transforms the Way We Live, Love, Parent, and Lead*. B fore this talk, I had not really considered how being vulnerable, auth ntic, and open took courage and great daring. But it does!

Brené Brown is curren ly a research professor at the University of Houston Graduate College of social Work, and much of her investigative studies have been done on sl ame and on wholehearted living. She has grown wildly popular through her Oprah interviews, Ted Talks, and public speaking over the last year or two. By chance, I met Dr. Brown when she was present to receive an honorary degree as my son graduated from Seminary of the Southwest in Austin, and she is a genuine, lively, vibrant individual.

Imagining how captivating Dr. Brown's instruction would be, I enrolled in a web-based Life Class sponsored by the Oprah Winfrey Network. Using her book *The Gifts of Imperfection*, thousands of us students learned to set intentions, get deliberate, become inspired, and take action. We worked in an art journal, painting, photographing, and writing about experiences; looked at ourselves as children; developed self-compassion; practiced gratitude; cultivated joy; and performed many other helpful exercises.

Through the process, we found out that: "Knowing that you can be brave and scared at the same time — that's what courage really is." One assignment was to generate a personal authenticity mantra and mine became: "Fear not. You are right where you should be." This saying helps me remember that whether I am succeeding or failing, I am learning and becoming more of my true essence, my soul child. Fear only gets in the way of moving along the path of life. As we did this exercise, we were also to find a favorite quote, and I rediscovered: "Be who you is, cuz if you be what you ain't, then you ain't what you is" from Joseph Campbell's *The Hero's Journey*.

More and more, through this class and continuing on my learning journey, I am discovering courage, valor, boldness, and fearlessness. I am discovering the deepest part of myself, and I am following.

February 1
"Why, what's the matter,
That you have such a February face,
So full of frost, of storm and cloudiness?"
Don Pedro to Benedick in William Shakespeare's *Much Ado About Nothing*, Act V, Scene 4

Here we are already into February, the second and shortest month of the year. This February first certainly did not dawn here in Birmingham full of frost and storm and cloudiness. After weather in the single digits and a paralyzing snowstorm this past week, the temperature in the lovely South is sixty-five degrees and the sun is shining brightly.

People are giddily wearing shorts and sandals and short-sleeved T-shirts. Everyone is out buying groceries and celebrating.

And there is plenty to make merry about this month: February is Heart Month, Black History Month, and I suppose since George Washington's Birthday is the 22nd, it is also National Cherry Month and National Children's Dental Month owing to legends concerning the Father of our Country cutting down a cherry tree and having a mouth full of wooden teeth.

Looking over the coming celebrations for the month fills me with reasons to feel silly and giddy and delighted that our freak weather has rolled on. People worldwide have created some improbable commemorations. February seventh is "Wave All Your Fingers at Your Neighbor Day," something I can hardly wait to do. The sixteenth is "Do a Grouch a Favor Day," which I already practice almost daily with a couple of people in my life. With grandchildren, I don't have to wait until February 26 for "Tell a Fairy Tale Day."

Many people here in Birmingham will be telling their descendants "Once upon a January 28th" snow tales for a long, long time. The "dusting" of snow forecast that turned into a three-day lock-in gave Birminghamians a chance to reach out and help one another. There are stories of pulling cars from ditches and people from ravines; folks traversing 20 miles on foot or in ATV and four-wheel drive vehicles to reunite with family members; neighbors sharing food, blankets, and supplies. Over 11,000 students were trapped in their schools with caring teachers and administrators who kept them safe. Employers opened executive dining rooms and set up bars for their stranded workers. The stories are heart-warming, surprising, funny, and touching. Most people are simply glad the month of January is behind us, with polar vortexes making people layer polar fleeces and pull out fuzz-lined boots that had not been worn in a decade.

I love January, named after Janus, the god of doorways — the month of resolutions and new starts. But this year, like many others, I am happy to say, "Goodbye January! Cheers! See you next year." As usual, we have no guarantees that February will have kinder weather. This month may be like Shakespeare's Benedick *"full of frost, of storm and cloudiness."* But we have so many goofy holidays to look forward to: Toothache Day (the 9th), National Umbrella Day (the 10th), International Dog Biscuit Appreciation Day (the 23rd), and Public Sleeping Day (the 28th). Even if the skies are full of rain, sleet, hail, and snow, we can lighten up just thinking about such momentous occasions.

February 2

In "Light of the World" from *Godspell*, Jesus sings words from Matthew 5:14: "You are the light of the world." (Listen to the work online or from your library!)

> Jesus and Chorus in Stephen Schwartz's *Godspell*

On a day like today, this very catchy tune from Stephen Schwartz's *Godspell* runs around in my mind. After all, it is Candlemas, that holy day between Christmas and Lent, that holy day that ends the arch we have been traversing since the first Sunday of Advent way back in very early December. When the rest of the country is holding its collective breath to see if a groundhog is going to see his shadow or not, I enjoy many aspects of the Candlemas celebration.

Today is a cross-quarter day, midway between the winter solstice and the spring equinox. Bringing up the rear of the Christmas season, this day, also called the Feast of the Purification and the Feast of the Presentation of Christ in the Temple, is 40 days after the celebrated birth of Christ. I have saved a Christmas cracker to pop open to remind myself that this is the tail end of our two-month observance of God becoming incarnate in the world, becoming one of us, taking on a human form, and sharing our joys and sorrows, highs and lows.

Candlemas remembers the early life of Jesus: Mary presenting the child to God at the Temple in Jerusalem. This offering of Mary's coincided with her purification ceremony after observing the traditional 40-day period of "cleansing" after his birth. Luke's Gospel tells the story of Simeon, an old man who was in the Temple waiting for the Messiah. He held the baby in his arms and praised God, saying, "Lord, you now have set your servant free to go in peace as you have promised; For these eyes of mine have seen the Savior, whom you have prepared for all the world to see: A Light to enlighten the nations, and the glory of your people Israel." This beloved "Song of Simeon" or "*Nunc Dimittis*" is read nightly by those devoted to Compline, an evening service in the traditions of the Episcopal and other Catholic and Orthodox churches.

During the Candlemas celebration at St. Andrew's, we often have a big pretzel of a procession around our nave, and the service is filled with singing, incense, and light. Our priest blesses the candles that will be used during the following year, which represent the light that Simeon saw early on in the eyes of the baby Jesus.

But Jesus said to his disciples and to us: You are the light of the world. YOU. You are the light of the world. We are. We ALL are. To live right, take the blinders off, undo the encrustation, put down the shield, peel off the covering, become vulnerable, become real, and show your light. Today is the day to unwrap the swaddling from your emergent self and present yourself as a Child of God!

February 3

In "That'll Be the Day" from *Buddy: The Buddy Holly Story*, Buddy sings his popular tune which warns his beloved that he will weep or even breathe his last if she says farewell. (Listen to the work online or from your library!)

Buddy Holly in Alan Janes's *Buddy: The Buddy Holly Story*

On this day in 1959, Buddy Holly did die in a plane crash. He was only 22, but he had made a huge impact on the budding rock and roll scene. February 3 was later called "The Day the Music Died" in the 1972 Don McLean's "American Pie." Along with Holly, Richie Valens, J. P. "The Big Bopper" Richardson, and the young pilot, Roger Peterson, were also killed when their plane went down near Clear Lake, Iowa.

The Beatles were just emerging and their first recording as the Quarrymen was a tribute to Holly, using one of his songs, "That'll Be the Day." The Rolling Stones also had a huge hit with Buddy's "Not Fade Away."

On January 2, 1990, saw a lively performance of the musical *Buddy* at London's Victoria Palace Theatre. When I heard all those old early 1950s tunes again, it took me back to my real growing up years. From the time I was five years old through my twelfth year or so, I often spent the night at my grandmother's house. My aunt Jackie, who was my mother's youngest sister and still lived at home, was just nine years older than I, but I to me she was the most worldly, enlightened person I knew.

Many times, I would sleep with her in her room and she was a night owl, so we would stay up late. She had a white AM radio on a bookcase that formed the headboard of her bed, and we would listen to all the great early rock ballads. We learned the words and sang along — she was actually a fantastic alto vocalist, so I was mesmerized by her

46

professionalism. At the time, Elvis was the King, but we tended to more enjoy the Everly Brothers, the Platters, and Buddy Holly and the Crickets.

The word "teenager" was actually devised in the 1950s to describe the burgeoning population in this age category. These teens were more mobile, had more time to socialize and spend leisure hours with friends, and were more likely to attend college than their parents or even older siblings. My mother and her other two sisters had grown up in the Depression and through World War II, but Jackie was part of a teenage society that was gaining independence. She was not rebellious, but she was forward-thinking and headstrong, and I learned those qualities from her.

Though my parents later enjoyed some of the rock music I was crazy about in the 1960s, at this time we did not listen to these artists at home. So when I visited Jackie and we heard "Peggy Sue," "Oh Boy," "Words of Love," and all the other great Holly hits, it was almost like a covert operation. It was something we shared that was not necessarily a secret I kept, but was special between the two of us.

So, on most February thirds, I mourn the early death of Buddy Holly, Richie Valens, and The Big Bopper who all left this earth too young. And this year, I am also remembering the loss of Jackie. She, too, passed away at an early age, when she was only 61 years old — three years younger than I am now. Wow!

February 4
"Do any human beings ever realize life while they live it? Every, every minute?"
Emily from Thornton Wilder's *Our Town*

Isn't it wonderful that almost every day is the anniversary or celebration of some thing or other? Today, in 1938, *Our Town* opened on Broadway, and it is one of my all-time favorite works.

I have know a number of people who disregard all the wondrous, small delights surrounding them and seem oblivious to the blessings received: fine houses, good jobs, pleasant families, nice trips. In contrast, I find myself often in a state of weeping with gladness — today for a lady bug on my rug this morning, appreciating the temperature rising past freezing, thinking of a professor who 44 years ago opened my eyes to the theatre, feeling blood coursing through my veins, discovering that the invention of beer was in 6000 BC in Mesopotamia, and I could go on and on. Continuously through the day, I am aware of the gloriousness of life and how miraculous it is.

Thornton Wilder is at least partly responsible for that. I studied *Our Town* in high school, and designed the costumes for the show twice. The truth of the play struck a chord within me. Emily Webb Gibbs dies in childbirth with her second baby and from the grave, longingly looks back at the life from which she has just been snatched. Emily eventually comes to the realization that few humans perceive the magnificence of life while they are living it.

The Stage Manager allows Emily to visit earth again and experience one day over. Advised not to make it one of the big days of her life (such as her wedding day), she asks to relive her twelfth birthday. Once back in time, she wonders at her mother's youth and can hardly stand the fact that no one is really paying attention to each other or absorbing the miraculous details of the world. Finally, she just cannot bear this wondrous grief any longer.

EMILY: [In aloud voice to the STAGE MANAGER.] I can't. I can't go on. Oh! Oh. It goes so fast. We don't have time to look at one another. [She breaks down sobbing. At a gesture from the STAGE MANAGER, MRS. WEBB disappears.] I didn't realize. So all that was going on and we never noticed. Take me back — up the hill — to my grave. But first: Wait! One more look. Good-by, Good-by, world. Good-by, Grover's Corners . . . Mama and Papa. Good-by to clocks ticking . . . . and Mama's sunflowers. And food and coffee. And new-ironed dresses and hot baths . . . and sleeping and waking up. Oh, earth, you're too wonderful for anybody to realize you.
[She looks toward the STAGE MANAGER and asks abruptly, through her tears.] Do any human beings ever realize life while they live it? Every, every minute?
STAGE MANAGER: No. [Pause.] The saints and poets, maybe — they do some.

And so, finding the experience unbearable, Emily returns to the grave and says to her mother-in-law, "That's all human beings are! — Just blind people." The experience has opened her eyes and allowed her, and some audience members, to recognize that our lives are fragile gifts to be experienced in the "now." Thank God I encountered this play when I did, stimulating early a perpetual gratefulness for just being alive.

February 5
Tiecelin: Caw! Caw! Caw!
Brun: Stop that infernal racket!
Ticelin: Caw! Caw!

Ticelin the Crow and Brun the Bear in Arthur Fauquez's *Reynard the Fox*

We produced this charming children's legend *Reynard the Fox* when I was in college. A satire, the play is filled with talking animals like a bear, a wolf, a marmot, a lion, a porcupine, and a fox. I loved Ticelin the Crow, played by a friend, Drucilla.

I often think about this show, because on my early morning walks in the neighborhood, I am greeted at every turn by crows cawing at me. *"Caw! Caw! Caw!"* they say. *"Stop that infernal racket!"* I call back. They never mind me, despite the fact that crows are counted as one of the earth's smartest animal. Sometimes they rattle, click, or gronk, but it is usually *"Caw! Caw!"* There is a roost down the hill from my house where hundreds of crows like to circle, gather, and sleep.

Though I realize crows and ravens are different birds, they are classified in the same genus, Corvus. I have always been fond of the captive ravens of the Tower of London. I understand from tours of the grounds that six of these black birds are required, with a seventh in reserve, to protect the Royal Family. A legend has grown up that if the ravens fly away, the Crown and all of Britain will fall. To assure their remaining, one of each of their wings is clipped.

Now, as often happens to me, an odd and synchronistic development has occurred as I have been writing this piece. The doorbell rang to inform me I have just received a late birthday present, conveyed by the UPS delivery man, from my dear friend, Joe Taylor who lives near Washington DC I opened the brown package, and what is inside but a black Eames House Bird?! I am writing about crows, and ravens, and I receive a magnificent black bird.

On the "Design Within Reach" website, I read that this object "rose to stardom in the 1950s when Charles and Ray Eames pulled it from their own living room and positioned it with a group of Eames ... chairs for a poster."

The prototype wooden bird was created some time around 1910 and was purchased by the Eames brothers as they journeyed through the Appalachian Mountains. Often embellishing design collections with items they found across the country, the charming and sleek black bird with its pointy beak and graceful tail, shiny finish and dark color was a prized addition to their collections. The current reproductions of the now famous original piece are made of alder wood in Germany, and fashioned using three-dimensional scans of the original.

"Synchronicity" is a term created by the remarkable Swiss psychologist, Carl Jung in his research on the unconscious. This happy happenstance concerning my black bird makes my heart very glad. I agree with Wayne Dyer in thinking that there is no such thing as coincidence. What we see as simultaneous events that seem unrelated are really subconscious messages that everything is totally more related that we could ever imagine.

February 6
"Solamen miseris socios habuisse doloris.
(It is a comfort to the wretched to have companions in misery.)"
Mephistopheles in Christopher Marlowe's *The Tragical History of the Life and Death of Doctor Faustus*

We cannot pass up Christopher Marlowe's birthday without a quote from *Dr. Faustus,* the mythic parable about all of us when we sell our souls to the Devil for knowledge, power, glory, fame, or success. Faustus is a highly esteemed German scholar who becomes bored with academia and decides to dabble in magic, substituting a dangerous dalliance for his usual, normal life. It is the ultimate clash of good versus evil. It is what we all battle every day when we know what is right and brilliant, and yet we choose what is wrong and stupid.

Having produced the play with a magnificent group of students, directed by Charles Reese (an alum), many lines from Faustus often come to my mind — the work is overflowing with gems. But I have chosen *"It is a comfort to the wretched to have companions in misery,"* taken from the writings of a fourteenth century Italian historian Dominici de Gravina.

We don't always subscribe to this philosophy. My theatre professor, WT Chichester drove around town with a megaphone advertising a comedy we were performing, proclaiming: "Laugh and the world laughs with you, cry and you cry alone!"

"Misery loves company" is how most people express de Gravina's idea. English naturalist and botanist John Ray, who lived from 1627 to 1705, not too long after Christopher Marlowe died in 1593, is credited with that specific rendering of the sentiment, along with an additional timeworn phrase, "Blood is thicker than water."

Two different Enneagram trainees with whom I am working are caretakers for their rapidly aging mothers who have dementia, as I had previously done. At our recent Enneagram retreat, one friend reminisced about how her mother had chastised her about her weight all her life. While taking her turn assisting her mom the week before our gathering, she was again upbraided about extra pounds.

Surprisingly, my friend's mother scolded her, and then immediately apologized (something she had never done before). She told her mom the remarks were forgotten. A few minutes later, her mom asked for pardon again, and again she was forgiven. Then later, her mother said, "I am really sorry about the comment." My friend broke down in tears relating the story of the trifold apology, and what amounted to a long overdue expression of regret for a lifetime of tongue-lashing, and a possible recognition of the pain she had caused.

I recalled to them why I had been so stalwart last August when I was training with them, and had gotten the call that my mother had died. Her actual passing from this life to another was really a calm and tranquil time for me, because I had left my mother's house a few months before her death, and had boohooed for three solid days. I woefully knew I had forever lost the person I had always called "Mama." She knew me, but she was literally fading like members of the McFly family in the photograph in Marty's wallet in the *Back to the Future* films.

As we all talked about reconciling (or not) with our mothers, and losing them at this stage of life, we definitely thought, "*It is a comfort to the wretched to have companions in misery.*" Sometimes they really do know very nearly what you are going through.

February 7
"*You can sit in some huge restaurant in Moscow and not know a soul, and no one know you; yet somehow you feel that you belong there... But here you know everybody and everybody knows you, and yet you don't feel you belong here, no not at all... You're a stranger and all alone.*"
Andrey in Anton Chekhov's *The Three Sisters*, Act 2

Very little really happens in Chekhov's *The Three Sisters*. More a study in the emotional development of the characters, the play reveals in an understated manner the ephemeral exquisiteness and melancholy of life's transitory nature. Chekhov wanted to portray commonplace, inconsequential times of life that occur between major events. Some critics deem this play the best drama of the twentieth century, with its deceptive clarity and universal themes: why are sensitive people defeated?

Is it best to live in the city or country? Is contentment possible? Are ignorant people better off than the educated?

So Andrey's quote about feeling at home in a huge public place in the city, yet feeling out of place here at home in the provincial town is very poignant, and brings to mind the question of how do we belong to a family, a group, or a city?

A good lesson I have learned studying online with and reading books by Dr. Brené Brown is that there is a difference between fitting in and belonging. Like other words we use all the time to describe ourselves, these two terms can be vague, and are many time erroneously used interchangeably. Fitting in involves adapting to the people in a group so they will accept you. Belonging, on the other hand, requires being present and authentic enough with a group to let others see who you really are, good and imperfect, intelligent and foolish, brave and anxious.

I think about the two concepts like this: during my high school years, I tried desperately to fit in. I wanted to be part of the "In Crowd." I cared very deeply about expressing myself in art. Was this okay with my classmates? I delighted in wearing the latest fashions using *Seventeen Magazine* as my guide. Did my peers dress like this? I adored the Beatles, romantic films, reading great literature, writing poetry, devouring the information from a class, putting movie popcorn boxes on my ceiling, and going to rock dances at the local armory. Did my fellow students do likewise? The answer to most of these questions is: not really, at least not openly. My high school was fairly conservative and traditional. So I masked enough of myself to fit in some, but not totally: I was "unconventional." I accepted myself, but I was pretty sure others wouldn't.

My college years at the University of Montevallo were just the opposite. The first time I visited and saw the tree-lined brick streets, beautifully designed campus by the Olmsted Brothers firm, and colorful medley of students, I fell in love. The years there were extremely important in my mental, emotional, and spiritual growth because, from the moment of my arrival I belonged. Art, diversity, theatre, a multiplicity of fashions, people who admired the Beatles, people who enjoyed classical music, film-lovers, science-lovers, math-lovers, people who wanted to tune in, turn on, and drop out. There were poets and dancers, athletes and home economics majors, students who wanted to be teachers and students who wanted to be doctors. Many professors, many books, many friends, and many ideas made impressions on me that have lasted a life time. The memory of the richness and opulent magnificence of my more authentic college years takes my breath away.

February 8
"All that glisters is not gold."
Morocco in William Shakespeare's *The Merchant of Venice*, Act II Scene 7

Speaking of my alma mater, at this time of year, along with red and pink hearts, my home is festooned with lots of purple and little tiny bits of gold. At Montevallo, we have an unusual Homecoming event in early February called College Night. The tradition is so unique, it was named a "Local Legacy" in the year 2000 by the Library of Congress. My daughter Elin helped create the exhibit that was accepted into their American Folklife Center.

No matter what other loyalties or disciplines, the entire campus divides into sides, either Purple or Gold, so designated for the school colors. Students participate in a noteworthy competition, and are ardently supported by alumni. For three weeks leading up to Homecoming Weekend, games of women's and men's basketball, soccer, volleyball, and other sports factor into the pre-production point scheme. But the center of the entire event is a contest between two original musical shows written and created totally by students. A College Night win is awarded by professional theatre and music judges and the victory is highly coveted.

I worked for the Purples all four years I attended the university, and was elected Side Leader along with my then-spouse. We were the first husband and wife team to be chosen for this extraordinary honor, and when our daughter Elin was a senior, she was chosen Purple Leader as well, the first time the child of a former leader was selected.

College Night is known as the oldest Homecoming tradition of its kind in America, but the exact custom is hard to explain. A former Leader wrote in 1931, "If you have never lived through one, never cried, laughed or sweated through one, know this. It is the crest of the wave of college spirit. It is the high spot that will stand out in your mind as meaning college when all the rest has faded." And that is true. College Night is a remarkably singular experience.

I discovered many things from my four Januarys and Februarys spent in the frenzy that helped brighten the post-holiday winter doldrums: collaboration, team spirit, imagination, stamina, determination, drudgery, organization, exhilaration, disappointment. I grasped the concepts of losing gracefully and winning elegantly. I discovered how to take something from an absolute zero, nada, nil, nothing to something tangible beautiful, expansive, even monumental. I found out how to work with all kinds of people.

I learned how to paint scenery, plan auditions, select cabinet leaders, deal with mean adversaries, curry the favor of faculty on the committee, and direct huge covert operations (neither side sees the other's show until a joint dress rehearsal before opening). All of these skills have helped me throughout my lifetime. One thing overseeing College Night did not prepare me for, however, was the heartache of a trio of losses sustained by Elin her first three years in school. I would so gladly have suffered the anguish she went through in her place. But the victory she garnered her senior year as Leader almost perfectly atoned for the prior crushing defeats. And as we Purples like to frequently jibe, *"All that glisters is not gold"* — purple sparkles, too — and Shakespeare is the first to have said that!

February 9
"A chipped glass is ruined forever"
Evelyn in Diane Samuels's *Kindertransport*

For one of my father's birthdays, my mother had saved up and purchased for him a really nice pewter mug. It was not terrifically expensive, maybe fifty dollars. But it cost more than she usually spent on one item for a special day. It had taken her fancy and she knew "he would have a fit over it." Pulling it out of the package, my dad, exclaiming over the mug, somehow dropped it putting a dent in it before he had ever used it.

I expected my mother to be furious or cry, but she simply said, "Well, now it's got some patina. And that dent, that's what memories are made of. Every time you use it, you will remember what happened the day you got it, and that will make it more special."

Wow! What a lesson I learned from her that day.

I know glass is a little different and a chip in crystal is not as forgivable in use as is a dent in pewter. However, Evelyn in Diane

Samuels's *Kindertransport* is a perfectionist. Understandably so, but still, a stickler for faultlessness. She sees the flawed glass as blemished, inferior, and below her standard.

What was called "the Kindertransport" saved thousands of Jewish children from Hitler. In the fall of 1938, Nazis burned synagogues, ravaged houses, devastated businesses, and cruelly mistreated Jews throughout Germany, Austria, and Czechoslovakia. His regime invented laws excluding Jews from public areas and from pursuing their careers. The Nazis saw the Jews as blemished, inferior, and below their standard.

These horrific happenings were only the beginning of the atrocities that was to come; but even then, some Jews realized the only hope was escape. The problem was how, and where could they go?

In the months leading up to the actual declaration of war, almost ten thousand unchaperoned Jewish children vanished from Germany. By train and boat, they entered Great Britain where most were adopted and survived; but, in the supreme sacrifice for any family, most never saw their birth parents again, many of whom died in concentration camps. Samuels's play *Kindertransport* traces the story of 9-year-old Eva, who changes her name to Evelyn and rejects her Jewish faith and culture, becoming a British citizen.

Who wouldn't want to put that past behind? Who wouldn't want to change her name and her nationality after losing her country, her home, her possessions, her family?

A few years ago in a spiritual discussion with my priest, I asked if we can pray backwards. He asked me what I meant, and I told him that I wondered if I offered petitions for people in Nazi concentration camps now, would it make a difference? He reminded me that God's time is eternal, not linear as we experience it; so, of course it would by some means have an impact.

So now, Monday is my special day to think of the Holocaust victims. Sometimes I fast. Sometimes I think of this play about a Jewish child who becomes Anglicized, or I research the history of the concentration camps, or I say the centerpiece prayer of Judaism: *Sh'ma Yisrael Adonai Eloheinu Adonai Eḥad* — "Hear, O Israel: the LORD is our God, the LORD is One." I hope somehow my thoughts and actions go back in time, and at least someone feels my empathy and senses that someone is entreating on her behalf.

February 10

Frihol: I'll buy your cow.

Jack: You? Have you money?

Frihol: What I have is better than money. See? (He spread the beans on the table.)

Jack: Oh-h! What beautiful beans! How smooth they are! What shining colors! I like them!

Characters in Charlotte B. Chorpenning's *Jack and the Beanstalk*, from the fairy tale

"What I have is better than money. See?" What is better than money to you? Probably not a handful of colorful beans, unless they really are somehow magic! What is better? Love? Life? Family? Friendships? Art? Health? Education? You probably have lots of items on your list.

For a long while, I have had a love/hate relationship with money. I remember being in graduate school in the early 1970s, living on about $200 a month. The apartment we lived in cost $50 a month. Utilities were included, but we had to be very creative at the grocery store. We could just about fill up a brown paper bag for $10, and one and a half of those had to last an entire week. One day, as I came home and unloaded our food, I dropped a big jar of mayonnaise. It was made of glass and it broke, spewing all over the floor. I could not afford to buy another one for a couple of weeks and I sat down in the middle of the kitchen floor and cried my eyes out.

I felt every bit as deprived and suffering as Scarlett O'Hara when she held up the turnip and declared to God that when the war was over, she and her family would never be hungry again. The mayo episode became a symbol of the temporary poverty I wanted to vanquish. And yet, I went into theatre, art, and nonprofit work, so I have always lived a life of what a friend of mine calls "genteel poverty" — rich in refinement, but fairly low on finances. Living this way, working on parish stewardship, and raising funds for charitable organizations have all taught me a good bit about money, however.

When I do have money saved up in an account, I am very loathe to spend it. Now I see why wealthy people stay that way: many do not spend without thought to where their dollars are going.

Except for the mortgage on my house, I have learned to have no debt. I don't like the rates of interest on credit cards, and if I don't have to pay creditors, I have more money to spend on things I may want.

Over the past few years, I have changed jobs a couple of times, and my income is slightly under what it had been. So I have lowered my expenses, because I have no desire to chase a high wage job. My current job gives me flexibility and I can work at home. It is amazing what you can cut out of a budget if you plan.

Money is like time. If I get a little more of it, I tend to squander it. If I am not careful, I seem to have even less cash than before. Money and time stretch to fit the situation, and if I have a little extra cash, it is so easy to find something I really "need."

What I now have **is** better than money — and it's not beans; it's the ability to stop struggling with the concept of the green stuff. As I endured the poverty of my graduate school and early marriage days, I nursed the philosophy of "Money Can't Buy Me Love." I was Bohemian enough to disdain wealth. But, I have learned that if I respect and welcome any funds that come my way, somehow they do. Money is energy, and can flow in and out of my life enriching others as it blesses me.

February 11
"The majority is never right. Never, I tell you! That's one of these lies in society that no free and intelligent man can help rebelling against. Who are the people that make up the biggest proportion of the population — the intelligent ones or the fools?"
Dr. Stockmann, in Henrik Ibsen's *An Enemy of the People*, Act IV

I was always taught never to say, "never," because something will always happen to change the never into sometimes, certainly, or always. Surely Dr. Stockmann is overstating his point. But, many historians and politicians tell us that America and the essence of democracy — the very foundations of our government and freedom — are built on the concept of sovereign majority. Our constitution upholds the concept and those who populate our legislative branches, both federal and state, rise and fall with the will of the majority.

My undergraduate days were so dazzling I could never decide on my majors and minors, so I had two majors and one minor, and was one class short of another minor. One reason for the minor I did complete was the professor: there was only one teacher in the Philosophy and Religion Department. The man we called Dr. van Tuyll was really a Dutch count, the Baron Hendrik van Tuyll van Serooskerken.

Dr. van Tuyll's family left the Netherlands during World War II and later came to North America, where he was assistant professor of philosophy at Acadia University in Nova Scotia for a couple of years. Amazingly, they settled in the town of Montevallo, where he taught at my alma mater from 1966 to 198 . His dissertation from the state university at Utrecht was on Immanuel Kant's Critique of Pure Reason, and he enjoyed teaching his students about Kant's structure of cognition. He knew, I believe, fourteen or more languages, including some medieval ones, and mentally translated his notes from Dutch as he lectured.

He also loved religion. He was an ordained deacon in the Church of England, a minister of the United Church of Canada, and he sometimes preached at the local Episcopal church.

Probably the most intelligent and most charming man I ever knew, Dr. van Tuyll would stroll across campus in a dark suit and delightful European boots. Even when it was not raining, he would have an umbrella, and he moved this staff in a precise motion like the figure on an animated clock: forward with a punch and straight bump down, forward with a punch and straight bump down.

One day, he asked our class, "How do you know the little gray animal scurrying about campus is a 'squill?'" as he called it.

A large provincial bovine-like male student replied, "Because we see it's a dang squirrel!"

"But how do you know" Dr. van Tuyll's eyes twinkled. And the entire rest of the class time was spent on a romp, with our attempting to understand how our minds constructed such knowledge out of images.

But back to the majority never being right. Dr. van Tuyll had lived and traveled all over the world, and he was one of those "free and intelligent" people who could not "help rebelling against" some ideas. Once he told us in a discussion about American democracy a nugget of brilliance I will never forget: "Just because in the United States everyone is entitled to their own opinion does not mean that everyone's opinion is equal in wisdom. Always remember, some people have better perspective and can think more intelligently than others. And what you say always tells your listeners more about yourself than the subject about which you are professing knowledge!"

February 12
"Flow backward to your sources, sacred rivers, And let the world's great order be reversed."

The Chorus in Euripides's *Medea* (410-414)

Medea is as tragic as it gets, so first let's have a joke from Andreas Nomikos, a wonderful Greek theatre designer and professor I knew in graduate school. In ancient Greece, a man goes to a tailor to get his trousers sewn back up. The tailor asks: "Euripides?" The fellow replies: "Yes. Eumenides?" Okay, it is corny, but Andreas thought the jest was hysterical, so I always laughed every time he told it because he was such a dear man.

Euripides crafted a powerfully startling work about regicide and infanticide with his *Medea*. In 1993, before I saw the production, I accompanied my then 16-year old daughter Elin to Wyndham's Theatre, London, to see Diana Rigg in the title role. When I picked her up, her eyes were as round as the full moon above us. "How was it?" I asked. "You'll just have to see it. I don't want to spoil it for you," she gasped.

Later, watching Diana Rigg's *Medea* was harrowing. The performance was full of everything you want in a Greek tragedy: banishment, blood, murder, revenge, deceit, the flaunting of male strength, the fierceness of a scorned wife, the rage of love, the violence created from the tension between maternal attachment and the desire to inflict utmost pain. And this production was etched in my memory through Peter J. Davison's intriguing set made of rusty corrugated metal panels that crashed and fell with alarming reverberations as the play drove to its unnerving end.

What I love most in a Greek tragedy is the Chorus. They are close to the ground and they know what is coming up and going down. Speaking in unison and individually, the Chorus goes right to the point of the moral issue at hand and expresses the emotions, ideas, and philosophy that guide those of us watching. They relate to the audience, control the atmosphere, comment on the action of the heroes and heroines, plead to the gods, and ask for their world to be righted.

In *Medea*, the Chorus tells the sacred rivers to defy their normal route and *"Flow backward to your sources."* This odd request, it seems, would lead dangerously to a deviant in the normal sequence of nature. But because of Medea's state of mind and the action she is setting in motion, having the rivers cascade backward might lead to wholeness. Reversing the world's great order might bring sanity, calmness, and peace. Let's go back and start all over again.

We have all had days like that. November 22, 1963: The assassination of John F. Kennedy. December 8, 1980: The martyrdom of John Lennon. September 11, 2001: Terrorist Attacks on New York and Washington. Days our parents died. Days our dogs were run over. Days our spouses or partners were rushed to the hospital. Go back rivers! Reverse! Go back hours! Please let us start the day over and, dear God, let it end differently this time.

February 13

"And this small part of me was then a whisper of the earth. When there was life, perhaps this part of me got lost in a fern that was crushed and covered until it was coal. And then it was a diamond millions of years later— it must have been a diamond as beautiful as the star from which it had first come... this part of me was so small it couldn't be seen — but it was there from the beginning of the world. And he called this bit of me an atom. And when he wrote the word, I fell in love with it. Atom. Atom. What a beautiful word."
Tillie in Paul Zindel's The *Effect of Gamma Rays on Man-in-the-Moon Marigolds*, Act I, Scene 1

Some years, Ash Wednesday falls this early in February. In my church, at this service, the Celebrant imposes ashes in the form of a cross on everyone's forehead, reminding us, "Remember that you are dust, and to dust you shall return. At Woodstock, Joni Mitchell sang about people actually being stardust. And humans apparently really are made of the particles of dust from stars, as well as water in the form of hydrogen from the Big Bang.

The fact is, the human body is made of so many atoms, the number is impossible to comprehend. In *The Effect of Gamma Rays on Man-in-the-Moon Marigolds*, Tillie marvels at the wonders of the atom revealed to her by her high school science teacher. Engineers at Washington University estimate there to be 100 trillion atoms in a human cell and 100 trillion cells in the body. So like Tillie, I am amazed that inside of us are millions and millions and millions of small bits of material, each "so small it couldn't be seen — but it was there from the beginning of the world."

First, Tillie thinks, the atoms inside her were nothing more than "*a whisper of the earth.*" Perhaps then those tiny building blocks — inside Tillie, or me, or you — got trapped into a fern, then coal, then a diamond "as beautiful as the star from which it had first come."

The thirteenth century Persian poet, Rumi wrote a poem about atoms, connecting science and spirituality through art:

"O' day, arise!
Shine your light, the atoms are dancing.
Thanks to Him, the universe is dancing,
Overcome with ecstasy,
Free from body and mind.
I'll whisper in your ear where their dance is leading them."

Many current theologians have begun to turn from our ancient concepts of the beginnings of life to offer a new human story informed by modern science. And a number of atheist and agnostic physicists and chemists believe that vital mysteries about the world can be best understood spiritually. I have attended conferences in which Christian wisdom teachers expound on chaos and complexity, biological evolution, quantum entanglement, and Big Bang cosmology.

I believe what twentieth century Jesuit priest and mystic philosopher Pierre Teilhard de Chardin posited: "We are not human beings having a spiritual experience; we are spiritual beings having a human experience." And yet, though I trust there to be much more to human existence than our molecular physical material bodies, once a year, at least, it is good to hear: "*Remember that you are stardust, and to stardust you shall return.*"

February 14
"Say what you will, 'tis better to be left than never to have been loved."
Mrs. Marwood in William Congreve's *The Way of the World*, Act II, Scene 1

Mrs. Marwood's line (performed first in 1700) is the earlier pronouncement of Alfred Lord Tennyson's more well known phrase, "'Tis better to have loved and lost than never to have loved at all" (from "In Memoriam," 1850). But is it better to be left, as she says, than never to have been loved at all?

Here it is Valentine's Day and the card companies, department stores, supermarkets, and flower shops would all have us buy into the romantic love market. And I must admit, my house is adorned with hearts and blooms. I'll eat strawberries and Valentine chocolates, have a nice dinner and some red wine tonight.

So what about romantic love? When I am going through love loss, whether from desertion, death, defection, demise, destruction, or any other word starting with a "D," I would not agree that "'tis better to have loved and lost." Facing the dissolving of any close relationship creates a devastating period of time where I find myself dumbfounded, dazed, and discombobulated — a time in which I might spit in the direction of either William Congreve or Alfred Lord Tennyson had they personally delivered their platitudes on love and loss to me.

When the first few months of single parenthood began to sink in for me — and I sometimes wept in exhaustion on the floor of the bedroom — my son Seth's new Springer Spaniel puppy Merlin would come up to me, sit as close as he possibly could, hold one paw up, and pat me. How he knew how to comfort me in that way, I will never know — he was a baby, and he was canine. But I grew extraordinarily attached to that dog over the next fourteen years until his death, beginning with this bonding that we had early in our relationship. And what a lost love that was!

I do believe that every experience we have makes us who we are today. Many years ago, I adopted one of Wayne Dyer's quotes as a daily affirmation: "In my world, nothing ever goes wrong." Yes, we go through horrendous experiences, sadness, wretchedness, suffering, grief, misunderstanding. That is human life upon this particular planet. As William Congreve would say, "it's the way of the world." But everything we face makes us grow, makes us stronger, and makes us more empathetic, more loving — or, if we refuse to grow, extraordinarily bitter. A dissolution or a death or a disease may not seem like a lesson at the time, but it can be if I can embrace life as life — the good, the wicked, the glorious, the unfortunate, the lucky, the grievous, all together.

Where would we be without love? So to answer my own question about Mrs. Marwood's statement, "Is it better to be left than never to have been loved at all?" I have to listen to this quote from *The Painted Drum* by Louise Erdrich. "Life will break you. Nobody can protect you from that, and living alone won't either, for solitude will also break you with its yearning. You have to love. You have to feel. It is the reason you are here on earth. You are here to risk your heart. You are here to be swallowed up. And when it happens that you are broken, or betrayed, or left, or hurt, or death brushes near, let yourself sit by an apple tree and listen to the apples falling all around you in heaps, wasting their sweetness. Tell yourself you tasted as many as you could."

February 15

"Who are you? What's your name?"
"Well, usually I'm Mortimer Brewster, but I'm not quite myself today."
Lt. Rooney to Mortimer Brewster in Joseph Kesselring's Arsenic and Old
Lace

In Joseph Kesselring's *Arsenic and Old Lace*, Mortimer Brewster is spending some time with his aunts, Abby and Martha in the home in which he grew up. He has just, on Halloween, married Elaine Harper who was the girl next door, literally. But the visit becomes a nightmare when he finds that his brother Teddy believes he is Theodore Roosevelt, his brother Jonathan tries to kill him, and his aunts have murdered a dozen or so old gentlemen as an act of charity. Mortimer realizes that his family has some very disturbing mental problems and thinking that insanity might be in his genes, he has fears concerning his marriage.

What finally happens is that Jonathan is arrested and Teddy is gently removed to a proper institution that can care for him. Abby and Martha decide to go along with him, but not before they reveal that Mortimer is really not related by blood to the Brewsters after all. He is actually the offspring of a steamship chef and the aunts' former cook, and had been taken in by the family. This knowledge delights him, for he realizes he is not destined to be a murderer or mad — but he, like Oedipus Rex, was really never quite himself before finding out a lengthily concealed secret.

I have no such case of elevated mistaken identity that would lead to the tragedy of Oedipus or the comedy of Mortimer. But I have days like his, when I absolutely do not feel like I am my usual self. Sometimes I am physically ill, sometimes my routine is upset, sometimes a crisis arises and I am still out of sorts. By the way, "sorts" are said to have been used to make up a font in press printing and the word describes the letters in a box (such as the "a" sort, the "b" sort, and so on). When sets of a type being used ran low, the printer was out of sorts, and so his work stopped, which would cause exasperation or displeasure.

Recently, I have been taking more responsibility for my feelings and doing something to dispel my doldrums. To get to the cause of being out of balance, I often have to write about what is going on. Apparently, the way I think best about something is to get my thoughts and feelings on paper by writing in my diary or work in my art journal or on a spirit collage.

63

Also, I have been reflecting more, experimenting with reflection, centering prayer, and *Lectio Divina*, a method of contemplative scriptural reading. As I have been taught, these deliberate practices of becoming quiet and slowing down really do calm the barrage of thoughts that my ego wants me to constantly tend. I seem to concentrate better and feel less stress, both emotionally and mentally, when I practice these methods. Learning detachment means little upsets sometimes fail to bother me.

So if a Lt. Rooney asks me who I am, at least I can say I am working on being my own true self more and more.

February 16
"What do I care how long I wait (Intensely sincere now) I'll think of her – and dream! I'd wait a million years and never mind it – for her! (He gives his sister a superior scornful glance) The trouble with you is, you don't understand what love means!"
Richard to his sister Mildred in Eugene O'Neill's *Ah, Wilderness!*

Ah, time! In *Ah, Wilderness!* Richard expresses the depth of his love by professing he could wait a million years for this love of his life. He doesn't care, in his youth, how long he waits. To him, a million years might be one or two months.

The best of times, the worst of times, time flies, in no time at all, a stitch in time, the time of your life, a matter of time, present time, past time, or future time. Humans are fairly consumed by our attention to time. We have watches, stopwatches, day planners, timers, and alarms. Our microwaves, stoves, televisions, radios, electronic devices, smart phones, and physical activity monitors all tell us the exact minute and second.

I remember distinctly my great-grandmother, my grandmother, and my mother all saying as they grew older that time began to fly past them. Does time speed up and slow down? Can we travel in time like characters in movies such as *Back to the Future, Bill and Ted's Excellent Adventure, Groundhog Day, Somewhere in Time, Time Bandits, Time After Time, The Butterfly Effect,* or *A Connecticut Yankee in King Arthur's Court?*

This idea of time fascinates me. When a number of sadly unexpected things happen in a week, or when I have numerous projects in a seven-day period, or when exciting adventures surface over and over during a short period, time seems to stretch. I look back and think last

Monday was at least a month ago. But when my life rocks on in its usual groove and everything is normal and blandly on schedule, weeks and months fly by like a finely oiled roller coaster. Suddenly another year has gone by, and what have I actually done in and with my life?

We celebrate the end of one year and the beginning of another. We are pressed by time into rash actions and time robs us of our youth. I have heard that before trains, we mortals were not so obsessed with time. But when locomotives began crossing countries and having schedules that had to be kept precisely, people had to catch those iron horses, or meet someone coming into town, so we had to become aware of hours and half hours and quarters. Then, if people arrive early at the train station, they have to kill some time.

Henry David Thoreau said, in *Walden* (1854), "As if you could kill time without injuring eternity." When I understand time best, I don't really comprehend it at all, but simply go through it in a way that explains the theory that God is eternal and humans are temporal. When I get lost in a creative project, I am present and in the moment – and then suddenly, I get out of the moment. When I let myself be absorbed in art, I lose track of temporal time and beat to a holy tempo. I create and wonder: where did that art come from? I look at a clock and can't believe it has been so long (maybe a million years!) – or so short – a time since I started. While the clock hands measured out the minutes exactly, my spirit went into a boundless, timeless space where I was able to touch something even our most modern electronic equipment cannot calculate or perceive.

February 17
"This isn't a game. . . One might almost believe that you're all guilty by the looks of you."
Detective Sergeant Trotter in Agatha Christie's *The Mousetrap*

When I was small, I was the most innocent, honorable, law-abiding child imaginable. But if someone at school did something wrong and the teacher questioned us all to get to the bottom of the situation, I always appeared to be culpable. I would blush and look ruefully contrite and blameworthy, never having participated in the wrongdoing at all. I believe I remember one adult even directly quoting Agatha Christie saying, *"You're all guilty by the looks of you."*

Wikipedia says that guilt "is an emotion that occurs when a person believes that they have violated a moral standard that they themselves believe in." I have enjoyed getting to know the difference between guilt and shame by studying books, Ted Talks, and taking that e-course by Brené Brown. Many Americans were reared by parents who shamed their children rather than kindling guilt. Guilt lets us know when we really have trespassed into territory we know is unethical, or even illegal. Shame, on the other hand, says we ourselves are rotten to the core. Guilt might even be categorized as a cerebral activity, where shame is definitely heart-oriented.

Most people probably use "guilt" and "shame" to mean the same thing, but mentally and emotionally, they are miles apart. In junior high school, I called a friend a disparaging name in front of the school bus crowd. Afterward, I felt guilty — and I should have. I cast aspersions on her reputation and breached my friend's trust. And, I also felt shame — I was embarrassed and disgraced to be the kind of person who would do such a nasty, hurtful thing.

When I was young and a classmate was at fault for some misbehavior, I was upset about how I might appear to my teacher. I felt shame, even though I hadn't done anything wrong. When I was older and I used unpleasant words to describe my classmate, that actually was erroneous judgment. My best plan would have been to acknowledge my action, ask for forgiveness from her, forgive myself, and release myself thereafter from believing I was a terrible person for acting this way.

But, that shame culture is hard to fight unless you recognize it. I am happy that today, people talk more about shame and guilt. I used to think that one day, I would once again become connected to what I did and find the nerve to ask my friend for mercy after all these years. And not long ago, I did so.

February 18
"Philly: Glory be to God! And who hit you at all?
Mahon (triumphantly): It was my own son hit me. Would you believe that?
Jimmy: Well, there's wonders hidden in the heart of man!"
Characters in John Millington Synge's *The Playboy of the Western World*, Act III

The Irish drama *The Playboy of the Western World* is filled with lovely, lively language and reflects a theme about the power of expression and imagination. As Christy Mahon snuggles into a clean and soft bed at the end of Act I, he contemplates his remarkable reversal of fortune. Having attempted to murder his father, he thought he would be treated as a criminal. But Christy is suddenly treasured in County Mayo as a hero. As the play progresses, what begins to set Christy apart is less his actions and more his growing ability to verbalize his own story. He discovers that with language, he can reinvent himself. Though he has little formal education, Christy hones a talent for rhetoric that at first makes him a hero in the eyes of the rural peasantry. As he becomes more and more sure of himself, his appreciation of his own abilities is reflected in the richness and power of his words. But by curtain fall, Christy has broken too many hearts with his deceptive fabrications, and has to flee the town with his still-living father.

As Jimmy says, "...there's wonders hidden in the heart of man." The word "heart" appears several times in the text. When we produced The Playboy of the Western World in 1980, we engaged an Irish director for the play. He pleaded for authentic Celtic touches for the set and one of his demands was a picture of the Bleeding Heart of Jesus to go over the fireplace. He said no Irish Catholic home or tavern of the time would have been complete without one. Never having seen such a painting around Birmingham — nor even heard of the Bleeding, or Sacred, Heart of Jesus — I was anxious, hoping that I wouldn't disappoint Sean. Amazingly enough, I found one in a junky antique store downtown — and it looked old enough to have come from Synge's original production! The painting was intriguing: Jesus, arms out, holding a heart dripping with blood and engulfed by flames. But his eyes were intent on viewers, inviting all to yield their own hearts likewise to him, to the power of his fiery love.

Marcus Borg, in The God We Never Knew, talks at length about the heart. A soft, open, malleable heart is receptive to God. A closed, inflexible, impenetrable heart closes out the Spirit. God wants to draw us into relationship — not by our following external commands, laws, and rules, such as honoring our father rather than attempting to murder him. The Divine calls us to expose and offer our yielding, pliant hearts — as Jesus does in the painting — to God's overwhelming, unwavering love.

As Christy learned in Playboy of the Western World, language and words have a huge influence on our lives. Listening for what God has to say often leads to change, to sacrifice, to relinquishment of our old, stubborn, obstinate ways. But if we surrender our hearts and listen to

Divine language, we can become part of a sacred reinvention of ourselves somewhat like Christy's, but more authentic and true.

February 19
"What, in ill thoughts again? Men must endure
Their going hence even as their coming hither.
Ripeness is all. Come on."
Edgar to Gloucester in William Shakespeare's *King Lear*, Act V, Scene 2

David Garrick must have been ripe for delivery, for he was born on this day in 1717. Best known as an actor, he was also a theatre manager and producer, literary critic, and even a playwright. Garrick became very influential in English and international theatre practice during the eighteenth century after playing Richard III in 1741. With this role, he captured the attention using a natural method, rather than the usual declamatory style. Just six years later, by September of 1747, he had gained such prestige and stature that he was able to partner with James Lacy to manage Drury Lane Theatre. As an actor, he was Lear, Macbeth, Hamlet, and more. For the next 27 years, as Garrick conducted the creative ventures at Drury Lane, he performed over 95 roles, appearing about 2,400 nights while maintaining a happy marriage.

This quote from *King Lear* is near the end of the play. The king has been defeated, and he and his daughter captured. Gloucester, one of his loyal noblemen, just wants to lie down and die at this turn of events. Edgar tells him that we cannot choose our time of death any more than our time of birth. *"Ripeness is all."*

In the South, we love our tomatoes vine-ripened and home-grown, so we don't eat many tomatoes in the winter. My dad used to call those round, red, off-season orbs "baseballs." If my mother brought a tomato home in January, he would look for the stitching on it. "Ripeness is all," he would say, adding "and winter tomatoes transported from western states taste like cardboard."

Most fruit is best when left to mature on the branch. Blackberries, strawberries, and peaches, when they mellow on their own, sop up more and more sun and moisture. Just the word "ripe" makes my mouth water anticipating a luscious, succulent, juicy, drippy bite.

John Keats once wrote a letter to his brother, with one hand holding a nectarine to his mouth. "Talking of pleasure," he penned, "... good God, how fine. It went down soft, pulpy, slushy, oozy — all its delicious embonpoint melted down my throat like a large beatified Strawberry." Fruit ripens to become more flavorful, more sweet, more full of its own true essence. As we age, we too can develop, mellowing into wisdom, aging into the beauty of our own quintessential self.

I remember when pregnant with both of my children, I would go for an appointment with my obstetrician, wishing for immediate hospital admittance. "Your cervical ripening is not complete," he would say matter-of-factly, sending me home. Dealing with the other end of life, an obituary reads, "Mr. McCoy died on Wednesday, but he lived to the ripe old age of 97."

So Shakespeare was right (at least, in the natural order of human life): both for our nascent appearance into this world, and our mature exit, a readiness is involved. Shakespeare himself was only 52 when his brief candle was snuffed out. David Garrick's career manifested triumph after triumph and he became famous all over Europe. Though he had reached no venerable age, dying at only 62, his funeral was mournfully suitable, and the inscription on his Westminster Abbey Poet's Corner monument near the Bard's proclaims, "Shakespeare and Garrick like twin stars shall shine / and Earth irradiate with a beam divine." Though fairly young in death, both reached a true ripeness of talent and spirit.

February 20

"Pop, I'm nothing! I'm nothing! Can't you understand that? There's no spite in it any more. I'm just what I am, that's all."
Biff in Arthur Miller's *Death of a Salesman*

As he delivers this line, the stage directions state: "Biff's fury has spent itself and he breaks down sobbing, holding onto Willy, who dumbly fumbles for Biff's face." The Loman household in *Death of a Salesman* is a fairly miserable one, full of blustering and delusion, deception and broken dreams. "Biff" actually means to strike someone sharply with the fist, and Loman means "low man," or, as Willy is always called, "the common man." Willy sees his son Biff as a failure and a loser. Biff, who doesn't quite know how to envision himself, is driven to find his own truth. In this scene, taken down to level zero, he admits his lack of achievement, no longer feeling enmity toward his father. He is desperately groping to retrieve his identity and rescue what is left of his life.

69

Once when a student of mine dropped four-year old Seth on his head in the theatre lobby, my son sustained a concussion. On doctor's orders, that night we waked him on the hour to ask him pertinent questions. "Make sure he can tell you his name," the doctor said. At 1:00 a.m. when I woke him and asked, he replied, "I don't know my name, but my sister is Elin Keith Olson," and he promptly fell back to sleep. Knowing our name, knowing the basics about who we are, is fundamental in life.

"I'm just what I am, that's all," says Biff. In some ways, that is the only thing any of us can say. One of my childhood demigods summed it all up, that crazy spinach-eating seafarer Popeye who sang about his name, and how he was who he was, and that was it! In his theme song, he boasts that he is tough and dislikes dumb oafs who he is likely to fight and win. He says he biffs them so hard, they never get anywhere!

I wonder if Biff Loman stole his line from Popeye, since his name is embedded in the cartoon character's lines. *"I'm just what I am, that's all."* In Exodus 3:14, God says to Moses, "I am who I am." Following God's lead, Jesus, according to John, picks up on the theme and declares: "I am the Bread of Life." "I am the Light of the World." "I am the Good Shepherd." "I am the True Vine."

In some configurations of spiritual development, at the ninth and highest stage, we finally say, "I am who I am." At last, we can remove the masks and armor we have used all our lives. At this junction, naked and revealed, we finally admit that we have nothing up our sleeves (we have no sleeves), nothing to prove, nothing to project. Like the Wizard of Oz, the curtain is pulled down. The Emperor recognizes he has no clothes. We have disconnected our self image machine and we are free to cast only God's original version of ourselves, our authentic and essential soul child.

Like Biff, at this point, we have been taken down to nothing, and we realize we are nothing. But this is the point at which, if we can comprehend it, we clearly recognize that we are also everything. We don't see it in the play, but maybe that is just where Biff is headed.

February 21

In "The Prologue" from *Into the Woods*, characters sing about not being afraid of the forest, for it is simply made of trees. (Listen to the work online or from your library!)

Characters in the "The Prologue" for Stephen Sondheim's and James Lapine's *Into the Woods*

Perhaps everyone has heard that in the Bible, the phrase "Fear not" appears 365 times, a reminder from the Divine every day of the year that we humans should not be anxious. Maybe the real count is only 79 or 123 or 37. (Part of the discrepancy depends on the translation.)

In *Into the Woods*, Little Red sings that no one should have fear. She doesn't. The forest is just filled with all these trunks and branches — and the trunks and branches just make up the forest — things we know, nothing to be afraid of. Is she being honest with herself, or is she optimistically affirming this platitude to keep her courage up?

In 1999, Barry Glassner wrote a book called *The Culture of Fear: Why Americans Are Afraid of the Wrong Things* in which he blasts the news media for stirring up and perpetuating anxiety in our country. Presently, a huge number of people are devoted to 24-hour news stations (conservative and liberal), and hang on every word the opinion hosts spew. Never mind that most of the stories are blown out of proportion, biased toward one political leaning or another, and are more entertainment or spectacle than real news.

I am rarely nervous about the future. I admit part of my serenity may come from a Beta Blocker I have taken for 26 years, used to calm former panic attacks and to lower my blood pressure. But I like to think it is more owing to the fact I quit my news junkie fixation cold turkey one day.

When my son Seth studied Henry David Thoreau in middle school, I took the Transcendentalist's advice to heart: "We should treat our minds, that is, ourselves, as innocent and ingenuous children, whose guardians we are, and be careful what objects and what subjects we thrust on their attention. Read not the *Times*. Read the Eternities."

Before that, I woke up to radio news, watched the morning TV news, watched the 5:00 and 6:00 evening news, and went to sleep with the 10:00 television news. I didn't realize it, but I had a subliminal drone of anxiety running through my being all the time. Luke tells us in the King James version of the Bible, "And the angel said unto her, 'Fear not, Mary: for thou hast found favour with God.'"

One day the same angel spoke to me by giving me holy support through the wisdom of Thoreau. That day I had the news habit; twenty-four hours later, I had stopped. I began to read and study things of an eternal nature: great literature and wisdom teachers. I now go to plays, concerts, ballets, operas, and out to dinner. I urban hike streets that are supposed to be "dangerous and savage." I live my life instead of being told how menacing and perilous it is. I have been much more peaceful ever since — because I have few fears, and I hope you don't either (nobody should!). I truly discovered the woods are just trees and the trees are just wood. But sometimes an acorn drops on my head.

February 22
Claire: "They said Dr. Dudley already called this number. He doesn't want to be called out of the theatre again."
Lenny: "I'm getting a new doctor. I'm not putting my life in the hands of the drama critic for Mt. Sinai Hospital."
Characters in Neil Simon's *Rumors*

Last night, after seeing the play *Grace* by Craig Wright, a friend who was also in the audience said, "This is the kind of play that gets into your DNA." I believe what she meant was that the haunting piece, which prompts many more questions than it answers, seeps into those molecules that render the blueprint of your life.

I don't think Neil Simon's *Rumors* transformed my genetic code, but I certainly appreciate Neil Simon's comedies. I recognize his droll genius. I am delighted at the multi-millions of people he has pulled into the theatre. I highly regard his corpus of works, the longevity of his career, and his energy. He certainly deserved his Tony Awards, Emmy Awards, Pulitzer Prize, New York Drama Critics Circle Award, and many others.

In the lines pulled from *Rumors*, Simon humorously gibes drama critics, who do hold in their hands the professional lives of actors and directors, designers and playwrights. Neil Simon has been both loved and disparaged by reviewers and theatre historians. *New York Times'* critic Clive Barnes once remarked that like his English compeer Noel Coward, Simon was "destined to spend most of his career underestimated," but very popular.

We used to have a reviewer for the *Birmingham News*, when we used to have a daily paper. (Actually we had two daily papers, in my city. The demise of these papers is fodder for another discussion.) Some of my theatre colleagues loved this reviewer Kenneth Paul Shorey and some of them loathed him. Some of them liked him when he gave their show a good review, but deplored him when he was not so favorable to their work.

And Shorey's reviews did reveal much about his own biases and beliefs. But what I loved about Kenneth Paul was that he continually urged the theatre community into boldness, risk, daring, and even adventurous audaciousness. He would rejoice when someone tried something difficult to stage like Carlo Goldoni's *Servant of Two Masters*. He would praise ensemble acting and refrain from using names to keep from being unfair to the collaborative composition. He would deplore the repetitive choice of kitchen table dramas from any theatre. He would applaud adventurous design decisions, valorous directing choices, idiosyncratic acting feats. He would encourage all of Birmingham theatre by assuming people would discuss productions for eons by saying something like "If you miss Reardon, you simply won't know what people are going to be talking about for the next year and a half."

Shorey took theatre seriously, and he desperately wanted theatre practitioners and audiences to do the same. In the days before the internet, cell phones, or other modern electronic forms of transmission, Kenneth Paul went down to the *News* offices and hand typed his review late at night to get the piece into the next day's paper.

I can remember the mixture of excitement, angst, apprehension, confidence, and foreboding I felt when I traced down a newspaper box that contained an early edition of the *News* inside. I inserted my quarters, shakily lifted the issue, and searched through the pages until finding Shorey's review. Sometimes my ego felt crushed, but more often my spirit was enlightened. No matter which way his review was slanted, it seeped into my DNA and made me a better designer and a better person having stood up to his scrutiny.

February 23

"If you refuse this offer, you will be the most ungrateful, wicked girl, and the angels will weep for you."

Henry Higgins to Eliza Doolittle in the musical *My Fair Lady*, book and lyrics by Alan Jay Lerner and music by Frederick Loewe based on the play *Pygmalion* by George Bernard Shaw

We performed *My Fair Lady* the second year I ran the box office at Parkway Playhouse, a summer stock theatre in the Appalachian

Mountains of North Caroline Henry Higgins tells Eliza Doolittle that to refuse his offer to be taught how to speak beautifully would be a most ungracious response. After all, she will have lots to eat, money for chocolate and taxis, and in six months, he bets he can pass her off as a lady of noble birth.

Sarah Ban Breathnach's book *Simple Abundance: A Daybook of Comfort and Joy*, which I read during 2000 influenced my life path. In order not to be a *"most ungrateful, wicked girl,"* I began a gratitude journal. Then, a few years ago, I encountered legendary Rabbi Meir's advice to utter one-hundred blessings a day. Not wanting to write all those down every day, I began the practice of coming up with 100 things to be thankful for on my daily morning walk.

Every day is not brimming with wondrous occurrences or glorious people and many days, my gratitudes are recapitulations of others. But I have learned that appreciation of life cannot simply be a response to having things always go my way or being showered with abundance. With practice, the "blessing search" helps me find value even in the worst of situations, remember wondrous things that have happened, and recognize worth in even cantankerous people.

So in thinking back with gratefulness about *My Fair Lady*, the film was released in October of 1964. Anyone who knows anything about civil rights knows that Birmingham was a hotbed of violent activity, bombings, campaigns, arrests, and marches in 1963. Birmingham schools were integrated that year, and someone threw tear gas into my favorite department store, Lovemar's, when management complied with integration rulings.

Unfortunately, I had grown up knowing few African Americans. In 1964, I was 14 and I went to see *My Fair Lady* at the Ritz Theater downtown with friends twice. I loved it so much, I begged to go one more time before the run was over. I am not really sure if this was the fall of '64 or the spring of '65, but, I could not drive. My parents were extraordinarily obliging and took me downtown on a Saturday night to see the show by myself. For some reason, I decided to sit in the balcony this time, and a black lady came and sat right next to me.

This encounter was one of the first times I had ever been that close to person of color — and certainly the first time alone — and I was mesmerized. My seat mate was very attractive and very personable, probably in her late 20s or early 30s. She told me she thought it was funny that she chose to sit in the balcony, since she was no longer required by law to do so. But she believed the upper tier gave a better view of the film. We chatted softly before the overture and I felt instantly comfortable with her. I am not sure why she even talked to me. People seated next to each other in a movie theater don't always strike up a conversation.

But I am grateful that she did reach out to me, a naive, guileless adolescent. Because of that encounter, I felt at ease around the next African American I met, and then the next, and the next. I often think back upon that evening and to my nameless three-hour friend and say, "*Namaste,*" I bow to the divine in you that reached something holy in me.

February 24
Puck: "*I go, I go; look how I go, Swifter than arrow from the Tartar's bow.*" Act III, Scene 2
Lysander: "*The course of true love never did run smooth.*" Act I, Scene 1
Theseus: "More strange than true." Act V, Scene 1
Hermia: "*I am amazed, and know not what to say.*" Act II, Scene 3
Characters from William Shakespeare's *A Midsummer Night's Dream*

When Samford University opened the then extravagantly priced $9-million fine arts center in the spring of 1976, we chose William Shakespeare's *A Midsummer Night's Dream* for the opening play. We moved into the building in the fall and did not present anything for a few months in order to settle in. So, we designers had a long research and preparation phase — months and months of planning. And the actors got to rehearse for quite a time as well. So it is no wonder that many quotes, and especially these four, from the play come back to haunt me time and time again.

In fact, almost every morning as I transition from my spiritual reading and journaling in my bedroom to practicing Yoga in my great hall, I say Puck's line, "*I go, I go; look how I go, Swifter than arrow from the Tartar's bow.*" Now Puck, being a fairy, could boast like this, since he was lightning fast. I may not always be as speedy as Puck, but the sentiment is there. And I get more and more rapid as I pick up a second cup of java in the kitchen as I pass the coffee pot.

In the very first scene of the first act, Lysander utters the famous words, "*The course of true love never did run smooth.*" Love certainly flowed boisterously and untidily in *Midsummer.* How often do we all hear this phrase, and how often does love run amok with ourselves or those we know and love. Life rarely runs smoothly, much less the passions and intense feelings of our amorous affairs.

Later in *Midsummer* when several sets of lovers have had as many adventures and misadventure as you could encounter in one evening, Queen Hippolyta tells King Theseus that the lovers are speaking of astonishingly strange things. He answers, *"More strange than true,"* meaning they are indeed telling curious tales, which he believes are made up. Lunatics, lovers, and poets, he believes, let their imaginations run wild, and fantasize about things that rational people cannot fathom. Any time I hear odd stories (why am I again thinking of the Alabama legislature?), this phrase immediately bursts from my mouth. It is a great short answer to someone who tells me something I am not quite sure is bona fide.

And likewise, when someone astounds me with brilliance, idiocy, treachery, folly, irrationality, beauty, inappropriateness, or insanity, my exclaiming *"I am amazed, and know not what to say"* at least gives me a few minutes to compose myself and think about the situation.

Actually, more and more I am aware of experiences that I cannot put into words. Scenes in nature, numinous connections to the Holy, deep contemplation or pondering all reveal mysterious truths to me that are almost impossible to verbalize. As William Countryman writes in *Living on the Border of the Holy*, "The deepest arcana are secret because they are hard to know, hard to reveal, hard to learn. They can be known only by experiencing them. Anything that can be fully conveyed in language, without remainder, is probably not of ultimate importance." So being still, amazed, and knowing not what to say is probably a good sign when the rest of my life is spent screaming, *"I go, I go; look how I go."*

February 25
"The violets in the mountains have broken the rocks."
Don Quixote in Tennessee Williams's *Camino Real*

Tennessee Williams passed from this life on February 25, 1983. He was found dead in his bedroom suite in New York City at age 71 at the Elysee Hotel (a fitting ending place, name-wise for him). The medical examiner revealed he had choked on the cap from a bottle of eye drops. I use saline eyedrops almost every morning upon waking and as I lie there,

I think of Tennessee Williams. I keep the cap far away from my mouth, but I can understand exactly how it happened.

The unfavorable reviews of and confusion over Williams's *Camino Real* astound me, because it is one of my favorite plays to have ever had the privilege of working on. No, it is not realistic. No, it does not take place in a modern kitchen. No, it is not based on linear time. No, it is not easy to follow. But it is lyrical, dark, illuminative, haunting, beautiful, chaotic, and theatrical — like life itself. Williams himself said the play is "nothing more nor less than my conception of the time and the world I live in."

I love the violet quote for many reasons: it reminds me of running spotlight on the play when I was a sophomore in college. Faculty member Charles Harbour directed the show, and several other favorite professors and many students filled out the large cast. Violets bloom this time of year, and are my favorite flower. My granddaughter's name is Emmeline Violet. My great-grandmother and grandmother both wore the scent April Violets, a perfume created in 1913 by Yardley of London. Yardley makeup and fragrances were wildly popular in America after the Beatles and other British rock stars invaded the US If you can remember Twiggy, the fashion model of the 1960s and '70s, her long eyelashes were made by Yardley. About this time — when I was working on *Camino Real* — I, too, had claimed April Violets as my scent of choice. The quote struck me with its note of triumph — and stuck with me.

The image of violets — those tiny, fragile, fragrant petals — even growing in the crags of a massive mountain — much less breaking apart its rocks — is fascinating. Modern life often causes us to be precautionary with others. In *Camino Real*, cold-hearted actions abound and people move about oblivious to other characters' misfortunes. This sterility is symbolized by a defunct fountain. But near the play's end, in reaction to a simple act of compassion, the water gushes and that is when Don Quixote proclaims, *"The violets in the mountains have broken the rocks!"*

Violets are symbolic of love and faithfulness. So if a violet can crack rocks, perhaps my casual, small acts of kindheartedness can pierce aloof detachment — or even hatred — as I travel the difficult journey down my own *Camino Real*. Maybe Tennessee Williams is right: it just takes a tiny loving action to split the fissure opening onto a more beautiful world.

February 26

"Well, he'd learned poetry and had kissed a girl. If he hadn't gone to school, he'd met the scholars; if he hadn't gone into the house, he had knocked at the door!"
Paul Shyre in Sean O'Casey's *Knock at the Door*

We knock on wood to protect ourselves from a jinx. Three knocks at the door mean ghostly spirits are outside. Kids still play the game of knocking and running quickly away so their neighbor opens the door to find no one there. In Sean O'Casey's biographical book and the play created from it, the last lines sum up the early part of the life of this inner-city-Dublin working-class poet with poor eyesight. He is making his presence known, even if he has not quite entered the arena.

One of my favorite verses from the Bible is Matthew 7:7, "Ask, and it will be given you. Seek, and you will find. Knock, and it will be opened for you." And even though I love the verse, I believe that proponents of prosperity theology misuse such scripture to promote the idea that economic blessings will materialize through such asking and seeking, through proper speech and positive thoughts, through strong faith and, particularly, contributions to the right televangelists who can assist with personal empowerment and the amassing of material wealth.

This year in my Education for Ministry (EfM) class, when studying a similar passage from Luke, I finally "got" what Jesus's words might really mean. Luke 11:9-13 reads, "I tell you, keep asking, and it will be given you. Keep seeking, and you will find. Keep knocking, and it will be opened to you. For everyone who asks receives. He who seeks finds. To him who knocks it will be opened. 'Which of you fathers, if your son asks for bread, will give him a stone? Or if he asks for a fish, he won't give him a snake instead of a fish, will he? Or if he asks for an egg, he won't give him a scorpion, will he? If you then, being evil, know how to give good gifts to your children, how much more will your heavenly Father give the Holy Spirit to those who ask Him?'"

So that is the key: *the Holy Spirit* will be given if I ask for it. Not mastery of the world or riches beyond compare. If I ask, search for, and knock at the door of the Divine, God is there. The Ultimate Reality is always there. The reason I sometimes fail to remember this truth is that often I am too afraid to ask the hard questions, too lazy to hunt for very long, too weak to keep rapping at the portal.

Since I believe in the Holy Spirit, I trust that that spirit is everywhere, all-pervasive, omnipresent, in the space that holds me together, this planet together, the universe together. But, I am not always

78

present to God. I ask the world for what I want. I seek in earthly ways. I knock on mortal doors in temporal time.

What I might do instead, because it really has worked over and over again, is to ask for the Holy Spirit to surround me, to seek the stillness where God is waiting for me, to tap into the deep spring of my own true Essence where sacredness dwells. I might start each day with this sentence from one of Marianne Williamson's fine prayers, "Please enter where You already abide." That kind of relationship is where I can draw real strength, energy, and vigor.

February 27
"We're regulars, we go there every year."
Delia to Ernest in Alan Ayckbourn's *Bedroom Farce*

Bedroom Farce is a fine comedy, well-structured, melancholy, funny, complex, entangled, full of interesting characters. But dear goodness, I did not want to design this Alan Ayckbourn piece. I was not particularly happy in my new job at a different university. I already missed doing big, bold plays that no one else in town wanted to tackle. I was out of my element, and I felt so much discomfort that my panic attacks returned. I longed to be a bona fide, established "old hand" in my new theatre community, but it wasn't happening.

"We're regulars, we go there every year." For some reason, that line stuck with me. Delia and Ernest, parents of one of the four sets of couples in the play, have made reservations for dinner, and Ernest is worried about their table. Delia reminds him they are "regulars," because they go to the same restaurant annually for their anniversary.

There is something charming about being a regular — but maybe with more frequency than Delia and Ernest. Roger is well-known at Lucy's Coffee and Tea, patronizing the shop several times a week. Lucy knows what he wants before he orders. He feels comfortable in the place, and he gets special treatment. He has made life-long friends with other habitual clients, and he hears all kinds of opinions from people of many professional backgrounds.

When my mother was still alive, she and my granddaughter Emmeline and I had lunch every Friday at our local country club, starting from the time Emme was eight-months old, so we had become "regulars." Our crackers and butter were already on the table when we got there. Rita announced that they did or did not have macaroni and cheese that day

(Emmeline's favorite), and brought my water and her chocolate milk without our ordering. We got royal treatment because we were appreciated as part of the club family.

I only stayed at the other university for 18 months before moving back to Samford in August of 1980. My first show upon returning was *East Lynne*, the 1860s old-fashioned melodrama, which kept me in the costume shop sewing bustle dresses 12 hours a day, cutting, draping, breaking sewing machine needles, and rubbing my fingers raw on the silky fabrics.

So, working hard on the production, I missed the opening of that 11-season television champion of "regulars," *Cheers*, a show set in a Boston bar where a bunch of local folks meet to sip suds, unwind, and share their lives. It premiered on September 30 and the theme song reflected an idea that avid fans believed: When work is hard, meeting friends to take a break at the end of the day helps!

I was happy enough at that point to be a regular back in my old costume shop. But I would have liked to break away at least occasionally to be a frequent customer at some pub where the staff was happy to see me. Because in places where people gather over and over to talk, we really do have a chance to see that we have similar problems and life challenges. When we have those rough days at work, it is a good feeling to leave, take a break, feel free, and walk into a familiar place to see folks who know you by name.

February 28
In "Joseph's Coat" from *Joseph and the Amazing Technicolor Dreamcoat*, Joseph boasts about how attractive he looks in his magnificent and shining in his many-hued tunic. (Listen to the work online or from your library!)

Joseph in Tim Rice's and Andrew Lloyd Webber's *Joseph and the Amazing Technicolor Dreamcoat*

In *Joseph and the Amazing Technicolor Dreamcoat*, the title character sings about all the dazzling colors of his coat — naming them all as if reading from a Crayola Crayon box. When I twice designed the show, I was taken back to the days when I learned ballet from a Birmingham master, Miss Nancy Lum. Her studio was right up the street from where I lived, and often my aunt Jackie, who was nine years older than I, would walk me to my class.

In the baby session which I attended, as I was only 2- or 3-years old at the time, we had to learn our proper arm positions. When we got to the fifth and final position, we rounded our arms over our heads with elbows slightly bent and palms facing inward. Miss Lum would walk around and inspect our ovals to see who was proper and who was not. She would ask us what color we were holding in our egg-shaped void, and other girls would reply yellow, red, orange, or blue. But Jackie would coach me on the way so that I could grandly reply, "Chartreuse," or "Lilac," or "Chocolate," or "Mauve," or "Azure," or "Lemon." How I loved my ball of many colors!

Until I was about 8-years old, Crayola Crayons provided me with 48 thrilling colors in a box of absolute wonderment. The distinctive sweet, earthy, waxy smell, which is now known to lower blood pressure, was enough to distract me for hours. But the names printed on the paper covers pulled me into other worlds: "Bittersweet," "Thistle," "Violet Red," "Salmon," "Orchid," "Burnt Sienna," "Prussian (later Midnight) Blue," and my all-time favorite, "Periwinkle."

In 1958, the boxes began to hold an amazing 64 colors with the breathtaking additions of "Copper" and "Mulberry" and "Forest Green" and "Goldenrod" (then the state flower of Alabama). I would sit and stare at the names, beguiled by the scent, and drift off somewhere far from the small bungalow where I lived in Tuscaloosa. Such a dazzling box of colors, how I loved my box of many colors.

I grew up, learned art in school, majored in art in college, and then jumped into theatre, designing costumes using watercolors, gouache, acrylics, colored pencils, inks, and Dr. Martin's dyes. I don't paint costume renderings as much anymore, but I still love to create visual pictures, and I sometimes get out the Crayolas. I recently found a discontinued "Mulberry" in my stash, and an inappropriately named "Indian Red" as well.

Joseph is a bit full of himself, boasting in his "Coat of Many Colors" song about how good-looking and stylish he looks. But I delight in the polychromatic story of Joseph: he is loved by his father (who gives him the cloak) and then naturally, hated by his 11 brothers. They decide to sell him into slavery and he is taken to Egypt. His brilliance wins the goodwill of his master and then Joseph falls from favor when he rejects the advances of Potiphar's wife. He is thrown in jail, he interprets dreams, he is elevated to a high position, and he is approached unknowingly by his brothers when famine strikes.

At first, Joseph treats them harshly and creates a little drama around them. But, eventually instead of revenge, he reaches out to his brothers in forgiveness. He weeps at the sight of them and, through compassion, reunites the family. Early in life, Joseph worshipped that coat of russet and grey and purple and white. But later he realized that it was the love of the many-faceted brothers that put the real color into his life.

February 29
"Fie on Vulcan, that fiery braggart of the Underworld! We met once in a challenge, Vulcan and I.
'Whose fire is hottest?' quoth he.
'Mine is!' quoth I.
'No!' quoth he.
'Yes!' quoth I.
'Show me!' quoth he.
'It will pleasure me greatly,' quoth I.
Then, Vulcan's temple erupted, he emptied his fire. The ocean bubbled, mountains crumbled and Pompeii was drowned. But I, a mere mortal against this mighty god, with a single exhalation of my breath, I leveled Crete and I leveled Alexandria, and the draft from the flaming ruins scorched the land and formed the Sahara Desert!"
Capitano in my own adaptation of a *commedia dell'arte* scenario which I called *The Artful Antics of the Disguised Gypsies*

What boasting the Capitano ("Cap-ee-tahn-o") lets tumble from his mouth! What imprudent, overindulgent, unrestrained, uncontrolled, lavish, extravagant crowing he does. He is one of the stock character of the Italian "comedy of art." Miles Gloriosus, a swaggering soldier of ancient Roman comedy, was his ancestor.

Though a loudmouth, the Capitano is anything but brave. In fact, in this Spring of 1980 production, the Harlequin servant character Arlecchino has sneaked off stage and back on with a hot coal that he places in Capitano's hat. When it begins the smoke, the captain, smelling something burning and realizing his headpiece is on fire, begins running about the stage screaming like a coward.

The servants or the *zanni* in this Italian improvisational theatre function as jesters, jacks and jills of all trades, confidants, and messengers. Both male and female characters are endowed with astuteness, acumen, and adeptness at practical pranks. The *zanni* also serve as a trickster, forming a terrific literary foil to the action. The role of both foil and trickster is to unveil the qualities of a character (Capitano). And whether in myth or in real life, the trickster uses keen observational skills to circumvent customs and put the characters (or ourselves) in proper place.

Most cultures give prominence to the mythology of the trickster. Carl Jung identified the character as part of the collective consciousness. Joseph Campbell said, "Almost all non-literate mythology has a trickster-hero of some kind... And there's a very special property in the trickster: he always breaks in, just as the unconscious does, to trip up the rational situation. He's both a fool and someone who's beyond the system. And the trickster represents all those possibilities of life that your mind hasn't decided it wants to deal with." The mischievous creature shows the shadow side of our ego selves that we usually ignore. And when the Universe is the trickster, it assists our squashed soul by mobilizing forces that wake us up to a new plan for our more enlightened lives.

When my daughter and her husband had only Emmeline, they discussed having more kids. David wanted three (as he has a brother and a sister), but Elin was fine with just adding a second one, repeating her family pattern of two siblings. Not wanting to give up working, she felt a third pregnancy and the accompanying young childhood days would be too demanding. They spent years talking back and forth about the "right" number. When they got pregnant with the second child, he turned out to be twins so they got the third child but with only one additional gestation period.

The Universe plays trickster for me over and over again, so I guess my shadow side is ever in need of revelation. One day, I fell and scraped my knees and tights when almost running in what was supposed to be a leisurely Sunday stroll to the opera. Every photo of a family event I didn't want to attend shows me with my slip showing. Almost every time I drive my car and begin shouting at someone for cutting in front of me or neglecting to use their turn signal, I do the exact same thing in a matter of minutes.

My rushing about, my feelings of inferiority, my true intent, and my temper were (are) all suppressed and in need of airing and disclosure. What the trickster does for us is free us from our ego.

March 1

"Daffodils that come before the swallow dares, and takes the winds of March with beauty."
Perdita in Shakespeare's *The Winter's Tale*, Act IV, Scene 4

In this scene, Perdita wishes she could conjure up spring flowers, daffodils and violets, pale primroses and bold oxlips, crown imperials and lilies of all kinds. Florizel asks if she wants all these blossoms to overlay a corpse, but she says no, to cover "a bank for love to lie and play on" — not like a corpse to be buried, unless he means buried in her arms!

On this first day of March, I have a mere three daffodil blossoms in my yard — well, now in my vase (it is bad luck to bring a single daffodil inside). It has been a harsh winter of ice and snow, cold winds and bitter temperatures here in Alabama and even the spring flowers are having trouble deciding whether to venture out yet or not.

I did see an entire bank of nascent daffodils on my drive to a contemplative workshop about Julian of Norwich this morning. The buttery trumpets were holding up fairly well in the brisk breeze of this early March day, their beauty as yet unspoiled. In England, because of the time they bloom, these flowers are known as "Lenten Lilies."

Daffodils are symbols of new beginnings, of rebirth, of stirrings of the soul after a long dormant period. From bulbs in the icy earth watchfully waiting for that first tiny hint of warming, they shoot up when the air is just right. With their return, especially after a harsh winter like we have had, I am reminded that after my setbacks and pain, beauty might follow.

So I was happy to see those blowing blossoms on my way to the Julian of Norwich conference I have read her *Revelations of Divine Love* both on my own and in a study class. Many of her amazing insights into contemplative life were planted inside me during those times, and a few of them began if not to bloom yet, at least to show fragile green shoots.

Julian talks about suffering and how we can better understand it by contemplating the figure of the incarnated God on the cross. For Julian, hardship and agony were not vengeance from an angry Spirit in punishment for sin. She saw instead that Divine love encompasses everyone, and she understood illness as a spiritual purification that can change our perspective, burn out excess, and make room for what is truly significant in our lives. She lived during the Black Plague and, in fact, in her younger life had asked God for a bodily sickness that took her to the brink of, but not entirely unto death.

Evening temperatures are supposed to dip into the 20s again this week. I haven't seen many swallows yet, but they are bound to be here soon — we do have several species that appear in Alabama in the spring. But I do hope the six-inch high flaxen-colored fronds of my daffodils don't suffer a setback from the freeze. Because when I see my side garden bursting with their mildly fragrant blooms, I see a sign that warmth is returning to the earth, and that gives me an expectation for a renewed life.

March 2
"Have you one word to say for yourselves?... Ah! don't irritate me, you there, or I'll lay my slipper across your jaws; and it's pretty heavy."
Leader of Women's Chorus in Aristophanes's *Lysistrata*

Lysistrata is a searing comedy about one woman's attempt to end the Peloponnesian War by persuading her fellow Grecian females to force peace by withholding sexual favors from lovers and husbands. The play is ribald, earthy, bawdy, and suggestive. Our *Lysistrata* in college was tall, able-bodied, and athletic, and yet about as proper and demure as a Southern young lady of the 1960s could possibly be. One of the most amazing transformations I ever experienced was to see her take on that role and fill it with robust ardor.

How many times do we women want to tell a man, *"Ah! don't irritate me, you there, or I'll lay my slipper across your jaws; and it's pretty heavy"*? I can name numerous times, and since I will no doubt find occasion to do so innumerable times again, I am committing the short quote to memory to have in my repertoire. Not that I would usually resort to actually throwing a shoe at someone, but the sentiment is so good that perhaps just the line would halt my adversary.

Thinking further along these pacifist lines (and *Lysistrata* is a peace-mongering show) I don't always have to physically throw that shoe. I could use my wit and cleverness to metaphorically launch a verbal knockout blow to bring my rival ("you there") to the ground, rendering him unable to defend himself.

I remember one time in a college English class performing such a spoken boxing blow. We had a swaggering braggart in the class who irritated everyone not only by his smart aleck remarks, but also by the electric blue shirts he wore. I honestly could not look at him for over a few seconds when he was so attired for fear of damaging my eyes. We were discussing Wallace Stevens's poem "Sunday Morning" and our classmate monopolized the discussion. Missing the point of the work, he attempted to insert Christian doctrine into it that is simply not there.

I didn't often speak out during such discourses, but somehow could not listen to one more of his ranting remarks. I loved the poem and had researched, studied and explicated it; so with a sword-like tongue, I swiftly slashed his presumptuous assumptions to shreds like Zorro's saber. It was one of those odd instances when I did something that prompted spontaneous applause, and the professor even patted me on the shoulder and said, "Well done, Miss Sloan!"

Many times, I think hours later of what I should have said in a situation. No matter how much I carefully consider items that might come up in discussions, I am not always quick on my feet with clever repartee or brave bantering. But now, I have a sharp-witted quote from a Greek play that I can heave on those occasions that warrant a slipper to the jaw.

March 3
[The English clock strikes 17 English strokes.] *"There, it's nine o'clock. We've drunk the soup, and eaten the fish and chips, and the English salad. The children have drunk English water. We've eaten well this evening. That's because we live in the suburbs of London and because our name is Smith."*
Mrs. Smith in Eugene Ionesco's The Bald Soprano

This passage which begins the very funny Absurdist play by Eugene Ionesco is one of those lines that I hear in my head nearly every night at nine o'clock: "There, it's nine o'clock. We've drunk the soup, and eaten the fish and chips,..." Unfortunately, I don't have a chiming clock, and if I did, it would be normal and strike only nine times. A great invention would be an Absurdist clock that would ding odd numbers of dongs for various hours — especially entertaining when you had guests over.

The first time I saw The Bald Soprano in college, I was disturbed by its presentation of life as meaningless and I was unnerved by its lack of emotional connection to the audience. These days, I relish the play for its circular quality, its farcical and yet melancholy slant on life, its delightfully delicious dialogue. As the curtain opens, a woman prattles on and on — for many, many minutes about many, many things — as if she did not know the man sitting next to her. He simply continues to read his newspaper and click his tongue, without an answer. They turn out to be Mr. and Mrs. Smith, man and wife, but you would never know it by their acknowledgement of or lack of affection for each other.

Then, two guests arrive for dinner (after the Smiths had already eaten, but admit to being very hungry) and the couple has an even more absurd exchange in which they discover that just today, they traveled on the same train and in the same compartment. Moreover, they live on the same street and in the same flat on the same floor, and both have a two-year old daughter, Alice.

Mrs. Martin says, "How curious it is! It is indeed possible, dear sir." Then there is silence and the clock strikes 29 times. After some reflection, Mr. Martin says in a monotonous voice, "Then, dear lady, I believe that there can be no doubt about it, we have seen each other before and you are my own wife... Elizabeth, I have found you again!"

I think the reason *The Bald Soprano* perturbed me when I was 19 is that despite many pains and wounds I had already suffered, I wanted to believe in the untarnished goodness and sanctity of life. I was impressionable, and I did not want the theatre of the absurd to underscore for me the preposterousness, the incongruity, the irrationality, or the pointlessness of modern life. The recurrent, fragmented, senseless dialogue that both the Smiths and the Martins participate (or fail to participate) in, the lack of plot or meaning to the structure, the bewildering and ambiguous circumstances — all pointed to a futility and hollowness of human existence that I did not want to acknowledge.

Fast-forward 45 years and I understand that sometimes life is good and holy, and sometimes it seems nonsensical and insignificant. As I am learning that to become an enlightened citizen of the earth, I have to rise above dualistic thinking. Life is not either good or bad, grounded or chaotic — it is the whole ball of wax, and to fail to embrace its everything-ness is to miss its beauty. Senseless heartache and jubilant delight are related, intertwined, and really, as Lebanese poet Kahlil Gibran wrote, "Your joy is your sorrow unmasked. And the selfsame well from which your laughter rises was oftentimes filled with your tears."

March 4
"What's here? a cup, closed in my true love's hand?
Poison, I see, hath been his timeless end:
O churl! drunk all, and left no friendly drop

To help me after? I will kiss thy lips;
Haply some poison yet doth hang on them,
To make me die with a restorative.
    [Kisses him.]
Thy lips are warm."
Juliet in Shakespeare's *Romeo and Juliet*, Act V, Scene 3

The timing of Juliet's awakening in the tomb — after Romeo has emptied the cup poison mere moments before — is devastating. Juliet has taken Friar Lawrence's potion which makes her appear lifeless. Romeo descends into the sepulcher, looks upon his beloved lying peacefully as if she were just sleeping (which she is, but he has missed communication of the plan), and he kisses her, drinks a bitter poison, kisses her again, and dies.

Juliet then wakes, sizes up the situation immediately, and seeing her sweetheart dead, hopes to ingest some of the toxin with a kiss. When that fails, she plunges his dagger into her breast. If things had not ended this way, we would not have a majestic tragedy, but a dull domestic drama in which Romeo and Juliet would live happily (or boringly) ever after.

One of my two or three addictions is my passion for microwavable heating pads. With a bad back, I go to sleep with one every night. Upon awakening each morning, and rummaging about the bed covers to find it, I think of Juliet's poignant and harrowing cry. Even after eight hours of inactivity, I still feel lingering heat in my little sack of dry rice. "Thy cloth is warm!" I cry out to it.

So almost every day I give a nod to this beautiful play and the genius of William Shakespeare. Being only 18 myself when Franco Zeffirelli's cinema adaptation was released, I was captivated by the youth of the actors, Leonard Whiting and Olivia Hussey who starred in the title roles. I delighted in the costumes, which won an Academy Award. I relished the cinematography (also Oscar-winning). I enjoyed the entire film, and I especially loved the music, although I thought it rather odd that so many people I knew who got married over the next few years used "A Time for Us" as their wedding song. Most of those unions met with just about as tragic an end as Romeo's and Juliet's did, probably because most of those people were scarcely older than this famous pair of lovers and made immature choices for life partners. Hopes for a good relationship crumbled in a terrifically short interval.

What haunts me about Juliet's *"Thy lips are warm"* quote is the sheer heartbreak of missing (or hitting) something by several heartbeats: coming in second by a second in a race, glancing at something in the car and rear-ending another vehicle, looking into a store window right as an old friend walks right past and not seeing each other. So much can happen in the blink of an eye.

March 5
"Rosemary Sidney: Look at that sunset, Howard!
Howard Bevans: A sunset's a beautiful thing, all right.
Rosemary Sidney: It's like the daytime didn't want to end, isn't it? It's like the daytime was gonna put up a big scrap, set the world on fire to keep the night from creeping on."
Characters in William Inge's *Picnic*

Sunsets are almost as beautiful to me as sunrises. The colors can be so vivid: Byzantium to aubergine, coral to cerise, flame to tangerine. Or maybe subtle hues appear: peach, bittersweet, or mauve. Sunsets symbolize day's end, finishing up business, or even life's end.

"It's like the daytime was gonna put up a big scrap, set the world on fire to keep the night from creeping on." Rosemary Sidney's line from Inge's *Picnic* beckons an intriguing contemplation. Why are humans afraid of the dark coming upon us? The fear seems to stem from an innate reaction inherited from our ancestors who had to deal with dangerous, predatory, nocturnal animals that had the upper paw at night. An odd squeak in the floorboard, a scraping of a bough against the siding, the drop of a pinecone on the roof can startle us from a deep sleep and scare us because, in a stupor, we can't identify the sound.

One of my very earliest memories is stirring in my crib in my first apartment home. I loved to have my family members read fairy tales to me, but somehow, "The Three Bears" took hold of my imagination in a frightening manner. The way a streetlight shone into our bedroom through window mullions manifested upon the wall three round light patches in descending size. Night after night, I would wake and interpret those bright spots as the three bears coming after a little Goldilocks named Barbie. And I had trouble going back to the Land of Nod even at two years old.

Slumber itself makes some people apprehensive. Edgar Allan Poe summed up this unease by saying, "Sleep, those little slices of death —

how I loathe them." Where do we go when we relinquish our consciousness on our beds each night? We begin to disconnect from the waking world, we stop communication with the outside, and let our inner sphere have dominion. We begin to dream. And what are dreams? Do they signify something or mean nothing? Do they help us sort out our thoughts and emotions, or confuse them?

I have several recurring dreams. One is of taking a short cut on some very long and involved walk, and the alternative route is through a house belonging to someone I don't know. Occasionally I get caught, but usually I wind my way through the building without being detected.

Off and on, I also have insomnia. No wonder I respond to Rosemary's idea that the day might pick a fight and use its flames to halt the ebony sky. But we know the veil will be pulled nonetheless, and darkness will fall. So I have found succor in several balms to quiet my mind and induce sleep. My best help comes from sniffing the scent of lavender, sipping Sleepy Time tea, listening to soft music, and reading the somnolent office of Compline from the *Book of Common Prayer*. "Visit this place, O Lord, and drive far from it all snares of the enemy; let your holy angels dwell with us to preserve us in peace..."

March 6

"O, Creator! Why have I been tormented like this, to learn the truth about my birth? The Sun is still the source of light to the world! My mother is still a respected queen! Yet I, the result of their union, am a wanderer."
Karna in *The Mahabharata*

The Mahabharata is said to be the longest epic poem ever written, and is one of two ancient Indian Sanskrit compositions. Winding through tales of the princes Kaurava and Pandava, the work delves into sacred and philosophical discussions while also telling the story of the Kurukṣetra War. Part of the poem involves the *Bhagavad Gita*, (or the Song of God) which comprises the conversation of Pandava's prince Arjuna and the Lord Krishna, who is also his guide and charioteer.

In 1985, ingenious British director Peter Brook translated *The Mahabharata* into a cycle of three plays lasting a total of nine hours for the 39th Avignon festival. Many critics hailed the work as a phenomenal success, celebrating the translation of the Hindu myth into something modern audiences could understand.

Unfortunately, I didn't get to see the French production that year. However, Peter Brook, Jean-Claude Carrière, and Marie-Hélène Estienne worked for eight years to create a script, and in 1989, that work was developed a six-hour television mini-series, and later, a three-hour DVD. Though I was never a mini-series devotee, I missed none of the PBS-sponsored *Mahabharata* programs. The series won an international Emmy for best televised performing arts presentation.

Part of the action of the tale involves Karna's mother, Kunti a very young girl, who much like Mary, the Mother of Jesus, becomes pregnant in a mystical union with the Sun. Then, like the parents of Moses, Kunti puts her newborn son in a basket and pushes him down river. And, like Moses, the child is rescued and adopted, in Karna's case by the king's charioteer.

This action complicates both families' lives later. Just before the quote for the day, Krishna has explained to Karna the truth of his birth, because he wants the great archer to join the Pandavas in the impending Kurukshetra war. Karna turns down the offer to switch sides, but subsequently enters a temple by himself and says, *"O, Creator! Why have I been tormented like this, to learn the truth about my birth? The Sun is still the source of light to the world! My mother is still a respected queen! Yet I, the result of their union, am a wanderer."*

Whether we are brought up by our birth parents, step-parents, adoptive parents, grandparents, friends, godparents, or someone else, we all wonder about our birth. When constructing a spiritual biography for a small group discussion, I began to think back on my debut into this world. What did the Divine have in mind when I was pointed toward Earth? Why was I born right smack in the middle of the twentieth century on January 24, 1950?

Why was I a fifth generation Birminghamian and not a twentieth generation Mumbaian? Why was my family English Presbyterian rather than Indian Hindu? I hope you don't feel tormented about your birth like Karna did. But what do you wonder about the year, the family, the city, the culture you were born into?

March 7

"I suppose I think that the highest gift that man has is art, and I am audacious enough to think of myself as an artist — that there is both joy and beauty and

illumination and communion between people to be achieved through the dissection of personality."
Lorraine Hansberry in Robert Nemiroff's *To Be Young, Gifted, and Black: A Portrait of Lorraine Hansberry in Her Own Words*

Last year I read Joan Borysenko's wonderful *Pocketful of Miracles* as my morning inspirational book. I am always interested in what people say about art and creativity. She had read the Gospel of Thomas, which I have also studied from the Nag Hammadi library of Gnostic Gospels. She quoted Jesus from this source as saying, "If you bring forth what is within you, what you bring forth will save you. If you do not bring forth what is within you, what you do not bring forth will destroy you."

Then she explained those words like this: the artistic urge is similar to the flow of electricity. If you use creativity, she said, "it will bring great benefit to life. If you obstruct it, it will burn out your circuits and cause depression, malaise and illness." I was floored by this idea, and so were some attendees at a conference when I related that idea to them in a presentation on the about the Arts.

Some of my participants remarked that they had done that very thing: stuffed their painting skills for law school, entombed their acting bug for the corporate ladder, and submerged their musical gifts to make ends meet. After a while, they felt depressed or developed high blood pressure, were stricken with ulcers or succumbed to despondency. Some of them had embraced their artistic gifts again and had recovered. Others wondered if doing that would help.

I agree with Lorraine Hansberry that art is certainly a high and wondrous gift, and great sculptors, musicians, composers, dancers, singers, painters, writers all connect us to something that is beyond us until we find their special portal. She was a great playwright herself, taken from us way too early at age 35.

But great artists aren't the only talented humans. Everyone is. Our Maker is creative and humans are made in God's image. Therefore, we are all creative beings. Period. When we create, we can get in touch with our Soul Child. Producing or experiencing art puts us in the now, and can help us drop our ego fixation as we use all our senses to communicate with others.

This concept is what Hansberry at her young age meant that through art *"...there is both joy and beauty and illumination and communion between people..."* Those people can be a jillion miles or eight centuries apart, and yet there is still the transmission of something exciting and important. Don't you want to create something to keep your circuits from burning out today?

March 8
"It's funny. It's all mixed up. There's something in you, and you don't know anything about it because you don't know it's there. And then suddenly, one night a little girl gets bored and tells a lie, and there, for the first time, you see it. Then you say to yourself, did she see it? Did she sense it?"
Martha to Karen in Lillian Hellman's *The Children's Hour*

The Children's Hour is an intriguing play, not just because it was controversial when first staged, but because it reveals such deep parts of the human psyche. The tense drama takes place in a boarding school. One day, Mary Tilford, a spoiled, ill-tempered student runs away from the all-girls institution. To avoid returning, the conniving Mary tells her doting grandmother that Martha Dobie and Karen Wright, the two headmistresses, are involved in a love affair. As the action unfolds, the two women's professional and personal lives are destroyed.

Almost unbelievable to a citizen of the twenty-first century, when *The Children's Hour* was produced in 1934, even the allusion to homosexuality on stage was illegal in New York State. Nevertheless, Hellman's play opened at Maxine Elliott's Theatre on November 20 and ran for over two years. Critics so highly praised the work, which was also a commercial success, that its subject matter was disregarded. Early on, the work was prohibited in Boston, Chicago, and London, but did open in Paris as *Les Innocents*.

In the scene featuring this quote, Martha reveals to Karen that she actually has been attracted to her in excess of a conventional relationship, but that she did not recognize it herself until Mary's false accusation compelled her to look deeply and truthfully into her own soul. This revelation disturbs Karen who encourages Martha to lie down. Believing herself to have ruined both of their lives by the confession, Martha then shoots and kills herself.

A peculiar part of our self awareness is that many things are in flux on a day to day basis. Many of us don't take a lot of time to delve regularly into our minds, our emotions, our spirits. Then, one day something happens that brings out either our shining beings or our shadow selves.

Our shadow self is woven together using our undesired thoughts and feelings — and some of our good features. When we are little, our parents caution us to behave, so we stuff our exasperation and our fury and even our true selves deep inside us to get along, to please, to survive. Recovery takes a lot of work, and many of us don't want to do it. In *The Children's Hour*, Martha commits suicide rather than face who and what she might really be.

Breathing deeply, chanting, finding a confidant, journaling, painting, employing a spiritual director or counselor, using reiki touch therapy, and many other techniques can help us all face our shadow selves and grow. I have recently been incredibly enlightened by my work with the Enneagram. I wish Martha had been able or willing to access such a powerful method of spiritual growth.

March 9
In "Life Upon the Wicked Stage" from *Show Boat*, Ellie sings to the Girls about what her life as an actress is really like. (Listen to the work online or from your library!)
Ellie to the Girls in Edna Ferber's *Show Boat*

Edna Ferber's *Show Boat* was one of the first plays for which I actually fulfilled a technical position and got listed in the program at the University of Montevallo. I was majoring in both Art and English, and somehow, to me, theatre put them both together. Before I began to work backstage, I knew very little about the inner operations of production work; but just a couple of plays educated me very quickly.

So, I agree with Ellie in the show that people who don't work "on the stage" may have misconceptions about those who do. If I had had a formal time of conjecture before I was somehow mysteriously pulled into the theatre, maybe I would have fancied that life in the theatre was glamorous, exciting, illustrious. That's what the stage struck maidens in *Show Boat* believe, that actors are happy day and night, sipping bubbly wine from a stylish shoe.

We can blame the scurrilous reputation of theatre folks on the English Puritans, really, and our American ancestors who immigrated here during the seventeenth century. On September 2, 1642, the predominantly English Puritan Parliament prohibited the performance of plays and not only closed the theatres, but in 1647, ordered that all stage galleries, seats and boxes be destroyed. At the same time, they proclaimed all stage players to be rogues and anyone found to be acting would be publicly whipped, with spectators subject to five shillings fines.

With Charles II of England's coronation in 1660, theatres were reinstated. These days, I am not sure what people who don't work in the theatre actually "suppose" deep in their hearts about the people who do. But I can tell you what life upon and behind scenes of the wicked stage have been to me. Because of all the personas I have had to creep into the skin of, I am a more empathetic person than I would have otherwise ever been. Because we can produce plays from Greek times all the way to the present, I feel connected to people of other centuries and places, and I get energy from these associations.

Because theatre is a collaborative art, I am more sociable and socialized than if I had pursued a studio art career and created art alone. Because performances involve so many people coming together to share talents and to work extremely hard, I have learned to cooperate with numerous different personalities and have gotten to really know many people very intimately. Because plays begin with a written script, my mind has been expanded, my literacy enhanced, my psychological skills sharpened, and my education expanded in this business. And because the written word then becomes spoken in the theatre, I have learned to listen, to be influenced by what the characters are professing, to think about my own life and principles and conduct, and to perhaps change.

March 10
"Job's Comforters. Every time they play this play Job's Comforters must come . . . to comfort him."
Mr. Zuss to Nickles in Archibald MacLeish's *JB*

"Every time they play this play..." I love the theatricality of the play within the play of *JB* In it, Mr. Zuss and Nickles once again, as if having done so thousands upon thousands of times before, pick up their masks and play God and Satan. We all impersonate God and Satan, don't we? Sometimes every day.

And we take on the role of Job, too. Job is Everyman, and I am Everyman as well. We performed this play in the spring of 1995. I had myself been through a rough couple of years, so I could feel a tiny measure of the anguish of this JB character.

The Job of the Old Testament owns lots of camels, sheep, and oxen and is blessed with wealth and a large family. He praises God for his lot in life. MacLeish's JB is an affluent New York banker who believes God has given him success as a reward for his faithfulness. Both Job and JB lose everything and are reduced to the dung pit, the ash heap of life.

Neither man is prepared for what happens to him, and both question God and cry out for justice, for understanding, for meaning from the universe. MacLeish himself wrote, "And it is in those repeated cries of his that we hear most clearly our own voices. For our age is an age haunted and driven by a need to know. Not only is our science full of it but our arts also. And it is here, or so it seems to me, that our story and the story of Job come closest to each other."

In the biblical version of the tale, Job is visited by three friends who want to console him, but they deeply believe that Job's suffering is retribution for his sins. They counsel him to confess what he has done wrong, and seek God's compassion. Three friends also call upon JB in the play, but in the modern version, the Comforters epitomize Science, Religion, and History. When all offer conflicting reasons for his circumstances, he sends them away in disgust.

Turning to God for an explanation, JB wants to know: where is justice and why do bad things happen to good people? The God-like Mr. Zuss asks JB who he is to ask such a question of the Creator of all? He promises that if JB will abhor himself and repent, he can save himself and go back to his old life. Like Job, he had always heard of God, but now he has seen him, "the mystery of the universe, beauty beyond the feel of fingers..." At first, JB feels remorse, but then, he asks, "Repent? For crying out? For suffering?... Must my breath, my breathing, be forgiven me?"

JB doesn't want to accept the idea that humans will never know why we suffer and why God is mute on the matter. "He answered me like the stillness of a star that silences us asking... We are and that is all our answer. We are and what we are can suffer."

MacLeish does not elucidate the reason for human pain any more than the author of Job does. He simply portrays a human grappling for the meaning of life, asking the hard questions. "Why suffering? Why me? Why life?" I have to find the answers myself, as I explore the role of Job. Job is Everyman, and I am Everyman, too.

March 11

"But I don't need to tell you, Madam, that life is like that; it's made up of absurdities, things which don't make sense – and which, like it or not, don't need to be credible, because they are true."

96

Father (hurt, using his 'mellifluous' voice) to Eliana in Luigi Pirandello's *Six Characters in Search of an Author*

Living in the South and studying English in college, I have always perceived that, as peculiar as some Southern literature is, truth really can be stranger than fiction. As Father tells Eliana in Pirandello's work, life is made up of absurdities, but they don't have to make sense to be believable, because they are what happens in living color. Creative writers have to compose a reasonably plausible plot to persuade their readers to stay engaged.

A Southern novel can begin, "The night the pig got loose in the wake of the tornado, Alva was delirious with the influenza, so she couldn't hear Mama on the phone telling Ida Pearl her plan to put poison in the collard greens." But it is not hard to find true stories or incidents much more far-fetched: In Alabama, it is illegal for a person to be blindfolded while driving a vehicle. During the summer of 1992, a child was playing outside, when she was carried off by a whirlwind and deposited uninjured in the top of a tree almost two miles away. After ingesting antifreeze, a dog was rescued from certain death by veterinarians who fed him copious amounts of vodka.

We have a metro columnist for the *Birmingham News* who keeps lawmakers and citizens on their toes by publishing the almost unbelievable antics of just about everyone around the state. Some people scold him, "What is to be gained by taunting and ridiculing a man for Pete's sake?" But other Birminghamians are glad to have his watchful eye and quick wit reporting the folly going on around us daily. Recently he admitted, "It was a wacky, wacky week in the Legislature. You just can't make the stuff up." And he told of four bills passed making it tougher and more bureaucratic to have an abortion, thus saving lives. In the same three-day period, the legislature passed a bill making it easier to kill people, keeping confidential the names of companies that make and supply drugs used in Alabama lethal injection executions.

Even prominent scientists agree with the idea that life is full of almost unbelievable absurdities. Lawrence Krauss is a Foundation professor in the School of Space and Earth Exploration and the Department of Physics at Arizona State University. "Truth is stranger than fiction," Krauss said at the 2014 annual meeting of the American Association for the Advancement of Science in Chicago. "The imagination of nature far exceeds the human imagination, which is why we constantly need to probe the universe via experimentation to make progress."

Maybe that is the answer after all. Nature, reality, the forces of the universe, even life itself all have a more overwhelming creative power than even the best William Faulkner could ever hope to channel.

March 12
"I swear, if you existed, I'd divorce you."
Martha to George in Edward Albee's *Who's Afraid of Virginia Woolf?*

Many people have heard the story of how Edward Albee got the title for his play. In a New York bar, he was "having a beer one night, and I saw 'Who's Afraid of Virgin a Woolf?' scrawled in soap, I suppose, on this mirror. When I started to write the play it cropped up in my mind again. And of course, who's afraid of Virginia Woolf means who's afraid of the big bad wolf . . . who's afraid of living life without false illusions. And it did strike me as being a rather typical, university intellectual joke."

Virginia Woolf was a fascinating character who lived from 1882 to 1941. Not only influential in society as a women's rights advocate and openly bisexual female, she was an intellectual, a brilliant writer, and, unfortunately, a sufferer of mental illness. In addition, she sought to live her life and write her literature by facing reality, even though much of her existence was painful.

Ralph Waldo Emerson once said, "The most dangerous thing is illusion." But we all have to live with a little chimera, something wished for and hoped for desperately, but which is probably impossible to attain. So when Albee's Martha says, *"I swear, if you existed, I'd divorce you,"* she is caught up in the game of delusional fantasy that she and George seem to be experts at playing.

Like George and Martha, all of us have little *trompe l'oeil* tricks in our bag, distractions that we pull out from time to time — some of us most of the time. Illusions cause many of our personal conflicts. Because reality goes on around us all the time, but what actually happens and the way we interpret real life are not always equal. My misperception or veiling of truth may be the only way I can sometimes make it through the day — or night.

For the first six years after my marriage dissolved, I continued my work in the drama department with my former husband. Our offices were on different floors, but theatre is a collaborative art and we were thrown together much more often than I could sometimes handle. We Enneagram Ego Type Fours often use our imagination to heighten our emotions, or to get through difficult situations — it's a coping mechanism.

So sometimes at night, I would imagine in great detail that my ex had magically figured out how to transport himself by balloon to another habitable planet. I could see him lifting off, rising in the dark, smiling, waving, and having a wonderful time, looking every bit like the Wizard when he leaves Oz.

The vision was so real to me at times that I was terribly surprised when I would go to work the next day and he would be there! He existed — and we were divorced. Reality, not illusion.

March 13

In "Deep Purple" a singer in *Showtime: A 1930s Radio Show* sings about how she remembers a former lover when the violet evening deepens to show stars in the sky. (Listen to the work online or from your library!)

Lyrics from "Deep Purple," written by pianist Peter DeRose and performed in *Showtime: A 1930s Radio Show*

The 1930s: Burns and Allen, Milton Berle, Jack Benny, and Fred Allen made their comedic career debuts in this decade. Little Orphan Annie, Buck Rogers, Amos 'n Andy, and Fibber McGee and Molly were widely popular radio shows. Tommy Dorsey, Benny Goodman, the Andrews Sisters, and hundreds more sang their way right into the American living room every night.

Over the decade of the 1930s, radios went from 12 million American households to more than 28 million. Radio was king that decade following the 1929 crash of Wall Street. Families, both children and parents, gathered around the central feature of American living room furniture, the radio, and its endless cheap entertainment and its stars brightened the lives of millions during the gloom of the Great Depression.

In the 1980s, I was part of a revue that pulled songs, comedic sketches, and drama from those days. One of the numbers was the nostalgic "Deep Purple." Its words talking about a memory returning at evening time remind me of my continuing relationship with the radio. Right now, I shuck out the costly fee to listen to Sirius XM classical and jazz music in my car since our local public radio station broadcasts news most of the day, and I need a restorative background for driving. Other than the brief shudder when I pay my annual bill, my drives everywhere are heavenly.

When I was a young teenager, our local rock 'n roll AM broadcasting station was WSCN and I had a bedside radio. But what was really sophisticated was my white plastic transistor that fit in my pocket or purse and went everywhere with me so I could listen any time to "the Good Guys," the disc jockeys who were local celebrities and household names. I became a station correspondent for my high school, and often got to visit their headquarters "on top of the city" in the City Federal Building penthouse.

I took my radio to Camp Winnataska when I was a leader. I listened miserably on the morning of June 5, 1968 to the report that Robert Kennedy had been shot as he walked through the kitchen of the Los Angeles Ambassador Hotel. In the early 1970s, I spent a couple of summers at Parkway Playhouse in Burnsville, North Carolina and depended on my radio for nightly bedtime sleep-lulling and for way-too-early wakeup alarms. One of the endearing qualities of the local station was that we got daily updates from the hospital, listener birthdays, and call-ins from natives who were concerned about lack of rain.

Unbelievably, when I spent a number of Januarys at Samford University's London Study Centre, the same sort of folksy bulletins came through the built-in radio in my room. I could hear, from a nearby British station, first names of who was "in hospital," birthday and anniversary greetings, and call-ins from natives concerned about too much rain.

Much like the internet today, radios used to be the method by which people all over the country, or even the world could be effectively connected. Wouldn't it be great if that sentence read "virtually united"?

March 14

"Lord High Executioner: As some day it may happen that a victim must be found,

I've got a little list – I've got a little list

Of society offenders who might well be underground,

And who never would be missed – who never would be missed!

Chorus: He's got 'em on the list – he's got 'em on the list;

And they'll none of 'em be missed – they'll none of

'em be missed."

Lord High Executioner and Chorus in WS Gilbert and Arthur Sullivan *The Mikado*

A daily task list, a bucket list, a list serve, a price list, a dream list, an address list, a grocery list, a passwords list, a best-dressed list, a play list, a 10-Most Wanted List, a control list, a rule list, a list of nice things to do for myself. Lists are endless! Do lists keep us on track? Protect the social order? Keep us focused on a goal? They can.

I have heard that there are two kinds of people: those who make lists and those who don't. Some people think those who make lists are mentally strong and visionary. Others think they are forgetful and disorganized. And nowadays, there are so many ways to make a list: real sticky notes, computer sticky notes, pre-printed notebooks, iPhone Notes, Covey Franklin planners, sync notes for email, apps to keep you organized.

The Mikado was originally staged at the Savoy Theatre in London on this day, March 14, 1885. One of my favorite songs in the show is Ko-Ko, The Lord High Executioner of Titipu's, "Little List Song." I am a list-maker, par excellence. I have a weekly list of tasks, a bucket list, an accumulative grocery list, a queue of films I want to see, and many assorted other lists. These lists are usually written out by hand, but I also use electronic devices. Very often, when I am composing my wondrous lists, the words to this song from *The Mikado* invariably come into my brain and I start singing this G&S patter song.

Lists help me organize and even break down jobs. Though I realize I really have very little control over my world, I do feel that a list can help me plan my day and week and month without leaving a bunch of things to chance. And, though I always test as a pretty high "J" (liking strategies, schedules, and decisions) on the Myers-Briggs Type Indicator, I am very flexible when plans change and I am extraordinarily open to new information.

Sometimes, we can all feel conflicted when we don't follow our list, or when things get in the way of accomplishing our goals for the day. Just a glance at a list might make us procrastinate seeing all that boring stuff to do. If a list looks too daunting, I sometimes make short lists from the longer ones to help my concentration for a day. And I have fun with the process: I cross out chores in different colored Highlighter markers so I can still see the job I have carried out, giving me visible proof of my industriousness. *"She's got 'em on the list – she's got 'em on the list;*

And they'll none of 'em be missed – they'll none of
'em be missed" because she's got 'em on the List!

March 15

"Caesar: Who is it in the press that calls on me? I hear a tongue shriller than all the music

Cry "Caesar!" Speak, Caesar is turn'd to hear.
Soothsayer: Beware the ides of March.
Caesar: What man is that?
Brutus: A soothsayer bids you beware the ides of March."
Characters in William Shakespeare's *Julius Caesar*, Act I, Scene 2

"Beware the ides of March," a soothsayer tells Julius Caesar, the emperor and perpetual dictator of Rome. He was too carried away by grandiose delusions of his own power to discern that the fortune teller's words might be true. His bloody assassination in 44 BC forever marked March 15 as a date of notoriety. In response, every year on this evening, I have a dinner in his honor. Not that I particularly put Caesar on a heroic pedestal, but he is an intriguing character.

Caesar tried twice to invade England in 55 and 54 BC At the time, Britain was in the midst of Iron Age culture. Though the Romans made no conquests in Britain those two years, Caesar enthroned Mandubracius, a friend of Rome, who helped bring the island into the political influence of Rome. Historian Tacitus remarked that Caesar "revealed, rather than bequeathed, Britain to Rome."

Ten years later, a group of Roman statesmen deemed Caesar a tyrant and, calling themselves "the liberators," quickly plotted his murder. Tragically — and maybe this is what grips me concerning the political homicide — even his friend Brutus got involved in the conspiracy.

There is really no historical evidence of Julius Caesar uttering Shakespeare's famous "Et tu, Brute?" or "And you, too, Brutus?" But, he had to be surprised and pained by the unexpected duplicity of his friend. That double-dealing may have hurt him more than the 23 stab wounds given by the daggers of the Roman Senators. Some critics have contended that perhaps he uttered the words as a curse, meaning something like, "Just wait, your time will come next." Brutus committed suicide two years later after being defeated in a battle with Mark Antony.

Brutus is near the top any list of the biggest traitors of all time, with Benedict Arnold, Tokyo Rose, Julius and Ethel Rosenberg, Guy Fawkes, and, needless to say, Judas Iscariot. I have been betrayed and I know what it is like to have a partner, a priest, a friend, and a trusted associate violate my faith or confidence, the turmoil it put me in, the hurt, the agony. I wish I had encountered a soothsayer on the way to at least one of these chicaneries — but would I have listened?

A quick response to infidelity is to want revenge or to proffer pseudo forgiveness. I learned a better reaction is to take a little time, acknowledge the breach in the relationship, grieve it but not too long or too deeply, talk the matter over with someone wise, and resist being obsessed with the past.

During his murder, Julius Caesar had little time to realize being literally stabbed in the back, and no time to recover. And so, for all those who have been betrayed, take this day to honor one of the towering treacheries of all time. I'll cook my Roman recipes of Chicken Fronto and honey-fried stuffed dates and give my own toast, "Hail, Caesar! I have no regrets about my past, for even the betrayals encountered brought me to this now!"

March 16
"I have come to the conclusion that one useless man is called a disgrace; that two are called a law firm, and that three or more become a Congress! And by God, I have had this Congress!"
John Adams in Sherman Edwards and Peter Stone's *1776!*

The first words I ever heard on a Broadway stage were, *"I have come to the conclusion that one useless man is called a disgrace; that two are called a law firm, and that three or more become a Congress! And by God, I have had this Congress!"* They were so eloquently vocalized by William Daniels that I immediately fell in love with him, with New York theatre, and with the profession of "the stage."

On this day in 1969, *1776!* opened in New York. Could you get any better than William Daniels leading a brilliant cast, a set and lighting by Jo Mielziner, and costumes by Patricia Zipprodt? The musical had been running for a little over a year when I saw it on spring break in 1970 with about 20 of my college buddies. Later, I watched Daniels as the endearing but acid-tongued Dr. William Craig in the television series *St. Elsewhere* and my children adored him as the voice of Knight Rider's talking car "KITT" His name was uncredited in the latter, but his recognizable vocal instrument gave him away.

Each individual's voice is unique because of his or her special vocal cords, body size, and speech habits, but Daniels' range and timbre are unmistakable. I so appreciate the fact that William Daniels' voice was my introduction to Broadway. His New Englander accent is particularly strong and pleasant. What a range. What expression. What resonance.

Once I was at a convention of my Episcopal diocese and on the last day, I happened upon the wife of a former priest. She was taking down a book display, and soon, her husband came in to assist her. He was my priest for almost 13 years, from exactly three weeks before my wedding in August of 1971 to precisely four months before my son was born in September of 1984. I had not seen either of them for several years.

As usual, the reverend father was bustling around, attempting to help his wife and mincing words with another lady packing up books. The moment I heard his voice, I leaned up against the wall, just listening. What a comforting sound struck my ears! I stopped everything just to drink it in. I could not get enough of it — those familiar tones which I had heard ever so rarely in almost a decade.

This was the voice that officiated at my wedding, the voice that baptized my daughter, the voice that counseled and cajoled, uplifted and scolded, whispered and screeched, conversed and cried with me for 154 months of my life. I heard this voice celebrate the Eucharist from the 1928 and the 1979 *Book of Common Prayer* over one-thousand times, his voice echoing and rebounding off the plaster walls and wooden reredos. The crackly tones, rising and falling, pulled me out of the everyday and into holy mysteries, into fellowship with the blessed company of all faithful people.

In much the same way as a favorite actor's vocalizations impress upon our memory, a priest's voice creates a groove in our mind after hearing it wrap so many times around each word of the liturgy. The voice takes phrases from the page and the voice transmits them into our ears, whether we are consciously listening or not. The special tones, the peculiar accent, the singular inflection, each breath, each glottal stop becomes inextricably linked with the comfortable and inspiring words we go to church to hear.

March 17

"It is not the literal past, the 'facts' of history, that shape us, but images of the past embodied in language."
Hugh to Owen in Brian Friel's *Translations*

Today is St. Patrick's Day, that time to wear green, enjoy parades, drink Guinness, hope to happen upon a pot of gold, and hunt for trinity-leafed (rather than the usual four-leaf) clovers. But it really is much more, and for me, is a time to ponder the "images of the past" that the saint himself conjures up for me.

Having helped produce Brian Friel's *Translations* in 1998, this line has stuck with me. Obviously, *Translations*'s title indicates that the play concerns language, specifically English, Irish, Latin, and Greek. But Friel's work also deals with communication, colonialism, and history. Near the end of the piece, Hugh tells Owen that history helps mold language. Words make sense when we understand the vestiges of the past embedded in them.

James Cahill's *How the Irish Saved Civilization* reveals that at the very time the Roman Empire was collapsing, a youthful missionary named Patricius, born in 387 AD, was taking Christianity to Ireland. The Irish of his day were primitive, having sprung from Celtic tribes — pagans and mercenaries who practiced human sacrifice and dealt in slavery. In fact, Patrick himself as a teenager was kidnapped by a gang of Irish slave-raiders and taken from his homeland of England to Ireland. Coerced into service as a shepherd, he was able to break free when he was about twenty-one.

After he returned to Britain, Patrick was educated and later ordained a priest and bishop. He had a vision around 431 that, oddly enough, beckoned him back to Ireland, where he energetically preached the Gospel, and loved the people into conversion. As he built chapels over old holy pagan sites and put wells under the protection of Christian saints, he also transformed the entire culture, encouraging in the Irish a love of learning.

The monk scribes who came out of this new religious zeal took it upon themselves to copy all the books that were threatened to be lost as the Roman Empire collapsed. "Without this service of the scribes," Cahill concludes, "our own world would never have come to be... Twelve centuries of lyric beauty, aching tragedy, intellectual inquiry...and love of Wisdom... would all have gone down the drain of history."

I have pondered this quote from *Translations*, "*It is not the literal past, the 'facts' of history, that shape us, but images of the past embodied in language.*" Studying scripture not as literal facts of history, but as images of the incarnated God embodied in its words, is a good practice for me this holy day. And I will honor the saint who went back to serve the people who had enslaved him blessing those who had cursed him. I will bind unto myself today some of the power of that kind of love.

March 18

"*Estragon: (having tried in vain to work it out). I'm tired! (Pause.) Let's go.*
Vladimir: We can't.
Estragon: Why not?
Vladimir: We're waiting for Godot."
Characters in Samuel Beckett's *Waiting for Godot*

Tonight, as I was contemplating what to write about this passage, I read my horoscope in the *Birmingham News*, which said, "You'll be waiting in a line of sorts. Instead of getting antsy, read the faces of the people around you." The horoscope suggested to me imagining stories about these folks. It was good advice, because waiting (for Godot, or just wasting time, holding on, staying put until something happens) has never been one of my best skills.

I began to think, there are different kinds of waiting. Last night, tornadoes, once again, tore through Alabama. My daughter Elin had just persuaded me to get a weather radio "app" for my phone, which went off continuously all night long. I thought, "I am actually waiting for God, the Universe, Fate, or whoever to move this weather along." I anticipated, uneasily, the end of the "midnight to 6:00 a.m." tornado warning.

When I used to drive 35 minutes each way to work, I got hooked on listening to audio books by Eckhart Tolle. This exercise distracted me from the frequent stops and stalls of traffic on the expressway. Most of us don't like to wait. We get anxious when stuck in traffic, stressed in long lines at the DMV, frustrated with a plane delay. We check watches. We grumble. We pace to dissipate some of our anger — unless we are in the car and then we can settle for listening to something enlightening.

Tolle suggests a good way to handle a wait — or anything out of my control: be in the moment. If held up by something, wait without "waiting," discover what the stillness is for, understand that this moment of suspension may actually mean something in or to my life.

In Beckett's play, Vladimir and Estragon wait and wait unceasingly and unsuccessfully for a character named Godot to arrive. Because the play never really explains who this Godot is, some people have speculated that the playwright was suggesting that humans wait for God who never shows up in their lives. Beckett once admitted, "It would be fatuous of me to pretend that I am not aware of the meanings attached to the word 'Godot,' and the opinion of many that it means 'God.' But you must remember – I wrote the play in French, and if I did have that meaning in my mind, it was somewhere in my unconscious and I was not overtly aware of it." The French word for "God" is "Dieu" – but if you say, "Godot" just right, it can sound like Go-Dieu!

Whoever Godot is to Vladimir and Estragon, the characters interminably wait for someone. Thinking about the angst during their anticipation and yearning, I remember the advice of Eckhart Tolle. A very good practice for life might be to allow myself first to be in the moments of waiting, so that they become more than just waiting. And then, to melt into the stillness of the Universe to hear what is speaking through, in, and beyond the waiting.

March 19
"Do you think I will be made a fool of, in front of myself!"
Romain Tournel in Georges Feydeau's A *Flea in Her Ear*

A good farce, with its roots in Greek and Roman comedy, always makes me laugh uncontrollably. And A *Flea in Her Ear* is a great farce. When I costumed the play in 1999, the director Don Sandley set it in a New Orleans French Quarter hotel and it worked beautifully. A farce's improbable plot is full of extraordinary situations, disguised characters, mistaken identity, flirty language, naughty innuendos, exaggerated characters, stylized acting, physical humor, and double entendres. Seemingly impromptu action builds to a final crescendo, with lots of doors opening and closing and slamming, and with the final action often involving a wild chase.

In this farce, the dashingly handsome Tournel is an arrogant, self-obsessed lady's man. If he were less concerned with his own circumstances, he would be more aware of what is happening around him. But then, what fun would that be? We like to laugh at a fool like him on stage.

Reality is a bit different, however. I remember being at a family reunion when I was five or six. It was held at a farm, and a cousin and I went off to play on his land. After an hour or so, we came back very importantly to tell what we saw while rambling across the fields. But as we rounded the corner where our relatives were gathered on the porch, we were met with huge gales of laughter. Apparently, we had played so hard that we had become dirty and disheveled ragamuffins.

Never before had I been the center of so many people's attention, nor the focus of so many bellows and cackles. If they were aiming for a bullseye, they hit the target causing a great wound. That moment is the first time I remember blushing, or feeling mortified, humiliated, or self-conscious. The expression wishing the earth would swallow you up made perfect sense to me that day.

For way too many years, I was hounded by that memory. Afterward, I would carefully tread a path through life, avoiding situations that would unexpectedly put me into such a disconcerting limelight: no raising of my hand in class, no venturing an opinion in an uncertain situation, no taking of a speech course where I had to perform. When I fell in love with theatre, my childhood recollection subconsciously enticed me backstage rather than encouraging me into an acting stint behind the footlights.

I always knew I was not the only person ever laughed at ... BY HER FAMILY! But it took me a while to deal with what happened, because I buried the event and wrapped layers of shock absorbing insulation around my heart. Once I took the memory out of the dark and revealed its power over me, I was able to heal, gain self-confidence, forget about the hurt, and move on. Now, I feel only the smallest twinge of pain when I think back to the day I was "made a fool of, in front of myself!"

March 20
In "Opening: The New World" from *Songs for a New World*, the singers belt out an exciting tune about how, just out of sight, a fresh realm beckons. (Listen to the work online or from your library!)
Singers in Jason Robert Brown's *Songs for a New World*

One of our theatre students at Samford University directed a very satisfying *Songs for a New World* in the early 2000s. A rather abstract musical review, or "song cycle," the show's tunes are woven together by a central theme concerning the moment of decision-making.

In this opening number, change is represented by the image of a "new world." Change can be frightening, crashing like thunder. Change can also be exciting, charging the air with energy. Such evolution can be hidden, waiting silently behind a metaphorical hill, or it can be loud and unnerving. But a time comes when transformation is inevitable. I have had times when the magnetic pull to refashion my life has gotten more powerful day by day, beckoning metamorphosis.

When my marriage dissolved in 1995, I searched for a meaning for my life on the other side of what was then a 24-year old union. My former husband and I had been theatre design partners, so not only was I severed from my spouse, I no longer had my close collaborator. And I had also lost myself in the years leading up to the breakup.

I made a decision: I wanted to recover; and more than recover: I wanted to grow and find new birth. I read books, I talked to wise friends and counselors, I formed new friendships, I exercised more. I also began listening to books on tape (before the advent of compact discs or streaming). One day, I went to the university library and chose an inspirational audio book randomly, and it turned out to be Dr. Wayne Dyer's *Choosing Your Own Greatness: Your Life, Your Choice.*

Wow, what a fortuitous, synchronistic selection! Dyer told me to stop focusing on the challenges in my life, and instead to discover solutions to problems; stop dwelling on what happened to me outside of myself, and rather begin to look inside. He said that life would become more fulfilling if I gave up negative emotions and stopped blaming others. Once I began to love myself, he counseled, dramatic change and good habits would naturally occur.

Either in this audio recording or a subsequent one I listened to, Dyer suggested dropping the word "try" from my vocabulary. Try to pick up a pencil, he said. Just try it. You can't do it. Now, pick up the pencil. See, straightaway you can. Or as *Star Wars's* Yoda would say, "Do, or do not. There is no try."

As this wisdom seeped into my soul, I began to feel like a snake shedding her skin. A serpent accomplishes this molting by rubbing its head against a stone or other hard objects, more and more until finally allowing its stretched skin to burst open. As the snake proceeds to rub and chafe, it finally slithers out of its old skin, turning this outer layer inside-out in one piece.

I couldn't describe the process of my unfolding self any better than this. Being rubbed and prompted by one hard situation after another, I began to see a new world calling to me, louder and more vibrant every moment!

March 21

In "Fancy Forgetting" from The Boy Friend, Mme. Dubonnet and Percival Browne sing about a love affair from long ago. (Listen to the work online or from your library!)

Mme. Dubonnet and Percival Browne in Sandy Wilson's The Boy Friend

Despite the frothy trivialities of the plot of The Boy Friend, I thoroughly enjoyed being part of a run of this show. A tongue-in-cheek look at 1920s musicals, the characters are charming, the costumes are colorful, and the score is sunny and catchy. After opening in London in 1953, the next year's New York production was the American Broadway debut of 19-year old Julie Andrews.

Set against the backdrop of the French Riviera, this romantic spoof takes place at the Villa Caprice where Maisie, Polly (played by Andrews in the Broadway show), and a number of other girls attend Mme. Dubonnet's School for Young Ladies. Polly, who is looking for a beau, has a widowed millionaire father, Percy Brown, who drops by to visit. After a few minutes with the headmistress, he and Mme. Dubonnet realize they were lovers many years ago, and as they sing this charming song, "Fancy Forgetting," the old flame is rekindled.

Such reawakened affection stirs a tender place in my heart even now. I have read that people reigniting youthful romances have a better chance of staying together than the rest of the population. However, for most people, such a reconnection is a fantasy.

As I think back on it, The Boy Friend revolves around a number of idyllic illusions, if not delusions, of the 1950s: the young ladies are "perfect"; boy friends are a necessity; if you don't have a guy, your dreams won't come true; once married, you live happily ever after. And maybe the most enticing fantasy to me: the sweet bohemian ideal expressed in "A Room in Bloomsbury." The song imagines a tiny London Bloomsbury abode, with a bright fire, cozy seats, books, dinner cooking on the stove — a picturesque idyllic attic flat for two young lovers.

When this musical was written in the 1950s, families were booming with babies and technology was soaring. There was an abundance of many items due to excess production from World War II, and the nation was optimistic having helped win the war and defeat the Great Depression. Some people look back on that decade as a Golden Age when everything was good and honorable, neighborhoods were safe and society was stable, the "Fabulous Fifties" they call it.

But that is make-believe as big as the ones you find in this musical. Many serious issues were bubbling under and over the surface: the civil rights movement, flight to the suburbs, poverty, the Cold War fueling a constant threat of nuclear attack, and the Reality goes on and on.

Nevertheless, maybe we have to retreat into our rosy memories, or snuggle into a seat in a theatre to experience a musical every now and then. Life can become dreary, monotonous, overwhelming, and frightening sometimes — and a little fantasy can help.

March 22

"Today I brew, tomorrow I bake;
And then the Prince child I will take;
For no-one knows my little game
That Rumpelstiltskin is my name!
Rumpelstiltskin is my name,
Rumpelstiltskin is my game!
Is my name, is my game!
Rumpelstiltskin is my name!"
Rumpelstiltskin in an original play from the Brothers Grimm's *Children and Household Tales*

Surely everyone knows the story of Rumpelstiltskin: the lovely Miller's Daughter is imprisoned in a room full of straw with orders from the king to spin it all into gold or she will die. A curious little man appears and promises help her for a price. On the first night, he asks for her necklace, and then spins the gold in return. In a larger room, the next night he demands her ring. The third night, in an even bigger chamber, and with nothing to give, she desperately promises him her first born child.

The king is amazed and marries the girl and they are happy until a son is born. When the imp appears to exact his due, the queen begs to keep her child. He gives her three days to guess his name or he will claim her son. The first two days, she guesses to no avail. She has a messenger go all over the countryside attempting to discover his identity, and before the third day's question, she has the answer. She asks, "Is it Jemm?" "No!" he replies. "John?" "No!" "Can your name be Rumpelstiltskin?"

The little man flies into a rage. In the children's theatre production that I costumed, the diminutive actor playing the role fumed and thundered and screamed. He jumped up and down, he turned red and his eyes popped wide open as he thrashed, and writhed, and spun around. It was a sight to behold and the children loved it. As you would expect, he was always the character they wanted to meet after the show was over.

I used to get mad while driving. First of all, I learned to drive from my dad, and he would get vexed at "dumb drivers." And, I am told I am competitive, so I suppose I viewed traffic as a contest and got angry when I was cut off or I saw road manners violated.

This is a true story that I am not making up. One morning, I decided I had had enough of the bad-tempered car behavior and resolved to learn more self control. That very afternoon when I checked my mail, I had an uninvited envelope from a Catholic organization containing a card you used in your car. It had a picture of Jesus on it, and it contained a prayer about driving safely.

Well, I turned a corner on my car madness that day, but I still got excitable about various upsets. Many forms of calming my mind have helped immeasurably. But one day, I got furious about something (probably losing something again) and, by myself at home, started jumping up and down and carrying on. Suddenly, I thought: I am Rumpelstiltskin! This kind of response is ridiculous.

Now, when I do feel like rage is bubbling inside me, I sing, "Rumpelstiltskin is my name, Rumpelstiltskin is my game! Is my name, is my game! Rumpelstiltskin is my name!" Sometimes I do a strong little tap dance with it, stomping the floor a tiny bit. But realizing that I am acting like a fuming, apoplectic fairy tale character is usually all I need to compose myself.

March 23:

In "Ol' Man River" from Show Boat, Joe sings about being worn out with his work, and yet the nearby stream simply keeps flowing and running its course. (Listen to the work online or from your library!)

Joe in *Show Boat*, a two-act musical, with music by Jerome Kern, and book and lyrics by Oscar Hammerstein II, based on Edna Ferber's 1926 novel *Show Boat*

I feel a bit like Joe today. I decided to daily attack my early spring gardening for 30 minutes, and I have been diligent. Every morning after my walk, while the temperature is nice and cool, I have been pulling weeds, digging up monkey grass, and getting ready to plant new fledglings when the weather warms up.

But I always overdo it. And my 30-minute periods stretch to 45 or 50. My shoulders ache, my lower back tightens, my arms cramp, and I just simply tuckered out. And I always sing Joe's song as I near the end of my work.

I was enlightened by working on that *Show Boat* in the spring of my sophomore year. It was my introduction to collaborating with African Americans in a show, to working on a full scale musical comedy, and to having an actual place on the running crew. For the first time, I was trusted running the spotlight, and I took my post in the balcony very seriously. I practiced several times before lighting rehearsals so I would know how to aim and control the instrument just right.

"Ol' Man River" is sung from Joe's point-of-view as an African American stevedore on the show boat. One night before rehearsal, our Joe was warming up, running through his song with the orchestra. He had a towel around his neck to mop sweat, and I thought this would be a perfect time to test some different colored gels to see what sort of effects the spotlight might be capable of. I tried rose pink, I tried bastard amber, straw, special lavender, and blue.

To my horror, at just that moment the wonderful curmudgeonly director, Mr. WT Chichester strolled in and yelled up at me, "Baaa-bra! Get that dreadful blue light off that stage. Don't you know that blue is a hideous color for a black actor?!?!" No, I did not know before, but I have never forgotten that piece of advice! Joe, thinking he might get chided for the towel draping his shoulders quickly threw it into the wings.

"Keep that towel!" Mr. Chi roared. "It gives you charisma."

So today, I am remembering the spotlight and Mr. Chi and our Joe singing with his charisma around his neck. As I struggle in from my self-appointed toil in the garden, "Ol' Man River" is in my mind and on my lips.

The song juxtaposes the suffering of the black race with the endless, constant, unsympathetic current of the mighty Mississippi River, and the words of "Ol' Man River" speak to me. Cultivating the almost unrelenting earth and weeds of my garden, I perspire and struggle, toting fertilizer, lifting pine straw bales till my body is sore and achy. This work is my own choice, but still I get weary — and sometimes want to give up. I am really not sure what keeps me laboring on, but singing Joe's song helps.

March 24

"Dottore: (Noticing Pantalone crawling) Pantalone! Antiquas non est cavortium!
Pantalone: Huh?
Dottore: The opening line of my new book, Pantalone... the one I'm translating from ancient Greek to ancient Latin... it means 'a man in his declining years shouldn't cavort.'"
Characters in James Fisher's The Bogus Bride, a two-act farce based on the characters and traditions of the Italian commedia dell'arte

Probably my favorite kind of humor is spun from the scenarios of commedia dell'arte and it physical comedy, so I truly enjoyed producing my friend James Fisher's TheBogus Bride in the spring of 1992. This exchange between Dottore and Pantalone somehow reminds me of a conversation between Marianne and Elinor in Sense and Sensibility. At one point in Chapter 8, Marianne confesses that Colonel Brandon is not quite to the point of expiring, but insists a man of his age (35) should hardly be thinking of marrying a young girl. Elinor agrees that maybe an older lady of 27 would be suitable.

Marianne supposes that such a match might work out, for after all, a lady that old is far past her prime and would only be marrying for convenience, so that the couple could provide some company for each other "in their declining years." What would these characters think of marriage in the twenty-first century, with so many women marrying for the first time past the age of 30? I have a friend who married for the first time at 69.

I remember giving my professor and mentor John Finlay, who shared a birthday with me, an "Over the Hill" card for his 30th birthday. Being over twice that age now, I must be over at least the seven hills of

Rome. But as someone who still feels young, I do protest that a man – or woman – in the declining years shouldn't cavort.

First of all, what are the declining years? A dictionary proclaims that declining years are, "a person's old age, especially when regarded as the time when health, vigor, and mental faculties deteriorate." American women's life expectancy right now is 82.65, and my personal span has been forecast as 100 years.

Just to keep myself active and open, I walk, ride a stationary bike, and perform Yoga every day. I read, teach, go to plays and movies, hear lectures, work in the development field, and take all sorts of classes. I have a large web of friends, socialize most weeks, and have a lifelong companion. I meditate and read spiritual works, and work with the consciousness training. None of this assures anything, but I really don't feel over the hill or past my prime.

And now to the word "cavort." What does it mean? Again, a dictionary definition is "To bound or prance about in a sprightly manner; caper; to have lively or boisterous fun; to romp." Keeping up with twin three-year-olds is quite enough to qualify me for cavorting every time I am with them. But I romp about in a sprightly manner most of the time even when they are not here.

Oh, wait! The quote says a "man" in his declining years shouldn't cavort, and nothing about a woman. Whew! I'm safe.

March 25

"Well. I thought I knew God. God, the Vengeful. The God of Job. That God, He was the one I set out to write about. Then you came, and tried to fit into what I know the things you said, the things you – It wasn't possible. I don't know God now."
Priest in Milan Stitt's *The Runner Stumbles*

Though I make a special effort to find joy and meaning in every day, even the bleak and hopeless ones, many a day rolls by and seems for all the world like any other one. Yet some days do stand out startlingly in the mind, etched in the recollection banks like designs on fine wine glasses. Before I went to college, like the priest in *The Runner Stumbles*, I thought I knew God, and He was a fairly vengeful, Old Testament character. I surely wasn't in love with that image of the Divine, so in school and away from home, I forsook my Presbyterian roots, and rarely attended Sunday services.

Thursday, March 25, 1970 is one of those days emblazoned in my memory. My Sophomore English professor, Mr. John Finlay, was an intense and compelling person, and a riveting teacher. Some students in my class were totally mystified by him, but some of us comprehended the fact that Mr. Finlay was a jewel, and we had better allow his sagacity to shine on us as much as we could.

This particular Thursday, Mr. Finlay had been characteristically late. But his lecture rumbled on, the clock neared 5:00, and the class still had minutes to go. Then suddenly, he asked us if we knew what day it was. No one did. He banged the literature book closed and said, "Anyone who wants to know, follow me." Three of us did.

Like puppies we scampered at his heels across a brittle, barren field where spring had not yet pushed up new green shoots. He was Moses. All he had to say was, "The sea will part for you. Walk out apace and I promise, the water will separate," and we would have flung ourselves upon blue waves never minding the danger. But here it was dry.

We came to a little brick place of worship and entered. He remarked that we would be taking part in a service, a rite of Maundy Thursday. So that was what this day was! It had a name.

A quiet hush filled St. Andrew's of Montevallo and my soul felt as if it had returned home unexpectedly. My shoulder touched John's as the four of us knelt. Our clothes absorbed incense as we took bread and drank wine from a common cup together. My heart, as the altar, was stripped bare. A different sort of God was present in this place.

John had come into class with an eagerness not only to teach his subject matter but also to enlighten (even evangelize) anyone awake and open. I am extraordinarily thankful that I was paying attention, and that I felt drawn to follow him. Otherwise, I may have never set foot in an Episcopal church. When I think of the incredible inheritance John gave me and my children, and their children, I feel satiated, glutted, and even overflowing with gratitude.

Every day, I thank my Maker that Mr. Finlay came into my life and that our souls are linked forever in this Maundy Thursday ceremony, all the more meaningful for the casual suddenness of the unfolding of events that day in 1970. As Emily Dickinson wrote, "To live is so startling it leaves little time for anything else."

March 26
"I pull in resolution, and begin

116

To doubt the equivocation of the fiend
That lies like truth: 'Fear not, till Birnam wood
Do come to Dunsinane:' and now a wood
Comes toward Dunsinane. Arm, arm, and out!
... I gin to be aweary of the sun,
And wish the estate o' the world were now undone."
Macbeth in Shakespeare's *Macbeth*, Act V, Scene 5

At this time of year, people in my neighborhood prune their bushes and trees and shrubs mercilessly. Well, in the South, things grow huge, so if we want our yards to look presentable, we really have to lop and shear and clip a little. I often see a neighbor, having accomplished an immense task of trimming, carting to the street what for the life of me looks like Birnam Wood advancing toward me, like Macbeth looking out of Dunsinane.

What an evil prophesy that was! The three destructive Weird or "Weyward" Sisters set a tone of gloom and foreboding for this Shakespearean play. In the very first scene of the play, they make a grand entrance amid thunder and lightning in a "desert place." They each have lines, and then together chant: "Fair is foul, and foul is fair: Hover through the fog and filthy air." From the start of the action, there is uncertainty about what is evil and what is good.

Shakespeare ingeniously employs the Witches to deceive Macbeth through duplicity and confusing vagueness. The Sisters prophesy thrice about Macbeth's future. The last prediction is that he will not die until the Birnam Wood moves to Dunsinane hill. Macbeth rejoices at this news, for how could acres of woods travel to his castle?

Ah, but the Witches prevaricate! They express the truth, but not all of it. In the lines quoted above, the woods have indeed changed position and progressed toward Macbeth's Dunsinane when branches are cut down and used as camouflage by the invading English forces. Soon Macbeth will be conquered. (He should have lived in my neighborhood and he would have saved himself some heartache, seeing how woods are constantly moving about, and he would have been prepared.)

Because of the Sisters and their misleading prophecies, deception is a major message in Macbeth. Or should I call this theme "beating around the bush" or "hedging"?

All seriousness aside, why do we — why do I — prevaricate, speak evasively, or mislead? I very rarely outright lie, but I do sometimes use vague language to soften impact. Many students read "The Ways We Lie" by Stephanie Ericsson to study ethics. In the essay, the author remarks that it is nearly impossible to tell the truth one hundred percent of the time to others. She says, "We lie. We all do. We exaggerate, we minimize, we avoid confrontation, we spare people's feelings, we conveniently forget, we keep secrets, we justify lying to the big-guy institutions." And I suppose to "avoid confrontation" or to "spare people's feelings" are mostly the reasons that I sidestep or waffle.

Through my study of the ego over the last few years, I have come to believe that lying is instigated by that inner false self, doing its damnedest to coach me into saving face or providing buffer. I am becoming prepared to do anything I can do to diminish my Ego. Maybe a good plan for me would be to remind myself I am turning into one of the deleterious Sisters when I feel a prevarication coming on.

March 27
In "I Won't Grow Up" from *Peter Pan*, Peter sings about being determined not to attain adulthood. (Listen to the work online or from your library!)
Peter and the Lost Boys in J. M. Barrie's *Peter Pan*, adapted as a musical mostly by Mark "Moose" Charlap, with additional music by Jule Styne, and most of the lyrics were written by Carolyn Leigh, with additional lyrics by Betty Comden and Adolph Green

I am a Baby Boomer, labeled as "the Youth Generation," and rebuked as an era of kids who never matured, who idolized the springtime of life with its enthusiasm and idealism, and who still do everything in their power to stay youthful. This point is most likely valid for many of us. But I have to complain that it is not our faults. Really.

Our parents put us in front of television sets every spring from 1955 to 1960 — at early and impressionable ages — and encouraged us to watch Mary Martin in *Peter Pan*. Every year, Peter asked us the same question: "Are you ready for today's lesson?" Along with the Lost Boys, we all replied breathlessly: "Yes, Peter!" Peter warned us not to wear ties or serious expressions, not to shoulder burdens with a worried air, or grow a fraction of an inch.

Because Peter Pan wants to stay young forever, so he doesn't have to face the pains and frights that come with adult life. We Boomers took this lesson to heart and tried very, very hard to remember. But one day, when it's been a while since that lesson, and life gets difficult — well, you have to grow up.

It happened to me that night of December 8, 1980. It was fifteen years after I was 15 and fell in love with the Beatles. They had disbanded in 1970. I listened to Mozart and Bach now, and classic jazz. I had a four-year old daughter. My life was jam-packed with teaching and designing theatre and the busy-ness of helping a child — well, grow up.

I heard the news, despite having drifted to disturbed dreams amidst the low growls of Monday Night football. Something about the tone in anchorman Joe Langston's voice burst into my unconsciousness. "Former Beatle John Lennon has been shot dead by an unknown gunman who opened fire outside the musician's New York apartment. The 40-year-old was shot several times as he entered the Dakota, his luxury apartment on Manhattan's Upper West Side, opposite Central Park, at 11:00 p.m. local time. He was rushed in a police car to St. Luke's Roosevelt Hospital, where he died. His wife, Yoko Ono, who is understood to have witnessed the attack, was with him."

With a bang-bang-shoot-shoot "my" Beatle was dead. Strangely, I then felt nothing as the world sat glued to their televisions. The next day, my mind defined my condition as glad — glad I had converted to classical music, grateful for the dull numb tone in my brain and in my bones, happy there would be no reunion with the other three to wring throbbing girl-hood thoughts from my memory. But rhythmically, in the grim rain that followed, pain seeped into every fiber of my soul.

I tried to dry blinking eyes and fill the odd hole in my heart that Mark Chapman, John's murderer, had expertly executed. And I mourned the loss of someone I had never known personally, but only communally, with millions of others across the spinning black discs that gave us something more than music.

And I suffered shortness of breath. A death like John Lennon's kills more than one body. A shining part of me was snuffed out on that otherwise ordinary evening.

John was 10 years older than me. He was supposed to go through each decade of maturing to teach me, through his music, what he did, how he felt, what he thought. He had just come back onto the music scene in 1980, to sing about how he loved his son Sean who was my daughter's age.

Since then, I have had to ripen and mellow, develop and age without the mentoring of that particular older guide who explored life before me and held a little flashlight backward to define my path. Under those circumstances, it was more terrible than all the awful things that ever were. But at 30, I realized I had to grow up.

March 28

In "Metaphor" from *The Fantasticks*, the young lovers Matt and Luisa sing about their love for each other. (Listen to the work online or from your library!)

Matt, Luisa, Hucklebee and Bellomy in *The Fantasticks* with music by Harvey Schmidt and lyrics by Tom Jones

First love is full of passion and panting and poetry. First love begins to define the kind of person you idolize and the one with whom you want to ride off with into the sunset.

The quirky musical *The Fantasticks* is a quintessential rite of passage tale in which two interfering fathers plot to trick their children into being attracted to each other. The story celebrates love — first love, lost love, and ultimately, true love.

Once I was assigned to write about first love, and, having designed this musical and many other plays that dealt with romantic themes, I tried to sort through my memories and go back to my initial crush or flame. Was it the fifth grade?

But our mentor told us to think outside the box. Our story didn't have to involve romance. So I wondered: what was my first love?

Every thing about my lessons with my Nannie made me fall in love with learning. From the time I could speak well enough (around 15 months), I would toddle next door to my great-grandmother's house almost every day. I climbed the stairs to her upper room and snuggled onto her lap. Everyone in the family encouraged me in my belief that this was the very most important part of my day. (I think it kept me occupied for a while so they had a breather.)

Nannie smelled of Yardley's April Violets. The wood in her room was fragrantly polished with lemon oil and the patterns on the linens and curios were very English, the details imprinting my idea of perfect design. The corner window overlooked a huge chinaberry tree where we watched the robins get drunk on the fermented fruit and fall off the branches.

We looked at calendars and clocks and old photographs. We sniffed fresh flowers in vases, listened to bees buzz or winds howl, touched eyelet coverlets, tasted Lorna Doones or bananas. But the real reason for my daily visits were my lessons, a learning extravaganza created by looking at a book that featured numbers, colors, and ABCs with pictures. Every day, using the same volume, we counted to twelve, named all the colors, and went through every letter of the alphabet, naming the objects for each letter.

We ended our time together by reciting the Lord's Prayer, and sometimes reading poems or singing songs. I was always a little melancholy when my lessons were over. When my family took me out to eat or to shop and we would run into friends, they would have me recite something that drew approving smiles or even applause.

And that was special, but that was outside approval, and at two, that was not what I craved. What was rewarding to me was the learning itself, the turning in my mind, the spark, the opening of doors; the grasp of letters and numbers and colors and objects and smells and tastes; the finding out that things had names and that names were spelled and that letters were used to accomplish that, and that pictures could be used to illustrate those words.

Oh, the giddiness of it all, the splendor, the miracle. My heart would lift and my mind would race. No wonder Eve wanted to eat the apple that would give her knowledge.

March 29
"Man is born broken. He lives by mending. The grace of God is glue."
William (Billy) Brown in Eugene O'Neill's *The Great God Brown*

What a great quote this is from a great American dramatist and winner of the Nobel Prize for Literature in 1936. Partly because of a chaotic childhood, wrestling with religion and God often find their way into Eugene O'Neill's plays.

I know I am a broken human, and used to be even more so 15 years ago. God has used a lot of glue and mending on me. I used to repeat every day: "I am growing closer and closer to the Holy," even though I did not feel a special intimacy at all. I knew that sometimes if you voice something, or act as if it were happening, eventually the desired result will manifest. I begged to be absorbed in Divine plans, and to know it without doubt.

My Sunday School class was reading *The God We Never Knew* by Marcus Borg. It is a great book in which Borg shows how to hold all together in our minds God, our faith, deeply held beliefs, science, logic, and the varying views of religious authorities. I was behind in my reading and felt like I needed to catch up, but the Saturday was cool and cloudy, portending a drizzle. The book was interesting, but I didn't really want to be reading it at the time. I really didn't want to be doing much of anything at the time.

Sitting on my bed in preparation to study, I realized I was actually mad at Life for some petty little disturbances and situations that were not going my way, so maybe that was why I was resisting reading about the Everlasting. As my mind ranted, I wondered why God never talked to us in the concrete ways he did to certain figures in the Old Testament, such as when he spoke to Moses through the burning bush — or to Noah, or Job, or Isaiah. And I pondered why spectacular miracles never happen any more, like the manna drifting down from heaven to feed the Israelites in the desert. What I wanted were tangible, substantial, genuine signs that God really does exist and that the Author of All Things speaks to us in some authentic, palpable way.

All of a sudden, I heard a splat and couldn't imagine what it was. A soft rain was now falling and I jumped up to look out on the deck off my bedroom. What did I see but a big, soggy piece of white bread lying on the boards? I couldn't believe it! Bread from heaven.

Okay, so maybe a bird dropped it from his beak. My next door neighbors are known to feed birds all sorts of delicacies on a frequent basis. But there it was: as big and real and undeniable a sign as anyone could have — and very prompt, too. This God definitely has a sense of humor. Ancient Psalm 78 says that mortals ate the bread of angels and the Lord provided them with food enough. Modern playwright Eugene O'Neill replies, "Man is born broken. He lives by mending. The grace of God is glue." Or soggy bread.

March 30
In *The Crucible* opera, Tituba sings to protect herself by proclaiming the blood she gave Abigail was not a baby's blood, but came from a chicken. (Listen to the work online or from your library!)

Tituba singing in the opera *The Crucible* with music by Robert Ward, libretto by Bernard Stambler based on the play by Arthur Miller

Today I am cooking dinner for 25 students from local universities as I do monthly. As I am preparing the chicken, I sing to myself Tituba's lines about fowl blood as I do any time I fix a poultry dish and a little red fluid seeps out of the flesh.

This warbling of mine always takes me back to the fall of 1977 when I designed the costumes for Robert Ward's opera The Crucible about the Salem Witch Trials, and spent many days in the costume shop sewing corduroy dresses and coats, and linen caps and aprons circa 1692. The students' practicing their music seeped into my being and has stayed with me.

I had earlier met Tituba, Reverend Parris' black slave from Barbados, when I worked in summer stock on the play The Crucible in the early 1970s. Tituba, who in the play and opera is a person accomplished in her native country's Black Magic, is said to have been seen with the Devil by the Salem girls when they are discovered in the woods dancing. Tituba ends up in jail, taking a lot of the responsibility for the witchcraft going on.

When The Crucible was first performed in January of 1953, many audience members and critics recognized the work as a blunt assault on McCarthyism. During the early '50s, when America was filled with dread about Russia and another world war, a little known senator, Joe McCarthy began accusing politicians, artists, and people in the entertainment industry of being card-carrying Communists. As in the Salem Witch Trials, he had no real proof. Nevertheless, he led special congressional committees to investigate hundreds of people in the attempt to unearth Communist leanings. Many Americans were blacklisted for years, finding it hard to find employment.

Finally, the hearings collapsed McCarthy's credibility and the Senate censured him, leading to the public's contempt over the whole affair. But right now, 60 years later, one of our Alabama congressmen is trying to ban portions of an Alabama high school textbook which contains The Crucible, convinced that McCarthy accurately targeted Communists. Really unbelievable.

A witch-hunt in modern parlance refers to a campaign to uncover covert actions involving a scapegoat — a targeted person or group — and the search for or creation of evidence that supports allegations. Such hunts play on the fear, creating panic or hysteria, in politics, business, organizations, or any group involving human beings.

Any witch-hunt, for "real" witches or for imagined communists, are nothing short of tragic. Just as in the real Salem event of 1692 — that the play and opera flesh out — people's lives are ruined by such action.

To sustain such a hunt, a community must be encased in delusion, suspicion, and particularly ego.

So I am cutting up a hen and singing about it being only chicken's blood and all these thoughts are bounding around in my head. Can we not learn from the past?

March 31
"How did it come
Our stars could mingle for an afternoon
So long ago, and then forget us or tease us
Or helplessly look on the dark high seas
Of our separation, while time drank
The golden hours?"
Tegeus to Dynamene in Christopher Fry's A *Phoenix Too Frequent*

The great Metaphysical poet John Donne died in London on this day, March 31, 1631. His deep love for Anne More and their secret marriage that effectively ended his political career are well known. I am always stunned when I read both his love poems, many to her, and his holy works.

But then, I am often astounded by poetry. The name derives from ancient Greek roots in the word "poieo," which means "I create." How lovely is that? One thing I appreciate about poetry is the way it can relay such emotion and imagery in a considerably succinct way. Humans have been reciting poetry since long before we could read. Epic storytelling, genealogy, history, and even law employed poetry in preliterate civilizations. Religious liturgy was drenched with poetry. Since temple times, a piyyut, or liturgical poem, often marked to be sung or chanted, has been part of Jewish religious services. Poetry is easier to memorize than prose for the most part, and interestingly enough, poems were written to be performed theatrically in these early societies.

Not many playwrights today exclusively or specifically employ poetry or poetic prose for their works. Tennessee Williams and many Irish playwrights, T. S. Eliot and Archibald MacLeish are twentieth century examples. And English poet and playwright Christopher Fry, whose life spanned December 18, 1907 to June 30, 2005, was best known for his 1940s and 1950s verse dramas.

In A *Phoenix Too Frequent*, a man and woman meet in the tomb of her dead husband in ancient Greece. They believe they might have briefly passed each other in childhood when Dynamene visited the village of Pyxa, where Tegeus grew up. Most of us would say something like, "Well, I wonder how our paths crossed in youth but we haven't seen each other since?"

Fry takes the experience beyond the mundane into a numinous and holy realm. Life itself is astonishing and magical. Why not express it as such? So his character asks, *"How did it come/Our stars could mingle for an afternoon/So long ago, and then forget us or tease us/Or helplessly look on the dark high seas/Of our separation, while time drank / The golden hours?"*

Unfortunately, some of us ignore the language of poetry, that subtle communication about love and self-awareness, about peace and introspection, about sadness, joy, loneliness, and caring. Like most artists, poets aren't paid much, unless they are musicians, and thankfully, people do embrace poetry in popular music lyrics. One encouraging sign is the sweeping popularity of regular poetry slams and poetry readings taking place throughout the county, well-attended by young people and old alike.

Poetry speaks to the human spirit too deeply to be ignored. Add some poetry to your life today!

April 1
"Whan that April with his showres soote
The droughte of March hath perced to the roote,
And bathed every veine in swich licour,
Of which vertu engendred is the flowr;..."
Geoffrey Chaucer, *Canterbury Tales* (ll. 1-4)

Translated, we might today say: "So today is the first day of April, a month of such plenteous showers that water overflows and even pierces dry roots, thirsty from the drought of March. Now, every vein of every plant will be so bathed in liquid that we will soon see an extravagantly unrestrained blossoming of flowers."

At such a beautiful time of year, according to Chaucer, folks yearn for travel, and religious pilgrimages. English travelers might decide to wander toward Canterbury to visit the site of Thomas Becket, "the holy blissful martyr." He might even cure their illnesses.

Chaucer's *Canterbury Tales* has been adapted for the stage several times, and on one occasion, I was able to see a workshop version of a dramatization. It was intriguing to see some of his characters come off the page of the medieval classic to vivid life on stage.

I actually feel like one of those characters myself. My strange tale and my fascination with Thomas Becket began when I was a freshman at the University of Montevallo. In the fall of 1968, *Murder in the Cathedral* was performed on Palmer stage by the National Shakespeare Company — a professional group that toured productions of classics to universities throughout America and Canada from the 1960s through '80s (the company that spawned the Shakespeare Conservatory). The play took my breath away.

I then took Chaucer my senior year, and we read, in Middle English, all of the *Canterbury Tales*. My teacher was Dr. Eva Golson, an amazing scholar with an encyclopedic memory who could recite long passages of Shakespeare or Chaucer by heart. She had been the first woman to earn a PhD from the University of Chicago, and she could mesmerize a class. As we studied the prologue, she told us of her own pilgrimage to Canterbury Cathedral and the way the steps were worn down by all the many people who had visited to pay homage to St. Thomas. Oh, how I longed to go!

According to scholars, Thomas Becket had not been a well-liked, saintly, or even very lovable man, but his murder in 1170 inside the cathedral stimulated a huge outcry. Within two years, a kind of Becket-mania pushed him to celebrity status and many miracles were attributed to him. By 1173, he was canonized. These wonders were illustrated in several whole window groupings in Canterbury Cathedral.

In 1538, Henry VIII's envoys from the Commission for the Destruction of Shrines demolished Saint Thomas' memorial in Canterbury Cathedral. Some say that 26 wagons were needed to convey the valuables taken from the shrine, including the gold crown of Scotland given by Edward I. That ego-centric Henry VIII was determined to teach Becket a lesson 368 years after his death. He demanded his bones be exhumed and "tried" in a court of law, where they were found guilty and burned. Henry also commanded the destruction of Becket memorabilia and portraits throughout England.

During World War II, all the cathedral's exquisite stained glass windows were removed for safekeeping from the bombing attacks of another ego-driven leader, when Hitler directed air raids on England. A large area of the town of Canterbury was demolished, but the main body of the cathedral thankfully remained undamaged. Well, here it is April and time for a pilgrimage to Canterbury — or at least a quick visit to their YouTube page for Morning Prayer or Choral Evensong.

April 2
"If every one were clothed with integrity, if every heart were just, frank, and kindly, the other virtues would be well-nigh useless, since their chief purpose is to make us bear with patience the injustice of our fellows."
Philinte in Moliere's, *The Misanthrope*

When Samford University Theatre produced *The Misanthrope* in the fall of 1985, we decided to design the set and costumes in black and white. For one thing, we liked the engravings of this play from the late seventeenth and early eighteenth centuries. And then also, the play deals with some dualistic, black and white issues.

Near the beginning of the play, Alceste, the cynical misanthrope, bellows to his friend Philinte that the reason he hates mankind is that everyone exhibits so much deceit and hypocrisy. He maintains that humans, to show integrity, must be completely frank, no matter if that honesty hurts feelings. Philinte asks Alceste to be more tolerant of people, even with their faults, because honesty should be balanced with manners.

My sixth grade teacher, Mattie Lee Jones, was a fiery redhead about four-and-a-half feet high. I was tall for my age, so at five feet already, I felt like I towered over her. But her lessons were certainly head and shoulders above those of many teachers I ever had and I fondly remember her as a person who greatly influenced my life.

One quote she drilled into our brains was by Thomas B. Macaulay, "The measure of a man's real character is what he would do if he knew he would never be found out." She wanted us to have integrity: that quality of being that makes people honest, gives us strong moral principles, strengthens our decency and our uprightness.

Every time I ponder doing something that is less than honorable or respectable, I hear Miss Jones reciting that Macaulay phrase in my mind. I was once privileged to hear Dr. Stephen Covey speak in Birmingham and he emphasized the idea of "true north" or an internal moral compass. As he once wrote, "Because the compass represents the eternal verities of life, we must develop our value system with deep respect for 'true north' principles. As Cecil B. deMille said about the principles in his movie, *The Ten Commandments*, 'It is impossible for us to break the law. We can only break ourselves against the law.'"

DeMille's words are intriguing. Laws don't literally break when I do something that is out of line with rules and regulations. But what happens is I weaken myself. If I cannot follow the speed limit, can I be trusted to not to steal something at work, or plagiarize when I write? Every time I ignore a law, or feel I am too superior to be bothered following a dictate, I manifest my ego, which wants me to win no matter what. I also demonstrate what mettle I am made of, and whether my moral fiber is strong or weak. "If every one were clothed with integrity," Philinte says. Maybe that is what I need to attire myself every morning as I roll out of bed.

April 3

Nell: Nothing is funnier than unhappiness, I grant you that. But –
Nagg (shocked): Oh!
Nell: Yes, yes, it's the most comical thing in the world. And we laugh, we laugh, with a will, in the beginning. But it's always the same thing. Yes, it's like the funny story we have heard too often, we still find it funny, but we don't laugh any more.
Characters in Samuel Beckett's *Endgame*

Endgame opened on April 3, 1957 in London. I dare say most of us would not agree with Nell's assertion that nothing is funnier than unhappiness. Twice, I have worked with student productions of Samuel Beckett's stark Absurdist play, in undergraduate school at Montevallo, and then with my Samford students. Both versions were wistfully evocative and yet poignantly amusing, and both followed Beckett's explicit instructions to set the play in an empty room with two high small windows.

Beckett himself admitted it is not a hopeful play. Two of the character, Nagg and Nell, no longer have legs and they live in "ash bins." The playwright was an avid chess player and "endgame" is a term used in the game during its final stages, indicating that the result is already known. So the play involves the end of life... maybe on this planet. Surely for these people. And yet, they fear that they are sinking into a sort of Dante's *Inferno* where they will have to go through their same desperate life over and over.

But is Nell right? Can unhappiness be the most comical thing in the world? Today, I found that I could send a "funny" e-card to someone proclaiming: "No one makes me less unhappy than you." Many droll Facebook messages come with frowning face emoticons, those relentless pictorial representations of our feelings. And emails and text messages are accompanied by :(sad faces made by punctuation marks.

Laughing at sad things is a coping mechanism, one way our brains find to deal with feelings of nervousness or awkwardness when tragic things occur. I remember being at the funeral home when a relative had died. I was around five or six years old, and my mother and her three sisters were very sad about the death of their relative. But they all got tickled when a family member brought a bucket of fried chicken into the somber and sepulchral room filled with black clothed mourners. "The Collins Girls," the moniker the sisters were known by, actually collapsed behind the coffin, attempting to control their guffaws. But the more they tried, the louder they hooted, and they finally snatched me up and left the room by a back door, attempting to twist their mirthful faces back into somber expressions.

Milton once wrote, "The mind is its own place, and in itself can make a heaven of hell, a hell of heaven." And that is actually what the characters in *Endgame* are doing: creating a Netherworld from life — maybe not a great life by some standards, but the only one they have. Nell is a dejected character in the play, but maybe on some level she understands Milton's point when she says, "Nothing is funnier than unhappiness."

April 4
In a song from *Rags to Riches*, the chorus sings about how in America, people can be anything they want to be — even going from poverty to millionaire status — if they just work and have luck. (Listen to the work online or from your library!)
Chorus in Aurand Harris's *Rags to Riches*

The first terrible illusion about this cheery curtain call song is that for many people, even making a minimum wage is not so easy today, and working to amass a million dollars is nigh impossible. The second misconception about luck and the American Dream — or serendipitously rising to the top — is not so viable any more either. Economic inequality and the freeze concerning intergenerational mobility has made the Land of Perpetual Opportunity almost a dream itself.

We performed this musical for children while I was at the University of Montevallo, and despite its chimera, I do enjoy tales about people rising from miserable surroundings. Aurand Harris, who wrote something like 36 lively plays for young people, based his melodrama *Rags to Riches* on two Horatio Alger stories, *Ragged Dick* and *Mark the Match Boy*.

In this play, a poor little shoeshine boy named Ragged Dick is charged with a task and given a two dollar bill by a rich banker. Taking change to the man's home, Dick meets the banker's daughter, who gives him a sense of purpose. During a stirring climax, Dick rescues a poor little match boy from a fire, impressing the banker who sets him on his own road to wealth. And, as fortune would have it, the little match boy finds he is an heir to a fortune, so both go from rags to riches.

Real versions of this fictional tale have certainly happened. But a very small one-percent of the US population commands something approaching 90 percent of the nation's wealth. And many of the most prosperous Americans are born into their wealth, though a few famous rags to riches biographies come to mind: media mogul Oprah Winfrey, actor Jim Carrey, Xerox CEO Ursula Burns, and wisdom teacher Wayne Dyer.

Does the pursuit of money and its acquisition always bring happiness? What if I turn this legend inside out and apply it to my everyday life? How have I gone from rags to riches in certain areas? How are other Americans doing so? I am excited about several movements in this country: the trends toward tiny houses, thriftiness, recycling, and local food. Many ideas have undergone scrutiny in these lean years, and at least some people are glad to exchange bloat and glut for a luxurious simplicity.

And what is richness anyway? One change that I have implemented is my view of time. I used to think there was never enough. Though I am still often busy, I have slowed my life down a bit lately and learned to say, "No" in a kind but firm way. So on some days, I find myself teeming with time: time that, with meditation or art projects, can turn eternal. With pluck and luck, my outlook on the clock has gone from tatters to treasure.

How have you learned to go from rags to riches lately? Can you think of something to do today to change?

April 5
"Memory is the mother of all wisdom."
Prometheus in Aeschylus' *Prometheus Bound*

Prometheus was the champion of human struggle to understand science and to fashion art. In this ancient Greek tragedy by Aeschylus, Prometheus takes pity on humans and gifts our race with fire. This act enrages Zeus, the chief deity of the pantheon, and he has Prometheus bound by chains to a rocky crag.

Eight months ago, as I have already written, my mother died of complications of Alzheimer's disease or some other equally despicable form of dementia. Her command post of all wisdom was compromised and most of her long-held recollections swept away. She eventually even had trouble navigating simple daily routines, and her exit from life was not as graceful as she would have liked.

My friend Tom Walker, founder of The American Village, talks about the importance of history by recalling a story with his grandmother. She had Alzheimer's and since he dearly loved the woman, he would frequently visit her. She gradually deteriorated so that she did not recognize him, which was understandable. But he was devastated the day he went to see her and she did not know herself. This, he recalled to audiences later, is what happens if we don't learn our national and personal history. We might as well have Alzheimer's, because we don't know who we are.

Year by year, America is growing older. New census figures indicate that by 2030, more than 20 percent of Americans will be over the age of 65, transfiguring the makeup of this country. Because more people will be older, more people will have dementia. Will they remember who they are? What used to be termed "senility," and was considered a customary component of aging, is now understood to be triggered by underlying health conditions that in some cases can be reversed with medical treatment or possibly prevented with attention to health and general well-being.

And something wonderful is that those Promethean arts can improve people's overall fitness, possibly prevent memory loss, and stave off dementia. Several studies over the past few decades have shown that when older people participate in cultural arts programs, they are likely to have less dependency on others. Overall health improves, doctor visits lessen, prescriptive drugs decrease, loneliness and isolation vanish.

Having been involved in dramatic careers for over 45 years, I have long known that theatre stimulates all four levels of a human's being: bodies are moving and reacting, minds are memorizing and analyzing, emotions are engaged and responding, and spirits are finding meaning and purpose. It takes a lot of courage to get up in front of people at any age, but especially when you are older, not looking or moving the way you once did.

And, there is a triumph in getting over self-absorption and fear. Audiences are enlightened by seeing the joy of older actors, and they themselves are exhilarated from watching the courage and talent of these elders. So I am encouraged by scientific studies that show cognitive stimulation through the arts. Participating in the arts can actually reverse memory decline and improve cognitive abilities.

It is true that memory can trick us or fail us. But I know from watching my mother's wealth of knowledge fade as her powers of recall became weak that Prometheus' words from the 400s BC are true: "Memory is the mother of all wisdom."

April 6
"There are more things in heaven and earth, Horatio,
Than are dreamt of in your philosophy."
Hamlet to Horatio in William Shakespeare's Hamlet, Act I, Scene 5

Horatio, a friend from the university at Wittenberg, has just said to Hamlet, "O day and night, but this is wondrous strange!" They, along with the sentry Marcellus, have just seen the Ghost of Hamlet's dead father. Hamlet begs the two men not to tell anyone what they have seen, and the Ghost makes them swear to obey Hamlet. Not the kind of scene we all go through on a daily basis.

I suppose everyone who lives upon this earth has days when the world seems like a foreign place, when things are off kilter, when we ourselves are out of sorts. Just last weekend, I spun a bit out of control around the house. For my Education for Ministry (EfM) class, I had listened to a dramatic reading of the entire book of Revelation in a couple of sittings. Let's just say that all of its scrolls, horsemen, devils, dragons, beasts, swords, plagues, falling stars, scarlet prostitutes, demons, judgments, imprisonments, and mass killings got to me.

For several hours, I staggered, with no firm ground under my feet. I was adrift, in another world, and swept up in a whirlwind. Then, I remembered a sermon one of my former priests, gave on "being *wazi-wazi*." I had first read about this term in 1990 in Gertrud Mueller Nelson's refreshing book *To Dance with God*. She actually got the term from anthropologist Colin Turnbull who wrote *The Forest People* in 1961, a highly appreciated and popular study of the Mbuti people of Zaire.

Nelson explains that, "The Mbuti see the person as being in the center of a sphere. In moving from here to there, the sphere moves too and offers protection. If movement in time or space is too sudden or vehement, we risk the danger of reaching the boundaries of the sphere too quickly, before the center has time to catch up. When this happens, a person becomes *wazi-wazi*, or disoriented and unpredictable."

So, in seeping myself in the apocalyptic imagery of Revelation, I really did find myself in a true *wazi-wazi* state. My awareness of time and space had been compromised, and, as Nelson says, "If you pierce through the safe boundaries of the sphere into the other world, you risk letting in something else which takes your place." I had become overtaken by someone who was not me. I wasn't thinking correctly, I didn't talk right, I couldn't make proper decisions.

"There are more things in heaven and earth, Horatio, than are dreamt of in your philosophy." When I realized that I was in an altered state because of the influence of the mind-boggling class preparation, I decided to assuage its assault and its jarring effect. What did I find as an antidote? A long listen to my collection of Cole Porter songs. Too bad Hamlet and Horatio couldn't have tuned him in!

April 7
"If you stick to the rules, then you never have to have a discussion about whether or not you were justified not sticking to the rules."
William in Kenneth Lonergan's *Lobby Hero*

I designed *Lobby Hero* a few years ago for one of our great local community theatres, Birmingham Festival. I say, "designed," but there was really not a lot to the costumes, as the "lobby hero" Jeff wears an apartment security guard uniform, as does his boss William. The other two characters are police officers on duty, so my job was to locate the authentic gear for these four individuals.

William is straight as an arrow, with very high ethical standards. Jeff is somewhat overwhelmed by a recent dishonorable discharge from the Navy for smoking marijuana. As the play unfolds, they both get snarled up in a local murder investigation pointing to William's brother. Along with the mysterious crime, Lonergan's play scrutinizes ideas of integrity, trust, and moral codes. Running underneath the action are found themes of police corruption, racial tension, and sexual competition.

Every character deals with fairly heavy matters. When William, the rule stickler, distorts his own private law to aid his criminal brother with an alibi, the audience realizes that he and all the rest of the characters have depth and complexity. Black and white distinctions vanish and ambiguity takes over.

Lately, I have been studying non-dualistic thinking, so, I am discovering that most things cannot be neatly divided into black and white, yes and no, good and bad, right and wrong. And I am practicing how to hold such diametrically opposed thoughts in my mind at one time.

But sometimes, life gets messy and borders are needed. Early in *Lobby Hero*, before the disorder caused by his brother, William says, *"If you stick to the rules, then you never have to have a discussion about whether or not you were justified not sticking to the rules."* Deep down, he wishes he could continue following those clearcut rules that a family challenge has rendered equivocal.

Like William, we all go through wildernesses in our lives, and maybe that is the time to find that clearcut guide who helps us follow principles and codes of honor. During the Prophet Amos's time, the Israelites became complacent and prideful. Amos 7:7-8 reads, "Thus he showed me and behold, the Lord stood beside a wall made by a plumb line, with a plumb line in his hand. Yahweh said to me, 'Amos, what do you see?' I said, 'A plumb line.' Then the Lord said, 'Behold, I will set a plumb line in the middle of my people Israel. I will not again pass by them any more.'" A plumb line is what a builder uses to make sure the walls are straight.

My dad was one of those plumb lines, as is my daughter Elin — both usually correct in their observations. I believe they are both Ones on the Enneagram: conscientious, ethical, moral, orderly, purposeful, rational — and almost always right. It is often beneficial to have such guides nearby when life is rough — those unequivocal folks who draw a hard line in the sand, giving the reassurance of rules and decrees to set our lives back on a straight path.

April 8
"Nothing forces us to know
What we do not want to know
Except pain."
Chorus in Aeschylus' Agamemnon from *The Oresteia* trilogy

Or we may say, "suffering" instead of pain. On a recent *Super Soul Sunday* on the Oprah Winfrey channel, author and American spiritual teacher Gary Zukav explained the difference between pain and suffering. Pain, he said, is really just pain. Your sister has died. That is painful. But, if you transform that pain, if you use it, if you, in fact, absorb it and hold it, then that pain is pressed into service for a worthy purpose which is your spiritual growth, and it can then be called "suffering."

Suffering alters the health of our souls. Our egos don't trust the universe. Our egos don't feel worthy, but they certainly want pain to have meaning, to be explained, and ultimately to go away. But our souls grow each time we experience agony.

Richard Rohr's email reflection today reminded me: "Don't get rid of the pain until you've learned its lessons. When you hold the pain consciously and trustfully, you are in a very special liminal space. This is a great teaching moment where you have the possibility of breaking through to a deeper level of faith and consciousness. Hold the pain of being human until God transforms you through it. And then you will be an instrument of transformation for others."

He explained that Mary at the foot of the cross of the crucifixion of her son is a perfect example of holding the pain. Most Jewish women would be wailing and grieving with their voices and bodies. But instead, she is still and quiet, "in complete solidarity with the mystery of life and death."

I remember the first time I encountered this truth in my own life. I had gotten myself to a wonderful state: physically fit, mentally alert, emotionally stable, and spiritually seeking and finding. At this very point, my then-husband announced that he wanted a divorce. The aftermath was agonizingly heartbreaking. And yet, I was at a place where I could hold the pain almost in my hands and feel the exquisite nature of suffering. Oddly, I embraced life as never before, and experienced a sudden recognition of its beauty and transitory nature. It was not a feeling or a realization that I would have actively sought.

But when it happened, I was grateful. And it did transform me. Curiously, the suffering led to a metamorphosis and new creation. My ego was totally crushed, and my divine self slowly began to emerge. I was in a numinous place where I was able to descend into a profoundly deep relationship with Grace. And it made me so much more aware of other people's agonies of illnesses, of brokenness, of cracked and shattered lives.

Aeschylus was right so long ago: *"Nothing forces us to know/What we do not want to know/Except pain."*

April 9:

The Shepherd: Ba-a !

Pathelin (feigning astonishment): Ba-a? The devil! What ba-a? Zounds! Art you crazy? Tell me your business.

The Shepherd: Ba-a-a!

Pathelin: How ba-a? Do you hear thy ewes a-bleating? Mind, it is to your interest.

Characters in the medieval play *The Farce of Master Pierre Pathelin* by Anonymous

Oh, how I loved directing and designing *The Farce of Master Pierre Pathelin* in the early 1990s. This French Medieval farce about a conniving lawyer is really quite funny. It is full of flawed characters, from Pathelin, the seedy pettifogger who steals cloth from the local draper; Pathelin's wife, Guillemette, who goes along with his schemes and receives the stolen fabric; the draper, Joceaulme, who is himself covetous and cunning; and the trial Judge, who cares so little about justice that he invites the accused Pathelin to dine with him. And then there is Thibault l'Aignelet, a ninny of a thieving Shepherd who gives Pathelin a dose of his own villainy and outmaneuvers the rest of them in the end.

At a funny trial, Pathelin defends the shepherd, and urges Thibault to say nothing but *"Baaa."* The judge totally muddles the proceedings and dismisses the charges, because the shepherd can only respond with a nonsensical *"Baaa."* Pathelin attempts to collect his fee, but Thibault continues to reply only with a soulful *"Baaa."* Pathelin finally just gives up, realizing his magnificent defense has helped the shepherd dupe him as well.

Our actors were fantastic, and I still laugh and laugh remembering our funny little Thibault baa-ing and baa-ing. I haven't been around sheep a whole lot. But one time, one very special, magical, shining time I was around a whole lot of sheep.

When my then-husband and I found out that we would be going to England for our very first January term class for Samford University in 1987, my mother and father decided to go with us, and insisted we take Seth, aged three, and Elin, aged 11. So we six went over early and spent Christmas in England. My parents wanted very badly to be with us the first time we experienced Stonehenge, so on December 22, the day after the winter solstice (so the crowds were gone), we all went out to the Salisbury Plain and soaked up the stunning, huge, mysterious prehistoric bluestone monument. Except for a couple of other tourists and thousands of sheep grazing nearby, we were alone.

It was around 3:30 in the afternoon, and beginning to get dark, which happens very early in the winter in England. I had been so absorbed in feasting my eyes on these stones I had longed to see all my life that I almost missed a totally different and yet equally transcendent event going on all around me. Something stirred, and I looked around at the meadowland that slopes up from the monument. All at once, the many thousand of sheep started bleating "baa" and began moving in a swirling pattern that swept over the plain.

Responding to a shepherd's voice, or a certain time of day, they all somehow knew it was time to stop nibbling and head for home. Slowly, in a protracted and choreographed manner, thousands of them, in a sedate and orderly way, followed each other off the hillsides and out of our sight.

"I am the good shepherd. I know my own, and I'm known by my own..." Every time I hear this passage in John 10 about Jesus as the Good Shepherd, I think of droll Thibault and her *"baa"* and I remember seeing the sheep who knew the voice of something calling. Was it the shepherd? Nature? The Holy One? Someone was calling those thousands of sheep by name and leading them back home.

April 10:
"The ordinary-sized stuff which is our lives, the things people write poetry about– clouds–daffodils–waterfalls–what happens in a cup of coffee when the cream

goes in—these things are full of mystery, as mysterious to us as the heavens were to the Greeks."
Valentine in Tom Stoppard's *Arcadia*

In 2006, The Royal Institution of Great Britain, that center of scientific education and research, named Tom Stoppard's play *Arcadia* one of the "best science books ever." On April 13, 1993 the intriguing work had opened at the Royal National Theatre in London. I saw a three-hour version at the Haymarket Theatre on January 4, 1995, and then went to a 4-hour *Hamlet* at the Gielgud Theatre right afterward. Talk about a day of play-watching!

A drama of mixed reviews, *Arcadia* is not easy to watch. You really must concentrate, as mathematical and scientific theories are woven throughout the action which simultaneously takes place in 1809 and the present. Stoppard entwines chaos theory, algorithms, landscape design, botany, determinism, and more into the plot — and what's fun, clues from the earlier period are interpreted by modern day characters.

Valentine's line about *"The ordinary-sized stuff which is our lives"* being full of mystery intrigues me. Most of us humans do all walk around day after day ignoring the spectacular miracles that surround us in reality. My son Seth and his wife Kim have a child Teddy who is three years old at this writing. If you want to be clear about the wonder in our everyday lives, just follow a toddler around for a day!

William Martin has an often quoted portion of his book *The Parent's Tao Te Ching: Ancient Advice for Modern Parents*. It goes like this: "Do not ask your children to strive for extraordinary lives. Such striving may seem admirable, but it is the way of foolishness. Help them instead to find the wonder and the marvel of an ordinary life. Show them the joy of tasting tomatoes, apples and pears. Show them how to cry when pets and people die. Show them the infinite pleasure in the touch of a hand. And make the ordinary come alive for them. The extraordinary will take care of itself."

Great advice, truly. But I also find just the opposite to be the case. Children teach me about the extraordinary mystery of daily existence. Youngsters experience new things all the time, and their amazement at what they discover is breathtaking. Teddy says, "Wow!" at blossoms that have opened since he last was here; "Whoa!" at a yard full of pine cones after a storm; and "Why?" at the bird who flew into the window and fell momentarily to the ground. Humans are born with an innate sense of wonder, and I realize that at some point — even a young age sometimes — we all begin to lose the sense that life is amazing, nature is wondrous, and people are remarkable.

But young children lead us to look at life with fresh and innocent eyes. We had put six big black bags full of pine straw in the back yard to mulch some flower beds. Teddy came running to me exclaiming, "BeBe, BeBe! Something is very wrong. You don't put garbage in your back yard! You have to put it by the street so the truck picks it up."

One thing my time with grandchildren the last few years has taught me is that every minute is filled with astonishing, breathtaking objects and events. So when we watch *"what happens in a cup of coffee when the cream goes in"* if we can recognize the act *"as mysterious to us as the heavens were to the Greeks"* we will look at life as the incredibly extraordinary experience that it is.

April 11:
"The great secret, Eliza, is not having bad manners or good manners or any other particular sort of manners, but having the same manner for all human souls: in short, behaving as if you were in Heaven, where there are no third-class carriages, and one soul is as good as another."
Henry Higgins to Eliza Doolittle in George Bernard Shaw's *Pygmalion*

Shaw's *Pygmalion* opened in London on this day, April 11, 1914, at Sir Herbert Beerbohm Tree's His Majesty's Theatre and starred Mrs. Patrick Campbell as Eliza and Sir Herbert as Higgins, running for 118 performances. As I said in writing about *My Fair Lady* — adapted from this play — I have always loved Henry Higgins for his complexity and contradictions: a tyrant and a sweetheart, brilliant academically and half-witted in social graces, unconventional and a voice of reason.

In this scene, Eliza has denounced him for his inconsiderate treatment, and he talks about having the same manners for everyone.

Funny I should have picked this quote for today, even though it is the 100th Anniversary of its London opening. Just two days ago, a friend of mine Bethe, spoke of her grandmother's good Southern manners, and her stressing of just how important comportment is. Grandmother had told the story of a gentleman who had invited his intended bride to dinner in his home to meet his family. When the first course was over, the servers brought in finger bowls. Not used to such practice, the young lady picked up the bowl and drank the water. Without missing a beat, the young man did the same. The grandmother said that manners not only include what a person should properly do, but how they have compassion and act with respect.

This tale was given as part of the introduction of another friend Sandra, who was performing a reading at our Speech Arts Club of Birmingham. The introducer remarked that our reader treated everyone she met with the same genteel manner and open heart, no matter if it is a homeless person she serves at her parish's soup kitchen or the Bishop of Alabama when he visits her church.

Only the Gospel of Luke records Jesus telling the story of the Good Samaritan, in which Jesus answers a lawyer's question by telling him to love both God and his neighbor as himself. Then the lawyer asks "who is my neighbor." Then comes the parable of a traveller who is beaten, robbed, and left half dead along the road. A priest and a Levite pass by, but neither stops to help the injured man. Finally, a Samaritan journeys down the road, and although Jews and Samaritans generally spurned each other, this Samaritan goes out of his way to assist the wounded man.

What does this really mean, *"having the same manner for all human souls"*? I think we are called to do just what the young man at the dinner table did, what the Samaritan did, and what my friend Sandra does: treat other people with respect, empathy, and courtesy. I am happy that several times a year in the Episcopal Church, we reaffirm our Baptismal Vows. Part of that covenant is to commit, that with God's help, to seek and serve Christ in all persons, loving our neighbor as ourselves, and to strive for justice and peace among all people, respecting the dignity of every human being. It is *"behaving as if you were in Heaven, where there are no third-class carriages, and one soul is as good as another."*

April 12:
"Now is my way clear, now is the meaning plain:
Temptation shall not come in this kind again.
The last temptation is the greatest treason:
To do the right deed for the wrong reason."
Thomas Becket in T. S. Eliot's *Murder in the Cathedral*

Murder in the Cathedral, first performed in 1935, is TS Eliot's stunning verse drama that I have written about before. Using the writings of Edward Grim, a clerk who actually witnessed the assassination of

Archbishop Thomas Becket, Eliot portrays the events leading up to the murder in Canterbury Cathedral on December 29, 1170. I was on the team that designed and directed an amazing *Murder in the Cathedral* at Samford in 1979.

Becket's internal struggle about power, authority, loyalty, and serving self versus serving God is the crux of the play. Toward the end of the first act, Becket contemplates possible martyrdom, and what that might mean in the purpose of his life. This scene becomes more and more fascinating as three tempters appear one by one to test Thomas and entice him with similar seductions Satan used to attempt to beguile Christ in the wilderness.

The first tempter offers Becket a way to return to "the good life" of pleasure and favor that he once had with his friend, King Henry II. The second tester attempts to persuade the archbishop to return to serving the king with the accompanying power, riches, and fame. The third tempter appeals to Thomas's competitive nature and begs his establishing an alliance with the barons to betray Henry. These temptations are all fairly easy for Becket to forego.

Suddenly, a fourth and surprise tempter comes in and almost pulls Becket off course. The archbishop has expected the other three, but not this last test. This cunning spirit presses the archbishop toward actively seeking the role of martyr to win sainthood, coaxing, "What earthly glory, of king or emperor," he asks, could possibly compare "with richness of heavenly grandeur?" He says if Thomas doesn't succumb to this yearning, he will never be remembered for anything.

Becket responds to this last, and really to all of the tempters, by proclaiming the often quoted lines: *"Now is my way clear, now is the meaning plain: Temptation shall not come in this kind again. The last temptation is the greatest treason: To do the right deed for the wrong reason."*

He has recognized in the final lure something that has been hiding in his shadow self, a fatal weakness, his own self-seeking, his vainglory, his ego. When he can embrace vulnerability and turn down what he might gain by pride, he has won a major battle.

How many schoolchildren beg for a test? Teenagers dread exams for weeks and college students often go to great lengths to pump professors for exactly what will appear on a quiz. Adults hope to avoid any sort of trial as well. But Thomas has a thorough examination of the soul, and he passes.

A dictionary definition of test is "that by which the presence, quality, or genuineness of anything is determined." When you think about it, how else can we know our own personal score, see what is lacking in our lives, understand where we need cleansing and strengthening than by a trial or questioning?

A test shows how we are at the moment. Unless we are sorely tempted, we never know the limits of our transgressions – or our goodness. The powers of the Universe lead us up steep and rocky inclines sometimes not to have us lose our way, but to find it.

April 13:
"Father: I don't go to church to be preached at as though I were some lost sheep.
Vinnie: Clare, you don't seem to understand what the Church is for.
Father: Vinnie, if there's one place the Church should leave alone, it's a man's soul!"
Characters in Howard Lindsay and Russell Crouse's *Life with Father*

At Parkway Playhouse in Burnsville, North Carolina, in the summer of 1973, I was a part of this heartwarming story based on the memoirs of Clarence Day. My good friend James Fisher played the loving but irascible papa with five rambunctious red-headed sons in *Life with Father*. The original Broadway production, which opened in at the Empire Theatre on November 8, 1939, ran for seven years and over 3,000 performances, making it the longest-running straight (non-musical) play to ever be staged on Broadway, a record that it still holds as of this writing.

The perfectionist Clarence, or "Clare," Day constantly complains about things in life that fails to satisfy his unattainable measure. But he has a good heart, and his practical and understated manner are constantly revealed in wry comments on the myriad events that happen to his busy, boisterous family. His declaration about the church leaving people's souls alone is typical of his prickly but highly amusing over-statements. The Day family has been on an even keel until suddenly Mother chances upon the fact that Father has never been baptized. Clare fails to see it as a problem, but Mother is worried and screams in horror as the second scene ends, "Maybe we're not even married!"

When this play was written, church attendance was the norm. According to recent studies, the number of Americans who have no religious affiliation is currently at the highest peak it has ever been since statistics on the subject began being accumulated in the 1930s, when this play debuted. At that time, 95 percent of Americans claimed to be a part of organized religion. This Pew Research study showed that number to have dropped to 77 percent, and falling.

Today is Palm Sunday and I spent two and a half hours in a service, complete with palm fronds, bagpipe, procession, incense, chanting, readings, a sermon, and communion. So you might think I would disagree with Father. And I do to some extent. However, I know many people who were hurt by their churches, disappointed, browbeaten, intimidated, even terrorized or abused. In such cases, we do want organized religion to leave our souls alone. So I understand some people's reluctance to darken the doors of a place of worship.

I also know that to become a spiritual person, to encounter the holy, to happen into the mystery of life, does not require denominational membership. For a good long while, I have understood that religion and the transcendent life can be related, but are definitely not the same thing. Atheists and non-church-goers can all wander across the borders and into the Holy.

Religion does not equal the numinous experiences we all have that bring us close to what you might call Wisdom, Life, Wholeness, Love, Reality, or the Divine. Like many things, an encounter in a house of worship may suddenly open a door into a surprising and holy place. And religion serves as the repository for and preserver of terms, language, rituals, and traditions that help us interpret what we discover in a thin space — that often veiled spot where, without warning, we see meaning and undergirding for our everyday life. Such unexpected awareness can inform and form us for the rest of our days, whether it happens in a church, nature, a museum, or a bar.

April 14:
"The only people who ever get anyplace interesting are the people who get lost."
Henry in Jerome Lawrence Robert E. Lee's *The Night Thoreau Spent in Jail*

Just today on Facebook, a friend posted the following: "I chose the road less traveled and now I don't know where the hell I am... Lost, I suppose."

I really admire Henry David Thoreau, and I so enjoyed twice designing *The Night Thoreau Spent in Jail*. The play features the time

Thoreau actually spent a night in the Concord, Massachusetts jail for civil disobedience. He declined paying a poll tax to oppose a war.

So yes, I love Thoreau, but oh, me! *"The only people who ever get anyplace interesting are the people who get lost,"* he says. Those words are troublesome to a person who scores a pretty solid "J" on the Myers Briggs Type Indicator instrument. Do you prefer a more structured and decided lifestyle (Judging)? they always ask. YES! Or do you prefer a more flexible and adaptable lifestyle (Perceiving) in your orientation to the outer world? NO!

Although I am getting better and better at letting things flow, I am a fairly entrenched "J." I like to have things established in advance, so that my mind is clearly settled. I don't mind if plans change or metamorphose, but I want to start the day with a strategy. I am a bit task oriented, make lists of things to do, get my work done before playing, plan jobs to avoid rushing just before a deadline. Just about everything on the Myers Briggs website that deals with a "J" fits me to a "T."

My fiancé Roger is a true "P." He occasionally makes lists, but is more often open to what is happening minute by minute. He is relaxed and prefers to keep plans to a minimum; in fact, sometimes my goals and blueprints for a day ruffle him a bit. An environmentalist, he connects deeply to nature and greatly admires Thoreau, so he absolutely believes, *"The only people who ever get anyplace interesting are the people who get lost."*

Traveling together can be a challenge, but we have come to realize that if neither of us is totally rigid, we can fill in gaps for each other and not only get somewhere, but have some unstructured fun as well. Most people of my type like organized vacations, like trips to a resort or a cruise, and I am actually more adventuresome than that.

Perceivers like Roger tend to travel off the beaten path and that is great with me. He enjoys hiking and river travel, fishing and talking to people at nearby tables at restaurants. I enjoy his finding little-known breweries on a hidden street or happening upon a music venue we had no idea about. He relishes the adventure more than the targeted sites, and I can definitely jump on board with that. Many of our journeys together allow time for meandering and soaking up the local ambiance.

So besides visiting specific attractions and restaurants that I research and yearn to see, when Roger and I travel, we also leave time to dawdle. He has admitted my destinations are usually attractive and enjoyable. And wandering about has become one of my favorite parts of our trips. After all, as Gandalf wrote in his letter to Frodo Baggins in JRR

Tolkien's The Fellowship of the Ring, "...Not all those who wander are lost."

April 15:
In "You've Got to Pick a Pocket or Two" from *Oliver!*, Fagin sings about figuring out ways to get untaxed wages through his petty thievery.
(Listen to the work online or from your library!)
    Fagin in *Oliver!* adapted from the Charles Dickens novel with book and music by Lionel Bart

    Oh, how those words of Fagin's song play in my head today, the deadline for filing tax returns to the Internal Revenue Service of the United States federal government. I really don't mind paying my fair share of taxes for safety, Social Security, health insurance programs, national transportation issues, and many of our other public services — although I do wish more of my money went to the National Endowment for the Arts.

    Finding some extra nontaxable cash is such a stirring idea! Not that I would pick a pocket, let alone two, to get such funding. But a nice benefactor who contributed the allowable $14,000 gift to my bank account each year would help me so much. And I would do such good with it!

    Alas! That is what people say when they buy lottery tickets and wish for the big break. They would have to pay a chunk of taxes on that earning — however, they promise they would save their family, friends, and even the world with what is left. People have a huge desire to fix their lives, and they think money will help that. And truly, money might help a few things, especially if you are in debt.

    But when a hankering for cash meets the fantasy world, you are ripe for buying that lottery ticket. One of my grandmothers, in her later years, was absolutely positive she was going to win the Publisher's Clearing House sweepstakes and have the Prize Patrol come to her door. Or she believed she might snag the give-away from American Family Publishers, whose spokesperson at the time was Ed McMahon. She would show me a packet of cards from American Family, with pictures of the celebrity, and say, "Just look what that sweetheart Ed McMahon has sent me this week!" — as if he were specially keeping up with what she was doing and what she needed. Every time she got a mailing, she bought a "trinket" or two until we finally had to slip the direct marketing envelopes out of her mailbox every time we found them.

Studies have shown that a good number of people who win large sums of money from lotteries and give-aways are fairly miserable afterward. Why? Because if my life is a mess to begin with, if I hate my family, if I don't have friends, or if I believe happiness comes from outside rather than inside me, then money is only going to exaggerate how far I am down the wrong path.

So no matter how much on this day of all days I wish to have a little untaxed income, I would be better served by sitting down to a deep reverie, thinking of how many riches I have in my life and how my happiness can well up from within when I count my many blessings.

April 16:
"John: (Blocking her way) I can see the scene going on just a tad longer, Mother.
Ann: How?
John: I think there's more to be said.
Ann: About what?
John: About you, Mother.
Ann: Me?"
John and his mother Ann in AR Gurney's *The Cocktail Hour*

Birmingham Festival Theatre produced a charming *Cocktail Hour* a few years ago and I was privileged to design the costumes for four really good actors. About an upper class family in the Northeast, the play concerns a really stretched out cocktail hour in which John, the son, reveals that he has written a play (also called *The Cocktail Hour*) about his family, which his parents Bradley and Ann find quite unflattering and very upsetting.

And to make the whole artistic foundation even more convoluted, A.R.Gurney actually based the play on his own relatives. After Gurney's mother saw *The Cocktail Hour* in New York, he asked her "Did you like it?" and she replied "Not much."

Gurney once said about writing plays, "I'm always conflicted; I think people who write plays are always conflicted. That's why they write plays. In the end writing is a psychological drive and not a drive for fame or fortune. It's a need to work out these issues in my own soul and drama seemed to be the best form in which to do it. I think I'd be a basket case if not for the theatre."

In the scene quoted above, John wants to know more about his mother. He wants her to reveal family secrets, naturally, but more than anything, he wants her to be genuine and truthful; he wants her, for once, to be transparent instead of hiding her true self with superficial gauze.

I agree with Gurney that writing helps work out issues of the soul. Just sitting down each day to compose these writings is a psychological, spiritual exercise that illuminates issues that have heretofore been smoldering beneath the surface.

One of the hardest spiritual exercises that I have been practicing lately is shedding my false self to find my true self. That is what John wants Ann to do. But she stays pretty concealed, and I can see why. I read, I listen to wisdom teachers, I study contemplations from sages, I meditate, I write, I talk to others on their spiritual paths. But it is hard, hard labor, and I have to exert myself mentally, emotionally, and spiritually every day.

We are drawing toward the end of Lent this week. During the entire 40 days, I have "altered my eating lifestyle." (I use that phrase instead of a "diet," because really, that is what it has been.) I have shed 20 pounds in that time span. It was not easy; in fact, this food routine has been arduous and austere physical work.

Peeling away the false self, peeling away my excess pounds. Both are challenging. But to be able to say I am having even a little success with them is a huge accomplishment for this past penitential season. And, I am feeling lighter and letting more light shine though me for Easter this year.

April 17:
"Oh, I've never forgotten for long at a time that living is a struggle. I know that every good and excellent thing in the world stands moment by moment on the razor-edge of danger and must be fought for – whether it's a field, or a home, or a country. All I ask is the chance to build new worlds and God has always given us that second chance..."
Mr. Antrobus in Thornton Wilder's *The Skin of Our Teeth*

I have already written some about *The Skin of Our Teeth* on January 28, but this quote is so good, and it is Thornton Wilder's birthday: he made his earthly debut on April 17, 1897. Though I believe life can be seen as a flow, and that we can look at even our struggles as meaningful learning experiences, the Antrobuses (their name means "human" in Greek) have been through a lot — more than the average person, because they represent "Every Family." So, they experience the ice age, refugees fleeing to their home, the break up of their family, a flood the size of Noah's, a devastating war, and the near destruction of the human race.

Mortals are continually beset by both natural catastrophes and man-made tragedies. In those peaks of drama in life, people do feel that, *"every good and excellent thing in the world stands moment by moment on the razor-edge of danger."* The things we believe in could be dashed forever. And people of courage step forward and battle for those shining, bright, right, and magnificent things that we all value in life.

Alabama has had more than its share of tornadoes in the last few years. And as well, our Southern Gulf coast has been beaten by huge hurricanes. And yet people jump right in after the last rain clouds have blown over and begin to *"build new worlds"* one more time.

And think of our everyday troubles. We have all heard some dreadful words: "Your biopsy shows signs of cancer." "You did not pass the bar exam." "I am leaving you." We want a do-over, a try-again, a re-wind to begin again.

Even though Mr. Antrobus makes numerous mistakes and slips, he and his family persevere. Despite — or perhaps because of — their struggles, he believes his life, and life itself, has significance. He spurs his kin to keep exerting themselves, to save the family, to advance the world, to leave a legacy for all future humans. Mr. Antrobus says, *"All I ask is the chance to build new worlds and God has always given us that second chance..."*

History shows over and over examples of people and nations who have had to reboot and grow anew. Even the Bible is packed with stories of folks who received, through no merit or labor of their own, second, third, fourth, and many more chances. Think of the disciple Peter, the barren Sarah, Jonah in the belly of the fish, the woman caught in adultery, Joseph who was sold into slavery, David the impetuous ruler.

Regret and wishing life had treated me differently will only weigh me down. What is best is to deal with the consequences of poor decisions, cross words, unfulfilled obligations, or heartaches; ask forgiveness, right a wrong, perform a duty, move on.

Really, the Universe, the Divine, the Holy, or whatever you call the undergirding of Life, gives us many more chances than two. Every day that we wake up, we have new opportunities to reconstruct our homes, our relationships, our outlooks, our selves.

April 18:

"There's no place like home."

Dorothy in film and play adaptations of Frank L. Baum's *The Wizard of Oz*

When I was a kid, I was introduced to the movie version of *The Wizard of Oz* in 1956 when CBS debuted the classic for the first time on television. We had a black and white TV at the time, and my mother bemoaned the fact that we couldn't see the transformation into color when Dorothy landed in Munchkin Land. But in a couple of years, we got a color set and CBS began broadcasting the show annually. It was a tradition for my family to watch it and wonder together about the idea of "no place like home."

When I designed an elaborate version of *The Wizard of Oz* for Birmingham Children's Theatre in the 1970s, that phrase about home kept coming back to me, and I pondered it, believing it had a deeper, more mysterious meaning than it seemed on the surface. Dorothy is violently uprooted from home, is miraculously dropped in the astonishing Oz, makes some remarkable friends, fights some formidable battles. But the whole time, she is trying to find her way to the Wizard, because all she really wants is to go home.

In the late 1980s and early '90s, as I lost my self and my life was disintegrating, I began searching, like Dorothy. I wanted a learned wizard to help me by waving a magic wand and making everything right again.

Several times, I happened to watch the movie version of *Oz* again, and slowly its real meaning dawned on me. Glinda the Good Witch of the North makes one final appearance, descending from the sky in her shimmering bubble and glides out of her ball of light. Dorothy cries, "Oh, will you help me? Can you help me?"

And Glinda kindly tells Dorothy that she has always had the power to go home. "You don't need to be helped any longer. You've always had the power to go back to Kansas." To which Dorothy asks, "I have?" The Scarecrow wonders why Glinda has not told her before, and Glinda replies, "Because she wouldn't have believed me. She had to learn it for herself."

Dorothy realizes that if she searches for her heart's desire again, "I won't look any further than my own backyard. Because if it isn't there, I never really lost it to begin with!" Of course, there is a little enchantment. Glinda says Dorothy has to click the heels of her ruby (or silver in the book) slippers together, and she will magically appear back in Kansas.

So it hit me: looking inside is the real thing that will help any of us. I might sometimes need some advice from books, counselors, or some perspicacious sages to get me on balance. But what I really must do is delve deep and find out what is happening right inside of me, in my home, which is my body where reside my emotions, my intelligence, my judgment. No matter how many discerning teachers I may consult, everything I really need is right here at home in my soul. And if I follow my soul, it will show me where to go.

April 19:
"The Regulars are coming out. The Regulars are coming out!"
Paul Revere in a reenactment of the events of April 18 - 19 at The American Village

Today is Patriots' Day commemorating the beginning and the end of the American Revolutionary War. In 1775 on this day, the Battles of Lexington and Concord were fought, being the first skirmishes of the war. The fight for independence finally ended in Yorktown on October 19, 1781, when Cornwallis surrendered to George Washington, and a formal treaty officially ending the war was signed in 1783.

The American Village is a historic replica site where tens of thousands of students and adults visit annually to discover the power and drama of America's journey for independence, liberty, and self-government. When I functioned as the Creative Director there, I assisted in the reenacting of many scenes from history, including the happenings on this date.

Last night, April 18, 1775, Paul Revere made his famous ride to let the Patriots know that the British troops were moving and he did not say, "The British are coming," but, according to eyewitness accounts of the ride and Revere's own writings, "The Regulars are coming out!"

At the Village, I loved helping craft scripts concerning American history to teach children about the country's many struggles and triumphs in our striving toward liberty for all. One thing that really impressed me while working so closely with characters from the past was that they didn't know how things were going to turn out. George Washington, Frederick Douglass, Abigail Adams, Patrick Henry, Phillis Wheatley: they all, just as I do, lived their lives one minute at a time. They had no idea if the

150

British or the colonists would win the War of Independence, if they would personally live or die in action, if the extremely long war would go on forever.

We sometimes read about and respond to history as if the people of that time should have acted differently, because we know what happened; but the colonists were not clairvoyant. As the Revolutionary War unfolds, just as any history develops, just as our own lives transpire, the early Americans have to think, listen, feel, talk, make or break relationships, hurry, slow down, ponder, wonder, make decisions, and operate without knowing what the consequences might be.

When Paul Revere was summoned to communicate to the colonists on the night of April 19, he had no idea that this one ride would go down in history as an important piece of the war puzzle. Revere had worked out a system of signals in case he was detained in Boston. During his journey on a borrowed horse, he confirmed that the "Sons of Liberty" had seen the two lanterns hanging in the Christ Church bell-tower. This indication cued patriots that British troops would approach "by sea" across the Charles River to Cambridge, rather than trooping "by land."

Throughout his trip to Lexington, Paul Revere notified every house he passed and didn't get to Lexington until midnight. When he drew near to the Hancock-Clark House where Hancock and Adams were staying, a guard cautioned that he be quiet, as he was making too much noise. "Noise!" cried Revere, "You'll have noise enough before long. The regulars are coming out!"

The least we can do on Patriots Day this year is to quote him correctly!

April 20:
"Jesus said, "Father, forgive them, for they don't know what they are doing."
from Luke 23:34

Jesus sings some very similar words in *Jesus Christ Superstar*, music by Andrew Lloyd Webber and lyrics by Tim Rice (Listen to the work online or from your library!)

Today is Easter Sunday this year, so my thoughts ran to stage depictions of the life of Jesus. I have always been fascinated with *Jesus Christ Superstar*, the rock opera by Webber and Rice first staged on Broadway in 1971, the year I got married, the year before I graduated from college. With a fairly untethered view of the Gospels, the work focuses on the last week of Jesus's life and ends with the crucifixion.

Andrew Lloyd Webber's *Superstar* music is stirring and appropriate for this 1970s rock pop treatment. When it premiered, the work was viewed as extraordinarily controversial, especially in the Bible Belt where I live. Religious leaders condemned the show as profane and the music as sacrilegious, thus prompting many theatre people to produce it just for this titillation factor.

After his father died, Andrew Lloyd Webber wrote a *Requiem* in his memory. When interviewed about it by Dennis Polkow for the 1987 cover story of *The Christian Century*, Webber is quoted as looking back and saying, "*Superstar* had a contemporary text by Tim Rice, and was never really intended to be anything more than a piece examining the story of Jesus from the point of view of Judas Iscariot. In that sense it is a dramatic work, and not specifically a religious work at all..."

Webber goes on to say, "But *Jesus Christ Superstar* was really not an irreligious piece, as has been so often suggested. In its own way and in its own time it was simply a work attempting to ask a couple of questions, the chief of which was stated by Bob Dylan some years ago: 'Did Judas Iscariot have God on his side?' ... *Superstar* never set out or intended to discuss anything at all like the resurrection. All it ever did was to declare itself to be a version of the last seven days of Jesus Christ."

I understand that this was all Rice and Webber intended for their rock opera, and I respect that. Thinking back on the work today, though, I realize why the ending seems empty to me. The crucifixion without the resurrection is like yin without the yang. All things on the earth – plants, animals, water, people – are constantly yielding to change: the death of the old and the rebirth of the new, the surrender to darkness and the reawakening to light, the concession to suffering and the revival in healing. The universe always offers the possibility of death transformed.

On our planet, we cannot have life without death; and we all die to something every day. Those of us who grew up and learned spirituality in the western world are steeped in duality. There is light OR dark, soft OR hard, life OR death. Eastern thought holds out the idea that these opposites don't rule one over the other, but sanction each other. And when we can hold death and resurrection together in our spirits, we can rest in the peace of the grace of life.

April 21:

"Buddha says, 'A child without courage is like a night without stars!'"

Punjab in the musical *Annie* based upon the popular Harold Gray comic strip *Little Orphan Annie* with music by Charles Strouse, lyrics by Martin Charnin and book by Thomas Meehan

The original Broadway production of *Annie* opened at the Alvin Theatre on April 21, 1977 and starred Andrea McArdle as Annie. It was still running in 1980 when I took a fun group of students to New York City on a theatre tour, and we saw the show. I heard "back in the day" that the creators of the work wanted young girls to have a musical comparable to what little boys had in *Oliver!* I am not sure if that is true or not, but it has worked out that way.

There are some fun quotes from the show: Annie's "Leaping Lizards!" Miss Hannigan's song about how other ladies have tons of jewels, while she is beset with a house-load of little girls. And Annie sings about how the sun will appear the next day.

I don't know if the Buddha really said, *"A child without courage is like a night without stars!"* The words don't seem very Buddha-like to me, and that child would be forlorn. But I know that most children do have courage because they really haven't learned to fear very much. The word "courage" comes from Latin "cor," meaning "heart." As Brené Brown reminded everyone who listened to one of her TED (Technology, Entertainment and Design) talks, "Courage originally meant 'To speak one's mind by telling all one's heart.' Over time, this definition has changed, and, today, courage is more synonymous with being heroic."

Being a spunky, optimistic, dauntless child, Annie certainly always speaks her mind by telling all her heart. An orphan, she wants to be reunited with parents she yearns to know, and that motivation guides much of her action in the story.

Throughout our lifetimes, we hear people say, "I am just speaking my mind" when they want to say something blunt or offensive. They are not using much heart when they do so. Southerners sometimes take the edge off such jibes by saying something like, "Well, isn't it the most puzzling thing that even though Thelma, bless her heart, has been on a strict low calorie diet, she's gained a healthy 11 pounds." The phrase "bless her heart" is intended to soften the blow of the most outrageous insult or put-down, and its use has little to do with the "telling all one's heart" that the original word "courage" intended.

One thing the Buddha did say is, "If you propose to speak, always ask yourself, is it true, is it necessary, is it kind." So sometimes I choose not to speak my mind. I don't always know something is truly true. Blabbing is often unnecessary. And I don't like being callous. I am empathetic and I want to protect people's feelings. Over the years, I have learned it is usually better to listen more than I speak — and to be loving more than protesting I am right.

April 22:
"I don't know what I am any more, or what I'm doing;
Now I'm on fire, now I'm freezing.
Every woman makes me change colour,
Every woman makes my heart flutter.
Simply at the name of love, of delight,
I am upset, and my heart beats faster
And I find myself talking of love
From a need I can't explain."
Cherubino in Wolfgang Amadeus Mozart's *The Marriage of Figaro*, Act I, scene 5

Cherubino is one of my favorite opera characters with his innocent, budding passion for women... Or is it her innocent, budding passion? I have designed costumes for Mozart's *The Marriage of Figaro* three times, maybe four. The comic feel to the work is strong, with its slamming of doors, hiding behind chairs, duping of masters, and implausible excuses. And even the characters are commedia-like: young lovers, bumbling but wily servants, a greedy old miser, and an ancient pompous scholar. Oh, and there is the gag of characters in drag: Cherubino is played by a woman, genders are confused with the prince and princess, and master and servant switch clothing at one point.

Ah, but it is all about love! Love, love, love. *"Now I'm on fire, now I'm freezing."* That description sounds like me going through menopause. And now, years after that passage of life, at the age of 66, Roger and I have become betrothed. *"My heart beats faster."*

Speaking of hearts beating, on April 22 last year, I went to check on my stepfather — it is almost three years since my mother died, and my brother and I are still tending to him. I fixed him an early supper, and lingered because he was lonely. I had left Roger pulling some English ivy

154

that was threatening to take over the front yard, and when I returned he was in a tub full of cool water. When I say full, I mean a couple of inches from the top.

This situation was odd because he is a water conservationist, and usually showers for a total of 30 seconds or so. I thought he was overheated from the yard work, but he said his chest felt tight. *"I am upset, and my heart beats faster."* Immediately, I was swept into a different realm, pulling power from something outside of me. Some people call this an automatic emergency response, but I prefer to think it is as a divine guidance system.

I asked Roger if he could get himself dressed. Yes, and he was going to call his doctor. This was late Friday afternoon, and I told him I was dialing 911. The paramedics came, checked him out, and rushed him to the hospital. As things unfolded, I was not thinking consciously and somehow leaped from my own little ego mind to the Big Mind of the Spirit, a place where I knew what to do and how to stay peaceful.

I calmly drove downtown, parked, found my way to the emergency room, discovered he had been rushed to surgery, and was guided upstairs by a helpful nurse at the very time a tech came out to find me. I wondered if he was going to say Roger is gone, or Roger is fine and is about to hop up and come home. He said they were doing some tests and would probably put a stent in.

After a 45-minute wait, a tall doctor came out, so ecstatic about the results he was beaming. He said Roger had what they call a Widow Maker heart attack with 100% blockage in his left anterior descending artery. "But," he said, "this is 2016, not 1990 and we can fix these things now. A few years ago, we wouldn't have had this result."

He also pointed out that the timing had been incredibly favorable. The heart unit has a skeletal crew on the weekends, because they schedule major surgery during the week. The techs had just gotten off work as Roger's ambulance arrived, but were still in the hospital when texted to return for an emergency. A 30-minute wait could have been disastrous.

Unlike *Figaro*, we didn't have a lot of slamming doors or hiding behind chairs. We didn't switch clothes or dress in drag. And the lovers in this drama are long past young. But hearts fluttering and hearts beating faster? Yes!

April 23:

"Put out the light, and then put out the light."
Othello in William Shakespeare's *Othello*, Act 5, Scene 2

Today, of this writing, is William Shakespeare's 450th Birthday! So we have to salute him with a quote from one of his masterful tragedies. I designed scenery for *Othello* in a class, and I have seen it performed several times, including at Shakespeare's Globe. In this scene, Othello enters Desdemona's sleeping chamber with a candle, and then blows out the flame. The setting is now shadowy, and he is about to commit the dark deed of murder, killing his wife who is beautiful, and filled with lovely brightness.

Othello ponders the idea that he can snuff out the blaze of the candle and relight it when he wishes, but he can only extinguish Desdemona's life once. Light and darkness are interwoven throughout this play, and back we are to the theme of resurrection. Ancient people saw the daily setting of the beaming, life-giving sun as death, followed by the enigmatically wild and mysterious night, followed then by the soaring again of the bright orb the next day. The sun symbolized our souls to our ancestors, in its daily ascending and falling, and it signified immortality in its continual rising from the "dead."

In Shakespeare's play, Othello's friend Iago lies, telling him that his wife is unfaithful. Iago has fallen in love with Desdemona himself, and knowing Othello's jealous nature, he easily instills doubt about her constancy in Othello's mind. What a foul and heinous action. But times of gloom are familiar to anyone who has inhabited a body on the planet Earth.

Sixteenth century mystic St. John of the Cross wrote a poem entitled *La noche oscura del alma* or *The Dark Night of the Soul*. The work specifically explores the spirit's pilgrimage toward unification with the Divine, and the poet encourages descending into a very dark place as a conscious practice of spiritual discipline. In John's starless downward decline, the soul is purged and emptied so that union with the Holy is possible.

Going through inky mystery is a hard exercise, whether I choose to look at the hidden parts of myself, or a sudden tragedy thrusts me into some sort of examination of my soul. To get to a deep spiritual life, however, I know that I must explore the dark side. If I neglect that investigation, my whole self will be seriously impaired. I tend to be a positive and upbeat person, but staying in a naively cheerful state all the time will never help me heal the wounded parts of my self.

Profound spiritual transformation is not for saints and mystics only. I, too, can uncover wholeness in myself. When I grapple with times of suffering and discontent and find meaning and a new reconciliation with life, then I can transform. Often, it is only through the "dark night of the soul" that I look at my life honestly and then find that there is a light that leads to a brighter and fuller, more dimensional and stronger self, a self that can then hold that light and darkness together as one.

April 24:
"Listen – look –
What is it, this that has captured me? This 'now,'
This exact truth of time – certainly truth –
The moment we're now crossing. Can this truth
Vanish? Look, your shadow thrown over the chair,
That dog's jerking bark, the distance of whistling,
A gate clanging-to, the water thrown into the yard,
Your fingers traveling your bracelet, my voice – listen,
My voice – your breathing —
(Teusret – his sister – is heard calling Rameses.)
And Teusret running through the empty rooms.
It is true for us now, but not till now, and never
To be again. I want it for myself.
This is my life.
(Enter Teusret)
It has gone."
Rameses talking to his aunt Anath from Christopher Fry's *The Firstborn*

I have never designed or directed Christopher Fry's play that features Rameses, the son of the Pharaoh Seti, but I have used this quote in some of my arts and spirituality workshops. This section of the play deals with the fragility of life and the pure brilliant truth of a present moment. In thirteen lines, in 99 words, Fry is able to capture the fleeting beauty of the here and now.

Over the years, I have been attracted to films, literature, and plays that deal with a character's realization of the poignancy and ephemeral exquisiteness of life on earth. This deeply moving drama by Fry is set in Egypt before the Exodus of the Jews, led by Moses. Rameses is a child growing into puberty. Moses, his hero, had been a part of their family, and had been absent for some time. Now Moses is back and Rameses wants to restore their relationship.

But Moses is busy with his mission. The sign to launch their march to freedom is conveyed by the very last Plague — the Death of the Firstborn. Jewish boys will be spared, but all the eldest sons of Egypt are to perish. Not until the plague starts its odious scourge does Moses comprehend that his beloved Rameses will die with the rest. And though he tries to save him, the boy, the child with the prescient vision about the delicate quality of our time on earth, the Pharaoh's privileged son succumbs to the curse.

Though I had delved into this subject, written papers about it, given workshops that utilized the theme, I really had never studied the full meaning of the present moment until November of 2003 when I listened to the CD version (yes, that was the state of audio then) of Eckhart Tolle's *The Power of Now: A Guide to Spiritual Enlightenment.*

That swiftly passing moment is all we have in life. ALL. The past is gone and should no longer torment us. The future has yet to dawn and should not make us anxious. Fear of what has happened or what might be is only the false fabrication of our ego selves.

I greatly appreciate Tolle's writing, and even more enjoy listening to him voice his ideas through audio, television, or video. But Fry's words about this idea are so full they are fragrant: "*What is it, this that has captured me? This 'now,'/This exact truth of time — certainly truth — The moment we're now crossing. Can this truth Vanish?*"

And Rameses, living in pure awareness, particularizes what he is experiencing by enumerating details: his aunt's shadow on a chair, a dog barking, someone whistling, a gate clanging, the sound of water, fingers tapping a bracelet, the aunt's breathing, his own voice, and his sister's feet pattering on the floor outside.

The child who will too soon leave this earth realizes Tolle's observation that the present is true for us now, but not until now. And our next now will never again be just like this one. Claiming this truth, Rameses cries, "*I want it for myself. This is my life.*" Then, when his sister Teusret enters, his contemplation evaporates with the disturbance. His insightful musing is as cursory as the now itself is.

April 25:

"No, this is false,
This can never be.
Your eyes fail to show you
What you truly see."
Sameth in Barbara Sloan's *The Cry of the Cockatrice*

These lines are from a play you have never heard of and will probably never see. I was on the team that wrote and fashioned it as a multi-arts piece, full of original music, dance, poetry, movement, choral odes, optical effects, lighting, sound, and every other aspect of performance and visual art that we could pack into a couple of hours. Brilliant students played the parts and executed the tech: Brent, Sherrie, Laura, Mildred, Autumn, Billy, Penny, Michelle, Lisa, LeAnne, and so many more.

The Cry of the Cockatrice opened on this date, April 25 in 1991, written for a salute to Great Britain in Birmingham's then-yearly Festival of Arts. We incorporated the idea of a bog sacrifice, having been fascinated with the Lindow Man in the British Museum, the preserved body of a human found in a peat bog in North West England in 1984. Into this story, we wove the myth of the cockatrice, a legendary beast that had appeared in English myths for many centuries.

Some of the production was startling, engaging, and successful, and some of it did not work so well. It gave me a great lesson in how to accept something that was partially good and partially a failure. And a very interesting thing happened during this production. In the midst of exhaustion, I received a life clarifying moment.

I was working hard, writing, directing, designing, and building costumes for *Cry*. This toil resulted in my being tired, and edgy, and sleep deprived. I had begun to tire of designing costumes because I had to turn right around and build them with mostly student labor. So, on this day, I was frantically working on the hero Sameth's costume by myself in the shop. I dozed off or went into a waking dream about an older lady who was a costumer at a summer stock theatre who fell in love with the costume she was working on, dancing with it as if in a number from a Broadway show.

When I came out of the reverie, I actually had the same experience and fell in love with the costume I was sewing. My whole attitude toward my work transformed in front of my eyes. The love of the costume moved to the Sameth actor, to the rest of the cast, and then to everyone working on the show.

I became aware of the little moments of every single thing we did from then on. I went from feeling burdened by the work to joy. Despite the long hours and the incredible strain, I came to love every second of everything I did on the crazy production.

From the time of the dream onward, I formed a different idea about creating for the theatre. I realized that the costume designer of a play has a different role than the other designers, the technicians, and the director. Though I believe that everyone working on a show can serve the playwright and the text of the play, I think the costume designer is the position most closely associated with the idea of "servant leadership," tending not only to the writer and the text, the director and the period of the play, but also to the very bodies of the actors who bring characters to life.

It is a very holy job, and I am so thankful that I had a conversion experience to remind me of how lucky I have been to work with fabric and with the people of the theatre.

April 26:
In "If I Could've Been" from *Working*, the Chorus sings about how things might have turned out differently with another job. (Listen to the work online or from your library!)

Chorus in *Working, the Musical* with a book by Stephen Schwartz and Nino Faso with music by Schwartz, based on the book by Studs Terkel, *Working: People Talk About What They Do All Day and How They Feel About What They Do*

I rarely look back on my life with regrets, wondering what would have happened if I had done this or that or the other. But this song always makes me cry when I hear it or even think about it. We produced *Working, the Musical* in the fall of 1988 and I really connected with the show. Seventeen actors portray 40-some odd characters.

The musical, as the Studs Terkel's research upon which it was based, looks at all sorts of working people and professions, people who love their jobs and those who are stressed, employees with hardships and bosses who want to be something else.

"Rich man, Poor man, Beggar Man, Thief, Doctor, Lawyer, Merchant, Chief!" So goes the familiar formula by which a child, counting off buttons on a shirt or petals from a flower, proclaims he has found, "What I'll be when I grow up!"

Many of us only wish it were that easy. But, school days are when most of us dream about our calling in life, conjuring visions of exciting missions, images of romance, and scenes of adventure and success.

Ask a group of five-year olds what they want to do with their lives and you might hear:

"A ballerina, because it's such fun to run on your toes."

"A banker, so I can see the money from the inside."

I asked my three-year old grandson Teddy the question and he wants to work in a garage, because he loves cars so much.

In high school and college, we see an array of jobs. Some have more money, some more security, some more glamour, and some simply a better location — near to or far away from family. We make a choice, and then plow ahead and concentrate on doing our best, leaving the little secret ambitions hidden in our hearts.

I once did a story for *Birmingham Magazine* called "Dreams of Another Calling," and interviewed well-known residents about their hidden ambitions. Some seemed connected: The lively arts newspaper editor saw himself as an orchestra conductor, the raspy country music disk jockey wanted to be a nightclub singer draped over a piano in a slinky dress. But others were startling. An elementary school principal wished to be a chef with his own restaurant. A modern dance choreographer dreamed of being a fire fighter. A funeral home executive envisioned herself as a judge. And race car superstar Bobby Allison desired to be an aviation engineer and inventor.

I talked to a priest at my church, but she declined to be interviewed for the article. The year was 1982, and she was one of the first women to have been ordained in the Episcopal Diocese of Alabama. She said that she had worked far too hard for this desire of her heart to be thinking about what other career she might have hidden deep down inside. Then, she related to me her whole struggle for holy orders. After hearing the details, I gave her a copy of *The Little Engine Who Could* because her story was so amazing.

Thinking about that gift, I did have one thing I always wanted to do as a child, and that was to write and illustrate a Little Golden Book. So maybe after all, I can sing with the best of them about what might have happened had that little wish been granted.

April 27:

"This Great God,
Like a mammy bending over her baby,
Kneeled down in the dust
Toiling over a lump of clay
Till he shaped it in his own image;
Then into it he blew the breath of life,
And man became a living soul."

The Preacher Man in God's Trombones, poems by James Weldon Johnson and music by Roy Ringwald

One thing I get very enthusiastic about is the interrelationship of the arts, and the connection between arts and spirituality. So, when we produced God's Trombones in the spring of 1993, I was captivated by the James Weldon Johnson poetry and the marvelous variety of music by Roy Ringwald.

"The Creation" is a dramatic monologue accompanied by a stirring undergirding of orchestral music and choral voices. This section tells the story of the Creation from Genesis. We produced the show in the large colonial-style chapel on campus, and this magnificent work filled the entire building with sonorous, reverberating, impressive sound. God's Trombones is a fine piece of art, but was certainly a transcendent and sacred experience as well for many of the audience members.

Art and spirituality are so closely interwoven, at least for me. Genuine spirituality, like art, is open and dynamic, and both help us transform our selves. As I grow spiritually, I am constantly challenged, but each provocation helps me get to a different and higher spiritual level.

Art offers me a way to genuine spirituality. Art is an affirmation of life, not simply a way to bring order to chaos, but the means by which I wake up to the very life I am living, like Emily in Our Town when she went back to relive her twelfth birthday. Poet Gerard Manley Hopkins tells us that the world is "charged with the glory of God." If I don't read passages like this, I miss resonating with such an observation. If I don't create poems and plays and paintings, I fail to closely observe this earth in all of its beautiful, stunning, terrifying, and amazing glory.

What is powerful in the greatest art is not just what it tells us or portrays, but what it points to, something unspeakable, a mystery, a silence, a meaning beyond its very words or images —something we cannot even verbalize, but can only experience and become one with. Listen to

Fred Waring and the Pennsylvanians recording of *God's Trombones* with Frank Davis as the Narrator and you will be carried away. Good art always reminds us that life is stranger, more beautiful, more demanding, more joyous, more tragic — more exquisite even — than our day-to-day brains would lead us to believe.

Some aesthetic urge for expression, and for exploration of what it is to be human, seems to be universal. Art, whether we create it or appreciate it, helps us find meaning in our everyday experiences. Art reminds us of what we know but may never have recognized fully. Art, like spirituality, digs deep under layers of reality, opens a door beyond physical existence (through the wardrobe, maybe) so that we can experience truth, so that we can stray into the borderlands between our earth and another dimension where we find the Holy.

April 28:
"(Grand angry) Oh very well. Hoity-toity! I'll look for my pistol. (Searches as they continue.)"
Highwayman in David Rogers's *Tom Jones*, based upon the novel by Henry Fielding

"Hoity-toity" is such a fun word — and it means haughty, disdainful, or conceited, snooty, stuck up, or uppity. In the mid-17th century when the word was coined, it meant "boisterous or silly behavior," which definition describes the play *Tom Jones*.

During the summer of 1974, we produced *Tom Jones* at Parkway Playhouse in Burnsville, a wonderful little North Carolina town that I have referenced before. My friend Jimmy Fisher, who often got the big roles, was cast as the lowly Highwayman.

But that placement failed to daunt him. He came out on stage and swashbuckled his way into the hearts of every single audience member. He took a minor role and made it something to chuckle at, something to admire, something to remember. He was energetic and charming, and every night, when he delivered the "Hoity-toity" line, he got an applause and guffaw break. And I truly learned the lesson that summer that (like the old saying goes) there are no small parts, only small actors: no matter what job or task you get, you can shine in it.

Meanwhile, during this monumental teaching, other things were moving under our feet. Here we were working in the theatre while on the world stage during June, July, and August, the World Football League played its first games, John Lennon was ordered to leave the United States, the "Flip Wilson Show" aired its last programs, the Episcopal Church began ordaining female priests, Philippe Petit walked a tightrope strung between the Twin Towers of the World Trade Center, and several of serial murderer Ted Bundy's victims disappeared.

I know these happenings must have impressed me as I kept up with world news on my radio. I am a huge John Lennon fan, I am an Episcopalian, I am a football lover, I thought Flip Wilson was funny. Interesting news items: some amusing, some disturbing, life going on as it always does with tragic things mixed with hilarity.

But all of that was blasted away by the August revelations concerning the Watergate scandal. Richard Nixon's August 5 admission that he withheld information about Watergate break-in, and his August 8 announcement that he was resigning his office rocked our world even in the deep Carolina woods. For most people, this news wiped all the other headlines away. Nixon performed a number of positive Presidential feats, but he is mainly remembered for this disgraceful Watergate mess.

In our little protected Playhouse sphere, we were sometimes peacefully, sometimes frantically, putting on this series of summer stock plays, a new offering opening each weekend: *Tom Jones*, then *Picnic*, then *Night Watch*, then *Ah, Wilderness!*, then *Arsenic and Old Lace*, and finally *My Fair Lady*. The time was idyllic and lovely, artistic and full of camaraderie. But as this major political scandal unfolded, a pall began breaking over our joyous summer activities. We realized that this was an event that would change our politics and our view of the Presidency forever.

As we all departed for our homes or universities, we wept our goodbyes, knowing we would never all be together again, knowing we would miss each other bitterly, knowing we would have no more Hoity-toity hilarity together, and most of all knowing something about our innocence was ruptured and would, like this beautiful time, never be captured again.

April 29:
"(Kneeling on the ground) God. Where are you? I wish you would talk to me. God. It isn't just me. There's a general feeling... You see, I tell you, it's this perpetual absence – yes? – this not being here – it's that – I mean, let's be honest – it's just beginning to get some of us down. You know? Is that unreasonable? There are an awful lot of people in a very bad way. And they need something

beside silence. God. Do you understand?"
Reverend Lionel Espy in David Hare's *Racing Demon*

I saw the fine David Hare play *Racing Demon* in London in the early 1990s, and then I designed the costumes for a student-directed version in the spring of 2001, shortly before I left my work there to go to the American Village. The British production gained universal acclaim as the first of a trilogy of Hare plays about current events in the British Isles.

This particular work concerns the challenges of four members of the clergy of the Church of England, and how they attempt to make sense of their work in the modern post-Christian world. Against a backdrop of disturbances about gay ordination and inner-city evangelism, the *Guardian* reported, "*Racing Demon* emerges as Hare's masterpiece... a humane, compassionate study of the eternal battle between the individual conscience and the institution."

We all have consciences, that judgment inside our minds that helps us distinguish right from wrong, divine choices from devilish ones. As a Baby Boomer, I heard lessons about forming my inner compass over and over from the oddest of places: the television, thundering out to me the words of the venerable Jiminy Cricket.

As he told Pinocchio in the Disney version of the story, life is full of allurement, and if he wants to be a "real boy," the puppet must learn to make right decisions. Virtuous things may seem unsound sometimes, and wrong things may seem right. Pinocchio, having already gotten in trouble by associating with a rough crowd, vows to exemplify proper behavior, and Jiminy pledges his help in song, telling Pinocchio to give a little call if he gets in trouble or meets temptation.

After some dancing on the violin, Jiminy ends by reminding Pinocchio to find the high road and if he starts to slide, to warble for help and be guided by a sense of right and wrong.

I admit this version of conscience is a bit juvenile. "Real boys" and "real girls" cannot whistle and have a cricket appear to save the day. Nor to me is conscience the simplistic idea that I feel guilt when I break a secular or holy law. It is really much more complex. I must listen to an inner voice, or what I might discern as a feeling in my heart, or a deep whisper in my soul, or the wisdom of the universe moving me, or my spiritual GPS system kicking in.

To realize that Spirit is talking to me, I have to be quiet and listen. Despite The Reverend Espy's complaint that God is silent, it is in silence, in quiet concentration, in peaceful prayer, that the Divine talks to me. I AM respects my free will, and does not call me on my i-Phone to make sure I understand what I might or might not do. I have to interpret the urges or inspirations I get after pondering things in my heart. If I am battling a dilemma in my mind and give myself just a little hush-time, a very distinct spark is lit that tells me which way to go, a trustworthy luminescence that lights the intimate path to my destiny.

April 30:
"...So we grew together
Like to a double cherry, seeming parted,
But yet an union in partition,
Two lovely berries moulded on one stem..."
Helena in William Shakespeare's A *Midsummer Night's Dream*, Act III, Scene 2

Helena is here talking about her best friend Hermia who she suddenly mistrusts in the madness of this midsummer's eve; but this quote reminds me of my twin grandsons, George William and Arthur Jackson, my daughter Elin's boys. They are on the brink of being fifteen months old and they are two busy whirlwinds.

On just about every Tuesday since they were a couple of months old, I have looked after these *"Two lovely berries moulded on one stem..."* They are identical twins who look very much alike, but are not really hard to tell apart. For one thing, George has always been a tad bigger than his sibling. But really, their personalities are so different that distinguishing the parted "double cherry" is easy. George is a little demanding; Arthur more daring. George likes to laugh; Arthur likes to do things to make his brother laugh. George enjoys dancing around in circles; Arthur prefers climbing up on as many things as he possibly can, and as high as he can.

One thing they have just started doing is discovering dish towels, and tottering about as if intoxicated, screaming, laughing, wobbling, falling, but all the while waving the cloth in their hands as if playing an embryonic form of "capture the flag." They get especially hysterical if I chase them a bit.

The twins have an older four-and-a-half year old sister, Emmeline Violet who is quite a character herself, and who stays with me on Fridays. The day she was born, she looked around the room in the hospital as if thinking, "Oh, so this is what it is like on the outside. I like it. I approve. I am going to belong here just fine."

I loved both of my grandmothers, and my one living grandfather for as long as I had them. And I always anticipated having grandchildren. Many of my friends crow over their grandchildren, swearing how different and more special the relationship is than with their own children, joking about sending home at the end of the day when they are tired and cranky. I don't think this way, because I was very close to both Elin and Seth as they grew up. I treasure the relationships I have with them singly, together, and with their friends through them.

So, I love my grandchild relationship "more" or "more remarkably" than my children, and even refrain from comparing the two and thereby diminishing my love for Elin and Seth. I do love Emmeline, George, and Arthur — and now Seth's son Teddy — greatly, and I realize more each day that love is not a limited product that you portion out. The more people I love, the more kinds of love I share, the more my heart expands, and the more love I can give.

In each of the grandchildren, I see something of myself, or of their parents or our grandparents. They are the little depositories of many genes and quirks, family traits and characteristics. And they are their own selves as well. Hopefully on their days with me, they are assimilating some of the wisdom my great-grandmother, grandparents, and parents taught me, because hopefully, their lives will go on long after I am gone.

May 1:
In "Lusty Month of May" from *Camelot*, Guinevere and the Chorus sing about what a light-hearted, lusty month May is. (Listen to the work online or from your library!)

Chorus and Guinevere in the musical *Camelot*, with book and lyrics by Alan Jay Lerner and music by Frederick Loewe

I can't help but sing the countless lyrics from this merry Broadway tune on this first day of May. I feel absolutely dreadful with three straight nights of no sleep: a tornado in the area Monday evening, a half hour pollen-induced coughing fit Tuesday midnight, and a stomach bug last eve. I am draggy, drained, and bone-tired, but if you could hear what is going on in my head, you would swear I was as light-hearted and vigorous as the chorus that sings and dances this happy spring song in *Camelot*.

May, that lovely, robust month when we all feel the windy breath of new life, days lengthening, flowers blooming, the air perfumed with their blossoms. Love is on the move, and even the birds and bees are scandalized at the frivolous and unrestrained passions of human love affairs.

May is full of celebrations — of mothers, of graduations, of impending weddings, of the winner of the Kentucky Derby, of the close to kids' soccer seasons. Swimming pools open and bathing attire and flip flops come out of storage. Vegetable plots are planted and more time is spent outside.

The dawn of spring encourages me to take layers off my body and house, throw away old clothing and dust-catchers, scrub windows, paint woodwork, rinse lawn furniture, and scour many items that need a bath in the brighter light. I can't wait to throw open all my windows at this time of year, despite the fine yellow powder from all those pesky male flower parts and pine pollen that blow in and cover my newly cleaned furniture. During the night, with no glass to buffer him, our resident mocking bird often wakens me with his endless stream of swaggering and scolding trills.

We might have a cold rain or two this month, but warmer weather is definitely defeating the long cold winter we endured this year. May beckons me to strolls in the park, reads on the deck, beers at the cafe patio, dawdles in the garden, and wades in the creek.

May is a magical month when everyone feels a little younger, a little friskier, a little perkier. I relish in the fact that each year offers several times for renewal: January's resolutions, August's reflections on a year three-quarters gone, and May's fresh starts and hopeful joyousness. Anything is possible in May. As Elizabethan dramatist Thomas Dekker wrote, "O, the month of May, the merry month of May, So frolic, so gay, and so green, so green, so green!"

Green is the color of freshness and fertility, of growth and healing, of creativity and abundance. The fourth chakra, I have recently learned, located near the center of the breastbone is associated with green. This heart chakra causes balance between feelings and thoughts, and regulates our interactions with other people.

So no wonder this green, green month is associated with ardent love. May, May, where it seems fine that we make mistakes in quests to pursue our own true loves. Leave it to Lerner and Loewe to capture this

168

bright emerald jewel of a month with unforgettable music and lyrics that run through my brain the whole month long.

May 2:
"Can't you see in my eyes that I'd rather die than cause you a minute's pain?"
Gloumov in Alexander Ostrovsky's *The Diary of a Scoundrel*

When we performed Ostrovsky's great play in the fall of my senior year in college, we were drenched in the aura that it had originally been directed by the innovative Russian theatre director Konstantin Stanislavsky at his Moscow Art Theatre. Our director was fairly new to the University of Montevallo, and he had begun some special studies in the Stanislavsky method of acting with any student who wanted to participate.

Constructed on the idea of using emotional memory to realistically portray a character, Stanislavsky's technique uses an evolution of practices to coach actors to develop a wide range of feelings, and to act as if they were real people living a life before and after the scene being delivered onstage. The method was first pursued in Russia, and later in America beginning in the early 1920s, with the most famous practitioners creating the well-respected Actors Studio in New York City.

So the tenderly moving monologue beginning *"Can't you see in my eyes that I'd rather die than cause you a minute's pain?"* is a perfect example of the kind work that fits this kind of acting technique. Though a farce, *The Diary of a Scoundrel* has plenty of passion and the play shifts between drama and humor. But how do I achingly remember that production with a quiver in my heart and a gasp in my breath?

Well, I wouldn't if I hadn't kept my own scoundrel diaries and journals myself. It was a fairly painful production to work on, because so much other drama was going on in my life. Besides having just gotten married and adjusting to a new life style, I was laboring over senior art and English projects, taking an overload of classes, and experiencing the sad departure of some close friends and professors. I was also working on our College Night production, full of its own turbulent theatrics and grievous shenanigans among participants.

I believe what Eckhart Tolle says is true about old emotional pain living inside you and me, which he calls a "pain-body." This unhappy throbbing is an accumulation of painful life experiences that were not fully faced and accepted. The pain lives in us as an energy, and becomes the emotional aspect of egoic consciousness.

Oddly enough, our pain-body, with a mind of its own, delights in our goading the people we love best. This pain-body inside us thrills at knowing exactly how to rankle, rile, and ride our partners or spouses, siblings or children to get the most hurtful retaliation. When I get the response, and I react, an upsetting cycle begins. As Tolle says, "And the pain-body loves it! Give me more drama, please!"

A few years ago, I thought of this play and what was going on in my life at the time, and having the knowledge of Tolle's theory, I recognized the pain-body arising. I have learned that when I can perceive when the pain shifts from dormant to active, when something triggers a very strong emotional reaction, when I can name it and observe it, then I can work through and dismiss it. Almost always, even with the people and situations who have wounded me the most, I can now say with Gloumov, *"Can't you see in my eyes that I'd rather die than cause you a minute's pain?"*

May 3:
"Hello – out there! (Pause) Hello – out there! Hello – out there! (Long pause) Nobody out there. (Still more dramatically, but more comically, too.) Hello – out there! Hello – out there!"
Young Man in William Saroyan's *Hello Out There* and the opera adaptation with the same name by Jack Beeson

Both the play by Saroyan and the adaptation by Beeson are tough one-act pieces full of menacing uncertainty and desperate yearning. While I admire both the 1941 drama and the 1953 chamber opera, I found both of them hard to produce. The costumes were not difficult, as the two main characters are a drifter and Emily, a teenager who becomes attracted to him.

The young man is imprisoned in a Matador, Texas jail because a promiscuous married woman cries rape. He and the unhappy Emily, who works at the clink as a cook, fall in love and decide to flee to San Francisco to escape their tiny hole-in-the-wall nightmare. Even at the 2020 census, Matador only recorded 579 residents.

Fearful in the vacant prison of revenge by the aggrieved husband, the young man persuades Emily to fetch her father's rifle. After she leaves, the husband and a mob of his friends appear. Not believing the young man's tale about his wife's seduction, the suspicious husband shoots him. Emily enters heartbroken as the explosive crowd drags the body away. In circular, existential fashion, as the curtain lowers Emily from the cell cries hopelessly, *"Hello out there!"*

So the works are bleak, as desolate and windswept as a treeless wasteland. When sitting in the dark theatre during rehearsals, my mind would conjure up tumbleweeds and dust blowing across the screen in Western movies and television shows I watched as a kid. Just thinking about the productions now gives me a sinking, murky feeling.

From the time I was about five years old, I would become overwhelmed with motion sickness when traveling. Both of my parents were addicted to cigarettes, and when riding in the backseat of the car with all that puffing and its ever lingering fog, I would come down with what I called "feeling smoky" — a horrendous condition consisting of a sour stomach, numb headache, a throbbing in my nose, cold sweats, bleary eyes, and a befuddled mind, even at that young age. Obviously, I must have had an allergy or at least a sensitivity to the cigarette fumes, but in the early 1950s, parents knew little about such reactions.

What made my smoky feeling worse was the inescapability of the situation. I couldn't jump out of the car, I couldn't persuade my parents to liberate me to the fresh oxygen beckoning to me from the roadside, and I surely couldn't persuade them to stop their habit. I was trapped, and that confined imprisonment only made my affliction more disagreeable and my fate seem as if it would ever be as unfortunate as it was at that moment.

I suppose somehow the predicament Emily and the young man find themselves in echoes my miserable compulsory rides in the roily backseat. Only, once the car was parked, I was liberated to fill my lungs with clean air. The two young lovers are forever imprisoned in their play and their opera, never to escape to their California freedom.

May 4:
"For God's sake let us sit upon the ground
And tell sad stories of the death of kings . . .
For within the hollow crown
That rounds the mortal temples of a king
Keeps Death his court; and there the antic sits,
Scoffing his state and grinning at his pomp . . ."

Richard II Character in *The Hollow Crown*, passages from Shakespeare, by John Barton

In 1961, John Barton created *The Hollow Crown* for the Royal Shakespeare Company as — the *British Theatre Guide* says — "a celebratory entertainment by and about the kings and queens of England." The RSC has repeated the work a number of times, with over 70 actors in the various roles. The quoted passage is from Shakespeare's Richard II. Samford University Theatre produced Barton's work in the spring of 1991. It starred several students, a couple of theatre alumni, and some professors.

I ran box office for the show, and delighted in watching rehearsal where I found that many of England's monarchs had both similar, yet very different lives. As Richard II goes on to say, some were slain in war, some deposed, some haunted by the ghosts they deposed, some poisoned by their wives, some sleeping killed, but all murdered. Not all of England's kings and queens were murdered — but like all of us, all crowned heads die a human death. One ruler, according to rumors, accidentally killed himself by overindulging in peaches and beer. What a way to go!

Interspersed with actual speeches, Shakespeare lines, tall tales, and period music, the readers theatre production tells the lives of potentates from William the Conqueror to Queen Victoria. Why are so many of us fascinated with the lives of kings and queens, whether on the stage or on our televisions showing Victoria or The Crown? After all, they are just ordinary people, right? These mere mortal puts their pants on one leg at a time, just like us, right?

Well, no, they do not. Kings and queens have dressers and servants who do that for them! In fact, records indicate that Queen Elizabeth II has one-thousand staff members working for her. Do you know what I could do with that number of helpers? With half? With one-tenth? With one? Wow! No yard to tend to, no supper to cook, no errands to run. And I would always have someone on hand to play live music, write thank you notes, and reset the clocks when my power blinks off momentarily.

Queen Elizabeth has someone to break in her shoes, check her art collection, and hold her long velvet train. The vehicle she is riding in can legally ignore speed limits, and she is the only person in the world who doesn't have to travel with a passport. I would have no more dreams about trying to get on the plane without one!

But then, the queen has responsibilities as Head of State, Head of the Armed Forces, and Head of the Church of England; she has a desk full of documents and reports to tend to; she represents the nation for great celebrations or tragedies; and she spends a lot of her time visiting schools, hospitals, factories, and other spots.

If we think about it, many ordinary people in the free world live a life that others on earth would call regally splendid: water flowing into our homes, warm (and cool) houses, safe and comfortable beds, plenty of clothing, an abundance of food, entertainment with the click of a remote. Do we realize we lead a royal existence? No, not until we meditate on it deeply and give thanks.

May 5:
"I can't stand a naked light bulb, any more than I can a rude remark or a vulgar action."
Blanche Dubois in Tennessee Williams's A *Streetcar Named Desire*

Oh, my. I know this line is really about much more than a stark bare light bulb. It conjures up the theme of fantasy versus reality running rampant in A *Streetcar Named Desire*. Blanche is a woman who wants to cover things up. So on their first meeting she asks Mitch, a possible candidate for marriage, to put a little colored paper lantern over the naked bulb. It will be more festive, more colorful, more fanciful, less real.

Later Blanche cowers, terrified of light and what bright light might reveal about her. She says, "I like it dark. The dark is comforting to me." She is desperate to maintain a mask, to let shadows hide her flaws, her lies, her fears, her insecurities, her past. And when Mitch tears off the paper shade he so obligingly put round the lamp earlier, she wails, "I don't want realism. I want magic! Yes, yes, magic. I try to give that to people. I do misrepresent things. I don't tell the truth. I tell what ought to be truth. And if that is sinful, then let me be damned for it! Don't turn the light on!"

Blanche doesn't want Mitch to see how old she is (around 30!), but she also doesn't want to face the verity of life itself. For so long, her image of the truth has been so blurred that she cannot tell what is in her imagination and what really happens any more. This fading Southern belle might believe she is still virtuous and refined, but she is drowning in alcoholism and delusions of grandeur.

All of this is fascinating and deep, but I keep going back to *"I can't stand a naked light bulb,"* because really, I can't. I can hardly stand the light coming out of any sort of standard ceiling fixture, but a bare bulb is about as odious as anything can get (and I am speaking of minor irritations here) in a house, hotel, apartment, store, cafe, or other establishment.

I don't understand ceiling fans with horrible lights attached to them, even with the little glass shades. I don't understand standard UFO-type fixtures attached to upper interior surfaces in builders' spec homes. I especially don't understand fluorescent fixtures. Fluorescents are cheap and durable, but cause health problems, migraines, eye strain, sleeping problems, depression, hormonal imbalance. And besides, they are even uglier than regular overhead lights. Thank goodness most of them are being replaced by newer, more efficient (though not necessarily more beautiful) bulbs.

Working for so long in the theatre, and using light to create just the correct mood for a love scene, just the right color for a sunset, just the perfect atmosphere for midnight must have either ruined me or so finely attuned me to lighting that it is one subject about which I have violently adamant feelings. Glaring overhead lights, be they incandescent, fluorescent, or any of the new breeds, are aesthetically unacceptable. I agree with Blanche. At least put a paper shade on it and mute the frightful unsightliness.

At night, turn on some lovely table lamps, a reading gooseneck, some wall washers, the kitchen task lights. Create an atmosphere to relax in, to feel good about, to enjoy. In the evening, after a long day, I too "want magic! Yes, yes, magic" that the right kind of light can conjure.

May 6:
"Let us be very strange and well-bred:
Let us be as strange as if we had been married a great while;
And as well-bred as if we were not married at all."
Millimant in William Congreve's *The Way of the World*, Act IV, Scene 5

Before this quote in Congreve's *The Way of the World*, Millimant says, "Good Mirabell, don't let us be familiar or fond, nor kiss before folks, like my Lady Fadler and Sir Francis; nor go to Hyde Park together the first Sunday in a new chariot, to provoke eyes and whispers, and then never be seen there together again, as if we were proud of one another the first week, and ashamed of one another ever after. Let us never visit together, nor go to a play together, but let us be very strange and well-bred..."

This Restoration romantic comedy of manners concerns a lot of conniving and infidelity, with timeless social commentary and very adult conversations. Oddly enough, I created the costumes and taught design to high school students at the Alabama School of Fine Arts in 1978 as we produced this play that mocked mores of the 1700s. The plot involves the inner workings of upper-class English courtship mainly between a self-confident gentleman named Mirabell and a strong-minded young lady, Millimant.

Being called *The Way of the World*, its plot hinges on the worldly themes of love and marriage, faithfulness and philandering. Mirabell and Millimant seem very modern, amidst the backdrop of jealousy and deceit, to have a plans prior to marriage. Congreve sets this ideal couple against a society filled with deception and infidelity to illustrate what is ideally possible in engagement and marriage.

An equal partnership is a relatively novel concept in my lifetime, much less in the social world of the eighteenth century. When I got married in 1971, the feminist movement was just beginning to be a force of change. Yet in this play, Millimant asks for a prenuptial agreement with Mirabell, remarking that if married, she does not want to "by degrees dwindle into a wife." Therefore, she wants to visit whom she pleases, wear what she wants, converse about her own interests, come to dinner when she so desires, even eat in her dressing gown whenever she is out of humor "without giving a reason."

The playwright Congreve's mistress, actor Anne Bracegirdle, enacted the original role of Millimant and was known as a very freethinking individual. Mirabell was originally played by John Verbruggen, a "natural" actor of some acclaim. So even though audiences were jolted a bit by this newfangled concept of partnership, they saw it acted in real life by two theatre celebrities. Since both Millimant and Mirabell are strong and self-actualized, they create an ideal couple who love and respect each other. Their union was less the usual contract marriage and more of a vow of true collaboration based on mutual affection.

I was too green in judgment to form any sort of before-matrimony agreement prior to my marriage, but if I ever even think of tying the knot a second time, I won't hesitate to formally lay some ground rules so that I don't "diminish into being merely a wife" once the ceremony is over. Maybe I will start with the list that Millimant created almost 315 years ago. I like the idea of eating supper in my pajamas without even giving a reason.

May 7:
"I would not wish any companion in the world but you."
Miranda to Ferdinand in William Shakespeare's *The Tempest*, Act III, Scene 1

During the 1990-91 season, we produced *The Tempest* and I loved every minute of the work on it: shipwrecked set, tattered Elizabethan clothes, thunder and lightning effects. It was a good show.

The young Miranda has been living on an island in the sea for twelve years, long enough that her father Prospero is the only human she remembers ever knowing. Then suddenly, a ship wrecks in a tempest, and one of the survivors is Ferdinand, son of the King of Naples. In no time at all, the two young people fall in love.

Ferdinand delights in her beauty, which he believes surpasses that of anyone he has ever seen. Miranda says she doesn't remember seeing any woman's face except her own in the mirror, nor has she seen any men's visages except her father's and now that of her good new friend, Ferdinand. She cannot imagine what other men might look like, but she vows, "I would not wish any companion in the world but you, nor can imagination form a shape besides yourself to like of." Heavy praise for only the second male she ever recalls putting her eyes upon.

But what a wonderful way to express love! She says nothing about irresistible desire, heart throbbing, passionate kisses, or fervent sensuality. All of those feelings are vital components to lifelong partnerships. But companionship is such an essential part of a romantic relationship. Companionship is a feeling of well-being, just finding yourself in another's company. The word conjures up camaraderie and intimacy, fellowship and closeness.

A companion is someone who will walk with you in silence and not feel restless; someone to whom you can really reveal secrets; someone easy to talk with, eat with, sleep with, travel with, snuggle with, read with, laugh with, cry with, pray with. A companion is someone who will accompany you through life without fabricating a lot of drama, because there is enough commotion every day without creating more.

A companion drinks coffee in bed with you in the morning amidst a riot of pillows and covers, and then sips wine on the deck in the late afternoon as long shadows slant across the lawn. A companion comes through the door whistling to let you know he or she is the one making such a racket. A companion dumps the wheelbarrow for you after you have weeded the herb garden, chops the vegetables for the stew you are making, bandages the finger you just crushed with the hammer.

Passion and erotic enthusiasm punctuate the sentences of our lives with the excitement and pleasure of exclamation points. But we live those long paragraphs of daily existence between those interjections just experiencing the little details of our earthly time: the fragrance of freshly cut grass, the sad news of a close friend's sudden death, the satisfaction of a newly straightened closet, the harsh squeal of tires on a wet pavement, the flavorful delight of a basket full of ripe strawberries.

I want someone close by me who can appreciate such seemingly trivial moments as the extraordinary parade of earthly being that they truly are. And I have found that person in my companion, Roger.

May 8

"A strange weight oppresses heart and tongue. Could the house speak, it might have much to tell. My lips will open, with my good will, only to those that know."
Watchman in Aeschylus's *The Oresteia: Agamemnon*

When I was in graduate school at the University of North Carolina at Greensboro, the theatre department produced all three plays in Aeschylus's trilogy *The Oresteia* for competition in the American College Theatre Festival. The production was stunning, with actors scantily clad in open-weave chitons. They wore gold makeup as masks, and bald caps that made men and women look alike. The chorus clenched huge staffs, which they repeatedly beat upon the floor in rhythm to generate dramatic effects.

When the Watchman talks of the house speaking, he means the cursed House of Atreus and its long, loud, clamorous fall. Throughout five generations, the family is involved in an attempt to trick the gods, cannibalism, torture, deceit, treachery, a rigged chariot race, curses, rape, murder, cooking the children of a rival, mistreatment, vengeance, war, more murder, and still more murder.

All my life, I have heard the phrase, "If these walls could only talk," and I have always been fascinated with the idea of a house revealing something. I am the third owner of my house, which was only built in 1967, so there are not a lot of ghosts in the closets, treasure chests in the attic, or important authentic documents behind the wallpaper. There isn't even any wallpaper. No one has died here, nor been born here.

But I do remember a startling incident that happened on the evening of a big storm on August 20, 1995, eight days before my 24th wedding anniversary. My then-husband and I had been battling for many months. As rain pelted the huge glass windows of the great hall, nature mimicked my interior world. After 288 months of marriage, my husband was leaving, certainly and absolutely. My eyes were cried out, but my gut was still churning, my brain still reeling from the inconceivable enormity of plain, cold facts.

The house was the same, the furnishings, the lamps, the rugs were all the same, Seth was the same, Elin was the same — but nothing in the world was ever to be the same again. Elin was at a friend's house, busily planning her sophomore year at college.

But ten-year old Seth was at home with a good friend Jon, pretending to be weathermen watching the impending storm. Oblivious to the turbulence about to shake his stable and steady family life, Seth was chattering into a tape recorder, giving updates to an imaginary audience as each peal of thunder grew closer.

We were standing near the rear window slashed with raindrops, me quietly searching in desperation for words that would not come. Suddenly, a majestic bolt of lighting swirled around the trunk of a huge oak tree, ripping off the bark in a sudden, intentional slash, signaling the end of a marriage and design partnership.

Two and a half decades of collective memories, of crafting plays and nurturing children together, teaching, learning, and discovering life together was abruptly finished. The electrical discharge made it clear that I was now utterly and completely detached. Not only did the lightning make an incisive gash in the tree, I was cut from my role and thrust into single parenthood in a flash.

Seth and Jon bounded up the stairs. "Did you hear...?" "Did you see...?" overlapping each other in squeals and questions, shrieking in delight about the howling weather, still unaware of the real storm swirling inside the house. And, though I was mystified about what the future might hold, the bolt made the transition as final as an exclamation point at the end of a sentence.

"Could the house speak, it might have much to tell."

May 9:
"I'm not young enough to know everything."
Ernest Woolley in JM Barrie's *The Admirable Crichton*

Happy birthday, JM Barrie! Thank you for writing *Peter Pan*, *The Admirable Crichton*, *What Every Woman Knows*, and all your other works. Sir James Matthew Barrie was born in 1860 and is best known for the creation of Peter Pan, Wendy, Neverland, and all the other wonders of that book, play, film, animation, and a myriad other manifestations.

The Admirable Crichton is a play about a super-efficient butler in 1905. Crichton, the butler, is employed by the Earl of Loam in Mayfair. A progressive man, the Earl believes humans are created equally, and sets up an experiment during which at tea one day, his daughters are asked to treat the staff as guests to the discomfort of all, especially Crichton.

But later, the family and butler are shipwrecked on a deserted island for two years and the social order reverses, because Crichton is the only one of them who knows how to survive under such uncivilized circumstances. The family members become his servants, and call him "the Guv." After they are rescued and go back to London, the social order goes back to "normal," but with several interesting and surprising twists.

In the first act Ernest Woolley, Lord Loam's nephew, says, "encouragingly" to his cousins Agatha and Lady Mary, *"Don't you see? I'm not young enough to know everything."* Agatha thinks that is a clever but ever so puzzling statement. Mr. Treherne, a clergyman, can shed no light on the utterance, thinking Ernest means he is not old enough to know everything. Only Crichton grasps Ernest's meaning that so often, young people think they totally comprehend the world and all its workings. Only as humans mature are we aware that there is always more and more to decipher and understand.

At least, some humans realize this verity. I remember talking in Philosophy class about a man named Thomas Young who lived from 1773 to 1829. Our professor told us that he was the last human who knew everything. He was a genius, skilled in math, physiology, energy, and many other fields. Even he did not know absolutely everything. But after the early 1800s, knowledge, learning, scholarship, and information grew so exponentially that no one person's mind would be able to grasp or hold it all.

Another aspect to the idea of *"I'm not young enough to know everything"* is the concept of the Enneagram's soul child. When we are young, we live in our being's essence or real nature. We feel connected to reality, the universe, and the Divine. As we grow up, the world becomes painful and demanding, so we lose contact with this precious being and put on an ego to protect ourselves.

As children we are not only emotional, mental, and physical beings, we are living souls, full of life and vigor, adventurous and curious, joyous and lighthearted, but also capable of exploding in rage and frustration, or going into fear and terror. Factually we might not know everything when we are young, but in our essence we are aware of the major reason people come to Earth: to love and to be loved. So the declaration of *"I'm not young enough to know everything"* may be a good phrase to ponder in this light.

May 10:
"I'm Charley's aunt from Brazil – where the nuts come from."
Babbs Babberly in Brandon Thomas's *Charley's Aunt*

Sometimes you feel nutty. Sometimes you don't! In the fall of 1987, I designed costumes for the old "chestnut" farce *Charley's Aunt*. In the play, Lord Fancourt Babberly is an undergraduate college man whose chums, Jack and Charley, persuade him to impersonate the latter's aunt. The original London presentation of the play broke historic records running from February 1892 at the Theatre Royal, Bury St. Edmonds for 1,466 performances.

Most of the comedic situations in the play arise from the young man, Babbs Babberly, cross-dressing as an honorable older woman, but acting not a bit like a lady. He smokes cigars and reveals trousers under the tug of a skirt, yet also acts coquettish with other men. In fact, the playwright Brandon Thomas gives a direction that the actor playing Charley's aunt must in no way "act the woman," but proceed with masculine behavior that makes the evolving situation funnier and more ridiculous as the play progresses.

When Babbs says, *"I'm Charley's aunt from Brazil – where the nuts come from,"* he – or is it she? – is correct that the Brazil nut (or really seed) comes from South America. This particular nut tree is native to Brazil, as well as other neighboring countries of Venezuela, Colombia, Peru, Bolivia and the Guianas.

In Britain from 1785, to "be nutts upon" was to be very fond of something, so in the late 1800s when Charley's Aunt was written, people often said they were "nuts" about something they really liked. They might also say they were "crazy for someone" they were fond of, so perhaps the two bits of slang got intertwined: to be nutty about something was to be crazy about it. Around the same time, the word "nut" was jargon for "head," so the phrase "off your nut" meant to be a bit loony.

In his line about being from Brazil *"where the nuts come from,"* Babbs/Charley's Aunt is also saying that she — or is it he? — is a bit mad, a bit quirky, a bit zany — as an older relative has every right to be. Look at Violet Crawley, the Dowager Countess of Grantham in the Downton Abbey series. Despite her prim and proper upper class breeding, she is full of wacky zingers and curious behavior.

When the Peter Paul candy company in the 1970s employed the cute little tune about sometimes desiring a nut candy bar and sometimes not, the play on words intrigued me. In television ads, feeling like a nut involved people participating in outlandish exploits. In one version, fun-loving high school students were eating the Almond Joys while the more studious kid was eating the Mounds Bar.

People have classified me as a bit unconventional all my life. My high school senior class prediction was that I would "return to normal," which I am happy to say has not happened. But eccentricity can be a good quality if it means someone is being authentic, marching to her own drummer, open to new experiences, going against the flow, and fully embracing life. I guess when it comes right down to it, I just about always feel like a nut.

May 11:
"You swam the moat?"
Queen to Winnifred in *Once Upon a Mattress*, with music by Mary Rodgers, lyrics by Marshall Barer, and book by Jay Thompson, Dean Fuller, and Marshall Barer.

Once Upon a Mattress opened this day, May 11, 1959 at the Phoenix Theatre off-Broadway. The musical is famous as the Broadway debut of Carol Burnett, who originated the role of Princess Winnifred, and who later became a huge television star and stage actor. Our Winnifred was expertly played by a Freshman named Amy, and our beloved departmental secretary Judy sang in the chorus.

When you teach theatre and constantly create costumes and scenery for plays, you work a lot. Through a four or five year period, I got terribly stressed and began to disintegrate personally and professionally. I became over-involved in design work, and developed a terrible workaholic habit. Though theatre is fun, enlightening, exciting work, it is still work.

In 1984 when daughter Elin was eight and Seth was born, a complex layer was added to our family. One child in the costume shop or backstage is workable but two are somehow triply or quadruply more complicated to maneuver. I somehow allowed the boundaries between work and personal life get totally blurred, and got so involved in the theatre that I never gave myself any time for relaxation, personal development, hobbies, fun, or distraction.

I knew all this was very wrong, but on a level I could not yet grasp. The fall of 1991, a student directed *Once Upon a Mattress*. I designed the costumes, and, as usual was overseeing the building of the medieval clothing. We decided to use huge period headpieces that were fun and fairly simple to construct.

One whole week, I had some activities that I absolutely had to tend to with Elin and Seth. Since I could hardly be in the shop at all, I left some students in charge, thinking I would come back and have to catch up and construct all of the headdresses.

Lo and behold: they did the work without me! In fact, Michelle, Lisa, Joe and the whole crew did a marvelous job. The theatre department did not fall apart; Samford University did not sink into a great dark hole; and most amazingly, the institution of theatre in America, in the world, and in the entire universe did not suffer a tremendous breakdown with my momentary lack of participation.

I began to give myself a little time outside work to grow and balance myself. I began to go into a library and to a shelf and let myself be led to a volume. A few weeks after *Once Upon a Mattress* closed, I was by chance drawn to Stephen Covey's *Seven Habits of Highly Effective People* in this way. Devouring this book helped me realize that I could plan some of my day for myself and develop a broad range of interests.

By giving myself permission to take some time for myself, I began reaching back to my writing and my art, reading for pleasure, walking and exercising, beginning a spiritual routine, and establishing new friendships. My panic attacks ceased, my head cleared, and my spirit began to soar as if I had been released from prison. I felt as if I could swim a moat and not despair if anyone thought that was odd or unladylike. I credit my experience with *Once Upon a Mattress* for this newfound freedom which has continued to morph and grow.

May 12:
"*(Holding him.) Poor child... poor child... poor child. (Huskily, faintly.) We must try to love one another. (Finally Eugene moves from her, picks up the valise, as the lights start dimming, holding a spot on her. Eliza seems to recede in the distance as into his memory.) Now for Heaven's sake, spruce up, boy, spruce up! Throw your shoulders back! And smile, look pleasant! Let them know up there that you are somebody!*"
Eliza Gant in Ketti Frings's *Look Homeward, Angel* adapted from the Thomas Wolfe novel of the same name

Every few years, Mother's Day falls on May 12, so Happy Day, Mothers — today or sometime recently or very soon. This year marks my first Mother's Day to have no mom with whom to celebrate, so not only do I feel like a motherless child, I am a motherless child, even at sixty-four.

Yesterday, our priest read a wonderful all-inclusive prayer for Mother's Day. It included blessings for women with their own birth children, women who wished for a child but were barren or who had miscarried, for women who adopted, for women who had lost children, for children who had strong relationships with their maternal parent, for children who had broken or non-existent ties, for children who had been mothered by men and for men who had acted as mothers to others, for single mothers, for poor and incarcerated mothers, for mothers forgotten by their children, for children forgotten by their mothers.

Eliza Gant is a strong-willed mother in Ketti Frings's *Look Homeward, Angel* and in the original, largely autobiographical and coming-of-age Thomas Wolfe novel. Maybe she shouldn't have even had children. A shrewd business woman, Eliza runs a boarding house, The Dixieland, and the play vividly portrays her as a woman obsessed by material security and who generally fails to form any sort of intimate bonds within her family. Eugene Gant, an alcoholic stonecutter, is dejected by his failures and unable to stand up to his wife.

Eugene Gant (aka Thomas Wolfe) has finally decided to leave the madhouse of theatrical characters, both in his family, and in the boarding house. Eliza holds him and says, huskily and faintly, *"Poor child... poor child... poor child. We must try to love one another."* But as the novel states so poignantly, "the terrible and beautiful sentence, the last, the final wisdom that the earth can give, is remembered at the end, is spoken too late, wearily." Wow. What we can learn from plays and novels!

We produced *Look Homeward, Angel* in the fall of 1976 when my daughter Elin was a two-month-old babe in arms. I didn't like cold Eliza very much, and vowed to be as little like her as I possibly could be. But her spunk reminded me of my very independent and hard-working mother-in-law who also had to deal with a similar husband, make a living, and raise three boys practically alone. Despite the hardships Eliza had to overcome, she seemed, to me, to be recalcitrant, bullheaded, and headstrong — not my picture of loving, forgiving, warmhearted motherhood, not my image of the kind of mother I hoped to be.

Looking back now, I know in mothering my children, as the *Book of Common Prayer* says, I left undone things which I ought to have done; and I did those things which I ought not to have done. Still, I have great relationships with my adult children who have been free to make their own choices, find their own dreams, build their own futures with all the support I could possibly give. In this year's Mother's Day cards, Elin applauded me for being a good role model and great mom, and Seth commended me for being "home" to him.

May 13:
"Tripping hither, tripping thither,
Nobody knows why or whither;
We must dance and we must sing
Round about our fairy ring!"
Celia and Chorus of Fairies in WS Gilbert and Arthur Sullivan's
Iolanthe or The Peer and the Peri

Today, on May 13 in 1842, Arthur Sullivan was born. Sullivan is probably best known for the fourteen operettas he composed with W. S. Gilbert, but also for operas, ballets, choral pieces, orchestral works, and hymns, the most famous of which is probably "Onward Christian Soldiers."

We produced *Iolanthe* in 1989, and had a grand old time with the immortal fairies who find themselves at cross purposes with the House of Peers. Like most of G&S works, the opera lampoons British politics, law, society, and tradition. The original production of Iolanthe in 1882 must have been spectacular, because the Savoy Theatre in which it debuted was the first playhouse in the world to have electricity, and the fairy wands, along with other special lighting, caused spellbinding effects.

Much of what I know about fairies, I learned from J.M. Barrie's *Peter Pan* and other literature for young people. When I watched Mary Martin's Peter Pan on television as a child, I would sob when Tinker Bell was about to die, and I would clap my hands raw when Peter would ask, "Do you believe in fairies?... If you believe, clap your hands!"

It was Barrie who taught me that, "... when the first baby laughed for the first time, its laugh broke into a thousand pieces, and they all went skipping about, and that was the beginning of fairies." The book Peter Pan also explains that though there "ought to be one fairy for every boy and girl," something terrible prevents that guardianship. "You see children know such a lot now, they soon don't believe in fairies, and every time a child says, 'I don't believe in fairies,' there is a fairy somewhere that falls down dead."

Maybe fairies and dragons are figments of writers' creativity rather than reality. But I have discerned — by keeping a journal — how much my imagination affects my memory of certain real events. I think a recall something quite vividly and distinctly, and then I look back and at least part of what I "remember" is a total fabrication.

Neuroscientists over the last decade have studied the connection between memory and imagination and are discovering that they are linked. Researchers on the "livescience" website say that, "We think parts of the brain used to actually perceive an object and to imagine an object overlap. Thus, a vividly imagined event can leave a memory trace in the brain that's very similar to that of an experienced event. When memories are stored for perceived or imagined objects, some of the same brain areas are involved."

I think I will just have to agree with one of my heroes on the issue of whether or not fairies are real or imagined. John Lennon once said, "I believe in everything until it's disproved. So I believe in fairies, the myths, dragons. It all exists, even if it's in your mind."

Our fairies in *Iolanthe* existed, dancing and singing round their fairy ring. *"Nobody knows why or whither,"* and looking as if they had been choreographed by Carol Burnette. Nevertheless, they were charming *"Tripping hither, tripping thither,"* and at least during the run of the show, they were real.

May 14

"Psha! there's no possibility of being witty without a little ill nature: the malice of a good thing is the barb that makes it stick."
Lady Sneerwell in Richard Brinsley Sheridan's *The School for Scandal*, Act 1, Scene 1

Richard Brinsley Sheridan's *The School for Scandal* is a comedy of manners which satirizes the behavior of England's upper classes, using witty dialogue, one-dimensional people, and stylized acting. Sheridan created a caricature of society in his time, cooking up a play with ingredients like intrigue, libel, gossip, defamation of character, and meddling. Humans today are as amused by scandal and malice as when this play debuted at the Drury Lane Theatre in London just a week or so ago on May 8 — in 1777.

What captivates me in this and other works of the eighteenth century is how the writers loved to give characters names that captured their personalities. Lady Sneerwell delivers the quoted line above, and some of her companions in *School for Scandal* include Snake, Lady Teazle, Benjamin Backbite, Uncle Crabtree, Mrs. Candour, and Careless. William Congreve's *The Way of the World* features Lady Wishfort, Sir Wilfull, and Foible. Inhabiting John Gay's *Beggar's Opera* are a jail keeper named Lockit, the squeamish servant Filch, the thieving Nimming Ned, the criminal Crook-Finger'd Jack, and members of Peachum's gang: Mrs. Vixen, Mrs. Slammekin, Suky Tawdry, and Molly Brazen.

Some people in real life have suitable names, at least for their professions. Tiger Wood is a golfer who uses woods, William Wordsworth gave us very worthy words through his poetry, and Larry Speakes was Ronald Regan's Whitehouse spokesperson. My grandmother's obstetrician-gynecologist was Dr. Cock and his nurse was Miss Carrie. We have a Crook Realty in town, my cousin used to go to a dentist named Dr. Polk, and my son graduated from high school with a fellow named Jim Gardner who opened a landscaping business.

I never used to believe my given name suited me. "Barbara" means "foreign or strange, or traveler from a foreign land." I wasn't sure about that. My college mentor John Finlay went around the room one day during Sophomore English telling us whether or not our names fit us, as we were studying literature with interesting monikers. During my college days, our professors called us by our last names and when he got to one classmate, he exclaimed "Miss Bonnet, your name suits you perfectly!" And, this girl had a bouffant hairdo, a favorite style of the day, that stood up six inches above her head.

Later in the library, he suggested my name should be something much more exotic, like Genevieve. A rose by any other name would smell even sweeter, maybe? But I looked up that name and when I found that it meant "tribe woman," and that the diminutive was "Ginette," I gave up on changing to that. Jeannette is already my middle name.

Lately I wonder if "Barbara" is not right after all. New research I have read about my name suggests it indicates deep gratitude for culture, especially theatre, literature, art, music, and the natural world, and that I draw peace from art and the outdoors. All true. I have also found that Barbaras are sensitive, long to be understood (but feel they aren't often), and have trouble verbally expressing inner thoughts. All true as well. Did my parents chose my name, or did that name somehow select me? Did my name shape my personality, or did my aloof artistic nature live into my name? Questions to ponder.

May 15:
"Epops, the Chorus leader: So what name shall we give our city?
Pisthetairos: Well, do you want to use that mighty name from Lacedaimon –
shall we call it Sparta?
Euelpides: By Hercules, would I use that name Sparta for my city? No...
Pisthetairos: All right then, what name shall we provide?
Epops, the Chorus leader: Some name from around here – to do with clouds,
with high places full of air, something really extra grand.
Pisthetairos: Well, then, how do you like this: Cloud Cuckoo Land?"
Bird Characters in Aristophanes's *The Birds*

Our Samford Theatre 1984 production of *The Birds* was so much fun! Masks created by pouring life masks of students' faces. Costumes with huge wings, gloved hands, and slipper-feet with claws! And our set had delightful clouds settling around its base.

Just across the street from me is a small five house cul-de-sac called Cloudcroft Circle. "Croft" actually means small holdings or a settlement of cottages, so that part of the word is apropos. A wonderfully uncommon name, the old English word "Cloudcroft" indicates something covered or shrouded in clouds. I live on top of Shades Mountain in a town called Vestavia Hills, so our neighborhood truly is often covered in mist and fog.

Cloud Cuckoo Land comes from the Aristophanes comedy The Birds. In the play, Pisthetairos (or "Mr. Trusting") and Euelpides ("Mr. Hopeful") decide to create a utopian city in the clouds called Cloud Cuckoo Land. Thus, the name has come to mean an idealistic realm.

I wouldn't call my own little kingdom across from Cloudcroft ideal, but I do love this house. I am only the third owner, and the second family stayed here only a year. A 1967-contemporary style, the original owners had an architect build the residence for them, and it is a peaceful space with huge windows looking out on trees on two sides and a fairly decent mountain view in the back, facing east. The sunrise each morning is viewable from my bedroom.

In May of 1998, I was able to buy out from my ex my portion of the house, making the place all mine. It was a back-breaking endeavor to find and save the money to do this. I wrote extra pieces for magazines and newspapers, took a play on tour to schools, did supplementary design projects, and finally also pulled some funds from life savings so that I could manage to break this last tie of marriage, cut this last legal joint holding, and put behind me this last vestige of a life together.

He had really only lived in this place for a scant 18 months before he decided to move on to a different life. So the house doesn't hold a lot of painful togetherness memories for me. I have lived here for 240 months without him — so many, many more than with him.

From the back yard, I look at the big puffy white clouds and see so many things: elephants, pirate ships, giants, dogs. My clouds rain and snow, float and race, turn menacing and blush with color at sunrise and sunset. And across them constantly race the birds. I appreciate my clouds up here — so maybe I should just call it "Cloud Cuckoo Land," a name *"to do with clouds, with high places full of air, something really extra grand."*

May 16:
"The costumes, the scenery, the makeup, the props,
The audience that lifts you when you're down.
The headaches, the heartaches, the backaches, the flops;
The sheriff who'll escort you out of town.

The opening when your heart beats like a drum...
The closing when the customers don't come...
There's no business like show business,
Like no business I know.
You get word before the show has started
That your favorite uncle died at dawn,
And top of that, your pa and ma have parted;
You're broken-hearted, but you go on."
Frank, Dolly, Winnie, and Company in *Annie Get Your Gun*, lyrics and music by Irving Berlin, and a book by Dorothy Fields and Herbert Fields

Annie Get Your Gun with its delightful Irving Berlin music premiered at the Imperial Theatre on Broadway this day, May 16, 1946, and ran for 1,147 performances. My then-husband and I designed the sets for the show at Music Theatre of Wichita (Kansas) in the summer of 1979, and with 10 or 12 separate locations in the show, there was a lot of scenery! Oddly, this musical is in the public domain in the USA since it was published here between 1927 and 1977, inclusive, and without a copyright notice.

"No Business Like Show Business" has become an anthem for theatre workers, summing up this world — and it is not wholly about "that happy feeling when you are stealing that extra bow"! Any career has delights, quirks, hardships, and rewards. But some people might be surprised to know that theatre takes a lot of labor.

"The costumes, the scenery, the makeup, the props." Theatre can be a dangerous profession. A colleague of mine stepped off the front edge of the stage and into the lowered orchestra pit one day injuring himself in any number of ways, and still suffers from his fall — and that was at least two decades ago. Batons are flying up and down all the time. Tons of weight are above the heads of actors and workers constantly. Power tools are the heart of set-making. Tall ladders, strong chemicals, and dark backstage areas.

"The audience that lifts you when you're down." Producing drama is dependent upon the people who pay money to watch the performance, and figuring out that angle is hard work. The tendency of modern audiences is to be capricious, preoccupied with technological devices, and unmannerly, but even a theatre critic in the eighteenth century deplored

the tendency of producers who "please the crowd" rather than produce quality work.

"*The headaches, the heartaches, the backaches, the flops.*" Theatre is physically and emotionally demanding. Whether onstage or backstage, actors and artists are moving constantly, lunging, climbing, walking, running, all of which can often produce every kind of bodily pain.

"*Everything about it is appealing.*" To me, the charm of theatre work is in the gain of so many varied talents: self discipline, creative problem solving, organizational strength, collaboration practice, interpersonal skills, respect for authority, flexibility, development of goals, working under stress, loyalty, leadership, nurturing, doing your best, giving your all, being involved, finishing tasks, cooperation, independence, and many, many more.

There really are "*no people like show people, they smile when they are low.*" I have known individuals who performed after cutting themselves severely during a scene, breaking a bone, vomiting between scenes, being filled with cold medicine. I have known crew members who gave the show their all after a tragic romantic breakup, after a wreck, after hearing that a "*favorite uncle died at dawn,*" and even after news that their "*pa and ma have parted.*" It might sounds wacky that "*You're broken-hearted, but you go on*" — but the ability to subjugate your feelings on demand makes you strong (if you can let them out afterward!). Later, after the last bow, the entire cast and crew mourn with you, but for the duration of the performance, you continue your role in the most professional manner possible.

Theatre is hard and draining work, but rewarding. "*Even with a turkey that you know will fold, you may be stranded out in the cold. Still you wouldn't trade it for a sack o' gold! Let's go on with the show!*" Wait! How big is that sack of gold? Just kidding — I love theatre work.

May 17:
"*I, Victor Robinson, on this 17th day of May, do hereby begin the diary of my family's strange existence in the place where we have been shipwrecked – a place somewhere to the south of Samoa.*"
Victor Robinson in *The Swiss Family Robinson: A Musical,* Book by Jerome Coopersmith, Lyrics by Annette Leisten, Music by Sheldon Markham, based on the novel by Johann David Wyss

It is mid-May, the day the fictional Robinson family was shipwrecked near an island where they stayed for several years before being rescued. While missing from their homeland, they learn about themselves, about the worth of familial ties, about survivorship, about cultivation, about the natural world, and about self-sufficiency. The Swiss novelist Johann David Wyss, also a pastor, wrote the book as a tribute to the teachings of Jean-Jacques Rousseau, and a large part of the Robinsons' adventures concern moral education based on the fundamental ideology of Christianity.

When I was on a team that created the scenery for this musical version of *Swiss Family Robinson* for Birmingham Children's Theatre in the mid-1970s, we had a delightful time creating a huge trunk with enormous limbs, and a tree house upon which the cast romped the entire show. Tree houses, exotic islands, faraway places, foreign shores: mid-May is the time to be planning a summer break away from the routine.

I work now from home, and if you have never tried it, maybe you shouldn't. I never fantasized about laboring from an office nestled in the nursery, about working in shorts and a tee shirt, or about being able to clean the house and put in professional time simultaneously. But I somehow ended up in this job that has no office attached to it.

I knew that I would be isolated, distracted, and interrupted. Though I am a driven and self-motivated person, for a large portion of my day professional hours, home routines and artistic stints blur together — and I often find myself working till 7:00 in the evening and wondering if I have done enough on my actual work.

So I miss the camaraderie of the office, the mutual support of fellow toilers, the team spirit of co-workers. What I really yearn for is the academic year. For professors and staff teaching theatre in a college or university, each semester is almost unbelievably full of teaching, designing, building, grading, researching, developing, and mentoring. Any week that holds only 40 hours of work seems like a wondrous breather.

But every May around this date, I would attend graduation, salute my matriculating students, celebrate their successes in our department, and then have an almost three-month break unless I taught summer school. So at this juncture, my thoughts drift toward vacations, sabbaticals, recesses, trips, holidays, relaxation, and sabbath — a time of repose and rest from hard labor.

Somehow, the idea of slowing down for the summer is ingrained in me and I struggle through my work while in my mind I am gardening, floating on the gulf, ambling through the art museum, swinging in the hammock. I don't want to be writing in my journal that I "hereby begin the diary of my family's strange existence in the place where we have been shipwrecked." But the part about "a place somewhere to the south of Samoa" doesn't sound so bad!

May 18:

"Place the shield upon the ground, Hector's shield so deftly rounded, a piteous sight, a bitter grief for me to see. O, you Achaeans, more reason have you to boast of your prowess than your wisdom. Why have you in terror of this child been guilty of a murder never matched before? Did you fear that some day he would rear again the fallen walls of Troy? It seems then you were nothing after all, when, though Hector's fortunes in the war were prosperous and he had ten thousand other arms to back him, we still were daily overmatched; and yet, now that our city is taken and every Phrygian slain, you fear a tender child like this! I do not commend the fear of one who fears but never yet has reasoned out the cause."
Hecuba in Euripides's *The Trojan Women*

Whew! Another play about war! In the spring of 1990, we were brave enough to perform this great Euripides tragedy about the women of Troy after the Greeks have entered their walls in the now-famous huge wooden horse. Their city has been destroyed and all the Trojan men have been slaughtered. With their husbands killed, the women and their remaining families are about to be shipped away as slaves.

The widowed princess Andromache hears of her daughter's sacrifice at the tomb of the Greek warrior Achilles, and then learns that her baby son will be thrown off the battlements so that he won't grow up to avenge his father Hector's death. She asks that at least her son's body be brought back so the family can give him a proper burial. My son Seth was five years old at the time of our production, and was cast as the child Astyanax.

Seth was an active youngster. He was very excited to play this part in the play, to have one of his favorite students Pistl (as he called her) make him up to first look like an adorable little Trojan, and then a bloody mess, to wear a tiny chiton (Greek robe), to stay up late at rehearsals, and to feel like an important part of the project.

Vic Fichtner, one of our alumni, directed *The Trojan Women*, and I totally respected his talent in this position. However, I had a tiny disagreement with the way he staged the scene toward the end of the play in which heralds return to the city bearing the body of Astyanax on Hector's shield. The scene was staged so that the shield was set down center in a spotlight with the grandmother Hecuba behind, and the chorus back of her delivering their ode.

Did I mention that the scene was nine minutes long? With a five-year old boy on top of a shield for that long, I might have staged the chorus around the body in a circle, but Vic was insistent that Astyanax should stay in full view of the audience the entire time. We practiced at home remaining immobile, we talked about how important the scene was, we taught deep breathing and relaxation exercises, and then we actually bribed Seth to be still for nine minutes. If he could do so for the final dress rehearsal and all six performances, we would all go to Disney World as a reward.

"How," I wondered during rehearsals, "did I ever agree to this? It is nerve wracking to the mother! Not only do I watch my tyke brought onstage as a lifeless corpse, but I have to worry about whether or not he decides to spring back to life in a Jesus-like resurrection." At every performance, I sat in the audience and held my breath. But before the show opened, I realized this scene was not about me, but about Seth as the tiny Astyanax, and if Vic was untroubled about it, I should let my anxiety go.

We did make a trip to Disney World. Funny thing, though: I was at a funeral recently at Samford and a colleague sat behind me. When the service was over, he asked how Seth was doing these days. "I'll never forget Seth in *The Trojan Women*," he said. "That little death twitch was so realistic!" So, my son wasn't flawlessly and absolutely corpse-like every performance, but I'll give him this: he was just about as perfect as a five-year old set down stage center for nine minutes could possibly be.

May 19:
"Mrs. Ralston! Mrs. Ralston! There's a terrible smell of burning coming from the kitchen!"
Major Metcalf in Agatha Christie's *The Mousetrap*

When I was two years old, Agatha Christie's murder mystery *The Mousetrap* opened in London's West End. The year was 1952. Twenty-six years later, we produced the show in the round on stage at the university. Now it has been an additional 36 years since our production and the original show is still running, having had it 25,000th performance on November 18, 2012. *The Mousetrap* is the longest running show of any genre in theatre history.

The enigmatic play takes place at Monkswell Manor, a large country house run by Mollie and Giles Ralston, which lends a mysterious mood to the action. A snowstorm brings several unexpected guests, and sets in motion several murders, many suspicions, alarms, an investigation by a police sergeant, and a surprise twist at the end. After so much tension, Major Metcalf has a humorous final line: *"Mrs. Ralston! Mrs. Ralston! There's a terrible smell of burning coming from the kitchen!"* To which Mollie wails, "Oh my pie!"

Smoldering pie would not be an appealing dessert, but today we love to eat grilled meats and vegetables, blackened seafood, darkly roasted kale, and nicely toasted marshmallows. We have be cautious, for now we are told that charred parts of grilled meats and poultries are the birthplace of carcinogenic chemicals. Our genetic DNA can be affected by eating such inky foods to the point of the development of cancer.

My mother always told the story of her mother's morning ritual: burning the first batch of toast. Mom related the habit with a bit of disdain, because she hated to waste food, and she was careful with her cooking. And the burned toast was thrown away with no mention of the poor children somewhere in the world who were starving and would have loved to eat anything. I am sure my grandmother, who took care of her mother and was a single parent to four girls, simply got preoccupied with getting all of them ready for school and work. But then, she was actually still burning toast when I lived next door to her the first five years of my life, so I got to experience the tradition myself.

Though I am known for being a fairly good gourmet cook, I take after my grandmother in many ways, and I can get distracted when I have something in the toaster oven or on the stovetop cooking away. Sometimes, I get so involved in a project that even when I hear the timer go off, I tune it out. Just recently, I have scorched the bottom half of some perfectly delightful zucchini, blackened the edges of some delicious sourdough bread, and turned a baked egg dish into fairly hard rubber. We ate the top portion of the squash, but the toast was tossed and the egg dish used in bouncing experiments.

Each time, I thought of my grandmother. She was born in 1900, fifty years before I was, and she died in 1987, so I got to spend 37 long years with her. A burning lamp who lit many of my paths in life, she is still an inspiration — if not in cooking, at least in sewing, in patience, in generosity, in leadership, in being a loving person. I must say I almost enjoyed charring the toast because just the aroma of the *"terrible smell of burning coming from the kitchen"* reminded me of her!

May 20:
In "Do You Love Me?" from *Fiddler on the Roof*, Tevye questions his wife Golde about whether or not she loves him. (Listen to the work online or from your library!)
        Tevye in the musical *Fiddler on the Roof*, with music by Jerry Bock, lyrics by Sheldon Harnick, and book by Joseph Stein, based on tales by Sholem Aleichem

In one of my favorite musicals *Fiddler on the Roof*, Tevye asks his wife if she loves him. She wonders what in the world he is questioning her for, but he presses on. Golde lists all the chores she has done for the last quarter of a century: cleaning, laundering, meal preparation, cow tending, child rearing. Doesn't this add up to something? she asks. By the end of the song, Tevye has determined Golde must be devoted to him, and he admits he loves her as well. If Tevye had never been brave enough to ask his wife such an intimate question, he would never have known for sure.

Not long ago, my granddaughter Emmeline went with me for a visit to my chiropractor. As we were checking out, she had noticed (being the extremely observant four-year old that she is) several rolls of labels on the wall. "May I please have a sticker, Sarah?" she asked. (She had also heard the doctor call her assistant by name, so she was able to make an even more personal inquiry.)

"Of course you may," Sarah said, allowing her to pick out a charming little bear.

"Why didn't I get a sticker?" whined a grown woman standing beside us. With as good a twinkle as I could muster in my eyes I answered, "Maybe because you didn't ask!"

So many people want things, but they don't ask, don't know how to ask, feel uncomfortable asking. I used to be that way, but in the summer of 1996, I read *The Aladdin Factor* at the beach on our family trip.

The book I choose for such summer illumination always infuses my vacation with its special aura.

Authors Jack Canfield and Mark Victor Hansen say anything is possible if you just dare to ask: from personal contentment to professional satisfaction, from creative accomplishment to finding time for relaxation. One exercise they suggest is to write out 101 wishes, and as I did so, the assignment was eye-opening. I still have the list and look at it from time to time. Many of the things I no longer care about, but some of them were good hopes and desires, some accomplished, and some still simmering in the imagination.

One day as I was going on my beach excursion amidst the riotous family activity on the trip, I told the Universe I wished for a fun solo adventure. I reveled in the blue sky. The tide came in and formed pools and I floated in one of the "lakes." I walked down the seashore accompanied by a big white "guardian angel" lab dog and saw a man wearing a bright purple thong. On the way back, I found numerous sea urchins and shells. A sandbar formed and I sat on it for a while.

I am not sure those incidents would have been observed by me if I hadn't asked for an escapade — just the petition for an enjoyable diversion made me receptive to what was happening to me, and helped me see the events unfold as a merry time. The book encouraged me to ask for a raise, for better seating at a restaurant, for the air conditioning to be turned down, for a hug, for a kiss, for a back rub, for a special dinner.

I have to admit, I don't always remember to think through what it is I want and then ask for it. But I agree with the writers that if you don't ask, chances are you are not going to get. What do you need to ask for today?

May 21:
"I'm doin' the best I can, Cora. Can't ya understand that? I'm doin' the best I can."
Rubin in William Inge's *The Dark at the Top of the Stairs*

I have not always been comfortable with a statement like Rubin makes in Inge's *The Dark at the Top of the Stairs*. In fact, when we produced the play in November of 1984, I had just delivered Seth in late September, so he was just short of seven weeks old when the play opened. Back in September, the afternoon and night before he was born, I supervised a dress parade for the opera *Susannah*, worked finishing the costumes, completed a story for *Birmingham Magazine*, made sure my daughter Elin got to school, dance, and piano classes, and went to her school's open house.

At the time, my tendency to aggrandize the importance of success and hard work was at a high point. Doing the best I could was never enough. I had to hold my standards as high as they possibly could be raised, compare myself to everyone else, and perform better than anyone ever could.

As I have gotten older, I am more lenient with myself and others. When I get perturbed at other people from time to time, my fiancé Roger says, "Just think, they are probably doing the best they can." A good followup quote is: "Success is doing the best you can with what you've got."

At my friend Father Bill's retirement from university chaplaincy, he said something of the same thing. He said one of his favorite movies is *Apollo 13*, the film depicting the planned third Moon-landing mission. During the flight, an explosion in the spacecraft depletes most of the astronaut's oxygen supply, as well as their electrical power. Not only do they abort the Moon landing, mission control scrambles to even get the three men home safely.

Bill said the scene he really loves is when all the smart guys at NASA's Houston Control throw all their books and information on the table and the flight director declares they are giving up the flight plan to devise a new mission. After some questions he says, "Well, unfortunately, we're not landing on the Moon, are we? I don't care what anything was designed to do, I care about what it can do. So, let's get to work."

That is just like campus ministry work, Bill said. You do the best you can with the people and the materials and the funds and the support that you have. That doesn't mean you don't have lofty visions, or that you don't set admirable expectations or that you don't get stellar results. But you have what you have, and you do the best you possibly can with that realization.

Rosalynn Carter once said, "You must accept that you might fail; then, if you do your best and still don't win, at least you can be satisfied that you've tried. If you don't accept failure as a possibility, you don't set high goals, you don't branch out, you don't try — you don't take the risk."

I like that outlook: Set goals. Take the risk. Make the concerted effort. If I fail, I have done my utmost. And I may succeed greatly.

Nowadays, I am much more apt to say, *"I'm doin' the best I can ... Can't ya understand that? I'm doin' the best I can."*

May 22:
"All right, listen, it's just a picture, we don't have to get bogged down with it, life's too short."
Serge in Yamina Reza's *Art*

Just before I left Samford University in the spring of 2001, we produced *Art* with an excellent trio of student actors. Having been an art major myself in college, I really enjoyed the deep discussion in the play about art. More than it answers questions, *Art* engenders debate about both friendship and art, involving a comic triangle of three close buddies, Serge, Marc, and Yvan. Serge appalls Marc when he purchases, for quite a bit of money, what he thinks is an evocative piece of modern art. The large totally white painting becomes a bickering point as Serge and Marc argue about what art really is. The rather indecisive Yvan attempts to mediate the conflict.

What people think or feel about art is subjective. Yet, great, and even good art is timeless, beautiful in some way, and makes a deep connection between you and the creator — within your heart and soul.

In a small group setting just last week, a bonding question was asked: "Tell us about a work of art that has touched your life." For me, it was a trick question, because so many plays, paintings, poems, and pirouettes have impacted me and changed my life. How could I pick just one?

But I did. Several years ago, Roger and I went to the High Museum in Atlanta. They had a special exhibit, but before we went, I had no idea what paintings were in the show. I got ahead of Roger, and orbited a special panel to behold Rembrandt Harmenszoon van Rijn's "Belshazzar's Feast." From the book of Daniel in the Old Testament, the work highlights the story of a feast that Belshazzar threw in which a disembodied hand wrote a message on a wall. Daniel interpreted the news as an end to the Babylonian empire, and indeed, that very night Persians invaded the city and killed Belshazzar. The painting was on loan from the National Gallery in London.

When I was an art major, I began to collect books of my favorite artists, and Rembrandt was one of those. I would spend hours pouring over his pieces, sketching some of them, reading about how he used light

198

and shadow so adroitly, learning how he organized his work to best use contrast, and discovering how he layered his colors and glazes to achieve unfathomable depths in his oil paintings.

This "Belshazzar's Feast" was not the first Rembrandt I had ever seen, having been to many museums in America and Europe. But when I rounded the corner and beheld that work, I burst into tears. Seeing that huge 5' 6" by 6' 10" canvas was a very spiritual experience for me, and the viewing somehow did break my heart. Robert Shimshak has said in "What Makes Good Art" that pieces and what we think of them is personal. "It is like a good marriage that completes a feeling inside you, something that lasts forever and grows with time."

Late nineteenth century French critic Emile Michel once wrote, "Rembrandt, in effect, belongs to the race of artists who cannot have descendants, the race of Michelangelo, the race of Shakespeare, of Beethoven; like these Prometheuses of art he wanted to ravish the celestial life, to put the vibrations of life into still form, to express in the visible, that which by its very nature is non-material and undefinable."

May 23:
"O God! that one might read the book of fate."
King Henry in William Shakespeare's *King Henry IV, Part II*, Act III, Scene 1

"O God! that one might read the book of fate." Really? Do we really want to know the future? Despite all our modern worries about what is to come, do we have to know right now if we get that promotion, how our intricate family situation plays out, when we die?

King Henry really doesn't want to know what the future holds either. In fact, he goes on to say that even if the most joyous young person came across such a volume, "viewing his progress through, what perils past, what crosses to ensue, would shut the book, and sit him down and die." Humans are not constructed in such a way that we can view eternal time. To read ahead about the magnitude of life, its immensity and its sorrows (and joys) would be too much to bear.

But I do like to read other kinds of books! So I was distressed the other day listening to National Public Radio that a series of studies shows a decline in teenage pleasure reading over the last few years, despite the success of the *Harry Potter* series and *The Hunger Games*. Almost fifty percent of 17-year-olds report they read for fun just one or two times a year, if that — probably due to spending time online and with social media.

What a shame! I remember the summer before I went to college. A high school English teacher gave me what was called "A Recommended Reading List for College-Bound Students" from a nearby university. (I actually still have it.) I busily checked off all the volumes I had read, and there were many, many more to go.

But I relished the thought of experiencing all those books: visiting the library and searching through the card catalogue — or even better, going to one of our locally owned bookstores and strolling amidst the shelves, leafing through pages, deciding which one I would choose that day. The library had the upper hand when it came to old books with intoxicating smells, but if I purchased a book, I would lawfully be wedded to the volume, to have it and to hold it, from that day forward!

On the list were classic titles, *The Bible*, *The Iliad* and *The Odyssey*; Middle Ages' selections such as Geoffrey Chaucer's *Canterbury Tales* and Thomas Malory's *Le Morte d'Arthur*; Elizabethan masterpieces from Shakespeare, Cervantes, and Sir Walter Scott; seventeenth, eighteenth, and nineteenth century works; and modern plays, novels, and poetry. What if I read every single volume? Did I have a chance in life to be a minimally knowledgeable person? A cultured woman? A human with an expanded awareness?

My favorite place to read at the time was in my room, on my bed, with a pool from the reading light falling across the rapidly turning pages. That summer, I devoured *Ivanhoe*, *Love's Labors Lost*, *Pilgrim's Progress*, *The Three Musketeers*, the poems of Robert Frost and Emily Dickinson, *A Farewell to Arms*, and Tolkien's *Lord of the Rings* trilogy. The discipline helped me prepare for college, and was a pleasure to discover the minds and the settings, the characters and the themes of the authors who wrote them. It developed verbal skills and memory, empathy and focus; it stimulated my imagination and improved my capacity to concentrate.

So, I am sorry that teenagers today don't use much of their free time to read. Such exploration gave me such a strong platform to begin discovering my own real self in college.

May 24:
"AHHHHHHHH CHOOOOO!!! (*Cherdyakov unleashes a monstrous sneeze, his head snapping forward. The main blow of the sneeze discharges on the back*

of the general's completely bald head. The general winces and his hand
immediately goes to his now dampened head.)
Ohhh, My goodness. I am sorry your Excellency! I'm so terribly sorry.
(The General takes out his handkerchief and wipes his head.)"
Cherdyakov in "The Sneeze" in Neil Simon's *The Good Doctor*

Almost twenty-five years ago, I designed costumes for Neil Simon's *Good Doctor* at Samford University. Based on stories by Anton Chekov, the script features an afflicted Chekov-like narrator who addresses the audience about a number of his stories. In "The Sneeze," an administrative clerical worker happens to sneeze on the head of his boss at the opera. He simply cannot stop apologizing, and even has a mental collapse over the episode. The choice of the show was a great one for student actors.

So Cherdyakov, begging forgiveness over and over, says that the sneeze was "unpardonable," "inexcusable," and "monstrous of me," making much more of an issue over the involuntary sternutation than it merited by constantly drawing attention back to the faux pas. No one was clocking that expulsion of air, but sneezes travel between 35 and a hundred miles per hour. A popular myth about this common bodily reflex is that your eyeballs pop out of their sockets if you sneeze with your eyes open since sneezes travel so quickly; however, our eyeballs are dependably fixed inside the skull cavity, so there is little chance of such a freak accident. And really, how many people do you know who have gaping holes in their faces from keeping their eyes open during a sneeze?

The polite courteousness of declaring "bless you" after someone sneezes possibly originated during the widespread and indiscriminately contagious Black Death, which triggered sneezing and coughing. The pope ordained that blessing a sneezer would defend others from the terrifying plague that ultimately resulted in the deaths of one-third of the Europe population in the mid-1300s. Another theory concerning saying, "God bless you," is that people thought that the soul temporarily leaves the body during a sneeze. Such an empty casing would surely lure evil spirits to fill it up quickly and take hold.

Unfortunately, in *The Good Doctor*, the general didn't have the modern convenience of antiseptic wipes on hand to disinfect his head, though he did pat it off with a handkerchief. And Cherdyakov didn't have our current medical advice about using a disposable tissue or achooing into the crook of his elbow.

I don't know about my soul taking a brief vacation from my body on occasions when I clear my nose of bacteria and virus, but I do know about contagion sneaking in when others sneeze on me. Once while watching *Les Misérables*, a woman seated right behind me sneezed and coughed on me so much that I was sick for a week afterward. And my twin grandsons have blown disease my way enough this winter and spring to bestow upon me three separate bronchial infections. Since a sneeze can dispatch something like 100,000 germs into the air from five to twenty feet away, it is no wonder I was felled by toddlers sitting on my lap.

May 25:
"Carefully on tiptoe stealing,
Breathing gently as we may,
Every step with caution feeling,
We will softly steal away."
Crew in William S. Gilbert and Arthur Sullivan's "Carefully On Tip-Toe Stealing" from *H.M.S. Pinafore*

H.M.S. *Pinafore* is one of the most enjoyable shows for which I ever designed costumes. It is silly and merry, making great fun of politics, social status, the English Royal Navy, promotion beyond capabilities, and many other aspects of Victorian society. I had wanted to be a part of a Gilbert and Sullivan comedy for a long, long time, but our Samford University opera director shied away from them for a while. Finally, some of us persuaded him to give *Pinafore* a whirl — and then he was hooked. It was the first of several G&S works we produced over the years.

The original performance of *H.M.S. Pinafore* opened this date, May 25, 1878 in London at the Opera Comique. Though ticket sales were slow after an enthusiastic opening, by the end of its 571 performances, it was the second-longest running theatrical musical piece to that time. Audiences thought it joyous and witty. As Harry Benford noted in *The Gilbert & Sullivan Lexicon*, "Even the title of the piece is silly, applying the name of a little girl's garment, a pinafore, to the fearsome symbol of a naval warship, which usually bore names like Victory, Goliath, Audacious, and Minotaur."

This funny scene and song "Carefully on Tiptoe Stealing" features the crew of the ship assisting Ralph and Josephine as they make a bungled attempt to leave the ship to elope. It is a stage-blue nighttime, and the sailors and lovers move about the deck with some pretty clever choreography. Ray Bolger's villainous "Barnaby" in the 1961 film *Babes in Toyland* offers another humorous rendering of "tiptoe stealing." Spying on everyone, he does a hilarious dance, pussyfooting around Toyland twirling his cape. If you have never seen either of these tiptoe scenes, check them out as soon as you possibly can!

I remember thinking I might be able to tiptoe to bed and not disturb my parents when sneaking in after curfew on high school nights out. That never worked! One or both of them always waited up for me and checked me in, late or on time. My senior year, Tiny Tim recorded his unusual version of the song "Tiptoe Through the Tulips," and if I ever endeavored to creep in the front door, my dad would start singing the crazy tune.

When I myself was a parent, I decided not to tiptoe around the house for my sleeping babies. Wanting them to get use to normal household, neighborhood, and outdoor noises, I walked and talked normally when they napped or went down for the evening.

Inspirational speaker Bob Proctor has been quoted as saying, "Most of us tiptoe through life hoping to make it safely to death." For some that means hiding what they really believe; for others, failing to take a risk; for others, freezing at decision-making. Or being afraid that they will be rejected in a relationship. Or fearing that someone will break into their business, abduct their children, steal their car, take over their job.

I am realizing more and more that if I go a-tiptoeing through my life, it must be in a bold pussyfooting endeavor, complete with big tall black boots and a dark cloak: fearlessly, exuberantly, joyously, stepping into some sort of humorous escapade befitting a stage rendition by none other than Gilbert and Sullivan!

May 26:
In "So In Love" from *Kiss Me, Kate*, Lilli Vanessi (playing Katherine) sings about how she is still deeply in love with Fred Graham. (Listen to the work online or from your library!)

Lilli Vanessi from *Kiss Me, Kate*, with music and lyrics by Cole Porter, book by Samuel and Bella Spewack, based on the play *The Taming of the Shrew* by William Shakespeare

I am so in love, so in love, so in love with Cole Porter. It all started in 2004 when my friend Beverly Brasell directed *Anything Goes* for the spring musical at our local Vestavia Hills High School. My son Seth had graduated the year before, but had friends he wanted to see in the show, so he came back from his studies at Sewanee, and we went with some of his buddies.

Before seeing *Anything Goes*, I knew Cole Porter's music. I had designed costumes for *Kiss Me, Kate*, I had seen films with his scores, listened to his tunes on the radio and television — so I was not incognizant of his work. But something about the vigorous performances of beautiful songs like "Anything Goes," "You're the Top," and "I Get a Kick Out of You" sung by those exuberant and masterful high school singer-actors caught my attention in a startling way.

Four months later almost to the day, I saw that the film *De-Lovely* was at a nearby movie house. On a Sunday afternoon, I went by myself to see the story about Cole Porter and his wife Linda. Thank goodness attendance was light and few people were sitting near me, because as I recognized in the film themes from my own life, I began to feel tears spilling from my eyes and down my cheeks. By the end of the show, I was sobbing uncontrollably, shoulders shaking, breath coming in spurts — in the darkened theater.

I got the compact disk of the "De-Lovely" soundtrack, and another CD collection of Porter's best known songs by different artists. I couldn't stop listening to them: something in the love songs touched me like nothing else had ever done. Soon, I began, after almost ten years of single hood and no romantic attachment, feeling like I wanted to be part of a couple again.

The next spring, I decided to go to Cursillo, a spiritual retreat at our Episcopal diocese's Camp McDowell and had to have a sponsor from my church for the event. I was given the choice requesting my old friend David or my newer acquaintance Roger Conville. I decided to ask whoever I saw first, and soon ran into Roger. Everything that unfolded after that was life-changing.

At the time Roger was married, but going through rocky and desolate times. On May 26 of that year, he told me that he was going to get a divorce and, since I had so recently been reliving my split with its decade anniversary, I coached him through his proceedings. Over a couple of years, we became closer and closer and my Cole Porter songs began wrapping round and round me as tightly as a hug from the composer.

Still I wasn't sure this was right. But lyrics from Porter's songs flowed in and out of my mind and soul constantly, and I don't know if Cole's music prepared me for falling in love anew, or mesmerized me, or beguiled me, or charmed me. But there was a definite connection, and when I listen to my Porter collection, as I am doing now, I weep with the remembrance of how de-lovely and bewitching the whole experience was.

May 27:
"Why, Mr. Avonzino, you're like the author of this book I've been reading – Dr. Kennick. He says babies are regular geniuses in their first fourteen months. He says: you know why babies sleep all the time? Because they're learning all the time, they get tired by learning. Geniuses, he says, imagine!"
Millie in Thornton Wilder's *Infancy*

A pretty hysterical sight is to view grown college students playing infants in huge perambulators in Thornton Wilder's one-act play Infancy, which we produced in the spring of 1988. Huge bonnets adorned their heads, ruffly gowns peeked out of their frilly white blankets, and they learned to cry and make humorous tot faces.

Babies really are unbelievable little sponges, soaking up new information minute by minute, sprouting new neurons, learning how to communicate, move, and make sense of their families and the vast world around them. Having two fifteen-month olds right now in identical twins, George and Arthur, I observe just what smart little boogers they are every Tuesday when I keep them.

Right now, they are talking in streams of sentences using words that make absolutely no sense to anyone but themselves. But they can understand almost perfectly what I say to them. Arthur was carting a bib around the other day, and I told him to wipe his drippy nose with that bib and he immediately did so. I asked George today if he wanted more macaroni and cheese and he answered, "Ummmmmm!" Arthur shook his head, "Nooo."

It is interesting having four grandchildren who visit me often enough that I can intertwine with their lives some, and watch them become savvy beings. When Emmeline was a baby, I took a test online to help me discover a name for her to call me. From the quiz, I discovered I am a sophisticated and artsy grandmother, and my best name in this role was "BeBe," so that is who I have become. The test revealed I would be most likely to engage grandchildren in activities like going to a museum, creating an art project, fixing a gourmet meal, picking flowers from a garden and arranging them, or going to a play or puppet show.

One time a friend said I was her model for child raising because I was a lenient parent. I was horrified, because I had rules and presupposed good behavior and manners. I took my children's thoughts and feelings seriously. But I had high expectations of them: I expected them to do chores and they did them. I expected them to act responsibly and they (mostly) did so. I expected them to behave in public and they lived up to those hopes.

One thing I did do was treat my children with respect as another person, and not as little people or "objects" that I could order around to do what I wanted. I listened to their points of view and engaged them in intelligent conversation from the time they could talk. We read together all the time. We listened to all kinds of music. We painted and sculpted and they both made their own works of art from fabrics in the costume shop.

I read somewhere that during the first decade life, the brain forms trillions of connections, and as they develop talents and skills, their brains generate inner connections so they are able to understand math, verbal skills, empathy, and all kinds of academic and life lessons. Babies really *are regular geniuses in their first fourteen months,* but they need a little coaxing, prodding, urging, and expectations to keep on developing from fifteen months till they leave your home.

May 28:
"Unbar the door! unbar the door!
We are not here to triumph by fighting, by stratagem, or by resistance,
Not to fight with beasts as men. We have fought the beast
And have conquered. We have only to conquer
Now, by suffering. This is the easier victory.
Now is the triumph of the Cross, now
Open the door! I command it. OPEN THE DOOR!"
Thomas in T. S. Eliot's *Murder in the Cathedral*

"Unbar the door! unbar the door!" I yell down the stairway to my Vestry co-worker at church on the day we have to count money from the collection plate and lock up the Nave and parish hall building. "What was that?" he calls back up. *"Unbar the door!"* I shout again, and though

he cannot hear me, I continue, *"We are not here to triumph by fighting, by stratagem, or by resistance, not to fight with beasts as men."*

Oh, those theatre quotes that will not depart from my gray matter. With a mind of their own, they struggle to pop out at what they think are appropriate junctures in my life. So, we have a push bar on the door in the parish hall that leads to the side street, and we have to use an Allen wrench to wrest it open or closed.

I always think of the opening action as unbarring and the closing up as barring the door, and of course we have to bar it at the end of services. And my lockup partner is downstairs using the wrench to bolt the door while I wonder why we cannot leave the doors open even for our enemies. And the barring action takes me right back to the gripping scene in *Murder in the Cathedral* when Thomas Becket's priests are trying to save his life as the murderous barons pound on the doors to come into the cathedral and assassinate him.

Back my mind goes to Eliot's poetic historical play based on fact. Henry II advances his old friend and fellow carouser to the position of Archbishop of Canterbury, expecting Becket to tow the party line against the Church. Having accepted the role, however, Becket takes his part seriously and realizes his devotion to God is greater than his allegiance to the King. Thomas has faced his tempters and he has come to understand his life's path might lead to martyrdom.

"We are not here to triumph by fighting, by stratagem, or by resistance," he tells his fellow clergy. He was not going to get out the armor and the swords, the battle plans or the reinforcements, as an army leader might have done.

"We have fought the beast and have conquered." The beast he conquered was his own selfish ego; that was his hard battle. Now he simply has to go through the pain of a hideous slaughter. But he is the hero here — not the bullies with the broad swords. *"This is the easier victory. Now is the triumph of the Cross, now open the door!"* he cries. "I command it. OPEN THE DOOR!"

Confucius once said, "He who conquers himself is the mightiest warrior."

"What were you yelling about?" asks my Vestry partner, coming up the steps after wrestling with the metal doors and wrenches. "Don't worry about it," I say. "I was just wondering if we really should bar the door."

May 29
"Well, I've wrestled with reality for 35 years, Doctor, and I'm happy to state I finally won out over it."
Elwood P. Dowd in Mary Chase's *Harvey*

Probably every one knows the story of the 1944 Pulitzer Prize-winning play about the six-foot tall "pooka" or humanlike rabbit buddy of the congenial Elwood P. Dowd. To everyone else, "Harvey" is invisible and possibly make-believe. Elwood's pretentious sister Veta wants to have Elwood committed to a sanitarium, but stops at having him injected with a serum that would make him "normal." In fact, Veta finally confesses that she has seen Harvey a time or two. And toward the play's end, she asks why Harvey chose to "speak to him in the first place? With the town full of people, why did he have to bother Elwood." So Harvey is real to her, even if she hates to admit it.

On May 29, 1987, Jay Herman came into our lives. He was Seth's imaginary friend, who was quite real to my son and became fairly existent to me as well. A three-year old Seth would bow very gallantly when Jay came into the costume shop, and he would introduce all the students to his wonderful companion. So I have lived with a creature very much like Harvey.

At one point in the play, Elwood says, "Years ago my mother used to say to me, she'd say, 'In this world, Elwood, you must be' — she always called me Elwood — 'In this world, Elwood, you must be oh so smart or oh so pleasant.' Well, for years I was smart. I recommend pleasant. You may quote me." He tells the doctor that he has fought with reality for three-and-a-half decades and that he is ecstatic that he finally triumphed over it.

The theme of fantasy versus reality was a favorite of mine when I was a student of literature in college and graduate school — and I even wrote a play about it. A pooka in Celtic folklore was a shape changer that often appeared as a goat, black horse, or **rabbit**! The spirit-like animal could be helpful or harmful, and like sprites, fairies, elves, and hobbits, pookas used to be very numerous in times when people were, like Elwood, more open to believing what they saw — maybe in their imaginations, maybe something more.

Though thoroughly grounded in reality, Seth always perceived things about life in a very spiritual manner. He somehow was able to balance "oh so smart" and "oh so pleasant." I find it significant that on the 26th anniversary of Jay Herman's arrival, Seth was ordained a transitional deacon in the Episcopal Church. And Jay was there, beaming with the rest of us!

May 30:

"I could do without my warhorse; I could drag about in a skirt; I could let the banners and the trumpets and the knights and soldiers pass me and leave me behind as they leave the other women, if only I could still hear the wind in the trees, the larks in the sunshine, the young lambs crying through the healthy frost, and the blessed, blessed church bells that send my angel voices floating to me on the wind. But without these things I cannot live; and by your wanting to take them away from me, or from any human creature, I know that your counsel is of the devil, and that mine is of God."
Joan in George Bernard Shaw's *Saint Joan*

Jeanne d'Arc, nicknamed "The Maid of Orléans," was burned at the stake today in 1431. She is an acclaimed hero in France, but she might serve as the patron saint of teenagers, because she was only 19 when she died, after living a full and adventuresome life.

Born at Domremy in north-east France of peasant lineage, she was a religious child who heard voices and had visions (speaking of yesterday's spirit-like creatures) of St. Michael, Saint Margaret, and Saint Catherine. She believed these saints urged her to support the uncrowned King of France, Charles VII to recover France from English domination in the Hundred Years War.

Charles dispatched Joan to lead an expedition to the besieged Orleans. According to legend, she wore white armor and brandished a banner with the insignia of the Trinity upon it. When the siege was lifted in nine days, other victories followed and Charles VII was quickly crowned at Reims. But on May 23, 1430, Joan was captured by the Burgundy forces and sold to the English. Later, she was put on trial by Bishop of Beauvais, convicted on May 30, 1431 of having "false and diabolical" hallucinations, and burned at the stake. Twenty-five years after her death, Pope Callixtus III authorized an inquisitorial court to investigate the trial, and seeing nothing to convict her, pronounced her innocent, and declared her a martyr.

George Bernard Shaw's play *Saint Joan* was published in 1924, just four years after she was finally declared a saint. She had been beatified in

1909. Shaw utilized actual records of her trial to create what is called his only tragedy. In a preface to the drama he stated:

"There are no villains in the piece. Crime, like disease, is not interesting: it is something to be done away with by general consent... It is what men do at their best, with good intentions, and what normal men and women find that they must and will do in spite of their intentions that really concern us."

Socrates wrote an essay called "No One Knowingly Does Evil," which posits that people do evil things out of ignorance, and not intent. He reflected that no one consciously decides to perpetrate an immoral deed, because such a choice damages the wrongdoer perhaps more than the person harmed. I am going to have to continue pondering this idea in my heart and mind, though I do believe a number os people go through life in a fog of unawareness.

When I read or hear onstage the beautiful passage quoted above beginning *"I could do without my warhorse..."* I realize that Shaw empathized greatly with this young woman of strong convictions. But I am not sure about there being no villains in the case of Jeanne d'Arc. Like Jesus, she was forced into a premature and torturous death, burning at the stake being one of the many brutal methods of killing that we mortals have devised for each other over the years.

Neither Jesus nor Joan experienced their suffering to tell us that such disregard for life is right and appropriate action. But perhaps through remembering on a day like today one such despicable act, at least some of us in the human race can move forward and listen to one another with open hearts, open minds, and open spirits. And let each other be.

May 31:
"What they could do with round here is a good war. What else can you expect with peace running wild all over the place? You know what the trouble with peace is? No organization."
Mother Courage in Bertolt Brecht's *Mother Courage and Her Children*

Some years, Memorial Day falls on May 31, when we remember our fallen in battle. Most mothers deplore war. Though the conflict in *Mother Courage and Her Children* concerns the Thirty Year War of the 1600s, this 1939 anti-war epic was written by German dramatist and poet Bertolt Brecht in protest of Nazism and Fascism.

Mother Courage concerns the picaresque fortunes of Anna Fierling, or "Mother Courage," a woman resolved to use the war for profit as she pulls a canteen cart through the countryside to trade with soldiers. On January 1, 1994, I saw an intimate production of the play at what was then the Cottesloe at London's National Theatre.

The epic structure of the twelve scenes reveal the shocking fright of war, as the audience comes to realize that when society has degenerated, such virtues as honor and decency, integrity and justness are abhorred. Mother Courage is created by Brecht to be an unsentimental figure, so even when her children, Swiss Cheese, Eilif, and Kattrin, are killed during the course of the battles, she is not seen as an empathetic hero.

"What they could do with round here is a good war. What else can you expect with peace running wild all over the place?" Theatre is built on conflict. Without strife and complication in a play, there would be very little drama to get excited about. Theatre mimics life to a great extent.

War continues to be a constant part of the makeup of this earth. Leaders of countries seem compelled to show other nations their strength, their superiority, their power and glory by invading, bombing, and annihilating. And many people, in their marriages or partnerships, professional life and friendships, are likewise drawn to conflict.

When my daughter Elin was at the University of Montevallo and engaged in the school's annual tradition of College Night (where two sides compete in athletic and dramatic events), she experienced an annual series of battles both on her Purple side, and between the Purples and the rival Golds. One year, the Purple playwright was charged with plagiarism, one year the Purple director quit, one year she was deviously left off the ballot for the leadership position, and every year there were squabbles and altercations with the Golds.

Much of the sparring was mild and done in the spirit of competition, but some of the episodes were gut-wrenching, and I would have much preferred to go through the melee myself rather than watch my daughter involved in such a war. And though she has become a stronger person, a more visionary leader, a more empathetic overseer of projects, surely there is a better way to do that than the raw rubbing of such encounters.

"You know what the trouble with peace is? No organization." When he returned to his native India in 1915, Mohandas Karamchand Gandhi did organize peace. Employing nonviolent civil disobedience, he was the

211

leader of the movement toward Indian independence after 200 years of British rule. He famously said that we should become the change we wish to see.

Fifty-six years later, Beatle John Lennon imagined the world being one, with everyone living in peace. That is the vision I would like to uphold. I am making a pledge to organize peace by becoming more and more conscious, recognizing my anger triggers, and loving myself and others by fighting less. How about you?

June 1:

In "June Is Bustin' Out All Over" from *Carousel*, Nettie and the Chorus sing about how the month of June is sprouting and shooting up everywhere. (Listen to the work online or from your library!)

Nettie and the Chorus in *Carousel* with music by Richard Rodgers and book and lyrics by Oscar Hammerstein II adapted from Ferenc Molnar's play Liliom

Richard Rodgers thought *Carousel*, with its lyrical and haunting music, his pinnacle musical. Set in a Maine coastal village toward the end of the nineteenth century, the story deals with misdeeds and redemption, revolving around Billy Bigelow who, much like Emily in *Our Town*, asks to go back in his life for one day. In this case, he wants to atone for his earthly faults and omissions. Billy had worked in a carnival as a carousel barker, and there met Julie. Their troubled romance and its consequences form the backdrop of this 1945 classic, called by *Time Magazine* the best musical of the twentieth century.

Today is June first and I feel it in my heart, see it in the ground and trees, smell it in the breeze: June really is suddenly surprising us with its appearance. I am so grateful for June, because my day lilies and gardenias, my wild and French hydrangeas, my perennial bed and freshly planted annuals — all are blooming abundantly.

June starts picnics and beach trips, school breaks and the neighborhood ice cream truck, lake floats and long fragrant afternoons that never seem to end, outdoor musical events and parks with carousels that ride children round and round in the fresh summer air. Oh, and weddings. Like Billy's and Julie's.

June is the month of marriages: some that will weather the storms of life and last 75 years, and some that will wilt immediately in the hot sun of real life. The *Huffington Post* reported recently that America's marriage rate is 31 marriages per 1,000 unmarried women. In contrast, during the 1920s, 92.3 percent was the average nationally. Some researchers estimate that at least half of all marriages dissolve into ruin and rupture. The median length for a marriage in the United States today is 11 years with ninety percent of all divorces being settled out of court.

Such statistics make me wonder why people get wedded in the first place. But oddly, I do think matrimony might be more apropos than ever before, because people don't have to tie the knot anymore: a couple can choose to take vows, and can choose to take them seriously. That fact contributes to the reason why many people wait to get married until their thirties or later these days, and why others choose legal partnerships.

In a civil marriage, love birds can forego the religious content. But in a religious wedding, two beloveds express their devotion before God, friends, and family. This declaration takes its place in a long, time-honored line of such oaths: millions of couples before this day have plighted their troth, and millions of couples after this day will do so as well.

So, now that June has leapt into our lives, surely I can find a wedding to attend soon, just to hear the lovely words (even if they don't stick): "to have and to hold from this day forward, for better for worse, for richer for poorer, in sickness and in health, to love and to cherish, until we are parted by death. This is my solemn vow."

June 2:
"They say that in your country If a butterfly [with an expression of fear] is caught by man, He'll pierce its heart with a needle, [with anguish] And then leave it to perish!"
Butterfly to Pinkerton in Giacomo Puccini's *Madama Butterfly*

I have been tending my garden, making sure there are plenty of flowers for the bees and the butterflies. This year, I have seeds to grow a refuge of lush milkweed for Monarchs on their pilgrimage to other lands. I have been instructed to cut off the top of the plant to create more stalks and leaves for the caterpillars to eat, but I haven't gotten that far yet.

Never would I pierce the heart of a butterfly or any creature with a needle. Even the thought of that makes me shudder. But in the opera *Madama Butterfly*, the miscreant Pinkerton responds to his new wife's fear about stabbing an insect, agreeing she may be right. "You're mine now. Ah! come, come you are mine now," he tells her as he catches and restrains her. This exchange takes place at the end of Act I as the two newlyweds embrace under the stars. Being the intuitive young woman she is, Butterfly feels a sudden sense of foreboding.

The nineteenth century story is the classic heart-breaker opera showing how a trusting woman's love is tragically betrayed. The American sailor, Benjamin Franklin Pinkerton on duty in Japan, marries a native 15-year-old named Cio-Cio-San, or Butterfly. She is blinded by love, disregarding family, friends, and faith. While she pins all hope upon their union, he regards their romance as a fleeting affair, with no intention of taking her home to the States. If you have never seen the opera, I won't spoil the ending now.

Its music makes me weep. Tears start falling at the overture and continue the whole way through, whether I am experiencing an actual performance, or my triple set of record albums. Part of the reason for my weeping is that the music is exquisitely emotional and expressive, and part is my enchanting memory of my graduate school experience when my then-husband designed the lights for *Madama Butterfly*.

Our scene designer at the University of North Carolina at Greensboro, Andreas Nomikos, was Greek, and he had created operatic scenery for La Scala, London, and many wondrous locations. He insisted that the scene at the end of the first act have stars in the sky. This feat was not as easy as it might sound to technicians today: it was spring and no one in town had any sort of Christmas tree lights in stock — nor was there an internet to search.

In the early 1970s, there was no internet, and no easy way to search long distance for such supplies. There were no strings of lights in the theatre store rooms, either. We finally thought to try our local Sears and through some sorcery, they were able to deliver a number of sets of lights (with white wiring — just what we needed!). The finished look of the show was spectacular. Another of the opera's special lighting effect is a morning scene when Butterfly is discovered still waiting for Pinkerton's arrival. During a long, six-minute instrumental interlude, the sun rises imperceptibly. And our crew pulled it off!

Each time the music plays, all of these adventures and more rush back to me. So though I would never attack a butterfly with a tiny sword, my own heart has certainly been pierced by the music and the magic of Puccini's Madama Butterfly.

June 3:

"My dear young man, don't take it too hard. Your work is ingenious. It's quality work. And there are simply too many notes, that's all. Just cut a few and it will be perfect."
Emperor Joseph II to Mozart in Peter Shaffer's *Amadeus*

And to this impertinently audacious comment, Mozart replies, "Which few did you have in mind, Majesty?" This remark by the emperor comes to mind so often. Sometimes the comment creeps into my thoughts sarcastically, like when someone on a news channel blabs on and on, and I think, "Simply too many words, that's all. Just cut a few..."

Sometimes the phrase sneaks in when I am overwhelmed as I look at a Julia Child recipe, and I declare, "Simply too many steps, that's all. Just cut a few..." Often in jest, when we hear Mozart or Bach, my partner Roger and I will marvel at a passage and then nod in jest, *"It's quality work. And there are simply too many notes, that's all. Just cut a few and it will be perfect."*

When I was in art classes, we students had to critique each other's work at the end of each day. Dealing with such evaluations of our own work and assessing others was a crucial part of our aesthetic education. The practice honed our analytical skills and appreciation. Appraisals were not always easy to hear or to voice; but the process was invaluable. Sometimes, we get so connected to our work that we cannot see how to improve it or transform it — we lack detachment, neutrality, or objectivity.

In the intimacy of an art class — where students began to trust each other over a day, a week, a semester, or a year — hearing my work assessed built courage and improved technique. So I was very used to this process when I got into theatre and had my theatre designs critiqued in public. I admit, it is a hard pill to swallow to see your name in the newspaper connected to a show that is reported as a flop, or failure. It is even more difficult when the critic's criticism is directly aimed at what you created in the production.

The process of working through this kind of artistic judgment, however, led me to what I might call an early phase of ego taming. My philosophy professor Dr. Hendrick van Tuyll, in our Aesthetics Class, urged us to understand that what you say about a piece of art, a concert, a ballet, or a play has a lot more to say about you, your knowledge, your taste, your experience than it does about the work itself.

So, if someone critiques a work of my art based on personal taste, her words are worth listening to only in the sense that I realize she really likes or dislikes what I have created. The art itself has not really been evaluated. On the other hand, if a critique comes from someone whose remarks are based on details about the art itself, from an informed point of view, and presented from an impartial critical perspective, I take what he says more seriously.

From my art and Aesthetics classes, I learned to see the value in great art, and even good art, without having to like it. For example, I am not overly fond of neoclassical art, but I appreciate it, and could list its wonderful points and delights for hours without ever referring to my own biases. So what do we think? Is Emperor Joseph a critic to be taken seriously? Just how many Mozart notes are too many?

June 4:
"How's he gonna find any water whin he won't even touch it? He don't wash, he don't bathe. The boy's dirt head to toe. I mean, Basil, he's not even baptized."
Luella in Jim Leonard, Jr.'s *The Diviners*

I couldn't resist using this quote and this story about water and Baptism on the anniversary of my own Christening. I don't remember it, since I was only four months and ten days old at the time, but I was initiated in grand style with water that my great-great-grandfather had brought back from the River Jordan from his travels thirty years before I was born. Yes, my family kept it!

In the spring of 1989, we produced Jim Leonard, Jr.'s *The Diviners* which takes place in Zion, Indiana in the 1930s, a Great Depression town in need of water and someone to care for their spiritual longings. It is a memory play, a slice-of-life drama, an ensemble piece culminating in a dramatic conclusion centering on Buddy Layman, a likable, mentally challenged teenager who almost drowned when he was a child.

This shock of nearly perishing in the water, together with his mother's death in the same accident, has made Buddy hydrophobic, terribly afraid of water. And time under the water without oxygen affected his brain. But, being a sort of idiot savant, Buddy is able to divine water and predict rain, and seeks a source of underground springs for a nearby farmer, Basil. Luella, Basil's wife doesn't think he will be successful. *"How's he gonna find any water whin he won't even touch it? He don't wash, he don't bathe. The boy's dirt head to toe. I mean, Basil, he's not even baptized."*

Early in the play, a disillusioned and formerly Bible-thumping reverend named C.C. Showers wanders into town and Buddy becomes friends with him. Wanting a new identity, C.C. has left his ministry and starts to work as a mechanic for Buddy's father. Because the village is without a minister, townspeople beg C.C. to preach for and pastor them, but he refuses. When Buddy's dirty skin fosters ring worm, Showers persuades the boy to get into the river to bathe. Townspeople see the preacher in the river with the unbaptized boy and assume it is the ceremony for which they have been waiting. In their excitement, they cause such a commotion, C.C. loses hold of the boy and Buddy does drown.

Everyone in this complexly poignant water play is divining for something: Buddy literally for water, Showers for a new identity, the townspeople for hope and for a spiritual guide. The experience of working on the show was extraordinary in several ways. We opened on a Thursday in early March and the next day, over five inches of rain fell, flooding highways and the street in front of Samford's campus, causing a number of patrons to skip our water show because of Nature's water show. By our Monday performance, there were warnings of icy flurries, and snow did fall a bit, but didn't close the streets.

Like the people of this play, I was certainly searching at this point in my life: Why did my marriage seem off the track? Why was I suddenly so drawn to the interviews of Bill Moyers with Joseph Campbell? Why did a routine pap smear call for cryosurgery to destroy a precancerous condition? Why did I never seem to have time for myself? Why did I feel like a snake just before it sheds it skin?

June 5:
"No arrow flies back to the string, the child does not return through the same passage that gave it birth."
The Praise-singer in Wole Soyinka's *Death and the King's Horseman*

When Samford University Theatre produced *Death and the King's Horseman* in 2000, it was directed by a dedicated African American student, and I designed the costumes. It is a poetic play filled with proverbs, and is derived from a true episode that occurred in British colonial Nigeria. According to tradition, when a king dies, his horseman, horse, and dog must also undergo a ritual death. After exuberantly living out his last day, the Horseman Elesin is blocked from the ceremonial suicide by the British colonial ruler. The intrusive breaking of this ritual

217

releases unsettling energy in the universe, so the entire community is disturbed and broken.

The people of the play speak using Yoruba proverbs. An interesting character is the Praise-singer who, like a Greek Chorus, acts as the Horseman's conscience and spiritual advisor. He warns Elesin about not fulfilling his duty by flinging to him this proverb: *"No arrow flies back to the string, the child does not return through the same passage that gave it birth."* Mythology would term this feeling as a desire to return to Paradise, and psychology would label it a wish to crawl back into the womb.

We all probably feel like retracting at times, pulling back, drawing in, hiding in our shells like turtles. Hit the snooze button and turn over. Hit the snooze button and totally cover our heads. Hit the snooze button and stay in bed all day. Running from instead of facing challenges. Staying involved with busywork instead of tackling the crucial deadline. Courting indecisiveness rather than pursuing our heart's passion.

I have made huge decisions numerous times in my life, and what I have learned is that some of my choices were perfect, some were so-so, and some were downright terrible. But I don't look back on the bad ones, or even the mediocre ones, with remorse or regret. If I could make choices based on what I will know in the future, I could be one-hundred percent flawless in my judgment on what to do all the time. And often, even without a crystal ball, I follow the right path.

For instance, my leaving the university, my teaching career, my designing profession, my students, the academic timetable, the yearly trips to London — saying goodbye to all of this was a painful choice I felt compelled to make. Sometimes, my feelings of sadness are as strong today as when I packed up 25 years of memories and memorabilia as I left. My life there served me very well, and I appreciate the times, the plays, the students, the friendships I had.

But if I had remained, I could not have grown into the person I was being called to become. The specter of a deteriorated marriage and design partnership cast a shadow too strong to foster any future blooming on my part. I knew what I was giving up, and it was a lot; but I also perceived that change was inevitable. I was aware that the end of that life had come, and I needed to let the curtain fall and move myself into a future free of the pain wraiths that haunted me. And though at times tempted, I have not gone back. *"No arrow flies back to the string..."*

June 6:

"Wonders are many, yet of all things is Man the most wonderful."
The Chorus in Sophocles's *Antigone*

Antigone was written by Sophocles near the end of his life and career. Along with other plays in his trilogy, *Oedipus the King* and *Oedipus at Colonus*, *Antigone* was produced in Athens, Greece. Though I designed *Oedipus Rex* and Jean Anouilh's *Antigone*, I have never had the pleasure of designing the Sophocles version except in classes.

In the play written around 441 BC, the Chorus sings this famous ode to human beings: *"Wonders are many, yet of all things is Man the most wonderful."* The Greek word "deinon" is hard to translate into English, because it can mean "wonderful" or "terrible." So the Chorus may be saying that humans are wondrous but at the same time strange and pitiable beings.

Nonetheless, the above translation by H. D. F. Kitto reminds me of Psalm 139, which was written about 600 years before the Greek tragedy. Verses 13 and 14 praise Yahweh, as the writer recalls "For you formed my inmost being. You knit me together in my mother's womb. I will give thanks to you, for I am fearfully and wonderfully made."

Each summer, when my daughter Elin, son Seth, and I direct a traditional summer camp at Winnataska, we choose a theme, and this year for our all-girls session, it was "I will thank you because I am marvelously made." We think it is an expression that young girls need to hear.

Some translations read, "marvelously made" or "wonderfully made" or "awesomely made." I must say that before contemplating this theme, I had rarely prayed every morning: "Thank you, God, for making me such a magnificent being!"

How many of us say that about ourselves — how many of us actually believe that we are amazing phenomenons? Do you think of yourself that way — like a work of art, carefully sculpted and created? Or do you worry about your weight or your intellectual abilities, your singing voice or your athletic prowess, your ability to swell your bank account or your knack for conversation?

Used to be, I did wonder sometimes about why I didn't have this talent or this physical attribute, a more detailed mind or less turbulent emotions. But I am coming to accept myself as "marvelously made." I no longer fret over my weight. I decided to do something about it and I am going to stay thinner for the rest of my life. I can't sing, but I can draw and paint. I am not the greatest marathon runner, but I love to walk every day.

I recently read a story about a Russian rabbi named Zusia. It is an inspiring story to me, and I hope you will benefit from it as well: One day some students were talking with him and the first said, "Rabbi Zusia, I am afraid that when I appear before the Holy One he will ask me, 'Why did you not have the faith of Abraham?'" A second student said, "I am afraid that when I am before the Holy One he will ask me, 'Why did you not have the patience of Job?'" Then a third student said, "Rabbi I am afraid that when I stand before the Holy One he will ask me, 'Why did you not have the courage of Moses?'" Then they all asked Zusia, "Rabbi, when you appear before the Holy One which question do you most fear?" Rabbi Zusia answered, "When I appear before the Holy One I'm afraid he'll ask me, 'Zusia, why were you not Zusia?'"

June 7:
"Doubt. Doubt can be a bond as powerful and sustaining as certainty."
Father Flynn in John Patrick Shanley's *Doubt*

I am right and you are wrong. This is in and that is out. He is evil and she is good. A dualistic approach to life makes us believe we have at least some control over life's uncertainties. But many people in this world cling to this dichotomy of light and darkness to create a false sense of security. Mystery, doubt, uncertainty: these are fearful words that put us into some sort of precarious fringe existence.

The play *Doubt* was originally produced off-Broadway in 2004 and moved to the Walter Kerr Theatre in 2005, running for 525 performances. Later made into a movie starring Philip Seymour Hoffman and Meryl Streep, the stunning work opens with Father Flynn's sermon in which he professes: *"Doubt. Doubt can be a bond as powerful and sustaining as certainty."* A cherished and progressive Catholic priest, Flynn becomes embroiled in conflict with the parochial school principal, Sister Aloysius. Austere and conservative, the sister harbors an extreme, dualistic view of the world.

After a dramatic series of events in which Sister Aloysius accuses the priest of misconduct, the audience itself is left in doubt at the curtain fall about what really happens behind the scenes of the play. Ever since becoming familiar with Shanley's work, I have contemplated doubt. In 2013, *The New Yorker* ran a story by Malcolm Gladwell on Albert O.

Hirschman, an economist who died in 2012. Hirschman and his brother-in-law, Eugenio Colorni (an Italian intellectual killed by Fascists during World War II) were extremely close and purported that doubt is the innovative factor that lets people see alternatives in the world.

Doubt, they believe, can activate, stimulate, impel, and inspire, because it frees humans from accepting at face value what they believe, from deferring to the limits placed on them, from being bound by ideological restrictions. Doubt can allow us to continue to search, create, open up vistas. What Hirschman and Colorni really desired to do was to "prove Hamlet wrong." They thought Hamlet should have been freed, rather than paralyzed, by his uncertainty.

Maybe Hamlet, but certainly Sister Aloysius is a perfectionist who looks at the world with black and white lenses, taking life and herself very seriously. Colorni wrote that courage calls for a person "to always be on guard against oneself." Once the sister has formulated a judgment about Father Flynn, she buys into it so deeply, she cannot give it up — despite many opinions, facts, and revelations to the contrary.

I have been reading books and listening to lectures by enlightened people so much lately that my last vestiges of a dualistic belief system are finally being broken down. My soul is ever searching, ever sifting through doctrines and wondering about that picture of the entire universe being built on opposing powers of good and evil. For recent months my Education for Ministry class has grappled with these concepts. I think we have come to agree with Father Flynn: *"Doubt. Doubt can be a bond as powerful and sustaining as certainty."*
June 8:
"High in heaven he shall be crowned;
Unto which place God bring us all thither
That we may live body and soul together.
Thereto help the Trinity,
Amen, say ye, for saint Charity."
Doctor in Anonymous's *Everyman*

The Day of Pentecost has come! In our parish, many of us dress in red, hang our festive red banners, sling the incense thurible, sing some grand old hymns, eat cake for the birthday of the church, and say goodbye to the 50-day Easter season. Before we knew better, we used to release red helium-filled balloons thither heavenward after the service.

I love this reference at the very end of the medieval play Everyman that every one of us is going "thither" into Heaven so that we can all live with our bodies and our souls together helping the Trinity. This reference to "thither" is the second for me in as many weeks. The word, which was already being used before the twelfth century, means "going to or toward a specific place." It is sadly not used much nowadays.

My ideas about Heaven have been growing and shifting thither over the last couple of years. When I was a child, I believed the hereafter consisted of a place in the clouds, paved with golden stones, and filled with angels and all our dead friends and family members floating about in eternal joy. As I matured, Heaven became a state of mind here on earth, a high and holy centering of life capturing the sacred, while Hell was the lowest Underworld the imagination could muster. But was there a Heaven after death?

As I began studying the Enneagram, and going through training, Dr. Raymond Moody briefly joined our staff. Dr. Moody is the leading authority on the "near-death experience," and coined that phrase in the late seventies.

Classically and scientifically trained, Raymond has degrees in medicine and philosophy. He told us that he did not grow up in a religious family, because his father was a surgeon who had a typical scientific outlook. So though Raymond has been interviewing people and researching their near-death experiences since 1965, he wasn't sure what to believe. The individuals he talked to were genuine, but felt his job was to record what they said, not to be convinced by them.

However, several years ago, Raymond gave a lecture and an artist came up afterward saying the usual, "I've never told this to anyone before, but..." The fellow had lost both legs in a horrific car crash that instantly killed his wife. The night of the accident, he went into emergency surgery, and died but was resuscitated. While "out," the artist saw his dead wife and family members who encouraged him to go back. Raymond advised him to write the story, and as he was about to publish his book, the artist realized he had mentioned the doctor who saved his life by name, but had never told him his story.

The man invited his world-renowned surgeon to lunch to relate his experience and his book. To his surprise, the doctor said he hadn't planned on ever telling anyone, but he knew his patient wasn't going to die that night. In the operating room, an entire, different dimension opened up, and the doctor also encountered the man's experiences, including seeing his dead wife and family encouraging him to live.

When Moody heard about this shared episode, he knew that two people could not have come up with the same story, so he now wonders about "heaven." Is rational proof of an afterlife possible? He now he believes it is within the realm of possibility. I am glad I have worked with Raymond, and perhaps someday I will go thither heavenward with him, body and soul, to help the Trinity!

June 9:

In "Anything Goes" from *Anything Goes*, Reno, Passengers and Crew sing about how today, all things are acceptable in behavior, fashion, or speech. (Listen to the work online or from your library!)

Reno, Passengers and Crew in *Anything Goes* with music and lyrics by Cole Porter and original book by Guy Bolton and PG Wodehouse, revised by Howard Lindsay and Russel Crouse

I know I talked about my love for Cole Porter on May 26, but he was born this day in 1891 to a wealthy family in Indiana — so I can hardly pass up this occasion. He thwarted the dreams of his authoritarian grandfather by following his bliss and becoming a musician and composer. Even though he was classically trained, he loved theatre and wrote a number of works for the stage.

For people living through the 1930s and '40s in America, Porter's music defined their era. At the same time sophisticated and optimistic, his tunes had a style of their own. His *Associated Press* obituary stated that, "Mr. Porter wrote the lyrics and music for his songs, and to both he brought such an individuality of style that a genre known as 'the Cole Porter song' became recognized. The hallmarks of a typical Porter song were lyrics that were urbane or witty and a melody with a sinuous, brooding quality."

Anything Goes, a classic hummable musical produced in 1934, delighted audiences years before *Oklahoma* brought a serious side to Broadway. The song of the same "Anything Goes" name is sometimes called the American anthem to naughtiness. It extols unfettering from social standards, and humorously exalts the virtues of such risqué behavior as spouting four-letter words, octogenarian romance, nudist parties, and divorce.

Somehow the bawdy behavior of the song (the scandalous peep at hosiery, for instance) seems a bit tame today when an awful lot of people don't care how foul their language gets, how revealing their clothes, how misinformed their opinions, how objectionable their aggression, how selfish their actions and motivations. Oh, and who even wears stockings? On the other hand, even now Americans lift an eyebrow at deviant behavior. Though our Constitution's First Amendment gives us freedom of speech, still our Puritan roots cause us to bristle at things that offend.

Anything Goes actually starts with words about how things have changed in America since the Pilgrims landed. And the song unfolds to say times are crazy with virtue being wicked, dark being light, and even daytime and evening having swapped places. When I was in college during what some critics call the "anything-goes-1960s," some of us did offend our elders by questioning authority, doubting bureaucracy, opposing the status quo, and deriding the American Dream. Though the greatest disturbance at my university was a brief food strike, other students in the country burned flags, pushed their presidents out of administration buildings, confronted police officers, and stormed buildings until campuses looked a bit like war scenes in *Les Misérables*.

John Lennon and his music spoke to my age as Porter did to his. Lennon once put our era into perspective, conceding, "The thing the sixties did was to show us the possibilities and the responsibility that we all had. It wasn't the answer. It just gave us a glimpse of the possibility." Some of the violence and lack of principles in the '60s was disturbing, but the liberal energy hastened such "possibilities" as civil rights, gender equality, a call for peace in Vietnam, and a reckoning of political, economic, and life priorities. It didn't quite happen, but the anything we wanted to go was bigotry, discrimination, and hate.

June 10:
"Abby: You mean the lightning? Are you really going to catch the lightning?
Ben: Someday... if I keep trying, Abby. Someday I'll send this kite up and up
and up... and I'll capture it. Then we can start to learn the secrets of electricity!"
Characters in Faye Parker's *Young Ben: Franklin's Fight for Freedom*

Today, in 1752, Ben Franklin carried out his kite experiment during a thunderstorm in which he collected a charge in a Leyden jar to demonstrate the electrical nature of lightning. In 1975 as a prelude to the huge celebrations of the American Bicentennial commemorating the Revolution and the colonists' break with Great Britain, Birmingham Children's Theatre produced this young people's play about Ben Franklin.

The story of Franklin's involvement in America's fight for freedom certainly started when he was a young boy, and that thrilled me when I was in the fifth grade and began to read juvenile biographies of interesting people. This patriot was born on January 17, 1706, on Milk Street in Boston Massachusetts. One of ten children of Josiah Franklin and his second wife Abiah Folger, Ben's father wanted him to be trained as a clergyman, but the family could only afford to send him to school for a couple of years.

I yearned to be like Ben who was sent off at age 12 to be an apprentice to his older brother James at a printing shop. That was just a few years older than I was at the time! He loved to read, as I did, and this appreciation for learning was enhanced by his printing trade. When Ben was only 15, James started printing his own newspaper, the first really independent publication for the colonies, the *New-England Courant.*

Franklin was a printer, a statesman, a patriot, an author, a humorist, a diplomat, a musician, a political cartoonist, a philosopher. And the number and variety of his inventions were phenomenal: bifocals, a stove, lightning rod, a long-arm reaching device, the glass armonica, the odometer, a catheter, swim fins. He was full of life and love and jests, and died at a good age of 84.

Franklin was a favorite character of mine in the musical *1776!* and when I worked at the American Village historic learning center. Franklin conducted his kite-flying experiment when he was an adult, but he and Abby speak of as children in the play. *"Someday I'll send this kite up and up and up... and I'll capture it."* Several times at the Village, we reenacted the kite flying, thankfully without the lightning.

But one Fourth of July at the Village, we experienced a huge summer storm, complete with torrential rain, rolling thunder, and slashes of lightning. We herded all of our thousands of visitors into the buildings to safely wait out the tempest.

Thirty minutes after the last lightning strike, we began to let a few people wander about, but a stray bolt of lightning flashed down from a cloud and struck the sound system and a patron. He was eventually fine, but I was about 20 feet away from him, facing away, when the lightning made contact with the earth. I felt as if I actually caught the lightning.

The hair on the back of my head stood out, my spine felt seared in a streak, and I ambled about for a half hour — and later remembered nothing of the stroll.

Since then, I am very respectful of lightning. Like Franklin, I have started *"to learn the secrets of electricity"* and one of them is that it can be very dangerous!

June 11:
"That love is childish which consists in words."
Iarbus in Christopher Marlowe's, *Dido, Queen of Carthage*, Act III, Scene 1

Unfortunately, the only Christopher Marlowe play I have ever been part of was *The Tragical History of Doctor Faustus*, but in my English studies in graduate school, I read all of his plays for one course. His dramatic work *Dido*, based on Virgil's *Aeneid*, tells the heartbreaking tale of the Queen of Carthage. She has a wonderful suitor, Iarbus, but the gods lead her into a fruitless pursuit of Aeneas.

At the close of the action, she fools Iarbas into thinking she is building a fire as a "private sacrifice to cure my mind that melts for unkind love." But after cursing Aeneas' sons — and their sons — she throws herself onto what becomes a funeral pyre and her appalled lover, Iarbas kills himself as well.

Midway in the play, Iarbus tells Dido *"That love is childish which consists in words,"* and the phrase makes me recall a study we had at church on Love and its various meanings. One section of the class, taught by our priest's wife, a psychologist, impressed upon us that love is really a verb, and what I do matters maybe even more than what I say.

That doesn't mean I should never tell people that I love them, because that is important, too. Also, the more I talk about loving someone, the more I begin to feel that I really do. So love is about verbalizing and activity rather than emotion. If I act as if I love someone, a wayward child for instance, eventually I will start to love him.

Some wisdom teachers push the concept even further by asserting that love is not as much what we say, feel, or do, but more who or what we are. Love is inside us, around us, below us, beside us if we just clue into the benevolence of the Universe.

In *The Story of a Soul*, the autobiography of Therese of Lisieux, the saint tells a wonderful tale to illustrate this idea. She said that a certain nun irritated her in every possible way, but determining not to give into natural antipathy, she told herself "that sentiments of charity were not enough; they must find expression, and I set myself to treat her as if I loved her best of all."

Every time they met, Theresa very earnestly offered up a devotion of the nun's virtues and merits to God. But even more, she did everything she possibly could for the sister. "And when tempted to answer sharply I hastened to give her a friendly smile, and talk about something else." Finally, one day, the nun said radiantly to Theresa, "What do you find so attractive in me? Whenever we meet you give me such a gracious smile."

Theresa said that she inwardly realized that what captivated her was "Jesus hidden in the depths of her soul, Jesus who makes attractive even what is most bitter." Hindus say, "Namaste" or "I bow to you, for I see the Divine reflected in you." The other day a man got furious at me when I tried to merge into his lane on the freeway. He even came up beside me honking his horn. Remembering Theresa and "Namaste," I gave the driver a sign of blessing instead of the single finger I really wanted to shoot off. He looked deeply perplexed, but calmed down. Love. Love my neighbor. Show that love to my neighbor. Be that love to my neighbor. Maybe I am finally beginning to get it...

June 12:
"This miry Slough is such a place as cannot be mended; it is the descent whither the scum and filth that attends conviction for sin doth continually run, and therefore is it called the Slough of Despond."
The character "Help" in a stage adaptation of John Bunyan's *The Pilgrim's Progress*

When I read Bunyan's Pilgrim's Progress both in undergraduate and graduate schools, and then designed costumes for Tom Key's *Pilgrim* in the late 1970s, I was fascinated with the idea of a Slough of Despond, a swamp of despair. In the allegory, the main character "Christian" descends into this swamp with the heaviness of his sins and the burden of his guilt for them.

First faced with the Slough of Despond, I wondered how to pronounce it. Is the "gh" an "f" sound or is it silent? It is silent. And is the "ou" a long "o," a double "oo," or an "uh" sound? None of these, it is "ow" as in ouch! Maybe it is almost the Slaw of Despond, a miry place that cannot be restored, all mingled with lost conditions and fears, doubts and discouragements that look a bit like chopped cabbages and carrots that can never be put back together again.

Bunyan was sure to have seen similar bogs in places near his Bedfordshire home, like the Squitch Fen or the Souls' Slough. However, his envisioned marsh is not a real-life natural wetland, but a place of spiritual desperation, of depression, of hopelessness, and of misery, due to sin and self-reproach. "Sin" is a word that modern folk wish to erase, believing the notion to be quaint, demeaning even. Certainly doctrine about sin and some religious leaders have browbeaten and tyrannized humans throughout history, so it is no wonder that some people today want to reject not only the concept of sin, but even places of worship.

I wonder about the idea of sin, and I have doubts and misgivings about what it has historically meant. Must people, like Christian in *Pilgrim's Progress*, really feel so encumbered with sin that they slip into a morass of despondency? Must we fret and worry about our lack of judgment and our tendency to repeat bad habits? No, I think not.

But I am pretty sure we need not throw out the concept. One of my former priests used to say that sin is really an estrangement from God, or our Life Force. I've heard sin described as "missing the target." I need to practice, and at least hold my bow in the direction of the bull's eye! Sin is indulging my Ego Self in the belief that I am in charge, I am all powerful, I am the Creator, and all the world revolves around me.

For me, it is helpful to know that all world religions have some sort of confession of faults. When I can remember that all people fail, we all hurt each other in large and small ways, we all harm our planet, we all reject the Holy, then I can both understand that this is what sin is, and remember that God's grace and forgiveness is also for all of us.

In the Episcopal service of Holy Eucharist, we make a communal confession of our offenses by telling God we have sinned "in thought, word, and deed, by what we have done, and by what we have left undone." Out loud, we together confess our individual and corporate sins and concede that we — all of us — could benefit by renewing our lives. And together, we are all forgiven — those present with me, and also everyone on our huge earth and beyond.

June 13:
"Courage, friend. You're a stranger in a strange land, you poor man."
Chorus in Sophocles's, *Oedipus at Colonus*

Early in the play *Oedipus at Colonus* (written around 441 BC), Oedipus is struggling with his blindness and his daughter Antigone says, "Come, father. Follow me. This way. Follow me with your blind feet." And the Chorus supports him, and yet reminds him of his plight: he is in a foreign land, and he knows no one. *"You're a stranger in a strange land, you poor man."*

Likewise, Moses, when he flees the Pharaoh in Egypt, ends up in Midian and helps the seven daughters of a priest water their flock of sheep amidst some unruly shepherds. The father is so grateful that he asks Moses to live with them, and he gives him his daughter Zipporah in marriage. She bears Moses a son, and he names the boy Gershom ("a sojourner there"), for he said, "I have been a stranger in a strange land." Exodus predated Sophocles's work by about 1,000 years, so the concept of being an alien or sojourner in another country is an old idea.

Over the last few years, Americans have heatedly and repeatedly debated immigration. Over the past half a century, the immigrant population in the United States has burgeoned. In 1960, when I was 10-years old, there were 9.7 million foreign-born people residing in America, but today the number is over 40 million.

Just recently, hundreds of unaccompanied children from Central America found their way through Mexico to cross over into the United States, overwhelming border authorities. The young people are mostly fleeing El Salvador, Guatemala, and Honduras, where long-standing poverty and escalating violence, drug wars, and gang activity are becoming unbearable. Most of them are determined to find safety in America despite the danger of rape, human trafficking, and death during their journey north.

I know this has been a huge strain on border patrols, that illegalities are involved, and that resources are exhausted; but these kids are five- to 14-years old, and have journeyed dangerous miles to our country, hoping to reunite with relatives here. My granddaughter will turn five next month. I cannot imagine her traveling with other children and young teenagers for 1,500 miles with nothing more than a prayer of meeting up with family members. No money, no food, no adult supervision, no proper identification. But maybe they have a hope of more than survival.

My son Seth went to Sewanee with three of the Lost Boys of Sudan. During the Second Sudanese War (1983 to 2005), they — with over 20,000 boys between the ages of seven and 17 — were displaced and orphaned, and they traveled enormous distances in an expansive African wilderness to escape the fighting. They had an amazing devotion to education.

In fact, they told the story of how they were tending sheep in the fields and hid when attackers killed everyone else in their villages. Then, they escaped, and as they left home, they grasped precious books. The boys used the volumes to teach each other in the years they roamed the wilds. One of the "boys" who graduated with Seth in 2007, returned to South Sudan in 2011 to help establish a new nation. Though these Lost Boys started out in America as strangers *"in a strange land,"* they ended up precious friends and beloved scholars.

June 14:
"Work never hurt anyone. It's good for them. But if you're going to work, work hard. King Solomon had the right idea about work. 'Whatever thy hand findest to do,' Solomon said, 'do thy doggonedest.'"
Clarence Day (Father) in Howard Lindsay and Russell Crouse *Life with Father*

Even though I quoted *Life with Father* before, it is around the celebration of Father's Day, and Clarence Day is such a comical patriarch. The more tyrannical and outrageous he acts, the more lovable he becomes. When he quotes historical figures like Solomon, he puts absurdly preposterous words in their mouths.

Work actually hurts someone every day: back discomfort from lifting, neck pains from computer work, headaches from overloads, flu or sniffles from fellow workers, injured fingers from hand tools. But Father is right that hard work can be a satisfying way to occupy time.

I enjoy work. In fact, I can find pleasure in whatever I am doing, whether dusting the furniture or creating a graphic for a publication, interviewing possible donors for my nonprofit or even applying for a grant online. And I love to exert myself in the yard.

My uncle Ham Perkins was a longtime builder in Birmingham, developing many subdivisions and homes in the wealthier sections of town. He had a supervisor named Roosevelt who oversaw all the landscaping, gardening, and yard maintenance at some of his many holdings. One summer, my cousin, Ham's son, worked with Roosevelt and he learned a life lesson from him.

The crew would toil all day long at some homs for sale or at an apartment complex, sweating in the muggy Birmingham heat, caking themselves with the red mud of the Alabama earth. Here, all day in the summer is from about 7:00 in the morning till 7:00 at night. For the first few days, Boo pushed himself until he was exhausted and almost sick. Roosevelt, observing his pattern, enlightened him with the words, "Son, the best way to tackle a big job like this is to work a while, and then rest a while. Then, we come back and do the polishing."

I heard this sagacious suggestion over 50 years ago, but every time I work in the yard, I still think of Roosevelt's wisdom. I begin by working extremely hard, doing my "doggonedest," so Clarence Day would approve. After an hour or two, I take a break, drink some water, and cool off. Then I polish. In terms of yard labor, that might mean picking up sticks or pine cones, raking a little mulch around newly planted herbs, trimming a few dead branches, or watering.

The polishing makes each little vegetable patch or flower bed look cultivated and well-cared for. And the hard work at the beginning is manageable because the break can come at any time and the polishing is easy and fun.

June 15:
"The flame of friendship ought to burn brightest in matters of the most concern."
Arsino in Molière's *The Misanthrope*, Act III, Scene 5

The Misanthrope, an oft-quoted play by Molière, is filled with wit and wisdom, satirizing the flaws and foibles — and at the same time, upholding the good qualities — of human nature and society. I resonate with the idea that, *"The flame of friendship ought to burn brightest in matters of the most concern."*

We have just ended our year of Education for Ministry, which is a program of theological training, mainly for lay people and their ministries, administered by The University of the South (Sewanee) School of Theology. I am finishing my second of four years of intense reading and discussion. Our eight-member class meets weekly from September through early June on Tuesday nights for about three hours.

To start our session, we light a candle to invite the presence of the Holy Spirit to be with us in our reflections, and then we "check in" with each other to see how our week has gone. Though the primary focus of EfM is explore the Christian faith through researching the Old and New

Testaments, Church history, and theology, we also learn to care for each other. Reflecting on and connecting faith with life experiences encourages our spiritual growth, but sometimes it is a rough ride. So we check in each week so that we can leave our daily burdens and joys at the doorway in order to create room for our germination, growing, and sprouting.

In our check in, we have created an open, supportive, and nurturing environment that promotes mutual interactive care and ever deepening friendships. When I hear about a fellow student's funny and painful insights into caring for a 90-year old father, or another's midnight trip to the emergency room with a spouse experiencing an excruciating headache, or another's heartbreak with the loss at a trial, or another's intriguing incident with a powerful piece of art, then I have lived part of their life with them.

I have heard stories of hysterical funerals and of tragic graduations, the bullying of gay members and the rupture of heterosexual relationships, the trauma of celebrations and the delight of minor daily drudgeries. My classmates have become vulnerable and courageous, forthcoming and transparent. We have shared and admitted, revealed and owned up, disclosed and divulged our lives to each other.

I have walked in their shoes. I can experience their challenges and their joys. I understand where they are coming from. I can release my judgments about them. I can appreciate their points of view. I can empathize with how they are living their lives. I can begin to see how we humans really are the same deep down; how we all really are one and the same. And the flame of friendship really has begun to burn brightest as we share what most concerns us each week.

June 16:
"My valour is certainly going, it is sneaking off! I feel it oozing out as it were, at the palms of my hands!"
Acres in Richard Brinsley Sheridan's *The Rivals*, Act V, Scene 2

I am a fan of bravery and daring fearlessness. But sometimes stoutheartedness is hard to keep hold of, as Acres reveals in *The Rivals*. It slips away furtively, right when I need it the most, dripping from my fingertips and leaving me in a cold sweat.

I was going to call that businessman about being on my advisory council, but when I found his number, finally, I realized I had so many other things to do. Not really! I chickened out. Same with speaking up in that meeting to the person who always monopolizes the time. Same with sending that letter to my old friend asking her forgiveness for my misdoings in front of a high school icy beverage stand.

Courage was the quality the Cowardly Lion in *The Wizard of Oz* hoped to gain from the old charlatan. When Dorothy and her new pals the Scarecrow and the Tin Man come across the Cowardly Lion, they think he is full of mettle. But after Dorothy smacks his nose for bullying her little dog Toto, the Lion weeps and frets.

"Why, you're nothing but a great big coward!" Dorothy tells him, and he agrees. "You're right, I am a coward! I haven't any courage at all! I even scare myself."

The Cowardly Lion learns over the course of their adventures that he has spirit and boldness deep down inside him after all, and comes to understand that courage means taking action even when you are afraid. There is a reason the Lion is the King of the Forest! The Wizard gives him a medal as an outward and visible sign of this inward truth. Like the Lion, many people are paralyzed by fear, and by failing to live up to their own importance and significance. As Marianne Williamson has said, "It is our light not our darkness that most frightens us. Our deepest fear is not that we are inadequate. Our deepest fear is that we are powerful beyond measure. It is our light not our darkness that most frightens us."

Valor really is a choice we make, just like a lot of things in life. In 1996, I read *Man's Search for Meaning* by Viktor E. Frankl, an Auschwitz concentration camp survivor. In it, I learned his incredible theory that, "Between stimulus and response there is a space. In that space is our power to choose our response. In our response lies our growth and our freedom." From that time forward, I have pondered the incredible human spirit of people like Frankl who lived through such horror with valor — and came out of it with hope and a buoyant spirit.

Valor, be done with your sneaking off and oozing away! Today, I am deciding to choose backbone and grit.
June 17:
"Oh, you weak, beautiful people who give up with such grace. What you need is someone to take hold of you — gently, with love, and hand your life back to you, like something gold you let go of — I do love you, Brick, I do."
Margaret (Maggie the cat) in Tennessee Williams's *Cat on a Hot Tin Roof.*

I once saw production of this play at our Virginia Samford Theatre directed by a good friend, Jack Mann. As I was fiddling with my wallet to pay for my tickets, Jack came up beside me, forced my wallet back into my purse and escorted me to my seat. "You do enough for theatre in Birmingham," he said, "that you are going to be treated to this play today!" And what an absolutely beautiful treat it was.

This quoted line just before the final curtain of *Cat on a Hot Tin Roof* was changed in the original Broadway show, but quoted above as restored by the playwright. To make the bleak ending a little more palatable for audiences, the director, Elia Kazan asked Tennessee Williams to soften and re-craft the third act. Maggie fibs telling Big Daddy she is pregnant. In this last scene, she invites Brick, her dissipated and impotent ex-athlete husband, to go to bed with her "to make that lie come true."

Kazan wanted to show that the marriage had some real affection, so the audience would have more empathy for both Maggie and Brick . Williams's first and later revised versions end with a grating conversation between the alcoholic husband and the unfulfilled wife that makes more sense than Kazan's fiddling. On the surface, the man's rejection concerns remorse over the suicide of Skipper, Brick's old friend. But what Brick manages to keep hidden below the floorboards is the real dilemma: his and Skipper's dormant homosexuality.

Lying, or "mendacity" as it is called in the play, is a major theme in *Cat on a Hot Tin Roof*. Except for Brick, the family lies to Big Daddy about the his incurable cancer; Gooper and Mae are deceptive in trying to acquire the estate when he dies; Maggie creates a fabrication about pregnancy; Brick exiles his homosexuality to an alcoholic state. In fact, the last line of the play as restored by Williams is a repeated phrase that Big Daddy has said to Big Mama earlier. Maggie claims, *"I do love you, Brick, I do,"* to which Brick answers, "Wouldn't it be funny if that were true?"

The specifics of the lies (illness, greed, desire, alcoholism, sexual orientation) in *Cat on a Hot Tin Roof* are not as important as the universal truth that we conceal our innermost being, our most sincere wants and desires (our true selves) from the people we might be most truthful and vulnerable with: our relatives. So many people, in this play and in reality, are so ardent about creating the idyllic illusion of a perfect life that they never actually live the life they have.

The mendacities they create to deal with imperfection cause disease, burgeoning misdeeds, and self-medication to the point that they are numb to sadness and joy alike. Maggie might actually be on to something when she utters her last line, *"Oh, you weak, beautiful people who give up with such grace. What you need is someone to take hold of you – gently, with love, and hand your life back to you, like something gold you let go of..."*

June 18:
"A certain Greek told the Emperor Augustus, as an axiom as useful as it was true, that when any accident puts us in a rage, we should, first of all, repeat the alphabet; so that in the interval our anger may abate, and we may do nothing that we ought not to do."
Arnolphe (aside) in Molière's, *School for Wives*

One year, I studied Molière's *School for Wives* in preparation for designing the costumes, but we decided on another show. The play was first performed the day after Christmas in 1662 at the Palais Royal in Paris. Never one to shy away from daring subject matters, Molière placed in the center of the comedy the 42-year old Arnolphe who wants to groom his very young and guileless ward to be the wife who will never cuckold him.

So Arnolphe says in this aside to the audience that he is being cool-headed about his plan for the young lady, Agnès. He may be conniving and clumsy in the beginning of the play, and frustrated and disappointed in the end, but he is civil. If only we could all follow this "certain Greek's" advice and recite the alphabet when we are upset *"so that in the interval our anger may abate, and we may do nothing that we ought not to do."* Etiquette is a customary code of polite behavior, either in society at large, or among members of a certain group, and it delineates expectations for social behavior according to conventional norms.

The summer before I went to work at The American Village, a fellow staff member, and I went to Colonial Williamsburg for research, and I was so very impressed with the behavior of the crowds at the landmark. Because the site's historical characters who bring the stories of America to life are so steeped in the manners of the eighteenth century, visitors "catch" that civility and act in a more genteel way than I have seen tourists behave elsewhere.

As we created our programming for the Village, we incorporated eighteenth century manners in our character and vignettes. Similar to this quote from *School for Wives*, Thomas Jefferson was famous for saying, "When angry count to ten before you speak. If very angry, count to one hundred." And George Washington, before the age of 16, transcribed *Rules of Civility & Decent Behaviour In Company and Conversation*, a booklet filled with proper conduct. Some of his 110 entries, which can be found on the Colonial Williamsburg website, include:

- Every Action done in Company, ought to be with Some Sign of Respect, to those that are Present.
- Shew Nothing to your Freind that may affright him.
- Let your Countenance be pleasant but in Serious Matters Somewhat grave.
- Speak not Evil of the absent for it is unjust.

While some people might look at Washington's list and think it rather quaint, civility is still important. Maybe more than ever, we need manner instruction in our rapidly changing twenty-first century, because in social and professional circles, norms do make a difference. And you can find new rule books that are filled with proper ways to make cellular phone calls, to create propriety in the workplace, to leave messages on answering devices, and to decipher how to address envelopes to unmarried couples. And most importantly, someone should include in their list of manners Arnolphe's advice to "repeat the alphabet" when we are in a rage. That suggestion is pertinent counsel, particularly in a section for automobile driving decorum.

June 20:

"That light we see is burning in my hall.
How far that little candle throws his beams!
So shines a good deed in a naughty world."
Portia in William Shakespeare's, *The Merchant of Venice*, Act V, Scene 1

Shakespeare might be happy about the fact that next-door to the reconstruction of his Elizabethan-style open-air Globe playhouse on the Thames in London, there is a new indoor venue. And, the staff uses hundreds and hundred of candles flickering in chandeliers and sconces rather than electric lights in an attempt to give audiences an idea of what theatre was like 400 years ago.

I have actually experienced an experimental one-man show that was lit by one candle, and it was extraordinary how much we spectators could see once our eyes got accustomed to the dimmer-than-expected performance. *"How far that little candle throws his beams!"*

I am getting ready today and tomorrow to go out thirty miles east of Birmingham to direct a traditional summer camp at Winnataska, along with my daughter Elin and son Seth. Elin tells the story of the first time she graduated from being on the college staff to assisting me in the actual direction of a camp. Since she had worked in outdoors some of the time she was on staff, she volunteered to hike about a mile with the campers up to an overnight campout site. Once there, everyone realized they were missing some supplies, so Elin and a male staff member volunteered to go back to the main camp to get them.

Always prepared, she had a flashlight. The night was wonderful. Just cool enough for a long-sleeved t-shirt, and no moon, so many stars were visible. About one-third of the hike is in open pasture and the rest is on a wide, tree-covered trail. On the way down the hill, they encountered some counselors who needed a flashlight to make it to the campsite, so Elin loaned them hers.

"Bright idea (pardon the pun)," she says, "but now my friend and I have no light whatsoever. It was dark. I mean pitch black, after we got a little further onto the trail. I asked my friend if we should call the leaders back and rethink our plan. I was told that I was acting old and should lighten up (ha ha) a bit. We decided to let our eyes adjust to the dark. Slowly they did, and the gravel on the trail stood out ever so slightly from the brush lining the sides."

As they made their way slowly down the hill to the main camp, Elin became surer of herself and actually enjoyed the trek. With her sense of sight removed, the tree frogs croaked louder, the pine needles smelled fresher, and the night breeze felt cooler on her face. She and her friend talked much more deeply than they might have in a normal brightly lit conversation. Since then, although they seldom see each other, their friendship has been enriched; all from doing something together that neither of them may have done alone.

She often thinks about this experience when she has a difficult task facing her, realizing that the dark days are much like that dark trail. She recalls, "I've come to camp since I was nine years old. I've walked that trail many times before, but the darkness on that trail that night made something so familiar different, almost daunting. Isn't it odd how the removal of one sense can lead to fear, a fear of the unknown. But that you can overcome it when walking beside another."

June 21:

"Oh, sisters, sisters!
I want to show you
where a sunbeam
has entered the cloister!
Look where it falls,
there, there among the greenery!
The sunlight is upon the sweet sedge!
So begin the three evenings
of the golden fountain!"
Sister Genevieve in Giacomo Puccini's *Suor Angelica* with a libretto by
Giovacchino Forzano

Suor (or Sister) Angelica is a one-act opera by Giacomo Puccini that
we did a couple of times while I was designing costumes for Samford
University. The melodic piece tells the sad tale of Angelica who was sent
to a convent in punishment for having an illegitimate child. During the
course of the opera, her feelings of guilt and pain dealing with her child's
life and death are exposed. Though most of the opera is fairly sad, in this
scene, Sister Angelica has set about hoeing and watering the flowers.
Sister Genevieve calls attention to the way the light is hitting the sedge as
it does annually for just a short three evenings in May.

When first reading *The Hobbit*, I became attuned to the idea that
light shines in varying manners at different times of the year — in fact,
daily sunlight shines in changing ways. In Chapter 11 of Tolkien's work
about Middle Earth, the dwarves and Bilbo reach the Front Gate of the
Lonely Mountain and see the ruins of the city of Dale. At first, the
dwarves are discouraged, but soon bang about noisily attempting to force
the door open. As they bluster, the unassuming hobbit, Bilbo sees a
thrush nip a snail, and when he knocks it against the stone floor, Bilbo
remembers that they should be looking for moon-runes and a secret door.

Bilbo yells for his companions, and they all gaze amazed as a ray
of the setting sun glints across the wall, whereupon the stone breaks open.
At this time and this only, the light discloses a keyhole — and then,
Thorin's key opens the door.

Ever since reading that passage, I have looked at light differently.
My bedroom windows face due east, looking out over a valley and a small
mountain range beyond. The sun rises right in front of my bed every
morning. But it moves from left to right and then back again as the earth
journeys around our fiery orb. To me, the sun is like an actor finding the

right spot upon the stage, and ever moving to a better one. But in this case, the actor is also the light!

Today, June 21 is the longest day of the year, the summer solstice beginning of the astronomical summer. During the Northern Hemisphere summer, the sun climbs high in the sky and its rays hit the Earth more directly, making the sunlight more intense and the air warmer. I am delighting in the extraordinarily long days when the sun rises at 5:30 and doesn't set till 8:00, with the light lingering long after the official setting time. Today's daylight is 14 hours and 22 minutes long.

Every day, a sharp beam of light through various trees and buildings will fall on an odd arch or sudden doorway and I wonder about Sister Genevieve's excited remark, *"So begin the three evenings of the golden fountain!"* Or Bilbo's guidance to find the keyhole to Front Gate of the Lonely Mountain. Might I find a hidden entrance to some exquisite or dangerous place? Might I be on the threshold of a special span of time that lasts just a day or two? Might I be!?!

June 22:
"(All is dark save the flame of the candle in Don Giovanni's hand. Slowly, with heavy footsteps that re-echo, the statue enters. It speaks.) Don Giovanni, you have invited me to sit at table with you. Lo! I am here."
Statue of Don Pedro, the Commendatore in Mozart's *Don Giovanni*

In a translation in one production I worked on, this line was rendered, "Don Giovanni, I come to supper!" Don Giovanni is a mess and he is about to have some retribution thrust upon him. A pompous and licentious young nobleman, the don insults and mistreats everyone he meets.

At the end of the opera, however, he stumbles across an entity he is unable to master, murder, or outsmart. He happens to meet his servant Leporello in a graveyard at about two o'clock in the morning. They encounter a new statue honoring the Commendatore, an important knight commander who Don Giovanni has killed in a duel. Lightly, Giovanni proposes supper at his palace, and unnervingly, at least for Leporello, the statue accepts.

In the last scene, they hear a threatening knock. The stage grows dark and the music swells ominously and reverberates with turmoil. Too scared to answer, Leporello steps aside so the don can open the door revealing the statue of the Commendatore. He tells Giovanni he has taken him up on his dinner invitation, *"You invited me and I have come!"* And then, he repeatedly asks the rogue to repent, but Giovanni steadfastly spurns the offer. "No! No! NO!" In a dramatic conclusion, the statue descends into the smoking earth, dragging Giovanni along with him accompanied by a mournful choir of demons.

You really might not believe what is happening as I write this piece. I have been absorbed in the remembrance of the opera and putting down my thoughts on paper, but in the background, I have been hearing a knocking, knocking, knocking! The sound finally broke through into my consciousness. Is it a visit from the Commendatore?

I slip over to the window from whence the noise is emanating, and find not the Commendatore, and not a raven quothing, but a huge pileated woodpecker about 20 inches long with a 30-inch wingspan. He is attracted to my siding and pounding very loudly at the wooden frame around my window! Fortunately for me, this was no magic statue of a bird, and he flew off when he caught sight of me instead of dragging me down into a hellish place below.

So back to my thoughts: every time I have people over for dinner and I hear a knock at the door, this part of Don Giovanni comes rushing back to me. "Donna Barbara," I hear a very deep bass voice singing, "I've come to supper!" I hear the singing in my head. Not that I am frightened or think that some of my guests will have turned into gruesome carvings that will carry me away.

For me, this playback of a song from an opera or lines from a play is the normal course. Happenings throughout my days and weeks are accompanied by segments from great performance pieces that have set grooves in my mind, sounding off when appropriate. Nor is it unusual for some odd little force of nature, like the woodpecker, to combine with the music or words to create a something really dramatic and synchronistically new.

June 23:
"Lord, what fools these mortals be!"
Puck in William Shakespeare's A *Midsummer Night's Dream*, Act III, Scene 2

Today is Midsummer's Eve, the time to celebrate the longest day of the year, and I wish Americans commemorated it more heartily. All over Europe, this summer solstice period between June 19 and June 24

240

brings festivals and dancing, bonfires and picnics, fairs and parties. Since the thirteenth century, people in Great Britain have celebrated June 23 as Midsummer's Eve, which is also the eve of the feast day of St. John the Baptist. Feasting and merrymaking are part of the tradition.

William Shakespeare's great comedy *A Midsummer Night's Dream* portrays the magical things that can happen in a forest in the middle of the summer. The center of the plot is the occasion of the wedding of the Duke of Athens, Theseus, and his bride Hippolyta. But all around that nuptial ceremony swirl the escapades of Hermia and Lysander, Helena and Demetrius, four young Athenian lovers, plus a rustic set of amateur actors. All of these folks are pulled into hilarious and bittersweet situations by the fairies who live in the enchanting forest where most of the play is set.

Since producing the play in 1976, Puck's line *"Lord, what fools these mortals be!"* has run through my mind many and many a time. Over and over, I have pledged not to think of people as fools remembering that once Jesus remarked, "Whoever says, 'You fool!' will be in danger of the fire of Gehenna." (Matthew 5:22). But just listening to the news some days, it slips right out, *"Lord, what fools these mortals be!"*

Many clever and memorable fools fill Shakespeare's plays. Many times, they are ordinary people who use common sagacity to outwit their "betters." Much like the jesters popular in courts of the Middle Ages and Renaissance, the bard's fools appealed to both the groundlings (audience members who stood on the ground to watch the play) and the members of court. Ever since they appeared on the boards of the Globe Theatre, fools like Touchstone in *As You Like It*, The Fool in *King Lear*, Feste in *Twelfth Night*, The Gravediggers in *Hamlet*, Clown in *Othello*, and Nick Bottom in *A Midsummer Night's Dream* — all of them have mesmerized, amused, delighted, and informed audience members.

Shakespeare's clowns seem witless, and yet, they have much wisdom hidden in their jesters' caps. They often appear to provide comic relief after a truly tragic scene. Some sing and tell stories, like court jesters, but they also advise on morality or mortality, speak of love or despair, or pick up on emotional confusion and offer guidance.

So on this Midsummer's Eve, why not give into some foolish lightheartedness? The day will be long, so have an evening picnic, take a long afternoon walk, blow bubbles, drink in the scents of the flowers in bloom, visit an English-like pub, listen to Felix Mendelssohn's score for *Midsummer Night's Dream*, buy a popsicle from the neighborhood ice cream truck, find a pool or creek for an evening swim. Take a break from the worries of your own drama and have fun!

June 24:
"Once and for all you must know that there's a universe of people outside, and you're responsible to it."
Chris Keller (to his mother) in Arthur Miller's *All My Sons*

In 2001, Arthur Miller was awarded the National Endowment for the Arts "Jefferson Lecturer Honor." In a biography crafted for their website concerning the award, Rachel Galvin wrote, "Throughout his life and work, Miller has remained socially engaged and has written with conscience, clarity, and compassion. As Chris Keller says to his mother in *All My Sons*, *"Once and for all you must know that there's a universe of people outside, and you're responsible to it."* Miller's work is infused with his sense of responsibility to humanity and to his audience."

Galvin quoted Miller himself as saying, "The playwright is nothing without his audience. He is one of the audience who happens to know how to speak."

Found in Genesis 4 is the intriguing story of Cain killing his brother Abel because the Lord had accepted Abel's offering, but not his own. God asks Cain where Abel is and we get an answer that has been debated ever since: "Am I my brother's keeper?" Paul, writing much later, says in Romans that none of us lives to himself.

Are we our brothers' keepers? Are we responsible to the whole universe of people outside ourselves? No, I am not my brothers' keepers if by that phrase I mean their forewoman or manager. When Seth was four and his sister Elin was a whopping 10, she would act ever so much like his second mother. His standard answer to her was, "You're not the boss of me!" He recognized early on that Mother or Father might be his overseer, but Sister was his sibling peer even though eight years his senior. That rendering of the "keepers" phrase is not what I believe it means.

In our era, many people refuse to be anyone else's keeper, believing that being responsible for themselves is all that is required in life. In fact, a large portion of our population is barely accountable at all — even to themselves. But around the nation, there is also talk these days about being our brothers' keepers. Barack Obama as President launched "My Brother's Keeper," an initiative to assist young men of color. Some denominations support a "Brother's Keeper Ministries" for the incarcerated or the homeless. And many individuals work hard for social justice and equality.

India.Arie is a wise songwriter and performer who has experienced a lot of pain, but has emerged a healthy and enlightened woman. One of her songs, "Brothers' Keeper" is about caring for someone who is desperate, broken, and needs to hear the message that our messes, slips, and blunders aren't who we are. And her chorus asks the very question about are we our fellows' guardians? She answers affirmatively with a resounding exclamation point. Listen today to her wonderful song.

More and more, I have come to see that all humans are brothers and sisters. We are all one race, and even more. We are all part of a huge creation that includes plants, other creatures, and other universes, and even more. We are all made up of energy manifested in different forms and shapes, and even more. We are all part of the Holy, the Creator, the Divine Space that holds us all together.

So nowadays, I listen to Chris in Arthur Miller's play and take his advice: *"Once and for all you must know that there's a universe of people outside, and you're responsible to it."*

June 25:
"We die to each other daily. What we know of other people is only our memory of the moments during which we knew them. And they have changed since then."
Unidentified Guest in T. S. Eliot's *The Cocktail Party*, Act 1, Scene 3

In our lives, we know some people very well, and for a long time we have regular interaction with them. Others, we are familiar with for finite periods: in a class at school, in a job, in a social club, and we may or may not know them very deeply. Still other people we meet only briefly, with compressed communication.

No matter how we know people, I believe TS Eliot is right. We do in essence perish to each other daily, because we ebb and flow out of each others' lives. In the present moment, when I encounter someone, he is alive to me. When that person is gone, I only have the recollection of the time we had together. I know only that aspect of him that I was able to glimpse and glean during our interaction, only what I was able to soak up in that brief juncture we shared on our earthly pilgrimage.

I think of all the students I encountered working together in the theatre. For the time it took to audition, rehearse, and build a show, a small — or sometimes large — group of us would be intimately involved. For those six or seven weeks, students would daily assist me in the costume shop or box office. Others who were acting in the play would visit the shop for measurements and costume fittings. Theatre majors would arrive to check in and check progress. The costume shop functioned as a safe place for students to drop by and discuss with me relationship problems and family joys, academic challenges and hilarious incidents.

Also, in Speech and Theatre, I formed close relationships with fellow faculty members, and with Judy, our department administrator. Music and Art teachers grew into friends as we worked on projects together. Professors from all over campus interacted in numerous academic meetings and schemes — and many were theatre supporters and part of a faculty patrons group.

Our diocese appointed a priest, Fr. Bill, to be the chaplain of the three Birmingham universities: University of Alabama at Birmingham, Birmingham-Southern, and Samford University, where I taught. Being an Episcopalian at a Baptist college, I was thrilled to begin a new adventure of having Eucharists and an Anglican presence on campus, so I became as supportive of the new ministry as I could. I knew Fr. Bill casually, but not well at all, so forming this new relationship was delightful as we began to share communion and stories, plans and projects.

And that was all 20, 30, and 40 years ago. Through social media, I keep up with many of my former students, and often see some of them who remained in Birmingham. A couple of times a year, I have lunch with theatre and speech professor mates. And I sometimes see Fr. Bill. I would say we are all still friends — but I see them all much less frequently. So now, I poignantly think of these Eliot words, *"We die to each other daily. What we know of other people is only our memory of the moments during which we knew them. And they have changed since then."*

June 26:
"If I'm ever to reach any understanding of myself and the things around me, I must learn to stand alone. That's why I can't stay here with you any longer."
Nora in Henrick Ibsen's *A Doll's House*, Act 3

In these post-feminist movement yet still patriarchal days, some people actually have the audacity of saying *A Doll's House* is "something of an all-too familiar feminist tract." But when it was first produced in 1879, it was banned, given alternate endings, criticized, and despised for its notion that a woman might leave her family to discover who she really is, causing great controversy for its condemnatory tone toward marriage norms of the nineteenth century.

Just thinking of the play reminds me of how I would have never grown to be the person I am had my then-husband not said, *"I can't stay here with you any longer."* That Monday morning, he had taken clothes out of closets, books off of shelves, and car out of the port. He had planned to come back after school so that together we could tell our children what was happening. Six o'clock came. Seth was relaxed, doing homework and Elin was out with friends. Seven o'clock. Eight o'clock, still just Seth and me. Eight thirty came, and it was close to bedtime. Elin was still out.

The phone rang and he was not able to make it back. Here was the truth of the situation: things were different now. No more joint nurturing. No more shared responsibility. So I sat Seth down in the great hall for a little chat.

The August glow was finally drained out of the evening sky and the light was dim — except for great pools of amber below the reading lamps. Seth sank into a couch and I perched opposite him and calmly told him that his father was never coming home again. I suppose I expected tears, maybe even an explosive outburst. After all, he was a highly expressive and active child. That didn't happen. He sat there, a calm veil drawn across his features. Deep down in his feelings, he had a certain knowing informing his conscience and restraining body movement. So, I just sat, waiting for a response, wondering what, on this doorstep of a new life, he would say to escort us through the portal that would take us to the reality of being a family of three.

He remained silent for many long, thoughtful, soulful minutes, his expression more like a monk in prayer than a child who had just been informed that his life was turned upside down. We used to call Seth "Mister Twister" because he was always in movement. But that night, he did not fidget or squirm. His big eyes wandered back and forth across the shadowy room and the dusk beyond the window panes.

I glanced at the clock: five minutes went by — five long minutes, then six, then seven. Suddenly, he smiled engagingly and his eyes began to twinkle. "Well," he said. "Does this mean we can get a dog?" His dad didn't want a canine addition to the household: too much mess, too much interruption, too much unpredictability.

"Yes!" I answered decisively and without a moment of hesitation. "This means we can get a dog!"

In an instant everything changed from tragedy to adventure. Everything that had happened in the past was past, and what might happen in the future was still hidden. This was now. Every present moment is perfect. Everything before and after that moment may be falling apart but the poignancy and beauty of Seth's attitude overrode everything. The worse that could happen in a family had already happened and we didn't melt; we didn't split into fragments; we didn't evaporate; we didn't burst into flames. So, everything from then on would be okay.

What an incredible embarkation onto uncharted ocean waves! Although we faced an end to life as we knew it, it was also passageway to discover untold riches that were denied us in the past. And Seth suddenly became the navigator — as I steered — to help find them, not at all afraid of this new journey. Not crying and angry, not explosive or depressed — but almost ebullient, and infectiously so.

June 27:

In "On a Wonderful Day like Today" from *The Roar of the Greasepaint, the Smell of the Crowd*, Sir sings about all the different things in nature that make this day fabulous. (Listen to the work online or from your library!)

Sir in *The Roar of the Greasepaint, the Smell of the Crowd*, Book, Music and Lyrics by Leslie Bricusse and Anthony Newley

We produced *The Roar of the Greasepaint, the Smell of the Crowd* in the fall of 1990, and I thoroughly enjoyed the experience. And, I do find myself singing a version of this song almost every day, because I expect each day to be wonderful, and many times, the day complies with me.

This is a funny story about one of my daily neighborhood walks several years ago. Usually, during the last third as I walk the down stretch toward home, I look for a "sign" for the day. I don't always get one, but sometimes I find a coin or a label from a bottle or a little object that gives me a hint about the day or reveals a message from the Universe about a question I have been pondering.

To set the stage, a few days before this walk, my son Seth had been pondering his slight materialistic bent versus contemplation of life as an Episcopal priest. We had chosen some new speakers and a receiver for my sound system, and when we got home, he grew very concerned that as a priest, he could never keep up with the technology he was (is) so infatuated with. He actually worked himself into a tizzy for five hours about it! When it was finally time to go to sleep, I was so tired from the drama, I just sat on my bed and wept and told him I didn't want to be the grownup anymore!!! And I meant it!

The next day at work, our staff met with a professional guide about teaming up to do character education. My boss was looking at an inventory of things that you can do in character education and he said, "Oh, Barbara, number 23 on the list is to create a personal mission statement." Well, he said it sort of jokingly and then two coworkers who knew I had such a mission statement teased me into revealing it, which at the time was: "To influence the world positively, leading people to grow spiritually, intellectually, emotionally, physically, and creatively through arts and education."

Then I told them I was in the process of revising my mission, which I really needed to do since I had had this one for about five years. And they asked me what my new mission was and, off the top of my head, I blurted out: "Girls just want to have fun."

The exclamation came from some deep desire for freedom from carrying the load of single motherhood, single house ownership, single bread winner-dom. But the idea began to grow on me.

So, back to the walk: I looked down in a yard about seven or eight houses from mine, and found a black Barbie doll boot. I said, "Oh, that's fun!" Then, suddenly rushing back to me, I remembered having one of the first Barbie dolls when they appeared in 1959. Members of my family, especially one of my grandmothers, called me "Barbie." Then, school friends used to call me "Barbie doll" — which was nothing terribly bad — but I was a very earnest fifth and sixth grader. Barbie seemed so frivolous and fun-loving, and I was determined to be taken seriously in my life.

In fact, my drive to be successful, hard-working, and active in every single class or club activity in high school led me to make friends much more with boys than girls. And I really totally buried the girly side of myself. Though I always have fun and am happy doing just about anything, that is not the same appreciating girly fun. That boot just explained so much to me.

I decided then and there, on that wonderful day, to challenge every cloud not to rain on my parade. I resolved to embrace my femininity more, and enjoy it. I bought a new purse with colorful hearts all over it, had a manicure, listened to romantic CDs, and began climbing at least part-way out of a position I had imposed on myself for too long.

June 28:

"Oh, Campers of Winnataska, knighthood is not dead. The pomp and pageantry are mere symbols of the ideals that still exist in the hearts of man. In our troubled world, the flames of knighthood are burning low. Let us, like knights of old, go forth in search of our Holy Grail. Let us keep the purity and courage that are the ideals of knighthood, and dedicate ourselves to a Holy Cause. Let us so live that we may be worthy of attaining the realization of our dream."

King Arthur in Camp Winnataska's *The Quest of the Holy Grail*

Unknown to most of the world, King Arthur and Queen Guinevere, Sir Bors and Sir Percival, Sir Lancelot and Sir Galahad are alive and healthy, dwelling in the middle of a steamy Alabama forest. These knights of yore come to life in a jewel-like play each summer — shielded from modern civilization by a never-changing ritual. In 1922, four years after the founding of Winnataska, an interdenominational Christian camp, the pageant of the Holy Grail was first performed, becoming an instant tradition. The words and actions tell of the Round Table's noble knights' search for the Holy Grail — the cup Jesus used at the Last Supper.

This particular Arthurian tradition arose because of a hymn called "Follow the Gleam." Written by Sallie Hume Douglas, the composition won the Bryn Mawr Silver Bay Prize for a song in 1920. The idealistic words and haunting tune, exhorting modern listeners to accept the spiritual challenges of medieval knights, captured imaginations across the nation in the early 1920s, and the song was in hymnals throughout the twentieth century.

A staff member at Winnataska encouraged campers to dramatize the words. For many years, parts were learned strictly by word of mouth until someone finally transcribed, by hand, the script. And still today, lovely characters from the old English legend, enunciating in decidedly Southern accents, come to life six or seven times each summer for a thousand Alabama young people.

As the play evolved, "Grail" was saved for the final evening of camp and parts became rewards for jobs excellently done by leaders and staff. Certain colors for the tunics and capes are traditional for particular knights: deep blue for Bors, green for Gawain, red for Lancelot, and pure white (emblazoned with a red Maltese cross) for Galahad. After the pageant, campers and leaders wind down a slope from the chapel holding candles in the pitch-black night, singing "Follow the Gleam." Once they reach a set of hillside bleachers overlooking the waterfall, everyone squints patiently into the inky darkness until the camp bridge bursts into flames as the admirable Galahad seems to be carried to heaven with the Grail in hand.

What the campers, leaders, and staff perceive through the repeated performances throughout the summer is that these knights attempted to live true and pure and sacrificial lives. They were human beings with frailties; some failed, but they struggled to succeed.

To some, the search for the Holy Grail symbolizes seeking Christ in their lives; to others, exploring God's plan; to others, searching for authenticity; to others, following their bliss. Through watching the pageant, campers are challenged to search for their own Holy Grail.

Younger children seldom get that message, but are drawn into the mystery of the colorful costumes, candlelight, and a burning bridge. Slowly, as they return year after year, they grasp the honor of being chosen, the challenge and sacrifice of a call, and the hardship yet acceptance of loss. And, at home in depths of winter, they recall the knights' goodness and perhaps think of the words that St. Paul wrote in his letter to the Philippians, "Finally, brothers (and sisters), whatever things are true, whatever things are honorable, whatever things are just, whatever things are pure, whatever things are lovely, whatever things are of good report: if there is any virtue and if there is any praise, think about these things."

June 29:
"Besides, now that I know you to be a confirmed Bunburyist I naturally want to talk to you about Bunburying. I want to tell you the rules."
Algernon in Oscar Wilde's *The Importance of Being Earnest*, Act I, Part 1

I was so honored today to see eight of Birmingham's finest seasoned actors in this "Trivial Comedy for Serious People," as Oscar

Wilde called *The Importance of Being Earnest.* How fun to see 60-, 70-, and 80-year olds playing all the parts, but especially the ingenue roles!

The play concerns, well, the importance of being sincere or truthful – a trait greatly appreciated by Victorian society. But Algernon says, "I have invented an invaluable permanent invalid called Bunbury, in order that I may be able to go down into the country whenever I choose." Oscar Wilde originated the word "Bunbury" to mean "leading a double life" or "hiding secrets." So what could be more deceptive and less earnest than to indulge in such lying and false living? And Algy has even invented the rules and protocol to follow when Bunburying.

Last year about this time, my granddaughter Emmeline turned four. Taking a bath as she spent the night with me, I asked her what was special about being this age. She said, "Oh, BeBe, now you get to know the Rules." I asked her, "What Rules?" Looking around the room, she said, "Bubble bath rules, towel rack rules, mirror rules."

Then she proceeded to rattle off a long list of regulations and edicts invented on the spot by her own imagination, and here are some of her best ones:

Light Rules: If the power goes out, so do the lights. Don't go in the bathroom. It's scary. Bubble Bath Rules: Don't use too much: it'll hurt your bottom.

Tall Towel Rack Rules: Don't try to touch it till you are 15 or at least 11.

Fish Rules: If a fish bites, your skin will grow back.

Mirror Rules: If you look in a mirror and see Emmeline, it might not really be the real one. Washcloth Rules: Don't spin around with one, you might fall.

Princess Rules: You don't ever, ever get near one if she is busy.

I am happy Emmeline shared her rules with me. Last year, our Vestry (the ruling "board" of our parish) did a year-long study with a consultant. At our first session with him, he said, "Okay, take out your Book of Rules. What? Don't look so puzzled. We all have one!"

Then, he talked some about the idea that each of us has a "Rule Book" that we have developed over our lifetimes. We know the regulations: what makes us happy, what makes us mad, what lifts us up, what drags us down. We have polished our guidelines through all sorts of crises and crossroads, crunches and critical points. The problem is, all of our friends and relatives have their own sets of statutes as well, and we rarely share what is in our governing books until we are forced to do so after a blowup. And at that point, we begin beating our spouse or partner, sibling or parent, child or best buddy over the head with what we think the guidelines happen to be in this case.

This consultant encouraged us that if we have a "rule" about something, it is best to share openly so we can avoid confrontations. Genuine rapport is then created and communication becomes real and clear. I believe what he was really trying to get across was the importance of being earnest.

June 30:
"O, he will dissolve my mystery!"
Mrs. Malaprop in Richard Brinsley Sheridan's The Rivals

Richard Brinsley Sheridan wrote the Restoration comedy, *The Rivals* in 1775. In the play is an amusing lady named Mrs. Malaprop. Her name comes from the French phrase mal à propos, or inappropriate. Self-taught, Mrs. Malaprop continually exchanges a similar-sounding word for the one she wished to use, usually with humorous consequences. Her name, or the word "malapropism," now means using the wrong word, or a having slip of the tongue.

When our Sophomore English class studied *The Rivals*, we loved her expression, "She's as headstrong as an allegory on the banks of Nile," really meaning "alligator." In fact, we guffawed at all of her funny expressions as we read the play aloud. I was finally able to design costumes for *The Rivals* at Samford University in 1985, and looking back over the play I really treasure Mrs. Mal's phrase: *"O, he will dissolve my mystery!"* She was trying to say, "solve or resolve my mystery," but I really like "dissolve."

The January 4, 2012 London paper the *Guardian* stated about Stephen Hawking, the former Lucasian professor of mathematics at Cambridge University, that, "his career has shed light on the secrets of the universe, from the nature of space-time to the workings of black holes, but there is one conundrum that still baffles the world's most famous scientist. In an interview to mark his 70th birthday this weekend, Stephen Hawking admitted he spent most of the day thinking about women. 'They are,' he said, 'a complete mystery.'"

When I was a Flaming Four on the Enneagram, mostly in my high school and college years, I loved the drama of wrapping myself in mystery. No one knew who I really was — I was special. And I was melancholy because no one understood how unique and uncommonly noteworthy I really was. Surely, a knight in shining armor would someday come and rescue me, decipher me, appreciate me, recognize me for my own authentic self.

But until that person came along, I would wrap myself in an enigmatic mystique. Only if some very remarkable equal to me could travel the maze, say the magic words, find the keyhole, discover the entrance, and rescue me from the sway of the dragon would I ever drop the veils and the disguises to reveal my true self.

Women are a conundrum to many men, and a few men are puzzles to women as well. As I am becoming a bit more integrated and balanced, I have let go of most of the hazy covering around me. Well, I don't think women should ever totally let go of all of their swathes. Life is a riddle. The Divine is, thank goodness, a mystery, the center of uncertainty and truth and beauty and love. And when I finally see God face to face, I believe the first thing out of my mouth will be: "O, *he is dissolving my mystery!*"

July 1:
In "Oh, What a Beautiful Mornin'" from *Oklahoma!*, Curly sings about the magnificent start to the day. (Listen to the work online or from your library!)
Curly McLain in *Oklahoma!* with music by Richard Rogers and book and lyrics by Oscar Hammerstein, based on Lynn Riggs' play *Green Grow the Lilacs*

Oklahoma! is the first great creative work by the legendary musical team of Richard Rogers and Oscar Hammerstein II. Set in the early 1900s in the Oklahoma territory, the 1943 work is based on Lynn Riggs' play *Green Grow the Lilacs*, and tells the story of cowboy Curly McLain and his love for Laurey Williams. A monumental landmark in theatre history, the musical marked the first truly cohesive piece where the drama, songs, and dances were all integrated into a narrative that evokes a wide range of emotions.

Not finding another quote from any play that would so beautifully open this luscious month of July, I settled on this heartbreakingly lovely tune. When I began my exercises at 6:00 this morning, there actually was a brilliant flaxen mist across the mountains that I can see from my back windows. I don't have any corn growing, but the tomato plants in the pots on my deck are almost shoulder — if not pachyderm-eye — height. Some of the thorny smilax vines that are trying to take over my yard don't just look like, they **are** rising right up to the heavens.

After my completing my routine at home, I took a walk and enumerated one-hundred things I am grateful today, starting with thanking the universe for the oh-so-lovely morning. The air was fresh and fragrant with earthy, summery smells. Hundreds of birds were singing and flitting about. With no school, there was very little traffic, so the neighborhood was unbelievably quiet at 6:25.

Often on walks or in the yard we see snakes, hawks, box turtles, and raccoons. One day not long ago, a mother possum and four of her children marched through my garden as I passed the window. One evening, I came home at dusk to see four or five deer resting in some indentions in the back yard. On an early walk one day, Roger and I saw a rabbit hopping as fast as he could down the center stripe of the road. A few seconds later, out of a wooded area came a red fox chasing the bunny, both looking just like they had freshly jumped off the page of a Beatrix Potter book. My remembrance of the fox was that he had on a velvet tail coat and vest.

When I steep myself in the magical natural world around me, whether in the heat of summer, color of fall, chill of winter, or blooms of spring, I center myself, I embolden myself, I fill myself with the splendor of the creation of the earth. Though tragedies still befall me, puzzles perplex me, vexations irritate me, surprises shock me, during my commune with the animal and plant world, I can always sing along with Curly about having a lovely sensation that today is going to move along fabulously.

July 2:
"Memory's like a policeman. Never there when you want it."
Norman in Ronald Harwood's *The Dresser*, Act 1

The Dresser is a play well-beloved by many theatre folks. Usually every town has a shared recollection of the production done by a couple of the great actors of the area. The story revolves around a dresser (an actor's costume assistant) during a production of *King Lear* during World War II's London blitz. The playwright, Ronald Harwood, actually functioned for a while as dresser to Sir Donald Wolfit and he used his experiences to create the play and the character "Sir."

The aging Sir has grown disheartened with his senility and is on the verge of mental collapse, though he carries on with his career, touring the English countryside with the troupe. All his actors are worn out, elderly, and disabled, qualified to entertain audiences in the throes of war only because they are all exempt from military duty.

My memory is about as funny as Sir's is. During my divorce 20 or so years ago, I lost a lot of my powers of recall, which had been fairly strong all my life. Before 1993, I could remember every play I had ever produced, the cast and crew members, the dates of its run, and just about every detail about the drama that occurred both onstage and backstage. After my marriage and theatre partnership dissolved, I had trouble even recalling all the plays, much less pinpointing the year we created them or the people with whom I labored so very intimately.

Medical research indicates that going through a critical mass of suffering and the accompanying lack of attention and concentration lead to such memory loss. An increase of cortisol in the bloodstream shrinks areas of the brain responsible for short-term memory. This explains why I had trouble processing and storing new information, but I think I also blocked a lot of my vivid old recollections.

Somehow, writing these pieces for the last few years have stirred up and brought forward a huge number of memories that I thought had been lost for good. I had wondered about my ability to reminisce, since my mother died of complications of dementia.

A couple of months ago, I drove down a county highway south of town on my way to a day retreat. On the way, I saw a road sign of an antlered deer leaping in the air, cautioning drivers to watch for the vaulting animals. The simple sight of the warning sign brought immediately to mind a large group of deer on the hillside that my then-husband and I saw as we drove past that very spot on that very parkway and deer sign one evening at sunset.

In the past, something inside me would have squelched that vision before it ever actually reached my cerebral cortex and would have blocked me from revisiting that pleasant experience. This writing, my spiritual work for two decades, and the growing realization that being single for ten years was the best thing that ever happened to me has allowed me to again recall many incidents I had suppressed. So while I can empathize with Norman and Sir about *"memory never being there when you want it,"* I delight that some of my data is again retrievable.

July 3:

"This made for a kind of harmony and a kind of confidence. It related the fortuitous and the ordained into a reassuring union, which we recognized as nature. The sun came up about as often as it went down, in the long run, and a coin showed heads about as often as it showed tails. Then a messenger arrived. We had been sent for. Nothing else happened. Ninety-two coins spun consecutively have come down heads ninety-two consecutive times...and for the last three minutes on the wind of a windless day I have heard the sound of drums and flute..."

Guildenstern in Tom Stoppard's *Rosencrantz and Guildenstern Are Dead*

I love a theatrical play like *Rosencrantz and Guildenstern Are Dead*, and it is Tom Stoppard's birthday, so what better way to celebrate than contemplating this funny, sad, intelligent work? The Absurdist play was first staged at the Edinburgh Fringe Festival in 1966 when the playwright was not quite 30 years old.

The two title characters are courtiers from *Hamlet*, and through the course of the action, major players from Shakespeare's tragedy enter from side stages, reenacting snippets of scenes from the original work. But what is so interesting is that in the space separating these overlapping scenes, our heroes ponder what is going on around them, having little way to conceive of the bigger panorama of events.

A major theme of the play, as evidenced by the quote above, concerns human control over our lives. Is what happens to me planned, or random? Planned by whom? If things go my way, is it because I am in control, or is there no pattern to life at all?

Rosencrantz and Guildenstern are certainly confused most of the play, even about their own identities. And they believe that the universe is random, equivocal, and mystifying. The haphazard appearances of other characters are so accidental that their lives seem to have no meaning, leading to a confused and frustrating despair.

But in pondering this motif, I have been enlightened by a conversation with a friend recently who was about to celebrate his 70th birthday, and he said that more and more, he subscribes to an idea broached by philosopher Arthur Schopenhauer in an essay called "On an Apparent Intention in the Fate of the Individual."

And, as fate or chance would have it, the very next week, I was watching again Bill Moyers' interviews with Joseph Campbell on the Power of Myth. Both my friend and Campbell are fascinated by

Schopenhauer's notion that, as Campbell states, "when you reach an advanced age and look back over your lifetime, it can seem to have had a consistent order and plan, as though composed by some novelist. Events that when they occurred had seemed accidental and of little moment turn out to have been indispensable factors in the composition of a consistent plot."

Naturally, the question arises: Who composed the plot? Some people see the Divine as a great playwright. Schopenhauer seems to believe that the will within us unconsciously composes our drama, just as dreams evolve by themselves, unsolicited in our sleep. We meet people through synchronicity who change our lives incredibly, and likewise we unwittingly give extraordinary messages to people we meet in the most casual of ways.

"The whole thing gears together like one big symphony," Campbell says, "with everything unconsciously structuring everything else. And Schopenhauer concludes that it is as though our lives were the features of the one great dream of a single dreamer in which all the dream characters dream, too; so that everything links to everything else, moved by the one will to life which is the universal will in nature."

So, not one, but two playwrights literally did create the characters and the worlds of these protagonists, Rosencrantz and Guildenstern. Stoppard's intriguing play highlights the intricate interconnection of real life and theatre. In fact, in bringing Shakespeare's characters back to life in another work, he enjoins the audience to believe in their actual physical existence: two cameo performers who merit major roles so their tale can play out from a different point of view.

July 4:
"How quiet, how quiet the chamber is; How silent, how silent the chamber is."
Spoken prelude to "Is Anybody There?" from *1776!*, John Adams sings about how silent the Chamber of the Continental Congress is, and wonders if anyone can hear him. (Listen to the work online or from your library!)
John Adams in Act II, Scene 7, *1776!* music and lyrics by Sherman Edwards and book by Peter Stone

What better show to highlight for Independence Day than the musical *1776!*? John Adams sings about how silent the room is where the Second Continental Congress is meeting. Quiet is not what a lot of us will have today. We have boating, parades, and swimming to rush off to; barbecue to spread on the grill and special dishes to scoop up; flags to fly and bunting to string; and lots of noisy fireworks to listen to as we watch. When I worked for the American Village, this day was constant activity for me from 7:30 in the morning to 9:30 at night. I never thought I would have a quiet July 4th in my life ever again.

Dramatizing events leading up to the signing of the Declaration of Independence, 1776! focuses on the relentless work of John Adams before he receives enough support from colleagues to sign a declaration for American independence. In this scene set in the empty Continental Congress chamber, a disheartened Adams re-reads a disappointing dispatch from General George Washington. But, in that quiet chamber, he has a premonition of how his future countrymen will celebrate this day of independence. In this haunting and stirring song, he envisions pyrotechnics, shows, processions, spectacle — and the future freedom of Americans.

As he marvels about the contrast of the hushed assembly room, suddenly, Georgia's Dr. Lyman Hall returns, giving Adams the good news that he is amending Georgia's vote from "nay" to "yea." Hope returns.

Okay, we all know it is going to happen, anyway. All the congressmen are going to sign the Declaration of Independence on that auspicious date of July 4, and yet Edwards and Stone build up such a struggle, based on the true history of these characters' quarrels and dissension, that the audience can hardly bear the suspense of watching 1776!

But back to John Adams alone in that soundless chamber of the Continental Congress. He enjoys a brief respite from all the political wrangling and squabbling about details, a breathing space where he can imagine the future, envision celebrations, and actually conjure up the fruits of the labors that he and his cohorts have been planting.

When I creep out of bed early in the morning before anyone else is up, and every room of the house is hushed, the words of Adams about the still room come back to me. I have heard that our current addiction to the wired world makes it possible to lose our inner selves. So, I enjoy the tranquil part of the day, the minutes before the sun rises, when everything inside and out is still dark, untroubled, and still. Even the birds haven't commenced their chirruping. Nothing has clothed itself in colors yet. It's a secret, peaceful, sleepy time. The next twelve or fifteen hours of my life may be as chaotic as the action leading up to signing of the Declaration of Independence, but this part of the day is conflict free.

I've enjoyed this practice since long before the advent of fancy telecommunication devices. And now, these few hours have no iPhone, no internet, no television, and not even any music. The external stillness gives me internal quietude and equanimity, a clear mind, a relaxed body, and a placid soul. I have come to highly value this contemplative life of early morn, a place where there is no asking or answering of questions, no news, no mind filling, no mind numbing; just unruffled, unembellished serenity in the silence of my Great Hall.

July 5:

"After they had explored all the suns in the universe, and all the planets of all the suns, they realized that there was no other life in the universe, and that they were all alone. And they were very happy, because then they knew it was up to them to become all the things they had imagined they would find."
Johnny Young (the unseen student) in Lanford Wilson's *Fifth of July*

So, here it is, July 5, the day after the big national holiday saluting our country's founding and marking the emergence of the American Spirit. After picnics and barbecues, swimming and fishing, leisurely strolls and the flash of last night's fireworks, today is back to normal. *Fifth of July* is a play in a Talley family trilogy by Lanford Wilson, written in 1978, and taking place the year before. The other plays in the series are *Talley's Folly* and *Tally and Son*. This particular play about the Talley family is set in rural Missouri. The work achingly demonstrates my generation's disenchantment with America as a consequence of the conflict in Vietnam, and its title reflects the letdown (as we all have after a big celebration) of American ideals after that hopeless war.

If you can — if you were alive then — think back to 1977. When I do, my brain feels like scrambled eggs. It was the year President Jimmy Carter pardoned Vietnam War draft evaders; there was a gas crises; the first *Star Wars* movie opened; Elvis Presley died; the World Trade Center was completed; my daughter, Elin turned one-year old. In the play Kenneth Talley, a gay paraplegic Vietnam veteran, inhabits his childhood home with partner and botanist Jed Jenkins. Talley has considered teaching English at his former high school, but now prevaricates.

Though filled with the ache of squandered life in a futile foreign war, *Fifth of July* concerns deep and painful and manifested love. Kenneth, like other homosexuals dealing with parents' rejection, put himself in harm's way, and was injured. So this is a play concerning a specific Vietnam vet. But, it is more about love and how humans try to avoid it, catch it, hold it, throw it away, reclaim it, and wring life out of it. As Ken's Aunt Sally says of life, "It goes on and then it stops. You can't worry about the stopping; you have to worry about the going on."

Several people in the play (Ken, his sister, and her husband) were passionately involved with antiwar protests, but through the course of the play, they realize life itself involves the same sort of dedication and attention they gave that cause. People must claim the power given them to make choices, to lose dreams, to generate amends. What do we learn from life-changing events like wars, pandemics, social upheavals? When the past can be laid to rest and the future embraced in the present moment, then all things are possible.

This theme comes out powerfully through an unseen student of Ken named Johnny Young, a brilliant, but almost incoherent young man. Ken has persuaded Johnny to record a story onto a tape, and then Ken reads aloud a transcription of some of the tale: *"After they had explored all the suns in the universe, and all the planets of all the suns, they realized that there was no other life in the universe, and that they were all alone. And they were very happy, because then they knew it was up to them to become all the things they had imagined they would find."*

As a director once said of these lines, "In these two beautiful sentences, we see acceptance of the future, happiness in that acceptance, and commitment to fulfilling one's potential. This is the essence of *Fifth of July*."

July 6:
"It was as though God kissed my hands when I first pulled the fabric through the sewing machine and held up a finished garment. I discovered all I need in these fingers."
Esther in Lynn Nottage's *Intimate Apparel*

Lynn Nottage has said that *Intimate Apparel* was inspired by her great-grandmother, Ethel Boyce, a plain and deeply religious woman who arrived alone in New York City in the early 1900s. "She was an amazing seamstress," says Nottage, "who specialized in intimate apparel for women." In the play, which takes place in 1905 Manhattan, Esther Mills stitches together lovely corsets, and is so good at her work that she has gained financial freedom, an unusual circumstance for a single African American woman of her day.

When I designed the costumes for the play for Birmingham Festival Theatre in 2006, we used my grandmother's pedal-operated sewing machine for Esther's work, and she actually operated it during the course of the action. My great-grandmother did tatting, handcrafting lace through a series of knots and loops. I have some of her placemats that she made especially for me before she died when I was 13-years old.

After I moved back to Birmingham after graduate school, sometimes my mother, my aunt Marge, and I would go to my grandmother's house and embroider. It was one of the few times I have ever been part of a women's sewing circle, and it was glorious. My grandmother made bibs for children out of bright juvenile fabrics, and somehow I inherited some of her fabric and, having some bibs she made for my children, I occasionally sew some for infant gifts or church bazaars.

My mother was a lovely seamstress and constructed a number of my mini dresses when I was in high school and college. If I close my eyes, I can smell the fabric section of Loveman's department store in downtown Birmingham where we carefully selected flowery fabrics to mock the London frocks we researched during the British Invasion during the 1960s. For my wedding, Marge and my mom helped me pick out a wonderful gauzy flowered voile for my bridesmaid dresses and they sewed many of them for the twelve female relatives and friend attendants I had.

I never thought of myself as a very good seamstress, at least not as good as my female relatives; but after spending 26 years in a costume shop, I got fairly decent at the job. One of my very favorite shows for costuming was *East Lynne*, a play we had produced when I was in college, and then we staged at Samford in the fall of 1982. I had just returned to that university after a brief career at a neighboring school, and I was so happy to be back in that costume shop, I became totally absorbed in the work.

As Esther in *Intimate Apparel*, my crew and I created corsets for all the girls in the show, along with the bustles, and petticoats, and lovely silky dresses. I had never worked so painstakingly on a period show, and the results were exquisite. The experience was holy — and wholly satisfying. It was one time I felt Esther's exhilaration when she exclaims, *"It was as though God kissed my hands when I first pulled the fabric through the* sewing machine and held up a finished garment. I discovered all I need in these fingers."

July 7:
"The test of an adventure is that when you're in the middle of it, you say to yourself, 'Oh, now I've got myself into an awful mess; I wish I were sitting quietly at home.' And the sign that something is wrong with you is when you sit quietly at home wishing you were out having lots of adventure."
Dolly Levi in Thornton Wilder's The Matchmaker, Act 4

Thornton Wilder is one of my favorite playwrights, and though I have never worked on The Matchmaker, I helped guide a glorious high school production of Hello, Dolly! while I was in graduate school. The rollicking comedy set in nineteenth century New York concerns the perennial duo of love and money, and features the exuberant meddler Dolly Gallagher Levi whose artful schemes bring together several improbable lovebirds.

Dolly is definitely always in the midst of an adventure, and I love one myself. When I was a toddler of about three-years old, disliking my naps, I slipped away from my sleeping mother and walked up to the corner fire station where the chief was the father of a family friend. Thankfully, some of the firemen recognized me and delivered me back home.

Later, I was a tree climber, loving to ascend leafy branches as high as I possible could rise. And I was a bike rider who loved the freedom of the breeze blowing through my hair and the thrill of the open road. As a teenager, I was a radio correspondent for my high school, a department store model and teen board representative, a rock and roll reviewer for the Birmingham News, and a leader at a traditional summer camp, Winnataska.

When I was at a theatre conference in Pensacola during graduate school, I was watching a production of Peter Weiss' play The Persecution and Assassination of Jean-Paul Marat as Performed by the Inmates of the Asylum of Charenton Under the Direction of the Marquis de Sade. Very Brechtian in style, with relentless assaults on the audience, this production unfolded inside a very hot and muggy restaurant in the historic section of this old Florida city, with the actors moving about the tables.

Seated at the end of a bench next to the wall, I suddenly had a terrible spell: my heart raced, I felt numb and sweaty, and I thought I was going to either faint, lose my mind, or immediately die. Some friends opened up their close by hotel room, and I finally felt better after lying down for a while. However, at the fresh young age of 23, my adventures were over for a while.

What had made me feel trapped was the first of several hundred anxiety attacks with the ominous name of "agoraphobia." Like others with this insidious condition, I began to be wary of crowded public spaces. I sometimes had to get up and leave classes or church services. I drove certain roads which I knew to have places where I could stop if I "lost control."

My mother who had suffered similarly suggested anti-anxiety pills ("Give me Librium or give me death!" I used to cry) but they didn't agree with me. I tried counseling, exercise, books on the subject, talking it out, but nothing worked extremely well until almost 14 years later, I chanced upon a doctor who prescribed a beta blocker for my high blood pressure, but who said it might cure the anxiety as well. I haven't had but a couple of panic attacks since then.

Actually, Dolly's quote from *The Matchmaker* could be re-written to describe agoraphobia: "The test of agoraphobia is that when you're in the middle of it, you say to yourself, 'Oh, now I've got myself into an awful mess; I wish I were sitting quietly at home.' And the sign that you have agoraphobia is when you sit quietly at home wishing **could be** out having lots of adventure." Such an illness, over which you feel such little control, can really squeeze the life out of you. Being symptom-free for 26 years now, I've returned to my own adventuresome self, and believe I am healed.

July 8:
"Moonlight and a gentle, misty veil.
The perfect setting for a fairytale.
Here, for an hour, you and I will climb
The silken threads of 'Once upon a time'..."
Narrator in Michael Elliot Brill's *The Masque of Beauty and the Beast*

In Hebrew, the phrase is *"Hayoh hayah pa'am..."* in French, *"Il était une fois..."* in modern Greek *"Mia fora ki enan kairo..."* in Welsh *"Amser maith yn ôl..."* *"Once upon a time,"* those magic opening words of works by the brothers Grimm, Hans Christian Andersen, Charles Perrault, and all of our grandmothers. These words foretell an anecdote that comes from oral folk tales, an escapade from literary geniuses, or an exploit from our own family history.

My granddaughter Emmeline, who just turned five yesterday, loves to hear stories of the great dog Merlin. He was the precious Springer Spaniel we welcomed into our home when my son Seth wanted to add a canine family member. Merlin's life with us spanned from the day Seth turned 11 until Emmeline was almost a year and a half — over 15 years. Emmeline can remember him a tiny bit. Photographs help, but the stories bring him back to vivid life every time we begin, "Once upon a time..." With such an awe-inspiring wizardly name, Merlin was bound to be the center of a number of escapades.

Merlin somehow snagged three hotdogs out of a hot pan on the back burner of the stove. Merlin somehow jumped up on a fully set table to look out the kitchen window without breaking a single Christmas plate. Merlin somehow found and neatly folded two towels and a blanket onto the cold slate floor to make himself a warm bed when left home by himself one night.

Merlin learned a little twirling dance he did to welcome us home every evening. Merlin discovered how to fly by running very fast at the top of the lawn and then jumping up in the air just as the yard sloped downward. Merlin once made a turtle run about 10 miles an hour. Merlin loved to put a string of Indian ankle bells around his neck at Christmas time.

We have Merlin narratives for each holiday, and for every plain old day as well. Emmeline loves the dog tales best, but also enjoys hearing family stories about when I was young, when her mother was little, when my mother and my grandmother were babes, what happened last Christmas, last beach trip, the time the tornado blew the attic door ajar, the time Hurricane Opal came up the power line right-of-way and destroyed the trees in my back yard.

I have read that children whose families chat daily about what they have done and who recall ancestral history can form stronger concepts of themselves and how they fit into the world, develop heartier characters, deal better with common situations, and even have less trouble with melancholy and stress. I simply began telling tribal tales because my mother and grandmother did, and I loved to hear the same anecdotes over and over and over again — and rightly thought Emmeline would, too. "Once upon a time..." "Der var engang..." "Noong unang panahon..."

July 9:

"Is that the fan you give a widow? (Throwing the fan on the floor.) Give me a black one and learn to respect your father's memory."
Bernarda in Federico Garcia Lorca's *The House of Bernarda Alba*

Costume, scenery, and lighting designers are not at liberty to simply read a script for fun, or for the literary content, plot, and theme, or for the excitement and thrill of the storyline. That is to say, we have a lot more to do than reading for pleasure when pouring over the words in order to get ready to design the work. Not that millions of people read plays for pleasure everyday anyway. There was a time when thousands of people belonged to Fireside Theatre (later Stage and Screen), a book club established in 1950 that specialized in sending patrons a new script every month. This institution that shut its doors in 2003 was the way I built up a fairly decent library of plays.

So, when getting ready to design the costumes for Lorca's *The House of Bernarda Alba*, I might read that Bernarda says, *"Is that the fan you give a widow? (Throwing the fan on the floor.) Give me a black one and learn to respect your father's memory."* Dang, I think. Not only do I have to find a bright and gaudy lady's fan, AND a black Spanish fan (probably lace) from the mid-1930s, but the first one has to be sturdy. It is going to be thrown on the floor. Every night.

Later, I read that Amelia tells Magdalena, "Your shoelace is untied." Magdalena then says that Adela has "...put on the green dress she made to wear for her birthday." Later, the green dress is a big deal. Just after the funeral for her husband, Bernarda Alba declares that her five daughters will strictly respect eight years of mourning in which they will dress in black and be confined to their house. Needless to say, the young women are crushed and distressed.

In searching for how I need to create these women's costumes, I discover that each divulges components of her character as she speaks. Magdalena seems to have been fond of her father and accepts the terms of the mourning. She implies that Adela should curb her defiance and give into the matriarchal subjugation. Adela responds with a flash of individual mettle. Flying in the face of her sisters, she rejects such a plan, claiming the color of nature, growth, harmony, freshness, and fertility. Wearing her green dress will symbolize her own unique identity and she

264

can thereby contemptuously disregard cultural constraints that keep women dressed morbidly.

Later, I also read that Angustias has dared to paint her face the day of their father's funeral. That Martirio is carrying lace for a nightgown and that Angustias has a beautiful ring with three pearls. That Adela enters in a white petticoat and corselet. That Bernarda wears a black shawl. That Adela enters covered with straw and that she also breaks her mother's cane in two.

As I concentrate on all these details, I begin to understand that *The House of Bernarda Alba* is the tale of a tyrannical woman whose cruel repression of her daughters converts their home into a flashpoint of pressure, envy, rage, and angst. And, after all, I am reading for pleasure because this method of noting the characters' remarks about their clothing and personalities is an enjoyable way of discovering what the play is really about!

July 10:
"Would you do me a favour, Babbybobby? Would you not call me Cripple Billy any more long?"
Billy in Martin McDonagh's *The Cripple of Inishmaan*

I know people named Bug, Killer, Kap, Mo, Barrel, Cookie, Mugs, Rook, and Queenie. My grandmother Dorothy was known as Little Dot and her sister Lillian was Toots. My granddaughter calls me "BeBe" and her other grandmother "Pat-Pat." Roger is "Rah-Rah." My mother's older sister always called her "Stinky," a name she despised from her childhood.

Names are funny, when you think about it. Our given name or first/second name, or so-called "Christian name" — that many of us have officially conferred upon us at Baptism — is a legal part of our identity. "Barbara," along with my surname or last name "Sloan," pinpoints me as particular person. Sloan, and my maternal connections to surnames like Collins, Bowron, and the paternal Aycock and Musgrove, identify me as part of a family or clan.

But, unless we change them, we have no power over our names at all — and especially not those epithets bestowed on us congenially — or unpleasantly — as nicknames. These monikers substituted for our proper names derive from love, ridicule, intimacy, or attachment, especially in families, classrooms, or places like summer camp. Bug, Killer, Kap, Mo, and Barrel are all camp friends of mine. We call one friend "Marty," another "BL," and another "Weezie," and I was sometimes called "Moose" during my time at Winnataska. My son was called "Cuss Cowboy" one year for a string of expletives he let loose when, at age 10, his horse ran away with him.

In Martin McDonagh's *The Cripple of Inishmaan*, Billy Claven has had enough of being called "Cripple." He is ready for a new image of himself and a new life, yearning to break away from his small, petty, poor hometown of Inishmaan. He auditions for a role in a documentary on the neighboring island, and the lame orphan surprises everyone by his spunk and gamble.

And yet, people have power over us when they know our names, when they dub us Barbara, Babs, BeBe, or Moose. Bobby asks what his friend would rather be called and Billy says, "Well, just Billy." And when Bobby says okay, Billy extends the understanding by asking him, "And would you rather be called Bobby and not Babbybobby?" But Bobby is fine with his sobriquet: "I do like being called Babbybobby. What's wrong with it?"

Some nicknames are fun and fine. Others, like "Cripple Billy" are enervating and devitalizing. They drain the person of any energy or vigor they might possible muster. Don't remind me of the cripple bit, Billy is saying. My shriveled arm and my bum leg are obvious: let's not dwell on that. I can take a boat to another island. I can audition for a film. Let's wipe out the paralyzing label of endearment. *"Would you do me a favour, Babbybobby? Would you not call me Cripple Billy any more long?"*

July 11:
"Our world is just like yours. The only difference is, we got caught."
Jules to Felix in Samuel and Bella Spewack's *My Three Angels*

In the summer of 1973 at Parkway Playhouse, we performed *My Three Angels*, a warm family comedy that takes place during the Christmas season of 1910. In it, there is no snow, no jolly carolers bundled up in warm clothing, and no "Baby, It's Cold Outside."

The play is set in the Ducotel family parlor in a sweltering French Guiana penal colony, where Felix and family have fled, penniless, because he is an idealist with no business sense. Felix wants to succeed in this new environment having been hoodwinked in his French enterprise by a deceptive cousin, Henri Trochard. He feels as penned in by his life as the three convicts in prison stripes who literally float above their house, fixing the thatched roof.

When the smooth-talking Henri turns up in the tropical colony hoping to cheat Felix again, the three jailbird angels hear everything going on below them. Feeling sorry for the Ducotel family's suffering right here at Christmas, they resolve to perform divine intervention, winning the affection of the audience and prodding viewers to consider what "criminality" really means.

I ran the box office for the two summers I worked at Parkway, and I dealt with the theatre's angels, those patrons who gave extra contributions to keep the Playhouse running. A few of our benefactors would "summer" in the mountains of North Carolina to escape the heat of this or that place. Several families were from Florida, the warm state they moved to in order to flee the cold and busy-ness of northern metropolises. They were like the Ducotel expatriates to some extent, I suppose; not for the same reasons, but in their migrating to different climates for portions of the year.

Parkway was the place I really learned to appreciate angels, those lifelines of any theatre enterprise. And Mr. Koch was my favorite angel. He called himself a Miami Jew, originally a successful businessman in New York, and he was congenial, charitable, and constructive. Having seen numerous Broadway and other professionally produced plays, he was quite knowledgeable about theatre, but was one of the biggest boosters of our university-produced season. He encouraged neighbors to attend and fill out our audiences, he bought season tickets, and he frequented our concession stand to expand our extra income. One year, he held our end of the year party at his lovely hideaway in the woods next to an ice-cold creek.

Theatre angels are somewhat like real angels: rarely seen by the multitudes, but serving as guiding influences; messengers who spread the good word about a show; beings with powerful minds who watch over the doings of us mere mortals. When I look back on my brief interludes with Mr. Koch, I remember him with bejeweled wings and glowing clothes.

July 12:
"Jabez: What does it mean here, about my soul?
Mr. Scratch: Why should that worry you? A soul? A soul is nothing. Can you see it, smell it, touch it? No. This soul, your soul, are nothing against seven years of good luck. You'll have money and all that money can buy."

Jabez and Mr. Scratch in *The Devil and Daniel Webster*, with Libretto by Stephen Vincent Benet and score by Douglas Stuart Moore

Oh, how I loved creating the costumes for *The Devil and Daniel Webster* when we produced the 1939 one-act folk opera in 1982. The story takes place in 1840 in New Hampshire where a farmer, Jabez Stone, struggles to keep food on the table for his young wife and his mother. After calamity and misfortune happen to the Stones, Jabez, in a deeply Faustian echo, determines to sell his soul to a mysterious stranger in return for seven years of good fortune.

Who else would the buyer be but the incarnation of the Devil, a Mr. Scratch who wanders about New England searching for hopeless victims to entice? Naturally, things change for the better and the worse after Jabez gets his wish. He does achieve wealth, but it makes him inconsiderate and heartless, and he is not only unfaithful to his wife, but he is disloyal to friends and fellow country folk.

Just when his seven years are almost over, he repents and calls upon the famous lawyer and politician Daniel Webster to use his golden tongue to present a case against Scratch. The only way the Devil will consent to a trial is if he can choose the judge and pull a jury of infamous sinners up from the depths of Hell. Both Jabez and Webster must forfeit their souls if Scratch wins.

What is this thing we call a soul? Is Mr. Scratch right? *"A soul? A soul is nothing. Can you see it, smell it, touch it? No."* Well, he doesn't even subscribe to his own philosophy, as he is gathering up souls just as fast as he can.

In one of my Philosophy and Religion classes, we devoured Ralph Waldo Emerson's essay "The Over-Soul," and the author's transcendental views about the human soul being immortal. Emerson talked about what I have been discovering in my consciousness research and teaching, that my ego self is insignificant and limited when juxtaposed beside our expansive and limitless souls.

My soul is my essence, an indwelling consciousness that watches my ego mind and my emotions and my dramas come and go. I constantly misinterpret myself, believing my ego is the real thing. When I am balanced and centered, my soul connects to that innate goodness or Divine which is in each of us, who forms the sum of all our parts.

My soul, not my ego, is the real me. I can find it by being present, and when I let intuition lead. It comes from a place of beauty, peace, and love, where dreams originate, where visions lead to hope, where I realize that I am connected to every thing and every person in the whole universe. What intrigued me in my college days and to this day is that Emerson was convinced that at some point, all of our souls are connected – that we are all really one; and, despite Mr. Scratch's rejection of the idea, the soul is something, something expansive and beautiful.

July 13:
"All rooms are lonely where there is only one person."
Alma Winemiller to the traveling man she picks up in Tennessee Williams' *Summer and Smoke*

In the winter of 1986, we produced Tennessee Williams' *Summer and Smoke* and built the life-size statue of an angel that sits in the middle of the set for the show. The story focuses on the sensitive and restless Alma Winemiller who is the daughter of a minister, and who has an unrequited love affair with the young and wayward Dr. John Buchanan next door. She – and Buchanan, who challenges her with the scientific anatomy chart, are never able to connect either with their spirits or their bodies.

Toward the end of the work, the two switch roles. She discards her spirituality and makes it obvious that she wants an intimate relationship, telling him "..now I have changed my mind, or the girl who said 'no', – she doesn't exist any more, she died last summer – suffocated in smoke from something on fire inside her." But he is already engaged to another, younger woman and, finding this spark too late for that matchup, Alma detains a young traveling salesman in the park. She says to him, "The life of a traveling salesmen is interesting ... but lonely."

The young man replies, "You're right about that. Hotel bedrooms are lonely. [There is a pause. Far away the train whistles again.] To which Alma replies, *"All rooms are lonely where there is only one person."*

Maybe you have been in a situation where you were at different points in a relationship from your beloved, and the connection collapsed before the consummation of love and intimate communication ever got started. Or perhaps you have lost a loved one through estrangement or death. I certainly found myself in many a room with only one person in my big old house after my marriage crumbled. I had lived with my family until I went to college. Then, I lived in a dorm for three years with dozens of sibling-like girls. Never having a sister, this life was heavenly for me.

269

Before my senior year at the University of Montevallo, I got married, so I never had a chance before I was wed to dwell unaccompanied. The first few months on my own, I felt awkward, self-conscious, and at a loss. My identity for 25 years had been as one-half of a couple and a design partnership. When I dined alone, even at home, I endured edginess. Going to arts events or movies made me feel stiff and gawky. I thought everyone was looking at me thinking, "Oh, poor thing. She has no one to hang out with."

As I worked my way through the months, I got stronger and braver. I went to an event at Montevallo and Mary Lou, the alumni director proclaimed, "Now see, you are traveling solo with flying colors." I cannot even remember the point at which I began to disagree with Alma and think that rooms are just fine for only one person.

Now, I value alone time significantly, and guard it carefully. I have come to realize a great truth: solitude and loneliness are two different things. Being lonely is negative, a state in which we experience isolation and believe we are missing something. But in solitude, I can be by myself without feeling unloved or unwanted. Such seclusion can be affirming, a most productive time when I can engage with myself.

July 14:
"James Keller: Sooner or later, we all give up, don't we?
Annie Sullivan: Maybe you all do, but it's my idea of the original sin.
James Keller: What is?
Annie Sullivan: Giving up!"
Annie Sullivan and Mr. Keller in William Gibson's *The Miracle Worker*

Living in Alabama, I grew up having Helen Keller as a hero and role model for life. I was 12 when the diminutive 15-year old Patty Duke played Helen in the film version of William Gibson's *The Miracle Worker*, and I was enthralled that someone — and from my own home state — who was deaf and blind could lead such a rich and adventurous life as an author, lecturer, political activist, and compassionate humanitarian.

Recently at a Speech Arts meeting, a fellow member presented a program on her work several summers when she was a student acting at the outdoor *Miracle Worker* presented annually on the grounds of Helen Keller's Birthplace in Tuscumbia, Alabama. She played Annie Sullivan, Helen's teacher who opened the world of communication to the child who could neither see nor hear. My friend had had a difficult childhood,

270

and had blossomed when she became part of the nurturing network of theatre, playing the role of a woman who refused to give up.

When Anne Sullivan was 21, she traveled to Alabama to teach the child of Arthur H. and Katherine Adams Keller. A responsible educator flexible enough to use her inventiveness and draw upon her own eye infirmities, she worked to make Keller understand the link between words and actual entities. Her tenacity and perseverance are wonderfully displayed in Gibson's play and film in the actual, historic lesson in which Sullivan repeatedly finger-spells the word "water" as she pumps the liquid over her headstrong pupil's hands.

I agree with Ms. Sullivan that resignation could be the original sin. Sometimes I can drive myself crazy when I continue to look for a lost object, or persevere into the night on a project, or press on searching for resolution to a dilemma. I would have probably made a good professional athlete, for I often rise to unbelievable heights to avoid surrender and defeat.

But another definition of "giving up" is the act of forsaking, renouncing, sacrificing, or surrendering. This meaning of the phrase is an undertaking I am attempting more and more these days. Putting divine order into my life requires my release of many possessions I have held onto for decades. Taking on the belief that all of us humans are really one demands that I renounce my desire to always be right. Realizing that love is an action and not an emotion necessitates that I sacrifice part of my paycheck to give to more causes and relief efforts, purchase more nonperishable goods for Greater Birmingham Ministries, and volunteer more of my time for favorite missions.

I am going to continue in my resolute determination and indefatigable doggedness. Because my dad had great strength of purpose, I don't think I can change my genes. But I am not giving up on my giving up either — fewer objects in the house, fewer dollars to spend on more objects for my house, less time to shop for those objects I don't need for my house. That sounds like a plan.

July 15:
"This royal throne of kings, this sceptred isle,
This earth of majesty, this seat of Mars,
This other Eden, demi-paradise,
This fortress built by Nature for herself
Against infection and the hand of war,

This happy breed of men, this little world,
This precious stone set in the silver sea,
Which serves it in the office of a wall
Or as a moat defensive to a house,
Against the envy of less happier lands,
This blessed plot, this earth, this realm, this England."
John of Gaunt in William Shakespeare's *Richard II*

In Shakespeare's *Richard II*, the terminally ill John of Gaunt is talking to the Duke of York, waiting for King Richard to arrive. Gaunt's deathbed wish is to positively influence the irresponsible young king. But the duke says Richard's sycophants have swayed him too far with the reckless imprudence of worldly pleasures. Gaunt then prophesies that the king is on the road to destruction in a "rash fierce blaze of riot" that will soon burn out. In one of Shakespeare's most memorable passages, Gaunt deplores the fact that the holy, happy, fair kingdom of England has been leased to a loser.

I have a book simply entitled *This England* which was published by the National Geographic Society in 1966 and purchased by my dad. It is full of photographs of this *"This earth of majesty, this seat of Mars"* that I love so much and is the home of my ancestors, all divided by sections like the Cotswolds, the Midlands, and the West Country. Every year or so, I go back through the entire volume, soaking up every picture and bits of the text.

My house has a number of artifacts from the *"sceptred isle"* collected from my trips there, and several of my walls are adorned with tapestries from Liberty of London. I recently bought some new chairs that, to me, have a medieval sort of design filled with birds and flowers. When the interior designer delivered the furniture, she enthusiastically praised the decor in what I call my "great hall," a room I had never seen as particularly outstanding, just comfortable and enjoyable.

But apparently, something about the room resonated with her and before long, she was telling me about visiting her ancestral home in Scotland, and how stunning it was to connect to her past. Then she said she was going to tell me something she had told very few people, but that she knew I would somehow understand. She felt that she sometimes caught a glimpse in her mind of herself dressed in a gown with wide sleeves and a cone-shaped hat with a veil trailing behind it. She wondered if it were a memory of a past life, or just a figment of her imagination.

I told her that I often have a sudden vision of myself tramping up a winding stone stairway or running across a flower strewn meadow with a castle in the distance. When I go into old cathedrals in England, I am overtaken by a melancholy for the time I seemed to have spent there long ago. And when I am working to put a tapestry on a wall or some similar task, I have a déjà vu sensation that what I am currently doing I have experienced in another lifetime. I have often wondered about reincarnation, or past lives, and I have also mused over whether my DNA carries with it memories lodged in its molecules, encoding my ancestors' experiences that are mysteriously delivered to me.

We were both a little surprised about our revelations to each other. But, the conversation was a lovely and a lively one, simply sparked by my relics from *"This other Eden, demi-paradise... This blessed plot, this earth, this realm, this England."*

July 16:

"Margaret: Shall I tell you my farthest back recollection? (In some awe.) I remember the first time I saw the stars. I had never seen night, and then I saw it and the stars together. Crack-in-my-eye Tommy, it isn't every one who can boast of such a lovely, lovely, recollection for their earliest, is it?
Dearth: I was determined your earliest should be a good one.
Margaret (blankly): Do you mean to say you planned it?
Dearth: Rather! Most people's earliest recollection is of some trivial thing; how they cut their finger, or lost a piece of string. I was resolved my Margaret's should be something bigger. I was poor, but I could give her the stars.
Dearth and Margaret in JM Barrie's *Dear Brutus*

The title of this play comes from Shakespeare's *Julius Caesar*: "The fault, dear Brutus, is not in our stars but in ourselves that we are underlings..." In that work, Cassius reminds Brutus that any failing of the Roman political structure was not due to the stars or Fate, but that they, and all humans, have weaknesses that lead to our destinies.

And with the title from *Julius Caesar*, *Dear Brutus* also draws upon *A Midsummer Night's Dream*, with themes of remorse, chance, and personal choice. Would we change things about our lives if we could?

With some sort of regret at their core, the characters of this story take an imaginative trip, reaching into their past to recover a thing so vital it could have reshaped their lives. The group is spending a weekend at a country house in midsummer with a Puck-like host named "Lob."

273

Walking into a nearby magical, ancient forest, each person lives out the situation of the person they would have been if they had taken a different path.

I once did a reflection that asked me to go back in memory and find my very young self, and to reassure that soul that everything was going to be fine in the future. What I saw was myself on the front porch of the Malloy cottage at Seagrove Beach at age three, surrounded by the cadre of tiny toys I took everywhere.

About ten of us had piled into the late 1940s Ford to make the trip, which at that time took most of the day on two-lane roads down the center of Alabama. The names of the towns we traveled through mesmerized me: Verbena, Luverne, Opp, Florala. They all sounded so exotic — and we were passing through them! I remember there being a big concern that the cake in the trunk did not tip over. My dad was driving and the rest of the crew consisted of females: my great-grandmother, my grandmother, my mother, myself, my aunts Patsy, Margie, and Jackie, and several chums. Our destination was an old-style Florida cottage owned by friends.

The tiny cinder block bungalow had a screened-in porch across the front. The space between the house and the cliff that led down to the beach was covered with aloe yucca, saltgrass, Saw palmetto, wild lantana, Southern bayberry, and, toward the edge, sea oats. Scattered about were spurs that stuck terribly in my feet. Down by the old-time store (with a cooler filled with ice-cold root beer) was a huge, sprawling magnolia past blossoming time, but fragrantly hypnotic with an earthy lemon, spicy sandalwood smell. And then there was the Gulf of Mexico, a body of water that took my breath away, so greeny-blue and sparkly, so vast, so mysterious — reaching out forever to the sky and yet lapping back to the shore toward me with skipping friendly white-capped waves; so filled with things not seen, not even imagined — such a vision of the inexplicable, the unfathomable, the incomprehensible.

All of this I remembered as I went back in time, the adventurous ride down, the family celebration, the warm and inviting sand, the earth alive with chirping crickets and buzzing bugs, the invigorating and briny air, the water. As I stood before that child to reassure her, I distinctly recalled being that child and seeing a vision of a person who came and spoke to me soothingly and comfortingly.

It was an uncanny experience, this glimpse into the eternity of time — and it has haunted me ever since. I don't remember if the grown-me offered the child-me a different path, but maybe she did. Maybe I took it. Maybe that is why I am where I am today.

July 17:
"Aeschylus and his Greek contemporaries believed that the Gods begrudged human success and would send a curse of hubris on a person at the height of their powers; a loss of sanity that would eventually bring about their downfall. Nowadays, we give the Gods less credit. We prefer to call it self-destruction."
James Reston in Peter Morgan's *Frost/Nixon*

Never having produced Peter Morgan's *Frost/Nixon*, I have no personal anecdotes about the show, but it is an intelligent and thought-provoking play and film that comes from a series of televised talks between former President Richard Nixon and up-and-coming English journalist and broadcaster (and later Sir) David Frost in 1977. Through the course of the story, the audience learns much about Nixon's character, his administration, and his role in the Watergate Scandal.

I agree with James Reston that, *"Nowadays, we give the Gods less credit. We prefer to call it self-destruction."* Why blame this responsive disorder on the poor gods? At some time or other, even fine folks succumb to the lure of good press, lavish praise, or an unbeaten record – all on our own accord. Then comes the over-confidence, the arrogance, and the self-adulation that makes me now seem invincible.

What the Greek playwrights revealed was that hubris or extreme pride, like that of Oedipus, will usually lead to haughty and abusive behavior that not only challenges our human moral guidelines, but also transgresses divine order (that's where the Gods come in). A little hubris can actually be a good thing if it leads to healthy self-image, an honorable challenge of authority, or striving for big, bold, brilliant goals.

But hubris can lead to a skewed view of life. Swiss psychiatrist and psychotherapist Carl Jung put it this way, "Through pride we are ever deceiving ourselves. But deep down below the surface ... a still, small voice says to us, something is out of tune."

If in this sweep of events we could only listen to that voice, be sensitive to that sudden squealing out-of-tune screech, heed that desire of our Divine Self to save us from ourselves, we might take a pause and dismount from our high horse. Most politicians have strong egos or they wouldn't reach the office to which they climb in the first place. When they get there, all the glory, laud, and honor make their vests seem bullet-proof.

The King James version of Proverbs says, "Pride goeth before destruction, and an haughty spirit before a fall." Those words of wisdom often prove to be true. When hubris is out of control, it upsets the natural order of life. When Nixon's associates stole documents, and then found out they had been taped, they went to the President. At that point, Nixon had a choice, and he opted to aid in the coverup that became Watergate. He thought as President of the United States, he was untouchable. In the Frost interviews, he says, "...when the President does it, it's not illegal." A good topple to the bottom always helps shrink the ego down to its rightful proportions.

July 18:
"Careless rapture at this stage would be incongruous and embarrassing."
Ruth in Noel Coward's *Blithe Spirit*

I have worked with the delightful *Blithe Spirit* by Noel Coward both as a fully directed play, and as a reading with seasoned actors. The play centers on novelist and society man Charles Condomine who invites the eccentric clairvoyant Madame Arcati to his house. In our reading, this part was given to one of our venerable male actors, and the results were hysterical.

Condomine doesn't believe in channeling spirits, he just wants to find some great material for a new book. However, his little plan miscarries when during the séance, Charles' tiresome and temperamental first wife Elvira materializes and begins to act up. During the rest of the play, Elvira meddles with Charles's marriage to his second wife, Ruth, who comically cannot see or even hear the ghost.

In Act I, Coward sets the stage for this humorous encounter of the two wives. Charles remembers Elvira as physically attractive, but "her spiritual integrity ... was nil." He also says, "I remember how morally untidy she was." Ruth surmises that there had been a good bit of physical electricity in her husband's former marriage, and she reminds Charles that they are not adolescents. *"Careless rapture at this stage would be incongruous and embarrassing,"* she notes with English restraint, explaining the calmer nature of a second marriage when partners are more mature.

It is curious that I had previously selected this *Blithe Spirit* quote for this day and just a couple of nights ago, I watched a third season episode of *Downton Abbey* in which Maggie Smith's character, Violet Crawley, who is the Dowager Countess of Grantham, remarked in a similar vein, "At my age one must ration one's excitement."

As I am maturing, I hope my careless rapture and excitement about all sorts of things in life are not "incongruous and embarrassing," because I can sometimes hardly contain myself from getting passionate about all sorts of things. Marriage may be a different matter. Just now, when so many of my gay friends my age are finally tying the knot with the dissolution of gay marriage bans in so many states, I am not sure a wedding is my desired design. And Roger agrees for now.

Maybe it is the second weddings of our parents. After his mother died, Roger's father married a peculiar woman who, after his dad died, purloined his and his brother's inheritance and promptly married again. Just months after my father died, my mother married a longtime family friend, but someone who really confused and confounded her last years as her dementia overcame her.

I believe deeply in the concept of second marriages. I agree with Ruth that subsequent relationships can be more serene if the partners can remember how the dramas of their first unions only led to discord and despair. Whenever I start thinking I need to prove something is right, I recall the conflicts that attitude can foster, and I choose love. After all that popular song proclaims that romance is "romancier" the next time: It may or may not lead to a trip down the aisle.

July 19:
"There is no present or future, only the past, happening over and over again, now."
James Tyrone in Eugene O'Neill's, *A Moon for the Misbegotten*

I once for a class designed the earthy 1920s costumes for Eugene O'Neill's tragedy, *A Moon for the Misbegotten*, the play that continues the tale of James Tyrone just short of a decade following the end of *A Long Day's Journey Into Night*. His mother and father are deceased, and there is no mention of other family, so Jim is left with guilt about what he has done in life, a shattered spirit, and a constant stream of lifeless days. For him, much like Bill Murray's character in the movie *Groundhog Day*, *"There is no present or future – only the past happening over and over again."*

I have a favorite day in the past that I like to revisit occasionally. I fell in love with the Beatles the first time W-S-G-N radio played the Fab

Four's "Please Please Me" in late February 1963. Two years later, I had cultivated the Beatle Girlfriend Look: long, straight hair and short skirts made of English chintz. Lots of black and white with "Carnaby Street" bursts of color. Just the name of a Beatle song was a portal into another world.

My two best sister-friends across the street and I took crazy photos like we saw on Beatle trading cards. I chose John as my Beatle, one sister took George, and the other Paul, and my mother, who was the cool mom of the neighborhood, happily settled for Ringo. The summer I was 15, I wrote a letter to the editor of the *Birmingham News*.

That year, 1965, the *News* published letters to the editor blaming the mop top band for the declining morals of teenagers. Since my adoration has blossomed into full-blown Beatlemania, I wrote a thoughtful criticism of these foolhardy grown-ups, praying for my astute views to be published on the op-ed page. Something even more wonderful happened: the editor called me and said if I wanted to do something about changing the judgment of my elders, I could cover the August Beatle concert in Atlanta for the News. Whoa!

I traveled to Atlanta with several friends, staying in the Victorian home of one girl's grandmother. To my great astonishment (I felt so very adult and powerful in my new role), I cried my way through the performance, calling: "John! John! John!"

But I soon recovered and back at the house, and while the other juvenilely immature girls were still screaming over seeing the Beatles in person, my friend Sandra and I sat on the side of a claw-foot tub with the bathroom door closed. In longhand, we wrote a review in a small notebook. I led with: "Help! The Beatles didn't need any help last night in Atlanta..."

The budding reporters could not drive, being only 15, so a mother took us at 1:00 in the morning to Western Union to telegraph the story to the News. Even though I felt so very professional, I doubted my piece would be published. I might have been young, but I had had my share of rejections in life already. On the way home the next day, we stopped at the first place that might have a Birmingham paper and bought the *News*. I searched through the all sections from back to front — nothing.

Then, flipping finally to the front page, there it was! — with a by-line and an Associated Press photo! Help! After all, I didn't need any help either — except from my collaborator Sandra.

July 20:

In "Marathon" from *Jacques Brel is Alive and Well and Living in Paris*, the singers compare life to a long-distance race. (Listen to the work online or from your library!)

Singers in *Jacques Brel is Alive and Well and Living in Paris* with Music by Jacques Brel; Lyrics by Jacques Brel, Eric Blau, and Mort Shuman; and Book by Eric Blau and Mort Shuman

When I was 20 years old, I went with a group of college drama majors to New York City on a theatre tour. One of the eye-opening shows for us newbies to the City was the experience of seeing *Jacques Brel Is Alive and Well and Living in Paris* at the Village Gate. And yes, there were hippies alive and well and living in Greenwich Village. As we walked down the street, free spirits would pass by and, in a sing-song falsetto, offer, "A-cid?"

The adventure of this musical revue which originally debuted on January 22, 1968, started as we entered the space and got to order a cocktail to drink during the show. I felt very grown up with my Manhattan, as the drinking age at the time in New York was 19 — and the bartender did not ask for an ID. *Jacque Brel* ran for more than four years, hitting 1,847 performances, and ranking third-longest-running show in off-Broadway history.

The revue, a sort of a musical character study of Brel, is interpreted by two men and two women vocalists, who perform 25 cabaret-type songs, consisting mostly of Jacques Brel tunes originally written to be sung in French and Belgian clubs and coffee houses. We saw the original cast, and they were edgy, sophisticated, and urbane. In France's popular music scene, Brel was comparable to America's Bob Dylan composing and performing profoundly individual and moving songs that are witty, heart-wrenching, theatrical, or serious.

According to Scott Miller on newlinetheatre.com, the revue *Jacques Brel* is known as "the world's first libretto-less musical," as it has no real storyline, though themes of love, death, and the passage of time shine through all the lyrics. "Eric Blau, one of the creators of the show, said that Brel writes about the way we live in a world we did not create." The words have all the complexity and beauty of poetry, and yet they also work as lyrics.

The opening song "Marathon" is a droll, absurdist catalog of twentieth century history and an extract of the whole show, Miller muses, previewing later songs about politics, popular attitudes, social mores, and the continuing capacity of human survival despite war, oppression, depression, and obsession.

Like many of the words and tunes in the revue, the phrase about joining the singers in an extended 26-mile competitive heat often haunts me, especially when I am running in circles doing several jobs at once: my actual work: "marathon," watching my grandchildren: "lengthy race," keeping on top of house tasks: "far, far, far race," carrying out committee work: "long-drawn-out race," taking care of family business: "marathon," researching my next consciousness presentation: "far, far, far run!" But like the singers, I continue, pirouetting through my mornings, afternoons, and evenings to complete my own marathon.

July 21:
"Oh, my childhood, my innocent childhood! This is the nursery where I slept and I used to look out at the orchard from here! Look, Mother's walking in the orchard. In a white dress."
Ranevsky in Anton Chekhov's *The Cherry Orchard*, Act I

Ranevsky has just gotten to the family home after five years as an expatriate in France, where she lived to escape the pain of her lover's suicide attempt. She and a small mob of friends and relatives gather in the nursery, where she and her brother Leonid spent much time in their youth. In this scene, Ranevsky peers at the titular cherry orchard. The branches are full of flowers, and as she glances out the window, she sees her deceased mother walking among the trees. But, no; alas, it is only a branch of white blooms that deceive her.

Some critics say Ranevsky grasps for the past and a romantic childhood to block the tragedy of her adult life. This yard of cherry trees viewed from the nursery window symbolizes untroubled times long ago, and she dives headlong into a vision of security that includes her mother. She is fairly disconnected from reality, and unable to find that elusive concept called "happiness."

First let me say that I have had a similar experience. When I was about 25 years old, my mother and my aunt Marge and I decided to visit my great-grandmother's house to look around. It had become the offices of a law firm, and had been nicely converted, leaving all the rooms as they had been, walls intact, but repurposed as a business space.

This is the house I lived next door to from birth to age five, whose rooms were lodged in my memory, whose doors I flung open almost every day since I resided so closely, whose windows I had peered out for the first time to discover that there was a world beyond our family, a world filled with trees and birds, automobiles and delivery trucks, and people with different skin color. In other words, this dwelling place was a center of life and learning for me.

As we walked around, I felt no connection at all with the space. My mother and aunt rattled on and on about how this room was this, and that pantry had the such and such resting in it, and this powder room was their baby sister's bedroom, and the pet (NOT!) mouse would run along this board.

I pondered my lack of bond, my total disassociation with the structure, until suddenly I realized I was now about three times the size I was when I daily frequented the residence. I got down on my knees and moved about the entire house, upstairs and down, and THEN I identified with the feelings and freedom, the awe and delight I had experienced as a tiny tot in Nannie's house.

Going back to a nursery, a kitchen, a living room, a study can bring such a rush of forgotten thoughts and experiences. That day, I was overcome by nostalgic smells that seemed to linger in the place: a fragrant cedar Christmas tree, my sweet-scented plastic doll "Jane," pork pie baking, musty sofa pillows, lemony wood polish, the coal that provided heat, Ivory soap.

I adored that house: its exterior round local rocks, its wide front porch, its creaky wooden floors, its genteel furnishings, its hundreds of books, its staircase, its nooks and crannies, its deep shadows, its bursting with life, its stories. And on that visit, like Ranevsky, I had to exclaim: "*Oh, my childhood, my innocent childhood!*"

July 22:
"I sometimes wonder if I exist myself."
Berenger in Eugene Ionesco's *Rhinoceros*

It's the middle of summer and I miss my Education for Ministry class! As I have written, the participation encourages theological study and reflection through Scriptures and traditions. We read a huge amount of material every week when we are in the midst of the course, and that can sometimes get tiring, but the philosophical and theological discussions we have really enrich my life. We talk about uncertainty and wonder, about challenges and practices, about life and death and beyond.

Ionesco's *Rhinoceros* would be worthy of one of our discussions. What the main character Berenger articulates by stating, *"I sometimes wonder if I exist myself"* is that existential doubt that so many modern people experience, and which pops up in so many Absurdist plays. It disputes seventeenth century philosopher Rene Descartes's famous phrase "I think, therefore I am," or the idea that thinking itself is the evidence of actually being or existing.

At the beginning of the play, Berenger finds little purpose in life other than alcohol. He wonders if life is really a dream, meaning he doesn't actually exist. Though he is relatively passive throughout, in the end, Berenger finds something of consequence to commit to. As others around him physically evolve into rhinoceroses, Berenger has an astonishing transformation of his own: he overturns his feeble strength of character and lack of purpose to preserve his fellow humans' subjugation by the rhinos. For him, his body and mind are not adequate equations of true existence; he must be drawn into a passionate cause.

Last year, along with my mom's dementia and other personal losses, we had a true crisis at my beloved church. Our priest, possibly inadvertently, divided the entire parish into dueling factions, making my life seem like a really bad dream — or, an Absurdist play. At the apex of confusion and conflict, I began my EfM studies. The first year is a lot of digging into the Old Testament, getting a huge dose of an angry and impetuous Santa Claus-like Deity. I really had a Dark Night of the Soul in which I doubted both my existence and God's as well.

But that parish dissension and my work in EfM was like a plow preparing the earth of my spirit to have some new seeds planted. That March, my friends invited me to an Enneagram workshop at our diocesan Camp McDowell. Roger had introduced me to the Enneagram in 2005, but I had not studied it in depth, and I not only went to the conference, but also selected the Training Track.

At about the same time, I started watching *Super Soul Sunday* on the Oprah Winfrey Network. Oprah's remarkable interviews with wise people have helped me think about the Divine and the soul in many different and illuminating ways. With that reinforcement, I have also been working with a remarkable group of colleagues in the Institute for Conscious Being performing special "Ego Recognition" work. These supports have drawn me, like Berenger, out of doubt and passivity into a passionate cause: a journey toward higher consciousness.

July 23:
Will: "And how shall I make order of the contrarieties in me?"
Sir Thomas: "By giving up parts of yourself, as all men do; it is called self-mastery."
Will: "Which parts?"
Characters in William Gibson's A Cry of Players

Many people are familiar with William Gibson's *The Miracle Worker*, but *A Cry of Players* is less frequently produced, and less well-known. That is a shame, because it is a lovely play based loosely on Shakespeare's life early during his marriage in Stratford — before an acting troupe visited and discovered the stage. The show debuted in New York City on November 14, 1968, and ran through February 15, 1969. In the 1970s, I saw a local version with a stunning set which I remember featuring a sweeping platform that came from a height of twenty feet or so stage left, and twirled in a spiral to stage right, and then to floor level back at stage left.

In the play, the twenty-year old Will is rather bored in a marriage to Anne, eight years his elder. Restless with the wonder of life, he feels stifled dabbling in his father's uneventful business. *Variety* has said about the play: "But when a troupe of itinerant actors arrived and he heard the flowery poetry of the stage, it was the siren cry of players in his ears, and he determined to be himself thereafter, even though it meant life away from home, family, comfort and security... None of this is explicitly about Shakespeare or Stratford — neither name is used, although the characters are called Will and Anne..."

William Gibson had precious little to go on for even a fanciful biographical play about Shakespeare's days on earth, for there are few records of the playwright's actual existence. Because of the paucity of documentation on life events, some critics in the last few centuries have questioned Shakespeare's penmanship. As Sarah Pruitt considers on history.com, "In the absence of such 'proof' of authorship, some skeptics have posed the question: How could a man of such humble origins and education come by such wealth of insight, wide-ranging understanding of complex legal and political matters, and intimate knowledge of life in the English court?"

However, like me, Pruitt questions the assumption that Christopher Marlowe, Francis Bacon, or Edward de Vere, the 17th Earl of Oxford must have penned the plays due to superior education, travels, worldliness, or social standing. People of "Will's" hometown of Stratford argue that such beliefs "reveal not only misguided snobbery but a striking disregard for one of the most outstanding qualities of the Bard's extraordinary work — his imagination."

I've experienced firsthand this kind of condescension; after all, I come from Alabama, but no, I don't have a banjo on my knee. When I was in a graduate school class, and handling literary discussions extremely well on daily basis, my professor asked me where I had done my undergraduate work. When I said the University of Montevallo, just south of Birmingham, Alabama, his jaw visibly dropped. He mumbled something about never having heard of it, but that I was doing very well despite my humble beginnings.

As one famous Alabamian (Forrest Gump) once said, "Stupid is as stupid does." Likewise, clever is as clever does. It really doesn't matter where you come from, or if you are born into a brilliant family, or a thriving business, or a state at the top of the IQ ratings. If you don't make smart decisions and surround yourself with bright people, you are doomed.

On the contrary, if you can make order of the contrarieties in yourself, by giving up parts of yourself and learning self-mastery; if you can move to London and immerse yourself in the bubbling life of theatre; if you can converse with the learned minds you find around you, and yourself have an open one, then perhaps even if you are from Stratford-on-Avon, you can learn to write a pretty good play.

July 24:

"I read somewhere that everybody on this planet is separated by only six other people. Six degrees of separation. Between us and everybody else on this planet. The president of the United States. A gondolier in Venice. Fill in the names. I find that A) tremendously comforting that we're so close and B) like Chinese water torture that we're so close. Because you have to find the right six people to make the connection."
Ouisa in John Guare's *Six Degrees of Separation*

Any parent with young children who has visited Disneyland, Disney World, or a Disney Park worldwide has probably been sweet talked into a special musical boat ride in Fantasyland filled with bright audio-animatronic child-like dolls dressed in costumes of the world. Once through that frolicking experience, the song "It's a Small World After All" is bludgeoned into your brain forever, and it resurfaces at extremely odd times. Like this morning when I was researching the actual history behind American playwright John Guare's 1990 play and 1993 film that popularized the phrase *Six Degrees of Separation*, and posits that it is indeed a small world.

His play was actually based on a true story that happened in 1983. David Hampton was a charismatic con artist whose claim to fame was hoodwinking a number of wealthy New Yorkers out of large amounts of money by pretending to be the just-mugged son of Sidney Poitier. John Guare's play delves into the idea of identity, using a young African American named Paul to crash into the lives of a New York art dealer Flan Kittredge and his wife Ouisa. Also introduced in the play is the notion of connections, and the playwright credits Guglielmo Marconi with the main hypothesis of the show. Marconi was the Italian pioneer inventor who worked on long-distance radio transmission and a radio telegraph system, receiving the 1909 Nobel Prize for Physics.

Apparently inspired by Marconi's work, Hungarian author Frigyes Karinthy developed a game in 1929 with friends during a heated debate about communication and the way the earth was, through the speed of transmission, growing ever smaller. Karinthy writes, "One of us suggested performing the following experiment to prove that the population of the Earth is closer together now than they have ever been before. We should select any person from the 1.5 billion inhabitants of the Earth — anyone, anywhere at all. He bet us that, using no more than five individuals, one of whom is a personal acquaintance, he could contact the selected individual using nothing except the network of personal acquaintances." Thus, with a relationship graph, the entire human population is intertwined by a chain of something like a mere 5.83 intermediaries.

The idea fascinates me, and working in fundraising, I have to make those kinds of connections happen all the time. My dad was one of those people who would go anywhere in Birmingham, the state of Alabama, the Southeast, and even oversees, and see someone he knew, or someone he knew of through a close friend or family member — so I believe there is some truth in the idea. Our hero from yesterday, Will(iam Shakespeare) has a character in *All's Well That Ends Well* say, "Love all, trust a few, do wrong to none." And, if I ponder the last part of the phrase "do wrong to none," how can I harm someone who is intimately associated with someone only five friends away?

July 25:
"Zach: But you're special.
Cassie: No, we're all special... I'll take chorus. If you'll take me."
Zach and Cassie in A *Chorus Line* with music by Marvin Hamlisch, lyrics by Edward Kleban, and book by James Kirkwood, Jr., and Nicholas Dante

When A *Chorus Line* opened at the Shubert Theatre on Broadway July 25, 1975, after some workshops and an Off-Broadway opening, the musical turned the theatre world upside down. Conceived, directed, and choreographed by Michael Bennett, the show's groundbreaking format and its fearless consideration of a number of social issues made it a revolutionary critical and box office success.

Running for over 6,000 performances, the musical gained twelve Tony Award nominations and won nine, as well as the 1976 Pulitzer Prize for Drama, one of just a few musicals to take this honor. The show revolves around an audition to fill the chorus of a Broadway musical, and is based on real stories of dancers and actors who were interviewed to create the script, and who bare their souls, putting everything on the line to get cast.

My daughter Elin was born in 1976 in the middle of theatre's love affair with the musical, and she felt deep affection for the show, even as a young child. She turned my parents into huge fans as well. I remember a New Year's Eve when she was four or five when we made a chain of choristers high kicking it through my mom and dad's house singing "One" to celebrate the dawn of a new year. Somewhere around 1981 or '82, we all went to see the show when Broadway came to Birmingham.

In the musical, Cassie had earlier performed in chorus lines before gaining principal dance parts on Broadway. During a relationship with Zach, the "director" of the show, she left for California to pursue a film and television career. Now, after some disappointments, she wants to return to the Great White Way. Zach doesn't think she can manage simply being in the chorus after all her work in leading roles. He says she is too "special" for the ensemble. Cassie protests. "No, we're all special."

When I began to study the Enneagram, I was led straight to some mirrors similar to the ones in *A Chorus Line* — only mine were spiritual looking glasses. As I started to examine myself through this wise and transformative teaching, I encountered in the reflection my false ego. I got to know that self — and it was a strong and stubborn self.

A Chorus Line is all about the struggles in life that these young people have gone through. Studying the Enneagram, I realized that through my grappling with life, my type Four spirit lost the awareness that I was intricately bound to the One True Source. I longed to be authentic. I believed my creativity was my own invention. I yearned to be special, and to have people notice me for that.

What I had to learn was that I am special — and so is everyone. I am artistic — but not because of my self. The Holy Force of creativity flows through me all the time. When I can savor being in union with the Creator, my own Divine Self comes out of ego darkness and into a sacred and life-giving spotlight center stage, shared by everyone. *"No, we're all special... I'll take chorus."*

July 26:
In "Mack the Knife" from *The Threepenny Opera*, Macheath sings about how the lovely incisors of the shark are similar to his hidden blade. (Listen to the work online or from your library!)
Macheath in *The Threepenny Opera* with musical elements by German dramatist Bertolt Brecht and composer Kurt Weill

I am packing for the beach today, and this song about the shark having beautiful fangs keeps rolling through my mind. Not that I am particularly worried about sharks in the Gulf of Mexico near Grayton Beach where we vacation. I am careful about watching what is in the water or checking the flags to make sure there are no undercurrents. But my stepfather is pouting about my leaving him for a week, and he pointed out several dire stories he had heard on his 24-hour entertainment — I mean news — television station about women having their legs eaten off by sharks this past week.

Drama critic Walter Kerr said, "I think the most wonderfully insulting music I have ever come across was composed by the late Kurt Weill for Bert Brecht's *Threepenny Opera*." The music is satirical and edgy and acerbic — not something you are ever likely to hear in an elevator.

When I was in my twenties, I found it somewhat odd looking back to when I was eight in 1958 that Bobby Darin had such a hit with "Mack the Knife." The rock and roll guru Dick Clark warned Darin about using a song from an opera for the popular music crowd, but the recording hit number one on the Billboard Hot 100 and won a 1959 Grammy Award, which made Clark later humorously rue his advice. I remember as a 3rd-grader hearing Darin's snazzy chart-topper over and over on my mother's car radio when we would drive to the grocery store or to visit relatives. At the time, snapping my fingers to the music, I had no idea it had come from such a raw and gritty piece of theatre.

I have designed conceptual costumes for *The Threepenny Opera* and for John Gay's *Beggar's Opera* upon which the more modern work was based, and I think both are amazing performance pieces. Brecht's epic musical theatre production opened in Berlin on August 31, 1928, just a half month before my mother was born, and two-hundred years after Gay's ballad opera debuted in London on January 29, 1728.

Both works are anti-operas with anti-heroes, both named Macheath. *The Beggar's Opera* is a forceful plea for libertarian principles in reaction to the governing Whig's burgeoning conservatism. Similarly, Brecht's socialist characters jab at the foibles of capitalism in the twentieth century. Both works challenge society's beliefs about property, populism, poverty, politics, and punishment. And both works are daringly different in their music and in their performance style. Listen to both operas all the way through and you will feel both mocked and moved by their uncanny ability to elicit from you strong thoughts and feelings about life.

But back to my thinking toward our annual trip to the beach and some shark showing me his pearly white teeth. I went ahead and checked, and found that according to the International Shark Attack File, only one documented shark assault on humans has been recorded in Walton County, Florida in the last 130 years. My stepfather could have frightened me more with foreboding forecasts about lightning strikes or panicked driving in the crazy vacation traffic or shellfish food poisoning. However, it doesn't matter what he comes up with, I'm leaving at 8:00 in the morning!

July 27:

"But a miracle is an event without an explanation. That's why people like you fail to believe, because you demand an explanation, and when you don't get one you create one."

Mother Miriam Ruth to Dr. Livingstone in John Pielmeier's *Agnes of God*

John Pielmeier's *Agnes of God* is an intriguing play that we considered producing, but self-censored our choice for its subject matter at a historically Southern Baptist university. In the play, a young nun is charged with killing an infant she gave birth to in a cloistered convent. A female psychiatrist who is assigned to the case is challenged by the convent's Mother Superior, and through the course of the story, all three women, as the playwright says, "...explore questions of Faith, Memory, and the meaning of Sainthood." Today's Samford could handle the work, but we didn't feel empowered to give it a try in the 1980s.

Many people today would fall into Dr. Livingstone's camp concerning miracles, demanding an explanation, believing there is no such thing. But I think the Mother Superior is right, a miracle can simply be a surprising and either disturbing or favorable event that is not easily accounted for using natural or scientific laws. Spiritually oriented people see such occurrences as the work of divine intervention.

Take for example this series of events that recently happened to me. First, I watched a *Super Soul Sunday*. In this particular segment, Oprah talks to legendary NBA coach Phil Jackson, "The Zen Master."

She reads from his book *Eleven Rings: The Soul of Success*. In it, he quotes a work he had read that gave him the idea that anything you do for yourself, any gesture of kindness or honesty, will affect how you experience the world. What you do for yourself, you are doing for others; what you do for others, you are doing for yourself. Jackson uses this idea in his work as a professional basketball coach. "We had a statement we repeated so many times to the players," he said. "'No man is an island. No man goes his way alone. What I put into the lives of others will come back unto its own.'"

The first part of the statement comes from one of my favorite authors, seventeenth century English metaphysical poet and priest John Donne, "No man is an island, entire of itself; every man is a piece of the continent, a part of the main." So, I had the coach's lovingkindness manifesto in my mind and that night, Roger and I decided at the last minute to go to a nearby Mexican restaurant for supper. The place was crowded, so we sat at the bar. We couldn't find chairs together, so we asked two men who were talking if we could move the stool that was between them. One gentleman stood up and gave me his tall chair — he said he was just waiting for take out. So we thanked him profusely and struck up a lively conversation with them.

Then, the take-out fellow left with two big bags of food, and we ate our dinner. As we got ready to pay for our meal, our waiter told us the gentleman we had been talking to had already taken care of our bill. A small gesture, maybe. You might not call that a miracle, but thinking about Coach Jackson's mantra had been a powerful tool in opening my heart, and must have somehow radiated good will. And now I am putting the experience into words, *"But a miracle is an event without an explanation."*

July 28:
"Sometimes I buy something that isn't black and I put it on and I am so sorry."
One of the Women in *Love, Loss and What I Wore*, adapted for the stage by Nora and Delia Ephron based on the book by Ilene Beckerman

Writer Nora Ephron passed away in June of 2012 at the age of 71. My friend and co-worker Ellise directed *Love, Loss and What I Wore* the following November. Birmingham Festival Theatre put the show in their season long before Ephron's death was eminent. A series of monologues make up the theatrical evening created by Nora (*Sleepless in Seattle, When Harry Met Sally*) and her sister, Delia, based on the book by Ilene Beckerman.

The Ephron sisters and Beckerman understood fashion, and the play's soliloquies explore the significance of clothing to women. Clothes can be a connecting tie or dividing line in a female relationship between friends, sisters, cousins, or mothers and daughters. Traditionally, the cast dresses in black and performs the play as a dramatic reading.

Black is the color for movie stars, fashion designers, and people working backstage in the theatre (so they won't be seen changing scenery). Black is not the universally flattering color; that distinction goes to the color pink. Pink compliments almost all complexions and hair colors. But black is fashionable, durable, dramatic, mature, figure-flattering, dressy, and chic. Black is always in style and you can dress it up with colorful accessories or sensational jewelry.

Aficionados of the modern Goth post-punk subculture have an interesting affinity for black clothing, the traditional color for mourning. Believing the morals of society dead, and what makes people civilized dying, Goths, in their dark and esoteric garb, seem ever to be mysteriously grieving for most people's lack of understanding and tolerance for all humans.

We actually all wear clothes, at least sometimes, that are symbolic in nature. A police or military uniform denotes power, an expensive suit indicates wealth, a round white color signifies clergy, scrubs characterize the medical profession, a ring on the left hand designates marital status. When I designed costumes for ten or 12 plays a year, I enjoyed creating clothing that got a character's personality, status, profession, psyche, emotional tendencies, mind-set, and temperament across to the audience at their first entrance.

Try this experiment yourself: sample dressing in clothing suited to a prostitute one day, or a nun, or a professor, or a painter, or a lab technician. How does your attire make you feel? Sanctioned? Sexy? Smart? Seedy? Strong? Studies have been done on why, when we dress in a certain outfit, we take on a role and that change affects our actual abilities. What would a Goth be in a frothy yellow dress and matching Mary Jane slippers? What would our doctor be in a sailor uniform? What would our gardener be in a clown costume?

One summer when my son was the supervisor at the Ropes Course at our summer camp, Winnataska, he and two other male staff members started the day in tuxedos. This camp is in Alabama, where the heat and humidity are high, and the usual raiment is shorts and sleeveless shirts. They wanted to show the campers and other staff they were serious enough about their jobs that summer that they would sacrifice comfort for the start of one day.

Of course, they wore black. Black is my favorite clothing color, too. *"Sometimes I buy something that isn't black and I put it on and I am so sorry."*

July 29:

In "Summertime" from *Porgy and Bess*, Clara sings about how people pass their days in summer in an uncomplicated way. (Listen to the work online or from your library!)

Clara in George Gershwin and Dubose Heyward's *Porgy and Bess*, based on Heyward's novel *Porgy*

The hauntingly expressive aria "Summertime" was composed by George and Ira Gershwin, with lyrics by Dubose Heyward, for their 1935 opera Porgy and Bess, based on Heyward's novel *Porgy*. The later consummate composer and lyricist Stephen Sondheim called the words to "Summertime," along with "My Man's Gone Now," "the best lyrics in the musical theater."

This particular tune has been performed and captured by so many groups and soloists, that it is one of the most recorded songs of all time. Just think of Billie Holiday, Janis Joplin, Frank Sinatra, Miles Davis, Ricky Nelson, John Coltrane, or Louis Armstrong with Ella Fitzgerald.

It's easy to see why the calming song is so popular. The first of its four appearances in the play, it functions as a lullaby, and it is a comforting and mollifying melody, suitable to lull any child to sleep.

Summer calls for docile actions. In the South, it's scorchingly hot, so things have to become a bit effortless, slowed down, and unhurried in summer. Mullet are the only fish that jump much in our part of the country, but it sure is fun to see them flash and splash out of the water. We are able to do that right now, as we are vacationing at Big Redfish Lake in Blue Mountain, Florida, and the mullet seem to flourish in this warm lagoon.

South Walton County, where we are staying, is famous for its sugar white sands and turquoise Gulf of Mexico waters. Until we started staying here four years ago, I didn't realize the area boasts over a dozen phenomenal coastal dune lakes, a geographical characteristic so unusual it only appears in a scattering of spots worldwide. Constantly evolving and changing, "our" Redfish Lake, like the others, was fashioned by wind and waves thousands of years ago. Fairly shallow, its water is brackish, with a mix of salt water from the Gulf and freshwater from an impressively gushing inland spring.

Roger is a bit worried about the frogs. Four years ago, he recorded on his phone a resonant, booming symphony of their evening croaks. Now, we hardly hear any at all. He notices such things, as he is a Thoreau naturalist at heart. He picks up worms from the middle of the street and nestles them back into the grass. He has rescued a Virginia Rail bird who was exhausted from migration, a baby squirrel who fell from his nest, turtles stranded and confused about their best path. And he coaxes koi fish to jump into his hands from outdoor ponds.

He is wild about the environment for what it is, every smelly, alluring, tasty, squishy, pulpy, velvety, satiny, harsh detail of it. I am infatuated by nature for what it does to me spiritually.

My trip to the beach always encompasses some staring at the horizon, which is supposed to reduce blood pressure, and a yearly assessment of what is going on with and in my life. Something about the waves rushing to shore and receding, the crashing sound, the sea birds' calls, the salty water, the clean wind off the sea — all send me back to a place where I was newly born, where I could rest, where I could loll and let go and bask in the sound of a summertime lullaby during those summer days when our actions become tranquil and unhurried, languid even.

July 30:
"Grace: I'm sorry, Mister, but you're just left out in the cold.
Virgil: Well... that's what happens to some people."
Characters in William Inge's *Bus Stop*

Ward, a friend of mine directed *Bus Stop* a few years ago at a local community theatre, and it was well done. In the play, a group of mismatched characters winds up together in the café of a small Kansas town when a bus driver is compelled to pull over due to icy road conditions. Almost like a reverse Canterbury Tales, this group of quirky and mismatched travelers is going nowhere, and all reveal their conflicts to the audience as the night progresses.

With the name Virgil Blessing, this one character is bound to be fatherly and protective. Additionally, Grace has a little grace about her beneath her resistance to trust.

An online review of the play by Wade Bradford remarks that, "Virgil Blessing, perhaps the most admirable character in *Bus Stop*, is the one who tugs on our heartstrings the most. In the conclusion, when the cafe is closing up, Virgil is forced to stand outside, alone in the dark, frosty morning... It's a line that makes us wish that the Virgil Blessings and the William Inges of the world would find comfort and solace, a warm place to take off life's chill."

Blessing is literally left out in the cold, but the phrase commonly means "being on the outside, not part of a group or an activity." Do I ever know that state of affairs? During the past few years, my wisdom studies have given me such insight into the pitfalls, agonies, avoidances, vices, and virtues of my ego.

Until integrated or redeemed, Fours like me sense we are defective and out of step with the norm. Longing for something – though we don't know exactly what – we idealize being part of a group that we know we don't fit into. Envying what others seem to have, we are achingly conscious of what seems to be missing from life.

We say we don't care being "left out in the cold," and heighten that flare, that originality, that unique quality. Hey, we don't fit in because we are too special to be part of the rank and file. And yet, we are melancholy knowing something about this charade is inauthentic.

I wanted to be a writer and a serious artist, but thankfully I was led – through many turns in my path and bumps in my road – into the theatre. Had I stayed in a study writing or in studio painting, I would have become a mercurial recluse and a peculiar eccentric. Theatre pulled me out of myself and into a world where all are accepted for what and who they are, for where and how they can contribute to the whole. Theatre brought me together with other people – some like me, and some very different from me – all working toward a meaningful end.

Theatre made me empathetic. When I designed costumes as a living, I created clothing for over 100 characters every year. I had to creep not only into their shoes, but into their entire wardrobes to see how they lived and what made them tick.

So Virgil might not be hard for me to understand in this play *Bus Stop*, but Bo the macho cowboy, or Cherie the nightclub singer, or Dr. Gerald Lyman the retired academician – I had to stretch to relate to and identify with such characters. And as that elasticity grew, I was extended, lengthened, expanded myself – and ultimately, thankfully drawn out of my Four shell.

July 31:
"I know you become such a coward that you'll grab at any lousy excuse to get out of killing your pipe dreams. And yet, as I've told you over and over, it's exactly those damned tomorrow dreams which keep you from making peace with yourself. So you've got to kill them like I did."
Hickey in Eugene O'Neill's *The Iceman Cometh*, Act 3

I survived watching a production of Eugene O'Neill's *The Iceman Cometh* in the late 1970s when a sister university produced it when

Birmingham hosted the Southeastern Theatre Conference. It was a fine production, but this is a gloomy, long, depressing play. A young Marlon Brando turned down a role in the original 1946 debut, saying even reading the script put him to sleep. He later called the work "ineptly written and poorly constructed."

One thing that made the show I saw intriguing was working draft beer equipment in Harry Hope's Greenwich Village saloon. Inhabitants of the pub are regulars, all broken boozers who drink to make life go away. The only highlight of their purposeless lives is the occasional visit of a salesman named Theodore Hickman, or "Hickey." O'Neill might have named the play *Waiting for Hickey*.

Hickey holds in his adept hands a fairly large sales territory that stretches across the East Coast. When the curtain rises, the bar flies are waiting for him to surprise them by attending pub owner Harry's birthday party. The bar really comes to life only when Hickey shows up to sermonize and enlighten them.

"I know you've become such a coward that you'll grab at any lousy excuse to get out of killing your pipe dreams. And yet, as I've told you over and over, it's exactly those damned tomorrow dreams which keep you from making peace with yourself. So you've got to kill them like I did," Hickey pontificates. This quote not only crystallizes his philosophy, it reveals his despair. And later we find he has not only assassinated his life's desires, but he has murdered his wife.

Even though I don't agree with all of Hickey's doctrine, something actually rings true in sometimes killing your pipe dreams. At an Easter Vigil one year, our bishop posited in his sermon that sometimes our dreams have to die. A young lady started weeping and ran from the service. I could relate to her. I have had many unfulfilled goals in and for my life. And I have had to come to terms with what our bishop meant: sometimes some dreams, hopes, or visions for the future are eventually impossible. Holding on to an expired aspiration is futile.

I read a quote on the internet recently, "Some people come into your life just to teach you how to let go." People do that, and so do events, moves, job changes. All of us are often myopic when conceiving grand plans for our lives with certain people or in particular professions, with hoped for talents or in magical circumstances. What our bishop reminded us is that sometimes God and the Universe have greater plans that don't include the people or things in our present situation. To develop, we have to let those ambitions go. In doing so, we grow stronger and more resilient as we move on.

As Elsa sings in the Disney movie *Frozen* (where the Iceman **has** cometh), free yourself. Don't be held back by schemes that have gone awry or by strategies that didn't work. Make a 180 degree turn and let your life recharge.

August 1:
In the song "Camelot" from the musical *Camelot*, Arthur sings to Guinevere about how ideal the atmospheric conditions are in his kingdom. (Listen to the work online or from your library!)

Arthur in the musical *Camelot*, with book and lyrics by Alan Jay Lerner and music by Frederick Loewe

Today we remember Joseph of Arimathea on the Holy Calendar, a saint who has always fascinated me since he is part of the legend of King Arthur that we perform at Winnataska during summer camp. When the film version of the musical *Camelot* came out in October of 1967, I immediately fell in love with Richard Harris. Later, I was even fond of his top ten recording of "MacArthur Park," with its mysterious reference to a cake left out in the rain, its sweet green icing flowing down, and the baffling loss of its recipe.

But, back to the movie. The law that was made that faraway moon ago, by the past queens and kings, concerning pleasant weather in July and August unfortunately does not stretch to the Camelot we create every summer at Winnataska. The temperature is as hot as blazes nowadays — and it was just as steamy in 1967 when I was a leader for the summer.

Camelot was a fairly popular movie, and I was enamored of the film. By the time I was 17 — the fall it debuted — I realized how quirky it was that a summer camp in Alabama performed a play several times each summer about the medieval English legend of King Arthur and the Knights of the Round Table. The fact that anyone in the world went to see the film somehow validated my camp and my life.

Summers at Winnataska were peaceful, yet enlivening. I was in high school, and my passion was centered in England, where a fashion sensation named Twiggy was the rage, where mini skirts got shorter, and the Beatles reigned supreme in the rock and roll world with the release of "Sgt. Peppers Lonely Heart Club Band." Some of my camp friends and I drew Twiggy eyelashes below our own lower ones, made up camp songs, and basically escaped from what was happening in the outside world: Israel's Six Day War; the Vietnam conflict; and tens of thousands of peace protesters marching in Washington, DC and San Fransisco.

And these events were fairly mild considering with the next year, 1968, came the assassinations of Martin Luther King, Jr., and Bobby Kennedy, protesters at the Chicago Democratic Conventions, and so much more. 1967 was hopeful that Camelot might return; 1968 was the cake left out in the rain, my innocence melting along with that sweet green icing.

After the crucifixion, when all the disciples left Jesus, Joseph takes the body away, wrapping it with spices, and placing it in his own new tomb. Later, a number of legends evolve about Joseph, and my favorite is that he wanders north until he arrives at the ancient town Glastonbury, taking with him the Holy Grail cup used at the Last Supper, still containing the blood and sweat of Jesus — found at the foot of the cross.

Over time, the cup disappears, and a tradition grows that only a person pure in heart can hope to find this Holy Grail. Many years pass, and when King Arthur becomes the ruler of England, he gathers about him the truest men of the kingdom, called the Knights of the Round Table. This band of knights decide to find purpose in life by searching for the Holy Grail.

Most of them are unsuccessful. But the interesting and still applicable idea that develops is that the person who finds the Cup has to have certain qualities. For what the Grail turns out to be is really our own authentic self, our soul, our essence — found deep inside of us. Through unbearable betrayals, dry deserts, disappointing dragons, and painful encounters, we are forced to drop the mask and be real, and what we find is our own pure, gentle, true, unselfish, courageous, and kind self.

August 2:
"And, lo! some rumour of this peace, being gone
Forth to the Greek, hath cursed me. Achilles' son,
So soon as I was taken, for his thrall
Chose me."
Andromache in Euripides's *Trojan Women*

Achilles lives next door to me. He has a childish lisp and is ecstatic that he can now spell his name. This boy can run fast and throw a ball fairly far, and loves to dress in a super hero cape. I am not sure how weak his heel is. I doubt his mother attempted to give him immortality by immersing him in the River Styx (or maybe the nearby Cahaba) when he was younger.

His grandfather, with whom he lives, was born in Greece and immigrated to Alabama to work in the food business, as many of our Birmingham Greek friends have done. He encourages us to pick the Italian figs from his tree whose branches dangle heavily over our yard when filled with delectable fruit in July.

Probably the strongest rendition of the ancient hero Achilles can be found in Homer's epic poem *The Iliad.* In this work, Achilles reveals characteristics of perception, steadfastness, bravery, and superhero strength. But the Trojans saw another, more arrogant side of this warrior. In this quote from *Trojan Women,* Andromache is mourning not only the death of her husband Hector, who was killed by Achilles during the Trojan War, but also the truth: being conquered by the Greeks, she will become a concubine for Achilles's son.

The little boy next door is a charming child, and a big talker. I can barely exit my back door before he is at the fence between our yards asking how I am doing today. He chats about his school friends, the little car that he drives around the backyard, or the rabbit that has come to visit earlier. Sticks are swords to him; nuts are missiles; pinecones are rocket ships.

I don't know how much my Achilles yet knows about his namesake. The Greek hero's heel was left defenseless when his mother dangled him in the magically powerful Styx River to prevent an early death, holding him by the heel. But one day in battle, a poisonous arrow shot right into his vulnerable spot, killing him.

Obviously, my Achilles is mortal. His body doesn't seem immune to arrows or other slings of life, as he often sports scrapes and bruises. But, at some point, maybe the ancient hero will live within him. I just hope his future grasp of the Greek myths of his grandfather-land move beyond our modern products that echo their power, such as Trident gum, Ajax cleanser, the Odyssey van, or amazon.com.

August 3:
"Argon: (shouting) Come quick. I'm dying!
Toinette: (off) Dying?
Argon: (shouting) When I can get my hands on you, I'll give you what for.
Toinette: (off) What for?

Argon: (shouting) Stop talking like an echo, and come here. (He pauses) Can you hear me?
Toinette: (off) No?
Argon: Aaaah! (He shouts) Come here, come here, come here. Drop whatever you're doing; and come here."
Characters in *The Imaginary Invalid* by Molière

The Imaginary Invalid, or *The Hypochondriac*, was the last comedy written by Molière. Even as he wrote the masterpiece, Molière was himself extremely ill. It premiered at the Palais Royal Theatre, on February 10, 1673. The playwright acted the lead role of Argan for four performances and collapsed on stage, dying soon after, so he was anything but an imaginary invalid.

In the first scene, Argan — not only a formidable hypochondriac, but also a curmudgeon —is checking his receipt from the apothecary for each and every single pill and mixture he has received. A miser too, he approves only about half the bill, and then he calls in his maid, Toinette, demanding, *"Come here, come here, come here. Drop whatever you're doing; and come here."*

Just a few minutes ago, my stepfather's present caretaker called me in tears. As I may have indicated, he is at least as cantankerous as Argan, and he told her she was fired (for the second time in so many weeks). She is wonderful, gentle, helpful; but something she did offended him and he spouted off at her just like a Molière character come alive in the present day.

Okay, my stepfather is not an imaginary invalid. He will be 94 this year and is almost blind, hard of hearing, so hoarse all the time he can hardly speak, and he has to get around with a walker. He is a real, actual invalid, with aches, pains, and the suffering of someone who has really outlived his body.

I have known people all my life who were abnormally anxious about their health, and he never used to be one of them. I knew a woman in a club with me who always said in the early fall: "Well, it's just about allergy time, and I know my girls and I are about to come down with sinus infections. It always happens about this time of year, and I am sure I will be the sickest of us all."

Sure enough, soon all of them would be sick — and she with the worst case — and I couldn't help thinking that she was a magnet, drawing illnesses toward her rather than attempting to repel maladies with not only attitude, but also precautions, sleep, exercise, vitamins, fresh foods, and other such balms. She seemed to enjoy her sicknesses though. They gave her an identity and, as a patient, she could command some caring consideration.

The Atlantic online, June 11, 2013, featured an article by Richard Gunderman entitled, "When People Seem to Want to Be Sick." In it, the author wrote: "Ironically, some people are so starved for attention and sympathy that they would rather make themselves sick than carry on feeling so ignored and under-appreciated. Regardless what syndrome we call it, there is something deeply sad in the fact that a person's life could be so empty."

Back to my Real Actual Invalid. My stepfather fell seven years ago and fractured his hip. Until that day, he worked out with weights four or five times a week at a gym, drove himself everywhere, walked in the neighborhood, swam, and was basically very active for someone 87-years old. But oddly, after the fall, he settled for being debilitated for the rest of his life.

But maybe this stance is working for this Invalid after all. Any time he wants something, he, like Argan, can call, *"Come here, come here, come here. Drop whatever you're doing; and come here."*

August 4:
"I love inscriptions on flyleafs and notes in margins. I like the comradely sense of turning pages someone else turned and reading passages someone long-gone has called my attention to."
Helene Hanff in James Roose-Evans's *84, Charing Cross Road*, based on the book by Helene Hanff

Helene Hanff published the book *84, Charing Cross Road* in 1970, and the volume was later made into a stage play, television play, and film. The delightful work dramatizes a real series of letters between Helene, a striving young New York writer, and Frank Doel, an established chief buyer for an antiquarian book store in London. So the communications are both business correspondences, and also love letters — the love being of great literary texts. But, over a twenty year period beginning in 1949 when Hanff first writes Marks & Co., the story follows a burgeoning long-distance friendship that only ends in 1969 with the death of Doel.

Charing Cross Road is a London street running from St. Martin-in-the-Field to St. Giles Circus, named in honor of the last of the "Eleanor crosses" that King Edward I had erected in memory of his wife Eleanor of Castile. As I mentioned in a January entry, when she died in Harby in 1290, Queen Eleanor's body was sent to London, taking twelve days to reach her burial spot at Westminster Abbey.

Crosses were erected at the places where her funeral procession stopped each night. The original wood crosses were later replaced by splendid decorated stone monuments. Romantically, every time I see a flowery cross on the interstate marking the tragic car death of someone's precious loved one, I think of Edward marking the spots where his beloved's body lay.

Charing Cross Road is chock full of second hand and specialist bookstores. I poked around in a number of them on a trip to London in 1992 when I took a group of students to Samford University's London Study Centre. I randomly selected a 1951 book by Desmond Dunne called *Yoga for Everyman: How to Have Long Life and Happiness* — and, as often such chance choices do for me, the volume changed my life.

I did not start doing Yoga immediately after reading that the practice can keep you flexible well into your older years, assist with graceful posture and balance, contribute to your overall health, and make you feel and look younger. But it was not long before I added Yoga to my morning routine.

Yoga is one exercise that keeps me focused in the moment. My thoughts very rarely race to what I need to do that day, to what I should accomplish at work, to what is for supper. I am pretty grounded while performing my workout.

But every now and then, at the very end, my mind wanders back to that little Charing Cross shop that was crammed full of the intoxicating aroma of old books, leather, ink, and paper. I think about that little red book I came across. It was marked up. Someone long before me noted several passages that jumped out at him. When I first read the volume, I felt a kinship with someone in England who had poured over the pages before me. I wonder if he is still walking the streets of London with the elastic, springy step of youth, having continued his daily routine of Yoga, cultivating the natural health God gave him. I like to think he is.

August 5:
"Berniece ain't gonna sell that piano."
Doaker in August Wilson's *The Piano Lesson*

When I taught Theatre Appreciation, I loved to turn my mainly white Anglo-Saxon students onto August Wilson, with whom they fell in love. *The Piano Lesson*, written in 1990, is the fourth play in Wilson's Pittsburgh Cycle. That series of plays, each set in a different decade, portrays both the humorous and the dramatic turns of African-American life throughout the 1900s.

In January of 1998, I took around ten of my group to see *The Piano Lesson* at the Alabama Shakespeare Festival. Set in Pittsburgh in 1936, right after the Depression, the play deals with the idea of gaining a sense of self by denying — or accepting — the past. Exploring some of Doaker Charles's family history, the plot revolves around an heirloom piano intricately hewn with likenesses of their enslaved relatives. The piano symbolizes several themes of the play as Berniece strives to keep the heirloom while her sharecropper brother Boy Willie struggles to sell the instrument to purchase the very land their family had labored on as slaves.

My paternal grandmother Jessie was the third in a family of six girls from Winfield, Alabama, where, like most Americans, they struggled through the same Depression that the Charles tribe survived. When Jessie graduated from high school, she went to business school, got married, and moved to Birmingham, filling a series of jobs that ultimately led to her being the "right-hand woman" of one of the Magic City's most respected Jewish lawyers.

Much like Boy Willie wants to do, Jessie put her small town roots behind her and carved out a respectable living and career during a time when few women worked. She always had a change purse filled with dollar bills and quarters for taxis. The floor of her closet was filled with the most glamorous shoes I have ever seen. She bought herself a wardrobe full of the nicest business dresses she could find. And she always helped any of her kin who needed a boost.

However, the one family tradition she never gave up was music. Her father had played the guitar, and the entire clan were fabulous singers. One of her sisters who had a slight intellectual disability lived with my grandparents, and sometimes when I spent the night, Jessie would play her ukulele and she and Myra would sing tunes by Hank Williams, Eddie Arnold, Ernest Tubb, and the Andrews Sisters.

When my grandfather died in 1968, Jessie moved to a new apartment near her office, which had relocated from downtown to the

Southside of Birmingham. With whatever benefits she had inherited, along with her own savings, she outright bought a Hammond organ and proceeded to take lessons and learn how to play what had always been her favorite instrument.

Even though it was brand new, it filled a spot in her heart much like the piano did for Berniece: it tied her back to her roots. On it, she played the gospel music and old-time hymns of her youth. She never wanted to move back to Winfield, but she liked to connect to it daily traveling a road engineered by her music.

August 6:
"I know death hath ten thousand several doors
For men to take their exits."
The Duchess in John Webster's *The Duchess of Malfi*

Today is the Christian day of the Transfiguration. On August 6 in 1945 during World War II, an American B-29 airplane unloaded our human world's initial atomic bomb. Dropped on the Japanese city of Hiroshima, the detonation annihilated about 90 percent of the city, killing over 80,000 residents immediately, with thousands more expiring later of radiation exposure. Just three days later, another plane dropped a second A-bomb, this time on Nagasaki, killing approximately 40,000 people.

Being burned to oblivion by an atomic bomb is certainly one way to take your exit from this earth. I remember growing up in the 1950s and wondering just when America's enemies were going to decimate our cities. We learned about the dangers of radiation and fallout, and schools rehearsed "duck and cover" drills — much like practice for a fire, only we did not run outside. We crouched under our desks and held our heads with our hands, as students do today rehearsing an intruder with a gun.

Death, just like life, has ten thousand, ten million or billions even, manifestations: one, I suppose, for every single human being who ever lived. I studied English dramatist John Webster's 1612 *The Duchess of Malfi* in graduate school. Though it begins as a love story, concerning a Duchess marrying beneath her station, the play is all about death, and concludes as a gruesome tragedy in which the heroine's brothers obliterate each other trying to exact revenge.

Most modern Americans not only fear death, they deny it or at least refuse to even think about their own end. What happens to me after

I die? Where do those *"ten thousand several doors"* take us? I don't really know, do you? I can listen and either believe or question people who have had near-death experiences. I can observe people as they make that transition from life to death and log what they say.

During a eulogy to her brother Steve Jobs, Mona Simpson disclosed that his final words, were: "Oh, wow. Oh, wow. Oh, wow." While part of me desperately wishes I could know what so wowed him, there is such a quality of astonishment and mystery about his utterance that maybe I don't want to fully grasp it quite yet.

Once a former priest of mine, said that, in his profession, he felt honored to have been present at the death of so many people. At the time, that statement was disquieting. I absolutely get the willies every time I see a dead animal in the road, be it dog, cat, squirrel, or even mouse. And I grieve every single time a bird flies into my huge picture windows, which is sometimes daily. I couldn't imagine sitting at the bedside of a dying person.

But, when my dad took a turn for the worse, my mother called me to come over as quickly as possible. My son Seth was about to go off to college and my daughter Elin and I had gone with him to a pizza party for several Sewanee freshman who lived in town. We three rushed over to my parents' home and were actually holding my dad's hands when he breathed his last exhalation.

The experience was not scary. It did not make us uneasy or anxious and I suddenly grasped what my priest had meant. It was actually a very holy moment, as we almost detected a spirit rising from him as he gently transfigured from this life into what I can now only perceive as the Great Unknown.

August 7:
"Catherine, what world were we waiting for?"
Anna in Paul Zindel's *And Miss Reardon Drinks a Little*

Notice Anna does not say the usual, "What **in the** world were we waiting for," but *"what world were we waiting for?"* The three Reardon sisters get together for a dinner seven months after the death of the mother who had cared for them after their father's abandonment. Paul Zindel's 1971 dark comedy-drama set in 1960 delves into the challenge of sororal relationships and the struggle of deciphering life when a bitter and controlling mother is out of the picture.

Zindel alternates humor and despair in this botched-up family life, revealing how very differently the siblings deal with the pain. All three women are involved in their local school district: Anna Reardon is a chemistry teacher, Catherine Reardon is an assistant principal, and Ceil Reardon Adams has climbed her way to the top, becoming the superintendent.

Catherine (the "Miss Reardon" of the title and the butt of school gossip for her closeted imbibing) becomes dependent on alcohol before the eyes of the audience. Anna, suffering from a near nervous collapse, has just been accused of molesting one of her students, but insists that her problems arose during a recuperative trip to Europe where a stray cat infected her with rabies. Ceil, a glacial control freak, attempts to dominate her sisters professionally as their school supervisor, and personally, having "attended" to their mother's belongings to her own advantage.

Without three superlative actors, this play will bomb terribly, and the script will seem dated. A recent review of a revival in Arizona drew this comment out of a reviewer: "Paul Zindel's 1971 play has aged as well as leisure suits and eight-track tape players..."

Recently, one of our local theatres, Birmingham Festival, posted some old commentaries online, and a 1975 critique of this play by Kenneth Paul Shorey was among the archives. Now, this production was staged just a few years after the play was written, but Shorey remarked about the three actors who were both "individually talented" and yet were able to "combine to repress their respective egos for the sake of an ensemble effect: The interplay of forces in itself exciting."

This review has lived famously, or in infamy, in Birmingham theatre lore for his comment, "If you're a BFT supporter who hasn't been turning out lately or if you've never been to BFT, this is the show to see. I mean, this is it: This is the one. If you miss Reardon, you simply won't know what people are going to be talking about for the next year and a half." (People are still talking!)

He goes on to say, "...in Ginger Marsh's mouth, the concluding line, 'Catherine, what world were we waiting for?' becomes approximately the equivalent of watching Kane's sled burn." That reference recalls the end of the film Citizen Kane and the stored toboggan Kane had loved as a child. To him, it symbolized a happy, carefree childhood, but to his staff at the Xanadu estate, it is deemed junk and burned in a basement furnace.

The blazing sled and Anna's line come at the finale of emotional roller-coasters. What world were the two unmarried sisters waiting for? Are you wasting time, hoping for a life to appear to you, ready-made, to take you out of your misery? Don't linger. Your world is of your making, and you daily have a shot at making this life great. "I mean, this is it: This is the one."

August 8:
"In a good shoe, I wear a size six, but a seven feels so good, I buy a size eight."
Truvy in Robert Harling's *Steel Magnolias*

A play can split theatre people right down the middle: they either absolutely love it and want to do it over and over or really loathe the idea of having to be a part of it at all. I believe *Steel Magnolias* is like that. And yes, it was a play before it became a sensational 1989 film hit directed by Herbert Ross. At Samford, a student directed it in the spring of 1995, and I enjoyed working on the periphery of it, even though I am not usually drawn to kitchen dramas or situation comedies, of which this is a blend. (Okay, I know the work is set in a beauty parlor.)

At the beginning of the play, situated in northwest Louisiana, a group of women are arguing about magnolias. In a recent interview with *Garden and Gun Magazine*, playwright Robert Harling said that as a child, he recalled that a lady in his neighborhood "had a large metal floral paperweight on her kitchen counter that served as a receptacle for change, keys... it weighed down the check for the milkman or the dry cleaner receipt... She called that thing on her counter 'the steel magnolia.'

"In her sweet drawl, she'd say, 'Take a quarter from the steel magnolia and get us some ice cream.' I found it interesting that the thing was neither steel nor a magnolia, but that's what she called it. And the imagery stuck. Something beautiful made of very strong stuff." The phrase has since come to typify a soft-spoken Southern woman who is at the same time feisty and independent, as delicate as the fragrant blooms and yet as durable as metal.

For the plot, Robert Harling used the story of his own sister's diabetic complications following the birth of his namesake nephew. She died when a family member declined to donate a kidney. He originally composed a short story both to work through the experience and to allow his nephew to get a first hand word-portrait of his deceased mother.

In that same interview with *Garden and Gun*, Harling recalled the play was written in just over a week. His sister and her death had so influenced him that when he found that playwriting was the best way to capture her life, the work flowed in an unending stream to the finale. "I had no idea what I'd written. I asked the first person I gave it to if it even looked like a play. I wasn't really sure. All I knew was that I felt it portrayed my sister's life and spirit accurately, and that was enough for me."

I like the play because it was written by a Southerner about Southerners. It has some great, natural-sounding native lines in it, like "I should've known Louie had problems when his imaginary playmates wouldn't play with him," and "The nicest thing I can say about her is that all her tattoos are spelled correctly."

And I often think of Truvy's *"In a good shoe, I wear a size six, but a seven feels so good, I buy a size eight."* Same exact saying can be used for ladies underwear. It is such a gently humorous way of admitting my own conceit at desiring to appear smaller, daintier, or more delicate than I actually am, and yet revealing my authenticity by telling the truth at the same time. Humble vainglory. Like a steel magnolia.

August 9:
"Until one loses today, and wins tomorrow. I say to myself, years of planning, and I get what I want. And then I don't get it... But I'm not discouraged. The world's open for people like you and me. There's thousands of us all over the world. We'll own the country some day. They won't try to stop us. We'll get along."
Ben Hubbard in Lillian Hellman's *Little Foxes*

Lillian Hellman's *Little Foxes* is an Alabama story about the small-town Hubbard family, drawn from Hellman's own family history, growing up Jewish in the early twentieth century south. Like Regina Giddens in the play, Hellman's grandmother was successful, manipulative, and disparaging.

In the above quote, Regina is considering why her brother Ben is a "good loser." He admits he has learned from experience that life has its ups and downs. One day you lose, the next day you win, but if you can ride that ebb and flow without losing spirit, you can find a way to succeed.

While I am not a scheming cutthroat like Ben, striving for ruthless control over weaker people in the community, I can understand his idea. Taking it outside of a struggle for power, his words can shed light on the rhythms of daily patterns.

Both the Buddhist philosopher Daisaku Ikeda and Spanish writer Miguel de Cervantes have reminded me that, "They who lose today may win tomorrow." I have a fondness for the word "vicissitude," a mutable change in life, those sudden and unexpected shifts in fortune or life.

I have mentioned before that keeping journals are part of my morning routine. Writing about the day before reduces stress and helps me quiet my mind. I can note important thoughts and inspirations, remind myself how long a certain trip takes, record health tips I have found. Journaling aids my focus, bolsters my memory, helps me document major and minor events in my life, and assists me in processing my achievements as well as my struggles.

"Until one loses today, and wins tomorrow. I say to myself, years of planning, and I get what I want. And then I don't get it... But I'm not discouraged." Keeping journals guides me toward this same perception that Ben Hubbard had: the realization that today might be spectacular, but tomorrow might bring sorrow — and to just accept both ups and downs are part of life. My present troubles might clear away for a fantastic future — in fact, they might help bring about that brighter destiny.

Journaling helps me seek appreciation for and comprehension of any situation I am having, any moment of the day. Life is one huge roller coaster ride. A glance back through my diaries reminds me that Seth had a bike wreck the week Elin received a dance instructorship; I got a university promotion just after an IRS note arrived announcing that I was due for an audit; the very day I did my first book signing for my first book, my grandmother died; Seth won a soccer tournament the week Elin lost her competition in College Night; the day a book deal was snatched from me, I planted a garden full of chrysanthemums and ate chocolate muffins. As the saying goes, "Life is good."

August 10:
"All I wanted was to sing to God. He gave me that longing... and then made me mute. Why? Tell me that. If He didn't want me to praise him with music, why implant the desire? Like a lust in my body! And then deny me the talent?"
Salieri in Peter Shaffer's *Amadeus*

Peter Shaffer's *Amadeus* is a fascinating play from which came a great film. In January of 1999, I was privileged to hear David Suchet as

Salieri deliver these very lines at the Old Vic in London. Through television, Suchet is famous for his portrayal of the titular character in Agatha Christie's *Hercule Poirot*.

Amadeus, sometimes categorized as a historical fantasy, reveals an interesting relationship between the young upstart Mozart and the famous musician Salieri as it explores an exaggerated rivalry between the composers in the musical city of Vienna. Shaffer takes liberties with their battle for dramatic effect, matching mortal aspiration against divine inspiration.

In the play, Salieri, envious and covetous of the younger genius's talent, manipulates the destruction of Mozart's career. Though Salieri holds a very respectable job as court composer for Emperor Joseph II, he laments his lack of God-given talent in comparison to Mozart, *"If He didn't want me to praise him with music, why implant the desire?"*

As Shaffer demonstrates in this remarkable conflict, self-doubt can be devastating. As director of Italian opera by the Habsburg court, Salieri was crucial to the development of this art form in his time. During his career he wrote 37 operas, as well as instrumental and sacred works, and also devoted time to being a teacher and conductor. So he was far from lacking talent — though he did not have the kind of celestial spark that infused Mozart's work. But (in the play) he believes in his inferiority and he stubbornly strives to eliminate the competition.

According to this scenario, self-doubt can paralyze your own life, or tempt you to ruin someone else's. But what if questioning yourself is really a by-product of training and innate ability? Salieri was not denied talent, and, in fact, he was able to recognize a greater gift in Mozart. In shepherding college-age actors during my years in university work, I found that the ones with less skill tended to believe they were great, while the really brilliant ones had humble reservations and were compelled to improve and work at their craft.

"All I wanted was to sing to God." So a natural ability and desire like Salieri's can lead to education and awareness. When I learn, I begin to care and to yearn to be better. *"He gave me that longing..."* And then I go through a period of doubt: *"...and then made me mute."* But if I can work my way through that uncertainty about my own ability, instead of focusing on someone else who is at a higher level at the time, I can continue to work and practice, to assimilate and absorb — and to improve.

I use to tell my students: There is always someone better than you in your work. And there is also someone who is not as good as you. Take any given talent and we are all lined up in a spectrum from "not-so-hot" through "mediocre" to "brilliant." What matters is that you authentically let your own genius shine through, and you will furnish the world what is uniquely yours, and yours alone, to give.

August 11:
"It's Galinda, with a GA."
Galinda in *Wicked: The Untold Story of the Witches of Oz*, with music and lyrics by Stephen Schwartz and book by Winnie Holzman, based on the novel *Wicked: The Life and Times of the Wicked Witch of the West* by Gregory Maguire

Today is my daughter's birthday. Last night was a full moon, just like the year she was born. She was to be induced on August 10, but my obstetrician's office called me at 4:00 a.m. on the appointed date and said I had to wait until the 11th. A full moon had flooded the delivery rooms at the hospital and there were new mothers living on beds in the hallways it was so crowded.

I did not know the gender of my baby until she was born. But I thought she was a girl and a couple of months before her birth, I realized that the names I was considering really didn't fit her: Catherine Bowron or Ada Barrett. I searched a number of baby name books in the library (long before the days of the internet), and I discovered a lovely Swedish and Welsh-Irish version of Ellen or Helen, names of which ran in the family. So we decided on Elin and Keith (which was my mother's middle name).

At the time, I didn't realize the name was fairly rare, and people never could get it quite right. From the time she could speak, when people asked her name, she would say, "Elin. (then spelling) E-L-I-N. Elin." Growing up in the theatre at Samford University, she has always loved musicals, so we went to see *Wicked* the first time it came to Birmingham.

Wicked: The Untold Story of the Witches of Oz was a smash hit on Broadway by the inimitable Stephen Schwartz. It is based on Maguire's novel that parallels some of the fictional history of L. Frank Baum's 1900 archetypal story, *The Wonderful Wizard of Oz*. Elin and I went to see *Wicked* during a Broadway tour to Birmingham while she was pregnant with her daughter Emmeline, named for my great-great-grandfather's sister (and containing her mother's name within her own!).

The musical *Wicked*, streamlined and changed from the novel, reveals the backstories of the Oz witches, both before and after Dorothy's arrival in their fair country. In *Wicked*, Galinda, later Glinda, the Good Witch of the North, and Elphaba, the Wicked Witch of the West, are unlikely pals who nevertheless struggle constantly because of their antithetical personalities.

Wicked jumbles up these two characters. Though we recall from the story that Glinda is "good" and the Wicked Witch of the West is "bad," in this musical, they are far from being diametrically opposed or dualistically simple. The Wicked Witch is given the moniker Elphaba and at first despises the popular Galinda, but as the one-dimensional Galinda makes a crucial shift in identity, the two become more connected friends.

"It's Galinda, with a GA," she says early in the musical. But her growth is later symbolized by the removal of the "A," and she remarks, "It's Glinda, the GA is silent." (Yes, she is still a blonde.)

Names mean something, and names can shape your path. The novelist Maguire formulated the name "Elphaba" using the phonetic pronunciation of the initials L. Frank Baum. So, L.F.B became El-pha-ba. Baum surely knew that the name "Glinda" actually means "fair or good." "Elin" means "light" and "Keith" means "from the battlefield," so I suppose being armed to withstand the struggles of life with a gleaming brilliance give her a fine way to cope with people who question her name.

August 12:
"I love to write. . . I love writing you . . . I feel like a true lover when I'm writing you. This letter, which I'm writing with my own hand . . . comes from me and no one else, and is a present of myself to you . . . You can tear me up and throw me out, or keep me, and read me today, tomorrow, any time you want until you die."
Andrew in AR Gurney's *Love Letters*

Love Letters is one of those plays that can be easily performed (or even read) by illustrious actors, as it has been done by famous duos through the years since AR Gurney wrote it. Debuting with the playwright himself along with Holland Taylor, the work was first performed at the New York Public Library, before opening in 1988 at the Long Wharf Theatre in New Haven, Connecticut, this time with Joanna Gleason and John Rubinstein.

Two characters, Melissa Gardner and Andrew Makepeace Ladd III, begin an enduring habit of writing each other as young kids passing notes in school, and penning summer camp messages and thank you memos. Staged with actors sitting side by side and perusing cards, invitations, Valentines, missives, and letters, the sweep of events covers almost 50 years of living separate but intimately connected existences.

Andrew becomes a dashing senator and Melissa a disheveled artist. But their letters evoke the hopeful dreams, the crushing disappointments, the touching and funny incidents that two longtime friends reveal only to each other, giving the audience two revealing and informative character studies of people linked spiritually and emotionally in true affection. Ultimately, the two are sideswiped by a brief affair, but the romance doesn't work in person as well as the sparks fly in the letters, and Andrew is devastated by the loss of Melissa through an untimely death in her 50s.

I have had long letter-writing relationships with a few people. One was John Finlay, my college English professor with whom I corresponded after he left the university. I have a series of letters from my mother and from one of my grandmothers. For a long time (before email), my friend Joe Taylor and I often wrote poems and letters to each other, all of which I have carefully preserved.

The one other person with whom I communicated by mail was my high school boyfriend, Drew. He never finished writing a page in our yearbook which he had claimed all for himself, saying he would return to finish it someday. He went to Auburn when I went to Montevallo, and we really tried to maintain a relationship long distance. For a high school graduation present, I created a box of stationery for him, decorated with original artwork, and he was very faithful about sending me letters.

Our connection slowly concluded, all from my end. I was so excited to be in a place where I could relate to other people on a higher intellectual level than I was used to in high school, a greater emotional depth, a more collaborative creative scale. But, I stopped answering his letters. I stopped returning his calls. Later in life, I hoped we would meet again and he would finish writing in that annual.

Last November, we had our 45th high school reunion, and I was looking forward to seeing him again. About two months before the event, we all received an email that literally wrenched my gut: Drew had died after a seven-year battle with cancer. *"You can tear me up and throw me out, or keep me, and read me today, tomorrow, any time you want until you die."* Most assuredly, he had torn up and thrown away all my notes to him. But I have kept his to me, and I will read some of them today, and can continue to do so until I die.

August 13:
"It's all so hard to balance – the was and the is and the what may be."
David and Gillian in Michael Brady's *To Gillian on Her 37th Birthday*

We produced Brady's *To Gillian on Her 37th Birthday* in January of 1996 at Samford, just a year shy of my 47th birthday. Gillian had been developed in 1984 by the literary department of the Ensemble Studio Theatre, a method of creation which snagged the play some scathing reviews for both its literary allusions and its evolution by committee, so to speak.

The play takes place in August on a small island off New England on the weekend of both Gillian's birthday and her death two years before in a freak boating accident. Gillian's husband David loved her and deals with his sorrow by preserving their romance with frequent walks on the beach with her spirit, or ghost, or memory. All of this involvement with his dead wife is detrimental to David's relationship with their daughter Rachel – and his brother-in-law Paul and sister-in-law Esther visit to relieve the situation. Called a "romantic drama," the play was made into a 1996 film – just after we produced it – starring Michelle Pfeiffer as Gillian.

A strange aspect to working on a play featuring undying love was the awareness that my own wedded bliss had so recently gone awry. The quoted line *"It's all so hard to balance – the was and the is and the what may be"* was exactly how I felt at the time. I had trouble dealing with the present, the past was a mess, and the future was unsettled and unsure. My church, my old friends, my family, my community, my college buddies, my parents' neighbors all aided in my wedding, but very few people gathered round me to help sort out the other end of the marriage.

Like many others in my position, I was anxious and wondering about the future. I went through counseling and other therapeutic ways to maneuver through my new life. And I was adjusting – but as the divorce was actually proceeding during the preparation and run of this show, I was sorrowful and totally exhausted.

I wanted my friends or my parish family to, if not celebrate, at least recognize that an era had come to an end. I needed a ritual or ceremony to go through. Some religious groups have since that time developed such observances, and I hope they help people dealing with so many odd things that happen at the closure of a long marriage: photographs that have lost all their meaning, a shared history that is now in shreds, holidays that have a new twist, friends and acquaintances who – not wanting to take sides – abandon you both. The "was" of my life was gone, and at the time, the "is" was hard maneuver.

But not very long afterward – through studies, reading, and talking to my priest – I realized I had a couple of choices: I could clutch my past, moan and be miserable in the present, or I could, as the Beatles say, "Let it be," release everything that was no longer relevant, and accept my new status. In performing this incredible feat of compliance with Reality, I discovered that the *what may be* can became more spectacular than anyone could ever imagine.

August 14:
"Life is very nice, but it lacks form. It's the aim of art to give it some."
The count to his actors in Jean Anouilh's *The Rehearsal*, Act I, scene 2

When Birmingham hosted the Southeastern Theatre Conference annual meeting in 1975, one of our theatres produced a stylish performance of Anouilh's *Rehearsal*. The world of the play, set in 1950, is brimming with artifice and devices. For a dinner party, the count and his friends are rehearsing Marivaux's 1700s play *The Double Inconstancy*, alive with *commedia dell'arte* characters and matters of the heart.

The interesting twist to the play is that the audience finds it nearly impossible to detect exactly where Anouilh's creation ends and Marivaux's begins. Events in *The Rehearsal* correspond eerily to those of the earlier play. And besides, the count and his coterie enjoy play-acting, seeing life itself as a cultivated theatre piece in process.

In many of my art and philosophy classes in the past, we debated the idea: Does art imitate life, or does life imitate art? I think it is an interesting question. TED talks and conversations have dealt with the idea of art borrowing from nature, capturing the experiences or emotions of humans, and wondering if the opposite may be true. As an example, some science fiction writers have fabricated elaborate technical inventions that were later created. Online debates seem to side with the concept that art can imitate life, but life does not imitate art.

If I really want to delve into the subject again deeply, I will need to reread Aristotle and Plato, George Bernard Shaw, and modern aesthetics books. But I do like to think about Anouilh's posit through the count that, *"Life is very nice, but it lacks form. It's the aim of art to give it some."* In ancient Greece, the term "mimesis," or imitation, was used to describe art which mimics the real world, and was understood as a prototype for truth, beauty, and worthiness.

In the late 1800s, the playwright Oscar Wilde wrote an essay "The Decay of Lying" which proposes an idea that Life mimics Art much more than Art copies Life. He wrote that anti-mimesis "results not merely from Life's imitative instinct, but from the fact that the self-conscious aim of Life is to find expression, and that Art offers it certain beautiful forms through which it may realise that energy."

Wilde's philosophy further maintains that art creates aesthetic truths which help humans understand life. "Things are because we see them, and what we see, and how we see it, depends on the arts that have influenced us." He talks of the fogs of London, proposing that, "At present, people see fogs, not because there are fogs, but because poets and painters have taught them the mysteriousness of such effects. There may have been fogs for centuries in London. I daresay there were. But no one saw them, and so we do not know anything about them. They did not exist until Art invented them ..."

So in the debate, I suppose I sit on the fence throwing my arms about both ideas. I do think art sometimes imitates life — or at least the artist or playwright or composer takes bits of her life (or someone else's) and makes sense of them through art. But I am also intrigued by Wilde's idea that Life itself is motivated to communicate to us, and it does so through our art. I think the ideas are so inextricably linked that it may be impossible to know which is influencing which at any one time — sort of like Anouilh's *Rehearsal*.

August 15:
"Stop that. Stop that. Stop it! No more bloody singing!"
Herbert's Father in *Spamalot*, with book by Eric Idle, music by John Du Prez and Eric Idle, and lyrics by Eric Idle, "lovingly ripped off" from the cult classic movie *Monty Python and the Holy Grail*

I have talked at length of my experiences with King Arthur and the Knights of the Round Table at Camp Winnataska when I was a camper, leader, and on staff. Just this month, I wrote lovingly of the musical *Camelot*, and how the film version enriched my life. So now I have a confession to make. For many years – dozens, maybe more – I shunned watching *Monty Python and the Holy Grail*. I am one of the biggest fans of true comedy in the world. I thought John Cleese, Michael Palin, Eric Idle, and the other Flying Circus comedians were hysterical. Their blend of slapstick, theatre of the absurd, and stream-of-consciousness could only have come out of my beloved Britain, and their association with David Frost, Marty Feldman, and others of their ilk only increased their value in my book.

But, because I so loved my Grail traditions, I was reluctant to watch *Monty Python and the Holy Grail* for years. I suppose I thought it was sacrilegious! The show definitely is a cheeky satire of the Arthurian Legend, but Roger and I recently ushered at a local production of the musical *Spamalot* ("lovingly ripped off," as they say, from the cult classic movie *Monty Python and the Holy Grail*). This production of the show was hysterical.

Why would Herbert's father yell at the end of the show, "*Stop that. Stop that. Stop it! No more bloody singing!*" It is a musical. People are going to sing! And Lancelot obligingly whacks him on the head while the Chorus sings about the ending of the musical. Such delightful slapstick!

My daughter Elin enjoyed the fact that her father and I worked in the theatre. She never minded sitting in rehearsals with us, doing homework in the costume shop, taking a role in a play every now and then, or going to productions with us. Her brother Seth was a different child. He resisted going to rehearsals. He just couldn't sit still and stay out of trouble. Interesting predicaments he encountered during rehearsals were getting a child's umbrella handle stuck in his mouth, crashing the wardrobe cart when he used it as monkey bars, and turning his fingers black sticking a safety pin into a floor socket. Though he didn't mind playing under the sewing table in the costume shop, he found it hard to sit through a long play, even a musical.

Elin was in four choirs in high school and loved to learn the lyrics to show tunes and sing them night and day around the house. Often, Seth would get "Broadway song overload" after a half hour or so and follow her around crying, "No singing! No singing!" She would respond singing louder and into his face, and he would continue with Herbert's father's sentiment, "No singing! No singing!"

Since this was real life and not *Spamalot* or another musical, I would usually intervene and quieten the fracas by moving them apart. Seth later learned to sing, and also to appreciate his sister's musical talents. But I have had several people tell me of children or siblings they had who also insisted on the "No singing!" rule.

August 16:
"Whoever you are, I have always depended on the kindness of strangers."
Blanche DuBois to the doctor in Tennessee Williams,'s *A Streetcar Named Desire*

Lots of people repeat this line. I suppose some of them know where it came from, and perhaps they have even seen the play or the film version of *Streetcar* with Vivian Leigh as Blanche and Marlon Brando as Stanley. I believe many folks who say the words have no idea about their origin.

In Williams's work, Stella goes to the hospital to have her baby, leaving Stanley and Blanche in the apartment alone. No one knows for sure, but there is a strong insinuation that Stanley rapes Blanche causing her to finally break down mentally. Many scholars believe that Blanche is fashioned after the playwright's sister, Rose Williams, who, after years of battling mental disease, was totally disabled through an experimental lobotomy. Just before the final curtain, Blanche voices her famous line to a compassionate doctor who coaxes her down the hallway. Stanley has insisted on putting Blanche in a psychiatric sanatorium, and an unwilling Stella has agreed.

Today is the birthday of Andreas Nomikos, a glorious man, a gifted scene designer, an accomplished teacher, a hospitable host, and the lovely person I got to know in graduate school at the University of North Carolina at Greensboro. I was studying English, but was an assistant in the auditorium that held the concert and lecture series, and I hung out with theatre graduate students.

When we first got to Greensboro, Andreas was a stranger, but I soon got to know him very well. All the graduate theatre students did. He invited us over to his house for dinner on numerous occasions. "Let me put some pizza rolls in the oven," he would say as we entered his gracious home. Beer and wine were plentiful. He knew we were all on very limited budgets. Our monthly stipend in 1972, '73, and '74 was a few hundred dollars that barely got us through the month.

Andreas was from Athens originally, and he moved to America after World War II. His specialty dish was Pastitsio, and he made it so lovingly, with that wondrous béchamel sauce, that I have never had any as good as his anywhere. I grew up in Alabama, surrounded by Southern hospitality, but I have rarely experienced courtesy, generosity, or kindness from strangers that even begins to rival what we all encountered in the home of Dr. Nomikos.

We may have started out as strangers, all of us, the students, the faculty, and Andreas. But because of his warm nature, his love for teaching and influencing young people, his brilliance, his humor, his wisdom — we all became acquaintances, and then friends, and then comrades. He bound us all together in love and companionship. So on this day each year, in some small and festive way, I honor my memory of Dr. Nomikos, this kind stranger who charmed everyone he met and took many of us in as family.

August 17:
"Bohr: It was a fascinating paradox.
Heisenberg: You actually loved the paradoxes, that's your problem. You reveled in the contradictions.
Bohr: Yes, and you've never been able to understand the suggestiveness of paradox and contradiction. That's your problem. You live and breathe paradox and contradiction, but you can no more see the beauty of them than the fish can see the beauty of the water."
Bohr and Heisenberg in Michael Frayn's *Copenhagen*

I really wanted to think about this play today. In 2003, we buried my father on August 16 (a day already packed with anniversaries). On the 17th, the very next day, my son Seth drove off to college at The University of the South in Sewanee, Tennessee. In two days time, I said goodbye to the two most important male family members of my life.

For their freshman reading, Seth's class was assigned Michael Frayn's play *Copenhagen*, concerning an actual mysterious 1941 meeting in Copenhagen between the physicists Niels Bohr and Werner Heisenberg. The "historical" drama had premiered at the National Theatre in London in 1998, five years before Seth studied the intriguing work.

The play takes place not at the meeting, but after their deaths, where the spirits of Werner Heisenberg, Niels Bohr, and Bohr's wife

Margrethe gather to debate an issue she raises early in the play, "Why did he come to Copenhagen?" Both scientists concoct a number of impressions about their secret 1941 interchange. Each version has ever-changing motives as they argue about the atomic bomb, nuclear power, control of such energy, and the ethics of scientific behavior.

One of the most interesting ideas to jump from the lips of the actors involves the "uncertainty principle" that the younger man had stumbled upon in 1927 while in Denmark working on quantum theory at Niels Bohr's research institute. While Bohr took a quick skiing trip, Heisenberg had time for deliberation and came to an astonishing awareness: at the subatomic level, the actual act of observation alters whatever is being scrutinized.

For the centuries before this theory, scientists had thought that all things in the universe were knowable and even anticipatory because nature worked repeatedly and predictably. Frayn, after reading about the theory, got to thinking about "How we know why people do what they do, and even how one knows what one does oneself... I wanted to suggest with *Copenhagen* that there is some kind of parallel between the indeterminacy of human thinking, and the indeterminacy that Heisenberg introduced into physics with his famous 'uncertainty principle.'"

For years, I have been giving up my inborn desire to be sure about everything, so I am subscribing to the "uncertainty principle." But even Heisenberg fails to live it. Bohr says to him, "You live and breathe paradox and contradiction, but you can no more see the beauty of them than the fish can see the beauty of the water." "Paradox" is derived from the two Greek words: "para" and "doksos," really meaning "contrary to expectation." G. K. Chesterton once wrote that, "a paradox is often a truth standing on its head to get our attention."

Daily, I realize more and more that most of life is a series of paradoxes — and they are beautiful, as Bohr points out. When I can remember to hold in my mind the "both" and the "and," I can grow, I can expand my thinking past determinacy, I can unite seeming conflicts, I can enjoy the mystery and the uncertainty of life.

Spiritual writers talk about the way we can overcome seeming opposites by discovering a reconciling third. In this view, we have active, passive, and neutralizing forces. When the third is brought in, a holding tank is formed. In that place, the veracity of the active and passive are embraced without booting the one or the other. So in my holding tank today is my profound sadness that my dad is gone and that Seth is no longer my little ward, but also effusive thankful joy for the gifts these two gentlemen have been in and to my life.

August 18
"I am in the business of putting old heads on young shoulders, and all my pupils are the creme de la creme. Give me a girl at an impressionable age and she is mine for life."
Miss Jean Brodie in Jay Presson Allen's *The Prime of Miss Jean Brodie*, from the novel by Muriel Spark

That time of year has come, that time to go back to school. I truly miss the academic routine since I haven't taught at the university for a dozen or so years. That cycle where everyone is excited at the first of the semester, slumped during the middle, and thrilled again at the end, just before the holidays; huge amounts of work, research, and study; watching students go from disinterest to appreciation.

Spark's novel *The Prime of Miss Jean Brodie* was dramatized by Jay Presson Allen, with a 1966 London opening starring Vanessa Redgrave, a 1968 Broadway debut featuring Zoe Caldwell, and a 1969 film with Maggie Smith in the title role. Miss Brodie is a charismatic teacher at the Edinburgh Marcia Blaine School for Girls in the 1930s. She dedicates most of her energy to the "Brodie Set," a group of 12-year old girls who become enthralled with her highly idealized view of the world, art, theatre, and literature.

Over the years, Jean Brodie makes a dazzling rise to a zenith, and ultimately a dramatic crash as well. Most of the staff and faculty at the conservative institution resent her fascist beliefs and her coterie of "favorites," and are happy to see her fall.

My granddaughter, Emmeline, is going off to five-year old kindergarten this year, so last Friday was my final one to have her stay at my house as she had done since she was about three months old. The day was emotional for me, and yet now, the twins will move from Tuesdays to Fridays and I will have a stronger work week, which is freeing in many ways. Emmeline has been in daycare and preschool for a while, but actual school is different.

"Give me a girl at an impressionable age and she is mine for life." Emmeline is definitely in a pliant period, and I hope she has gathered something about how to live a good life from her time with me. We

undertook a series of "life lessons" this summer and learned a little bit about how to do many things. We visited local attractions, landmarks, art galleries, and parks. We went swimming and walking, and we cleaned the house. We learned sewing, shoe tying, time telling, napkin folding, phone calling, yard stick navigating, and bug identifying.

But now Emmeline's teacher is in *"the business of putting old heads on young shoulders."* With the formidable name of "Ms. Snodgrass," I am counting on a good year of enlightenment and edification. I expect this teacher to have passion, affection for educating, love for children, understanding, patience, courage, and strength. I pray that she enjoys putting in long hours, pinpoints the best approach to get Emmeline to grasp and discover, finds the forbearance to hear over and over, "But why?" "But why?" "But why?"

Maybe Emmeline will look back when she is my age and recall Ms. Snodgrass as I do Mrs. Burns, Miss Jones, Mrs. Myers, Mr. Clayton, Mr. Finlay, Mr. Triplett, Dr. van Tuyll. Teachers who shaped not only my academic years, but my very life.

August 19:
"Leave no stone unturned."
Eurystheas in Euripedes's *Heraclidae*

Heraclidae or *Herakles' Children*, is a tragedy by Euripedes that was first performed in 430 BC The plot concerns Hercules's offspring who want protection from Eurystheus the king who was responsible for many of the difficulties experienced by the now dead Herakles. To keep the children of Herakles from seeking revenge, he endeavors to kill them; but they flee under the protection of Herakles's close friend and nephew, Iolous.

I cannot find a record of a performance of this patriotic play anywhere, and I have certainly never worked on it or seen it. Maybe I haven't been diligent enough, because I have probably left many stones turned and unturned in looking for some evidence of a production. But I love to know that the phrase *"leave no stone unturned"* comes from this fairly obscure Greek play.

In 1983, the actor Diana Rigg assembled a selection of theatre critiques that lambaste productions and directors, actors and playwrights in some of the funniest, but also the most appalling reviews ever published. The name of her book is a spin of this phrase, and is entitled

No Turn Unstoned! It is a delightful book, but doesn't mention an evaluation of *Heraclidae*.

"To leave no stone unturned" is a phrase used to mean doing everything possible to find something or someone, or to solve a problem, to achieve a good result. I have to leave no stone unturned quite frequently. I don't lose my glasses since I am nearsighted and have had to wear a pair since I was eleven. And I don't generally lose my keys, because I have a hook to hang them on by the back door to the carport. But other stuff? I don't know why I lose things so often, but I have several theories.

One idea, which I know science and most people in the world would discount, involves my belief that inanimate objects actually can and do move themselves. Why else would I look for a sock in its box in my storage bin by dumping out all the pairs, painstakingly looking at them, putting them back, looking elsewhere all over the house, under the dryer, in the floor of the closet, in other drawers — only to go back to the bin and find the sock sitting right on top of the pile, almost waving at me?

Another hypothesis, also probably not verifiable empirically either, is that there is an alternate universe that bumps up to ours and even, at times, overlaps it. So I place something where it should be, but the bubble separating our universes happens to be so thin at that time I actually place my VERY IMPORTANT PAPERS on a table resembling mine in that other space.

Yet one more conjecture is that the universe is telling me something about paying more attention, being in the now, being present. I admit I am often distracted by things going on in my mind and heart, and okay, maybe I put things down in odd places. Then, there is also the problem of being a visual person. So I often picture the lost book, for instance, in my mind as being red, so I feverishly look for a red object that is six by nine inches, and then, after days of searching, I find the volume in full view — and it is blue.

"*Leave no stone unturned*" should probably be my motto, however, for no matter what theory I subscribed to about lost objects, I don't seem able to settle down until the dad-gum thing is found!

August 20:
"It's not necessary to be there in order to BE there."

Henry in Jerome Lawrence and Robert E. Lee's *The Night Thoreau Spent in Jail*

As I said in April, I hold Henry David Thoreau in high regard, and really had fun with the play's costume designs both times Samford University Theatre produced *The Night Thoreau Spent in Jail*. In this particular scene, Henry is in jail, and is telling his cellmate, Bailey, who has been accused of burning down a barn, that he (Thoreau) might not actually be present in Walden, but he can nonetheless BE there because he can always access past experiences.

I have never been to Walden Woods, though I would love to go there some time. But I do have places I drift off to at a moment's notice. If I want to be energized, I am on the streets of London, moving with the vigor of that city. If I want to relax, I am floating in the perfectly clear, lake-like calmness of the Gulf of Mexico. If I want to be inspired, I am at what we call "Hillside" at Camp Winnataska.

Just the other night, I was talking to my fiancé Roger about how we, like Thoreau, can learn so much from nature, and I recalled one early evening at Winnataska, at Hillside, a small semi-circular amphi-theatre made of native rocks. Every evening during camp sessions, as the sun is setting, campers gather there to hear an inspirational talk.

When I was a young camper, around nine-years old, I absolutely loved to go to Hillside. The tier of seats is about the best place in camp to view our iconic waterfall. I have to admit, at this age, the brilliance of the speaker and the guiding light of the message were sometimes lost on me. The voice seemed to be a drone, much like the teacher in the Charlie Brown movies.

But that does not mean that the time there was for nought. For one thing, something seeped into my brain, because I now love to listen to spiritually uplifting presentations. Probably such communication reached me on a level I hardly realized, and formed a groove in my brain that I now have to fill with recordings of wisdom teachers.

Anyway, this one afternoon stands clearly in my mind like few other memories I have of anything or anyone. I sat below the seats on a little concrete jut-out and the waterfall was roaring so loudly after some recent rain that I had trouble hearing the speaker. So I turned my attention to the ground I was sitting on.

I was suddenly aware of some very large black ants. Now, I had seen house ants before, and had understood that they were to be sprayed and not tolerated. They were after your sugar. But these ants were different — bigger and somehow more observable. And what I discerned really changed my life — maybe more than if I could have heard what the speaker was saying.

These ants were carrying a dead companion on their backs. From my kid's-eye-view, I was suddenly overcome with the realization that it was very much like a hearse in our own human funerals. I was struck with the idea that something as tiny as these ants in some way cared about their fellow species, had intelligence and cognizance, and acted in a respectful way. I have borne this image in my heart ever since, and I even when I am not at Hillside, I can BE there with this memory.

August 21:
"*Mary: I have always traveled solo hitherto.*
Fanny: As have I.
Alex: As have I.
Mary: Occasionally encountering a sister sojourner on a trek —"
Mary, Fanny, and Alex in Eric Overmyer's On the Verge, or The Geography of Yearning

On the Verge is a clever literary play that professionally premiered in January of 1985 at Center Stage in Baltimore. Eric Overmyer's wordplay and vision have been compared to SJ Perelman, Caryl Churchill, Tom Stoppard, and Thornton Wilder. I read the play over Labor Day weekend in 1988 and was intrigued by the three Victorian lady explorers who are, as the book jacket says, "equipped with dialog as pithy as their helmets," and who "thwack their machetes through the wilderness while telling tales of past jaunts among the natives." It is a happy feminist play, even a joyous one.

During their adventures, Mary, Fanny, and Alex discover a rain forest containing a myriad of objects from the future. And even though the heroines adapt to numerous emergencies, they become a bit bewildered by the modern times they come upon. Overmyer has said that he based his characters not upon particular individuals, but on actual historical details gathered from books about Victorian lady travelers. He says, "The spirit of the lady travelers inspired On the Verge, and that spirit is the play's true concern: the quality of yearning, courage, and imagination."

I am in the middle of a 21-day web-based meditation experience called "Expanding Your Happiness," introduced by Oprah Winfrey and led by Deepak Chopra. The current program is the third time I have joined these two on what they call a "journey." This particular meditation series is intended to spark joy, overwhelming peace, and playful bliss inside of me — much like Overmyer's characters have. I have realized for some time that I am responsible for my own happiness, and to avoid stress, I would do better to rejoice in the way things are than to grumble every time the world doesn't go my way.

Not that everything around me is perfect — certainly not; but that life is unfolding as it will and, as Deepak said this morning, if we can get to high level contentment, "Anxiety and Insecurity are not our companions" any more on this adventure called "life." It reminded me of this quote from On the Verge, "I have always traveled solo hitherto."

Companions are important when planning a trip. So, if I have to travel solo to exclude unwanted sidekicks, so be it. I would like to embrace Joy as a companion on my journey, or Peace, or Grace; but I must quickly say goodbye to Anxiety and Insecurity if they want to tag along. I am hearing more and more people talk about Happiness being a choice. Not when you are clinically depressed, but when you are healthy, you can select Delight to be your escort rather than Misery. New scientific studies have shown that meditation alters us genetically. Through contemplation, I find Peace, and Focus. Then, I can encounter sister sojourners Hope and Optimism on my trek, and allow Worry and Self-Doubt to be left behind.

August 22
"True hope is swift, and flies with swallow's wings;
Kings it makes gods, and meaner creatures kings."
Richmond in William Shakespeare's Richard III, Act V, Scene 2

Richard III died on this day, August 22, in 1485, killed in the Battle of Bosworth Field only two years after becoming King of England. Just a few days ago, the news reported "Tests on the long-lost skeleton of Richard III reveal the medieval monarch had a taste for rich foods such as peacock, heron, and swan, and that his liking for the finer things in life — including wine — increased significantly after he became the king of England." But obviously, his intensification in appetite was as short-lived as his reign as a god.

Shakespeare's play about this king is fun to watch, because Richard's character is so very nefarious. In fact, Richard's line, "I am determined to prove a villain" signals Shakespeare's intention: to manifest evil incarnate. Shakespeare was a playwright, not a historian and he took plenty of liberties with the king's story.

These lines about hope are spoken by "Richmond" or Henry, the Earl of Richmond. Though he doesn't appear until the end of the play, he challenges Richard for the kingship. By defeating Richard in the final battle and claiming the throne, he affects the entire outcome of the play. His words indicate that the miraculous quality of hope can expand your power and influence.

In the Renaissance, kings and queens had "divine rights" because they were thought to be ordained by God. So the monarchy was just a tiny step below the Creator. A Great Chain of Being — supposedly mandated by God — ranked angels, then humans, then animals, plants, and on to minerals. So this quote is saying that hope can push kings up a rank, and ameliorate "lesser folk" as well. In other words, with hope, I can rise above my present life's situation.

Hope is often described expectantly by writers: "Hope springs eternal in the human breast" (Alexander Pope). "Hope is a thing with feathers that perches in the soul" (Emily Dickinson). Or even not so encouragingly: "Hope in reality is the world of all evils because it prolongs the torments of man" (Friedrich Nietzsche).

Hope is actually an attitude that encourages faith in a positive outcome. Such states operate almost like filters, coloring my impressions of what is happening, which then impacts my feelings about those events. I can be in other states; for instance a mesmerized state, or a reverent state, or a dithering state. If I am mesmerized, the world is enthralling; if I am dithering, all around me is agitated and indecisive. And, I will respond differently to similar situations because of the filter I am using, which explains why some people complain that optimistic folks are wearing rose-colored spectacles.

When I am feeling downhearted, when things are not going "my way," what I must ask is: How did I get here? What turns did I take on that path that led to this despair? I am responsible for my choices, and for my thoughts. So if I can employ hope, I can stop using the microscope of angst that zooms in on the small problems and employ the lenses that encompass the panorama of my life. Then I can creatively anticipate and work toward a brighter future.

August 23:
"And now, since you've talked me into this,
  I'll proceed into my palace, treading
  on this crimson pathway as I go."
Agamemnon in Aeschylus's *The Oresteia: Agamemnon*

As I recalled on May 14, the theatre department at the University of North Carolina at Greensboro, produced all three plays in Aeschylus's trilogy *The Oresteia* while I was in graduate school. The Greek hero Agamemnon has a family history that includes treachery, rape, incest, reprehensible crime, curses, murder, mayhem, and misfortune.

Agamemnon has been off fighting the Trojan War for a decade, and comes back home to his wife Clytemnestra who professes to be ecstatic that he is home (though she has taken a lover in his absence). Putting pretensions aside, she later murders him, but in this scene, she literally rolls out the red carpet, inviting him out of his chariot and into their home by walking on this expensive pathway so that his feet never touch the ground. At the time, purple dye cost a small fortune (the source of which was a rare sea-snail), so the color indicated rank in society.

Agamemnon fears that walking on the dark red-purple fabric would be a display of pride, for only a god would be allowed such a walkway. But Clytemnestra insists and he finally gives in. The translation used in the UNCG production was a translation by Richard Lattimore: "Now since my will was bent to listen to you in this, my feet crush crimson as I pass within the hall." In this version, I really like the blatant action that Agamemnon takes once his mind is changed.

Here it is, the end of August again, and football preseason games are on television. I am a Southeastern Conference college football fan, and I will tell you one reason why. Some of my theatre colleagues and I have had conversations about the similarities between American football and Greek tragedy. The game is played in a huge arena, somewhat comparable to Greek amphitheatres. For very different reasons, the players being watched on the field or stage wear padding: either for safety (in the sport) or for visibility and legendary mystique (in the theatre). Both the game and the tragedy are gripping and compelling, and the story unfolds as you are right there watching it, always in the now.

The players in football and the cast of Greek tragedy are all male, though the audience of both is mixed gender. Greek tragedies were created to be part of religious festivals, but they were also a time for civic pride. All citizens of Athens, often even slaves, gathered together to see their ancient myths unfold before their eyes.

Though the reason for football games is not to delve into the stories of our nation or state or city, the sport is a modern secular religion for many people. Everyone chooses up sides and pulls for their team, despite the singing of the National Anthem at the beginning, which might remind fans that we are all still part of the same country.

Monday Night Football sports broadcaster Howard Cosell always made the game seem akin to Greek tragedy. Probably the most compelling similarity is the catharsis of emotions that both a Greek tragedy and football bring, that wonderful process of being able to release and be relieved of our strong or repressed emotions.

So just whose feet are going to "crush crimson" as they pass this fall? I hope no one, as I am a huge University of Alabama fan, whose color is crimson. Roll, Tide, Roll!

August 24:
"Believe me, my young friend, there is absolutely nothing half so much worth doing as simply messing about in boats. In them or out of them, it doesn't matter. Whether you get away or you don't, whether you arrive at your destination or whether you never get anywhere at all, you're always busy."
Ratty in Alan Bennett's *The Wind in the Willows*, adapted from the novel by Kenneth Grahame

For Christmas in 1990, the National Theatre in London produced Alan Bennett's version of Kenneth Grahame's *The Wind in the Willows*, directed by Nicholas Hytner. The production turned out to be tremendously popular with all ages, so the play was revived in 1991 and 1993. In the fall of 1993, my then-husband took a mini sabbatical, traveling to London for a work-study program at the National Theatre, so he worked with Mark Thompson, the set designer in getting the scenery ready to go again.

That December with me, my mom, dad, and children, Elin and Seth all went to London a second time for the holidays and saw this enchanting production. Every character of the captivating story came beautifully to life: Mole, Mr. Toad, Mr. Badger, and Ratty (who is really a water vole). But he is a very cultured gentleman, fond of literature and of the good life — especially the irresistibly fascinating life on the river.

My fiancé Roger was involved in the formation of Alabama's Black Warrior Riverkeeper in 2002, and though he is no longer intimately connected to that group, he loves rivers — and lakes, ponds, gulfs, bogs, bays, creeks, and just about any other body of water. He would agree with Ratty that, "...there is absolutely nothing half so much worth doing as simply messing about in boats."

Like Ratty, he is also very much a "P" or a "Perceiving Person" on the Myers-Briggs Type Indicator. In daily happenings, he prefers a flexible and spontaneous way of life. He enjoys understanding and adapting to the world rather than organizing it, and is constantly open to new experiences and information. So, he like Ratty, would probably say, *"In them or out of them, it doesn't matter. Whether you get away or you don't, whether you arrive at your destination or whether you never get anywhere at all, you're always busy."*

I like water as well, and I like boats. I simply like to know more about whether we are going to get somewhere or not, and maybe even who all is going! I like to have a destination, and perhaps even an estimated time of arrival. Actually, because I have worked in the theatre where you often have to adapt to alterations at the last minute, if the plans change, I am totally fine. Something in my mind just works better if I have a design or outline for the day.

I do see there is something romantically alluring gliding in a boat from river to canal to channel throughout England with no particular port of call in mind. And I have become intrigued with the Alabama Scenic River Trail, a connection of blue-ways from mountain streams to river deltas to the salty waves of the Gulf of Mexico. People can paddle or use powerboats to explore about 3,000 miles of accessible waterways in this state, including a long-distance tour.

With the waterways in England, or the rivers in Alabama, I might actually believe Ratty's proclamation about messing around in a boat. And I might be persuaded to put my maps, planners, and itineraries aside and just drift a while.

August 25:
"The sun, the splendid herald of the morn,
will soon set off upon his golden course –
soon will doubts disappear,
soon the wise man will triumph! –
O sweet contentment, descend upon us,

return to human hearts;
then earth shall be a paradise
and mortals be like Gods."
The Boys in Wolfgang Mozart's *The Magic Flute*

Samford University Opera performed this last opera of Mozart in the fall of 1998, and I greatly appreciated the opportunity to design its fantastical costumes. The fairy tale concerns Prince Tamino and Princess Pamina, young lovers who battle many forces of nature using the awesome powers of a magic flute. In the beginning, when a serpent assaults Tamino, three ladies appear from nowhere and save him. Claiming to be assistants of the Queen of the Night, they show him a picture of the Queen's daughter Pamina, who has been stolen away by the evil Sarastro, and he immediately falls in love. The imposing Queen appears and gives Tamino a magic flute to aid him on his quest to rescue the princess.

Tamino has a sidekick, an innocent bird-catcher Papageno, who travels with him. When the prince finally encounters the kidnapper Sarastro and his temple-goers, they are quite lovely. They have actually kept the princess from her evil mother who is trying to take over the world. Pamina is attracted to Tamino, but before they can marry, they must undergo trials engineered by Sarastro, such as walking through fire — but they are aided by the magic flute.

The Queen of the Night appears, commanding her daughter to kill Sarastro in one of all of opera's most famous arias. Not only does she push the human voice to it ultimate peak by climbing to the highest of notes, she conveys her volatile and possessive personality. The Queen of the Night and her compatriots attack the temple but are defeated and banished, her voice reverberating into the night as if forever. Sarastro blesses Pamina and Tamino and everyone revels in the triumph of bravery, honor, and wisdom.

Ah, me, that mad, shadowy thing called a "sleepless night" must truly be ruled over by this wicked Queen. She haunts me every few months, or even weeks, and it happened just the other evening. I was talking to two of my girl friends and told them I had been awake for a couple of hours the night before, and they had, too. We wished we had known, so we could have called each other up for cheer and enlightenment.

All three of us confessed to being plagued by mysterious doubts and curious uncertainties during the agonizing tossing and turning. Sleeplessness used to make sense when I "had" to worry about teenagers spending the night out, making soccer teams, driving, dating, getting into college — or during family deaths, tornadoes, 9-11. Sleeplessness even made sense during menopause, when I was a furnace blazing all night long.

But the other night, I fretted over my life's import. I felt worthless, as if I had heretofore had a meaningless and futile existence. The more I talked to myself about how wrong that was, how beautiful life is, how much the Divine shows up every day, the more useless and hollow everything seemed.

I think I understand why people have personified evil into beings such as Satan and the Queen of the Night. In the depths of those midnight trials, I certainly feel as if I am being overtaken by someone else's thoughts, someone who does not have my well-being uppermost on her agenda. I long for *"The sun, the splendid herald of the morn"* so that my doubts will disappear and my wisdom will triumph.

August 26:
"Don't cut up your wedding dress, Mommy... Please don't cut up your wedding dress."
Linda to Rosina in Arthur Giron's *Becoming Memories*

To close out our season in 1994, the theatre produced the emotive work *Becoming Memories* which Arthur Giron crafted with members of the Illusion Theatre of Minneapolis. He pulled together five families' stories to fabricate a montage of American small town life throughout three generations. When I worked with The Seasoned Performers, we created several plays using this same method with very interesting results.

Today is my daughter's eighth wedding anniversary. *"Don't cut up your wedding dress, Mommy... Please don't cut up your wedding dress."* That line reminds me of the months leading up to her nuptials. She didn't want to use my groovy tiered 1970s wedding dress that my mother had crafted for me. But, being the sentimental person she is, she became infatuated with using my mother's gown.

Mom had been very thin in 1948 when she and my dad got married, and Elin was never going to fit into the bodice. We decided to cut the dress apart and have the indomitable former United States Senator from Alabama, Maryon Allen, expert seamstress and wedding ensemble specialist, design a frock from the various pieces of satin and lace.

"*Don't cut up your wedding dress, Mommy*" might have been the very words from my lips. I had sewn hundreds of costumes for every character imaginable in every sort of theatrical production, but I just could not bear to carve up that gown — and I certainly couldn't put it back together. The task was too emotional for me.

From the time I was a tiny tyke, I had watched my maternal grandmother sew. When the had Depression hit, she, who was a meticulous and talented seamstress, began to make extra money stitching tutus and ballet costumes for Miss Lum's Dance Studio. Then, in 1942, her husband Jack, who traveled in his business, died of pneumonia in New York City — literally months before penicillin was introduced to kill infectious bacteria. My grandmother had to travel up and bring his body back on the train, and was left a youngish widow with four girls sixteen and under — so she sewed more and more to make ends meet.

As I have said before, until I was five, I lived next door to my great-grandmother, Nannie, my grandmother, and my mom's three sisters. One of my earliest memories is walking through the door one morning to discover a magical path through dozens of pale-toned tutus scattered across the floor. Ready to be tried on and adjusted for a recital, they were on every inch of floor and piece of furniture: pale yellow, carnation, lavender, pastel blue. It looked like an enchanted indoor garden with huge blossoms swirling through every downstairs room.

The night I was going to cut apart my mom's wedding dress, it took Elin and three of my cousins to give me the strength and nerve to take scissors to the satiny fabric and lace to snip it into pieces. My grandmother had lovingly sewn my mother's wedding dress on her treadle sewing machine, and my mom loved her dress. But she loved her granddaughter more, and wanted her to have what she wanted. Elin's gown turned out wonderfully, and I found out that sometimes it is fine to cut up a wedding dress.

August 27:
"*Wait a minute, boss. Let me get this straight. You mean I'm canned?*"
Zero in Elmer Rice's *The Adding Machine*

332

Most plays, I delight in seeing on stage. Many plays, I am smitten with as I read them. Some plays, I love after I have agonizingly slogged through them. Elmer Rice's *The Adding Machine* is an example of the latter category. I can't skim through a text as dense as this one is, so scrutiny is the only choice. But what a headache I have after such a study!

A perfect example of 1920s Expressionism, the extremely non-realistic play depicts a characterless man named Mr. Zero, his atrocious wife, and people named One, Two, Three, Four, Five, and Six. The action features a series of episodic and disagreeable adventures, beginning with an amazing three-page monologue by the wife. Then, Zero, an accountant for a quarter of a century at a large vacuous company, goes berserk after finding out he is to be replaced by an adding machine, which prompts him to murder his boss. There is an arrest, a trial, a hanging, and a meaningless excursion to an after-life setting, the "Elysian Fields."

Throughout the events, Mr. Zero elicits no sympathy from the audience, as he is a shallow character full of self-blame, indirection, and malice. In fact, in watching the play, or even reading it, I am overcome with a sensation of suffocation. It is the same feeling I have when, either actually or figuratively, I am canned, booted, rejected, spurned, rebuffed, or otherwise given the thumbs down signal. It is hard to take, being dismissed from a job, deserted in a partnership, betrayed by a friend, repudiated by a child or a parent.

There was the time that, for four months, I had researched and painstakingly written part of a book on Birmingham law only to be told an attorney was taking over the project. Puff! Cough! Gasp for air! There was the time a new director took over the state soccer association and informed me I was no longer the editor of the youth soccer magazine. Wheeze! Sharp inhalation! Oh! There was the time my motives were questioned for asking a board member a simple question that was utterly and convolutedly misinterpreted. Gulp! Choke! Really?

"Wait a minute, boss. Let me get this straight. You mean I'm canned?" Elmer Rice uses a mimetic style of writing which elicits in me the very physical and emotional sensations I would have in such a situation. The air seems to be lacking oxygen. My lungs are being squeezed and deprived. I feel disoriented, trapped, oppressed. *The Adding Machine* may not be a pleasure to read or watch, but it certainly causes a physical and emotional reaction.

August 28:

"I've always liked Jerry. To be honest, I've always liked him rather more than I've liked you. Maybe I should have had an affair with him myself."
Robert in Harold Pinter's *Betrayal*

Betrayal, Harold Pinter's 1978 play, has an innovative structure as the action unfolds in reverse chronology. Only 40 pages long in script form, its dialogue is fairly sparse, the action is restrained, and the characters hide their feelings while also cloaking intentions. Film critic **Roger Ebert** reviewed the 1983 movie saying, "*The Betrayal* structure strips away all artifice. It shows, heartlessly, that the very capacity for love itself is sometimes based on betraying not only other loved ones, but even ourselves."

In the story, from 1968 to 1975, Jerry and Emma engage in an affair without the knowledge of Emma's husband (and Jerry's best friend) Robert. Committing adultery against both Robert and Jerry's wife Judith, neither are very passionate about their love for each other. In Venice in 1975, Emma admits the intrigue to her husband, but fails to clue Jerry in that she has done so, thereby being disloyal even to her lover.

When I was in London for a 1999 January term, Don Sandley, my theatre department chair, and I, along with some of our students, stood in line for the National Theatre revival of the show and were able to get tickets for Trevor Nunn's excellent direction of Douglas Hodge, Imogen Stubbs, and Anthony Calf in the Lyttelton Theatre. We were so close we got spit upon by the actors. Don was so excited about the show, he wanted to produce it at Samford, and asked if I was up to designing costumes for the show. I assured him it was too good an opportunity to pass up, and we performed Pinter's piece in the spring of 2000.

Going through the show night after night, I did wonder: Is any situation in life as painful as betrayal — treachery from a friend, a spouse, a partner? The word "betrayal" itself resounds with echoes of rage and despair, humiliation and defilement. Trust and faith, which had been freely and tenderly given, are lost, desecrated, disgraced. How can something so desperate transpire?

For a long time, I wondered about many betrayals in my life and sometimes even agonized over them. Then, one spring, I studied the theology of Jurgen Moltmann. In one of his books, he wrote: "God will save everyone." We don't know how, but in the end, the Holy One will gather everyone up. And why would God save wretched people like Hitler, Jack the Ripper, Jeffrey Dahmer, or Judas? Because we are all made up of good and evil. I may not murder anyone, but I have betrayed people, too. I have lied and cheated and swindled — and yet I also build people up, tell the truth, help, and soothe.

I understand that concept fairly deeply, and believe it to be true. And yet, sometimes I still awake with a gasp in the dead of night, wondering why certain pledges are ripped so violently apart. Like the London production, we used this W.B. Yeats poem in our *Betrayal* printed program, and it says oceans about such treachery:

"Others because you did not keep
That deep-sworn vow have been friends of mine;
Yet always when I look death in the face,
When I clamber to the heights of sleep,
Or when I grow excited with wine
Suddenly I meet your face."

August 29:
"What, What?"
King in Alan Bennett's *The Madness of George III*

I would love to say I had designed this wonderful Alan Bennett play about the British king that Americans enjoy abhorring. I did get to see the National Theatre production of *George III* on December 29, 1993, with the delightful Nigel Hawthorne in the title role. The work is based in history, though the playwright strayed a bit from the truth for dramatic reasons. Both riveting and humorous onstage, the play was well transformed into a 1994 film. In both, we see the King's struggle with something like a psychiatric disorder which makes him seem very human rather than pompously royal.

What, what is the play about? It is really a reflection on the authority and control of the monarchy and Bennett uses an actual bout of derangement that George III encountered, possibly a symptom of the blood disorder "porphyria," or possibly real madness. His decline into insanity and the resulting loss of abilities causes opponents to jump at a perfect chance to depose the unpopular king. But the audience grows fonder and fonder of the crotchety old fellow the more illness, inhumane treatment, and back-stabbing he has to undergo. Doctors attempt to cure the King by blistering him, purging him, and finally through restraining him by strapping him into a waistcoat, while family members and friends scheme to overtake the throne.

Alan Bennett has said that George's actual historical recovery was only slightly less dramatic than when he rallies in the play. "In this process of recovery," Bennett has said, "the 'what-whatting' was crucial. This verbal habit of the King's was presumably the attempt of a nervous and self-conscious man to prevent the conversation from flagging, always a danger in chats with the monarch as the subject is never certain whether he or she is expected to reply or when." So, while ill, King George dropped the familiar refrain, and began to speak rapidly and almost continuously.

As he gained peace of mind and came to himself, back came the "what-whatting," as Bennett says, to show his recovery. To others, it served as a symbol of the King's return to wisdom. In England, the old-fashioned expression is still used sometimes to end a question that doesn't really need an answer, such as, "That was a spectacular football match we won, what, what!"

"What, What?" echoes from the King on many occasions before the madness, and during the final unfolding of the drama. It is a great exclamation to have added to my vocabulary. With quizzical tone, it can mean, "What the bloody heck, really?" With a suspicious timbre, it can express, "Hmmmm, you don't say!" With a spirited tenor, it can suggest, "All right, old chap!"

If you have never experienced the play or film, why not find a disk or streaming service to watch tonight. *"What, What?"*

August 30:
"With your foot you tap, tap, tap;
with your hands you clap, clap, clap;
right foot first,
left foot then,
round about and back again!"
Gretel in Engelbert Humperdinck's opera *Hänsel and Gretel* with libretto by Humperdinck's sister, Adelheid Wette, based on the Grimm brothers' fairy tale *Hänsel and Gretel*

I know, I know. Everyone else in the world who knows anything about the opera Hansel and Gretel claim as their favorite song from the work to be *"Abendsegen"* or the "Evening Prayer" the children sing before they fall asleep while lost in the forest: "When at night I go to sleep, Fourteen angels watch do keep." But having watched rehearsals for weeks while in graduate school when the UNC-G School of Music performed the work, the foot-tapping tune is the one that more often runs through my head.

Sometimes when I am feeling anxious about waiting for my name to be called at the doctor's office, or getting antsy about time slipping away from a project, or fretting about a missed phone call, I will rap the toes of my shoes against the floor. The second I do so, I begin to laugh because this little dancing song comes to mind.

In the first scene of the opera, Gretel sings as she sews while Hänsel makes brooms for their father's business. Hänsel is so hungry he can't work well, and Gretel reveals some milk a neighbor brought them. This news excites Hänsel so much, he drops his work for a merry dance as they imagine the rice pudding they will eat for supper.

Last November, granddaughter Emmeline was in the chorus of the opera at Samford University. Her father David works in the theatre department where I used to spin fabric into costumes day by day, and she often gets tucked here and there into ensembles when children are needed in a production. Again, the lighthearted song and foot tapping with its "tralalas" made it almost impossible to stay in my seat for wanting to dance and enjoy the frivolity the children were experiencing.

Dancing was sometimes a bittersweet experience for me, as one who worried about appearances and wanted to learn things properly. I studied ballet as a very young child with Miss Lum, the woman who owned the studio for which my grandmother sewed costumes. She was a demanding older grand dame who carried a cane to point out mistakes with posture, foot position, arm movements, and skipping.

As a teenager, the sweet foot-tapping and hand-clapping came in dancing the Frug, the Mashed Potato, the Twist, and the Watusi, for which I hung out at local armories where bands played every Saturday night. That practice was better than the bitter foot-tapping of going to school dances where I felt awkward. In college, after an abysmal grade in badminton, I took Modern Dance, Ballroom, and Square Dance to bring my PE average up to a respectable level. One of my partners Frank Cruz, who later sang and danced on Broadway, helped immensely with that swing in assessment of physical abilities, and I really enjoyed and improved my dance moves.

Today, my dancing is usually confined to weddings and evening activities when I direct summer camp. That is, unless I find my foot tapping in the waiting room or the line at the grocery store. Then, I remember *"With your foot you tap, tap, tap"* and *"with your hands you clap, clap, clap"* and I can hardly refrain myself from *"right foot first, left foot then, round about and back again!"*

August 31:
"When the sharks the sharks devour
Little fishes have their hour."
Singer and Chorus in Bertolt Brecht's *Caucasian Chalk Circle*

Bertolt Brecht's epic plays are not easy to watch; they aren't supposed to be. They fill your mind with conflict and questions and you go home from a production with a lot to consider. Samford University Theatre recently produced his *Caucasian Chalk Circle*, and the child who was supposed to play Michael, the pivotal role, dropped out during the last weeks of rehearsals. This departure allowed my little fishes grandsons to have their hour, because 5-year old George and his twin Arthur took alternating nights of rehearsals and performances.

They had no idea what the piece is about, and they didn't have to in order to perform their role. A cool aspect of this student production is that *Caucasian Chalk Circle*'s world premier was a student production at Carleton College in Northfield, Minnesota, in 1948. Brecht had written the work four years earlier while living in America during World War II.

The theme of the play echoes the Biblical story of Samson in 1 Kings judging between a child claimed by two mothers. Solomon orders, "Divide the living child in two, and give half to the one, and half to the other." The real mother screams, "Oh, my lord, give her the living child, and in no way kill him!"

When the other woman shouts, "Divide him," Solomon proclaims, "Give her the living child," and pointing to the first woman, he says, "She is his mother."

Caucasian Chalk Circle, is a theatrical work concerning a dispute over a valley amid the ruins of a war-torn Caucasian village after Nazis came through with tanks and guns, leaving only rubble. A singer and a group of players organize a play within the play to shed light on the dispute. Through songs and dramatic scenes, they introduce the audience to a situation which ultimately ends with a very unorthodox judge chosen to decide the real mother of the abandoned Michael. Brecht based his play on a fourteenth century Chinese play *The Chalk Circle* by Li Xingdao, which drew from archetypal folk tales found in the East and the West.

A test is ordered, and a circle is drawn in chalk. The child is placed between two women, and the judge reckons the real mother will be able to draw Michael from the ring. Like the baby in Solomon's dilemma, if they both pull hard enough, each will get half a boy. When told to begin, the surrogate mother declines to injure the boy by tugging. She gets two chances, but cannot bear to hurt the child she has nurtured during their ordeals.

Like Solomon, this judge also sees who is the true (if not birth) mother and lets Michael go with her. Is this a play about a wise judge? A test of compassion? A hypothetical question? A detective tale? A parable to shed light on the dispute between two communes, the Collective Fruit Farm and the Collective Goat Farmers, concerning which will inherit a valley of farm land after Nazis march through and then abandon it?

The Singer, at the end of the real play, says, "And you who have heard the story of the chalk circle bear in mind the wisdom of our fathers: Things should belong to those who do well by them, children to motherly women that they may thrive, wagons to good drivers that they may be well driven, and the valley to those who water it, that it may bear fruit." But Brecht's anti-realist, expressionistic, audience assault leaves watchers wondering – and that is such a good thing.

September 1:
In "Try to Remember" from *The Fantasticks*, El Gallo sings about thinking back to a certain sort of dulcet divine September. (Listen to the work online or from your library!)

El Gallo in *The Fantasticks*, Music by Harvey Schmidt and Book and Lyrics by Tom Jones, loosely based on the play *The Romancers (Les Romanesques)* by Edmond Rostand

Eventually running for over 42 years, *The Fantasticks* premiered Off-Broadway on Tuesday, May 3, 1960. Right up my theatrical alley, the allegorical musical combines conventions of *commedia dell'arte*, romantic fables, and Noh drama with a sparse set and simple costumes – all of which beg audience members to use their imaginations. The plot entwines neighboring fathers who pretend to feud so their children, Luisa and Matt, will fall in love. As young folks do, they fall in love – but become disenchanted with each other until they discover that going through pain and sorrow creates a richer and stronger relationship between them.

To get ready to write this piece, I sat down to listen to a YouTube version of "Try to Remember" by The Brothers Four, and I broke down and sobbed uncontrollably. I have designed the show two or three times (once creating a dress for the future Broadway star Rebecca Luker), and I immensely enjoyed the experience each time.

But my closest tie to the tune is singing it with friends at Camp Winnataska in the mid-1960s, just a mere half-decade after the play debuted. The lovely rendition I just experienced brought the same emotions to my heart and thoughts to my head that I had when I was 15, 16, 17.

"Try to Remember." Just this past weekend, I attended my 50th High School Reunion, so remembering back to that slower and more mellow era in my life has been a major part of the last few days. Our Algebra teacher attended the event — it was his junior high math class I was in the day John F. Kennedy was assassinated. But other memories are happier: creating banners for the football games, getting called to the office for mini skirt measurements, participating in Beatlemania, painting wonderful projects in art class, being escorted to the senior prom with someone I really liked.

"Try to Remember." Some of the lyrics of the song talk about only a willow weeping way back in this memory, but in high school, so did I — I am a weeper. And looking back on that era, I cry. Not because I want to relive it or be back there; but because my high school friends and I were all such fragile and naive fellows, so innocently unpolished, so caught up in our budding egos, so often phony. We pigeon-holed each other: cheerleader, brain, football captain, student governor, beauty, wallflower, stud. Classmates called me "hippie," not because I really was one, but because I was artsy, I was different, I was unique. I had dreams of great things for my life in that little dream box beside my pillow.

"Try to Remember." Fifty years later, we're all like Matt and Luisa. We've gone through suffering and loss. Our hearts are full. One high school leader has had three failed marriages. My date to the prom has died. Many have knee replacements, substitute hips, stents, hearing aids, glasses. Some of my dreams have come true, and some never will.

"Try to Remember." But, when classmates spoke, they were genuine, soulful, authentic. Egos are shed pretty much now. Much love was shared. We all remembered — our hearts remembered — those high

340

school days, and we followed those memories; and can now look back at our brash young selves with wisdom, experience, and understanding.

September 2:
"Things are not always what they seem to be."
Don in David Mamet's *American Buffalo*

In 2006, two friends of mine, Jonathan Fuller and Alan Gardner, forged a new professional theatre in Birmingham called City Equity, and they opened with *American Buffalo.* They both starred in the production, Jonathan as Teach and Alan as Don, joined by a student, Tobie Windham, who played Bobby. The audience squeezed into a tiny storefront-turned-audience-chamber on a busy downtown street to view the provocative drama up close. It was a perfect shell for the set: a crowded and disheveled junk shop.

"Things are not always what they seem to be." The performances were across the street from the Alabama, a jewel of an old movie theatre. Alan told me that movie patrons one evening were amazed to see what they believed to be a holdup taking place when, as part of the action, Teach fiddles with a gun. Thinking a real stickup was going on, several people called the police. Five squad cars blared to the theatre only to find it was a play, not an armed robbery, unfolding.

"Things are not always what they seem to be." Does art mimic reality, or reality art? Where is the line? Who's to say? The night Roger and I attended *American Buffalo*, an older, possibly inebriated, man saw lights on and came in to see what he might buy cheaply in what seemed to be a store. Audience members weren't sure if this was part of the action or not until Alan (as Don) took a menacing step toward the man and yelled, "Get the f— out of here," or something Mamet-like.

"Things are not always what they seem to be." This play's style itself might fall into that category. Someone attending *American Buffalo* by chance, and who knew nothing about the playwright might be offended by its crude vulgarity, in large quantities. But the characters not only speak as these people would really talk, the playwright is a mastermind of realistic, yet poetic dialogue. When Seattle Rep did the play in 2013, their website explained: "Mamet's plays usually contain terse dialogue that is chock-full of profanity. At first it might seem as if anyone could master Mamet speak just by spewing curse words, but Zachary Simonson, who plays Bobby, pointed out that the language in *American Buffalo* is actually

very precise and measured. 'There's a term called "profane poetry" which very well describes what's going on,' he said." He explained that many lines are written in iambic pentameter, the same verse meter that Shakespeare used.

"*Things are not always what they seem to be.*" The story of the play is also not really what it appears to be. The three characters are plotting to steal back an American buffalo nickel Don sold to a customer for ninety bucks. Now he thinks the coin is worth a lot more, and he wants them to commit a burglary to retrieve it. But the audience can tell from the beginning that these three, plus an accomplice we don't see, are never going to pull anything off, much less a heist.

Alan, who taught theatre with me for a few semesters at Samford University, was a big burly fellow who might look threatening in a dark alley. A gregarious guy, he would try to be serious, but a laugh was always bubbling under the surface. His twinkling eyes showed he was full of life and humor, and an undying passion for theatre. I thought a person so full of vigor and enthusiasm would go on creating Birmingham theatre forever. But, my friend Alan died in November of 2016 at the age of 48 after a really hard 6-year struggle with cancer and its many manifestations. As Mamet writes, "*Things are not always what they seem to be.*"

September 3:
"*Because hell, Señora, is a place for the wicked. The wicked are quite comfortable in it: it was made for them. You tell me you feel no pain. I conclude you are one of those for whom hell exists.*"
Don Juan in George Bernard Shaw's "Don Juan in Hell" (Act III of *Man and Superman*)

I saw *Man and Superman* (all four acts) on a cold Wednesday in January 1979 in New York City at Circle in the Square Theatre and it was fantastic. My *Playbill* reminds me that, "A confirmed bachelor is pursued by a woman in George Bernard Shaw's play depicting the eternal battle of the sexes. The play's controversial third act, "Don Juan in Hell," features a debate between a Puritanical Don Juan (played by the same actor who plays the bachelor) and the Devil."

I cannot remember where we sat with students we had escorted on a theatrical trip to NYC, but it was fairly close to the actors since the audience seating is only 10 rows deep, and on all sides of the stage. The next time I came face to face with the play is when I was executive director of The Seasoned Performers and we performed "Don Juan in Hell," the portion of the play that was not even performed when it premiered in London on May 23, 1905.

Working on even this one act of the show is a tedious, though joyful task because of its deep philosophical message and social satire. In the "Don Juan in Hell" section, the main character Jack is dreaming, and this Hades of his reverie is filled not with sinners, but people bored with life. He is Don Juan, and tells a woman "there is no mistake: you are intentionally damned." When she asks why, Don Juan replies, *"Because hell, Señora, is a place for the wicked. The wicked are quite comfortable in it: it was made for them. You tell me you feel no pain. I conclude you are one of those for whom hell exists."*

But Don Juan wearies of the woman, this tedious netherworld, and even the genial and intellectual Devil he debates when he delivers a skeptical opinion on how humans are evolving. Don Juan departs for Heaven to further meditate on his (Shaw's) ideology: that to create a race of healthy and moral geniuses, people will have to eradicate mediocrity.

Now that is an interesting idea. I forgot to mention that in the audience with us in New York was Steve Allen, first host of *The Tonight Show*, and a great American composer, actor, comedian, and writer. Seated right in front of us, he turned around to chat for a long time during intermissions. About ten years later, he wrote an intriguing book called *Dumbth*, inspired by his view that, "The American people are dumber now than they have been in a very long time."

I read the book not long after it was published and was both entertained and appalled by his examples of American's "combination of ignorance and stupidity." "Dumbth," he says, "is a tendency toward muddleheadedness, or willful stupidity appearing in all segments of American life." I translate that to be the very mediocrity that Shaw hoped to eradicate. And clearly, even now — thirty years after Allen's book first appeared — we are still a far cry from evolving into a race of healthy and moral geniuses.

While writing this entry, I found this quote by J. Heinrich Arnold. He wrote, "My father used to say that stupidity is the greatest sin. He did not mean simplicity of mind, but spiritual dullness... Very few people today have any idea of the riches of the human heart. Our hearts are created to experience great things; most of us have no idea of what could happen in our lives if we would overcome our stupidity and dullness." Wow.

September 4:
"And remember
The truth that once was spoken
To love another person
Is to see the face of God!"
Direct quote from Victor Hugo
Valjean, Fantine and Eponine in *Les Misérables*, with music by Claude-Michel Schönberg and original French-language lyrics by Alain Boublil and Jean-Marc Natel, with English libretto and lyrics by Herbert Kretzmer, based on the novel by Victor Hugo

If you don't know the history of the musical *Les Misérables*, it is worth a quick trip to Wikipedia or some other source to discover the twists and turns of its real life plot. Since opening in London on October 8, 1985, it has continued for over 30 years, making it the longest running West End musical ever.

The show, as the Hugo novel, follows the nineteenth century French tale of Jean Valjean who has endured prison for almost twenty years for stealing bread for hungry family members. When released, no one will help him except an angelic bishop who inspires him to a transformed life. However, Valjean is mercilessly hounded by a police inspector, Javert. After the intertwining of many characters and events, the hero is engulfed by a student uprising during a general unrest in Paris. The young visionaries construct a street barricade where most of them perish in a fight for their ideals.

The first time I saw *Les Misérables* at the Palace Theatre in 1988, I sat with Bruce, an art professor colleague. It was our first night in London with a bunch of students, and we had settled for some fairly cheap tickets. They were in the upper part of the upper balcony, and the warmth from the heating system rose, baking us. Pillars blocked three-fourths of our view. We had been walking all day exploring museums and we were exhausted, and couldn't help falling asleep. A few minutes into the performance, my colleague leaned over and groaned, "I see why they call it *Les Misérables!*" It really was a miserable experience. The next time I saw the play, I had seats in the middle of the stalls, and the experience was fantastic.

Shortly before the finale, Valjean sings Hugo's quoted line about love and truth and divinity with the spirits of Fantine and Eponine. Like the rest of the music in the memorable score, this song is haunting and romantic, mimicking the script and its action. I have often thought of those words.

And what a week I have had to be thinking again about this quote about love from *Les Misérables*. On Saturday, I watched the electrifying sermon by our Episcopal Presiding Bishop, Michael Curry at the Royal Wedding of Prince Harry and Ms. Meghan Markle. The world was so charmed by his powerful words that the speech and his core message went viral. Of course, he referenced the love shared by Prince Harry and Meghan Markle. But he went way beyond that. "This way of love is the way of life," he said. And, "We were made by a power of love. And our lives were meant and are meant to be lived in that love."

The *Guardian* newspaper declared, "Michael Curry's royal wedding sermon will go down in history." And his impassioned words and animated delivery might be out of the norm in Britain, but we Episcopalians have been onto his charisma for some time. Since he is African American, no one blinked at Curry's reference to Civil Rights; but he brought past words of King's into focus for 2018, saying, "The late Dr. Martin Luther King once said, and I quote: 'We must discover the power of love, the redemptive power of love, and when we do that, we will make of this old world a new world. For love is the only way. There's power in love.'"

Or as Valjean says it, you see the face of God when you love another person.

September 5:
"Why then, can one desire too much of a good thing?"
Rosalind in William Shakespeare, *As You Like It*, Act IV, Scene 1

Renaissance writers used all sorts of euphemisms to suggest sexual double entendres: cocks, baubles, the beast with two backs, dying, Os, circles, flowers, plums, shafts, pipes, horns. John Basil, the artistic director of the American Globe Theatre says that Shakespeare is "never crude but he always reminds us of our humanity on every level."

Many ribald puns are found in Shakespeare's works, including this one about desiring *"too much of a good thing."* *"Thing"* was a sly reference to either male or female genitalia. The humor in this situation is even funnier as we remember that even though Rosalind and Orlando have huge crushes on each other, at this point, she is disguised as

Ganymede, a young man. When she chances upon her sweetheart in the Forest of Arden, she conceals her true identify and then, with Orlando, takes on the "role" of Rosalind to instruct him in the subtleties of courtship. With this little dramatic coverup, Rosalind can study Orlando's heart, testing his romantic ideas of courtly lovemaking.

In normal modern parlance, *"too much of a good thing"* translates quite cleanly into "hurting yourself by overindulging in something good." But as the bawdy vaudeville actress Mae West once quipped, "Too much of a good thing can be wonderful!" And maybe she was speaking Renaissance-talk!

Many Americans today either resist *"good things"* — believing themselves to be unworthy — or put way too many *"good things"* on their credit cards, running up huge bills. Either way, we are not, on the average, a very joyful bunch, even though the Declaration of Independence gives us the right not just to expect, but to pursue happiness. But, *"good things"* (or contentment) involve more than a quest or a striving after. Happiness is really in our true core, a part of our very source of being if we let it bubble up.

Most of us think that the *"good thing"* called happiness is the emotion we feel after we chase a dream and achieve what we want. When I worked more regularly on plays, I designed and built three or four or more each semester. Though I enjoyed my work, maybe it was *"too much of a good thing,"* like eating too many sweets or listening too long to rock and roll. I had a false notion that once this one particular play was over, I would be relieved, I would be happy about its outcome, it would be finished, and I would enjoy a life of doing exactly what I wanted, when I wanted to.

Somewhere along the way I thankfully began to approach happiness in a different way: I realized no one and no thing could externally fill me with bliss if it were not bubbling up from inside me. Rather than seeking that temporary joy when the show was accomplished, I explored the limitless delight that comes from process rather than outcome, from collaboratively working on a creative project rather than seeing the curtain rise on a finished piece or fall on the finale of one. Once I uncap such inner bliss, joy and fulfillment become evident in all my actions. And as I find happiness, it overflows to others. So can anyone ever *"desire too much of a good thing"* like this?

September 6:

In "I'm Calm," the funny servant in this Roman musical comedy sings about being serene and unflustered when he is anything but tranquil. (Listen to the work online or from your library!)

Hysterium in *A Funny Thing Happened on the Way to the Forum* with music and lyrics by Stephen Sondheim and book by Burt Shevelove and Larry Gelbart

In vaudeville, when audience members heard the oft-repeated line "A funny thing happened on the way to the theatre," they knew they were in for a comical story. This musical comedy by Stephen Sondheim is based on Roman farces — the precursors of vaudeville — mainly the works of Plautus who lived from 251 to 183 BC As most Roman comedies, this play involves the antics of a slave, this one named Pseudolus who wants more than anything to purchase his freedom. Originally played on Broadway by the irresistible Zero Mostel, Pseudolus toils toward his goal by encouraging Hero, his young master, to pursue Philia, the girl next door.

Chock-full of quintessential features of slapstick, the musical overflows with cases of mistaken identity, plot twists, exaggerated situations, social satire, puns, doors slamming, and broadly stylized performances — set amidst three domiciles on a Roman street. Hysterium is the anxious, frenetic head slave of one of the households, and Pseudolus swindles him into helping in all his complicated plots, including dressing Hysterium up as the corpse of Philia.

Hysterium has been left in charge by his mistress, and as everything seems to career wildly out of control, Pseudolus urges him to remain unruffled. Hysterium tries to motivate himself by singing this song. It is a great tune to chant to yourself when untoward happenstances arise from the universe, and you have to keep your cool.

I am not normally an apprehensive person, and something big has to ruffle my feathers. But, when things do go awry, I can be as loose-jointed, flustered, and rattled as Hysterium. Like last week when my hotel reservations were mishandled, my stomach coiled and billowed, my head felt light from shallow breathing and rapid heart rate, my body hair stood on end, and my brain went fuzzy.

To myself, I actually crooned Hysterium's lyrics about comforting objects in nature, jewelry, weather. Because really, situations like my hotel disaster are what playwrights use to draft their comedies. In times of kerfuffle, I fare best if I can just deeply breathe, count to ten, take my mind to another realm.

Hysterium's advice to himself falls apart when Pseudolus calls him and he screams like a frightened — well, me when I see a mouse. But his intent is to be unshakeable and prepared, indifferent to disaster, cucumber cool, and as in control as a cat.

All his witticisms are wise guidelines for handling the little shocks that life throws my way. As a matter of fact, my best choice toward integration is to cultivate the virtue of equanimity (composure, poise, equilibrium) in my life. My friends performed *A Funny Thing...* when I was in graduate school, and the lyrics are emblazoned in my brain. Listen to the words of this song — they really do help me not only get through a tumultuous situation, but hover above it and sometimes even laugh, as if what I am going through is part of a Roman farce itself.

September 7:
"Ah! if, if, if, if! If ifs and ands were pots and pans there'd be no need of tinkers."
Joan in George Bernard Shaw's *Saint Joan*

Yes, Joan herself says these words in a meeting with the Archbishop in the cathedral of Rheims in George Bernard Shaw's Saint Joan. Her fellow soldier, friend, and confidante, Dunois, who functions as Joan's voice of reason, takes up for her, saying, "But I know exactly how much God did for us through The Maid, and how much He left me to do by my own wits; and I tell you that your little hour of miracles is over, and that from this time on he who plays the war game best will win — if the luck is on his side." And Joan answers, *"Ah! if, if, if, if!"*

My mother used to have a rather crude proverb that expressed the same sentiment. Growing up, when I would say, "Oh, if only I had done this instead of that," she would reply, "Oh, if your aunt had — [the right equipment], she'd be your uncle." So even now, when I wonder if I might have taken a different route, or made a better choice, I can hear her saying to me, "Oh, if your aunt..."

But I rather like the idea of asking "What if?" in the way that Samuel Taylor Coleridge suggested in his writings: "What would you discover if you remembered to ask What if? What if you slept? And what if in your sleep you dreamed? And what if in your dream, you went to heaven and there plucked a strange and beautiful flower? And what if when you awoke you had the flower in your hand? Ah, what then?"

Rather than conveying regret for a bad choice, this version of "What if?" opens me up to possibilities I might have never have discovered if I hadn't asked. Coleridge is speaking metaphorically. But I have had incidents where I gained something from an encounter with the Holy which I could not explain, and, in fact, which I could not even put into words. The experience was like a strange and beautiful flower plucked from a mysterious source.

Joan of Arc claimed to hear the voices of St. Michael, St. Catherine, and St. Margaret at a very early age giving her personal messages at first, and later advising the young girl to go to the King of France and help him reconquer his kingdom. At age seventeen, Joan was given a small army with which she encircled the city of Orleans, and then scored a series of spectacular military successes. She never stopped to ask, "What if I get burned at the stake?"

So many of us have learned the bad habit of limiting ourselves, of being needy, envious, fearful, or greedy. "What if" as Coleridge wonders, I step out of my ordinary, petty, small self? "What if" I allow my boundless soul to dream? "What if" in that dream, I communicate with the immeasurable Holy Universe? "What if" I find that I am actually one with that unfathomable Cosmos?

Might I then expect inexhaustible resources? Might I then ask for synchronistic connections? Might I then anticipate extraordinary fulfillment? Why not? Ah if, if, if, if!

September 8:
"Some people build fences to keep people out ... and other people build fences to keep people in. Rose wants to hold on to you all. She loves you."
Bono in August Wilson's *Fences*

Fences is August Wilson's 1950s decade contribution to his intended 10-play cycle about the twentieth century African-American experience. This particular work won the 1987 Pulitzer Prizes for drama and is probably one of his most popular pieces. The vibrant and moving story is both universal and particular to the decade and the black family to which it belongs. Set in 1957, the play slowly reveals how Troy Maxson's disappointments in his aspiration to be a professional baseball player affect his ability to support his son Cory's application for a college football scholarship.

Now at 53, Troy, who has ended up in the garbage disposal business, and Cory work on a fence throughout the play. The "ain't got nothing nobody want." During the action, we see that Rose envisions the fence keeping her family safe rather than impeding burglars, and Troy begins to look at the enclosure as an attempt to maintain control over Cory.

I remember when a psychologist friend of mine noted all the railings, walls, and fence lines around yards in a fancy neighborhood near us. "Dogs? Security? Property value?" I wondered. Or did realtors tell them that adding a charming picket fence would bring immediate curb appeal while providing a private haven. Do fences make good neighbors? Do fences create great neighborhoods? The narrator in Robert Frost's poem "Mending Walls" declares, "...Before I built a wall I'd ask to know what I was walling in or walling out..."

My psychologist friend said that her theory, at least in this neighborhood, was that the delineations provided physical and psychological borders not only between the private and the public, but also between the neighbors. Unlike neighborhoods in the 1940s and '50s, where people sat on the porch and knew everyone who came down the street, today's suburban living quarters required privacy and distinct margins marking who lived where, exactly and precisely.

She went on to explain that in a successful relationship, each individual has a distinctly clarified sense of identity. If I don't understand myself, I can hardly participate in any sort of healthy bond that gracefully enhances both me and my partner. This action, she said, was creating boundaries, like the fences do in that fancy neighborhood. This action limited "enmeshment," as she called it.

I think I understand the concept, although I sometimes wonder — a bit like Frost's narrator who questions his neighbor's twice-given advice that, "Good fences make good neighbors." This raconteur asserts "Something there is that doesn't love a wall." He wonders if it is elves? But no, "it's not elves exactly."

Maybe it is his momentary vision that we are really all one, and putting up those walls is an attempt to deny the overwhelming evidence otherwise. I rather like a phrase I heard from Ilia Delio recently: quantum entanglement. In physics, the term describes two particles — but in theology, people — who share a common history that makes their futures intertwined.

Does your yard or apartment building have a wall or a fence to keep people in or out? If so, what does it symbolize to you?

September 9:
"Atheism is a sort of crutch for those who can't bear the reality of God."
George in Tom Stoppard's *Jumpers*

Jumpers is a high-spirited comedy by Tom Stoppard that was first performed at the Old Vic Theatre in 1972 by the National Theatre Company. The play pokes fun at the study of philosophy, asking questions about how we know what we know. And the playwright earnestly attempts to wrangle with the ideas of moral absolute and of the metaphysical reality of God.

In typical Stoppard style, the play is set in an alternative topsy-turvy reality, where British astronauts reach the moon, a new Radical Liberal party has taken over the British government, and energetic academicians sneak through evening London streets reveling in death-dealing gymnastics. Some recent revivals have caused some critics to wonder if the work translates to the twenty-first century, and others to enthusiastically claim it does.

But one review noted that, "with its eclectic blend of satire, melodrama, philosophy, cabaret and vaudeville... the concept runs away as if drafted by George Bernard Shaw and the Monty Python team on amphetamines." Stoppard has called his own work "indefatigably facetious." And some commentators complain that all of his plays go on five minutes (or more) too long.

Stoppard has always been enormously in love with language itself. He once said, "For a lot of writers the language they use is merely a fairly efficient tool. For me the particular use of a particular word in the right place, or a group of words in the right order, to create a particular effect is important; it gives me more pleasure than to make a point which I might consider to be profound."

So buried amidst the burlesque and mayhem of *Jumpers* is this minuscule scene between academics George and Archie. In discussing atheism versus a belief in God, George tells his colleague "there is more in me than meets the microscope." Then, Archie announces that rival philosopher McFee is dead and George delivers the line, *"Atheism is a sort of crutch for those who can't bear the reality of God."* Since usually we would hear something like "belief in God is a crutch for weak, pathetic people who haven't the power to take responsibility for their own lives," this utterance from a modern philosopher is not only surprising, it is, well, Stoppardian.

The thought is almost as unexpected as the assertion I have heard spiritual leaders say: that atheists may be more ready for spiritual transformation than most Christians because at least they have rejected the infantile idea of a bearded grandfather in the clouds who answers, or refuses to respond to, our prayers. So the disciple upholds the skeptic.

In the book *Tom Stoppard in Conversation*, the playwright is quoted as saying, "When I am asked if I believe in God, my answer is that I don't know what that question means. I approve of belief in God and I try to behave as if there is one, but that hardly amounts to faith... I am uneasy with religious ceremonials, because I think intellectually, and the case for God is not an intellectual one." And the unchurched champions the believer.

September 10:
"I have a dream sometimes there of you, dressed all nice and white, in your coffin there, and me all in black looking in on you, and a fella beside me there comforting me, his arm around my waist."
Maureen in Martin McDonagh's *The Beauty Queen of Leenane*

Oh, what a bleak and heart-rending picture of a mother-daughter relationship this quote and this play is! A 1996 black comedy by the Irish playwright Martin McDonagh, *The Beauty Queen of Leenane* was favored with nice runs at London's West End, on Broadway and Off-Broadway as well.

The play is set in a depressing Irish village where everyone knows everyone else and rumors run rampant. Forty-year old Maureen must tend to her corpulent, boorish, and domineering mother Mag, who is declining in physical and mental health, and the audience is pulled into the dark and destructive relationship between two people who can only move from downfall into destruction.

When I designed and taught at Samford University, Don Sandley, my department chairman had worked in Ireland as he researched materials for his doctorate of philosophy, so he was drawn to McDonagh, Brian Friel, Marie Jones, and other current Irish playwrights. We never produced *The Beauty Queen of Leenane*, but because of Don's interest in this genre, I read the play and it is both funny and horrifying, a bitter blend of curious melodrama and uncompromising tragedy.

This play, set almost solely in a dark and dilapidated kitchen, caught my interest through its ability to suck the reader or audience into a sense of choking confinement. A fine moment is filled with hope, only to be dashed by trepidation and dread. Mysteries, betrayals, enigmas, violence: the work contains almost everything you can, as an audience member, hope for except a happy ending — or a feeling of catharsis.

Like much Irish drama and poetry, this play draws me right into it, but it is a really hard play to experience. Sort of like real life. In fact, in a critique of a Philadelphia Theatre Company production of the play, a reviewer said he felt as if he needed to take a bath after watching it. He wrote, "I'm still left with a gnawing fear that McDonagh, the play's wunderkind playwright, is, with his precocious command of dramatic suspense, anticipation and reversal, maybe a little too skillful; that he is, perhaps, as passive-aggressively manipulative as his two principal characters; that he is, in short, doing to us what his characters are doing to one another."

Wow! The fact that a playwright is actually able to make that kind of magic through speech, action, characters, intention, movement, and all his other tools is amazing. Once, all of this action consisted of thoughts in McDonagh's head, then they became words on the page, then memorized dialogue by the actors, then action orchestrated by the director, then characters illuminated by the costumer in front of scenery created and lit by designers, then witnessed by the audience.

Some people believe a Divine Entity made the entire universe out of nothing. Others cannot understand how that could possibly happen. But just think, all the time, playwrights make this kind of life onstage where there was never life before. That is their job!

September 11:
"Death ends a life, but it does not end a relationship."
Gene in Robert Anderson's *I Never Sang for My Father*

Robert Anderson's moving play, *I Never Sang for My Father*, was made into a 1970 movie starring Gene Hackman as Gene Garrison, a widowed New York college professor in love with a California woman. His plan is to marry his girlfriend and move to the West Coast, and while

Gene's mother is encouraging and understanding, his authoritarian father expects his son to stay put.

Suddenly, Gene's mother dies and plans are thrown askew. Gene has always tried to love the unpleasant, selfish, stingy patriarch. So what should he do? In the end, the son really attempts to find inside him some warmth for his dad, but succeeds for only a moment. Gene realizes he can never "sing" for this parent, never really communicate, empathize with, or comprehend a person who cannot accept and appreciate — and love — him back, as his mother always did. He won't soon forget her.

September 11 is one of those days that make us remember the year 2001 with great clarity. On that clear blue morning, I will always, like you, remember where I was. I hopped into an SUV to carpool to work at The American Village and my friend and co-worker Linda had the radio news on. "Have you heard this?" she asked in wonder. "A commuter plane has flown into one of the Twin Towers (World Trade Center)." Later, we found it was not a commuter plane, but a commercial liner that had been highjacked in one of four coordinated strikes by the terrorist group al-Qaeda. The attacks in New York City, Washington DC and over Pennsylvania killed almost 3,000 people and damaged $10 billion worth of property and infrastructure.

Mothers and fathers died that day. Brothers, sisters, sons, daughters, friends, cousins, students, coworkers. We watched stunned on a tiny television in the office as the second plane crashed into the second tower, and as both unbelievably began to fall to the ground; as the Pentagon was hit; and as the plane went down over Pennsylvania.

Less than a month later, on October 1, my priest's 22-month-old son died during heart surgery. I was called out of a meeting at work to hear the news, and I went home weeping, even more heartbroken than I had been for the last 20 days. My priest and his wife miraculously taught us all how to grieve, mourn, lament, and yet somehow live through a tragedy like the loss of a child, and like the loss of the 3,000 people on September 11.

Our whole parish was devastated by all that had happened. But I will never forget how they viewed his short presence in their lives as a gift. He had almost died a few days after birth, and they were so grateful that they had known this precious person for the almost 16,000 hours they had him on earth.

They frequently talk about their departed child. Subsequently having two more children, they candidly tell new friends that they have three children, but that one is now dead. They still wonder about what their first-born might doing if he were alive. They fully understand the concept that Gene was expressing in I Never Sang for My Father: *"Death ends a life, but it does not end a relationship."* The boy is still part of their family, as I suppose most of those killed on 9-11 are to theirs.

September 12
"In memory everything seems to happen to music."
Tom as the Narrator in Tennessee Williams's *The Glass Menagerie*, Scene 1

Today is my brother Bill's birthday, and I think of the music of our childhood. Tom is right; music swirls through many of my memories. Ballads create an imagined film score to accompany certain impressions from my past. Right now I'm thinking of Frank Sinatra's "I'll Be Seeing You." When I was 13 and 14, just as the Beatles were stealing my heart and filling my days with their lively, lovely tunes, my nights were often spent in my room alone, doing homework, creating art, and listening (on my very own stereo record player) to a couple of albums belonging to my parents: "The War Years" and Sinatra's "Only the Lonely."

"The War Years" was filled with songs that were popular during and just after World War II, like "I'll Be Seeing You," "As Time Goes By," "There Will Never Be Another You," "I'll Get By," and "Autumn Leaves," among others. "Only the Lonely" featured "Spring Is Here," "Willow Weep for Me," and "Blues in the Night."

I am not sure why the melancholy music appealed to me so very much, not being a particularly sad young teen. But the songs affected me deeply. All involved great romance that I had not yet experienced, mostly concerning lovers who had been lost, or who were away at war.

The singers seemed to know so much more about life and love than I could ever hope to encounter: last evenings together, heartbreaking partings, mopping up tears, one last sip before leaving the bar. Here is spring where even gentle winds do nothing to charm. Summer kisses have vanished from the cheek. And abruptly, fall arrives blowing leaves across the window, hinting at more love lost. At the time, seasons dragged by so slowly for me, and these people watched them whizzing by in a sophisticated and knowing way.

A fairly recent study featured in the *New York Times* reports that when we listen to sad music, we improve our emotional system. I can cry at the blues, but still realize I am also appreciating the artistic experience. And in doing so, I actually undergo "vicarious emotions," fairly unencumbered by the distressing feelings of real life. I may feel temporarily melancholy but not genuinely heartbroken. However, my emotional capacity is enlarged and I can better understand myself and relate to fellow human beings.

I cannot find "The War Years" album, but I have both the "Only the Lonely" album, and a compact disc and the selections are easily found on You Tube. Any time I hear Frank Sinatra croon those songs, I become fifty years younger, forty pounds lighter, and a thousand heartaches freer. I am back in my old room painting, reading, or hugging my pillow and wondering if what the singers tell me is true. When I am older, will I only know the songs that the lonely know? Will each melody really recall a love that once was passionate? The songs would be countless. Will every one of those myriad tunes mirror romances that ended in this sadness that I at once desperately longed for, but somehow understood would be almost too painful to endure?

September 13:
In "Rose's Turn," in *Gypsy*, the mother of the famous Gypsy Rose Lee complains that her timing in life is off, both in her arrival on earth and in starting her career. (Listen to the work online or from your library!)

Rose in *Gypsy* with book by Arthur Laurents, music by Jule Styne, and lyrics by Stephen Sondheim, suggested by the *Memoir of Gypsy Rose Lee*

Gypsy is a well-loved show, which has been called "the greatest American musical" by audiences, reviewers, and theatre professionals. The expert theatre critic Clive Barnes once alluded to Rose's character as "one of the few truly complex characters in the American musical."

The 1959 piece, with music by Jule Styne, lyrics by Stephen Sondheim, and book by Arthur Laurents, originally starred Ethel Merman in the role of Rose. The work is partially rooted in the 1957 memoirs of the burlesque entertainer, Gypsy Rose Lee, famous for her striptease act. The musical highlights her obsessive mother Rose Hovick who, we might as well say, created the expression "stage mom." Rose is resolute about pushing both Louise (Gypsy Rose) and her sister June Havoc into the disappearing realm of vaudeville.

Rose blurts out near the end of the musical, that her life timing has caused her to fail to be a star herself. But like many stage parents, her actions were mostly about herself, rather than what her daughters really wanted.

Demanding tiger parents pressure kids for academic success; helicopter mothers and fathers take overprotective and excessive concern in their children' lives; and sports dads, pageant moms, and other pushy parents usually bend their offspring so much in their youth that they can turn into emotionally crippled adults. A study published in 2013 was the first to experimentally investigate pushy parents, and not surprisingly, researchers report that these moms' and dads' own unrealized ambitions drive their domineering style. All of them neglect very important boundaries. They see their child as an extension of themselves rather than as the separate human being they really are, so they see any of their offsprings' achievements as their very own.

Such parents, according to the investigation published in the journal PLOS One, are trying — like Rose in Gypsy — to mitigate their own failures by living through their children. That's not entirely surprising, but, as study co-author Brad Bushman, professor of communication and psychology at Ohio State University says, "Our research provides the first empirical evidence that parents sometimes want their child to fulfill their unfulfilled ambitions — for example, that they want their child to become a physician when they themselves were rejected for medical school."

"When parents see their child as part of themselves, they may experience the child's achievements as if they were their own," says Bushman. "They may bask in the reflected glory of the child's achievements. As such, the child's achievements may become a surrogate for parents' own unfulfilled ambitions."

Rose claims timing as an impediment to her own success. But the past can bog us down: our youth is gone, and living through our child will not bring it back. Whatever our boys and girls accomplish or botch is their own doing. And no matter how great the success or how disappointing the failure, their actions should never weaken who we are as individuals, or even as parents.

September 14:

357

"There is no wicked side: life is all one. And I never wanted to shirk my share in whatever evil must be endured, whether it be sin or suffering. I wish I could cure you of middle-class ideas, Dolly."
Barbara to Adolphus "Dolly" Cusins in George Bernard Shaw's *Major Barbara*, Act III

In our 1987 family Christmas trip to London, one evening, just as we entered a pizza parlor to relieve our hunger from traipsing all over the city, we were treated to a barrage of Christmas songs played by a small Salvation Army brass band with drum. In this Shaw play, Barbara Undershaft is a major in the Salvation Army. She says the above line to Adolphus Cusins after he remarks to her, "I thought you were determined to turn your back on the wicked side of life."

Until he was 30 years old or so, playwright George Bernard Shaw called himself an atheist. He was a eugenist, or believer in the philosophy of improving the genetic quality of the human population, and dipped into Communism while descrying the democratic system of the twentieth century.

Shaw's crusading nature and love of justice led him to embrace and firmly cling to a variety of causes, which he promoted ferociously. He called his own pre-vegetarian self a "cannibal." He believed that workers were too uneducated and indifferent to vote intelligently, and that poverty would be eradicated by giving equal wages to everyone. He staunchly embraced socialism and became a charter member of the Fabian Society, which aspired to spread socialism by peaceful means.

Major Barbara features the upper class Barbara Undershaft who is disappointed when the Salvation Army receives a donation from an armaments manufacturer and whisky brewer, even though it is her father. Later, she decides to take a healing message to the rich rather than try to transform the poor.

Shaw blended humor and charm with his social agenda, and enticed middle-class audience members, as critic Fintan O'Toole puts it, "into philosophical minefields and then exploded their most cherished assumptions. What makes *Major Barbara* the most terrifying ... is that it is most uncomfortable for those in the audience who might usually emerge from a Shaw play with the warmest glow of vindication. It attacks, essentially, Shaw's own side — the decent, progressive people who feel guilty about exploitation, slums, and misery and want to be nice to the poor. Shaw deliberately offends socialists, liberals, and muscular Christians."

"There is no wicked side: life is all one." When I think broadly like Shaw, I see that the underpinnings of most world religions point to the idea that reality and the universe are good, and yet paradoxically full of sin and suffering. We all make mistakes, and we feel pain. As I get older, I gaze upon positive and negative incidents in my life as tiny shards that are moving together to create a mostly magnificent mosaic.

One Richard Rohr quote I like is, "Wisdom is where you see it all and you eliminate none of it and include all of it as important training. Finally, 'everything belongs.' You are able to say, from some larger place that even surprises you, 'It is what it is' and even the 'bad' was good."

After the Buddha sat under the Bodhi tree for enlightenment — and was able to see life as it really is without projections or interpretations — the words he spoke to the first person he saw were, "In this blind world, I beat the drum of deathlessness." Maybe Major Barbara played the drum in the Salvation Army band of her day to say that somehow she (Shaw) was beginning to see life without all of its delusions and belief systems.

September 15:

In "The Beauty Is" from *The Light in the Piazza*, the mother sings about figures in Old Masters paintings who beckon to the viewer by stretching their arms forward. (Listen to the work online or from your library!)

Margaret in *The Light in the Piazza* with book by Craig Lucas and music and lyrics by Adam Guettel, based on a novella by Elizabeth Spencer

Though I no longer teach at Samford University, David Glenn my son-in-law does. He is the technical director of the theatre, and recently they performed *The Light in the Piazza*. In it, my granddaughter Emmeline, had a cameo appearance in the play and carried some balloons onto the stage, which thrilled her little drama princess heart. Set in the 1950s, the script and score tell the story of an affluent Southern lady, Margaret Johnson.

With Clara, her emotionally and mentally delayed daughter, she takes off for a summer in Italy. The 2005-06 Broadway debut of the show at the Vivian Beaumont ran for a respectable 504 performances. The score of the musical leaps beyond this century's Broadway convention of peppy pop music into the realm of opera, and several subsequent productions of the play were staged in opera houses as well as theatres.

The lines about paintings and the figures in them that Margaret sings about are haunting. In college, I had a double major in English and Art. One day, my Sophomore English class studied a poem, "Musee des Beaux Arts" by WH Auden. After we reviewed the poem in class, I went to the library and looked at the painting it refers to by Pieter Breughel. That day, my being was changed. In 21 succinct lines, the poet explains the ultimate and underlying meaning behind the works of the great classical painters, and about art and life itself.

If you do not know the Auden poem and the Pieter Breughel painting of the Icarus myth, please go today and find a photograph online of the painting and then read online or in a book the Auden poem. If you are not blown away by the experience, let me know and we can talk.

Back to the musical: when she sings this reprise of "The Beauty Is," Margaret feels like she is reliving the moment when the young Clara was kicked in the head and significantly injured by a rented pony on her twelfth birthday. Thinking back on the incident, she regrets that she ran to answer the phone instead of watching her daughter more carefully. Like anyone looking back on a past tragedy, she recalls how slowly the momentous affair seemed to unfold. And today, all she really wants is to reach out and have that one moment back.

Returning to the idea of art, she sings about painting the day differently. In the play, Margaret tries desperately to control Clara's life and keep her from falling in love to protect her. I suppose everyone reflects on past mistakes and wishes things had turned out differently. We blame ourselves and obsess over how we might have acted, or what we should have done. And we harm the people we love most by hanging on to the idea of what might have been.

But we must let these memories go, or they will have destructive power over us forever. In the play, Margaret finally reappraises Clara's fate, as well as her own life with all its hidden hopes and lost dreams. In the end, the mother allows her daughter to take a chance on love despite its many risks and potential pain. What do love and joy mean without the accompanying suffering anyway?

September 16:
"When we are born, we cry that we are come
To this great stage of fools."

360

If my mother were still alive, she would be 86 today. She loved birthdays — her own and those of her family members. Annual natal remembrances were always a cause of celebration with her. She loved to make the cake, purchase the gifts, choose a crazy card, cook a favorite meal of the honoree, and gather all her brood around to have fun and observe the special day with care.

And she would have agreed with the Bard that *"When we are born, we cry that we are come/To this great stage of fools."* What a wonderful line from *King Lear* this is. The King has certainly run the gamut of emotions in his life, and this utterance superbly captures the mood of his disenchanted weariness. His long life is almost over, and, nearing the end, Lear feels quite ready to leave the stage.

Shakespeare apparently enjoyed the idea of comparing life to the stage. "All the world's a stage, and all the men and women merely players: they have their exits and their entrances; and one man in his time plays many parts," says Jacques in *As You Like It.* And Macbeth opines, "Life's but a walking shadow, a poor player that struts and frets his hour upon the stage."

We do all take on roles and masks as we grow up and leave our essence behind. Our bodies become the costume for our souls. We perform, we act, we do our little song and dance — that ceaseless play of life that we enact on Earth. We are the star of our show, and everyone else has a supporting role in that wondrous libretto written specifically for us. Drama unfolds all about us.

Some people believe with all their hearts that they want the accompanying script! Maybe I could look ahead a page or two and see what booger boo is around the corner, what brilliant flash of joy I should be prepared for, what black unseen hole is looming — maybe, even, if I survive!

Seán O'Casey, the great Irish dramatist and memoirist, quipped, "All the world's a stage and most of us are desperately unrehearsed." And that is true. But how exciting that, like actors performing a Renaissance *commedia dell'arte* scenario, we are free to improvise the action as we go along, deciding day by day how to spontaneously play each scene as it unfolds before us.

Yesterday, I played the character of an anxious and unsettled worrier about that presentation I am giving tomorrow, but today I choose to be a valiant and unruffled paragon in front of 75 strangers. Before, I found myself rehearsing how I might fail, but today I practice humble triumph with great aplomb. But I, too, sometimes wonder exactly what part I am playing in this great eternal production.

When my mother died last year, she essentially exited our earthly stage, and we all wept. And yes, we also cry the moment we are born. But is it because *"we are come to this great stage of fools"* and tragedians — or do we cry because there was nowhere to hide that darn script of our life upon our bare little bodies?

September 17:
A member of the cast of *Hank Williams: Lost Highway* remembers Hank as a skinny young man rushing around, humming so much like a mosquito that they called him "Skeet." (Listen to the work — or any of Hank Williams recordings — online or from your library!)
Hank Williams' mother in Randal Myler and Mark Harelik's *Hank Williams: Lost Highway*

Some critics think Myler and Harelik's *Hank Williams: Lost Highway* is one of the greatest examples of a musician's biography ever written for the stage. The work starts at the rise of this star when he played at the Louisiana Hayride country music radio and television show on his way to conquer the Grand Ole Opry.

I love this piece and Williams' music not only because he is the father of contemporary country music, not only because his tunes are so haunting and joyous, but also because Hank Williams was born in my state of Alabama — on this day, September 17, 1923, — in the bucolic community of Mount Olive about 50 miles south of Montgomery. His bible-toting mother who called him "Skeet," (mosquito) moved the family to Montgomery when Hank was 13, and opened a boarding house, since Hank's father Lon spent a lot of time in a veteran's hospital.

She had presented her son with a guitar when he was eight, and his musical mentor became a Montgomery blues street singer named Rufus "Tee Tot" Payne. It was really from Tee Tot that Hank studied guitar and learned to sing the blues. Later, he formed a band called the Drifting Cowboys and was a regular on local radio station, WSFA. Hank Williams died way too soon at age 29 in the backseat of his Cadillac on the way to a New Year's Day performance in 1953. The official cause of death was cardiac arrest, likely brought on by a mixture of painkillers and alcohol.

His honky tonk spiritual songs are just about as wondrous as you can get: "I'm So Lonesome I Could Cry," "Your Cheatin' Heart," "I Saw the Light," "Cold, Cold Heart," "I Can't Help It." Mmmm, hmmm! How he could capture the gamut of life's tumultuous emotions in a life just short of three decades, I don't know: new love, lost love, no love, family anxiety, and the joy of being.

Some people call Hank Williams the most legendary recording artist of all-time, others call him country music's original bad boy, lots of folks call him both. Like me, like you, he was a combination of dark and light, sweet and peevish, intelligent and dopey, progressive and nostalgic. As the thirteenth century Sufi poet Rumi said, "Good and bad are mixed. If you don't have both, you don't belong with us." Williams' brilliant and enduring music, short time on earth, and meteoric career create an emanation from his life, a mythic trail of tears and beauty that even today call listeners to be part of the enduring genius of a man who once performed a record six encores at Nashville's Grand Ole Opry.

September 18:
"Walter Mitty lives in every town and city in our land. You have met him many times. Middle-aged, married, in love with the long ago and far away, he is the lonely wanderer in the crowd, the silent daydreamer, the fellow that stares out at sea long after the ship has sailed. Right now he is driving his wife to the hairdresser's in Waterbury, Connecticut – or part of him is, anyway."
Narrator in James Thurber's "The Secret Life of Walter Mitty" scene in *A Thurber Carnival*

The fun revue *A Thurber Carnival*, adapted by the author from his own humorous New Yorker stories and cartoons, is a fond memory of mine, having produced it in our 1974-75 season. As this quote from the Narrator indicates, Mitty is a mild-mannered dreamer, whose mind is often off in the clouds, envisioning himself as the hero of some exhilarating adventure.

I have always been a daydreamer and my mind often drifts into assorted imagined worlds and situations. That propensity can be a positive experience if I don't let myself meander into my ego's conversation. For a lot of my life, my brainpower was often fogged – as though a swirl of morning mist and clouds were enveloping my thinking-power.

This kind of cloud is made of the fumes of mental conditioning, and habitual patterns that make up my ego personality. This kind of cloud makes me believe my ego self is "who I am." Until I started listening to the audio recordings of wise spiritual teachers like Richard Rohr, Deepak Chopra, Eckart Tolle, and Wayne Dyer, I understood precious little about the ego, which tries to beguile me on a daily basis: "If you do that, you are a fool!" "Things don't work that way!" "You are so much better than she is!"

Before I understood this voice for what it is, I believed that I was a lone individual, separate from the whole of creation. My mind distracted me untold times each day with aversions and attractions, fears of failure, thoughts of rejection, visions of abandonment. My first great advancement was to understand the concept of the ego, and the second was to begin to notice what my tricky little ego was up to each day. Through working with a consciousness community, I am able to sometimes part the clouds and peer toward enlightenment.

Comically, this Thurber quote became very insightful last evening. *"Right now he is driving his wife to the hairdresser's in Waterbury, Connecticut – or part of him is, anyway."* I (and not Walter Mitty) was driving myself across town not to the hairdresser's, but to give my very first Enneagram seminar since being certified to teach last December. This entire presentation was an introduction to this ancient typology system, and how it can brush away those clouds or peel away the veils that our Egos continually use to cover our Divine Essence.

And do you know what happened? In a desperate attempt for my ego to assert itself, I heard: "You are going to be sick. Doesn't your stomach feel nauseous? Oh, and, there is a step on the front of that stage where you are going to be speaking. You probably will fall off it, so why don't you just tell the folks you can't speak tonight. You will be jittery in front of 75 people anyway."

I had actually been ignoring the voice, distracted by thinking through some of the talk, but I suddenly paid attention. "You have got to be kidding!" I retorted back. "Sorry, I am NOT going to listen to you! And you are pretty much going to be bashed tonight, so hush!"

The incident was actually helpful, although I didn't fully process it until after my workshop was over. But because I had gone through that little drama, I was able to lead myself into complete presence and equanimity while I was teaching, and it was a magnificent experience.

September 19:
"Do not bandy words with your father, nor treat him as a dotard, nor reproach the old man, who has cherished you, with his age."
Just Discourse in Aristophanes' *The Clouds*

The Ten Commandments urge us to honor our fathers and mothers, advice is very much like Aristophanes exhortation: *"Do not bandy words with your father, nor treat him as a dotard, nor reproach the old man, who has cherished you, with his age."* I have always believed that parents have a noble calling. I respected my parents and they trusted me, so we had a fairly affirming relationship that went both ways.

I can't say I never bandied words with my own father, for our political outlooks and life experiences were quite divergent. The two of us had many arguments and altercations when I was a teenager because we were both a bit hard-headed and fond of our own beliefs. But a lingering sadness for me is that he died at 78, not at all a dotard or what I would even call an old man. Because he took a certain blood pressure medicine for many years, his kidneys were affected and unfortunately, his doctor didn't monitor him carefully enough. He had passed the age for transplant eligibility before his medical advisors found how deteriorated his kidneys were. Though on dialysis for several years, his body grew less and less able to sustain his life while his brain and mind remained as sharp and active as ever.

My father's name was William Earl Sloan, but everyone called him "Buck." Once, not long before my daughter Elin was born, my parents ran into a longtime acquaintance and his friends at a restaurant. The man got flustered making introductions and called my father "Bu-bu-bu-bu-bu... Bubba!" We all thought it was so hilarious, that we sometime called him that, and Bubba became his grandfather nickname.

In the Air Force toward the end of World War II, my dad had such a distinctive walk that my mom, brother Bill, and I could always identify him in a veterans parade. And, like many men of his era, the military duty led his parenting style toward the maneuvers of a lieutenant colonel.

However, when my children were born, Dad became a softy with them, delighting in their several-times-a-week presence. Always a source of strength in our family, he was a wonder to Elin and Seth and they learned an abundance of Bubba Wisdom from him.

Another name for him was Tinkerbell, because he could fix anything, and showed them how to as well. Having been a pilot, he could identify every plane that flew overhead, calling to my mom or the kids, "Look, there's a Boeing 247 (or a DC-6, or an L-1011, or ...")." He taught them car safety, home security, weather patterns, bird watching, table manners, and keeping your word. He wanted them to look on the bright side, realize all problems have a solution, and to carry on even through losses. Taking up ham radio correspondence at a late age, Bubba encouraged them to open up to the world and to keep learning their whole lives.

Nowadays, when one of Elin's or Seth's children misbehave in school, or slip up on home chores, or pester a neighbor, we remark that it's regrettable that they missed being trained by Bubba. He was the grandfather with whom they rarely bandied harsh words, who they never treated as a dotard — and who in return, cherished and nourished the two of them in his older age.

September 20:
In "Tradition," Tevye sings about keeping Russian Jewish customs when times are changing. (Listen to the work online or from your library!)

Tevye in the musical *Fiddler on the Roof*, with music by Jerry Bock, lyrics by Sheldon Harnick, and book by Joseph Stein, based on tales by Sholem Aleichem

Fiddler on the Roof appeared on the boards for at the University of North Carolina at Greensboro while I was there working on my Masters in English. The show was a joy to behold. I have always loved this musical, which debuted on Broadway a couple of days from now — on September 22, 1964.

As a costume designer, I was grateful for the way the original Broadway costume designer, Patricia Zipprodt, textured and broke down the costumes to get a realistic look. I always heard this was the first Broadway show to age or distress outfits to get a specific patina. I am not sure how to check the authenticity of this idea, but I believe I remembering hearing Zipprodt herself say so once at a Southeastern Theatre Conference convention.

It is funny how we all try something once, like throwing dye on a costume and roughing up its edges, and suddenly it catches on. Then, shortly it becomes a... tradition. Many theatre costumes even today go to the dye room for a break down before making it to the stage.

Traditions are long-held customs or beliefs that are passed down from generation to generation. For instance, at Camp Winnataska, where I direct a session each summer, there is a tree growing through the boards of a footbridge we have to cross to get across the creek. When I was a leader, we used to jokingly say, "bread and butter" as we got split up going around the trunk.

As most people know, the blessing of "bread and butter" is called out by friends walking together when they are compelled to split up when an obstacle or pole comes between them. Some sort of bad fortune is prevented by both walkers saying the phrase at once. But what we used to announce casually has metamorphosed into an ironclad... custom. In fact now, no one even lets the tree come between them so that they would have to say, "bread and butter." Even under the most extreme and crowded conditions, campers go on only one side of the tree so as not to break their bonds of friendship.

I love such ritual habits, and we have plenty more at camp and wealth of them at my church including a book of Lenten devotions created each year with parishioners' writings, and the Red Egg Guild painting and decorating eggs for Easter. Family traditions include kissing every time the University of Alabama football team makes a touchdown — a custom started by my father, a huge Roll Tide fan. Among many other customs, we also celebrate the 12 Days of Birthdays between January 24, the anniversary of my debut on Earth, and Roger's on February 5.

Traditions are fun and quirky, eagerly awaited, and fondly greeted as they return daily, weekly, monthly, or yearly. Tevye is right: if we go without these historical conventions, our families and organizations become as wobbly as a fiddler on the tip of a housetop.

September 21:
"There are no big moments you can reach unless you've a pile of smaller moments to stand on. That big hour of decision, the turning point in your life, the someday you've counted on when you'd suddenly wipe out your past mistakes, do the work you'd never done, think the way you'd never thought, have what you'd never had — it just doesn't come suddenly. You've trained yourself for it

while you waited — or you've let it all run past you and frittered yourself away.
I've frittered myself away. . ."
General Benjamin Griggs in Lillian Hellman's *The Autumn Garden*, Act
3

This autumnal play about middle age examines the inertia certain people experience as they grow older. While living life, some of us acquiesce to what life dishes out without transforming. When we stop and examine what has gone before, it is often too late to make a dramatic shift. Set in September 1949 in a Gulf of Mexico resort one-hundred miles from New Orleans, the characters' unfulfilled lives unfold before their own — and the audiences members' — eyes.

When asked about the theme, Hellman said that she didn't mean to insinuate that people can't do anything about their lives, but just the opposite. Humans have a lot of control over their lives. What you do, how you let your being guide you, how you act or think or feel — all of these things have an influence on how your life plays out. For this work, the playwright got help from her long-time lover Dashiell Hammett, American author of detective novels and other works, who even received a percentage of the royalties.

This play implies that at middle age, our youth is fading, our physical self is declining, and we have certainly had our share of family troubles and work disappointments. When we encounter seminal points in life, the losses, missed opportunities, and regrets are often overwhelming, and point only to dwindling or even hopeless expectations. The Hellman-Hammett collaboration reveals that both of them understood that little moments of time throughout our lives count, or, as the general says, one day you find "you've let it all run past you and frittered yourself away."

Say you wanted to pursue a profession of painting, but got married, had kids, bought a house with a mortgage. You had to make ends meet, so you got a job that could immediately bring home a paycheck. You wanted to show the world you were a grown up and could take care of business. Obligations! But... you frittered your self away.

Say you were lucky enough to pursue that profession of painting. You married a well-to-do spouse, and had loads of time to create and express. But, you didn't have the right studio. You didn't want to make a mess of your house. So you didn't start painting, you added a studio in the attic. That took a while. Then, the studio was ready, but the brushes weren't right. Or the pencils needed to be sharpened. Or the attic was too darned quiet, or too hot, or... Procrastination! But... you frittered your self away.

As writer Paulo Coelho so vividly expresses in his international best selling novel *The Alchemist*, we all come to earth with a personal legend to fulfill. Joseph Campbell created the expression "following your bliss." You might talk about your life's purpose, and I might refer to it as a path God created for only me to tread.

Whatever term you use, when your realize you are off track, it is best to find your self's way quickly or remorse is sure to overcome you, just like the characters in *Autumn Garden*. You'll suddenly find yourself in Winter Garden, and there really will be no time left to write or paint or mold your personal legend.

September 22:
"Chip the glasses and crack the plates!
Blunt the knives and bend the forks!
That's what Bilbo Baggins hates –
Smash the bottles and burn the corks!

Cut the cloth and tread on the fat!
Pour the milk on the pantry floor!
Leave the bones on the bedroom mat!
Splash the wine on every door!

...That's what Bilbo Baggins hates!
So, carefully! Carefully with the plates!"
Dwarves in different stage adaptations of JRR Tolkien's *The Hobbit*
(Tolkien, J. R. R. 2012. The Hobbit. London, England: HarperCollins.)

This day is the birthday of both Frodo and Bilbo Baggins. I have never actually worked on a production of *The Hobbit*, or any other Tolkien work, but I saw a dramatic version in London on January 3, 2001. Since my senior year in high school, I have been a huge Tolkien fan. We studied *The Hobbit* in Miss Autry's class. Miss Autry. Now there was someone straight out of the mind of someone like Tolkien, CS Lewis, or perhaps even more likely, JK Rowling.

Miss Autry was an older lady about four feet ten inches tall, with enormous calves that puddled at the ankle and dripped over her sturdy black lace-up shoes. Brilliant, but very quirky, she ruled her classroom with ever darting and roving eyes that were always searching for some mischievous business going on. She had us read and then give reports on *The Hobbit*, and the research and sharing was going well until one student detailed the numerous Tolkien fan gatherings that were part of the youth movement of the late 1960s.

Something about the world view of Tolkien's imaginative works resonated with anti-war marchers, feminists, civil rights advocates, and others hoping to confront "the establishment." Professor Ralph C. Wood, a Tolkien scholar explains that Middle Earth was a literary escape hatch for a generation haunted by the Vietnam War and the atomic bomb.

Having never heard this news, Miss Autry was scandalized. "The very idea of taking a great work of literature to the dirty, filthy streets! Everyone put your books on your desk!" She proceeded to take up everyone's copy of *The Hobbit* (even though many of us purchased them ourselves), and said, "That is the end of the reading of this book. You will never speak of it in my presence again!" I immediately bought another copy and read it and *The Lord of the Rings* as fast as I possibly could.

The quoted passage above comes early in the book, on the day of an unexpected party at the home of Bilbo Baggins. Gandalf the wizard invites thirteen dwarves for tea, and a flustered hobbit has to pull all kinds of food out of his pantry. At the finish of the meal, the dwarves leap up and shakily carry great piles of plates to the kitchen. The dwarves are amused at the frightened Bilbo — fearing the ruin of his dishes — and they sing this song of breakages that never happen.

The food for the party is described as: "Some called for ale, and some for porter, and one for coffee, and all of them for cakes . . . A big jug of coffee had just been set in the hearth, the seed-cakes were gone, and the dwarves were starting on a round of buttered scones . . . 'And raspberry jam and apple-tart,' said Bifur. 'And mince-pies and cheese,' said Bofur. 'And pork-pie and salad,' said Bombur. 'And just bring out the cold chicken and pickles!'"

So every year on this day, to celebrate this auspicious occasion, I assemble as many of the named delicacies as possible. I make an old family English meat pie, adding to it cheese and seed-cakes, pickles and ale, and sometimes other delights. People who say English food is boring just haven't had a proper hobbit meal I suppose.

September 23:
"We haven't time – that takes all day. Besides, I haven't the black gloves."
Caroline in Thornton Wilder's *Childhood*

Caroline is answering her sister Dodie's plea to "let's play Funeral!... let's play Orphans!" In true Thornton Wilder fashion, the very short play *Childhood* is both thought-provoking and frightening in a funny sort of way. Presented from the point of view of the children, this revealing game of make-believe challenges family pretenses and traditional parental roles. We paired the play with Wilder's *Infancy* with great success in the spring of 1989.

I remember feeling joyous just about this time of year when my brother Bill and I would go out to play in my neighborhood in Tuscaloosa. I was six-years old, and times were fairly safe. There were dozens of nearby kids, and we loved to play make-believe en masse: cowboys, pirates, weddings, hospital, car crashes.

I was a tomboy and ran fast to keep up with the lads in dashes through forbidden back yards. We climbed trees, organized ball games in a nearby field, played hide and seek, and games like "Mother May I?" I also loved to play with dolls and my best playmate for that pastime was Barry, a good neighborhood pal, and probably my first gay companion.

Sometimes, I would run free by myself: wind in my hair, leaves crunching underfoot, azure sky up above. The entire world seemed to be at my fingertips. A withered-grass-and-chrysanthemum smell of autumn permeated the air. I was present, in the moment, delighted with life and myself. I had no agenda, no concept of time, no responsibility, no care.

But my amusement was not for naught. Play teaches children social skills, cooperation, communication, and other important duties of maturing. Experts in child development are finding that free play – away from grownups and coaches, technology and oversight – is an important counterpart to academics.

Play is fundamental to our becoming a functioning, well-balanced adult. It helps with learning and memory. Many families today over-schedule time and, with homework, children don't have enough freedom to be creative, entertain themselves, learn to think things out independently, and find talents and passions by exploring in leisure.

I know in my neighborhood play, my imagination was strengthened, my physical skills were improved, my emotional interaction was refined, and my confidence and self-sufficiency were built up while I remained part of a community. Just thinking about all this reminds me: if play teaches kids how to be grownups, surely play can remind adults how to be young again.

My grandson Teddy is with me today. I think we will go outside right now and run through the already crunching leaves. The sky is bright blue today, the amber sunlight is glinting angularly through the trees, the air is crisp: a perfect day to remember that I can still play and, in the moment, be that free and unencumbered self I was in Childhood. I may even take out that pair of elbow-length black gloves I have! What might Teddy think of that?

September 24:
In "Carry On," Miss Tweed, Hope, and Lettie support Lady Manley-Prowe in her alarm. (Listen to the work online or from your library!)

Tweed and others in *Something's Afoot*, with book, music, and lyrics by James McDonald, David Vos, and Robert Gerlach, additional music by Ed Lenderman

Disregard your feelings! the ladies counsel. Really? I am an emotional (some might say, "moody") person. I am sensitive. And one thing — going to my annual doctor's appointment where I have to step on the scales — makes me jumpy, high-strung, restive, anxious, and — well, skittish. Do I condone those feelings? No. I feel them, nonetheless.

But the British as a whole often place their emotions in a box they place on the shelf. They persevere.

Sometimes we Americans use the phrase "carrying on" to mean some sort of extended rambunctious behavior, such as when George and Arthur, my twin grandsons, come over for a visit and they continue to "carry on," acting like bear cubs wrestling in the woods. But in England, the expression means "keep on doing what you are doing." Supposedly, the idiom came from the British Navy where it meant to steer a boat to stay the course.

I had a small calendar a couple of years ago that was red, emblazoned with a crown and the slogan: "Keep Calm and Carry On." Originally, the phrase graced an inspirational poster aimed at bolstering the spirit of the Brits. In preparation for World War II, the British government created the placard in 1939 after frightening news of probable air attacks on their major cities. According to several sources, there were a number of posters printed, but only a few were actually displayed. One of the leftovers was found in a bookstore in England in 2000, and the expression has since become popular for mugs, posters, journals, and t-shirts.

But, at Samford, we produced *Something's Afoot* in 1983, seventeen years before the rediscovery of the poster, so the familiar words are firmly entrenched in English life. Wikipedia calls the expression, "Evocative of the Victorian belief in British stoicism – the 'stiff upper lip,' self-discipline, fortitude, and remaining calm in adversity..."

So even though I am a rather emotional person, I was brought up in an English family which, even living four generations on American soil, held self-restraint in high regard. I had to learn the hard lesson of keeping my upper lip from trembling when I felt the "slings and arrows of outrageous fortune" and wanted to boohoo in front of family members.

Stoicism is an ancient Greek philosophical idea that promoted the endurance of suffering with no display of emotion. Romans, such as Seneca, spread the practice, which continues through the Renaissance, the period of so-called Enlightenment, the Victorian Era – and even today. Seneca stated: "Two elements must therefore be rooted out once for all, – the fear of future suffering, and the recollection of past suffering; since the latter no longer concerns me, and the former concerns me not yet."

Which is similar advice given by modern wisdom teachers who caution us to live in the present, and forego much suffering we place upon ourselves through shame about the past and anxiety over the future. To hear the philosophy in a melodious way, you might find an online video of "Carry On" and listen to it today!

September 25:
"To smile at the jest which plants a thorn in another's breast is to become a principal in the mischief."
Joseph Surface, to Lady Sneer in Richard Brinsley Sheridan's *The School for Scandal*, Act I, Scene 1

I used to really despise having a splinter or sliver taken out of a finger or foot, and I still find it a very unpleasant experience, especially since I have to do it myself. But alas, I work outdoors a lot and have a number of hollies and roses that I tend, and smilax, greenbrier, and other vines that I attempt to eradicate from time to time. Invariably, I jam the tip of a holly leaf or the thorn of a blackberry bush or other needly plant into the tip of my right index finger. Since I am right-handed, my poor, underdeveloped left hand has to work clumsily at extracting the bothersome spike.

Using such an image from nature, Richard Brinsley Sheridan's character Joseph Surface comments disapprovingly to Lady Sneer, *"To smile at the jest which plants a thorn in another's breast is to become a principal in the mischief."* Unmoved, Lady Sneerwell retorts: "Psha! there's no possibility of being witty without a little ill-nature: the malice of a good thing is the barb that makes it stick." Which is true, but no fun if you are at the pointed end of the cutting remark or actual spine prick.

In 2 Corinthians 12: 7-9, the Apostle Paul coins a phrase about a thorn, "By reason of the exceeding greatness of the revelations, that I should not be exalted excessively, a thorn in the flesh was given to me: a messenger of Satan to torment me, that I should not be exalted excessively... I begged the Lord three times that it might depart from me. He has said to me, "My grace is sufficient for you, for my power is made perfect in weakness." Most gladly therefore I will rather glory in my weaknesses, that the power of Christ may rest on me."

Power is made perfect in weakness. Hmmm. If Paul is right, I must be getting pretty strong, because worse than splinters or even jabs at the heart are the people and circumstances that become annoying, long-lived spurs in my side — those continuous problems that not only irritate me but constantly pierce like a shard that no set of tweezers can dig out: the rolling rainbow ball on my computer, folks who don't realize the little stick by your steering wheel can indicate that you are turning, tangled hoses in my yard, people who use abbreviated texting language (2F4U OMG!), price tags that will not come off even with Goo Gone stuff, robot calls about my car warranty, pushy sales people, no tissue in the public ladies' room (found missing at the wrong time).

Okay, that series contains truly minor annoyances — but couldn't they be considered messengers "of Satan sent to torment me" or you? Some studies suggest that at least seven times in 24 hours, the average person is frustrated by similar little things totally out of their control. Such lists also reflect twenty-first century vexations that would never have been experienced by the 1777 characters in Sheridan's tangled and gossipy Restoration comedy of manners. But the rumors, disguises, affairs, and corruption in the play reflect the shallowness of the human spirit that is present today in these same vices — and also displayed by lists that show our irritation at such inconsequential frustrations.

September 26:
"Seven years we have lived quietly,
Succeeded in avoiding notice,
Living and partly living.
There have been oppression and luxury,
There have been poverty and license,
There has been minor injustice.
Yet we have gone on living,
Living and partly living."
Chorus in T. S. Eliot's *Murder in the Cathedral*

T. S. Eliot was born into a Unitarian family this day, September 26, 1888, in St. Louis Missouri. After graduating from Harvard and studying in Paris, he married in 1915 and moved to London where he converted to the Anglican Church. Over the next few decades, he became an admired and well-read modernist poet. Eliot said poetry "may make us from time to time a little more aware of the deeper, unnamed feelings which form the substratum of our being, to which we rarely penetrate; for our lives are mostly a constant evasion of ourselves."

In 1935, he was commissioned to write a play for Kent's annual Canterbury Festival. With few limitations on subject matter, he decided to dramatize the 1170 murder of Thomas Becket in a play he called *Murder in the Cathedral.*

In this chosen passage, the Chorus moans about a frozen, static, stationary life for the past seven years without their Archbishop, who had fled into exile to France to escape the disgruntled King Henry II. The women of Canterbury have dwelled in a "both-and" sort of existence: *"oppression and luxury, poverty and license."* Their prolonged communal life of suffering has unfolded in a jillion shades of gray, which they have borne stoically.

When I wonder about this kind of *"living and partly living,"* what comes to mind is parents of a kidnapped child, children of a mother who has wandered into the wilderness, a man suddenly arrested for something another did, a woman given a diagnosis of breast cancer — all of us in the deepest woundings of our time on earth. For days, months, even years, we then go through *"living and partly living."* Nothing is normal in our world, but the sun continues to shine, the rain to fall, the traffic to roll, the restaurant to serve food. We don't want the sun or the rain, to drive or to eat. Yet, something about our life has to continue on.

I love this Greek-tragedy Chorus. While *"living"* these seven years, they have refined a radar-like ability to detect the emotional pulse of their city: Thomas is coming with applause, and yet doom. And while *"partly living,"* something inside them has matured an obstinacy and the ability to doubt, a wisdom and the capacity to surrender to life as it unfolds, while still commenting on it.

Unlike these sage elders, our Samford students who wailed and lamented this and other Eliot passages were full of the vigor and promise of youth. And yet, they memorized these passages. They devoured the text and spit out lines about "the small folk drawn into the pattern of fate," "our hearts are torn from us, our brains unskinned like the layers of an onion, our selves are lost, lost," and being "afraid in a fear which we cannot know, which we cannot face, which none understands."

Confronted, in delivering the words of this play, with the perplexities of life, "a fear not of one but of many, a fear like birth and death," these students grappled with — at a young age — the challenge of making sense of it all: the meaning of who we are, and the reason for our being on earth. Such experiences are why theatre is such a spiritual space where we can cross over a line into the Holy, and a realization that we can no longer continue the "constant evasion of ourselves."

September 27:
"Sganarelle (alone): For the life of me, I can't figure it out. Why the devil do they all take me for a great doctor? But the change is not for the worse. In fact, I've half a mind to stick to my new vocation."
Sganarelle in Molière's *The Doctor in Spite of Himself*

French actor and poet Jean-Baptiste Poquelin, known more frequently by his stage name Molière, wrote the hilarious *The Doctor in Spite of Himself*: full of physical comedy, clever verbal jokes, implausible disguises, and ridiculous plot twists. Molière crafted a scathing attack on the medical profession of 1666 (and today) using two hypotheses: that most doctors worry more for money than their patients, and that patients are hopelessly enamored by the mystique of their physician.

Molière often took the role of Sganarelle, who features prominently in several of his plays. In this plot, Sganarelle appears in the opening scene as a penniless woodcutter who squanders any money he makes on food and drink for himself at the expense of Martine his wife and their children. When the curtain rises, the couple earnestly and playfully argue, but Sganarelle ends up pommeling her, and she plans retribution.

All at once, to her delight, a couple of servants pass by looking for a physician for their master's daughter who has suddenly been struck dumb. Martine persuades them that in the woods, they will find a peculiar but clever doctor, a miracle worker who can cure anything, but who will deny his profession unless they beat him. Delighted, they run into the forest.

There, they discover Sganarelle drinking and chopping down trees, and accordingly whack him until he says he will be anything they want, even a medical practitioner. Through twists and turns of plot, and many jibes at the medical profession, Sganarelle takes on the role of doctor, and then is discovered to be a quack. As with most comedies, everything turns out well in the end.

I've been wondering lately about the beatings in slapstick. Loud tomfoolery and coarse wit still pull laughs from twenty-first century audiences. But the clobbering in *The Doctor in Spite of Himself* mirrors a not-so-funny thread of human history: husbands and wives (parents and children) and even strangers verbally and physically assaulting each other. Just this morning, I read about a Pakistani woman who has accused her husband of beating her and shaving her head when she refused to dance in front of his friends.

But what if there is more to these thrashings in comedy. In one of his 1961 Charles Eliot Norton lectures, theatre critic and playwright Eric Bentley stated that on-stage beatings are about "revenge, justice, and bitterness" — and, in farce, unlike tragedy, grasping for power and pure-aggression instincts "lie beneath the surface... The one simple pleasure is hitting someone in the jaw without getting hit back."

According to Bentley, comedy has a deeper purpose than making us laugh. Farce hints at the serious side of life, and along with tragedy, has the goal of self-knowledge. "In comedy," he said, "the ego takes just as terrible a beating as in tragedy, even though knaves and fools are cut down, and not a hero." But comedy "veils its feelings with eloquencies, while tragedy is a long lament."

So if I can remember that the beatings on stage are pummelings of the ego, more than the real person, I can agree that we all need to wallop our egos a bit. And after all, the sound of slaps in Molière's time were performed on cold fish, not warm actors' cheeks!

September 28:
"Who controls the past controls the future. Who controls the present controls the past."
Winston Smith in a stage adaptation of George Orwell's *1984*

Just like the renowned 1949 novel by George Orwell, stage adaptations of *1984* tell the story of Winston Smith, an insignificant member of the massive machine state of Oceania. Physically and mentally observed by the omnipresent watch of Big Brother, Winston is compelled to confess Thoughtcrimes and is eventually jailed by the Ministry of Love. This quote, which recaps the party slogan, is part of Winston's remembrances to a member of the Inner Party, O'Brien, concerning the nature of his past.

In the spring of 1984, we performed this play while I was pregnant with my son Seth, whose birthday is today — so I thought it was appropriate to consider an allusion to this provocative work. The play is as intriguing and exhausting to sit through as the book is to read. Through thought control, the Party has generated a false history concerning a past time of human suffering, from which it supposedly liberated everyone. Using this slogan quoted above, the Party shatters psychological autonomy. If the Party can create a past that promotes their authority, they also maintain power over the future.

Since the Party has total control of the present as well, it is able to direct how its subjects understand the past by writing history books that communicate only Party tenets. Photographs and personal keepsakes are prohibited, so the memory-impoverished people of Oceania believe everything they are told. When O'Brien hears Winston say this created past has no real actuality except in the minds of human beings, O'Brien contends that since the Party history is what everyone regards as truth, that fake past has actually transformed into reality.

The Oxford Companion to English Literature says *1984* generated the adjective "Orwellian," which describes official deception, secret surveillance, and manipulation of recorded history by a totalitarian government. The book also coined such modern terms as "Big Brother," "memory hole," "doublethink," "Telescreen," "thoughtcrime," and "Newspeak," among others. Orwell was reacting to World War II, out of which he actually doubted that the British government would emerge, but later admitted events proved him wrong.

On a birthday, it is natural to think about past, present, and future. Though I am concerned about the ever-encroaching ways government and social media invade our privacy and occurrences of fake news, at least we now control our own personal records and photographs. Most years on Seth's birthday, I read over a journal I kept through my pregnancy and his birth. I got to the hospital at 5:30 that morning and it was really good we lived only five minutes away, because he was born at 5:58. Not much time for prep or numbing drugs, so I had him the natural way.

I recall the nurses tending to his fluid-filled lungs and his bright gaze that morning. And as he grew, I remember his lack of love for naps and sleep, his uncanny naming of every car brand by 20 months of age, his climbing ability, his humor, his Chip and Dale dancing style. To think, if controlled by the state of Oceania, I would have had none of those memories. But Seth did sometimes later complain of being physically and mentally observed by the omnipresent watch of Big Sister Elin.

September 29:
"Like the spiritualists try to use that stuff, are you enlightened, are you centered, channeled, whatever, this reaching out for a spiritual past in a country where no indigenous spirits exist – only the Indians, I mean Native American spirits and we killed them off so now, there are no gods here, no ghosts and spirits in America, there are no angels in America, no spiritual past, no racial past, there's only the political."
Louis in Tony Kushner's *Angels in America: Millennium Approaches*, Act III, Scene 2

What a masterpiece is this two-part *Gay Fantasia on National Themes*. It is funny, tragic, and compelling even with its difficult and comprehensive subject matter. Set in Ronald Reagan's 1985, the play reflects the grim reality that AIDS had started to drastically diminish gay communities in San Francisco, Los Angeles, and New York City. Two of the main characters have a crisis in their relationship when one of them is diagnosed with AIDS.

Today is "Michaelmas" or St. Michael and All Angels Day. Of the numerous angels mentioned in the Bible, only four are named: Michael,

Uriel, Raphael, and Gabriel. Michael, who we celebrate today, is the one who escorts God's people at the end of this worldly life, and helps ward off evil during our days on earth. Michael must have been heartbroken at his overwhelming task during the height of the AIDS epidemic. Louis's tragicomic dialogue quoted above denies any indwelling of holy presences in America since it is such a young country and we, as he says, killed off the Native Americans and their indigenous spirits.

American politics is a major influence on our national identity, as Louis suggests. But the playwright Kushner sees our state of affairs being infused with a feeling of spirituality, upheld by history and transcendent communal identity. Basically, Louis's philosophy is called into question during the course of the action: there is not only an Angel in America, but an Angel of America. At the end of *Millennium Approaches*, an actual stunning angel smashes through the character Prior's ceiling. Both tender and forceful, this bi-sexual creature, as such other-worldly creatures are wont to do, appoints Prior, a sufferer of AIDS, to prophet status.

The Angel in this play is called "the Continental Principality of America," and embodies that ethereal soul of the United States. I believe Louis is wrong in saying, "there are no gods here, no ghosts and spirits in America, there are no angels in America ..." Some might argue that the Angel is a hallucination of Prior's and that Louis is correct, but I have seen otherwise.

From numerous spiritually oriented books I have read and from experience, I have come to realize that words fail when attempting to describe a numinous experience — not only because there is precious little vocabulary for it, but also because what happens is beyond description. People who have near-death experiences, for example, rarely talk about them to others because they find the happening so hard to relate. Besides, they don't think they will be taken seriously.

A transcendent incident happened to me in the fall of 1985 (the year this play is set!), and I cannot report it here because, well, it happened in a little slip of eternal time and boundless space, and it is impossible to relay its truth through human expression. It concerned my Guardian Angel and his power, and his name. I understood so many things in the blinking of an eye and the falling to the ground that words really cannot do justice to the happening. I just knew for a brief second or two, there was not only an Angel in America, but an Angel in Alabama — and even an Angel on Cahaba Road.

September 30:

In "Fugue for the Tinhorns," one of the gamblers in *Guys and Dolls* believes a horse named after a Revolutionary War hero is the one to bet on. (Listen to the work online or from your library!)

Nicely-Nicely Johnson in *Guys and Dolls*, with words and lyrics by Frank Loesser and book by Jo Swerling and Abe Burrows, based on works by Damon Runyon

We put *Guys and Dolls* on the big stage at Samford in the spring of 1999 and just about filled the Wright Center up with audience. Set in the 1920s New York underworld, the musical is crowded with gamblers and gangsters, policemen and performers. These characters bump right up against the band of the Save-a-Soul Mission, led by a lovely, and also fervently devout lady, Sergeant Sarah Brown.

With the writer Runyon's fondness for juxtaposing street jargon with fairly formal language, the dialogue is humorous and the action is filled with the never-sleeping rush of New York City. In this song, "Fugue for Tinhorns," three minor-league gamblers, Nicely-Nicely Johnson, Benny Southstreet, and Rusty Charlie, wrangle over which horse will come in first in an upcoming race.

The song is a sort of round or counterpoint, starting with a theme sung by one voice (Nicely). Then, Benny joins, singing the same theme with different words, while the first voice continues on with a contrapuntal accompaniment. The third voice, Rusty's, finally enters crooning the same theme and his special words, and all are moving at their own time intervals. It is not the easiest of song types to perform, but I absolutely adore it.

"Fugue for Tinhorns" has been performed by the Muppets, and why not? It gets stuck in my mind like "Elmo's Song" or "The Rainbow Connection" do. Catchy ditties tend to go round and round in our heads. For centuries, music and the sung and spoken word were used as memory devices. Human brains have developed permanently connected circuits that pull up information formed with melodies on demand.

So, if I hear someone say, *"Can do!"* when I have requested something, my cerebral cortex begins to reverberate with the song about the horse named for Paul Revere! And not much is going to stop its round and roundness for an hour or so. I've tried the "cures," like singing another tune, thinking of other matters, counting from 125 backward skipping every third number. One suggestion I read was to listen to the song, but with "Fugue for Tinhorns," I remember the clever words, admire the singers on YouTube, and embark on the impossible preoccupation of attempting to sing all three parts in my head at once!

Sometimes, when I wake up in the middle of the night, I find my gray matter in the middle of a hymn or Beatle song. I suppose the tune was part of a dream that fades so quickly I don't make the connection, but the song continues to play out, and sometimes play over, in my mind until dawn. Beatle hits like "All You Need Is Love," "Across the Universe," "We Can Work It Out," "Within You and Without You," and "Let It Be" all formed my philosophical view of life while I was in my very formative early teens, and — unbeknownst to me unless I happen to stir in the wee hours — they must be persevering to keep me open-minded, joyful, and full of love through dreams.

October 1

"The spring, the summer,
The childing autumn, angry winter change
Their wonted liveries, and the mazèd world,
By their increase, now knows not which is which."
Titania in William Shakespeare's *A Midsummer Night's Dream*, Act II, Scene 1

This is early fall, I know, and not midsummer, but this quote does mention *"childing autumn,"* meaning "fertile or fruitful fall." Titania is offended at the actions of her husband Oberon. He creeps away from Fairyland in shepherd's clothing to sing to and dance with a new girlfriend. Oberon, not only unfaithful, but argumentative, has interrupted fairy life and in the chaos, the fairies cannot lend Nature proper support. In fact, Oberon prompts fogs and winds, and with all the rain, farmers' labor in vain and unripe grain rots before it ripens.

Playing fields are covered in mud, and the moon is mad, conjuring disease and causing ill moods all over earth. Even the seasons change places so that frosts "fall in the fresh lap of the crimson rose," and the icy winter dons a pungent "chaplet of sweet summer buds" in mockery. The disorder is caused by the argument between the King and Queen of the Fairies, and Titania is aggrieved. That word is from Middle English, meaning "to wrong grievously," to make heavy or worsen.

382

The same sort of crushing upset happened to our church family in 2001 as I wrote some about on September 11. October 1 will always bring to our minds the tumble of events. My priest and his wife had a 22-month old son with a heart defect that doctors thought could be corrected.

On September 30, he went into the hospital to have that operation. The baby was cheerful and named everyone in his hospital room the night before his procedure. But to everyone's complete shock, he did not survive the next day's surgery.

When we friends and parishioners heard the news, we were not so aggrieved as stricken with grief — not the exact same root word, but related. Our hearts were made heavy, so maybe we were both. Like the out-of-kilter world in *Midsummer,* we couldn't understand the upended circumstance of a child dying before his parents.

The two parents have subsequently managed being without him in an amazing way, like another mother and father I know whose grown son died. Some people, faced with such a loss, retreat and diminish their own living day by day. But these parents found ways to allow life to burgeon around the huge bundle of grief. With amazing affirmations of carrying on with their existence, they have all four allowed energy to grow and expand around the sorrow that was — and is still — so immense.

I am grateful, on this *"childing autumn"* day to remember what these families have taught me about love. Though I may feel in the shattering loss of a child — or any tragedy — that summer is winter and spring is fall and the entire earth is in disarray, if I can hang onto love through that suffering, I can pull through. If I can avoid becoming bitter and callous, my capacity for compassion, forgiveness, and love will increase.

Those great words of the *Book of Common Prayer* from the Burial Office come back to me: "For if we have life, we are alive in the Lord, and if we die, we die in the Lord. So, then, whether we live or die, we are the Lord's possession." Whether dead or alive, we are part of Life. I don't know how: it's a Mystery.

October 2
"Well, spring isn't everything, is it, Essie? There's a lot to be said for autumn. That's got beauty, too. And winter — if you're together."
Nat (Father) to Essie (Mother) in Eugene O'Neill's *Ah, Wilderness!*

Ah Wilderness! premiered on Broadway on this day, October 2, in 1933 (two weeks before O'Neill's 45th birthday), a "comedy in four acts." Set at the Fourth of July 1906 in a little Connecticut village, Richard, the sixteen-year old middle son of the Miller family, has numerous crises that move him toward adulthood. His escapades stretch from defending his "subversive" books of poetry to a surprise meeting with prostitutes, from a love letter by a girl friend to a sneak-out on the night beach. He ends up lovestruck, but realizing the dangers of drinking, older women, and other perils of grownup life.

O'Neill gave it the subtitle of *"A nostalgic comedy of the Ancient Days when Youth was Young, and Right was Right, and life was a wicked opportunity."* He once called the work "a sort of wishing out loud. It is the way I would have liked my childhood to have been."

He was born to the well-known romantic actor James O'Neill and his wife, Ella Quinlan O'Neill. Eugene Gladstone O'Neill was delivered in a New York City hotel on October 16, 1888, while his father was on tour. Since Eugene lived his first seven years on the theatre circuit, in hotel rooms with a mother addicted to drugs, it is no wonder he fantasized about a stable and loving family who cares for him in a conventional household.

A play penned some years ago by Birmingham writers for our Birmingham Children's Theatre was called *Backstage Baby!* It could have depicted the life of Eugene O'Neill — or of my children. They both spent much of their childhood backstage.

Working sixty-hour weeks for the seven weeks of rehearsal and a run is grueling. The creativity and collaboration are exhilarating, but also exhausting. In August, students return to campus, new faces appearing among the old. Through auditions and read-throughs, costume measurements and early blocking, the show begins to take shape. Undergraduates come and go in the costume shop, often helping, sometimes goofing off, usually confiding about life and challenges. The clothes for the characters grow in front of our eyes.

My time is split between teaching and overseeing the box office and the costume shop — running up and down stairs about twenty times a day. After school, Elin and Seth end up at my parents' house or my shop, and between students, their dad, and me, they get homework done, games played, food consumed, and rehearsals watched, with dashes to piano and dance or soccer.

By this time in October, we are in the last week of rehearsal, with costumes, scenery, props, and lighting added day by day. Outside is beautiful, golden air, leaf-turning autumn. I furtively glance out the car windows as I drive the kids to activities. Yes, red, and orange, and gold leaves are appearing. Look at that full moon rising! The afternoon shimmers with flaxen sunlight. I dash back to campus, and sit in a darkened theatre till the sun has long gone down and made the outside world inky as well.

"There's a lot to be said for autumn. That's got beauty, too"... if you can see it! But I don't regret all those falls spent in fabricating theatre with my students and my backstage babies. Because, in the theatre, you can generate September haze when it's summer time, and bright spring in the depths of December. Now that I am no longer on an academic schedule, I can relish autumn days like today. But presently, I am longing for a shadowy theatre, to create a play about the hoary frosts of wintertide.

October 3

"...Not to mention I might, I don't know, hate this baby, hurt this baby, throw the baby or something like that, I'm not kidding, what's inside me. Now, do you have some Bible quotes for that, or am I just beside the point, handcuffed to this bed..."
Keely in Jane Martin's *Keely and Du*

Though I prefer the nickname "Magic City," my hometown of Birmingham, Alabama has been known as both "Big Bad Birmingham" and "Bombingham." It has seen its share of brutality and political violence over the years, and during the Civil Rights era, as whites resisted integration, black homes were destroyed by explosives, and in 1963, a bomb detonated in the African American Sixteen Street Baptist Church, killing four young girls.

On the morning of January 29, 1998, I was listening to public radio in my office at the university when an announcer broke in to say that a grisly echo of the 35-year-old tragedy had just occurred. Just blocks from my church, someone later identified as Eric Rudolph devised an explosion that devastated the New Woman All Women abortion clinic.

Robert Sanderson was the off-duty officer working as the clinic's security guard. His body was blasted apart by the bomb. Emily Lyons, a counselor and nurse, was critically wounded. People in buildings at the University of Alabama in Birmingham and all over town experienced rumbling repercussions from blocks away. Windows of the clinic — and even some in an office building across the street — were shattered, scraps of building material were strewn everywhere, and sickening smoke poured from the building.

The following fall of 1998, our theatre department was gutsy enough to present to its predominantly Christian audience Jane Martin's *Keely and Du*, a Pulitzer Prize nominee and the 1994 winner of the American Theatre Critics Association Best New Play Award. Diligently directed by a delightful student Elizabeth, *Keely and Du* addressed this hot Birmingham issue: the still ongoing debate about abortion. The playwright conceives an interesting juxtaposition between the difficulties of a pregnant rape victim and the beliefs of zealots who fight abortion for religious reasons.

Strong pious persuasions can drive people to drastic actions that lead to ridicule on one end and to martyrdom on the other. In this case, Keely is kidnapped (or as her abductors say "rescued") outside an abortion facility much like our New Woman All Women clinic. Du, a registered nurse masked to hide her true identity, and Walter, a militant minister full of superior moralizing banalities and Bible verses, handcuff the defenseless woman to a bedpost, imprisoning her for the span of her pregnancy. Keely also gets a visit from the alcoholic estranged husband who raped her, but who is now born-again and remorseful, begging forgiveness.

In a very realistic way, the play explores an extreme form of criminal activism while showing the irreconcilable sides of a delicate, complicated, thorny problem that is as ancient as the human race. Keely's captivity shows how people with deeply held religious convictions can elevate themselves to false sovereignty, even to the point of controlling someone else's body and spirit. And how, although meaning to be righteous and godly, such individuals end up violating someone's personhood through acts as abhorrent as either the rape or the abortion.

October 4

"Look, Lucio, look! What a light shines on me! I am moonstruck: There she goes to make my fortune! I shall be Prince: the world shall hear of me! And for Assisi, I will make a name, – for fair Assisi."
Francesco in Laurence Housman's *Little Plays of St. Francis: A Dramatic Cycle from the Life and Legend of St. Francis of Assisi*

Today is the feast day of St. Francis of Assisi, who was born in Italy in 1181. He grew up in a wealthy household and had many friends, all of whom loved him. He was a happy, charismatic young man and a true leader, who really wanted to become a knight. Believing himself bound for glory and renown, as evidenced by the above quote, he got thrust into battle when his town of Assisi declared war on a town close by, Perugia, their perpetual enemy.

Francis was put in prison, but was ransomed after a year, and slid back to evenings of partying and drunkenness. In 1204, Francis, feeling another call to fight, was on his way to a battle when he had a vision that told him to return to Assisi. He suddenly lost his fondness for his lavish lifestyle and on a pilgrimage to Rome, he joined some poor people who were begging at St. Peter's Basilica. This trip drew the young man to a life of poverty. After Francis returned to Assisi, he began preaching on the streets, gathering a number of followers.

Never ordained to the priesthood, he founded the Order of Friars Minor for men and the Order of St. Clare for women, as well as the Order of Brothers and Sisters of Penance or the Third Order. His first Order was authorized by Pope Innocent III in 1210. In 1979, Pope John Paul II declared him the Patron of Ecology. Pets and animals are blessed on St. Francis Day, for he preached that the world and all creation were beautiful, God-given gifts.

One day on the road with companions, they passed a place with birds in trees on both sides of the road. Francis asked if they could wait a while "for me while I go to preach to my sisters the birds." As he spoke, the flock was mesmerized by his voice and sat and listened until he finished. That is why the saint is often pictures with a bird in his hand or on his shoulder.

I have had a number of St. Francis experiences, but here is a vivid example. One day, our Springer brother Merlin was barking and barking and I could not feature why. I looked out the front window and there was a little yellow lab-mix puppy walking around our yard, wagging up to the door, and just yelping. I gave him some food and water, but didn't want to do too much to entice him to stick around, because I thought his owners would be calling and looking for him.

So, my son Seth agreed and we just left him out all night – nice warm evening, so no problems there. The next morning, I got up to drink coffee at 5:00 and lo and behold, he was still there, just crying at my front door. I was trying to decide whether or not to bring him in when he went over to the St. Francis statue in my garden, put his paws on the saint's shoulders, put his nose straight up in the air, and began to howl. "Francis, please intercede for me!" I could hear him saying. Well, how could I resist? So we brought him in and Merlin was amazed by him for the several weeks he abided with us until we found him the perfect adoptive family.

October 5
"A baby is God's opinion that life should go on."
Merrill in *The World of Carl Sandburg*, a stage adaptation of Sandburg's work by Norman Corwin

In our 1985-86 season, we performed *The World of Carl Sandburg*, a staged reading of selections of Sandburg's poetry, chosen and arranged by Norman Corwin. The original production, which toured in 1959-60, starred Bette Davis and her husband Gary Merrill.

This line, *"A baby is God's opinion that life should go on"* is often reproduced on parents' newborn photos and cited in "favorite quotations" series. Less mentioned is a passage later in this staged Sandburg piece: "... Attila the Hun, he had a mother. Schicklgruber, too, had a mother. Michelangelo and J. Sebastian Bach, each sucked at a mother's breast — and not one of the mothers held beforehand sure foretokenings of what was to come..."

An interesting contemplation, that. During his reign, Attila was possibly the most feared enemy of the Western, Eastern and Roman Empires. Called the "Scourge of God" by the Romans, "the Hun" assembled one of the most formidable and feared armies of the ancient world. During and after his leadership, Adolf Schicklgruber has probably been the most despised tyrant of the modern age. Also called Hitler, "*Der Führer*" assembled a regime that was responsible for the extinction of at least 5.5 million Jews, and millions of other targets.

On the internet, I find an adorable photograph of Adolf or "Adi," as he was called in childhood, as an infant around 1889 or '90. Unfortunately, we don't even have an adult portrait of Attila, much less a newborn depiction, but this image of Hitler as a one-year old is as charming as any baby picture I have ever seen. Would any of us have children if we knew there was a possibility they would grow up to be known as the "Scourge of God" or that they would be responsible for eight million deaths? Whew!

But then, "*Michelangelo and J. Sebastian Bach, each sucked at a mother's breast.*" And look at how they developed: Michelangelo Buonarroti was one of the greatest artist of the Renaissance, and to many critics, one of the supreme creative geniuses ever. Johann Sebastian Bach was not only an extraordinary Baroque composer, he was one of the most sublime musical masterminds of all time.

"*Not one of the mothers held beforehand sure foretokenings of what was to come...*" Nor do any of us. Sometimes parents nurture dreams for their kids even before pregnancy, certainly during gestation, and unquestionably after birth: Maybe he will be just like me, only more handsome, more athletic, more intelligent. A Little Me! A Mini Me!

This sort of thinking can be a slippery slope, because the mystery of becoming a mother —or father — is that our kids upend and invert our plans for them. We hope for demure, she is shamelessly audacious. We aspire for Einstein, he is a Chippendale Dancer. Thankfully, I got and followed advice early that my livelihood as a parent was to discover my children's gifts and passions and to point them toward a road that could possibly help them on their way.

Now looking at my grandchildren Emmeline, George, Arthur and Teddy, I have no certain early manifestations of what is to come. And only if I make the effort to discover these children of God as who they truly are can I be a moving influence in their lives.

October 6
"*Isn't it amazing how the play lasted just as long as the lights went up and then down?*"
The Visitor in Steve Martin's *Picasso at the Lapin Agile*

Many playwrights, directors, and actors in the late 19th through the mid-20th centuries were deeply concerned with realism in the theatre. Their highest desire was to show a slice of life by actors who portrayed characters as genuinely and naturally as possible. As a drama aficionado, I delight in watching method acting where those onstage identify so emotionally with their character that it seems as if real lives unfold right before our eyes.

But I luxuriate in a play that uses theatricalism, with dialogue and situations that remind the audience that though the actors are real people, the play is a creation of the playwrights, directors, designers, technicians, and actors. I have followed Steve Martin from his early fame as a comedian and musician, to his roles as actor, and later playwright and screenwriter. In his zany *Picasso at the Lapin Agile*, Martin explores the odd nature of genius, setting his work in a Parisian Café on October 8, 1904. Pablo Picasso and Albert Einstein meet in the *Lapin Agile* ("Nimble Rabbit") bar, just before these 20-something year-olds each transform the world of physics and art with revolutionary theories. Wacky, absurdist, and anachronistic, the play offered a great evening of theatre a couple of years ago when I ushered at a local playhouse.

Using centuries-old devices of puns, pratfalls, and pranks "the play," according to Martin, "attempts to explain, in a light-hearted way, the similarity of the creative process involved in great leaps of imagination in art and science." The piece is also peopled by Charles Dabernow Schmendiman a simpleton inventor, Freddy the bartender, Germaine the waitress, Gaston the old gentleman, Suzanne Picasso's paramour, Sagot an agent, a Countess, a female admirer, and finally "The Visitor," a King of Rock singing phenomenon from the future, wearing blue suede shoes.

When The Visitor speaks his lines near the end of the play about the lights and the work's length, I am reminded of an insight once gained from Edward Albee on the evening in the early 1990s that I wrote about back in January. My recompense for helping host a writers conference in Birmingham was an invitation to a reception with some of the participants and guests. I was able to converse for a couple of hours at a kitchen table with Albee, who affably spoke about *The Ballad of the Sad Café* (which I was designing and directing at the time) and others of his plays, his ideas about the stage, and his philosophy on life.

One of Albee's convictions was about the length of plays. "I don't understand why people worry about the length of my works or anyone's plays," he confided. "When *The Zoo Story* and *The Sandbox* were first produced, critics said the plays were too short. Then, four years later when *Who's Afraid of Virginia Woolf?* ran for over three hours, that work was too long. A play is as long as it should be, a few minutes, or a few hours. That's the way they come to me... some are short and some are long. They are all just right."

"Isn't it amazing how the play lasted just as long as the lights went up and then down?"

October 7
In "Someone Else's Story" from *Chess*, sometimes Florence and sometimes Svetlana sing about another lifetime, and how a person with

her same name made a promise. (Listen to the work online or from your library!)

Florence or Svetlana in *Chess*, with lyrics by Tim Rice, and music by Benny Andersson and Bjorn Ulvaeus of the group ABBA

In the fall of 1984, the creative team that wrote *Chess* released a double Long Playing "concept" album of the music to critical acclaim. Tim Rice had long desired to create a story concerned with the Cold War, and this one captures a romantic triangle between players in a world chess game championship and the woman who is the manager of one, who happens to fall in love with the other.

While the album and two singles from this release were successful hits, and theatre producers scrambled to obtain the stage rights, the resulting West End 1986 musical was never the artistic or commercial success everyone would have desired. It was, however, the first theatre production I ever saw in London — and the event fell on New Year's Eve of 1987. The music was intriguing and Robin Wagner's tilted chess board set looked fantastic to me. My then-husband even caught one of the foam frisbees cast members threw out into the audience, and he graciously gave it to me.

We were still on good terms then, still a couple, a design team, parents in a family of four. I feel like that was so long ago, and it has been two and a half decades. Like the lyrics of "Someone Else's Story" suggest, when I remember back to that era, it seems like another person's life in an alternate universe or a fictional place, where I was a miscast player.

Sometimes I wonder why I married so young, before I had even graduated from college. Why, when I was such an independent, strong individual, I became reliant. Why I hid true feelings and thoughts. Why I got caught up in negativity and drama, just to keep a marriage together. It was like I was one person in high school and college, and then became a person with my same name, and who looked a lot like me, but who was different and unfulfilled.

It is intriguing that the game of chess incorporates mythic archetypes, symbolizes paths we take in life, and encompasses what it takes to conquer ego. The game involves the perpetual pairing of good and evil, spirit and substance, being and nonexistence.

Even the black and white squares on the board — and on the stage of this production — remind me of this duality. When we make a move in chess, our adversary reacts in a certain way, unlike action taken with a different move. Likewise, life often forces us to choose a position or make a decision. Some choices lead down strange paths. I won't say I regret my marriage, for it made me the person I am today. But I am joyous that now I can say I am someone with my name who looks a lot like me and who actually is me.

October 8

"Milt (seeing Harry on the bridge about to jump): ...How have you been doing, Harry? What's been happening? It must be ... why, at least fifteen years since I saw you last. We had that party after graduation, I said, 'Keep in touch,' you said, 'I'll call you in a few days,' and that's the last I heard of you. Fifteen years.
Harry: Is it fifteen years?
Milt: Fifteen years.
Harry: Hard to believe.
Milt: Fifteen years next month as a matter of fact...
Harry (slight pause): Who are you?"
Characters in Murray Schisgal's *Luv*

In the winter of 1974, my then-husband created the scenery for Murray Schisgal's *Luv* as part of his thesis production to obtain his Master of Fine Arts at our graduate school, the University of North Carolina at Greensboro. In this first scene in the play, Harry is about to jump off a New York bridge ostensibly to commit suicide, but it is a low bridge and the water is very shallow. Murray Schisgal, son of Jewish immigrants, was adept at such "black comedy," which darkly and humorously explored the irony and angst of his people with a distinctly American Jewish voice.

I am struck by the questions in this opening dialogue for this funny play. Maybe it is because I heard a sermon recently about asking the "right" questions. The preacher used to be a reporter in South America. When he taught journalism, he advised his students to ask provocative questions, ones that dug deep to get the information needed for a news story.

This former reporter also noted that if you ask a question, you need to be ready to accept the answer in some way or other. If you ask, as Milt does in *Luv*, "How have you been doing, Harry?" the responder might really tell you that he is suffering, that he is upset, that he is so depressed he is about to kill himself; so what are you going to do with that information? Sometimes the polite social greeting of "How are ya?" doesn't get a carefree, "Oh, just fine!"

Edgar M. Bronfman once wrote: "To be Jewish is to ask questions. Our *Talmud*, by insisting we question, allows us to doubt. As Jews celebrate Passover with the Seder meal where traditionally the youngest person at the table asks four questions; or as I think of it, one question with four examples: What does it mean to be Jewish?"

So many of us are complacent about life. We are satisfied with the pablum fed us by news media, movies, friends, coworkers, and television — we even cling to concepts pushed into our ears at a young age by our parents. Some of us were afraid to ask questions in school or temple or scouts, thinking we would be judged by our peers or humiliated by our teachers or clergy. And yet, when we become curious and ask a question, we admit we don't know everything. We allow a breathing place in our minds where we can take in new information and grow.

Why do people seek answers? Well, as Bronfman intimated, especially as we grow older and more conscious, we wonder about our life. What does it mean to be Jewish? Or Christian? Or Muslim? What does it really mean to be human? Who am I? Why am I here on this earth at this time in history? Do I really matter? What is my passion? Am I making an impact on the world? Who will remember me when I'm gone?

The scientist Carl Sagan once wrote, "There are naive questions, tedious questions, ill-phrased questions, questions put after inadequate self-criticism. But every question is a cry to understand the world. There is no such thing as a dumb question." So if you meet an old friend, who seems depressed and anxious — and who wants to jump off a squatty bridge in a tall city — and you ask "How are you?" be prepared to accept a deep and far reaching answer.

October 9
"Isaac: Dear father, I pray you, hide it not from me,
But some of your thought that ye tell me.
Abraham: Ah, Isaac, Isaac, I must kill thee!
Isaac: Kill me, father? Alas, what have I done?"
Characters in *Abraham and Isaac* by Anonymous, the Brome medieval manuscript

This quote is from a medieval mystery cycle play, a genre I studied in graduate school. When I taught Theatre Appreciation, I discovered a black and white British video recording of the *Abraham and Isaac* play and my students were amazed to see the story come to life.

In my church, we hear what is called "The Sacrifice of Isaac" from Genesis 22 every three years in our lectionary readings for Sunday services. We recoil at the beginning as God calls to Abraham and says, "Take your son, your only son Isaac, whom you love, and go to the land of Moriah, and offer him there as a burnt offering on one of the mountains that I shall show you." Is God suggesting child-sacrifice?

But, as always with scripture and with plays and great literature, the deeper we dive, the broader we scan, the longer we sit and cogitate and hold things in our hearts, the more meaning comes through. Abraham believes that God will provide, and Isaac trusts Abraham. Even today, in traditional Jewish practice, the Akedah or "Binding of Isaac" recounts Abraham's strapping of his son to the altar. On Rosh Hashanah at the beginning of the year, Jews pray to God to show them mercy as he did to Abraham. The story, often cited as a pattern for Jewish suffering, indicates that the Jewish people will give up life itself for the Holy Name.

In my Education for Ministry class, we learned that some theologians, both Christian and Jewish, see the narrative as a protest against human sacrifice, and the angel intervenes to prohibit a practice despised by God. In this interpretation, the narrative illustrates that God, differing from gods of nearby cultures, abhors human sacrifice.

What is sacrifice? Unless we are talking about an act of slaughtering a living being as an offering to a deity, sacrifice is the act of giving up something valued for the sake of something else regarded as more worthy. Using that definition, I forgo things often. For instance, I would enjoy sleeping later or tarrying in my comfortable bed every morning. But I follow a balancing routine: drinking coffee and reading spiritual nourishment, reciting affirmations, journaling, doing Yoga, and taking a 40-minute walk, often coming up with 100 gratitudes in my life. My practice is more important than a late rising time.

If I could follow my appetite, I would eat a sausage biscuit for breakfast, fried chicken and fixings at lunch, and roast beef with mashed potatoes topped off with a delightful trifle for supper. I would also be as big around as my breakfast table, so I eat vegetables and proteins and low carbohydrates. My desire for health eclipses my natural inclinations.

When I was a parent and, like Abraham's my children were small, I could have pursued a more aggressive theatrical career and left much of their upbringing to institutions and individuals who had much less interest in their well-being than I did. My family ranks higher than a professional high-water mark. So I took my children to the costume shop with me and worked shorter hours so that I was available for school pickups and field trips, friends over and music lessons.

I am not better than late sleepers, or carb eaters, or other mothers or dads who choose differently. My act of giving up "something valued" just differs — and the path up the mountain in Moriah is a divergent one from theirs.

October 10
"Sometimes it's necessary to go a long distance out of the way in order to come back a short distance correctly."
Jerry in Edward Albee's *The Zoo Story*

In the spring of 1989, we somehow sandwiched student-directed productions of *The Zoo Story* and *Sandbox* in between *The Diviners* and *Pierre Pathelin*. It was a hectic few months! But not as busy as Edward Albee must have been when he created this one-act play in just three weeks in 1958. It was his first. Maybe I should think more about this Albee quote when I daily set intentions or make resolves. Because really, the short, clear distance sets us on our true path. Instead of taking that, though, I often wander to remote areas, thinking that surely things have to be long and difficult to be worthwhile or true.

The play concerns a publishing executive, Peter who, sitting on a park bench one Sunday afternoon, is accosted by Jerry, a carelessly dressed transient who has just come from the Central Park Zoo. Peter tries to remain aloof, but Jerry begins to rattle, intent on a meaningful interchange, to Peter's great annoyance. The lonely, dispirited Jerry tries to give meaning to a story about his drunken landlady's "attack" dog.

Jerry first tried to kill the canine with kindness, and then to actually poison the creature. An honest attempt at connection failed, so getting the animal out of the way seemed the only measure Jerry could use to mount the stairs without being pounced upon. The dog grew ill, but didn't die, and since has remained mute and compliant. Symbolically, just as the dog first attacks, then simply leaves Jerry alone, the poor man is hoping that Peter will at least move a short distance to accept him. Unfortunately, this strange relationship devolves quickly from bonhomie to violence, and Jerry dies as he runs into a knife he has placed in Peter's hand.

"Sometimes it's necessary to go a long distance out of the way in order to come back a short distance correctly," says Jerry in the play. I suppose my

affinity for long, drawn-out, irregular distances are destined for me. Since a young girl, I have been fascinated with books and stories about quests, like *The Adventures of Huckleberry Finn* or *The Wizard of Oz*. If on Fridays, I could go to my elementary school library and find Bobbsey Twins or Nancy Drew mysteries, I would be in heaven all weekend.

In high school, I became infatuated with *The Hobbit* and *The Lord of the Rings* trilogy. In the 1980s, my favorite night on TV was Monday when the A&E mysteries brightened the start of the week with Dame Agatha Christie's Marple and Poirot, or other weeks Sherlock Holmes or Lovejoy. With my children, I fell in love in the late 1990s with the Harry Potter books. Nowadays, Roger and I are hooked on *Vera*. Not only do all of these works involve expeditions and adventures, they take you to all parts of the world!

It is funny: while I was thinking about this idea of such searches and distances today, my grandson Teddy, finding a beach treasure, said, "BeBe, what do you think of seashells? Don't you love them?" To which, unwittingly, I replied, "Yes, they are beautiful, but I would much rather look for them than to collect them." Hmmmm. Story of my life.

October 11

"As for those three pasty-faced card players – they are the guards, members of Creon's police force. They chew tobacco; one smells of garlic, another of beer; but they're not a bad lot."
Chorus in *Antigone* by Jean Anouilh, adapted by Lewis Galantiere, inspired by the original by Sophocles

Sophocles wrote the play *Antigone* in the fifth century BC When speaking of the Jean Anouilh version in English-speaking countries, people differentiate it from its ancestor by pronouncing the title more like the original French, an-ti-GONE, rather than an-TIG-oh-nee. Incredibly, Anouilh's *Antigone* was first performed during Nazi censorship at the *Theatre de l'Atelier* on February 6, 1944. In the 1949 Old Vic production, Vivien Leigh was Antigone, and Laurence Olivier played the Chorus role. At the time, German inspectors suppressed any new plays that suggested anti-Fascism, but Anouilh somehow slipped Antigone past censors as the harmless revival of an ancient tragedy.

As I recalled in my writing of June 6, we performed this play in 1974, in the "dungeon" arena theatre, set up in the basement of Reid Chapel. It was a cozy stage, and not a terrible audience space – unless you got seated behind one of the concrete pillars that held the building up! This underground Arena Theatre is where we breathed life into *Antigone* again.

Echoing politics of Anouilh's day, in the play, Antigone (a daughter of Oedipus Rex) refuses to compromise her moral and spiritual convictions. She demands the burial of her dead brother's body, in defiance of Creon's edict that his corpse remain on the field. Her sister Ismene fears the death penalty, but is powerless in discouraging Antigone from literally getting her hands dirty. Forging ahead on her own, Antigone becomes a powerful role model for anyone who faces repression, as happens all over the world every day.

The reason my brain is swimming with all the wonderful earthy imagery of this play right now, though, is the line, *"one smells of garlic, another of beer."* Just about every time I fry onions or garlic and swish a little beer into the sauté sauce, those words from the chorus come back to me. And I have been cooking a lot of the day.

Our parish is having an Italian dinner with operetta shorts tomorrow night, and I have been making a long and involved recipe of vegetarian lasagna. The event is raising funds for our deacon Gerri and a small team of Birminghamians to take a medical mission to Haiti. The Diocese of Alabama has been in a companion relationship with the Diocese of Haiti for almost a decade. Joined by Haitian nurses, pharmacy workers, and a physician, the group will set up mobile clinics in churches and schools in villages outside of *Croix des Bouquets* for a couple of weeks.

Haiti is one of those places, oh-so-close to the United States, which has lengthy history of repression and impoverishment. And it also has strong, but little known history of resistance. Like Antigone, it is the women of Haiti who have defied the government, reshaping the stability of social and state power. Like Antigone, they had to experience devastating state-sponsored brutality, abuse, rape, unlawful arrest, and political execution. And like Antigone, they are modern heroes. I am happy to be cooking my garlic and beer to raise funds to reach out to them and their children.

October 12
"What are kings, when regiment is gone,
But perfect shadows in a sunshine day?"
King Edward in Christopher Marlowe's *Edward II*

When Royal Exchange Theatre in Manchester, England performed Edward II in 2011, reviewer Charlotte Starkey remarked, "Five weeks after the murder of Christopher Marlowe, on the evening of 30th May 1593 in Deptford, the text of Edward II was entered in the Stationer's Register, as required by law, and it has been argued that the play itself was in existence as early as 1591 — a date recently argued for some of Shakespeare's English history plays, too." The full title of the first publication of the play is quite a mouthful: *The Troublesome Reign and Lamentable Death of Edward the Second, King of England, with the Tragical Fall of Proud Mortimer.*

Marlowe's play tells the tale of the short rule and meteoric downfall of King Edward II (who lived from 1284 to 1327). It was an unruly period in England during civil war. A weak king relied upon his favorites, and powerless nobleman stirred up trouble. Even Queen Isabella took a role in a conspiracy against her husband.

As he surveys the shattered remains of his kingdom, King Edward II becomes philosophical and compares himself to a perfect shadow *"in a sunshine day."* Starkey goes on to say about the quote, "The beauty of the paradox within that image belies the horror of Edward's death. This is a tragedy of a king, a queen, a country, a family, a man and a boy. This production at different moments gave Edward all these roles and, as in Marlowe's text, Edward simply could neither play nor resolve them all. Marlowe himself played a few and had the same problem and, tragically, an equally fateful, early demise."

Don't we all feel like that sometimes, though? A mere shadow of that something we were before, feeling less strong and less powerful than we were in the past, even a moment ago? One translation of Job 17:7 is, "My eye also is dim by reason of sorrow. All my members are as a shadow." Cancer may do it, illness, failed marriage, addiction, abuse, the death of a significant person in your life, or as in the case of Job, a number of these misfortunes.

Depression, postpartum, and even menopause can overwhelm a person to the point of leaving the old self behind. You can look at Marlowe's quote and take the word "regiment" to mean "to order or control," rather than its intended meaning of a king's battalion. Probably most of us find ourselves shadows when we lose our health or loved ones (or our kingdom). Our daily discipline is pulled out from under us, and we find ourselves mourning the life we once lived, grieving for the death of our self as we were.

I have become a shadow of myself a couple of times, after huge life losses and also when I was afflicted with agoraphobia. People who have experienced intense anxiety for several years often say they once felt personable, gregarious, humorous, and glad to be themselves; but living with constant panic attacks kills the individual we used to be. If you are struggling with something that makes you feel like a shadow, don't give up hope. Therapy, medication, support groups, and calming skills — depending on your situation — can all work to find not only your old self, but a better, stronger, newer one.

October 13
"Down in the valley, the valley so low,
Hang your head over, hear the wind blow.
Hear the wind blow, dear, hear the wind blow;
Hang your head over, hear the wind blow.
...Roses are red, love, violets are blue;
God and his angels know I love you..."
Traditional folksong in the public domain, recorded by many artists, and used in this opera
Chorus in *Down in the Valley*, a folk opera in one act with music by Kurt Weill and libretto by Arnold Sundgaard, from American folk songs

In the fall of 1993, I designed costumes for the Samford Opera's production of *Down in the Valley*, the one-act folk-opera composed by musician Kurt Weill and librettist Arnold Sundgaard. Originally written in 1945 for the radio, it was reconfigured for the stage and first produced in 1948.

The opera integrates famous folk songs including "Down in the Valley," "The Lonesome Dove," and "Hop Up, My Ladies" into Weill's original choral music. The chorus sings "Down in the Valley," entwined with the Leader's sung account of Brack Weaver killing Thomas Bouché over his beloved Jennie Parsons. The action begins in the Birmingham jail the night before Brack's execution and is told in flashbacks.

The ballad is sometimes called a traditional Ozark ballad, an Appalachian Mountain courting song descended from a British air, and a song sung by the Kentucky mountaineers in the early 1800s. Those versions with a reference to the Birmingham jail had to be later than the early nineteenth century, because Birmingham wasn't founded until 1871. Let's just say it is a Southern folk tune about a condemned prisoner and the woman he loves, and that it seems to have been first inserted into print collections in the 1910s.

I am not sure if *"hang your head over, hear the wind blow"* in the song is an actual catchphrase, but it seems to mean "resignation to what is." And boy, did I need that advice over this last weekend when I seemed to be down in one of those valleys! I thought I was having a perfectly fine Saturday — it was the first one in weeks that I didn't have appointments or special events to attend, so I did what I wanted: took a long walk, shopped for a new shirt, fixed a dish for friends, and worked on some craft items.

After a shower, I sat down to watch a late afternoon Alabama football game and they didn't play a stellar match, though they did win it. I was disquieted and fretful during the entire contest, and my behavior even less dazzling than the team's performance. I pondered why my ego seemed to suddenly subsume my conscious self and realized that the next day, Sunday, I was conflicted about two events that I wanted and needed to attend: a fundraiser I was helping plan, and a big race that involved my son, which I had failed to put on my calendar when I set the fundraiser date.

Nothing can make me antsier than feeling the need to clone myself. But I woke up Sunday determined to let the day play out as it would. I drove an hour to see Seth, had a meaningful exchange, drove an hour back to the fundraiser and got to the setting right on time. On the way back, I thought how pleasant the day had unfolded, despite my Saturday perturbation.

As I came to that conclusion, I saw the most beautiful mist rising over a river, with lightning flashing in my rear view mirror and the sun setting through dark clouds on my right causing the barely turning leaves to shimmer from beneath a peachy fog. "*...Roses are red, love, violets are blue; God and his angels know I love you...*" and they knew I needed a physical sign to sear that understanding into my visually oriented brain!

October 14

"I hate little notes on my pillow. Like this morning. 'We're all out of cornflakes. F.U.' It took me three hours to figure out that 'F.U.' was Felix Unger. It's not your fault, Felix. It's a rotten combination."
Oscar in Neil Simon's *The Odd Couple*

Surely, I don't have to tell anyone that after a 1965 debut on Broadway, Neil Simon's play *The Odd Couple* morphed into a very popular 1968 film and a well-liked 1970s television series, spawning numerous spin-offs and imitations, including Simon's own adaptation in 1985 featuring females. The plot revolves around an incompatible pair of guys who suddenly become roommates, the tidy and high-strung Felix Unger and the sloppy and carefree Oscar Madison.

I have been involved with the production of *The Odd Couple* several times, and there are some funny lines in this show. One of my favorite quotes is this: *"I hate little notes on my pillow. Like this morning. 'We're all out of cornflakes. F.U.' It took me three hours to figure out that 'F.U.' was Felix Unger. It's not your fault, Felix. It's a rotten combination."* It is funny because the audience doesn't immediately think the "F.U." stands for Felix Unger either!

I do love little notes, though: on my pillow, on my dresser, on my breakfast table. My son, Seth used to leave little messages all over the house and in the costume shop: "Please visit me in my fort," "Write me a note back," "Look in closet number three and see a prize!" One time, when he was 10-years old, he put one by the clock in the bedroom and wrote, "Don't forget to look at the clock later. Come to my party in my room at 5:00." Then, when I went down to his bedroom, he whipped up an instant celebration.

When my former husband and I were at the end of our counseling attempt and he told both me and our counselor that he was going through with his plan to leave, I wondered how he could give up the little daily family revelations I was so attached to — watching kids grow up hour by hour, homework, soccer practice, dance concerts, reading *The Chronicles of Narnia* on Sunday while we get the week's ironing done, seeing some wonderful little reward like the notes Seth would leave by the clock or dinner plate. I couldn't have cut those out of my life.

Seth began to excel at the notes. When he knew I had had a particularly hard day, he would even enlist the computer to create a banner, "Welcome Home to the Best Mom in the World!" strung up on the kitchen wall when I got home. By then, we had our dog Merlin, and Seth branded his creations "Ole Pup Publications." I often left him notes in response.

When he was older and going off with friends, or driving himself somewhere, he never failed to prop a message on the stairs: "Gone with David to see Brad. Back at 9:30. Love your son, Seth." After he was in college and would come back home during break, I would create banners to welcome him back. And in departing, he would leave a note on his pillow or the breakfast table: "Dearest Darling Mother: Thanks for the hospitality. I so much enjoyed the food, the fun, and the fellowship. See you soon! Seth (your son)."

I am sorry Oscar didn't get joy out of the little memorandum on his pillow. That Seth is a grownup now and on his own makes me happy, but also sad that we don't have the daily exchanges with notes. I do treasure the memory of this little custom we shared.

October 15

In "The Finale: The Mounted Messenger" from *The Threepenny Opera*, Polly sings happily about the stay of execution for Macheath. (Listen to the work online or from your library!)

Polly in *The Threepenny Opera* with musical elements by German dramatist Bertolt Brecht and composer Kurt Weill

Oh, my goodness, am I singing this song about being reprieved this morning! I had another quote set for today, but this one is ringing in my head. My sister-in-law called to say she was already tending to our stepfather and I got a pardon from going to his house. I spend so much time there, I enjoy amnesty every now and then. Today, I have been spared and rescued – reprieved!

I wrote about the satiric *Threepenny* operetta on July 26 when I was pondering shark's teeth as I was packing for the beach. Bertolt Brecht was contemplating adapting John Gay's *Beggar's Opera* the year my mother was born in 1928. According to the Threepennyopera.org website, right before writing *Threepenny*, "Kurt Weill and Bertolt Brecht were both regarded as 'enfants terribles' in the world of Weimar culture. They had one obscure collaboration under their belt, Weill's setting of five of Brecht's poems about an imaginary city called Mahagonny, and they were already hard at work on the full-length *Mahagonny* opera, which would cause a scandal and lead to Nazi riots in 1930."

Polly sings of the sparing of her beloved. Medicines can reprieve patients experiencing pain. Forgiveness can pardon tremendous personal hurt. Fall-like weather can rescue relentless summer heat. Condemned prisoners are sometimes given a stay of execution (as was Macheath in *The Threepenny Opera*). So reprieves run all through the fabric of our mutual human lives. But back to my own wonderfully temporary relief from

402

spending over one-twenty-fourth of my day with my stepfather and doing what I want today.

I usually take in good stride my "sandwich generation" responsibilities – though I do sometimes feel a bit like chopped up chicken salad, both (solemnly) tending daily to my elderly not-even-parent and (gladly) helping weekly with my young grandchildren. Maybe you take care of an aging relative or friend and know the daily mission involving a hot house, blaring televisions news, degenerating hygiene, and the same stories repeated countlessly, numerously. That's okay, it is to be expected of older people.

This man who has become my stepfather has always befuddled me. When I was a child, he would ask my opinion about something and then immediately tell me what was wrong with my view and how I should think in the future. A successful salesman, he always wanted to put his own spin on everything. A fortunate World War II pilot, he always believed he was as accurate about everything as his bombs were at hitting their Nazi targets (after Bertolt Brecht had left Germany).

A long time ago, I put him in an imaginary box on a shelf in my mythical closet. There, I would never have to deal with him again! Then, about ten years ago, after my dad died, my mother married him – and then she died, and now I care for him almost daily. At one point in my life, I would have lacked the ability to do this. Truly, it is a spiritual exercise and one that expands my compassion for everyone in the world almost daily. Except today. Today, I was reprieved.

October 16

"... I saw the Ghosts before me. But I almost think we are all of us Ghosts, Pastor Manders. It is not only what we have inherited from our father and mother that 'walks' in us. It is all sorts of dead ideas, and lifeless old beliefs, and so forth. They have no vitality, but they cling to us all the same, and we can't get rid of them . . . There must be Ghosts all the country over, as thick as the sand of the sea. And then we are, one and all, so pitifully afraid of the light."
Mrs. Helen Alving in Henrick Ibsen's *Ghosts*

Henrick Ibsen originally wrote this play in Danish, the language of the written word of Denmark and Norway in his day. However, according to Wikipedia, the word *"Gengangere"* (rendered "Ghosts" in English) is not Norwegian. "The Norwegian word is *'Gjengangere'* but the translation is reasonable, literally meaning 'again walkers.' Norwegians also use the term about people who frequently show up in the same places, be they pubs, parties or first nights or other places or occasions."

In the world of dramatic literature, there are a number of plays whose titles at least are reminders of Halloween, so I thought it would be fun to explore some of them in the next few days leading up to the holiday. And then, the haunting figures of both Nicholas Ridley and Hugh Latimer were burned at the stake in Oxford on this day, October 16, in 1555 – to be joined by Archbishop Thomas Cranmer a few months later. The fiery deaths of these three men are remembered by a Martyrs' monument in Oxford, which I have visited on several occasions, always palpably sensing the lingering effect of their spirits.

Ibsen's *Ghosts*, as most of his works, ferociously explores social concerns and the overbearing morality of the late nineteenth century. In this play, the audience glimpses the immobilizing effect of false obligation, the futility and harm of detrimental self-sacrifice, and the ruinous result of expelling all delight from life. The playwright is specifically addressing the oppressive role of wives in miserable marriages – but he is also concerned with individual growth and freedom which Victorian culture all but totally crushed.

In fact, Pastor Manders asks Helen, "What right have we human beings to happiness? No, we have to do our duty!" He is intent on saving souls, even if those very essences are being extinguished by the anguish and heartbreak of the repressed puritanical lifestyle he upholds.

Helen speaks of the Ghost "...we have inherited from our father and mother that 'walks' in us. It is all sorts of dead ideas, and lifeless old beliefs, and so forth. They have no vitality, but they cling to us all the same, and we can't get rid of them." I think of the way some acquaintances of mine are like what Helen calls, "Ghosts all the country over, as thick as the sand of the sea."

These Ghosts seldom question inheriting worn-out opinions from teachers, priests, or parents. These Ghosts see the same folks every day and feed on tired old notions they have fostered for years. They content themselves with television news and sitcoms. These Ghosts' orbits in the world are very small and they keep themselves insulated in a homogenized world. They rarely travel, read books, go to museums or films or concerts – or anywhere they might expand their minds.

These Ghosts would not even recognize themselves being talked about in Ibsen's *Ghosts*, because they would never venture to a play, especially a serious drama. Unfortunately for them – because at least our society allows individual development and independent thought – they don't want to be illuminated or transformed. Like Helen says, they are *"so pitifully afraid of the light."*

October 17
"This is the way the bat seeks revenge.
This is the way the bat seeks revenge.
Oh Fledermaus, O Fledermaus,
Release your victim finally;
The poor man, the poor man,
Has suffered too much."
Alle and Falke in Johan Strauss's opera, *Die Fledermaus*

Why are people so scared of bats? They are not blind, and they generally do not flap into your hair, because of the incredible sonar system that guides them. And yet, some of us freak out when these creatures get close by.

It is October, so *Die Fledermaus*, literally *"Flying Mouse"* or *The Bat*, is fair game for plunder. In this light-hearted story, Dr. Falke takes mischievous revenge on his friend Gabriel von Eisenstein for previously playing a practical joke on him. Mid-October in 1987, Samford Opera did a nice production of this Strauss classic.

A couple of years before the action of the opera, von Eisenstein, pulls the prank, abandoning a drunken Falke dressed as a bat in the town center, making him the target of mockery by Sunday strollers at the next day's light. Worse yet, he has since been christened "Doctor Bat." Falke has never forgiven this incident.

Falke interests Eisenstein in a party to be given that night by Prince Orlofsky, by telling his flirty friend "all the ladies from the ballet will be there." Falke has carefully orchestrated invitations for von Eisenstein's wife, maid, and others all wearing disguises to the party so they can all spy on how he acts. Eisenstein gets tipsy and alienates his wife by courting her (dressed as a Hungarian countess). At the finale, Eisenstein tells her that his terrible behavior was induced by the champagne. Since this is an opera, she forgives him.

Movies and modern culture seem to demonize the bat. For instance, in a 1940 film *The Devil Bat*, Bela Lugosi stars as a mad chemist also intent on revenge. He breeds some extra large bats, and then invents an aftershave lotion that causes them to kill anyone who wears it, ingeniously offering his product to his wealthy employers as a "test" product.

Originally, bats were associated with Halloween through the precursor to our modern celebration. At the Gaelic Samhain festival, people built large bonfires to chase evil spirits away and encourage protective ones. The holiday commemorated the end of harvest season and the start of winter. The October 31-November 1 date fell at just about the halfway mark between the autumnal equinox and the winter solstice. When flying bugs were drawn to the fire's illumination and heat, bats were not far behind, and the mammals became associated with this holiday as they flitted about in the blaze.

Instead of being fearful of bats, we might admire their role in our ecosystem. Though I agree they look a little creepy hanging upside down, covering their bodies with many-jointed membrane wings, bats are really cool. They are the only mammals that can truly fly. They help in the pollination of flowers and the distribution of fruit seeds — and bat excrement, or "guano," is a premier plant fertilizer.

"*Oh Fledermaus!*" I often cry out when I go out on my deck at dusk. Numerous bats wing around my neighborhood at nightfall, and I welcome their clearing the air — they can eat about one-thousand bugs each hour. Maybe the bats are just hungry. Or maybe they, too, are exacting some kind of revenge — protecting us, their fellow mammals, from the real nasty blood-sucking monsters, mosquitoes.

October 18
In "Memory" from *Cats*, Grizabella sings about her former glamour day, and about wishing for acceptance from the other cats. (Listen to the work online or from your library!)

Grizabella in the musical *Cats* by Andrew Lloyd Webber, based on *Old Possum's Book of Practical Cats* by TS Eliot

The original West End London production of *Cats* opened in 1981, directed by Trevor Nuun and choreographed by Gillian Lynne. Then, the same creative team guided the wildly popular extravaganza to an opening on Broadway, October 7, 1982, the anniversary of which was just eleven days ago.

As of this writing, *Cats* is the second longest-running show in Broadway history, the fourth longest-running West End musical, performed all over the world, and translated into more than 20 languages.

Setting all sorts of box office records, the London show ran for twenty-one years and the Broadway version for eighteen.

A college friend of mine, performed in *Cats* on Broadway and went on its national tour. My daughter Elin danced, in her final ballet studio recital, the role of "Macavity" when she was a junior in high school. My students used to create wonderful versions of Cats makeup in my theatre classes.

Though the musical is a bit dated, *Cats* — as well as *Starlight Express* — made waves in the theatre world at the time for the intense choreography, extreme athleticism, amazing spandex costumes, and clever makeup. *Cats*, maybe more than most musicals, is either intensely loved or hated with a deep-seated passion. I thoroughly enjoyed seeing the production in person when it came to Birmingham on its national tour. Just watching the movements of the actors was worth the purchase of the pricey ticket.

The song "Memory," recorded by Barbra Streisand in her 1981 Memories album, is sung in *Cats* by Grizabella, a once glamorous feline who has lost her glory, and is now nostalgically yearning for both the past and a new life. For many people, "Memory" is the song they fondly recall from Cats. I can't help but hear all the words right now. Because think back to the early 1980s and how different life was. If you were alive then, what can I say to put you back into that time? Madonna, Cabbage Patch Kids, the first Apple Macintosh, Hepatitis B Vaccine, hostile corporate takeovers, leveraged buyouts?

Cats premiered just two and a half months before the wedding of Prince Charles and Princess Diana, which happened on Wednesday, July 29, 1981, at St. Paul's Cathedral. Three days later, on August 1 at 12:01 a.m., MTV launched itself with the words "Ladies and gentlemen, rock and roll." This cable music television station promoted "Hair Metal" groups like Mötley Crüe, Van Halen, Def Leppard, and Bon Jovi.

In November of 1982, Michael Jackson released *Thriller* which sold one million copies worldwide per week at its peak. And he got to meet the President. Remember who that was? Ronald Reagan! Hippie was out, and Punk was in. Unisex clothing was the rage. The movie *Flashdance* and the aerobics craze encouraged everyday fashions like puffer jackets, leggings, and velour jogging suits. Television shows like *Dallas* and *Dynasty* encouraged "power dressing," shoulder pads, and the big bouffant hair craze.

How different I am from my Eighties self! How much more innocent I was, yet so encumbered with my ego! How married I was! How deeply involved in pushing forward my professional career! I am in a much better place now. But how I would love to sneak back just one hour to experience life as it was then, and sing with Grizabella about all the impressions and recollections I was able to gather.

October 19
"No man at all can be living for ever, and we must be satisfied."
Maurya in JM Synge's *Riders to the Sea*

In October of 2001, our Opera program performed Ralph Vaughn Williams's version of the *Riders to the Sea*, short opera based on John Millington Synge's play. Like so many Irish works, *Riders* is both gut-wrenching and achingly sad, both visceral and cerebral.

Before the story begins onstage, the elderly Maurya has already lost her husband, father-in-law, and four of her six sons at sea. Not long after the curtain rises, Maurya's daughters Nora and Cathleen hear that a body that could be their brother Michael has washed up on shore in Donegal — and this news turns out to be true. Then Nora, near the end of the play and opera, sees villagers carrying a load, which turns out to be the corpse of their final and youngest brother Bartley, who has fallen off his horse into the sea and drowned.

Earlier, Maurya had a premonition of this last son's demise, vowing she saw Michael's ghost riding behind Bartley as he rode away. Like any woman would, she laments the loss of the all these men in her family to the never-ending, all-powerful waves. But now that she has no male to lose, she actually conquers the sea and realizes that we gain understanding through suffering. In resignation to such a bereft life, Maurya says, *"No man at all can be living forever, and we must be satisfied."*

No, we none of us will ever live forever, except in a Halloween film or television series about zombies or the walking dead. We are rapidly approaching All Hallow's Eve, All Saints Day, and All Souls Day, that triduum when both the liturgical year and secular celebrations honor saints, martyrs, faithful departed, and everyone who has died.

And all of us souls and saints still living on earth are thought about daily by others, and will be remembered when we are gone. No matter how many people we interact with from week to week, we all influence others more than we know, and make a difference with our words, our deeds, our decisions, our care.

I heard a talk with a 32-year old movie box-office superstar the other day, and for his age, he was very grounded, balanced, and humble. He spoke with passion about all the other projects he has on the horizon, and others he wants to do in the future. He felt like he didn't really have time in his allotment on earth to accomplish all he wanted to do.

The interviewer said to him something like, "Stop! Look at how much you've done in your young life. If you are gone tomorrow, your work has been fantastic. You as a person are enough. You might achieve more, but look at the millions of lives you have already touched and be thankful for that!" And he agreed.

So even though we cannot sustain our human lives through eternity, we will all somehow leave our mark in the world. We were all put on earth for some purpose, and though some of us never uncover that reason for which we're living, we all impact other people, create a little art or music, provide some guidance, teach lessons, or in a jillion different ways make life better, or at least, altered for family, friends, acquaintances, and even strangers — and with that, "*... we must be satisfied.*"

October 20
"Lot 666, then: a chandelier in pieces.
Some of you may recall the strange affair of the Phantom of the Opera:
a mystery never fully explained.
We are told, ladies and gentlemen,
that this is the very chandelier which figures in the famous disaster."
Auctioneer's speech in *The Phantom of the Opera*, with music by Andrew Lloyd Webber, lyrics by Charles Hart with additions from Richard Stilgoe and book by Lloyd Webber and Stilgoe, based on *Le Fantome de l'Opera* by Gaston Leroux

Things fall. On earth, we deal with the law of gravity, so loose items make their way to the ground. At this time of year, leaves drift from trees, petals drop off flowers, needles descend from pines, rainwater cascades from roofs.

I hope I am not spoiling anything for you if you haven't seen the Lloyd Webber *Phantom of the Opera*, but the chandelier falls. Like many of the huge, spectacular musicals of the 1980s and 1990s, *Phantom* has numerous special effects — and this chandelier's crashing is the musical's signature. When some church friends rented a bus and went to Atlanta's Fox Theatre to see the show, we were all transfixed by this amazing spectacle.

The show gives nightmares, however, to the theatre to which it tours, since this one-ton hanging light fixture has to nosedive from the ceiling to a couple of dozen feet above the audience. Then, it suddenly changes direction and swerves toward the stage. Venues usually end up getting nearly half a million dollar's worth of exterior steel work, insurance, and safety permits just to allow this one prop to do its magic.

Symbolically, the musical begins with the Auctioneer dealing with "lot 666." In religious nomenclature, 666 is the diabolical number of the antichrist, an end-times enemy who will arrive to oppose God and God's people. In Revelation 13:17, the number is associated with the "mark of the Beast" and the "name of the Beast."

In this story, the Phantom is in love with a singer named Christine, and he functions as a Beast to her Beauty. At the end of Act I, as the cast within the cast at the Paris Opera house is taking bows for *Il Muto*, the Phantom brings down the chandelier, which lands at Christine's feet on the stage.

Falling objects can be beastly dangerous, indoors or out. I think of disasters that have happened involving falling objects. When a mile-wide F 4 tornado ravaged Tuscaloosa and the Birmingham area on April 27, 2011, entire houses were picked up *Wizard of Oz*-like, and dropped back onto the ground blocks away. And who can forget September 11, 2001, when terrorists struck the New York Twin Towers with airplane, causing a rapid collapse of the buildings.

Weird things fall from the sky quite often when wind, storms, and tornados are involved: worms, fish, meat, frogs, nondairy creamer, golf balls, spiders, bowling jackets, and mud have turned up miles from their "homes." Even beasts like cows and live sharks appear from the heavens when enough wind scoops them up. How mystifying! A little like *"... the strange affair of the Phantom."*

October 21
In "Pieces of Lives" from *Quilters*, the chorus sings about how little parts of our lives are like quilt pieces that make up the whole. (Listen to the work online or from your library!)

Chorus in *Quilters* by Molly Newman and Barbara Damashek, music and lyrics by Barbara Damashek, based on *The Quilters: Women and Domestic Art* by Patricia Cooper and Norma Bradley Allen

Seth, my son phoned last night. "Sorry to call so late," he began. It wasn't terribly late, but past the time he would usually call to converse. His voice was wooden and unnatural, so I knew something was wrong.

He asked if I remembered a certain good friend from seminary? And I surely did. I spent two partial weeks in Austin when they were in school there. "Well, he committed suicide today," he said sadly. In the last few days, Seth's school companion had been diagnosed with bi-polar disorder, and recently divorced. I can't even imagine how life must be for people who become so depressed, they feel hopeless and lose interest in pleasure and activities — and even life itself.

Until recently, I didn't realize that almost half the people suffering from bipolar depression attempt suicide at least once. In fact, comedic actor Robin Williams' tragic and untimely death two months ago focused public attention on bipolar disorder and depression. As I read about it, I started to understand how brain circuits and the imbalance of brain chemicals can cause a person to have an unusual range in emotions, moods, and energy levels. Then, I began to realize how desperate life sometimes becomes to those affected by the condition.

The sorrowful news about Seth's friend made me think how people, and places, and experiences make up the fabric shapes of the quilt of our time on earth. Our theatre department produced *Quilters* in the spring of 1992. A cast of seven female actors play the various characters in the musical, which consists of brief scenes sprinkled with musical numbers.

As the play unfolds, the audience gathers more and more about womanhood and life in pioneer America. The tableaux are named for quilt patterns, such as "Rocky Road" and "Butterfly." These "blocks" tell stories about school days and illness, marriage and childbirth, log cabins and twisters, the certainty of death and the pageantry of life, with all its joys and sorrows, laughter and tears. At the end, the pieces are sewn together into a large strikingly colorful and breathtaking set piece.

So this schoolmate was a bright and vibrant square on Seth's quilt of life. Like most people with bipolar, he probably thought he was a dark and unconnected shape, which friends and family would just as soon see ripped out. I am told that depressed people think they are helping free their friends or family members when they take their own lives.

Nothing could be further from the truth. In this case, Seth and all his seminary classmates are grieving the loss of this sweet soul. A friend posted on Facebook that she would miss him and his "funny spirit, and the love you showed so many!" And Seth himself said he cherished the fellow's "ability to make the reverent irreverent and the irreverent reverent, his enormous heart, his love of the practical, his passion for common prayer, and mostly his love of Our Almighty God."

The great quilt of life is forever being created, and, in some mysterious way, we all contribute our own curious, unique square to its pattern. In this sense, everyone's contributions are important and have great meaning, maybe even especially those who leave us too soon.

October 22

"...For what is not connected with her to me? and what does not recall her? I cannot look down to this floor, but her features are shaped in the flags! In every cloud, in every tree – filling the air at night, and caught by glimpses in every object by day – I am surrounded with her image! The most ordinary faces of men and women – my own features – mock me with a resemblance. The entire world is a dreadful collection of memoranda that she did exist, and that I have lost her!"
Heathcliff in Carlisle Floyd's *Wuthering Heights*, based on the novel by Emily Brontë

In the fall of 1994, I designed the costumes for Carlisle Floyd's wonderful opera, *Wuthering Heights*. Based on the Emily Brontë novel, the opera tells of two unforgettable characters who, during childhood, fall deeply in love. The setting is Wuthering Heights, the ancient Earnshaw mansion perched on a high ridge. Heathcliff is actually a dark-skinned gypsy orphan found on the streets of Liverpool, and raised by the Earnshaw family. Throughout the course of the story, the relationship between Catherine Earnshaw and Heathcliff destroys their lives, and devastates everyone around them as well.

After spraining her ankle at a nearby neighbor's home, Cathy stays with them a while and becomes close friends with Edgar and Isabella Linton. While there, she is influenced by their pretentious manners, and upon finding a scruffy Heathcliff when she returns home, she feels shame about their bond. Following this incident, Cathy and Edgar become closer, and then engaged. Yet Cathy still longs for Heathcliff, who has left

Wuthering Heights. Three years later, Heathcliff mysteriously returns with a fortune and wins the homestead in a card game. Heathcliff asks Catherine to marry him, but she refuses, and he marries her friend Isabella, who is also in love with him. By the end of the story, the conflicted Cathy professes that death would be better than the life she is living, and actually dies in Heathcliff's arms, as he asks the ghost of Cathy to haunt him forever.

Heathcliff then develops an obsessive preoccupation with his "departed idol," even excavating Cathy's grave. His whole being, body and soul, is chained to Catherine, and he perceives everything to be imbued by her presence: *"In every cloud, in every tree – filling the air at night, and caught by glimpses in every object by day – I am surrounded with her image! ...The entire world is a dreadful collection of memoranda that she did exist, and that I have lost her!"*

When I read the novel in my high school English class, I thought their affair was a wonderfully wild and bewitchingly unrestrained expression of love. I longed to find someone like Heathcliff, that mysterious archetype of the tortured romantic hero. I yearned to live in that otherworldly, time-worn manor house out on the moors in a barren, windswept landscape in the English countryside. That dream was never fulfilled.

However, here I was, designing costumes for this old favorite of mine and I was excited to delve into the work again. *The Wuthering Heights* duo had all-consuming passions – but that fervor also ruined their family and friends. When Catherine's cries, "I am Heathcliff!" I saw how empty her own soul was, and how she actually thirsted for him to fill her up, like a drug or alcohol addict. In fact, they both exhibit a kind of sexual dependency and a fierce need to possess each other.

To design this show and actually see Cathy collapse into a premature extinction was startling. And as I watched the action unfold on stage, I was horrified at how unhealthy the love between Cathy and Heathcliff actually was, and I realized that some of my past relationships were just about as enmeshed and as filled with intensity and dramatic conflict.

October 23
"I'm very good at integral and differential calculus,
I know the scientific names of beings animalculous ;
In short, in matters vegetable, animal, and mineral,

413

I am the very model of a modern Major-General."
Major-General in *The Pirates of Penzance or, The Slave of Duty*, with book by W. S. Gilbert and music by Arthur Sullivan

In the autumns of both 1986 and 1996, Samford Opera produced Gilbert and Sullivan's *The Pirates of Penzance*, both thoroughly enjoyable experiences. For the first one, I designed some of my favorite costumes ever, and we reused most of them in the revival. The operetta's premiere was not in London, but at the Fifth Avenue Theatre in New York City, on New Year's Eve of 1879. The topsy turvy story is about Frederic and his beloved, Mabel, daughter of Major General Stanley.

Frederick, son of a wealthy gentleman, was supposed to be apprenticed to a pilot at a young age, but his nursemaid was nearly deaf and indentured him to a gang of pirates. They were a kindhearted lot led by the Pirate King, and now that he is turning 21, Frederic is about to be liberated from his obligation, and promoted to full Pirate.

However, the poor dear finds he was born on February 29, and is technically only a little over 5 years old. His apprenticeship contract states that he must continue his work with the pirates until his 21st birthday, so now he must serve for another 63 years. Restrained by an uncommon sense of duty, he begs Mabel to wait for him till then. "It seems so long," she sighs, pleading that he not leave her.

Lots of crazy action ensues. One of the highlights of the show is Mabel's father's patter tune, the "Modern Major General's Song," which pokes fun at the notion of a fashionably educated British Army officer of the late nineteenth century. With its quick beat and difficult, alliterative lyrics, it is a crowning achievement to perform. Pondering this paragon of a modern Major General, I am thinking how interesting that the actor Johnny Depp claimed he modeled a large part of Jack Sparrow (the buccaneer in the Pirates of the Caribbean movies) after Rolling Stones guitarist Keith Richards, declaring, "Pirates were the rock stars of their day."

Though he can wield a sword and exchange blows when necessary, Sparrow usually survives by employing wit and charm, choosing flight over fight under treacherous circumstances. Disney executives were astonished at Depp's pirate interpretation, which was 180 degrees away from theirs. In a Vanity Fair interview, Depp said senior officials asked about his Sparrow: "What's wrong with him? ...Is he, you know, like some kind of weird simpleton? Is he drunk? By the way, is he gay?"

But it worked: Depp somehow portrayed Jack Sparrow as both virile and swishy, over the top, and ever surprising. Those Disney moguls might have been directed to recall the flamboyant and flashy appearance of Captain Hook in *Peter Pan* or the foppishly outlandish and campy behavior of these *Pirates of Penzance*, who were certainly precursors to this interpretation.

So, can you imagine if the Major General let Jack Sparrow sing his song, what it would be like? I gave it a try:

I can read a voodoo compass to steer Black Pearl all across the sea,
And fight you with a sword while drinking rum, now isn't that savvy?
In short, in matters bootying and shivering and timbering,
I am the very model of a modern of an "Arrgghhing" Pirate King!

October 24
"All my life I wanted to be somebody, but I see now that I should have been more specific."
The Character "Chrissy" in Jane Wagner's *The Search for Signs of Intelligent Life in the Universe*, a 12-character play featuring Lily Tomlin

This poignant idea comes from the character "Chrissy" in Jane Wagner's wonderful *The Search for Signs of Intelligent Life in the Universe*, a 12-character play featuring Lily Tomlin. There is a great 1991 filmed version of this one-woman stage show that won the Drama Desk Award for Unique Theatrical Experience.

Chrissy, like the others in this play, is a searcher, and a hopelessly cheery fitness maniac. She admits to having "gained and lost the same ten pounds so many times my cellulite must have déjà vu." Attending one seminar after another, Chrissy has tried expert and self-help advice so much that she has become skeptical of transformation.

I like her quote for two reasons: Chrissy wanted to Be Somebody in Life. That concept is something we all can identify with, surely. I know I do. Secondly, she finally realizes that just asking to be "somebody" is not enough when any of us need guidance from the Universe. "I want to be an accomplished artist" (healer, gardener, public servant — fill in the blank) is more helpful. "My company needs to generate $150,000 to set up a retirement plan." "I want my family to find concrete ways to make lifelong memories." Those statements start getting a little more specific.

I have learned from reading and listening to wisdom teachers, that a goal is hard to achieve in my life journey if I don't have a clue about where I want to go. To fulfill my deepest desires, I have to voice precisely what I want and focus on that intention. However, BIG POINT, at the same time, I must let go of my own version of how this whole thing might work out, and relinquish attachment to any single outcome. Only this two-pronged approach can open me up to abundant possibility.

Mark Twain once said, "The two most important days in your life are the day you are born and the day you find out why." My deep and soulful desires are like bright candles that show me the way and light a pathway to my true self and its providence. Whatever is going to make me "Somebody" is connected to my soul's mission to make a contribution to the world. American writer and theologian Frederick Buechner put it this way: "The place God calls you to is the place where your deep gladness and the world's deep hunger meet." As I follow my own heart's desire, I flourish, and from this overflowing, blissful place, I can be of great service to others.

In this sense, I create my own reality. Clear attention will energize my mind and help me form intentions that will transform my world, because the universe really does synchronistically offer me what I request, though usually disguised. If I can place attention on what I desire, my purpose ignites my intuition, and something takes over that begins to organize everything I need to accomplish my vision. If I can be receptive, the universe even works with me to buttress my plans.

October 25:
"This story shall the good man teach his son;
And Crispin Crispian shall ne'er go by,
From this day to the ending of the world,
But we in it shall be remembered.
We few, we happy few, we band of brothers;
For he to-day that sheds his blood with me
Shall be my brother; be he ne'er so vile,
This day shall gentle his condition;
And gentlemen in England now-a-bed
Shall think themselves accurs'd they were not here,
And hold their manhoods cheap whiles any speaks
That fought with us upon Saint Crispin's day."
King Henry in William Shakespeare's *Henry V*, Act IV Scene 3

Today, October 25, is the feast day of the twin saints Crispin and Crispinian who may have been martyred in the 280s. They are the patron saints of cobblers and leather workers, born to a noble family who fled Rome during persecutions and ended up either in Gaul or Faversham, England.

The day was made famous in Shakespeare's play *Henry V* when the King spoke to his men before the Battle of Agincourt, a major skirmish in the Hundred Years' War between England and France. This speech is possibly the greatest theatrical rendering of what leaders might to say to motivate their followers.

Before this battle, Henry and his English troops had traveled through the northern part of France, claiming Calais and a few other towns to win back former English territories. The ultimate goal was to take the French throne. Trying to outmaneuver Henry, the French slipped between the English troops and the port of Calais where the Brits would return to their homeland.

The English had lost men to death, desertion, and dysentery, and they were low on food. Tauntingly, the French accompanied them along rivers, impeding their progress, confident they would win any battle that ensued. The English army still fought mainly on foot, while the French used a cavalry as well. But, the English possessed a new weapon, the longbow, which had been successful in a couple of previous clashes.

When the French mustered enough troops to handle the threat, they refused to allow Henry to pass, prompting an inevitable fray. Numbers vary greatly, but there were many more French than English warriors on the morning of October 25. Some estimates are an army of 13,000 English and 50,000 French, so by this accounting, the English were outnumbered about four to one. Morale among the weary English soldiers must have been flagging, seeing an immense and fresh force of skilled French fighters.

Though Shakespeare's words to his men are from his own imagination, King Henry certainly gave them a rousing speech to raise their spirits. *"We few, we happy few, we band of brothers,"* he begins, celebrating the fact that there are not many who will have this glorious opportunity. *"He to-day that sheds his blood with me shall be my brother,"* he *continues, and will find himself in a much better spot. In fact, gentlemen who are right now sleeping back home in England "shall think themselves accurs'd they* were not here, and hold their manhoods cheap whiles any speaks that fought with us upon Saint Crispin's day."

Somehow, through the terrain, the disorganization of the opponents, and the longbow, the French casualties were stunningly estimated at a possible 400 to one. The French were trounced, and that so small an army overcame a much larger one makes this one of the most legendary battles in history.

I am a very peaceful person who abhors war and violence. But this play, this speech, this battle are all important to me. My 14th great-grandfather and his brother, Thomas and William de Bolron, were archers who fought in this battle and heard whatever speech King Henry gave to galvanize his troops. Give me an endeavor and tell me it is impossible to achieve, and I will usually accept the challenge and find a way to secure my own little Agincourt victory — after all, I have longbowmen's blood flowing through my veins.

October 26

In "Steal Me, Sweet Thief" from *The Old Maid and the Thief*, Laetitia sings asking the Thief to steal her instead of some goods. (Listen to the work online or from your library!)

Laetitia in Gian Carlo Menotti's *The Old Maid and the Thief*

In the fall of 2000, I designed the costumes for Italian-American composer Gian Carlo Menotti's *The Old Maid and the Thief*. Originally created as a one-act radio opera the work was commissioned by the National Broadcasting Company in 1939 to such acclaim that the composer later adapted it for the stage.

The story is about a small town oldish spinster, Miss Todd, and her youngish housekeeper Laetitia who wish for a man in their lives. Their desires become manifest in a drifter named Bob, with whom they both fall in love. A nosy neighbor Miss Pinkerton announces that a notorious robber has broken out of jail.

Everyone thinks Bob is the thief, but he is really just a respectable nomad. However, when challenged, Miss Todd accuses Bob, and he retaliates by plundering her house and running off with Laetitia in her car. And so, the message according to Menotti is: "The devil couldn't do what a woman can: make a thief of an honest man!"

To hear Dawn Upshaw or another fine soprano sing "Steal Me, Sweet Thief" is deceptively joyful, because Laetitia's aria certainly paints a frightening picture of the decay of girlhood, a rapidly approaching old age, the brevity of life, and death coming quickly to take her away. She begs the "thief" to carry off her mouth, her heart, her cheeks, her breath, herself. For, she sings, otherwise time is stealing them all away.

Laetitia has had enough of the feather dusting and silver polishing. Distraught that she may end up unmarried like her employer, she is desperate for the attention of this drifter she scarcely knows. She laments that time is snatching her youth. And yet, she seems to have done very little to fill her life with any sort of meaning, purpose, or commitment.

I sometimes wonder what has happened to all the minutes in my day. Though I mean to fill each moment with intention and action or being, I sometimes find myself drifting in thought, frittering away whole stretches with meaningless tasks, sneaking too many peeks at emails or Facebook posts. And so time marches on, one millisecond followed quickly by the next. Time hasn't evaporated or been stolen, I simply haven't used it properly.

German minister, theologian, and anti-Nazi dissenter, Dietrich Bonhoeffer once said, "Time is the most precious gift in our possession, for it is the most irrevocable. This is what makes it so disturbing to look back upon the time which we have lost. Time lost is time when we have not lived a full human life, time unenriched by experience, creative endeavor, enjoyment, and suffering. Time lost is time not filled, time left empty."

Don't let time's flight steal what youth you have left today. Seize and live in your moments so they have the power to fill your life with unbounded riches before all your time is gone.

October 27
"O this learning, what a thing it is!"
Gremio in Shakespeare's *The Taming of the Shrew*, Act I, Scene 2

The basic one sentence version of *The Taming of the Shrew* is: A hot-tempered, spirited Katherina, used to doing things her way, has let her biting wit keep men at bay until she meets Petruchio, who she eventually marries and lets "tame" her. The play is fun, and I love this line from Gremio, spoken when several male companions meet up, with one pretending to be a scholar. The satire in this line is that much learning still needs to take place, and most of it is not academic, but concerns how to navigate love and find worldly knowledge.

I am always on the lookout for powerful tutorials about life, and I got a strong one yesterday. Unbelievably, His Holiness, the Dalai Lama came to Birmingham — yes, Alabama. Mayor William Bell, met him in Japan and invited him to visit the Magic City, and, by golly, he came!

The Dalai Lama stepped onstage in his simple red monastic robes and presented Mayor Bell with a lovely white prayer shawl. As he sat to begin his intimate conversation with the 8,000 or so of us at the baseball stadium, he had one of his fellow monks hold an umbrella over him to give him some relief from the blaring, almost 90-degree late October heat. As he began to speak, a feeling of peace fell over the audience.

First, he talked about how all humans are alike, and that today's world demands we accept the oneness of humanity. Whether we like it, whether we agree, whether we accept it, every one of us has been born into the human race. We are now three or four minutes into the speech.

This man gets up at 3:30 each morning to spend time in prayers, contemplations, and prostrations, and gives hours each day to meditation, and has since he was a child. He has probably logged over 100,000 hours in such reflection. He is the exemplar of self-control, discipline, perseverance, and delayed gratification. Daily, he reads scripture, exercises, eats wisely, and catches up on the news (through the BBC). He is known as one of the great spiritual leaders of the world.

Needless to say, I admire this man very much. His followers believe when he dies, he will be reincarnated because he has so much love to give, one lifetime is not enough.

His Holiness continues saying that it does not matter if we are rich or poor, educated or uneducated, from this nation or from that religion, all of us just want to be happy. Now, we are about six minutes into the speech. But wait. He is stopping.

Even in the process of an address, the Dalai Lama halts the lecture in an act of concern. He rises, moves around, and gets his chair closer to Mayor Bell's, goes through a few maneuvers, and steers the umbrella to cover both of them. Everyone applauded! I was truly impressed that he ceased a speech to tend to someone else. What a vivid teaching of how our actions can be the manifestation of compassion. *"O this learning, what a thing it is!"*

October 28

In "Princess" from *A Man of No Importance*, Alfie talks to Adele about how wonderful acting is when you can be another human being and leave yourself behind. (Listen to the work online or from your library!)

Alfie in *A Man of No Importance*, a musical with music by Stephen Flaherty, lyrics by Lynn Ahrens, and a book by Terrence McNally, based on the 1994 Albert Finney film

The SiriusXM classical station has been throwing in a few "scary" pieces to get listeners in the mood for the upcoming Halloween holiday. Yesterday, the announcer reminded everyone that the sister Metropolitan Opera station would be airing Richard Strauss's opera *Salome* Wednesday afternoon. "Now listen to that if you want something frightening!" he told us.

The mention of *Salome* reminded me of a few weeks in October of 2003 when I was still mourning my father's death and feeling lonely for Seth who had gone away to college. I was working at The American Village and also missing my theatre work. At this point, I was still a member of Stage and Screen (formerly Fireside Theatre and now defunct), a book club that concentrated on sending me play scripts. That fall, one of the selections was *A Man of No Importance*, the musical by Stephen Flaherty, Lynn Ahrens, and Terrence McNally.

The work, based on a film starring Albert Finney, tells the story of Alfie Byrne, a middle-aged Dublin bus conductor who lives with his spinster sister, reads poetry aloud to the dismay of his passengers, and is passionate about his amateur theatre company which rehearses and performs in the basement of St. Imelda's Catholic church.

In love with Robbie who drives his bus, but unable in 1964 to speak of such homosexual affection, Alfie is a huge Oscar Wilde fan and is intent on staging a version of his play *Salome*, despite the objections of church authorities. I became as infatuated with the tender and beautifully written *Man of No Importance* as Alfie is with Robbie. The music is lyrical, and the tale features one of my favorite themes: Who am I and what am I on earth to do?

So I read the play, I listened to the music, then I read the haunting Wilde *Salome* (which was originally banned on the basis that it was unlawful to depict Biblical characters on stage). Then, I found in the library the Finney film that the musical was based on. I reread the biblical version of the story of John the Baptist and his demise at the hands of a teenager. I found my old book with Aubrey Beardsley's evocative illustrations created for the first English edition of Wilde's play in1894 and poured over them. And I listened to the Strauss opera *Salome*. It was an absolutely bewitching few weeks for me. I could not get enough of any of the pieces.

During that time, Seth came home for fall break, Elin broke up with her boyfriend Ben and had a date with her future husband David for the first time, I had a Yard Sale, my work computer had to be totally revamped, I painted and donated an art piece to my university's silent auction, I worked on camp and club projects.

But in my mind, I kept seeing the *Salome* setting, a great terrace in the Palace of Herod, a gigantic staircase, an old cistern surrounded by a wall of green bronze, and the moon, a full, scintillating, lustrous orb shining very brightly in the sky, just waiting to watch that dance of veils and see what it might bring. As I carried on my life, in my mind I luxuriated in the overlapping, interconnected, luminous works that formed and informed almost one-twelfth of my year of 2003.

October 29:
"*Mombi: Shadows are falling, screech owls are calling, Hobgoblins and Sprites appear!*
Hobgoblins: Booh-oo-oo-oo-oo!
Mombi: Booh! With pranks so bold, you shudder to behold, then creeping up behind you,
Should they find you, Then you'd better scoot, scoot, scoot!"
Mombi and Goblins in *The Woggle-Bug Words* by L. Frank Baum Music by Frederic Chapin

You have probably never heard of *The Woggle-Bug*, a musical based on L. Frank Baum's *The Marvelous Land of Oz*. The author himself created the book and lyrics and its music was written by Frederic Chapin. It opened June 18, 1905, in Chicago, and closed less than a month later, a failure artistically and financially. If you take a peek at the script or even at a synopsis, you might see why: cast of thousands (well, hundreds), complicated action, major changes to the original book, numerous settings, confusing characters.

If they were all still alive, today would be my grandmother's 114th birthday, and my parents' 66th wedding anniversary. I have always loved this golden day at the end of October when the sun's light is like pure honey, the leaves are just beginning to trade fading, yellowing greens for russets and ochres; shadows are lengthening; days are growing shorter. On this day, I always wander back to my grandmother's childhood. On this day, I always yearn to still be celebrating a wedding milestone with my mom and dad.

The Wonderful Wizard of Oz, Baum's first of many Oz books, was published on May 17, 1900, just five-and-a-half months before my grandmother was born. Her name was Dorothy — not named for the character in the book, but she adored Baum's imaginative tale of journey and friendship, and, as she would point out, of discovering that what you have deep down inside you is quite enough to get you through the adventures of life.

One of the most endearing characters my grandmother ever introduced me (in *The Marvelous Land of Oz*) is Jack the Pumpkinhead, a tall, tree-limb fellow with a pumpkin for a head. He is made by a little boy Tip who wants to scare his guardian Mombi, the old Wicked Witch of the North. Jack is not the brightest lantern ever created, but he often gives Tip curious pieces of advice and guidance.

When I still carved pumpkins each year for Halloween, my daughter Elin insisted we get out the old original 1904 edition of *The Marvelous Land of Oz* and carefully draw Jack's features on the front for us to take a knife to. We had to be sure to get the perfect fruity gourd: extra round, much wider than tall, nice creases, and just the perfect shade of butterynutty-orange.

When Seth was just a little over one year old, he called Jack "Boka," his attempt at "Pumpkin." He fell in love with that shining face and we had to have the candle inside him lit day and night. One day, we came in from work and Jack had folded in on himself. Seth dashed into the dining room to see him, and came running back to me crying desperately, "Boka! Boka!"

I had to make up a ceremony without hesitation, so we decided that we would find a woodsy spot where we could toss the jack-o-lantern as far as we possibly could. That hurl was the first ever of our "Pitch the Pumpkin" events which we hold to this day. Even though we always have to toss old Jack the Pumpkinhead away, I am ever grateful that somehow my grandmother and her love of Baum characters was passed down through my mother and me to my children.

October 30
"Harker: The sun! The stake, Professor – the stake! Hold him, Doctor.

423

Seward: I've got him.
(Dracula, with loud burst of mocking laughing, goes down trap on the word
'sun,' leaving the two men holding the empty cape.)"
Characters in Hamilton Deane and John L. Balderston's *Dracula*, based
on the novel by Bram Stoker

In early November of 1980, as my ex and I were about to leave
Samford University for what turned out to be a year-and-a-half departure
to a nearby university, we created the scenery and costumes for *Dracula*.
Working on the show and knowing we were soon departing was a bit
harrowing. I had intense love for a number of students we were leaving
behind, but the professional situation at the other school seemed to
promise so much more.

And I stress the word "seemed"! We left because — at the time —
our administration had yet to fully acknowledge affirmative action or the
women's liberation movement. It appeared as if the other college was
more advanced in modern egalitarian treatment and the acceptance of
women professors as equal to men.

As soon as we got to our new jobs, however, it seemed as if all the
assured goodness went down the trap door with Dracula's mocking
laughter, leaving the two of us holding an empty cape. A large chunk of
our increased salaries went for such items as parking passes and higher
benefit deductions.

In the first thirty days, my car was broken into, my purse was
stolen, my office was burgled, all of the food for a patrons' reception was
pillaged from the costume shop, a student was raped on the bridge
outside the theatre, and a campus policeman was mugged. When my
daughter Elin first walked into the costume shop, where she knew from
her Samford experience that she would spend a lot of time, she vomited.
Just in the first month!

By June, we were the senior faculty members in the theatre
department, as one professor became associate dean, one took a position
at another university, and the woman who recruited us went on sabbatical
and then changed careers without ever returning. Over the summer, I
served as interim department chair, and I had only been there five
months! We eventually hired a theatre chairman with whom we were
incompatible, and employed a series of temperamental guest directors.
The dance department rioted and threatened to secede from the

university. My blood pressure shot way up and my anxiety attacks returned. (And I was only 31 years old!)

Naturally, there were great aspects to the job: I had wonderful students. I learned that I enjoyed teaching. And we created a really good productions with fun designs and great student acting. However, we wanted to go home! I realize that just about anyone who accepts a new job goes through a transition period to acclimate to new people, new responsibilities, and new environment.

But our expectations were not fulfilled. We probably failed to ask enough questions going in, and we discovered that our previous academic life was not nearly as bad as we had thought. One really hard thing to admit is that you are wrong in your professional judgment, but that is exactly what we did.

Samford had not yet hired anyone to fill our positions, so we restrained that feeling of humiliation, swallowed our pride, and, though it was gut-wrenching, asked for our old jobs back. We admitted we made a mistake, and we were actually welcomed back with a better position for me, as a faculty member as well as costume designer. Was the U-turn worth it? Yes! Yes, it was.

October 31
"I did not believe in ghosts... I did not believe in ghosts..."
Arthur Kipps in Stephen Mallatratt's *The Woman in Black*, based on the book by Susan Hill

It is Halloween, the eve of All Saints or All Hallows Day. Time for Ghosties, and Ghoulies, and Things that Go Bump in the Night. I saw the incredible spooky story *The Woman in Black* on January 6, 1992, three years after its West End opening. The stretch between Christmas and Epiphany and a few days beyond was a magical time to be teaching Costume History in London, and my students looked forward to experiencing this ghost play.

The theatrical piece is famed for having only two performers, Mr. Kipps, a solicitor who employs the Actor to interpret a horrifying tale from his younger days so his soul will be free. The lighting is dark in the Victorian theatre where they rehearse, and as the story comes more and more to life, the duo are surrounded by the unfolding history of the curious deceased Mrs. Alice Drablow and her rotting house in the small village of Crythin Gifford near a marsh at the edge of the sea.

In order to settle the dead woman's affairs, the lawyer must examine piles of records, and he begins to uncover deep secrets and mysterious occurrences. If you haven't seen the play, I am going to let you ponder the questions of: Why is he staying and even delving into this secret? Why don't the townspeople cooperate? How is he tormented in later years? And really, who might the woman in black be?

"*I did not believe in ghosts... I did not believe in ghosts...*" I have always been open-minded about spirits, angels, ghosts, and other ephemeral beings. So has Bill Murray who helped write and star in *Ghostbusters*, the 1984 classic comedy, praised for its skillful mixing of just the right amount of terror, excitement, and comedy.

Not long after we saw the movie in the theatre, we put our house on the market. Seth had arrived in September of 1984, and we were rapidly outgrowing our 1920s classic bungalow. Like the lawyer in The Woman in Black, we researched the history of the house which was built and purchased by McLin J. Carter in the early 1920s. When the stock market crashed in 1929, sadly, he and his wife Lula had to auction the house on the steps of the courthouse.

We were intrigued with the story, and found an engraving in the attic that we believed was of the original owner, framed it, and hung it with a homey saying from one of McLin's real estate ads. For months, we had a series of people look at the house, but no one was ready to buy. So our realtor scheduled a caravan of real estate agents to take a peek. The kitchen floor was deplorable, so, since my mother-in-law was out of town, we borrowed two of her Persian-type rugs to add some warmth to the room.

Early on the morning of the caravan, I went into a dark kitchen to warm a bottle for Seth and stepped on one of the runners. It felt wet! How could that be — nothing was placed near the mats that could have leaked or dripped or spilled? I flipped on the lights and examined the rug: there was soggy green slime eating away at the edge of the fabric! I alerted the family and none of us could make any sense of it.

Upset that we had surreptitiously borrowed the rugs, we immediately took them to the oriental rug experts in town. The owner tested the substance and could in no way speculate what sort of gel or liquid might have suddenly appeared and then eaten the runner's border.

Our family has always gone with the theory that McLin Carter's ghost didn't want us to sell and leave his home and was attempting to thwart our deal by inhabiting the house, with the idea of blanketing objects with ectoplasm. *"I did not believe in ghosts... I did not believe in ghosts..."* But now I do!

November 1
"Good pilgrim, you do wrong your hand too much,
Which mannerly devotion shows in this,
For saints have hands that pilgrims' hands do touch,
And palm to palm is holy palmers' kiss."
Juliet in William Shakespeare's *Romeo and Juliet*

Here we are a day after Halloween in the middle of a masquerade party at the Capulets' home in fair Verona. Almost every significant citizen of the city has come to feast and make merry. Juliet talks of saints, and today is the celebration of All Saints, a commemoration of all the great people who have gone before us to light our way. Some of them may be hidden from us, and some not.

Usually, masks are for disguise, or perhaps concealment. Romeo is actually crashing the ball and, though all the partiers' faces are hidden, he especially feels more comfortable in his coverup. Apparently in a comic jester mask, since Tybalt calls it an "antic face," Romeo has accompanied his friend Benvolio to the soiree to see Rosaline, while Benvolio wants to persuade Romeo that he can do better.

Romeo is a Montague, a mortal enemy of the Capulets – and Tybalt, a Capulet, becomes infuriated that Romeo would attend uninvited (knowing he was unwelcome). On top of that, because of the comic false face, Tybalt jumps to the conclusion that Romeo is making fun of their celebration. Actually, the enmity and intolerance generated by the intense family feud are what is really covering the true character of both the Montagues and the Capulets.

But at the party, Romeo spies a beautiful Juliet and forgets all about Rosaline. The quote about saints and pilgrims depends on the audience's knowledge that many people in medieval and Renaissance times visited holy sites on pilgrimages, often traveling great distances to see the shrines of favorite saints. Just before, Romeo has likened Juliet to a "holy shrine." He has found the object of his reverence, and offers his "lips, two blushing pilgrims" to kiss away any profaning that his "unworthiest hand" may have committed in the process. In other words, he is flirting in a big way.

Juliet teases right back, saying that pilgrims often do touch the statues of saints, but that a pilgrim's proper "kiss" would be palms touching together — in prayer! Romeo asks if saints and pilgrims don't have lips too? And Juliet leads him on with the retort, "Ay, pilgrim, lips that they must use in prayer." As they quip back and forth, Romeo tells her that the thing he's praying for is a kiss from her, and she holds still while he gives her a big smooch.

I like to think of myself as a pilgrim on this day. I like to remember saints who have gone before me and saints in my life right now. Many of them — probably most — have not been formally canonized, but they have lent special light and guidance to my life. I hope I can think of all of them as the day progresses, from Shakespeare to Mr. Sunny Sunshine (who used to clear the dishes at my university), from the real saint Thomas Becket to David who cuts my hair, from both of my grandmothers to the many dozens of theatre students I mentored. Oh, and my dearly departed Springer, Merlin.

I think of them all with great affection, for they have somehow given me physical, emotional, spiritual, or mental enlightenment. Maybe by recognizing them as saints today, I can remember to reach out my palms to others and one day be remembered on this day as well.

November 2

"It is as if we only existed one at a time, combining to achieve continuity. I keep space warm for Higgs. My presence defines his absence, his absence confirms my presence, his presence precludes mine... When Higgs and I walk down this aisle together to claim our common seat, the oceans will fall into the sky and the trees will hang with fishes."
Moon in Tom Stoppard's *The Real Inspector Hound*

In the fall of 1995 when we presented this play at Samford University, my life was a bit out of control. Elin was at the University of Montevallo in frequent contact about many exciting escapades. Seth was involved in a traveling soccer team and training our brand new puppy. I was in charge of many community committees and teams while getting used to single parenthood. And among a jillion other real life theatrics, the hurricane Opal — with 75 mile-an-hour winds — blew through Birmingham knocking trees in our yard into power lines and cutting power off for a week or so right before opening of *The Real Inspector Hound*.

428

And I had to work on this play, just as if nothing special or harrowing was going on in my life. I was determined not to bring the spectacle of my life into the drama onstage. The students deserved more – a lot more – than that.

This short play within a play is really quite intriguing, and it took my mind off my strife, as well as somewhat oddly paralleling what was going on. As a spoof of "country house murder mysteries" – and in particular Agatha Christie's *Mousetrap* – *The Real Inspector Hound* introduces us to four theatre critics. Birdboot is a reviewer and lecher who gives glowing evaluations of young starlets, presumably in return for sexual favors. Higgs is another writer, the senior critic at his newspaper, and Moon is his second-string stand-in. When neither Higgs or Moon can go to a show, Puckeridge is on duty.

Stoppard himself had been a theatre critic in Bristol, and brings the action to a nice bubble as he explores a favorite theme of fate and free will. Moon laments the fact that he really only exists if Higgs is off duty. He answers the age-old question of "Who am I?" by identifying with his job, so if Higgs shows up, in essence, Moon doesn't exist.

At the time, I was just beginning to realize how unhealthy it is to closely enmesh myself in my profession. My work duties were difficult, but all of my own making. I so vividly saw myself as a Costumier. I remember our department chairman saying over and over, "You really shouldn't keep such long hours. This university will let you work as hard as you want, but you can give yourself a break."

I never gave myself time to know and understand myself. I never found the time to devote to a physical and spiritual regimen (which I knew I needed). I never even let myself have hobbies, or leisure time, or sabbaths, or repose. I tended to my children, the house, and my work.

Over the next few years after designing this play, I became more and more independent, authentic, and true to myself, through a whole lot of physical, mental, emotional, and spiritual work. When I look back at how I had been and what I am now, I do feel like *"the oceans [have fallen] into the sky and the trees...hang with fishes."*

When people ask now who I am, I hardly ever answer with my profession or my family role. I don't define myself by my relationships, my university, my work, my birthplace, or my family. Not that these aren't important to me, they just don't explain who I am. I hope one day Higgs and Moon walk down that theatre *"aisle together to claim [their] common seat."* A chance like mine should be granted everyone!

November 3
In "The Impossible Dream (The Quest)" from *Man of La Mancha*, Don Quixote sings about doing what you must to achieve your visions, even though the quest seems foolhardy and unachievable. (Listen to the work online or from your library!)

Don Quixote in *Man of La Mancha* with a book by Dale Wasserman, lyrics by Joe Darion and music by Mitch Leigh, adapted from Wasserman's non-musical 1959 teleplay, *I, Don Quixote,* which was inspired by Miguel De Cervantes' novel *Don Quixote*

The musical *Man of La Mancha* is bewitching — and bothersome... and bewildering — to borrow a phrase from Rodgers and Hart's musical Pal Joey. Some critics think the work is a commanding, solitary, masterwork of theatre, but to others, it is banal and schmaltzy. Some audience members love its ties to the 1960s experimental theatre movement, and others are uncomfortable with its jabs at authority and institutions, government and religion.

The musical departs heavily from the Cervantes book, and relates the tale of the "foolish" knight Quixote as a play within the musical. Taking place during the Spanish Inquisition, the interior play is actually performed by the author Cervantes and other inmates. The playwright Wasserman has always maintained that his work is not a musical rendition of *Don Quixote*, and he never intended it to be such a mammoth undertaking. The 1965 Broadway premier ran for 2,328 performances and won five Tonys, one of which was "Best Musical." Revived at least four times on Broadway, the show is popular with community theatres.

A number of people love the idea of this impossible dream, and I must admit, I am one of them. In the musical, the tune is first performed by Don Quixote standing mindfully over his armor when Aldonza asks what is meant by his expedition.

One of the professors at the University of Montevallo, Bennie Middaugh, played Don Quixote in this show many times, and sang a matchless version of "The Impossible Dream." I heard him belt it in performances of the play, in concerts, in classes, and in special fundraisers — and he almost always made me cry.

John Stuart Mill once wrote: "A man who has nothing which he is willing to fight for, nothing which he cares more about than he does about his personal safety, is a miserable creature who has no chance of being free, unless made and kept so by the exertions of better men than himself." Cervantes and Wasserman give us the antithesis of such a miserable man, Don Quixote, who thinks voices are calling him to transform the world and right all wrongs.

Don Quixote exhibits selective perception when he tilts at windmills he believes to be giants, or mistakes dust clouds from scurrying sheep as great armies about to engage in war. However, this idealist enters the fray of life, and fights metaphorical clashes while everyone else calls him crazy, and ridicules his attempts. Not one to sit on the sidelines while life passes him by, Quixote exemplifies people who dream and help create their own reality, and who, even when their bodies are exhausted, they grasp for the heavens.

Such a quest can seem hopeless, and it is definitely tiring: to conquer corruption, to strive with that last ounce of courage, to be willing to die so that honor and justice may live, to make the world a better place. Not many people choose this path, because they want to stay under everyone else's radar. Or at least be judged correct, and normal, sane. Don Quixote may be right, even though very idealistic, to think we should look at reality as it might be rather than as it truly is.

November 4
"You see, I haven't really thought very much. I was always afraid of what I might think – so it seemed safer not to think at all. But now I know. A thought is like a child inside our body. It has to be born. If it dies inside you, part of you dies, too!"
Rachel in Jerome Lawrence & Robert E. Lee's *Inherit the Wind*

I have never designed Lawrence and Lee's great play, *Inherit the Wind*. Every time I read it, I think: How in the world did this trial happen in Tennessee instead of Alabama? It seems like my home state is always the one caught up in battles over whether to teach scientific evolution or Biblical Creationism in our schools. And really, should we educate our children at all? Mightn't they begin to use their minds and slip into some progressive thought patterns?

431

Freedom of thought and the pursuit of Truth are the great themes of this play, based on the famous Scopes (or Monkey) Trial, actually called The State of Tennessee versus John Thomas Scopes which took place in 1925. In the dramatization, Bert Cates, like Scopes, is accused of violating Tennessee's Butler Act, a law that made it illegal to teach Darwin's theory in a state-funded school.

One of the great aspects of the play is the battle between the two lawyers, who somewhat resemble the famous attorneys on the actual case, Clarence Darrow (counsel for the defense) and William Jennings Bryant (counsel for the prosecution). In the stage version, prosecutor Matthew Harrison Brady (a three-time losing presidential candidate) is an arrogant, condescending, self-proclaimed prophet of God, who wants to impose what he believes religion to be on the rest of the world.

The *Baltimore Herald* newspaper steps in to hire an equally prominent attorney, recognized for his accomplished defense strategies, Henry Drummond to defend Cates. Serving as the playwrights' voices throughout, Drummond tirelessly upholds a human's right to think, and battles censorship of learning. At one point, Brady says that all Drummond wants is to destroy "...everybody's belief in the Bible, and in God." To this accusation, Drummond retorts, "You know that's not true. I'm trying to stop you bigots and ignoramuses from controlling the education of the United States."

Rachel, whose quote started this whole meditation today, is the daughter of the fire-and-brimstone fundamentalist preacher in town, Rev. Jeremiah Brown. A second-grade teacher herself, she risks the ire of her father by falling in love with Cates. In talking to Cates and Drummond near the end of the play, she says how she has come to understand that whether ideas are good or bad, they have to be uncovered. And people should be able to listen to all opinions, think about them, and perhaps change their minds about issues.

Through Rachel, Lawrence and Lee are able to illustrate how education can open humans to new thoughts. Fearful people in control, like the preacher Brown and the political figure Brady, would rather restrain the masses through ignorance, thinking that otherwise, their positions — and even all of society — will be threatened.

I was just reading yesterday about English priest and influential theologian Richard Hooker, the "saint" for November 4. From his masterpiece work *Of the Lawes of Ecclesiastical Politie,* published in 1594, came the Episcopal Church's idea that philosophy and personal theology should be based not only on the scriptures and tradition, but also upon reason and first-hand experience. Today, there are a number of really intelligent scientific people who talk about Consciousness as the Mastermind behind the Big Bang and a number of really insightful theologians who see evolution as part of the Divine's generation of creation.

November 5
"O brother, speak with possibility,
And do not break into these deep extremes."
Marcus Andronicus in William Shakespeare's *Titus Andronicus*

Titus Andronicus was sometimes banned during the Victorian era for its violence. For the same reason, audiences of the mid-twentieth century ate it up. Probably Shakespeare's first play, the tragedy is a bloody revenge piece. Nine people are murdered on stage and five off, there are multiple severed appendages, rapes, the burial of a live person, insanity, cannibalism, swords, spears, animals, blood. What a mess!

After ten years of fighting the barbarians, Roman general Titus returns home with four-fifths of his sons dead (he had 24!). He wants to be emperor, but he may rather retire instead. First he is venerated as prototype of holy tradition, then he is vilified as a damnable traitor. A tragic hero, Titus seems to take macabre pleasure in pursuing revenge to its utmost horror, and then he perishes in the process.

"O brother, speak with possibility." In this quote about feasibility, his brother Marcus begs Titus to be real, to give up living in excessive imagination. Marcus sees his brother's mind unraveling as Titus becomes less balanced and less focused.

Recently, I read on the "Shower Thoughts" website: "If there really are infinite universes with infinite possibilities, Batman is reading a comic book about me." Amedeo Balbi, author of popular science books, has said, "In an infinite universe, every possible event does happen. Not just that: it happens an infinite number of times." As you have no doubt picked up reading these reflections, I am no physicist. I am not sure if there are infinite universes, parallel universes, infinite possibilities, the repetition of history, alternate histories, or de-coherent histories. It boggles my mind just to consider it, but it thrills me, too.

And the idea of "possibility" is intriguing. I am participating in a contemplation series and the centering thought for today was: "My true self contains every possibility." I can agree with that. But at some point, I also believe we have to narrow down our chances.

One idea that I used to teach in theatre appreciation is that as an audience member, you come into the theatre with great anticipation. If you know very little about the play, the experience can be very exciting. You sit down with expectancy.

Then the curtain rises. At that moment, on the stage, there are infinite possibilities. Anything could happen in this play! But very soon, as you note the scenery, as you hear some music, as you are introduced to the first few characters, as you observe the costumes, as you pay attention to the unfolding action, probabilities start narrowing.

The play seems to be fairly realistic: there will be very few theatrical shenanigans. The actors appear somber and serious: there will be infrequent episodes of comedy. Large bouncy elephants are unlikely, as are multimedia effects, Brechtian placards, songs, or direct explanations to the audience about why the characters are eating supper. About ten minutes into the play, the possibilities become more finite.

Our lives are a bit like that. Though I do think my authentic self carries within me all possibilities, I cannot pursue every one of them. Titus was having trouble focusing, but that is just what I must do — and I have to act. The *Upanishads* reminds me of this concept as I read this message on an affirmation card every morning: "As is my desire, so is my intention. As is my intention, so is my will. As is my will, so is my deed. As is my deed, so is my destiny."

November 6:
"Do you see that tree? It is dead but it still sways in the wind with the others. I think it would be like that with me. That if I died I would still be part of life in one way or another."
Tuzenbakh in Anton Chekhov's *Three Sisters*

I just had three dead trees cut down in my yard this past week. They no longer sway in the wind, as I was fearful that if they did, one of them would topple onto my neighbor's house. *Three Sisters*, by Russian author and playwright Anton Chekhov, is one of his pinnacle stage works, along with *The Cherry Orchard*, *The Seagull*, and *Uncle Vanya*. Written at the turn of the twentieth century, the work debuted the next year at the Moscow Art Theatre in 1901.

Three Sisters concerns the Prozorov family, members of whom are discontent and annoyed with life, and hoping to find meaning at the fin de siècle. Opening on the first anniversary of their father's death, the naturalistic play exposes the aimlessness of the wealthy class in Russia as it deteriorates and begins to vanish. Konstantin Stanislavski, the Russian actor and theatre director who first staged Three Sisters once said, "Chekhov often expressed his thought not in speeches but in pauses or between the lines or in replies consisting of a single word... the characters often feel and think things not expressed in the lines they speak."

Roger and I last month enjoyed Birmingham Festival Theatre's production of Christopher Durang's *Vanya and Sonia and Masha and Spike*, a play that originally opened in 2012. Not three sisters, but a trio of siblings make up this family, with Vanya (the gay brother) and Sonia (the adopted sister) who live on their "family estate" in Bucks County, Pennsylvania, supported by their second-rate movie star sister Masha. They were all named for characters in Chekhov's plays by their now-deceased university professor parents who were community theatre aficionados.

Our play program noted that according to Durang, "My play is not a Chekhov parody... I take Chekhov scenes and characters and put them into a blender." The show depicts how the middle-aged but immature Vanya and Sonia while away their time quietly conversing about basically nothing, contemplating vanished hopes, and wondering if their grove of nine cherry trees is an actual orchard or not.

When the overly dramatic Masha shows up with her very young boy-toy Spike, she threatens to sell the ancestral home, evoking the theme of loss from *The Cherry Orchard*. These preeminent local actors were exceptionally good at evoking a Chekhovian mood of pensiveness with a subtext of discontent — in a very funny way.

But back to *Three Sisters* instead of Three Siblings. In the play, Tuzenbakh is a nobleman and Lieutenant who is admirable in his own cordial and sincere way. Leaving the army to marry the youngest sister Irina, he is a philosopher as can be seen in his line likening himself to the dead tree swaying with the others. *"I think it would be like that with me. That if I died I would still be part of life in one way or another."*

His idea in some way reminds me of the hymn "Lord of the Dance." The last verse, which is Christ talking, goes, "'They cut me down and I leapt up high, I am the life that'll never, never die; I'll live in you if you'll live in me; I am the Lord of the Dance,' said he." I think more and more that all of the universe, the stars, the planets, our earth, the creatures and plants, and we humans are all one, and remain part of life somehow, whether we are alive, or dead.

November 7:
"Hell is other people."
Garcin in Jean-Paul Sartre's *No Exit*

No Exit, which debuted in Paris's *Vieux-Colombier Theatre* as *Huis Clos* in the spring 1944, is probably Jean-Paul Sartre's most famous and most intriguing play. According to several sources, Sartre created the work in the one-act format so that the audience could get home before a Nazi-established curfew just before the French liberation toward the end of World War II. Plays and other entertainment were held under scrutiny by German censors, and *No Exit* was almost kept from its premiere several times during rehearsals.

Opening as a Valet escorts three newly deceased characters, Garcin, Estelle, and Inez, into a curious room (Hell), the play portrays a trio who can do nothing but create eternal torture for each other. Each of the people needs someone else to define their individuality and life purpose, but as often happens in real life, each attracts the opposite.

After the War, *No Exit* premiered on Broadway in 1946, to mixed critical reviews and varied audience appreciation. Critic Stark Young called Sartre's work "a phenomenon of the modern theatre," and quipped that, "It should be seen whether you like it or not."

The play was recorded in 1965, and Sartre gave a talk that explained his famous phrase. "'Hell is other people' has always been misunderstood," he said. "It has been thought that what I meant by that was that our relations with other people are always poisoned, that they are invariably hellish relations. But what I really mean is something totally different. I mean that if relations with someone else are twisted, vitiated, then that other person can only be hell. Why?"

Sartre explained that when we envision our self, we are often misled by other people's views of us. He insisted that he does not "mean that one cannot have relations with other people. It simply brings out the capital importance of all other people for each one of us."

Maybe too much importance — until we learn to rely on our own internal guidance system. To me, the play screams the need for each individual to do holy work, self-contemplation, self-discovery: to go inside themselves and find their true essence. Though we need other people and I believe in community, we do not have to be defined by other people, by the circumstances of our birth, by our bad life choices, by egoic behaviors.

One of the hardest lessons I had to learn when I became a single person and mother was that no one could make me feel bad or happy or mad or upset. I truly believed other people had the power to me miserable. One day, I heard Wayne Dyer on an audio book say: "No one can create anger or stress within you, only you can do that by virtue of how you process the world." I was mad at Dr. Dyer for almost a year until I was able to unravel that idea and realize how true and liberating that thought really is!

Hell is other people if we let other people's mirroring of us take us to that conclusion. And that is what Sartre was trying to say with his play.

November 8:
"As long as man can believe in music, I'll believe in the future of mankind."
Albert Einstein in by Willard Simms's *Einstein, A Stage Portrait*

When *Einstein: A Stage Portrait* premiered in 1984, the playwright Willard Simms directed the one-man show in Los Angeles. Simms, whose script has been performed all over the world from Italy to Zimbabwe, from Scotland to Argentina, has said, "The indomitable spirit of the man who was the greatest scientist in the world, yet believed that morality was always more important than science, will always be universal."

The action takes place in the year 1946. The atomic bomb has been dropped, impacting the history and future of the earth. Wanting to explain his part in and thoughts about the event, Einstein has asked the audience over for some personal time, spiced with soul-searching, violin music, and his impish humor.

He talks about the Germans (after immigrating to the United States), their discovery of properties of uranium, and his remorse for suggesting that American scientists explore the destructive power of nuclear fission. He later regretted a communication about this to President Franklin D. Roosevelt, and, in fact, said, "The release of atom power has changed everything except our way of thinking... the solution to this problem lies in the heart of mankind. If only I had known, I should have become a watchmaker."

Though Jewish by birth, Einstein chose to be labeled an agnostic. "My religion," he once said, "consists of a humble admiration of the illimitable superior spirit who reveals himself in the slight details we are able to perceive with our frail and feeble mind."

Being an amateur musician, playing both the violin and the piano, he thought science and art were closely aligned. *As long as man can believe in music, I'll believe in the future of mankind,"* he professes in the play. And he thought that the greatest of scientists are also artists.

To him, scientific insight did not rise from logic or mathematics, but — as it does for artists — from creativity, inspiration, and intuition. "The most beautiful thing we can experience is the mysterious. It is the source of all true art and all science," he said.

How true! I am no scientist, but I have worked in the arts all my life. When we are deeply absorbed in recasting verbs in a poem or brushing strokes on a canvas, performing a plié at a barre or sliding a bow across the strings of a viola, something happens to us. We fall into the mystery of eternal time, merging with the divine, becoming a conduit, discovering something beyond what we thought were our limits. We are freed from the mundane and move into a place where our souls soar, where our hearts open, and where our wisdom increases.

As Einstein put it, "He to whom this emotion is a stranger, who can no longer pause to wonder and stand rapt in awe, is as good as dead: his eyes are closed." It is a shame that school systems that have shut down arts programs so their students can concentrate the "more important" subjects of math and science don't listen to the greatest physicist of the twentieth century, and maybe of all time.

November 9:
"I think it's a mistake to ever look for hope outside of one's self."
Holga in Arthur Miller's *After the Fall*

In *After the Fall,* American playwright Arthur Miller surely seems to be working through the suicide of Marilyn Monroe, his former wife, though he vehemently repudiated that idea. A difficult play to produce in its three and a half hour length, theatre critics have not looked favorably on its performances, though it is an intelligent and well-written script to read.

Directed by Elia Kazan, the play debuted in New York City the day before my fourteenth birthday, on January 23, 1964, almost two years after Monroe's death. I think it takes a while and a lot of work to get through the suicide of someone you love. After just going through such a death with the family member of one friend, I have just gotten the dreadful news of the self-destruction of another friend's young nephew in such a grisly fashion it is hard to think about.

The title of Miller's work refers to the struggle to endure in a fallen world, echoing the biblical fall from Eden. The action takes place after the Depression, World War II, the Holocaust, and the Red Scare, so he is dealing with some twentieth century history that illustrates a massive plummet in the human condition. Quentin, the main character, has been a successful attorney, but after a self-appraisal begins to sense his own loss of innocence. He can find no God to adjudicate his life, and he feels estranged.

But then, Quentin and his fiancée Holga visit a Nazi concentration camp and he is horrified that so many humans were subjected to such savagery by fellow members of their race. What leads people to such shameful conduct? What could anyone have done to help?

"I think it is a mistake to ever look for hope outside of yourself," Holga says to him. I, too, believe that happiness and hope must come from inside. But what about someone whose mind is not functioning properly? If he has no hope, mightn't he seek it outside of himself? Mightn't someone lead him to a place, a person, a habit, a treatment, a chemical of help, and hope?

In the play, Quentin is steered like that. He has been rejected by first wife, Louise, and has lost his anguished second wife Maggie to suicide. Holga's calm presence and strength help him begin to see his own conflicted spirit and to realize how he affects other people.

She tells him about a disturbing recurring dream about an infirm child she had near the end of the war when she just wanted to die. The baby kept climbing into her lap, clutching her frantically. Holga eventually came up with the idea that if she just kissed the child, she would discover part of herself in that baby. When she could own that, she could sleep again. *"And I bent to its broken face,"* she says, *"and it was horrible. But I kissed it. I think, Quentin, one must finally take one's life into one's own arms, and kiss it."*

External life might be a beautiful sunrise and freshly baked cinnamon rolls one day, and a terrible house fire the next. If hope comes from the travails and delights of outside stimulus, faith and trust will be ever fading one day and surging the next. All of our lives are a blend of broken and beautiful, and we, like Holga, must finally just kiss and appreciate what we have. Hope really must come from my ability to accept life and embrace it, and then reach deep down and pull from the Divine Source that is flowing through all humanity if we reach for it.

November 10:
"Sally, I've been all over the country, and there is New York, isolated neighborhoods in Boston, and believe me, the rest is all the South."
Matt Friedman in Lanford Wilson's *Talley's Folly*

Lanford Wilson's second in a cycle of dramas, *Talley's Folly*, opened in 1979, and we mounted the play in the spring of 1997. Interestingly, the action is contained in one act, played without an intermission, and lasting just over an hour and a half, paralleling exactly the time spent in the action of the play itself.

Talley's Folly, which won the Pulitzer Prize for Drama in 1980, has just one setting, an old boathouse near Lebanon, Missouri, where Sally Talley and Matt Friedman sort out their romance in 1944. Most critics and scholars call the Victorian shed the third character in the play, and John Lee Beatty's original set for the romantic comedy is an icon of twentieth century stage design.

A "folly" in architecture is a structure built for decoration or exaggerated ornamentation in a garden or landscape. This one has louvers and lattice embellishing its Gothic Revival gingerbread design, and is, as the playwright notes, "covered by a heavy canopy of maple and surrounded by almost waist-high weeds and the slender, perfectly vertical limbs of a weeping willow."

So the setting, and even the lighting and sound, are supposed to be very romantic: a sunset at the opening, moonlight slanting through ceiling gaps later, and water reflecting its river ripples across the inside of the room. That description sounds very Southern and brings up Matt's line, *"Sally, I've been all over the country, and there is New York, isolated neighborhoods in Boston, and believe me, the rest is all the South."*

I live in the South, the Deep South. Along with Mississippi, Alabama falls dead last in so many lists and surveys that we who live here can hardly believe it. We love where we live, yet there are people in this country who truly believe Alabamians are barefoot and (if female) pregnant, living without running water or proper electricity. We are a very conservative state in many ways; yet, I wonder why almost everyone who moves here falls in love with us and remains here?

Edward L. Ayers, in a virginia.edu document, remembers that a Virginia native "who went to Harvard in the early 1980s fantasized about putting a sign around his neck to foreclose some of the questions he repeatedly faced, or imagined he faced: 'Yes, I am from the South. No, I do not know your uncle in Mobile. No, I was not born there. Both of my parents, in fact, are literate. No, I do not like Molly Hatchet. No, I do not watch "Hee Haw." No, I do not own slaves. No, I do not want any. Thank you very much. Have a nice day.'" He decided that the ploy would fail "because everyone would think someone else had written it for me, probably so I wouldn't have to memorize it."

It is interesting to contemplate that Matt, in *Talley's Folly*, thinks that only New York and isolated neighborhoods in Boston escape being designated "the South." If true, this notion might give Alabama some company.

November 11:
"Everyone knows it, everyone says it,
The regiment above all!
The only one to which everyone gives credit to
In all the taverns of France...
Over there, over there, over there, by Jove!
It is there, it is there, it is there,
The handsome Twenty-first!"
Marie in Gaetano Donizetti's *The Daughter of the Regiment*, with French libretto by Jules-Henri Vernoy de Saint-Georges and Jean-Francois Byard

When the Seattle Opera produced *The Daughter of the Regiment*, their short synopsis was: "Tomboy, unable to transform into snooty duchess, finds true love anyway." This quoted song is performed by Marie, who was adopted as an infant by a regiment who found her on a battlefield. Because of such an unusual circumstance, she has 1,500 fathers and no mother, and has become a "camp girl." In the spring of 1990, Birmingham Opera Theatre performed the French work at Samford and several of us faculty members assisted in the delightful production.

Today is not only Veterans Day, but also popular French saint Martin of Tours' feast day. The date for Veterans Day was picked as

November 11 because it is the anniversary of the armistice that ended the World War I signed in 1918. But it is interesting that the date also celebrates Roman soldier Martin, whose father had also been a veteran officer.

Martin did not serve long, because of a mystical happening. As he walked toward the gates of Amiens one day, he was confronted by an impoverished man. Immediately, he cut his military cloak in two and gave part of it to the beggar. Later, Jesus came to Martin in a dream, dressed in the partial cape and Martin overheard Jesus say to the angels: "Martin, who is still but a catechumen, clothed me with this robe." The saint later became a monk and bishop.

My maternal grandfather fought in the trenches during the First World War, and received gunshot in a shoulder that never fully healed, and complications from mustard gas. It is interesting that St. Martin's popularity climbed during the First World War, possibly because a number of priests served the French troops as chaplains. When the armistice was signed on this day, the French believed Martin was interceding for the affairs of their country.

As I wrote on October 25, my fourteenth-great grandfather and his brother (Thomas and Robert deBolron) fought for the English in the Battle of Agincourt in 1415, and were given land as a result of the victory. Longbow blood flows in my veins, and I call myself a Daughter of the Battle of Agincourt.

My paternal family name "Sloan" is a long-established surname in Scotland and Northern Ireland, and is an Anglicized form of the Old Gaelic "Sluaghadhan," leader of a military expedition or raid. My father, in fact, served in World War II, the Korean War, and Vietnam.

Despite all this warrior-like lineage, and maternal and paternal families of soldiers, I deplore war. The idea of a daughter adopted by a regiment is romantic. The sight of soldiers in their uniforms is attractive. The phenomenon of wartime camaraderie is intriguing. But why do leaders of nations continue to be led by their unconscious ego selves?

Presently, mental and behavioral psychologists, scientists, and health researchers believe that long-term consequences of war and violence can be transmitted as stress in humans for four generations. Americans today, then are able to feel in our bodies the effects of battles all the way back through current skirmishes, Vietnam, Korea, and the two world wars — even back to the Civil War. When can we break this chain of suffering?

November 12:

"Such an outrage! We two women
Suffer from this man of lust.
So insulting, all his scheming
Fills me only with disgust.
But our honest name, our honor,
Soon shall be avenged, my friend!
Woman, when the mood is on her.
Sure and artful means will find!"

Mrs. Page and Mrs. Ford in Otto Nicolai's *The Merry Wives of Windsor*, with a German libretto by Salomon Hermann Mosenthal, based on the play by William Shakespeare

In the fall of 1983, Samford University Opera produced *The Merry Wives of Windsor* a three-act opera by Otto Nicolai and I was fortunate enough to design the costumes. The opera is what is called in Germany a *Singspiel*, or "song play," a drama with not only interludes of ballads, songs, and arias, but dances and magical happenings.

This particular opera is based on a play by William Shakespeare and has several layers of comedic underpinnings. *Merry Wives* concerns two already married lady friends, named in German Frau Fluth and Frau Reich, and based on the original Mistress Alice Page and Mistress Margaret Ford. Both are courted by none other than the lascivious, exuberant, fat, destitute rogue Sir John Falstaff. Both women receive a love letter from the rascal, and as soon as they grasp the duplicitousness, they resolve to break his heart and drive him into contrition.

Many critics bemoan the characterization of Falstaff in this play and opera, believing him to be a wan ghost of the man he is in the history works. However, he still projects a bigger than life personality, brimming with great faith in his own attractiveness and ability to woo women. He needs money and thinks he can use his supposed irresistibility to finagle some of the wives' gold.

In some of my Enneagram presentations, I use Falstaff as the embodiment of the Ego Type Seven. He is jolly, gregarious, and a drinker who is hooked on the sack he uses to avoid pain. He is a great speechifier who not only loves to hear himself talk, but can also chatter himself out of most of the trouble he gets himself into. But Shakespeare, knowing that humans are a ball of incongruous opposites, created him as a complex character who habitually lies yet deludes himself as well as others, is boastful and yet humorous in self-examination, lazy and yet full of imaginative explanations, cowardly and yet unshrinking in his bravado, dishonest and yet able to see the humor in his own mischievous actions.

Having studied *Henry IV, parts One* and *Two* in college with my favorite English teacher, I learned to love Falstaff despite all his faults and foibles. In the history plays, the Prince at one point observes that his chubby companion "lards the lean earth as he walks along." But his sweaty fatness makes his rather unforgivable vices somehow endearing.

Theodore Dalrymple — an English doctor, psychiatrist, and cultural critic — wrote an *Arts and Culture* article in 2015 entitled "Why We Love Falstaff." In it, he says, "Falstaff in the abstract is abominable: a thief, a coward, a liar, a poltroon, an eternal sponger, and a parasite. We should hate and despise him, but we love him. He enriches our life. Reflection on this paradox by itself can preserve us from what George Orwell, in his essay on Dickens, called the smelly little orthodoxies that are now contending for our souls. To hate Falstaff is to hate humanity (to 'banish all the world'), for there is some of Falstaff in all of us."

November 13:
In "Remember Who You Art" from *The Lion King*, Mufasa and Simba sing about how we change over the years, but can recollect our true being. (Listen to the work online or from your library!)

Mufasa and Simba in Disney's *The Lion King*, with music by Elton John, lyrics by Tim Rice, and book by Roger Allers and Irene Mecchi, along with additional music and lyrics by Lebo M, Mark Mancina, Jay Rifkin, Julie Taymor, and Hans Zimmer, based on the Disney animated feature film of the same name

The Lion King musical premiered at the Orpheum Theatre in Minneapolis, Minnesota on July 8, 1997, and became immensely popular even before moving to the New Amsterdam Theatre for previews on Broadway October 15, 1997, and actually opening on November 13, 1997.

The work was directed and designed in part by Julie Taymor, whose work I had admired since seeing Juan Darian, A Carnival Mass off-Broadway in the late 1980s. That work — with her incredible masks, puppets, and unusual costumes and scenery — inspired my then-husband-design-partner and I to expand our vision of what could be done on stage and led to an experimental musical we wrote and designed called *The Cry of the Cockatrice*.

I didn't see *The Lion King* on Broadway until 2005 when my daughter Elin and I took a trip to New York City. We had hoped to visit with one of my all-time favorite students Sammy Ledbetter, who was the Company Manager when the musical opened on Broadway, but he had gone to London to manage *Sweeney Todd*. We thought the musical was as magical as we had imagined it might be.

Even today I remember sitting in the movie theatre with my kids on the day before Thanksgiving the year *The Lion King* film first debuted in 1994. Seeing a new magical film during this holiday season remains a favorite family tradition. Mufasa's Ghost in the movie — and the musical — tells his son Simba that by forgetting himself and his life's purpose, he fails to recall and honor his father.

This spirit of a lion might as well be talking directly to me, and maybe you, at points in our lives when we get so out of tune with our true self, we forget who we are and what we might be able to accomplish in our life times. Mufasa encourages Simba to affirm his part in life's great big moving wheel.

If you have given up your dreams, if your spirit has shrunk to the size of a sugar ant, if your best characteristics seem to have slipped away, take the advice given Simba and look inside yourself and claim your role. A great exercise we use in teaching the Enneagram for The Institute for Conscious Being is to remember yourself at age four or five in your backyard, room, or a favorite spot. See the child, remember the spirit of the child, talk to the child, listen to the child.

Can you go back? Can you find the person you used to be? Can you remember who you really are? Musicals and films like *The Lion King* can remind us to leave our shadowy selves behind and jump courageously into some new adventure.

Recently, a new photorealistic computer-animated remake of Disney's *Lion King* has been released. I haven't seen it yet, but maybe I should ask Elin and Seth to accompany me — for a sit through memory lane, and for a renewal of our engagement with life.

November 14

"*Ill the wind, ill the time, uncertain the profit, certain the danger.*
O late late late, late is the time, late too late, and rotten the year;
Evil the wind, and bitter the sea, and grey the sky, grey grey grey."

Chorus in TS Eliot's *Murder in the Cathedral*

I know, I know, I've already quoted *Murder in the Cathedral* several times and talked about the production we created in 1980. More than likely, I could write an entire day book using only quotes from this play! I loved it so much while working on it that the lines really do come back to me day after day after day.

Here it is fall in Alabama. It has been a rather balmy one, and the leaves have refused to turn color until just the last few days. And now, guess what! The weather forecast calls for twenty-degree weather tonight and several nights next week. *"Ill the wind,"* indeed. *"...And grey the sky, grey grey grey."*

It is so blustery out today that all of the freshly metamorphosed leaves will be off the trees before we have had a chance to soak in the flame red of the sumac and sugar maples, the buttery yellow of the mulberry and chestnut, the deep burgundy of the dogwood and sassafras.

"O late late late, late is the time, late too late, and rotten the year..." It is getting late in the year, but it hasn't been a rotten one for me, and I don't think it is ever *"late too late."* Sometimes I wake up in the middle of the night and my mind is whirling about not getting everything done that I want to accomplish in life, that I want to leave as a legacy, that I want to fulfill as my visions.

But, I keep a daily journal, and I was just thinking of all the new adventures I have had this past ten months: I lost 25 pounds; I went to a conference to hear Richard Rohr, Rob Bell, and Ilia Delio; I have explored several new crafts and art projects; I bought new furniture for my Great Hall; I helped raise money for a wonderful charity; and I have committed part of every day to write these musings. And that is just a few things off the top of my head.

A few weeks ago, Marianne Williamson was on *Super Soul Sunday* and talked about running for office in California's 33rd Congressional District last year. After a couple of decades at the front of what is sometimes called "a worldwide spiritual movement aimed at creating a global shift in collective consciousness," Williamson tried something new at age 61.

She talked about stepping out of our comfort zones, and continuing to do so no matter how old we are. Risks are tough at any age. "The challenge of age is not to skip life's disappointments but to transcend them," she said on the show. Doing something new is like giving birth. "It has to do with who your self is," she says. "Because spiritually, you know, enlightenment is a shift in self-identification from body identification to spirit identification."

"Uncertain the profit, certain the danger," the Chorus cautions me! But, you know, that is okay. At any age, life can be a scramble; however, it seems that the more I struggle, the more power I have to transform — and that brings joy and gladness. I have rarely been cautious about the uncertainty leaving my comfort behind. Why don't you step out and do something daring today?

November 15
"I am amazed and know not what to say."
Hermia in William Shakespeare's A *Midsummer Night's Dream*, Act III, Scene 2

A strong female character in this fairy play, Hermia stands up for herself in a patriarchal society. Her first gutsy move is to tell her father just exactly who she wants to marry, Lysander and not his preferred Demetrius — and she says so right in front of Duke Theseus. Thereafter, she flees to the forest with her beloved Lysander, but boldly, and for chastity's sake, won't let him settle down anywhere near her for their evening of sleep.

A *Midsummer Night's Dream* is known for Shakespeare's intertwining of four related plots: the preparations for the marriage of Duke Theseus to Hippolyta, the enchanted adventures of two sets of young lovers in the woods, the rehearsing of a crude play by some comical mechanicals, and the magical meddling of the fairies in the affairs of all these humans.

Hermia's line is said soon after her best friend Helena refuses to trust her anymore and her beloved Lysander calls her names. Well, what he actually says is, "Get you gone, you dwarf, You minimus of hindering knotgrass made, You bead, you acorn!" What a great putdown, and in itself worthy of memory to spout to someone at some point. However, these words are not what you want to hear from your sweetheart. The young lovers, all of them, are bewitched by the fairies, and when Helena and Lysander run away from her, Hermia cries, *"I am amazed and know not what to say."*

Of all the verbiage I have and will cite in this book, this quote is one of the most useful! We all have embarrassing moments every now and then. Some of us, every month (or week) or so. We knock on the wrong door in the condo when going to deliver a meal to a sick friend. Our mother bumps into a bundle of balloons at a restaurant birthday party and says, "Oh, excuse me, hon!" The cleaning lady, peering at the thin, blousy disguise of our overweight belly, exclaims, "Oh, I know what carrying a baby is like. Bless your heart!" My personal recent favorite was running into a glass wall that I thought was a free clear space. What to say when this happens is always a conundrum. Consider these possibilities:

Your coworker texts you, thinking you are his boyfriend. Just message back: *"I am amazed and know not what to say."*

You are checking out with a full buggy at the grocery store and realize you left your debit card at home by the computer while purchasing something online: *"I am amazed and know not what to say."*

At a function, the host is excited to introduce you to her guest of honor. You round the corner with her, and it is your ex: *"I am amazed and know not what to say."*

The imbroglio might not go away immediately, but at least you won't be at a loss for words. And, you are quoting Shakespeare!

November 16:

In "My Favorite Things" from *The Sound of Music*, Maria sings a catalog of her best-loved personal objects and natural observations. (Listen to the work online or from your library!)

Maria in *The Sound of Music*, a musical with music by Richard Rodgers, lyrics by Oscar Hammerstein II, and a book by Howard Lindsay and Russel Crouse, based on the memoir of Maria von Trapp, *The Story of the Trapp Family Singers*

It is 40 days till Christmas and already, holiday tunes have been playing on some radio stations and in malls and restaurants for weeks. In an early scene in *The Sound of Music*, the postulant for holy orders, Maria expresses regret for warbling in the garden. Only in a musical would the Mother Abbess then join her in singing another number, "My Favorite Things." Because the tune is filled with lovely winter visions of snow crystals, shiny kitchen pots, jingle sounds, gloves, and beribboned presents, the piece has become a hugely popular holiday hit.

But as Wikipedia, the free encyclopedia notes, "The happy, optimistic lyrics ... are just a counterpoint and cover up an undercurrent of fear... The song was written to be sung by a young woman scared of facing new responsibilities outside the convent."

Mary Martin and Theodore Bikel starred in the original Broadway show, which debuted this day in 1959. As the curtains open, Maria wonders if the life of a nun is right for her, and when she takes a governess job to discern what her future might hold, she becomes infatuated with her new charges, the von Trapp children — and later falls in love with their widowed father. A captain, he is commanded to assume service in the German navy. Because von Trapp is disillusioned by the Nazis, he leads an escape from their Austrian homeland.

My daughter Elin helped make costumes — many, many nuns' habits — for her high school's production of *The Sound of Music* during her sophomore year. She was too busy singing in four choirs to be in the production, but she would come home and croon all the tunes from the show, most of which even now remain highly popular after 60 years since the musical opened.

The refrain of this song is sung a couple of times and some people complain that it reflects a juvenile view of life using overly optimistic platitudes about staying positive even when a dog sinks his teeth into us. But I have learned in spiritual readings and practices that remembering the good, favorite things in our lives, or being grateful, quiets my ego, which, when rampant, is convinced that my red wasp attack is the worst anyone could possibly have.

As Wayne Dyer has said, "Gratitude and humility send signals to all who meet us that we're all connected to something larger than life itself." About this time of year, Oprah Winfrey comes up with an inventory of 80 or more "Favorite Things," glorious items to give as Christmas gifts. Right now, my own list of dearest items would include my sweet little FitBit step tracker, a small piece of fresh perfectly fried chicken, the azure ceramic lamp in my bedroom that used to be my grandmother's, the medieval tapestries on my walls snagged at several Liberty of London's after-Christmas sales, the amazing *Pocketful of Miracles* daybook by Joan Borysenko, my electric heating pad, a Bear Bryant Roll Tide frosted candle holder, my morning routine, an aromatic cup of French Press coffee, Mozart or Beatle music, tiny violets growing in my green grass. I could go on and on. How about you?

November 17:
"The three little kittens, they lost their mittens,

And they began to cry,
'Oh, mother dear, we sadly fear,
That we have lost our mittens.'
'What! Lost your mittens, you naughty kittens!
Then you shall have no pie.'
'Meow, meow, meow.'
'Then you shall have no pie.'"
Using the actual words from the children's book classic
The Narrator and Kittens in *The Three Little Kittens* with book and lyrics
by Jean Pierce and score by Jay Tumminello

Speaking yesterday of "whiskers on kittens," in 1999, I designed costumes and scenery for Birmingham Children's Theatre's fun production for wee folks, *The Three Little Kittens*. Then, a couple of years ago, I took my granddaughter Emmeline to see a new presentation of the same script. It is a great show for preschoolers, staged in BCT's intimate downstairs flexible theatre space.

In the show, the heroine, Katie Sue, seems to continuously lose some of her things: a lunchbox, her gym socks, a blue crayon. Hmmmmm. In a parallel to the kittens of Mother Goose fame, she loses her mittens, making her mother fairly upset. And like the kittens, if she can't find her mittens, she can't eat any pie. In an innovative plot device, Katie Sue enters the Land of Lost and Found and, with the help of her three furry kitten friends, discovers that most problems can be solved with a little bit of thinking.

In doing a little research on the poem when I created the costumes in 1999, I found that the story more than likely originated in folk tales of Britain. However, the poem as we know it today is credited to a Sunday school teacher and abolitionist from New England, Eliza Lee Cabot Follen, who lived from 1787 to 1860. As a member of a distinguished Boston family, she put her own genteel spin on the work. According to Janet Sinclair Gray, author of *Race and Time*, these kitties are not farm felines or alley cats, but domesticated urban pets who are accustomed to munching on pies and dressing in mittens and little suits of clothing. Mother Cat's authoritative training and demand of strict obedience definitely bespeak their middle class positions in life.

In the poem, the kittens are called "naughty," "silly," and "good." And while I must admit I have used all those adjectives on my own children, now that I am helping rear grandchildren, if I ever say, "good girl" or "good boy," the phrase grates on my very last nerve and if I hear it coming, I bite my tongue. Sometimes it comes out and I muddle through changing the phrase to something else very quickly.

I now know that qualifying a child – or even one of her actions – as "good" really fails to instill any sort of dignity in her self. Really, it probably does the reverse. Number one, if Emmeline hears "good girl!" when she performs in an outstanding way, she will think when she fails at something she is "bad." Secondly, if I call some deed "good," I am making an editorial comment on the action rather than letting her say whether or not it is "good."

These days I am more likely to simply thank Emmeline if she lends a hand or tell her how happy it makes me if she performs well on a task. When I own how I feel about her efforts, she actually gets feedback, and begins to understand how her actions impact other people. Though I am old enough to want to have my grandchildren do things simply to please me, I am also old enough to understand that is not the most supportive way to help them grow in a healthy way.

November 18:
In "Whatever Time We Have" from *Children of Eden*, Eve sings about trusting in new opportunities after failure. (Listen to the work online or from your library!)
Eve in *Children of Eden* with music and lyrics by Stephen Schwartz and a book by John Caird

Our Eve at Samford University had green hair – or was it blue at the time? This creative and engaging student changed the color of her long tresses quite often and I can't remember in the spring of 1998 what shade she used. The joyous and sweeping *Children of Eden*, with its cast of fifty or more and its derivation from the Old Testament, was a perfect choice for a university with Baptist ties.

The fellow who played the Father was new to the faculty and later a good friend, Alan Gardner. He was an energetic and powerful Equity actor who gave the role the punch it needed. Based on the book of Genesis, the musical starts in the first act with the Creation story, and continues with Noah and the Flood in the second. The play has an unusual history, originally created in 1986 for a youth theatre camp production in Illinois. Later, composer Stephen Schwartz reworked the script and music crafting it into a full-length musical.

451

In January of 1991, the show opened in London's West End after being developed further in workshops by the Royal Shakespeare Company. With less than stellar reviews, *Children of Eden* closed three months later, and never played Broadway, though it is popular with university and community theatres.

Shining through the work is a theme of family relationships, and parents dealing with willful, obstinate children who bring about catastrophic disasters — both earthly and heavenly. Near the end of the play, Father and Noah sing about the fact that once a seed starts sprouting, you can't push the greenery back into the shell, paralleling the growth of our children. The men decide that the most difficult part of the parent-child relationship is letting our kids go off on their own.

Which brings me back to Eve's idea of second chances. We humans are somehow prone to mistakes. Sometimes our errors are slight, sometimes our screw-ups are horrendous. We are imperfect beings, and I often wonder how we make it through a day or a week or a year without blundering and miscarrying more than we do.

A friend of mine had a wonderful partner who uncharacteristically and abruptly left him for someone else. After a year or so, my friend had several minor heart attacks and was in the hospital twice for treatment and medication adjustment. During the illness, his former partner came back into his life and asked for a second chance at the relationship.

I think both of them are very brave: the one for admitting a mistake and asking for forgiveness, and the other for taking a risk and opening back up his heart. So many people acquiesce to their egos rather than realizing that the hardest, the rarest, the truest part of love is letting go — not of the person. Letting go of the hurt, of the dispute, of the animosity.

My friend's heart attacks constituted a physical metaphor for what was going on in his life. His heart was broken, and yet it became a guide toward courage. The root of the word "courage" is "cor," which is Latin for "heart." His logical ego mind may have warned him to bolt from a restart. But the heart wants to move toward forgiveness and reconciliation. Eve, and my friend, are heart people. They believe in allowing relationships to be born again.

November 19:

"Why, Ma, you're good lookin'! We always said you were good-lookin' – and besides, you're the best ma we could ever have."
Beulah in Thornton Wilder's *The Happy Journey to Camden and Trenton*

In Thornton Wilder's short play presented on an absolutely bare stage, very little really happens. Arthur and Caroline accompany Ma and Pa to see their married sister Beulah in Camden. The journey is in a make-believe car created from four chairs, and the actors bounce and swerve around as if they are really riding in a 1930s automobile.

The family laughs and reminisces, the kids ask numerous questions as they pass road signs, they sing and joke. But mostly, they teach us how to live in the present moment. What if all family vacations could yield such a profound appreciation of little things in life: flowers by the roadside, hotdogs fresh from a stand, stars appearing in the sky?

Beulah, who has just lost a baby in childbirth, and her mother have a lovely exchange at the end of the play in which the daughter begs her mother to just sit a while. "You always get the fidgets when we try and pet yuh, Mama," she says. And Ma says it is foolish for them to want to cuddle an old bag of bones. Beulah protests, *"Why, Ma, you're good lookin'! We always said you were good-lookin' – and besides, you're the best ma we could ever have."*

I remember my son Seth once giving me a card on which he had written, "You are the best Mom I ever had." *Mommie Dearest*, Christina Crawford's tell-all biography about her famous actress mother Joan, was published in 1978, two years after the birth of my daughter, Elin. The ironic title has come to exemplify a self-serving mother with little inborn nurturing tendencies. Because the memoir was talked about for years, the concept of using an endearing term in spite of bad parenting was always in my brain. Partially due to the book, I never let my children call me "Mommy," but steered them to "Mama" or "Mom."

By the time Seth was three or four, and I had some mothering techniques down, I jokingly suggested they start calling me "Dearest Darling Mother." "Darling" to me was a reminder of Barrie's beloved family of *Peter Pan* fame, and I just thought it was a funny moniker. At the age of twelve, Elin was horrified by the idea and bristled about using the title, even in jest. But it somehow resonated with Seth and he began to employ it when he wanted something very badly, or when he wrote me notes. In fact, even today he starts off an email with "DDM."

I am certainly not sure about the mothering skills, or lack thereof, of Joan Crawford. But I truly hope I am more closely aligned with the mother in *The Happy Journey to Camden and Trenton* — the Ma who comforts the daughter who has just lost a child. The Ma who, despite tragedy, carries on with hope and trust. The Ma who, like my own mother, manages the family in crisis by making sure the trip is planned, the food is ready, and the practical matters are handled. The mother who exits the stage singing a song about the one sheep left in the dark when the ninety-nine were safe in the fold, but who was found by the shepherd and guided home.

November 20:
"Polonius: What do you read, my lord?
Hamlet: Words, words, words."
William Shakespeare's *Hamlet*, Act 2, scene 2

"Words, words, words," Hamlet replies to Polonius when asked what he is reading. A cheeky response to be sure. In William Luce's lovely play *The Belle of Amherst*, Emily admits: "Words are my life. I look at words as if they were entities, sacred beings. There are words to which I lift my hat when I see them sitting on a page."

Words have been a big part of my life. I certainly delight in writing and I relish reading, and, like Emily Dickinson's, my heart thrills when I see certain words: Ebullience. Gargoyle. Labyrinthine. Plethora. Vouchsafe. In this one-woman piece about Dickinson's life, the writer says she looks at words as if they are living creatures, and holy ones at that.

I spent a half a century working in the theatre, and I still even now design costumes, usher, attend, and support local theatres. Actors say lots of words in plays. Just for fun, let's look at the research and design of the 250 of the plays in my career. Let's assume those plays were on the short side and had only 7,500 words each. Still, I have dealt with over two million words studying those plays.

Hamlet says he is simply reading words. Emily Dickinson thinks words are holy, hallowed, blessed. What does that means to me? Why would a word be holy? What words are holy to me?

I remember as a two-, three-, and four-year old, I would visit the house next door to me every morning. In it lived my maternal grandmother, her mother, and three of her four daughters (my mother's sisters). I have mentioned lessons with my great-grandmother. With her, I learned the marvel that words were units of language that actually stood for something in the real world, or in your mind. That was holy to me.

That group of women in that house were all voracious readers who were drawn to words. It was a lively household and word-filled conversations flowed frequently. Scrabble and other word games were common. My mother was addicted to crossword puzzles, and my dad could talk for hours spouting many, many words about every airplane ever created. And he was a ham radio operator, talking and listening to words from all over the world.

I enjoyed English classes in high school and became an English major in college. I fell in love with the *Oxford English Dictionary* and got my own set when I graduated. I've used Word of the Day calendars and received emails furnishing me with a new term every day. All of the words I encountered over all those years blessed me.

Not all the words I use are consecrated. I have work to do to control some of the verbs and nouns that can — seemingly without warning — fly out of my mouth. But maybe curbing or reining in the propensity to cuss will be my new resolution. Maya Angelou never allowed anyone to swear in her home because she believed that words stick to the walls and become the home.

That needs to become my new mantra: "Words stick to the walls and become the home," so that my dwelling becomes as sacred as the "*words, words, words*" spoken here.

November 21:
"*Oh Mother! You should go out and see! There's never been such a sky. Damp clouds have shined it, and soft winds have swept it, as if to make it ready for a king's ball. All its lanterns are lit, all its torches are burning, and its dark floor is shining like crystal. Hanging over our roof, there is a star as large as a window; and the star has a tail, and it moves across the sky like a chariot on fire.*"
This work is in the public domain in the United States because it was published in the United States between 1927 and 1977, inclusive, without a copyright notice.
Amahl in Gian Carlo Menotti's *Amahl and the Night Visitors*

Tonight, we are all going to see my granddaughter Emmeline in the chorus of *Amahl and the Night Visitors*. While teaching and designing at Samford University, I worked on *Amahl* a half-dozen times. The short opera by Gian Carlo Menotti was commissioned by the National Broadcasting Company and debuted on Christmas Eve of 1951 in an NBC studio in Rockefeller Center. It was later on television as the original offering of the Hallmark Hall of Fame.

The opera is about a little lame shepherd boy Amahl, who lives with his mother in poverty. One night, the youngster is enthralled by the night sky, especially *"a star as large as a window; and the star has a tail, and it moves across the sky like a chariot on fire."* His mother accuses him of lying, as he often stretches the truth.

Soon, three strangers dressed in fabulous garments and bearing unbelievable gifts knock on their door. His mother doesn't believe Amahl when he says a king is at the door. They knock again, and then a third time, and finally his mother goes to the door exasperated with her mendacious son and is surprised that he is telling the truth. They ask to rest at their humble home.

While everyone is sleeping, and seeing all the precious cargo, the mother takes a few gold coins, but the page catches her. After hearing the kings are traveling Bethlehem to visit a newborn Child, a King, and the gifts are for him, the mother refuses to keep the money, even when Melchior presents it to her. Amahl then offers his only possession, his little crutch. Upon handing it to the Kings to take to the Child, he finds he can now walk — and skip and jump and dance. The visitors see the healing as a sign from the true King, and Amahl begs to accompany them and give his gift in person.

Menotti said in his notes for the original recording of the opera, "This is an opera for children because it tries to recapture my own childhood. You see, when I was a child I lived in Italy, and in Italy we have no Santa Claus. I suppose that Santa Claus is much too busy with American children to be able to handle Italian children as well. Our gifts were brought to us by the Three Kings, instead."

I love hearing about worldwide holiday customs. In Austria, Luxembourg, Portugal, Switzerland, other parts of Europe and South America, the *Christkind* ("Christ-child") brings gifts — a fairy-like boy with angel wings. Norway and Sweden are visited by *Julenissen* or *Jultomten*, a small Christmas dwarf or gnome. In Spain, it is *Papa Noël*, in the Netherlands St. Nicholas, and in England, Father Christmas.

When a tot, my daughter Elin and my grandmother danced to Christmas music all year long — they never waited for Christmas, or even Advent. Their childlike wonder about the season stretched across the months. Many people in my church favor the Twelve Days of Christmas, and celebrate from Christmas Day to Epiphany.

I celebrate the Twelve Days as well. But, being a pagan and a "saint" together, I also divide my December days between a raucous time of Christmas preparation, plays, and pageants — and a holy Advent quiet time. And I will begin that trek this evening, when I see Emmeline in *Amahl and the Night Visitors*.

November 22:
"Mirror, Mirror on the wall, who's the fairest of them all..."
Queen in a stage adaptation of *Snow White* at Birmingham Children's Theatre

I have designed costumes for *Snow White* at Birmingham Children's Theatre several times. The first couple of shows featured designs straight from my imagination, but the last time, the director wanted to base our work on the Disney film version. Though not totally thrilled with that concept, I did it, because it was not my choice. Directors sometimes listen to their designers, but ultimately, they have the final word on the look of the production.

Today was my day to clean mirrors. It popped up on my housekeeping chart without my even knowing ahead of time that it would correlate to the quote for the day. Before I did that polishing, I worked for an hour in the yard cutting down saplings and pulling honeysuckle, smilax, and other prickly vines. As I gazed into the looking glasses that I was shining, I honestly appeared a good bit more like the huntsman who took Snow White into the woods than the evilly vain Queen who couldn't tolerate having a rival beauty in her life.

Mirrors, those omnipresent functional and decorative objects, are fairly unforgiving reflections of our outer selves. We peer into them to brush teeth or apply makeup in the morning, check hair or tie before a business lunch, examine carbuncles on the back of the leg, wash and moisturize our faces before bed. They betray us at our worst moments and reveal us at our best.

Mirrors are used by barbers and dentists, in flashlights and telescopes, in follow spotlights and baby toys. We could hardly drive our cars without them, and just think what a *discothèque* would be without that shiny, turning ball hanging from the ceiling. The 1969 Apollo 11 spaceflight team deposited a mirror on the moon, still used to reflect laser

457

light from Earth, and able to measure the distance from the Earth to the moon as it computes the round-trip time of the light.

Reflective objects have always fascinated human beings, from Narcissus being captivated by his own image in the water to the magic mirror in the witch's kitchen in Goethe's version of the Faust story. When I created a stage version of an English myth about a cockatrice (who turns people to stone with a piercing glance), I found that the beast will die instantly if it looks at itself in a mirror.

Some people who stare too much in a glass have an inflated self image, and some a deflated one. After all, even though they are uncompromising, mirrors are artificial objects and simply reflect our outside self, not our inside one. If I am too dependent on external indicators, I can lose the grip on my true self fairly rapidly.

Jungian psychologist Dr. Nancy van den Berg-Cook has written about Snow White: "The Queen looks continuously into the mirror, no doubt hoping to get a sense of who she is. She asks it repeatedly about herself, asking in a way for reassurance. She is obsessed with looking because she has no stable sense of self. She doesn't know who or what she is, and thus keeps looking and asking."

Maybe today I will take a look at myself from the inside out, rather than focusing on my mirror image. How about you?

November 23:
"He is not here; he is risen, just as he foretold. Go, announce that he is risen from the sepulcher."
Angels in Anonymous's *The Passion Play*

The Vestry in the Episcopal Church is a group of elected parishioners who administer the affairs of the parish. After a Vestry meeting today, four of us questioned our priest about angels. Well, actually about some of the children being costumed as angels for our Christmas Eve service.

Today is the Feast of Christ the King. The last of the green liturgical hangings were taken down last week, and today the Nave was festooned with white banners and table hangings and the altar party was dressed in white. Next Sunday is the first Sunday in Advent — almost unbelievable.

Jesus is about to be born again. And yet, here is a quotation about his being risen from *The Passion Play*, an old medieval work that Samford produced in the spring of 1998. It was directed by a highly creative student and staged in the gym!

The answer in the quote above is given after Jesus's death and burial. The Angels ask the women coming to check on his body, "Whom do ye seek in the sepulcher, O followers of Christ?" And the Marys answer, "Jesus of Nazareth, the Crucified, O heavenly ones." This question in Latin is *Quem quaeritis?* "Whom do you seek?" and scholars believe the lines originally formed a short drama in the Easter service that later developed into a form of liturgical theatre performed in the church to clarify portions of the Christian story to a non-reading public.

Today, my daughter Elin gave a devotion to our Vestry. In it, she said let's slow down, and be quiet. It's Advent (almost). "What does that look like for you?" she wondered. "What does that look like for me? Some of us may wait and put up our tree on Christmas Eve. Some of us will put up decorations next weekend after Thanksgiving. Some of us will attend an Advent Quiet Day. Some of us have already sneaked a few Crooner Christmas tunes onto our electronic devices.

"I am willing to bet that our ways of commemorating the Advent season will all be different. And they will all be perfect." As Elin said, Advent is a time to make space — space in my home for presents. Space in calendars for times of fun and fellowship. And space in my heart for the new Christ child. "But what will I remove?" she asked. "Broken toys and outgrown clothes? Easy. Wasted time and endless shopping trips? I can probably handle that. Sin, guilt, self loathing? Yes, I think I'd much rather have room for the Baby Jesus."

In the Christian religion, God became incarnate in the flesh of Jesus, and in doing so, emptied the Godself. Knowing this incredible manifestation, Christians through the ages might have realized that everything in the created universe is holy — including us human beings. Everything is connected. Everything — planets, trees, dirt, dogs, and people — all are part of God. Not all churches give us that message. Maybe as we approach this Christmastide, we can look into that space inside and see that God is already there, ready with us to experience Jesus being born again.

November 24:
"He has wings — but he isn't free! I've been free, Father! For one moment — down here on earth — I have been free! When I did what I did, I was free! Free and not afraid!"

I spent the afternoon of January 6, 1994, in the Lyttleton Theatre at the National Theatre complex on the South Bank of London watching a gripping *Machinal* starring an incredible Fiona Shaw on an equally stunning set by Ian MacNeil. *Machinal,* written by American journalist and playwright Sophie Treadwell, was based on the true legal proceedings of murderer Ruth Snyder. Most critics call its 1928 Broadway debut the most significant production of Expressionism ever produced in America.

The Young Woman who is the heroine is living with her mother at the opening of the play, employed as an ordinary stenographer, plodding along with her life. The play's action sounds like the real life story it is — she weds her boss and has a baby, decides her husband is revolting, seeks pleasure with a younger man, decides to murder her husband, is caught and found guilty, and is ultimately put to death in an electric chair. But the style is very unrealistic: flat characters, rapid short scenes, repetitive dialogue, monotonous action, confusion between inward and outward truth, harsh and yet emotional sound effects.

The playwright said that the "Plan" for the show is to tell a story illustrating "the different phases of life that the woman comes in contact with, and in none of which she finds any place, any peace." Critic Paul Taylor wrote of this particular production that the Young Woman "is supposed to be a representative example of the way women are constricted and crushed by a system evolved to suit men. But she comes across, both in the writing and in Fiona Shaw's splendid, unsparing performance, as such a congenital martyr to nerves and high-strung fastidiousness as to constitute a special case."

The sight of Fiona Shaw being starkly electrocuted in the final scene is something that has stuck in my brain. As Taylor said of the unbelievable technical and mechanical resources used — evocative of hell — they were almost unbelievable. "...Truck-stages and hydraulic lifts, false walls, floors and all manner of traps work overtime to create a dark phantasmagoria. Ceilings that do everything but stay put... [and] the trial scene is brilliantly evoked when the huge collage-grid overhead tilts and descends to become a steep, oppressive incline rearing up behind the accused, the judge and officials poking through flaps in the cage. It looks more a prison than a courthouse."

Between the bold design of the scenery and the daring acting of Shaw, the production definitely exhibited the freedom the Young

Woman spoke of in the above quote: *"When I did what I did, I was free! Free and not afraid!"* Some plays don't call for such audacious action, but I remember our theatre design professor at the University of North Carolina at Greensboro saying that if you cannot create a set that gives the audience an experience that matches the script and the acting, then the play should be performed on a bare stage to allow the spectators to imagine the scenery themselves. This set did its job!

November 25:
In "The Trees on the Mountains" from *Susannah*, the title character sings about how nature reflects her disappointment in love. (Listen to the work online or from your library!)
　　Susannah Polk in Carlisle Floyd's opera *Susannah*

While writing this book, I have often had to look up for sure the dates and years that I worked on various productions, but not *Susannah*. Samford performed this Carlisle Floyd opera in early October of 1984, starring a young student named Elizabeth Futral. We had a dress parade on September 27. I was busy that day. Besides getting all those costumes ready for the director to see under stage lighting, I also wrote a story for *Birmingham Magazine*, went to our students' season ticket drive pep rally, picked up my daughter Elin at dance, and went to her third grade open house. None of that is so very odd except that at 5:58 the next morning, I delivered baby Seth. That was a lot to do the day before you have a baby, and probably is why he was born almost a week early.

　　Floyd wrote this music and libretto during the time he was on the piano faculty at Florida State University, adapting it from Chapter 13 of the apocryphal Book of Daniel. In the scriptural version, Susannah, alone bathing in her pond, is observed by two lecherous elders who say they will tell everyone she was involved with a young man if she won't have intercourse with them. Bravely, Susannah refuses to be coerced. Just when she is about to be executed for wantonness, Daniel interjects that the elders should be questioned. When their stories do not match, they are put to death instead of Susannah.

　　Floyd's adaptation moves the tale to the hills of Tennessee and, as in the original version, Susannah Polk, an innocent 18-year old is attacked as a sinner. When the town, not knowing the truth, turns against her, she faces the vigilantes with a shotgun, basically rupturing all connections with everyone she knows.

The New York Music Critics Circle awarded *Susannah* the prize for Best New Opera in 1956 and a production of the piece went to Brussels World Fair in 1958, as the epitome of American culture and music. The song "The Trees on the Mountain" is a hauntingly beautiful and sad song that tells of a false-hearted lover who deserted her, a fire grown cold, and a dark and lonely road up ahead. Even though untrue to her, she wishes her lover would return for just one day.

So, my baby was born, and given the name John Seth. The Seth was for my grandfather's brother. John was for about fourteen different people, including relatives, saints, rock stars, and friends. Every time I hear any of the music from this opera, I think of those few crazy days when I was so busy at work, then abruptly, so engaged in other ways.

Seth was so suddenly here! I knew (even with no testing) that he was a boy, but if for some reason, he had been a girl, I would have named him Susannah to honor the opera in which we were so involved. So here it is now, a couple of days before Thanksgiving, and like in Susannah's song, the leaves are off the trees and the weather is growing cold. And as I think back on that few weeks of activity so long ago, it might be fun if that time could return for 24 hours, as Susannah wishes her beloved could. I went through it in such a blur, I would like to relish the moments a bit!

November 26:
"I will live in thy heart, die in thy lap, and be buried in thy eyes, and moreover I will go with thee to thy uncle's."
Benedick in William Shakespeare's *Much Ado About Nothing*, Act V, Scene 3

Last night we watched a very smart black and white 2012 film version of William Shakespeare's *Much Ado About Nothing*, produced, and directed by Joss Whedon. We liked it quite a bit. It is clever and foolish, sophisticated and slapstick all at the same time. Rotten Tomatoes said about it: "Lighthearted to a fault, *Much Ado About Nothing's* giddy energy and intimate charm make for an entertaining romantic comedy — and a Shakespearean adaptation that's hard to resist." And Roger Ebert called it "one of the best films of the year."

One of the fun parts of this adaptation is that the Elizabethan language is maintained in a modern-day setting of the play. The juxtaposition makes for some funny scenes. Never having designed this play, I have seen productions of it several time over the years. This film brought out the zany verbal and physical wrestling match of the early combative relationship of Benedick and Beatrice more than any version I have ever seen.

The B characters form a second plot in this play which involves another love duo (Claudio and Hero) deceived by a villainous character named Don John. Beatrice, a strong and independent woman, and Benedick, her scornful chauvinistic male counterpart, are actually tricked into falling in love in the play – but fall in love they do, complete with affectionate letters.

More probably, they have loved each other all along and are finally convinced of the truth by all the antics in the play. Toward the end of *Much Ado*, Beatrice is asked to go to her uncle's house where Lady Hero has been falsely accused. Beatrice asks Benedick if he will accompany her, and he vows, *"I will live in thy heart, die in thy lap, and be buried in thy eyes, and moreover I will go with thee to thy uncle's."*

How affectionate that sounds! Some people call it one of the most romantic, poetic lines in literature. In fact, I begged Roger to memorize the line to pledge to me frequently, and he agreed! Humorously sunk into the middle of his sentence is the funny euphemism about dying: in the 16th and 17th centuries "to die" was a metaphor for sexual climax. Despite the clever double entendre, Benedict is truly expressing his amour – he has fallen for Beatrice and she for him; and through their affair, they shed some of their egos and become more well-rounded people; people who even decide to celebrate that love by being wed.

That is what moves us all to go deep inside and rediscover our true selves, right? Either deep love or great suffering. Through one or the other or both, we wake up to the fact that our ego maneuvering is no longer working and something has to change. And so we find things that put us back in touch with our essence.

At the end of the play, his friends tease Benedict about deciding to become a married man after vowing not to. He answers them: "I will think nothing to any purpose that the world can say against [marriage]; and therefore never flout at me for what I have said against it; for man is a giddy thing, and this is my conclusion." Then, he invites everyone to dance. And when you think about it, admitting past faults and letting your ego take a back seat is something to frolic about!

November 27:

"Good, good. Let's have something with plenty of gravy that we can sop the bread in. [A knock at the door.] Oh! someone is knocking. Smeraldina, see who it is."
Pantalone in Carlo Goldoni's *The Servant of Two Masters*

I was on the team that directed and designed Goldoni's *The Servant of Two Masters* at Samford University in 1977. We had intended to produce a different play, but found and created this comic piece. It sparked an over 40-year love affair between me and *commedia dell'arte*.

I didn't plan to put another play with a feisty Beatrice in it right after *Much Ado*, but here we are. In our *Servant* production, we used Italian pronunciations, so this female character was "Bay-a-tree-chay." She travels to Venice dressed as her dead brother. And, throughout the play the elements of *commedia* figure strongly: disguise, *lazzi* or physical funny business, masks. And stock characters inhabit the work, including wily servants, dopey fathers, and several sets of lovers.

Beatrice has a skinny little zany servant named Truffaldino who is always hungry and in search of food. Through the intricacies of the plot, he finds that he can be a servant to Florindo, a second master (thus the name of the play) and possibly find opportunities for more food! Truffaldino's double work keeps him on the move around Venice, and in his shenanigans, as he tries to fill the orders of both employers, his scheme is almost discovered. When various characters continually ask him to get a message or money to "your master," (and he is unsure of which one) the pressure makes him develop a nervous stammer.

A wonderfully famous centerpiece to the play is a scene in which Truffaldino has to serve a banquet to Beatrice and Pantalone, and also to Florindo in separate chambers. A parade of soups, boiled meats with gravy, rissoles, fricandeaus, and puddings are brought out and the servant constantly mixes the meals up. At one point when a bowl arrives, Truffaldino says, "I wonder if this soup is worth eating; I'll try it." Taking a spoon out of his pocket, he admits, "I always carry my weapons about."

Though this funny scenario is the main food focus of the play, Pantalone's line that I picked for today — *"Let's have something with plenty of gravy that we can sop the bread in"* — comes in the first scene. His is one of those play quotes that enters my brain frequently. My family is blessed — or some might call it cursed — in longing for food like Truffaldino.

I just love food — the smell of something cooking, the amazing array of textures, the sour or bitter or sweet or pungent tastes, the appearance, the everything. When my granddaughter Emmeline was the tiniest baby just beginning to eat actual food, she would murmur after every bite, "Mmmmm. Mmmmm! Mmmmm!!" And she would try everything, from salad to shrimp, and from sweet potatoes to spinach.

Happily, I love to cook, to plan meals, to shop for the ingredients, to find new spices and herbs to use, to discover a recipe and then loosely follow it. And at least weekly, as I am contemplating the menus for the ensuing days, I hear Pantalone pleading, *"Let's have something with plenty of gravy that we can sop the bread in."* And, well, this is Thanksgiving week, so I will have to give into him and make some of that delicious liquid sustenance.

November 28:
"Your table needs to be reglued, rescrewed, and renewed."
Paul in AR Gurney's *The Dining Room*

Samford Theatre opened the 1991 season with AR Gurney's *The Dining Room*. In18 episodic scenes, the comic drama focuses on the differing natures of the room where families do — or do not — eat. Any number of actors can play the 57 characters, and for that reason, it is produced often by high schools and universities. It takes place from 1935 to 1980 in a non-sequential order, and the table is actually a metaphor for change as characters come and go around its edges.

The work explores stories of American White Anglo-Saxon Protestant families. Some scenes concern the table and other furniture, some portray family celebrations enjoyed in the room, and others explore the upper-middle class culture of the late twentieth century.

A grandmother struggles with remembering who her family members are. A sister and brother fight about who gets the dining room set. A young man tries to decide with a real estate agent if he wants to buy a house with a (dining) room he will never use.

"Your table needs to be re-glued, re-screwed, and renewed," says Paul, speaking not only about the piece of furniture, but also of Margery the divorcee who is flirting with him under the table — as well as societal changes taking place in the early 1980s. The overall theme of Gurney's play echoes our culture in the rise of the women's movement and the ersatz decline of a patriarchal society, the ascendance of gender rights and

the move away from connected family meals around a symbolically central table.

I am thinking of tables, table settings, and food during these holidays. A tradition in my family is to use our silverware every day, not solely for special occasions. In fact, I don't have any other sort of flatware. I use one of my sets of china every day, and my antique, quirky, and greatly loved table linens as well.

My cousin, through her mother, the oldest sister in the family, inherited the 14-leaf dining table that was owned by our great-great-grandfather. It is a wonderful oak piece under which all twelve of my cousins and my brother and I played a game called "Butterscotch" as children. I use my breakfast room more than my more formal space, but I do often use the dining room.

On Christmas morning, it is where we eat pork pie, an English dish that has been in that same great-great-grandfather's family for at least nine generations. We make the crust with beef kidney suet as the lubricator when we can still find it, and then stack it ten or more layers thick, alternating sausage and fresh pork. The crust is stuck all over with cloves, and the pie cooks for six hours, making wonderful fragrances waft through the house on December 23. The recipe came from Stockton-on-Tees, the town from which my great-great grandfather emigrated to America. After cooking, it is refrigerated and served cold for Christmas breakfast. Yum!

During this time of holidays, or every day: do you still use your dining table? Does it need re-gluing or re-screwing or renewing? How about your life?

November 29:
"Do you know the country where the orange flowers bloom?
The land of golden fruit and crimson roses,
Where the breeze is fresh and the birds fly in the light,
Where in any season bees are seen foraging,
Where radiant smiles are a blessing from God,
An eternal spring under a deep blue sky!
Alas! Why can I not follow you
To this happy shore? Here the fates have exiled me!
There it is! This is where I want to live,
Love, love and die!"

Mignon in Ambroise Thomas' opera, *Mignon*, with an original French libretto by Jules Barbier and Michel Carré, based on Goethe's novel *Wilhelm Meisters Lehrjahre*

In the fall of 1985, I designed the costumes for the Samford Opera's *Mignon*. In the first act, Mignon is grateful for being rescued by some young men, and she divides a nosegay of wild flowers between them. She tells them that she had been kidnapped by Gypsies at a young age and in this aria, she recounts her childhood home in striking images. The song especially impacted me while watching rehearsals because our family was right in the midst of buying a new house.

What a crazy time to be moving! In fact, we loaded our belongings on December 20, unpacked the next day, and decorated our tree on the 22nd. Some professional movers helped with a few big items, but most of our possessions went into vans and cars filled, driven, and unbundled by several of my cousins, friends, and coworkers. Like Mignon, we had our rescuers.

I find it so comforting to have theatre quotes and lines from operas and musicals flow through my mind, helping form and inform my life. Like Mignon's remembrance of the place she grew up, our new house was a happy little cottage. When I first saw it, I thought it was a perfect late 1970s-style storybook home, maybe belonging to an updated Little Red Riding Hood or Jack Beanstalk and his mother or the lady who made the Gingerbread Man. There, my orange flowers were day lilies, and I had crimson roses and golden — not fruit but — chrysanthemums. Surrounded on three sides by woods, the breeze did blow freshly, and the yard swarmed with birds and bees.

Spring was not eternal, but the change of seasons in that spot was spectacular. With a room of his own, my son Seth learned, at fifteen months, to sleep through the night. And my daughter Elin had plenty of room to invite friends over to spend the night.

Probably I am recalling with too much fondness that little bungalow we resided in for eight years. Like Mignon, or any heroine from an opera or romantic story, I think of mostly the good memories, and not the bad: the house's coziness and fairly expansive storage, the large basement garage (I now have a carport) and the sewer water (I am now on a septic tank), the growing up of my children — Seth from fifteen months to age nine, Elin from age nine to high school.

I realize that retaining good memories probably aids my dealing with complications that come along. And they also support my affirmative attitude about this world.

I didn't want to move from that little storybook cottage, and the thought of Mignon's kidnapping by wanderers recalls a sad happening from the house we moved to, the one where I still reside: someone broke in one day and stole all my gold jewelry. The investigating police officer told me not to bother searching pawn shops; they were Gypsies who had equipment in their van to melt precious metals onsite. Funny, it was four or five years after my marriage ended and they nabbed my 18-carat wedding band. If I think about it, it makes me melancholy even today: maybe more sad for them than me. Who is so desperate that they would slip into someone else's house, rummage through their possessions, and, of all things, sneak away with a wedding ring?

November 30:
"I know it's terrible, trying to have any faith... when people are doing such horrible... but you know what I sometimes think? I think the world may be going through a phase the way I was with Mother. It'll pass, maybe not for hundreds of years, but some day... I still believe, in spite of everything, that people are really good at heart."
Anne in Frances Goodrich and Albert Hackett's *The Diary of Anne Frank*, based on the book *The Diary of a Young Girl by Anne Frank*

The stage adaptation of Anne Frank's book debuted on Broadway at the Cort Theatre on October 5, 1955, ten years after the historical setting. The production won a Tony Award for Best Play, as well as the Pulitzer Prize for drama. *Diary* remains a popular and remarkably uplifting way to delve into the heart of one of the darkest times in human history. And with Anne believing in the goodness of humankind, her writings luminously sketch the blueprint for maneuvering suffering in this life.

The work tells the story of a real 13-year old Jewish girl who hid from the Nazis with her family before they were discovered and taken to concentration camps. After Anne's father, Otto Frank was released from Auschwitz — the only family member to survive — he returned to the place where the Franks hid and discovered his dead daughter's diary. Since its publication, it has become the most read work about the Holocaust world-wide.

When the play was first performed in 1956 in Germany — not so very long after the end of World War II — at curtain, audiences remained still and soundless in their seats for quite a while before leaving silently. I, too, have been so overcome by a piece of work in the theatre that I wouldn't dared have ruined the spell by applauding.

I have often wondered how in the world a family could live in the tiny attic apartment for two whole years. I have written these thoughts about play quotes over the last decade, and some years before that. Now suddenly, in March of 2020, the entire world is being asked to self-isolate, or quarantine in our homes because of the novel coronavirus disease. In no way am I likening my weeks and months of being cooped up in my house to the years the Frank family hid from the Nazis. However, the experience does give me an insight into some of the challenges, but also a few joys, of such cloistering.

People all over the world feel fearful, stressed, overwhelmed, powerless. Stock markets have plunged and economies suffer. Locally, schools are closed and meetings first limited to 500 or fewer people, quickly lessened to 25 and 10, and now everyone is asked to shelter at home unless you work for a health related business or hospital, grocery store, or pharmacy. Restaurants and breweries give curbside service and take extra handling precautions to stay afloat. Churches and arts groups offer services and performances online. We thought the precautions were for two weeks, but now it looks like months — and even those are evolving into a year or more.

One of the joys of this experience is that we can all take a breath and slow down. If we treat the time as a Sabbath, it feels much better. We can read and write, paint and create, watch movies and converse by phone or online. We can develop a new skill or learn a new language or take walks in the fresh air. My most fervent hope for this period is that it brings us into a collective higher consciousness as we realize we — all of us, all over the world — are intricately interconnected. Because that is surely one-hundred and eighty degrees away from the way the Nazis thought. Through all this do we dare with Anne Frank to believe, *"...in spite of everything, that people are really good at heart"*?

December 1
"Why should proud summer boast
Before the birds have any cause to sing?
Why should I joy in an abortive birth?

469

At Christmas I no more desire a rose
Than wish a snow in May's new-fangled mirth;
But like of each thing that in season grows."
Biron in William Shakespeare's *Love's Labours Lost*, Act I, Scene 1

Here we are at the beginning of the end, the last month of the year. Winter: time for ice and snow. Advent: time for peace and anticipation. Christmas and Hanukkah: time for celebration and joy. During December, I love to go to heart-stirring holiday concerts and delicious plays, to pubs and cafes decked with greenery and lights, to family gatherings and on festive jaunts with friends.

"...But like of each thing that in season grows." To me, the thing that grows the very best in this season is love. And speaking of love, *Love's Labour's Lost*, an early Shakespeare comedy probably written in 1593, enjoyed its first recorded performance at Christmastime 1597. The actors put on a show for Queen Elizabeth at the Inns of Court. In the play, the young King of Navarre and three of his cohorts decide on a self-improvement program that has them mimicking a monastic lifestyle.

Though the King seems devoted to the plan, his friends — like modern fraternity brothers — are wary of a life concerned with fasting, the pursuit of learning, and — especially — the denial of distracting pleasures, even women. During a visit from the Princess of Acquitaine, the men find their resolve tested with an ensuing admiration of the queen and her fair ladies-in-waiting. True to Renaissance comedies, the humorous work unfolds at pell-mell speed involving droll buffoons, scholars of uncertain brain power, and multiple wooers adding color as the brotherhood secretly pursue various romantic interests.

Advent can be, despite the lure of the commercial world, a wondrously magical time of fasting, study, and denial of participating in the frantic rush of the season. If there is anything I have learned in my last few years of fairly intense spiritual practices, it is to savor the present moment, to appreciate whatever (good or challenging) is going on in my life, and to enjoy each season for its singular pleasures and even its annoyances.

Right now, *"I no more desire a rose than wish a snow in May's new-fangled mirth."* Today, I walked in a freezing mist with fog so thick that I moved over into neighbors' yards when I heard a car approaching so I wouldn't — unbeknownst to the driver — be hit. I was wrapped up in scarves and head warmers, gloves and fleeces, with thermal heat keepers as a base.

Maybe icy temperatures and low hanging clouds are not your idea of delight, and I admit I used to grumble when I had to walk in such weather. Or, I just chickened out and decided not to venture out. I have come to realize that when I appreciate the time of year for what it is rather than wishing it were blazingly sunny or pleasantly chilly, I have a much better day.

And if I can relish in it, all the better. From there, I count my blessings and name my gratitudes and admit my thankfulness just to be alive, to have skin that feels the chill, to have hands that can put on gloves and feet that can still get me over 5,000 steps on my FitBit from 6:20 to 7:00 each dawn.

December 2
Tiny Tim: "God bless us, every one!"
Tim Cratchit in *A Christmas Carol* adapted for the stage and based on the novel of the same name by Charles Dickens

A Christmas Carol is one play I would never tire working on December after December. I have always been a Dickens fan, and right now, I am gathering some of my costume renderings to hang in the lobby of the Hoover Library Theatre while a local company produces the musical *Scrooge* this week. The original designs were created for a Birmingham Children's Theatre production in the 1980s, but I reworked them about ten years ago using fabric collages for the clothing parts of the renderings.

One reason I am fascinated with Dickens is that he so deftly threads social commentary about Victorian England into his novels bursting with colorful characters, page-turning drama, vivid descriptions, and episodic style. Who doesn't know the story of Tiny Tim who represents a child of the lower classes dependent upon others for survival, contrasted with the wealthy, though spiritually bereft Ebenezer Scrooge? The youngest Cratchit child is crippled and ailing from an illness that will soon bring on his death unless better food and healthcare intervene.

To me, an irresistible aspect of the relationship between Scrooge and Tiny Tim is how their destinies are inextricably intertwined. Their connection is a shorthand portrayal of the interconnection between

London's prosperous and its impoverished. But the young child plays a huge role in the old man's transformation.

When the Spirit of Christmas Present takes Scrooge about London, Ebenezer actually sees first hand what is going on with his employee's family, and he suddenly becomes emotionally affected by the Cratchits' poor circumstances. Bob enters with the crippled youngster on his shoulders. Despite the obvious poverty of the household, the family happily celebrates their scant Christmas feast. Scrooge implores the Spirit to tell him if Tiny Tim will live. The Spirit retorts that given the current situation in the Cratchit house, an empty chair will darken next year's holiday dinner.

Scrooge's midnight experience is a true picture of any human's transformation. In this case, for many years, Ebenezer wrapped veil after veil around his heart and his soul, woven by a number of woundings in his life. He became a miser: a hoarder of money, Bob Cratchit's time, ill thoughts of others — allowing his ego to remain in charge of his life. When the Spirits of Christmas lead him to the past, present, and future, he realizes he is caught up in a critical mass of suffering, and he has an unanticipated desire for relief. Having gone through the portal of self-remembering (seeing himself as a child and young man), Scrooge returns to his essence and to a higher level of consciousness.

So, when Ebenezer awakens on Christmas morning after the three Spirits have departed, he decides to change his miserly ways. Tiny Tim has played a part in the drama, that of a synchronistic catalyst for this conversion, and then he benefits from the alteration of the old gentleman's character. In fact, by the end of the tale, Dickens clearly shows that not only does Tiny Tim survive, Scrooge transfigures into a "second father" to him.

December 3
"Lloyd: I'm starting to know what God felt like when he sat out there in the darkness, creating the world.
Belinda: And what did he feel like, Lloyd my dear?
Lloyd: Very pleased he'd taken his Valium."
Characters from Michael Frayn's *Noises Off*

English playwright Michael Frayn wrote *Noises Off* in 1982, but the concept of such a romp occurred to him a dozen years earlier as he viewed a performance from the wings, those areas flanking each side of a theatre stage accessible only to performers and technicians. The buffoonery that inspired him came during the showing of *The Two of Us*, a comedy Frayn wrote for Lynn Redgrave. He said, "It was funnier from behind than in front, and I thought that one day I must write a farce from behind."

On New Year's Day in 2001, I saw the hysterically well-done version performed by actors at London's National Theatre. An ingeniously crafted farce, Act One explores a theatre person's worst nightmare: a dress rehearsal during which nothing works. The actors miss cues and lines, are mystified by their own entrances and exits, and are totally befuddled by prop pieces and costumes. A recurring "funny bit" involving several plates of sardines is so like some rehearsals I have been through it is almost excruciating to watch.

In Act Two, which is a month into performances, Frayn exhibits pure genius by having the audience observe the manic activity backstage at a matinée performance at the Theatre Royal in Ashton-under-Lyne. This literal peek behind the scenes spotlights a decomposition of relationships between cast members, causing them to accelerate the hoopla onstage and to create pure chaos backstage. Before bows, the performance crumbles. Act Three, when they are almost done with a 10-week run, they are playing the Municipal Theatre at Stockton-on-Tees, the town in which my maternal great-great-grandparents lived. Though the actors' interpersonal rivalries have intensified, they have resolved to disguise an ever-escalating spate of calamities.

One of my own recurring dreams is that I am either in the balcony or backstage in a theatre and I cannot find my way to the place where I need to be to complete my creative work. In one dream, I seem to traipse under ten or twelve stages, each as big as the Metropolitan Opera, searching for my actors to dress. Maybe I didn't *"know what God felt like when he sat out there in the darkness, creating the world"* — but I was certainly in the dark and instead of creating, I was unable to fabricate anything.

But then, creative labor always comes from some unknown place. Often when we are — well, when I am — generating art, I watch as everything becomes as chaotic as a scene in *Noises Off*. It seems as if all is lost and nothing good or meaningful will come out of my work. Then, somehow, that storm moves into a sudden quiet calmness and the play, the costumes, the writing, the painting come together as the most beautiful expression of something I had no idea was inside of me.

December 4 is St. Barbara's Day
"I've always said, when asked the question, I'd never wed!
When I observe the married state, I'm grateful I've not found a mate!
For marriage seems, at best, sir, a sizable burden."
Danilo in *Die Lustige Witwe* or *The Merry Widow*, music by Franz Lehár
and libretto by Victor Leon and Leo Stein, based on the play *L'attaché
d'ambassade* by Henri Meilhac

Franz Lehár's *Die Lustige Witwe* premiered in Vienna in 1905. I
created costumes for the well-loved *Merry Widow* ninety-five years later
when Samford Opera performed it in May of 2000. The action is set in
an imaginary Eastern European territory, and involves whether a rich,
young, high-spirited widow Hanna will re-marry, and if it might be to a
Pontevedrian, so her money remains in the country to save the province.

How fun are these lovely period costumes that emphasize the tale
and exaggerate the contrast between the Parisians and the Pontevedrians?
Evening tails and beautiful early 1900s dresses, sharp military uniforms
and frilly petticoats for the can-can dancers. All so fun to find and sew.

Today is the feast day of St. Barbara, my name saint. Legends tell
of her beauty, and how Dioscorus her father kept her locked in a tower
for protection. As she became a Christian, she refused to marry. This
infuriated her father who dragged her to the provincial prefect. Locked
up, she was tortured and Dioscorus himself beheaded her. During his
journey home, flashes in a thunderstorm struck him and he was reduced
to ashes, so lightning is linked to this saint.

Barbara is the patron of artillerymen, gunsmiths, and anyone who
works with explosives, and is, in fact connected to a number of armed
forces, navies, and air forces. Though no one seems to know why, she is
also associated with brewers.

The merry widow Hannah wanted (eventually) to get married; the
fervent saint Barbara did not. Marriage has traditionally served as a
cultural custom to promote the common good by providing a safe place
to build and grow families to propagate the human species. From a
religious perspective, a wedding binds together male and female, male
and male, or female and female in physical, emotional, mental, and
spiritual ways.

Despite the good aspects of wedded life, this very day two friends
and I talked — for the time it took us to drive across four states — about
the freedom we gained through the dissolutions of our marriages. We

were traveling to an out-of-town conference and as we motored along, we realized that our egos had been so wrapped up in the creation and maintaining of our marriages that we had all become very inauthentic people in those relationships.

Marriage can be quite wonderful — or, a sizable burden if its participants are unconscious and insensitive to each other. And sometimes the only way out is to split and find your self again.

Ah! But, we said, we are none of us like the saintly Barbara who was satisfied with a lonely chamber in a tower. Just like *The Merry Widow* characters, we could be swept out to sea again by a wave of love. This time, though, we will let our souls rather than our false selves lead the way.

December 5

"I knew nothing about what happened to my old professor. I hadn't seen him since graduation day years ago. I promised I'd keep in touch, but I got busy dancing my own dance."
Mitch in Mitch Albom and Jeffrey Hatcher's *Tuesdays with Morrie*

The book *Tuesdays with Morrie* is further titled: *An Old Man, a Young Man, and Life's Greatest Lesson*. A decade and a half after graduating from Brandeis University, Mitch Albom, by then an accomplished journalist and musician, happened to see a former sociology professor on the television news. He found out that his beloved but long-separated Morrie was battling Lou Gehrig's Disease and decided to pay him a visit. That call evolved into a weekly holy journey during which the younger man was taught important life lessons best learned from someone about to leave this world.

The play adapted from the book was performed in the fall of 2008 at our local Birmingham Festival Theatre and I consulted on the costumes. As *New York Magazine* said about the original production: "Unforgettable! No matter how well you tell the story, the play makes it more vivid, more shattering, more humorous."

I have mentioned my own guiding mentor John Finlay before. A fiery visionary, he was my Freshman-second-semester and Sophomore-both-semesters college English professor. He was young and learned, formidable but approachable — a born teacher and a very fine poet as well. Given to dramatics, he sometimes slammed doors, peeked over eyeglasses in mock disbelief, or balanced on the back legs of his chair for emphasis. He had, in several private lectures, opened the mysteries of *The Odyssey* to several of us when the rest of our class grew bored with the piece. How you can get weary of *The Odyssey*, I am not sure.

After my Sophomore year, John left Montevallo to pursue his doctorate at Louisiana State University, and we would hear of some of his travels and exploits. Even when I graduated, I corresponded by letter with him and, in addition, would hear of his contacting another English professor with news. He sent me books of poetry as he published them, but I yearned to be in more consistent contact with him.

Once when I visited my alma mater for homecoming in the late 1980s, a mutual friend told me that John was very sick. As months progressed, I found that he suffered from AIDS, and had moved back to his family's farm in Enterprise so that his mother and sisters could care for him. I wrote him and talked to him on the phone once before I heard of his death on February 17, 1991. Though I knew that his prognosis was not good, I was stunned and stabbed with sorrow at the message.

Soon after, I went to confession to sort my feelings out with my priest. As the older version of the *Book of Common Prayer* prompts, I had "left undone those things which [I] ought to have done, and ... done those things which [I] ought not to have done." I felt I should have gone to visit John in person. I should have told him what an impact he had on my life. I should have read to him some favorite work since he had gone blind. My excuses were lame: young children, important theatre work, lots of volunteer duties.

When I first read Mitch Albom's book about Morrie, and then helped bring the play to life, I saw what I might have done had I had the courage to intrude back into the life of an ill professor. Both of us would have gained so much.

December 6 - St. Nicholas Day
"Welcome, friend! Saint Nicholas, welcome!
  Welcome to this merry band!
  Happy children greet thee, welcome!
  Thou art glad'ning all the land!"
Children in *Hans Brinker or the Silver Skates*, a children's play based on the novel by Mary Mapes Dodge

The early spring of my sophomore year in college, we produced the children's play *Hans Brinker or the Silver Skates*. I cannot find the script we used, so I was unable to pull a direct quote from the play. I worked on lighting the show, and I recall how interesting it was to watch the cast learn to move as if they were skating on stage.

But I vividly remember delighting in this book when I read it at about age 10 or 11. I come from a family of voracious readers on my mother's side. My grandmother's home was filled with shelves that brimmed over with books, and she often encouraged me to take one home and read it. All the classics were there: *The Wizard of Oz* and six or seven other Oz books, *Little Women*, *The Secret Garden*, *The Water Babies*, *The Little Prince*, *Heidi*, *Hans Brinker or the Silver Skates* — and that just scratches the surface.

The chapter in *Hans Brinker* about St. Nicholas captured my imagination and would not leave my mind. Something about this Dutch custom appealed to my emerging spirituality. As Dodge writes, "In Holland, Saint Nicholas visits earth on the fifth, a time especially appropriated to him. Early on the morning of the sixth, he distributes his candies, toys, and treasures, then vanishes for a year. Christmas Day is devoted by the Hollanders to church rites and pleasant family visiting. It is on Saint Nicholas's Eve that their young people become half wild with joy and expectation."

Reading the book as a young person who didn't follow this tradition, I searched my *World Book* encyclopedia at home, and many other sources in my school library, for pictures of this saint. He was dressed in long red or black robes with a tall hat upon his head. Little did I know at the time that he was dressed as any Catholic bishop would be: it was just that somehow, the costume seemed so much more faithful and truthful to the holiday for me than our Santa Claus.

I was smitten by the custom of his filling wooden shoes with candy, nuts, and fruit. I was fascinated that the evening of December 5 was *"Sinterklaasavond"* or St. Nicholas's Eve. *Sinterklaas* parties would distract children with treasure hunt games as poems and riddles gave clues to find little presents left by the saint. I dreamed of being in the middle of such a party, eating special baked goods and sweets, when suddenly a knock would be heard at the door and we would answer it to discover a sack full of presents!

Even only a decade old, I somehow resonated with the idea of separating Santa Claus from the arrival of Jesus and the miraculous birth that was the incarnation of God on earth. When my children were little, in our parish we celebrated St. Nicholas Day every year on December 6 —

and even had a visit from the saint himself. And St. Nick always left Christmas pajamas for my children as he came by for their letter on this day.

Even now, I follow my young self's desire to celebrate St. Nicholas and make sure my Santa Claus collection is out by December 5. Who knows when he might stop by and leave me a shoe full of cherished prizes?

December 7

In "Stars" from *Les Misérables*, Javert sings that the masses of celestial bodies in the night sky function as guardians who protect us. (Listen to the work online or from your library!)

Javert in *Les Misérables*, the musical by Claude-Michel Schönberg and Alain Boublil, adapted from the novel by Victor Hugo

On September 4, I talked about the first time I saw *Les Mis*, as it is affectionately known by theatre folks and fans, and how I was so far up in the atmosphere, I could have touched a star if I had been outside. Adapted from Victor Hugo's sweeping novel, the musical takes place in France in the early 1800s. In this song, policeman Javert vows to the stars that he will find the story's hero Valjean and recapture him. To him those celestial bodies symbolize order and light: they are protectors on the lookout for danger or trouble in the night.

In 1990, the Hubble Space Telescope was placed into orbit by a Space Shuttle. At the present time, it is still functioning and estimating hundreds of billions of galaxies in the universe. Not long ago, the number was thought to be possibly 500 billion by a German super-computer simulation. Scientists and astronomers believe many of the galaxies are much older than the Milky Way, which itself probably has 100 thousand million stars. Reality is so much bigger than the human mind can comprehend.

When the first "Blue Marble" photograph of Earth was taken by the Apollo 17 astronauts on December 7, 1972, we were all mesmerized by the sight. But the Earth, our island home, is tiny in comparison to the infinite cosmos. Human-like creatures have only inhabited our planet for about 2 million of its probable 4.54 billion years. Yet so many of us still believe we are personally the center of the entire universe.

To think how small humans really are is mind-boggling. When I was a tot, my mother used to attempt to lull me to sleep at nap time, but I was rarely sleepy. I would rather her tell me stories about places she had been or where we were going or what she did when she was little. I remember her recounting to me the time she and her friends were in high school and they stayed up all night thinking about the magnitude of the solar system and the tiny role of humans in Creation. They even debated whether humans were real, or were just a dream that God, or maybe even some giant, was having. What if, they wondered, God — or the giant — woke up, and that was the end of us?

I don't think I am the only one who gazes into an inky night at the stars and humbly marvels at the magnitude and splendor, feeling a draw as if the stardust in me wanted to go home. In the 1980s, astronomer Carl Sagan hosted a PBS show called "Cosmos," and in one episode he posited, "We are a way for the universe to know itself. Some part of our being knows this is where we came from. We long to return. And we can, because the cosmos is also within us. We're made of star stuff." So maybe as Javert posited, the stars are our evening (and daytime) protectors, both within us and way up in the night sky.

December 8
"Money? Who cares about money? This is art, you blockhead! This is great music I'm playing and playing great music is an art! Do you hear me? An [banging on piano] ART! ART! ART! ART!"
Schroeder in Clark Gesner's *You're a Good Man, Charlie Brown*, based on the characters created by cartoonist Charles M. Schulz's *Peanuts* comic strip

My Education for Ministry mentor says that everything you need to know about the true meaning of Christmas is contained within the 1965 television holiday classic *A Charlie Brown Christmas*, so I think a lot about Charles Schulz's characters at this time of year. In February of 1987, our Theatre Department performed Gesner's *You're a Good Man, Charlie Brown*, and do you know how hard it is to create costumes for actors who are over five-feet tall to even slightly resemble the oh-so-well-known comparatively two to three-foot figures from the Peanuts strip? The proportion is so wrong that you just have to settle for the best you can do.

However, my costumes were art, you blockhead! They were great costumes I was creating, and fabricating great costumes is an art! Do you hear me? An ART! ART! ART! ART! Money? Who cares about money?

I once interviewed the conductor of the Alabama Symphony for *Birmingham Magazine*, and he told me that he had recently been horrified by what a new board member had said at his first meeting. The conductor was asking for a raise for his first violin position, and this new member asked him, "Well, what does she do for a living?" As if the musician played music for a hobby and had a day job on top of the grueling work needed to be even a competent orchestra player.

The conductor said, "Being a musician is very demanding physically and mentally, emotionally and spiritually. She has to be physically fit and able to hold her instrument for three hours or more in a stretch. And that happens six to ten times every week for more than three-fourths of the year." There are rehearsals and individual practice sessions, there is working with a conductor and a number of other creative and sensitive people, there is stretching to "love" every piece and every style of music she plays.

Like people who work in the theatre, who dance, who paint, who sing, who sculpt, who write, most musicians would be terribly unhappy pursuing any other career, because their art gives them life. But that does not mean it is easy work. Artists of all kinds must continually practice their skills and constantly educate themselves in old and new ways. Performing artists also have to collaborate with all kinds of personalities.

This idea of the conductor was not relayed to me to denigrate those amateur artists who do have a day job and use theatre or dance, art or music as a release after their day job. But people who choose art as a profession should be paid well for their work. After all, their real trade is advancing humanity by communicating a personal sense of the world in a unique way.

December 9
"The Younger Son: How many of my father's hired servants have food to spare, and here I am starving to death! I will set out and go back home and say: Father, I have sinned against heaven and against you, and I am no longer worthy to be called your son. But take me back and I will be like one of your hired servants."
Lost Son in a dramatic adaptation of *The Prodigal Son*, based on the Biblical story from the Gospel of Luke

A great play for the historically Baptist Samford University was *The Prodigal Son*, which a student directed in the spring of 2000. The well-known story from Luke's Gospel of the "lost son" recounts the reversal of fortune of a younger heir who begs for an early inheritance from his father. After going to a distant land and squandering his wealth, he hires out as a swine herder. When he begins to long for the pig's pods to eat, the young man decides to return.

Nearing home, the son's father rushes to meet him and then holds a feast, which the older brother resents, because he had stayed and been loyal to the family. But the father insists that they should rejoice: the son who was dead now lives.

In Benjamin Britten's operatic version of the story, an interesting twist is a Tempter who comes unbidden into the younger son's life before he leaves home. The boy asks who this Tempter is, for he doesn't understand his questions. The Tempter tells the young man that he is not living his life to its fullness, to which he replies that this stranger has no right to tell him how to behave. Then, the Tempter reveals himself, saying he is no outsider, but the boy's own interior voice, and his very being.

Oh, that inner voice we have. That false self. That ego! I have just spent five days at a retreat exploring how to navigate around, under, above, and through the ego that traps us in infantile positions of failure and decline. In some of our training to teach the Enneagram, we looked at this parable.

The Younger Son is our unbridled Ego and our Id descended into disintegration. The Older Brother is our Ego plus our Super Ego, pointing out shameful wrongdoing. What is the space that allows the two to come together? The Father who represent the Soul and understands the unbalanced components of the human psyche.

Henri Nouwen, the Dutch-born Catholic priest, professor, psychologist, and writer, sat in a chair all day long in Russia looking at Rembrandt's painting of The Prodigal Son. At the end of the day, he realized that the Father's left hand in the piece is strong, muscular, and firmly masculine. And yet the right hand is refined, soft, and tender, with an elegant, feminine quality.

"The Father," says Nouwen, "is not simply a great patriarch. He is mother as well as father. He touches the son with a masculine hand and a feminine hand. He holds, and she caresses. He confirms, and she consoles. He is, indeed, God, in whom both manhood and womanhood, fatherhood and motherhood, are fully present."

Our mentors told us in this exploration of the Prodigal Parable that the Divine is in the spaces of our lives, coaxing us back to remember our own true nature. "Remember" in Greek is two words: one is looking back, and the other is bringing the past up to the present. So remembering is really bringing the pieces of our lives back together into the whole we were meant to be, like the Prodigal Son who returns to the welcome arms of home.

December 10
"To find that phosphorescence, that light within, that's the genius behind poetry."
Emily Dickinson in William Luce's *The Belle of Amherst*

My favorite English professor in college admired a great number of poets, and Emily Dickinson was at the top. Once for his class, we wrote a paper on her poetry, and though he liked my work and I got an "A," I will never forget a note he scribbled in the margins. To vary wording throughout the paper, I sometimes wrote, "Emily Dickinson," sometimes "Miss Dickinson," and once "Emily." Circling in red that particular citing, Mr. Finlay wrote, "Oh, you know Miss Dickinson personally?!" When I asked him about the note after class, he cautioned against overfamiliarity in formal academic work, a great assistance to me on my road toward graduate school.

Then, actually, I did get to know Miss Dickinson personally when I designed her costume for *The Belle of Amherst* in 1981. The actress, Jane Trechsel, a well-known and favorite Birmingham actor and Yoga teacher, is a poet herself. I was 31 and yearning to write professionally. I had sent several manuscripts to publishers with nothing in return but rejection slips.

So in June of that year, I got up my nerve to ask for an interview with Ray Martin at *Birmingham Magazine*. He was a wise and wary editor and was at first hesitant to give me an assignment since I had no published pieces. I somehow won him over in the end, pleading with him to let me try an article or two on theatre since I knew that subject.

My first mission was to interview Jane since *The Belle of Amherst* was opening in the fall and many magazine readers were looking forward to seeing her perform the role of Emily Dickinson. The chat with her was lovely, taking place on her sun porch with a terra cotta tile floor, comfortable cushioned chairs, copious plants, and afternoon light streaming in. She told me many things about the role, about Dickinson's writing and biography, about her own poetry and family.

One thing she recounted changed everything for me. Talking about her daily practices, she explained she did Yoga and spiritual work every morning to get herself centered and focused for the day. I said I wished I had time to do that, and her response was, "Oh, I find I have ever so much more time in the day when I do these exercises!"

So (either bold or foolhardy me) I jumped into the idea wholeheartedly. The very next day, I mentally prepared for my day by reading. Quickly after, I added physical walks, spiritual conditioning, and emotional journalling. In 1998, my daughter Elin gave me Jane's book and compact disc "A Morning Cup of Yoga" and it has become a component of my daily work ever since. Another part of my routine is to thank the Holy One for giving me my professor John and my friend Jane, two phosphorescent poets, each of whose *"light within"* radiated to me good and right things that transformed my life.

December 11
"They should put a tax on stupidity."
Stanley Bumiller in Ed Howard, Joe Sears, and Jaston Williams's *Greater Tuna*

I was always a bit surprised that we got away with producing *Greater Tuna* one year at Samford. The play was produced in 1997, sixteen years after the *Tuna*'s debut in Austin, Texas in 1981. And the work was a directed by a student which, perhaps since it did not appear on the mainstage brochure, slipped under the administration radar.

A spoof of the moral majority, *Greater Tuna*, as its official website proclaims, "is the hilarious comedy about Texas' third smallest town, where the Lion's Club is too liberal and Patsy Cline never dies. The eclectic band of citizens that make up this town are portrayed by only two performers, making this satire on life in rural America even more delightful as they depict all of the inhabitants of Tuna — men, women, children, and animals."

The dialogue is downright clever and adds to the hilarity. For instance, the above quoted line is ironically said by a reform school dropout. Stanley Bumiller is commenting on the collective IQ of small town Tuna when he says, *"They should put a tax on stupidity."* And though the playwrights give the characters a running commentary on how small towns are replete with small minds, there is a charm about the life in Tuna as well.

Critics call the original *Greater Tuna* the most somber of the series, since in it a male judge is discovered dead, wearing a Dale Evans swimsuit. Even that is humorous because one of the funniest features of the farce comes from the two male actors wearing dresses and heels to play women. In fact, the two performers each play ten characters. And those incredibly fast costume changes are a riot in and of themselves.

Greater Tuna is funny despite its dark side. Springing from a comic skit inspired by a political cartoon, the comedy grew into a series consisting of the original play plus *A Tuna Christmas, Red White and Tuna*, and *Tuna Does Vegas*. Different people respond to different kinds of humor. I really like most any kind of comedy: satire, highbrow, deadpan, burlesque, caricature, farce, standup — so the flamboyant thigh-slapping jests and sight gags in *Tuna* keep me guffawing. I also resonate with ancient Greek comedy, *commedia dell'arte*, Laurel and Hardy, the Three Stooges, Charlie Chaplin, Benny Hill, and lots of Saturday Night Live skits.

And, since it is December, I might add another favorite tradition of mine: the English Christmas pantomime, informally known as the "panto." Pantos are loosely based on beloved fairy tales gone awry, and the fun of them is the participatory aspect where audience members sing along and interact with performers by shouting out phrases or words. A family designed musical stage extravaganza, the shows are performed during the Christmas and New Year season and much like *Greater Tuna* include slapstick, cross-gender actors, and topical, often political humor. So though Tuna is a tiny hamlet in the great state of Texas and London is the 15th largest city in the world, broad boisterous comedy appeals across the globe. Maybe they should put a tax on that. On further thought, no "they" shouldn't!

December 12
In "Aquarius" from *Hair: The American Tribal Love-Rock Musical*, the Tribe sings about the emergence of a new pinnacle of peace, actually referring more to the Hippie movement than an actual astrological occurrence. (Listen to the work online or from your library!)

The Tribe in *Hair: The American Tribal Love-Rock Musical* with a book and lyrics by James Rado and Gerome Ragni and music by Galt MacDermot

The musical *Hair* had an off-Broadway debut in October 1967 at Joe Papp's Public Theatre, after which it had a brief stint at a New York nightclub and opened on Broadway in April of 1968. It subsequently ran for 1,750 performances. I saw *Hair* during Spring Break of my Sophomore year, in 1970. A group of 20 or so theatre students rode a bus to New York City with one of our professors, Charles Harbour — bless him! We saw *1776*, *Butterflies Are Free*, *Jacques Brel Is Alive and Well and Living in Paris*, *The Boys in the Band*, *Fortune and Men's Eyes*, and *Hair*. Though Montevallo is a small town right in the middle of Alabama, it is a (very) liberal arts university and my college days were a wonderful, liberating time for me. To be there in the late 1960s and early '70s during the days of the hippie counterculture and sexual revolution, women's liberation and civil rights, and the peace and anti-war movements was freeing for me — even if our school wasn't exactly the hotbed of any of these social upheavals.

Never having been to a city as large as New York, this theatre outing was filled with adventure. It started when about five of us piled into a taxi from the bus station to our hotel. The cabbie from Bronx was amazed by us Southerners and our accent, and as we were leaving and trying to settle up our fare, he told us, "Okay, I'm ona give you kids a break. It'll be free!" We students on no income were ecstatic. "Wow," we said. "Thanks! A free taxi ride."

"No," he corrected. "I said free (holding up three fingers), not free!" So we flustered children from Alabama came up with the dollar bills needed and thanked him immensely anyway. Just then, we encountered two men passing by asking, "Hash?" in high sing-song voices (but we declined). Later, we discovered basement Italian restaurants, purchased blown plastic flowers from street Hippies, tested Afro wigs in a store front, rambled around Macy's looking for souvenirs, viewed the just-out movie *Woodstock*, and ordered Manhattans in a hotel bar (well, we were in Manhattan where the drinking age was 19!).

We seemed so bohemian. Being an Aquarius myself, I felt like the Age of Aquarius was arriving. I truly believed that when Jupiter and Mars lined up, the War in Vietnam — in fact, all war — would be over. Long hair and funky, psychedelic clothing would stay forever! Peace really would be guiding the planets. Creativity and artistic freedom would reign supreme. Love truly would steer the stars. Communes and spiritual consciousness would grow! I could see it!

But you know what happened? The week we came back to our campus after our magical mystery tour, the Beatles broke up. The war dragged on. A month later, four students at Kent State University were killed. Next, race riots erupted in Augusta, Georgia. The drug culture burgeoned. Though many good things happened, too, I went into a half-decade melancholic decline.

Is any of that unconventional *Hair*-like optimism revivable in these retiring years of the Baby Boomers? I always have hope.

December 13
"They wrapped him in a comforter and laid him in an apple crate."
Narrator in *Cotton Patch Gospel* by Tom Key and Russell Treyz, with music and lyrics by Harry Chapin, and adapted from Clarence Jordan's *Cotton Patch* versions of the gospels of Matthew and John

In 1977, my then-husband and design partner and I got to know a fellow theatre person in town. He had enjoyed our design and direction of *The Servant of Two Masters* so much that he invited us to help create the designs for his *Pilgrim* (based on John Bunyan's Pilgrim's Progress) at our university. The next fall Tom Key played *Oedipus Rex* in our Samford production.

A few years later, after Tom had moved with his family to Atlanta, he collaborated with Russell Treyz to write a version of *Cotton Patch Gospel* for the stage. Delightful folk-rock singer songwriter Harry Chapin wrote the music and lyrics shortly before his untimely death July 16, 1981. Just three months later, the show premiered at the Lamb's Theater in New York City on October 21. For what became a popular musical, Tom and Russell adapted Clarence Jordan's *Cotton Patch* versions of the gospels of Matthew and John.

What a great story for this time of the year, as the action starts with a young lady Mary who is engaged to Joe Davidson (or Joseph, "David's Son") humorously reflecting Jesus's lineage. Set in modern Georgia, the story follows the Bible accounts of the child conceived in the womb of a virgin through the power of the Holy Spirit. Joe wonders if he should marry a pregnant girl, but an angel visits him and allays his fears.

In January of 1983, we hosted a three-week run of *Cotton Patch Gospel* at Samford and it was packed almost every night and matinee. One Thursday evening, snow poured down and the roads closed, so no one off-campus could make it to the show. A university administrator bought all the seats and 300 students were able to see the show for free. They loved the translation of the biblical narrative.

In *Cotton Patch* Mary and Joe have to travel to Gainesville for an income tax audit. When Mary suddenly goes into labor on the way, they find no vacancy at the Dixie Delight Motor Lodge. So the manager and Joe are able to open an abandoned trailer, where the baby is born, and *"they wrapped him in a comforter and laid him in an apple crate."* This Southern-ized Jesus Davidson had the enthused crowd rocking as he was baptized in the Chattahoochee River, preached to a Stone Mountain crowd, and even as he finally met his end through a lynching in Atlanta.

For this first month of '83, we made crock pot meals, cleaned house, attended PTO meetings at Elin's school, ran out of coffee, taught classes, designed future shows, and buzzed about town visiting relatives. George Wallace was inaugurated for the fourth and final time as Governor of our state, Tom Corts was announced as our university's new president, Alabama's Paul "Bear" Bryant died less than a month after his retirement as football coach, the Miami Dolphins lost to Washington in the Super Bowl, and the movie *ET* was running.

While the *Cotton Patch Gospel* played on for over twenty performances, Jesus was born, lived, and died nightly. And our sometimes mundane, sometimes extraordinary lives continued to relentlessly unfold as a continuing story as well.

December 14
"A man can't give up his business."
"Why not? You've got all the money you need. You can't take it with you."
Mr. Kirby and Grandpa Vanderhof in George S. Kaufman and Moss Hart's *You Can't Take it with You*

You Can't Take It with You opened at New York's Booth Theatre on December 14, 1936. Running for 837 performances, Kaufman and Hart won the 1937 Pulitzer Prize for Drama with this work. Many people interpret the expression to mean that we should maintain a steady buying spree and stockpile material treasures while we are living. Use that credit card, buy that palatial home, acquire that flashy car, possess as many jewels and electronics as possible, because there is no way that you can hang onto such things as you enter your grave and beyond.

The play *You Can't Take It with You*, however, is inhabited by a family of artistic dreamers led by "Grandpa" Martin Vanderhof. He has wisely given up the rat race of corporate life to enjoy life doing what he pleases, and encourages his family to do the same. The living room is described in the script as "an every-man-for-himself room." It is the place where "meals are eaten, plays are written, snakes collected, ballet steps practiced, xylophones played, printing presses operated — if there were room enough there would probably be ice skating."

So obviously, the delightfully unconventional family is fairly opposed to materialism. All of us must leave worldly wealth behind when we die. But what is "worldly wealth" and what do we do while we are here on earth? Do we find our calling, pursue our talents, fill up our hearts, souls, and minds?

Tony Kirby falls in love with Alice Sycamore, Martin's granddaughter and the two families are contrasted. The Kirbys have bought into the power and success of money and corporate life, while the Vanderhof gang believes that instead, the American Dream involves creating a span of days that they can enjoy, doing what makes them happy, zestful, and invigorated. Mr. Kirby tells Grandpa that if everyone acted the way they did, society would fall apart, nothing would ever get done. Grandpa posits that many people have a burning desire to work on Wall Street or become a CEO, so let them follow that dream. But for those people who are just working to make a lot of money to buy stuff, maybe they could try pursuing something that enriches their spirit.

In the end, the Kirby family members realize they are the crazy ones and that the oddball Vanderhofs and Sycamores see what is really important in life. Grandpa helps the Kirbys and the audience realize there are many avenues to fulfillment: just be sure you are on the right path for yourself.

So what might you do today? Perform on an accordion, train for a marathon, rescue Springer Spaniels, collect toys from the early twentieth century, go see a play? Maybe *You Can't Take It with You* is running in your town!

December 15
"Why, was there ever seen such villainy, So neatly plotted, and so well performed?"
Ithamore in Christopher Marlowe's *The Jew of Malta* Act III, Scene 3

In graduate school, I studied all the plays of Christopher Marlowe and worked very hard on a huge project about *The Jew of Malta*. We had decided to produce the play at Samford one year, but a Jewish director friend of ours persuaded us that it was too anti-Semitic for a nice Christian school like ours to do. And yet, *The Famous Tragedy of the Rich Jew* is so intriguing.

This particular quote goes to the heart of irony and droll self-adulation in the text. Literally, Ithamore is commenting on the favorable outcome of Barabas's conspiracy to murder Lodowick and Mathias. However, his observation is also an artful allusion to the playwright's own talent at writing a play *"so neatly plotted"* and now *"so well performed"* for its viewers. Theatre people love to find in a script such references to the cunning craft of playwright, director, designer, or actor.

Not long ago, I had a not-so neatly plotted nightmare in which I was asking the head of the theatre department if I could have my old costume design position back. In the dream, I had to literally jump through a number of hoops before I could talk to the dean about the possibility. I woke up before I ever found out if I made it or not.

For more than twenty-five years, my costume shop was in a windowless room in the bowels of the building. So for over a quarter of a century, I spent probably 75,000 hours of my life down in that recessed area of the theatre. I sewed close to 2,000 costumes for around 1,000 student actors.

When you are part of the theatre for any extended time, the work gets into your psyche and your bloodstream. It becomes so much a part of your life, that for some people, it becomes their life. It seduces them, comforts them, invigorates them, even defines them. It is a community with which they can identify. "Theatre is my life!" is sometimes the cry of such folks.

Even though I don't work daily in a theatre any more, I still feel part of that circle. Through all my friends who still act and direct, design and build, I keep up with most of the producing groups in town. And once or twice a year, I design costumes for a community theatre.

In fact, as I have remarked before, one of my recurring dreams is that I cannot find the costume shop for some show that I am working on. I wander through many tunnels, across several backstage areas, beneath stages being used for rehearsals, but I am very rarely reunited with the actors I am supposed to be clothing. I am lost, I am overwhelmed, I am stricken knowing I am not upholding my duty as a designer and seamstress of theatrical garments. Because *"was there ever seen such villainy"* as an actor having to go on stage undressed?

December 16
"Strange, isn't it? Each man's life touches so many other lives. When he isn't around he leaves an awful hole, doesn't he?"
Clarence in *It's a Wonderful Life Live*, (originally produced by Chicago's American Blues Theater), based on the film produced and directed by Frank Capra, based on the short story "The Greatest Gift," by Philip Van Doren Stern

A few years ago, my former student Marty Higginbotham, who had moved back to Birmingham, produced and directed *It's a Wonderful Life Live*, a play he helped develop, produce, and direct in Chicago based on what happens to be my favorite movie. In Marty's delightful version, just eight actors bring Bedford Falls to life, accompanied by live Foley sound effects, an original score, and a setting suggesting a 1940s radio broadcast.

Surely everyone knows the story: George Bailey is a frustrated husband and father who long ago relinquished his own dreams of traveling the world so that he could help others. When he is considering suicide on Christmas Eve, prayers intercede for him and prompt the appearance of a guardian angel named Clarence Odbody. Throughout the night, the somewhat bumbling but lovable divine messenger presents George with the realization of how many people he has positively influenced and how altered Bedford Falls would have been without his presence.

What Clarence did was to open the heart of George Bailey to see his how different life would be if he had not been born. Open-heartedness is a physical feeling as well as an attitude. Because the body, emotions, soul, and mind are so interconnected, when we can learn to create the physical sensation of open-heartedness, our thoughts shift to reflect the body's reality.

The other night, I tried this meditation at a Camp Winnataska volunteer meeting, and you can try it, too. Close your eyes and take a few breaths. Remember a time when your heart was truly open: seeing a beautiful sunset... hearing the crashing waves of the gulf... tasting a freshly picked peach... smelling a favorite home-cooked meal. Bring all your senses to the memory, recalling the sights... the sounds... the fragrances

... how your body felt and the emotional and physical sensation of your heart opening.

During our meeting, we sat with that sense of open-heartedness. I had handed out small paper hearts and asked them to write on the heart a camp person who helped their heart open up?

I wasn't sure how the exercise would go over, but they enjoyed it and when I asked if someone wanted to share their revelation, Paul spoke up. He said that he had not thought of this incident for years, but the first time he was a hut leader, he tried to pull a funny joke, but it backfired. He was 15 years old, and knowing nothing else to do, he ran to hide in his hut.

A little later, the camp director knocked on his door and Paul appeared, apologizing profusely. On his way to have a private talk with the director and his wife, he worried they would send him home. But, after talking to him, they decided he would simply lose his canteen privileges for the week.

My friend was so very grateful that he was not sent home and that they dealt fairly with him. Just think, he said, "If I had gone home, I wouldn't be sitting here tonight. I wouldn't be chairman of this group. I wouldn't have met and married my wife, because I would have never come back and spent another six summers at camp. I wouldn't have my two boys. My life would be totally different."

As Clarence would say, *"Strange, isn't it? Each man's life touches so many other lives. When he isn't around he leaves an awful hole, doesn't he?"*

December 17
In "I'm Not Throwing Away My Shot" from *Hamilton*, Alexander Hamilton sings about having a burning ambition to make something of his life. (Listen to the work online or from your library!)

Alexander Hamilton in *Hamilton*, with book, music, and lyrics by Lin-Manuel Miranda, based on Ron Chernow's biography

Hamilton opened off-Broadway at the Public Theater on February 17, 2015. The innovative production captured the hearts of audiences and critics alike, and was so popular that, on August 16, 2015, it moved to the Richard Rodgers Theatre on Broadway. After being nominated for 16 Tony Awards, Lin Manuel Miranda's Broadway sensation won 11 Tonies including Best Musical.

From its start, *Hamilton*'s tickets were expensive (in the $850-range) and extremely hard to acquire. With a unique combination of rap, rhythm and blues, hip-hop and jazz, along with more standard Broadway tunes, the play tells the story of historical American Founding Figures with a cast of many races and genders.

One reviewer complained, that even with the female cast members, the story remains patriarchal. Nevertheless, both the book and music are youthful, energetic, and refreshing, and the set, lighting, costume design, and staging are amazing. Barack Obama said *Hamilton* "... has not only become a smash hit, but a civics lesson our kids can't get enough of. One with fierce youthful energy. One where rap is the language of revolution..."

As of this writing, *Hamilton* is not yet available for licensing, so I have not been involved in a performance of the play. But about a year and a half after the Broadway opening, my granddaughter Emmeline established a campaign that the only thing she wanted for Christmas of 2016 was *Hamilton* tickets. She was seven at the time, and she dressed as Hamilton for Halloween that October. My daughter Elin scolded that her request was ridiculous for a child, but she was relentless in her petitions. (She wasn't going to throw away that chance.)

In *Hamilton*, Alexander sings "My Shot" near the beginning of the musical. I once heard Lin Manuel Miranda say this song is the "biggest meal" of the production, and, as an actor, once you've sung this number (it contains 1,080 words!), you've got the show. The young Hamilton wows other young revolutionaries with his way of speaking, and in this instance, it is through rap.

In the play, the phrase "throwing away my shot" not only means not giving up a chance at success and a legacy, but it also refers to his famous duel with Aaron Burr when — at the end of the musical and of Alexander's real life — Hamilton heroically turns his pistol towards the sky, effectively tossing his shot away and being hit and killed in return.

A couple of months before Christmas, I came into a little inheritance, so I decided to give Emmeline a certificate for tickets to *Hamilton*, saying that somehow, somewhere in 2017 we would see it. She and Elin and I were able to find third row seats at the Broadway production during the Veterans Day holiday that year, and we were all delighted that the child had insisted on such an extravagant gift. What shot are you not going to throw away today?

December 18

"Rootie: Most beautiful I ever seen. I feel like I should kneel or something.
Bev: You should only kneel for God, honey.
Rootie: Well, I'm not for certain God's there, but I know Elvis is."
Characters in Ellen Byron's *Graceland*

"Elvis has left the building!" He's left Graceland. In fact, he's left the world. But his memory lingers on in the minds of many fans. The King died on August 16, 1977. I was shopping in a Rich's department store when I heard the news.

Thirteen years after Elvis' final departure, in the fall of 1990, several Samford students directed the plays *Patio and Porch* by Jack Heifner and *Graceland* by Ellen Byron. The latter show, set in 1982, takes place at the front entrance of Graceland, the Memphis mansion belonging to the late Elvis Presley. Three days before the ribbon will be cut opening the manor to public visitors, two strangers meet at five o'clock in the morning. Each one hopes to slide over the threshold first.

So Rootie and Bev set up at the head of the line and dig in. From Wilmington, North Carolina, Bev has come equipped with a tent, chair, and cooler of junk food. She thinks she is the ultimate Elvis fan and should be first into the door. Rootie, an insecure, thin young Cajun from Louisiana, eats very little except hard-boiled eggs. They wonder about each other, but the more they talk, the more a relationship grows. By the final curtain, the good-natured Bev gives up her place to the gaunt girl from the bayou.

The music of Elvis Aaron Presley (1935-77), the King of Rock and Roll from the mid-Fifties until his untimely death at age 42, provided much of the soundtrack of my generation. His first big hit was recorded the year I was five-years old, "I Forgot to Remember to Forget." The year was 1955 and that song later remained on Billboard's Country and Western "Most Played in Juke Boxes" chart for five weeks. Even in these early day, Elvis' concert and television appearances pierced the hearts of teenagers, especially girls. They adored his handsome looks, wiggly hips, and sexy gyrations. Some fans, like these in Graceland, looked at Elvis as a sort of savior figure.

Even though I was little more than a toddler who was yet to face first grade, I myself developed a crush on the soon-to-be star. Every time we visited a five-and-dime or grocery store, I pleaded for a pack of flat pink gum that held a trading card with Elvis' visage. I had a very favorite card that I slept with under my pillow. Though my parents teased me some about my puppy love, they also bought a few 45 rpm records of his early songs: "Heartbreak Hotel," "Hound Dog"/"Don't Be Cruel," and "Shake, Rattle and Roll," which I would dance and sing to. But I profoundly fell in love with "Love Me Tender."

I was not obsessed, but definitely fascinated by Elvis. His music made me happy, and my infatuation with him waned by the time I was seven or eight years old. The butterflies in the tummy and warm hearted feelings I had for him definitely prepared me for the later huge maniac crush I developed for the Beatles, an enthusiasm that lives on today — though not quite as fervently as during my teenage years.

December 19
In "Ya Got Trouble" from *The Music Man*, Professor Harold Hill stirs up the parents in River City about the mischief of pool tables so he can later persuade them to let him form a boys marching band. (Listen to the work online or from your library!)

Professor Harold Hill in *The Music Man* with book, music, and lyrics by Meredith Willson, based on a story by Willson and Franklin Lacey

Don't you love it when people make up a concern or give something a wicked spin, causing anxiety and fear in the surrounding family, town, school, club, or community? When you look a layer or two deeper, the perpetrator may be a shyster, a con artist trying to sell you something. Such scammers think highly of themselves, are slick, and are assertive with their product.

Sometimes, I can be a sucker for such folks. Once, I let an aggressive salesman give me a "free home water test," and then did all he could to convince me the water was contaminated and that my entire house needed an expensive filtering system. Another time, I was close to purchasing a fraudulent vacation package until my gut told me there was something fishy about the deal. I did let a slick Panama City Beach attraction owner entice me to paint some scenery for him. As he put it on his truck and started to roll southward, he said he had forgotten his wallet, and that I would be paid "later."

In *The Music Man*, Professor Harold Hill arrives in River City, Iowa to perform his repeatedly successful routine of masquerading as a boys' band organizer. The town has just gotten a new pool table in the billiard parlor, so he latches onto the depravity of such a perversion and persuades parents that a marching band is the wholesome alternative.

The Meredith Willson musical opened on this day, December 19, 1957, at New York City's Majestic Theatre, remaining there almost three years. Don't you wish you had been in the audience less than a week before Christmas? It moved to The Broadway Theatre and finished a 1,375-performance run there on April 15, 1961.

"Professor" Hill is no teacher, and he is not even a musician. His plan has worked before: create a desperate need to buy band instruments and uniforms, promise music lessons, and then skip town. The ultimate shyster. Nevertheless, we, as the audience, along with Marian, the prudish yet attractive librarian, fall head over heels for this snake oil salesman.

And why is it that we love Harold Hill? This is musical comedy! Have you ever seen a version of *The Music Man* – in person, photographs, the movie, or recordings of any kind – in which Hill was not a handsome and charming guy? He is captivating, and he enchants us. On top of that, he wears great costumes, can sing, dance, and move about the stage in a lively fashion.

But there is more! When folks get agitated after finding out the truth about the fraud, Marian and her brother Winthrop advise Harold to leave town. But he decides to stay, for he has fallen in love. Hill is put into handcuffs, but eventually freed after the children astoundingly perform Beethoven's Minuet in G for the townspeople.

Marian tells her little brother that she believes in Hill, because the boys were transformed in the way they talked and acted that summer. Harold Hill is redeemed by the end of the musical by the love of Marian – and also of the kids who have learned to become a part of something in community, something bigger than themselves, and have gained something that the arts teach so well: confidence, camaraderie, and capability.

December 20
"You know what your trouble is, Willy? You always took the jokes too seriously. It was just jokes..."
Al Lewis in Neil Simon's *The Sunshine Boys*

On this date in 1972, Neil Simon's *The Sunshine Boys* debuted in the Broadhurst Theatre on Broadway for a 538-performance run, starring Jack Albertson as Willie Clark and Sam Leven as Al Lewis. Simon puts two aging vaudevillian actors together for a reunion and the play is filled with delightful over-done physical bits, whacky double entendres, one-line zingers, and prop schtick. After performing together for 43 years, the two have been estranged for over a decade when they reunite to rehearse for a television special on the history of comedy.

As a kid, I delighted in televised variety shows in which some sketch inevitably included a guy slipping on a banana peel, walking into a wall, or getting slapped. *The Three Stooges* shows brimmed with smacks on the head, slippery slides, double takes, and more. Experts think that the concept of certain human movements being funny probably predates our language, and thus verbal comedy. Maybe we are wired to see humor in other people's predicaments. But whatever the origin, even today, physical entertainment makes us chuckle.

Maybe it seems a bit cruel to laugh at someone falling down, but psychologist Peter McGraw thinks the best jokes are able to transform something dark into something silly. In quoting his work, *The Atlantic* in its February 27, 2014, issue explains how we are deeply wired to laugh at something a bit unsettling. "Our caveman ancestors lived in a world rife with physical threats. There was relief in discovering that a rustling in the darkness was a mouse rather than a saber-toothed tiger." Sigmund Freud, in 1905, posited that humor might just be the fun-loving id arising in spite of objections from the stuffed shirt superego.

My enjoyment of physical humor doesn't stop at what I see onstage or screen, however. In real life, I chuckle when I see someone trip, and I guffaw if I do so myself. I always wondered why I seem to stumble and bang myself a lot in my life. Recently in reading Sandra Maitri's *The Spiritual Dimension of the Enneagram*, I think I found the answer. She says my Ego Type Four has a tendency to feel our separation from our Holy Origin as a sense of disorientation in the world. She notes, "Some Fours constantly bump into things or people, lacking a physical perception of space that includes all of the objects within it."

Take two nights ago for instance. Please, take it! My now 10-year old granddaughter Emmeline went with Roger and me to an Alabama Symphony holiday concert. We decided to have a meal beforehand, and tried a new restaurant. I got in a hurry leaving, as the time for the event was rapidly drawing near. Seeing what I thought was a shortcut to the front door, I dashed toward the exit. Only there was a wall of windows there and no archway to freedom at all. I ran smack into the glass and then doubled over — not in pain, but in uncontrollable laughter. Roger and Emmeline, once realizing I was fine, joined me in the biggest belly hoots we had had in weeks.

Al Lewis's words come back to me, *"You know what your trouble is, Willy? You always took the jokes too seriously. It was just jokes…"* Thank goodness in a situation like that, I don't let my ego take itself seriously and get grievously bruised.

December 21 - Winter Solstice
"Thus sometimes hath the brightest day a cloud;
And after summer evermore succeeds
Barren winter, with his wrathful nipping cold:
So cares and joys abound, as seasons fleet."
Gloucester in William Shakespeare's *Henry VI, Part 2*, Act II, Scene 4

So, according to Gloucester, problems come and go like the seasons. Today marks the Winter Solstice, the shortest day of the year, harkening the dark, cold season of *"barren winter, with his wrathful nipping cold,"* at least in the Northern Hemisphere. And, we have a few more days of Advent.

During this season a number of years ago, I had something of a problem: I was awaiting the development of a relationship that I wanted to move ahead. But as with Advent, the relationship was paused as we both waited for something. As I discussed the situation with my priest, I told him I had to live in the present without forecasting the future, and also, having no history with this person, not caught in the past. "When I live in the now," I said to him, "I am able to relish everything I am going through, the exuberance, the sorrow, the wonder, the frustration."

So my priest asked if I knew the etymology of the word relish, and I didn't, nor did he. Together we looked the word up in two dictionaries, and here is what we found: relish comes from Old English and Old French, *reles* or *relais*, "something remaining." Then the instructions directed us to *relaisser* or "release." Release is from Middle English (*relessen*) and Old French (*relesser* and *relaisser*) meaning "to leave." And the instructions directed us to "relax" from Latin *relaxare*. "*Re*" means back and "*laxare*" means to loosen or widen. I had used the word relish in the sense of to enjoy, and the definitions — for the noun, at least — also have the overtones of "flavorful" or "distinctive." And so, "release" means to set free, as from a prison, to unfasten or let something that is snagged go. And relax means making something looser, less firm, less strict, less severe.

"Something remaining" from the first word "relish" — looking at my particular situation — began to mean to me that something from every one of those crazy, painful, joyous moments was being deposited in my psyche, or my soul. So as I savored each moment for being itself, I was building myself. I am a person who experiences moods and feelings deeply and frequently — and that is good, because that is me.

So, I was feeling during Advent the depths of all those emotions and not denying them or blocking them, and that was healthy. But to add "release" onto the definition meant to me that I could experience, and then free the parts that made me feel bad or sad, and let them go. And further, to add "relax" onto that meant to calm down, unwind, slow down, and let it be.

I finally came to terms with the idea that I could not do one thing to hasten or change my situation. So, on or about the day that fall turned into winter that year, when frosts bit and icicles dripped, I was able to abandon myself to the fine art of detachment. I learned to live life as it unfolded on its own, and not according to my plan. My thoughts, I realized, were just thoughts and not reality. By the way, that Christmas season was one in which — knowing the meanings of the word — I enjoyed with great gusto all the delicious cranberry, onion, piccalilli, and pepper relishes that people could pile upon my plate!

December 22
"One day Henny Penny was out in the barnyard pecking for corn when all of a sudden, something hit her on the head. 'Dear me, the sky is falling. I better go tell the king.'"
Henny Penny in Paul Sills's *Story Theatre*

I was never lucky enough to persuade fellow faculty members to produce *Story Theatre*, but the concept intrigued me from the very first time I heard about the show. Opening on Broadway at the Ambassador Theatre on October 26, 1970, the play closed after 243 performances on July 3, 1971. Our college spring trip to New York City just missed by a few months the run of the innovative-improvisational-theatrical show.

Eleven years earlier, in 1959, the playwright Paul Sills was a founder of Chicago's Second City, the historic improvisational theatre that birthed so many Saturday Night Live cast members. The theatre employed *commedia dell'arte* techniques, as well as embodying the theories of Paul's famous writer and teacher-mother, Viola Spolin.

She advocated — as did *Story Theatre* and Second City — story telling, dance, improvisation, transformation, mime, and music to bring to life to theatre, and, in this play's case, to energize some of Aesop's fables along with other myths and legends. What made the play so fresh and contemporary in 1970 was the use of folk and rock music. The band "The True Brethren" performed in the Broadway version. For instance, the "Henny Penny" sketch is interspersed with lyrics from the protest song "Vietnam Rag" by Country Joe and the Fish, a favorite "psychedelic rock band" who performed at the Woodstock Festival. If you would like to hear some of the music, search online for music from *Story Theatre*.

My college years fell right in the middle of the hippie countercultural era, and I was a fringe Flower Child, supporting many of the major philosophies of the movement that culminated in signs and slogans such as "Make Love, not War" and "Give Peace a Chance." I loved the long hair, round glasses, leather, head bands, filmy long dresses, tunics, beads, and other accoutrements of the time. But I was really stirred by the active rights movements for minorities and women, ideas of nonviolent change of the materialism and repression of society, environmental concerns, and the growing utilization of unprocessed foods. As protests of war swirled around us, my male friends sweated through the draft lottery held on July 1, 1970, and many were having to determine what to do about drawing lower numbers: enlist or dodge?

After Henny Penny presumes that since something hits her head, the sky is falling, the musicians encourage all the brawny young men in the audience to stop studying, grab a weapon, and go help Uncle Sam fight the war. They ironically add such action will be fun-filled! In the play, Henny Penny finally recruits all of her barnyard fowl to go with her to tell the king. On the way, they are duped by Foxy Woxy who lures them into a hole to eat them one by one — as the band sings the chorus of "Vietnam Rag," which not so reassuringly vows that we all go to our last resting place anyway (whether by Foxy's or War's foxholes).

December 23
"Our doubts are traitors,
And make us lose the good we oft might win
By fearing to attempt."
Lucio in William Shakespeare's *Measure for Measure*, Act 1, Scene 4

Supposedly, "Fear not" or an equivalent phrase appears in the Bible 365 times, once for each day of the year. Yet, many of us allow anxiety and mistrust to block avenues that open throughout our lives.

Healthy terror is needed, as it keeps us out of trouble. I have just recently learned to be cautious around red wasps, having been stung twice now, suffering with the accompanying pain, swelling, and infernal itching. (One would think that one attack would suffice!) Since long ago watching the movie *Thelma and Louise*, I have had derivative fears of driving off the side of the Grand Canyon (I've never been) or even small embankments, making me careful about such precipices. And after two friends fell down steps, one to her death and one to a badly broken shin, I now cautiously grip handrails going up or down inclines.

But when facing life decisions, fear and self-doubt can hold us back from taking risks and courageously following our dreams. As Lucio says in *Measure for Measure*, our doubts are traitors, and work against us, spooking us and impeding our judgement so that we are too frightened to try something new.

Recently, a friend vacillated over whether to begin a doctorate program in education or to take a different route like spiritual direction training or a counseling degree. She is easygoing and can feel incapable of selecting from among options, as we all do.

I asked her if she wanted to learn to "play" Purple Bowl, and she was intrigued, so I taught her. Once for a house warming gift, my good college friend Joe Taylor gave me a purple bowl. I wanted it to be useful for mixing food and for holding decorations; but it needed another more elegant, more dedicated purpose as well.

At the time I got the gift, I was facing some decisions of my own in life about whether to continue teaching theatre or go into an arts-oriented business, or even studio art. Like my friend who was wondering what career to follow, I can stall in my decision making — because I can see so many different possibilities, and I can creatively imagine how each and every one of them could play out.

I had to choose an option, however, so it dawned on me to put every single course of action I could think of onto equally sized pieces of paper. After days of brainstorming, I put all the slips into the purple bowl and said that whatever I drew out, I would pursue. A funny thing happened. On the first pull, I drew out the idea "Start the Heart Art Business," and I had an immediate gut reaction that the choice was terribly wrong. So I tried again: "Move to Florida and work for Disney." No! Why did I think that was even an option?

I realized that randomly picking a possibility and saying that I would follow through with it was a ridiculous way to resolve what to do. However, just drawing out the suggestion gave me such a clue to what I really thought that I was able to pare down the ideas rapidly. We now sometimes play Purple Bowl to answer where to go to dinner. But, beforehand, we have to decide to either go with our first draw, or continue fishing until we find the restaurant we really want to patronize!

December 24

"Now's the time a man who lacks what he wants might get hold
By secretly stalking into the fold... (seizes a sheep)
A fat sheep, I dare say,
A good fleece, I dare lay,
Pay back when I may,
But this will I 'borrow.' (takes sheep home)."
Mak in Anonymous's *The Second Shepherds' Play*

Just the thought of the medieval cycle plays stirs my imagination! Most of these jewels were mounted on decorated pageant wagons drawn through towns and presented by amateur theatre folks from various trade guilds. Taking over 24 hours to perform any number of theatrical episodes, the event stretched for two or three days around the Corpus Christi festivals in Europe, a feast that is celebrated on the Thursday after Trinity Sunday — so a fun early summer festival.

The Second Shepherds' Play comes from the Towneley-Wakefield cycle consisting of thirty-two plays written by a number of anonymous authors over a two-hundred-year period. In graduate school, I studied the interrelationship of the arts in the Middle Ages, and this play, along with some shepherds carols, was part of my research.

The cycle plays told the stories of the Bible to audiences who could not read, because they had little or no access to the written word. So, from the Creation to the Last Judgment, the scriptures came alive for all who viewed them. *The Second Shepherds' Play* is a funny exploration of the shepherds who hear angels sing and find themselves on an adventure to see the newly born baby Jesus.

A charming aspect of Medieval and Renaissance drama is that the space and time between Biblical and current events buckle so the audience could relate to common complaints of their own era. For instance, the shepherds grouse about fingers chapping from cold weather, being crushed from overtaxing, or enduring robbery from the rich. In this play, Mak visits the shepherds (Coll, Gib, and Daw), and while they sleep, he "borrows" a *fat sheep* to take home to his hungry wife Gill and their children. All the while, he anachronistically swears by St. James, St. Stephen, and Christ's Holy Name!

I was never good at stealing, deceiving, or swindling. If I ever took something, I would sneak the item back. Otherwise, I had wave after wave of remorse and shame nearly drown me. That instinct was strengthened in fourth grade when I attempted to pull a fast one on a math test. I didn't need to cheat — I knew very well the arithmetic lessons for which I was being examined. But I had heard schoolmates talk about slipping answers from their desks during tests, or pinning solutions to the inside of their sweaters. The concept intrigued my 10-year old mind, so before one test, I wrote some notes on my hand in ink. Naturally, my teacher caught me and called my mother in for consultation. The entire incident gave me a lifetime inoculation against dishonesty and a super shield of integrity grew from the time my mother and I left the school until the time my father got home.

In thinking of Christmas, celebrations of new birth, and giving presents, the remembrance of this sudden, ignominious failure stands out as truly one of the greatest gifts I ever handed myself. That day, I went through the depths of my small self, and all the way to my soul. Once recovered from the horrifying ramifications of the deception I had practiced, I eclipsed any burning need to cheat or dissemble again.

December 25
"Small cheer and great welcome makes a merry feast."
Balthazar, in William Shakespeare's *Comedy of Errors*, Act 3 Scene 1

Christmastide is one of my favorite times of the year. I delve deeply into the quiet and contemplation of Advent, even though I do partake in some of the pagan revelry and gift purchasing during December as well. Actual Christmas — or Christ Mass — is the liturgical feast of the Nativity of our Lord. It stretches from sunset on Christmas Eve, which in our little Episcopal church is honored with a late afternoon children's service, to Twelfth Night, the day before Epiphany, forming the Twelve Days of Christmas.

Balthazar in Shakespeare's *Comedy of Errors* is right in noting that all we need for a merry feast is a bit of food and a big dose of hospitality. In fact, the air and essence of cordial congeniality is much more important than the actual food — although at Christmas, even Dickens's poor Cratchit family indulges in a slightly more laden table than their usual fare. And, they exude the warmth of *"great welcome."*

Think of Christmases past and food you had once, or the recipes which have become traditions. As I recall bygone holidays, some delightful dishes were ruined by stomach-churning political or topical conversations. On the other hand, some first-attempt barely edible casseroles transformed into savory pleasures because of the charming ambiance of the company. Whether you have beef or goose, ham or turkey, cranberry sauce from a can or a pan, smashed potatoes or whipped sweet potatoes, squash or green bean casseroles, cake or pie for dessert — none of the time and prep, none of the taste or the flavor of any of the elaborate spread make up for neglecting the *"great welcome."*

My maternal grandmother who we called "Babaw" always threw a big noontime party for her fourteen grandchildren and their parents a Saturday or so before Christmas each year. Her hospitality exuded warm-heartedness and, though she was on a limited income, the table was nicely set, with goodies like egg and olive and chicken salad sandwiches, cheese rounds with pecans in the middle, chips, dips, and chocolate chip cookies — all homemade.

My brother, cousins, and I have such fond memories of the annual event that several years ago, we began taking turns hosting the "Babaw Christmas Party." It is now held at night with some beverages we wouldn't have indulged in as children. But the graceful embrace of the host of the year always makes the feast a merry one. All but one of my grandmother's four daughters are gone, and our uncles are all dead. So gathering together to remember we still are a family for this festivity is a highlight of our Christmastide, and of the whole year.

December 26 Boxing Day!

"Always on Christmas night there was music. An uncle played the fiddle, a cousin sang 'Cherry Ripe,' and another uncle sang 'Drake's Drum.' It was very warm in the little house. Auntie Hannah, who had got on to the parsnip wine, sang a song about Bleeding Hearts and Death, and then another in which she said her heart was like a Bird's Nest; and then everybody laughed again; and then I went to bed."

Dylan Thomas in his *"A Child's Christmas in Wales"*

When I was the Executive Director of The Seasoned Performers, Alabama's only senior adult theatre, we often produced a Christmas offering during December. Two of our best Birmingham actors alternated year by year delighting audiences with their own readings of this Dylan Thomas classic. Thomas actually wrote the piece to be recorded by himself in 1952, and according to Wikipedia, the original "recording of A *Child's Christmas in Wales* was a 2008 selection for the United States National Recording Registry, stating that it is 'credited with launching the audiobook industry in the United States.'"

Dylan Thomas was born in 1914, so his childhood remembrances about growing up in Wales happened somewhere in the mid-1920s. He recalled snow and fires in homes, "turkey and blazing pudding," "festoons and Chinese lanterns." There were Useful Presents, like zebra scarves and "tam-o'-shanters like patchwork tea cozies," and Useless Presents, such as "many-colored jelly babies and a folded flag and a false nose and a tram-conductor's cap and a machine that punched tickets and rang a bell."

In thinking of this reminiscence piece, I myself look back wistfully in two ways: one to the good times we had producing our Christmas readings each year. Once, the presentation was in an older Birmingham home converted into an event space, decorated with a large tree and lovely greenery laced with tiny lights. We had candles glowing and wine flowing and we gladdened the hearts of a good many friends and patrons. That event has never left my mental cache of best holiday evenings ever.

The other nostalgic recollection that this piece stirs in me is the era when I was about 10 years old, the age Thomas was in the sketches about which he writes. We lived in a suburb of Birmingham called Homewood, with its own little downtown jam-packed with stores of all kinds: toys, clothing, shoe repairs — a movie theatre even graced the middle of one street. Across from that establishment was my favorite place to visit: the five-and-dime store. To me, it was glorious, overflowing cornucopia of everything imaginable.

My mother would drive me to this store with my hard-earned two-weeks worth of allowance, and run Saturday errands by herself. Going inside was an awe-filled experience. The display tables and floors were made of wood that smelled wonderful when mixed with candy and all the other delightful odors. First I encountered a stand filled with books, turned a corner to see small boxes of toy dishes, round another bend to find buttons or gloves or electrical supplies or hats. If this place sounds reminiscent of Walmart or another big box store, think again. All of this wonder fit into a space of a few thousand square feet. It had no fluorescent lights, and no shelving stacked to a 40-foot ceiling.

My favorite counter was toiletries: tiny bottles of perfume, miniature flagons of lotion, wee cylinders of powder. I couldn't resist picking one of these every time I visited. Sometimes I would also get a handkerchief scattered with violets or a paper sack with pick and mix candies. If I had enough change, I would get licorice for my mother in appreciation for allowing me to solo shop for what my uncle called "all of Barb's balms and lotions." To this day, I still have bottles in my bedside drawer, and travel with a valise filled with small containers of ointments and unctions, which I use daily with much delight.

December 27
"Peter: I wasn't crying. But I can't get my shadow to stick on.
Wendy: It has come off! How awful. (Looking at the spot where he had lain.)
Peter, you have been trying to stick it on with soap!
Peter: (snappily). Well then?
Wendy: It must be sewn on.
Peter: What is 'sewn'?"
Peter and Wendy from JM Barrie's *Peter Pan or the Boy Who Would Not Grow Up*, adapted for the stage by the author himself

When I was young, one of my aunts and I could entertain ourselves (and others) for long periods of time making all kinds of shadow puppets on the wall with our hands and other objects in front of a slide projector. Then, when I got involved in theatre, I learned that shadow drama was an ancient, long revered form of storytelling. Ever since JM Barrie wrote the play entitled *Peter Pan, or The Boy Who Wouldn't Grow Up*, which first opened in London on this day in 1904, people have been enamored with the characters and Peter's shadow.

The author originally created stories about Peter Pan between 1897 and 1902 as entertainment for some friends, the Llewelyn Davies boys who lived in Kensington Gardens near Barrie, and where Peter Pan's statue now finds its home. The idea of a boy who never grows up probably came from Barrie's childhood tragedy when his older brother David died in a skating accident just before his fourteenth birthday. He and his mother always thought of David as eternally a child.

Even take-offs of the author's work put the nature of childhood front and center. Barrie — a diminutive man himself — was able to tap into the juicy reality of children's lives: their fascination with games, their fertile imaginations, their desire to both connect with and unhook from their parents. To the heart of the latter matter, in theatre versions of the work, the same actor plays both the charming Mr. Darling and the villainous Captain Hook.

Psychologists say Barrie was attuned to childhood psychoanalytic theory and some experts even look at Peter Pan as illustrating key stages of child development. Popular psychology uses the phrase "the Peter Pan syndrome" to characterize people unwilling to accept the responsibilities of adulthood. And psychology practitioners and spirituality teachers delve into the "shadow self," the part of our ego that holds parts of us — both good and rotten — that we have trouble acknowledging.

The idea in *Peter Pan* that a person's shadow can be unattached is an interesting concept, and a theme of Peter Pan is the interplay of darkness and light in our lives. On an earlier visit to the Darling home to hear stories, Peter's shadow was ripped from him when the window shut close, and the limp silhouette was placed in a dresser. During the present trip, he tries to reattach his shadow with soap, but finally Wendy has to sew it on for him.

Barrie's own stage directions indicate the shadow is "a flimsy thing, which is not more material than a puff of smoke, and if let go would probably float into the ceiling without discolouring it. Yet it has human shape (Act I)." And so, is the shadow that is now only mechanically and not naturally attached a symbol of Peter's inability to grow up? And could it also be an indication that the boy's incapacity to mature is a sign that he is already dead and a kind of ghost, like Barrie's brother? We could go on and on speculating about Peter and his shadow! What do you think about it?

December 28
"Some are born great, some achieve greatness and some have greatness thrust upon 'em."
Malvolio in William Shakespeare's *Twelfth Night*, Act 2 Scene 5

In just eight days, we will celebrate the Eve of Epiphany with Twelfth Night. Shakespeare wrote a play by that name and, well, where do we start with this quote? With the naughty joke about thrusting? With the error in self-judgement that Malvolio has about his own importance? With whether or not the prank being played on this character by others is just or unjust?

I have been composing these ideas about theatre for several years now, and some were penned long ago. As I am finishing up, it is early 2022 and we have been in the midst of the worldwide coronavirus pandemic for a couple of years. Many theaters, orchestras, operas, and art museums have been closed, but are streaming productions and art for free and for fee. Roger and I were lucky enough to see the National Theatre presentation of *Twelfth Night* not long ago.

Filmed live on-stage in 2017, the gender-bending production stars female actor Tamsin Greig as the loyal servant Malvolia, and what a wonder she is. As *Vogue* critic Sarah Crompton says, Greig "turns Malvolia into a woman who imposes order as a way of controlling her life and takes the audience into her confidence in ways that are both funny and ultimately heartbreaking." And she quotes the actor herself who explains, "It's very interesting how someone can be so universally disliked and not realize it."

In the play, Malvolio is the steward or chief servant to Lady Olivia. Sir Toby, Olivia's uncle and his friend Sir Andrew Aguecheek, scheme along with Olivia's other servants Maria and Fabian. Together, they devise a practical joke to highlight their boss Malvolio's arrogance and egotism. Maria carefully pens a note crafted to trick him into thinking that Olivia is in love with him. With Malvolia being a woman in this production, a new twist is added to the theme of unrequited love. The letter encourages Malvolia to appear in foolish yellow garb and to smile lavishly even though Olivia is in mourning for the death of her brother. By doing so, Malvolia will have greatness thrust upon her when Olivia shows favor to her. It's hard to believe she falls for the scheme, but self-seeking, she hopes to improve her standing any way she can.

England is a land of queens and kings who are born "great" and assumed to be future leaders of the land. In fact, all people, from princes to paupers, in Shakespeare's time inherited rank and social position from their parents. But whether poor or wealthy, some humans display natural talents and finesse that lead to remarkable lives. Many folks are able to attain distinction through labor, networking, or enhancement of natural abilities. And there are the lucky few who find themselves in the precise place at the proper time to "have greatness thrust upon 'em."

In previous productions of *Twelfth Night*, I have felt that Malvolio deserved his comeuppance, what with his prudish, narrow-minded, joy-dashing outlook. But Greig's interpretation of the character made me empathize with her despite her vanity and even the wearing of her unbelievably gaudy and comical costume. Maybe any time I am tempted to feel too big for my britches, as my mother used to accuse, I should remember Malvolia and her ruination. As the Book of Proverbs, 16:18 King James version, says, "Pride goeth before destruction, and an haughty spirit before a fall."

December 29
"Is the honor of God washed clean enough? Are you satisfied now, Thomas?"
King Henry II in Jean Anouilh's *Becket*

Today marks the martyrdom of Thomas Becket. Jean Anouilh wrote *Becket or The Honour of God* in French and it was first performed in October of 1959 at the Theatre Montparnasse Gaston Baty in Paris. Like *Murder in the Cathedral*, the play portrays the conflict between King Henry II of England and Thomas Becket, Archbishop of Canterbury, ending with Becket's assassination in 1170.

The most astounding three hours I ever spent in a theatre was on New Year's Day, 1992 at the Haymarket in London. Derek Jacobi and Robert Lindsay did not play the roles of Becket and Henry, they WERE the Archbishop and the King. I broke into tears when the curtain fell because I believed I had actually been viewing the deep and twisted friendship between these two men, had been a part of their lives — and I wanted the experience to go on and on.

I recently read a review of another revival in which the critic asked why anyone would "resurrect an old costume drama like this." Well, he obviously did not see the production I saw. I have spoken to four or five other extremely literate theatre aficionados who also saw the Jacobi-Lindsay production and who agree with me that it was the best theatre they ever experienced.

When I went to England for the first time in 1987, on this day of Becket's martyrdom, we called ahead to see if there were going to be services at Canterbury Cathedral in remembrance of Thomas, and there were. So we arose quite early and took a train to Faversham, and then on to Canterbury.

It was dark, and, as we rapidly passed by houses, we could peek into lace-curtained windows at men shaving, people putting on kettles, Christmas trees still lit. I felt like Chaucer's Wife of Bath myself on pilgrimage, and I even wore red tights for the occasion! After making our way from the train station to the Cathedral, we attended a 10:15 morning Eucharist with 25 other people in Trinity Chapel, and were served by Archbishop Runcie himself. My head was spinning, thinking of Thomas Becket, our production of *Murder in the Cathedral*, my English professor Dr. Golson, and others who had a Becket connection. I staggered about the streets afterward as though stunned.

I purchased a Thomas medal in the gift shop when we went to a second service that started at 3:30 in the afternoon, about the time of his actual murder. Hundreds of us processed with candles to the martyrdom site where we deposited our still burning remembrances. I was absorbed in reverie the whole train ride back, fingering my Thomas medal. We went to a pub in London for supper and some slick pickpockets talked to us while surreptitiously trying to lift my purse. I realized what was happening, and "accidentally" spilled my glass of water in the crotch of one of them, spoiling their attempt at robbery.

Ever since that evening, I feel protected when I wear my St. Thomas medal. Its locket bail is now very thin and worn, so I often pray not to lose my holy armor!

December 30
In "Somebody's Got Your Back" from *Aladdin*, Aladdin and Genie sing about how wonderful it is to have each other to help out. (Listen to the work online or from your library!)

Aladdin and Genie in Disney's *Aladdin* the Musical by Chad Beguelin with music composed by Alan Menken and lyrics by Howard Ashman, Chad Beguelin, and Tim Rice based on the film with music composed by Alan Menken and screenplay by Ron Clements, John Musker, Ted Elliott, and Terry Rossio

I remember when working on sets for *Oliver!* at Parkway Playhouse, some of us would paint in the scene shop, which was right off stage, during rehearsals. We couldn't hammer or saw, because we would make too much noise. After going through the practices over and over, we all knew the songs and lines by heart. And we got silly after hearing about who would let the other in front of them from the song "I'd Do

Anything," as it had to be choreographed and coached over and over again. We would mimic it when finishing up a drop: "I'll paint your drop. No, I'll paint your drop." Or trying to get out the door for lunch: "And I'll go last. No, I will. No, I will! No, I will!" Then it moved, for some reason, to "I've got your back!" "No! I've got *your* back." And on and on.

Having someone's back means you are willingly volunteering to help or defend them. This song from the musical occurs after Aladdin expends his second wish: to free himself and his buddies from their underground prison.

When my daughter Elin and granddaughter Emmeline went to New York City to see *Hamilton*, we also got tickets to *Aladdin*. Really good tickets. House tickets, which a former student of mine, David Redman Scott was able to offer us for purchase without going through an agency. Not only that, David gave us a lovely tour of the Disney studios office where he was working at the time.

The friendship that grows in the musical between the scruffy little street urchin Aladdin and the supernatural magical Genie is an interesting one. The spirit in the oil lamp hasn't had a master in ten thousand years, so perhaps he was starved for companionship. But he is also surprisingly encouraged by the question Aladdin asks him: What do you wish for? When Genie says he wants his freedom, the boy promises to use his last wish to grant it to him.

After a while, the two learn to trust each other, and in the end, Aladdin is true to his vow and he frees Genie from his tiny lamp home. I like to think of their story as a metaphor for how things work in the theatre. Except on the very rarest of occasions, the motley group of people – who come from all backgrounds, all races, all genders, all religious beliefs – who come together to create a production. Over several weeks or months, we all learn to trust and respect one another.

Theatre is a collaborative art, meaning all the players onstage and backstage have to cooperate. And each separate person also must contribute his or her own talents, skills, nuances, personalities, souls, and hard work to have the piece come alive for the audience. I have been part of productions where the cast doubted the director, where the designers and crew fought, where some actors wanted to steal the spotlight, where lighting cues were purposefully missed – but not many. I hope I never have to slog through one of those disasters again, echoing the disfunction of *Noises Off*.

When a production syncs correctly, egos fall away and souls shine through the characters on the boards and through the beautifully functioning technical crew behind the scenes. That scenario brings a spiritual *"I've got your back"* quality to the production which, as the audience appreciates the performance, becomes almost tangible, palpable, manifest.

December 31
"Love all, trust a few, do wrong to none."
Countess in William Shakespeare's *All's Well That Ends Well*, Act I, Scene 1

"Love all, trust a few, do wrong to none" has an inimitable English ring to it. Shakespeare uses the phrase early in *All's Well That Ends Well*, when the countess advises her son as he is leaving for a court visit following the death of his father. She is giving him a design for life that we all might adopt as good counsel. From reading Joan Borysenko's *Pocketful of Miracles*, I learned the Metta, or Lovingkindness Meditation. In her version, I sit in a comfortable, relaxed manner and take some deep letting-go breaths.

As I enter a still and holy place, I imagine a bright star just above my head with marvelous light that washes through me, unveiling the clearness of my heart. Then, the light expands beyond me, encompassing Divine Love. Metta is practiced first toward myself, since most of us find it hard to love others without first loving ourselves. Sitting quietly, I anchor myself and repeat: "May I be at peace. May my heart remain open. May I awaken to the light of my own true nature. May I be healed. May I be a source of healing to all creatures."

When I feel healed, I move on and bring a loved one to mind and repeat the same or similar phrases, using his or her name: "May she be at peace" and so on. As I continue the exercise, I bring to mind other friends and neighbors, colleagues or a stranger I saw on the street, animals or trees, and finally people who I hold in judgment, but to whom I am willing to extend forgiveness. For all of these, I can use the same phrases, or put words together that better represent the loving-kindness I am now feeling toward these beings.

Finally, I picture our beautiful "fragile earth, our island home" as *The Book of Common Prayer* describes it — seeing it from "the vast expanse of interstellar space," amidst the stars and other planets. The point is to hold up all of creation, dark and light, good and bad, up and down, male and female — and to open my heart to the balance of it all, to be spacious and kindhearted, to *"Love all"* — which, as you probably know, is the motto of the Hard Rock Cafe. "May there be peace on earth. May the hearts of all people be open to themselves and all others. May all people awaken to the light of their own true nature. May all creation be blessed and be a blessing to All That Is."

As we do such a deliberate heart and thought exercise, we realize we are all part of one big whole, and that we all belong to something huge, something much greater than our little selves. At some point in life, we can gaze back through the years and pardon people from the past. Even everything hurtful that happened somehow trained me and got me to the point where I am today. Even to beloved folks who betrayed and broke faith with me, I can let things go, and let things be as they are.

And so, as we come to the last day of the year, let us say: all is well that ends well!

Made in the USA
Columbia, SC
19 April 2023

15617115R00307